Kyoto CSEAS Series on Philippine Studies
Center for Southeast Asian Studies, Kyoto University

A Capital City at the Margins

Kyoto CSEAS Series on Philippine Studies
Center for Southeast Asian Studies, Kyoto University

A Capital City at the Margins

Quezon City and Urbanization
in the Twentieth-Century Philippines

MICHAEL D. PANTE

ATENEO DE MANILA UNIVERSITY PRESS

in association with

KYOTO UNIVERSITY PRESS

Ateneo de Manila University Press
Bellarmine Hall, ADMU Campus
Loyola Heights, Katipunan Avenue
Quezon City, Philippines
Tel.: (632) 426-59-84 / Fax (632) 426-59-09
E-mail: unipress@ateneo.edu
Website: www.ateneopress.org
ISBN 978-971-550-923-7

Kyoto University Press
Yoshida-South Campus, Kyoto University
69 Yoshida-Konoe-Cho, Sakyo-ku
Kyoto 606-8315, Japan
Tel.: +81-(0)75-761-6182 / Fax.: +81-(0)75-761-6190
E-mail: sales@kyoto-up.or.jp
Website: www.kyoto-up.or.jp
ISBN 978-4-8140-0243-6

The publication of this book is financially supported by President's Discretionary Budget of Kyoto University for Young Scholar's Research Results, International Program of Collaborative Research at the Center for Southeast Asian Studies (IPCR-CSEAS), Kyoto University and Asian Studies Fund at Kyoto University.

© 2019 by Michael D. Pante

Cover design by Nikki Solinap
Book design by Paolo Tiausas

All rights reserved. No part of this publication may be reproduced, stored in a retrieval system, or transmitted in any form or by any means, electronic, mechanical, photocopying, recording, or otherwise, without the written permission of the Publishers.

The National Library of the Philippines CIP Data

Recommended entry:

> Pante, Michael D.
>   A capital city at the margins : Quezon City and
> urbanization in the twentieth- century Philippines /
> Michael D. Pante. —- Quezon City : ATENEO DE MANILA
> UNIVERSITY PRESS, [2019], c2019.
>   xv, 367 pages; 22.86 cm
>
>   1. Quezon City (Philippines) —- History. 2. Urbanization --
> Philippines —- Metro Manila. 3. City planning —- Philippines —-
> Metro Manila. I. Title.

959.9214   DS689.Q48   P920190099

Contents

List of Figures	vi
List of Maps	viii
List of Tables	ix
Acknowledgments	xi
Abbreviations	xiii

INTRODUCTION
The Contours of a Capital at the Margins   1

CHAPTER ONE
From Cattle Rustlers to Cabaret Dancers   19

CHAPTER TWO
Quezon's City   61

CHAPTER THREE
Spectral Spaces beyond Balete Drive   103

CHAPTER FOUR
Jeprox Ambiguity   151

CHAPTER FIVE
The Submissive and Subversive Suburbs   205

CONCLUSION
Past, Imperfect, Tense   247

Notes	257
References	323
Index	355

List of Figures

Fig. 1.	An Addition Hills advertisement, 1931	53
Fig. 2.	Manuel Quezon at Kiya-machi, Kyoto, accompanied by Tomás Morató, 1938	68
Fig. 3.	The Quezons' Pasay residence	69
Fig. 4.	Editorial cartoon depicting Aguinaldo's search for Quezon's alleged properties	71
Fig. 5.	The 1941 Quezon City master plan by Harry Frost	81
Fig. 6.	Laying of the cornerstone in Diliman, 15 November 1940	82
Fig. 7.	An advertisement of the 1941 Philippine International Exposition	83
Fig. 8.	Artwork for Merrit's article comparing Quezon City and Washington, DC	84
Fig. 9.	An advertisement of Juan Ysmael & Co.'s New Manila subdivision	87
Fig. 10.	An advertisement of Gregorio Araneta, Inc.'s Santa Mesa Heights subdivision	89
Fig. 11.	Artwork depicting residents opposing road construction in Kangkong	97
Fig. 12.	Cartoon depicting a UP student surprised by his sudden proximity to cabarets	100
Fig. 13.	Quezon meets his cabinet at his Marikina home before the Japanese invasion	105
Fig. 14.	Construction of UP Diliman's main administration building, Quezon Hall	116
Fig. 15.	Laying of the cornerstone of UP Diliman's Gonzalez Hall	117
Fig. 16.	Quirino inspecting the 1949 Master Plan	125
Fig. 17.	Quezon City's general design based on the 1949 master plan	126

Fig. 18.	An artist's depiction of the proposed Constitution Hill	127
Fig. 19.	Editorial cartoon showing the "savagery" of Balara	141
Fig. 20.	An early design for J. Amado Araneta's proposed International Cockfighting Stadium	147
Fig. 21.	Street layout of the proposed Malaya Subdivision	161
Fig. 22.	The Santa Catalina Site of Gregorio Araneta, Inc.	171
Fig. 23.	An advertisement of Araneta Center's Farmer's Market	174
Fig. 24.	A two-bedroom bungalow in Philamlife Homes	181
Fig. 25.	Slums in Bago Bantay, 1952	192
Fig. 26.	A vibrant street scene in Bago Bantay	198
Fig. 27.	Metrocom officers in front of Quezon Hall during the Diliman Commune	209
Fig. 28.	The Marcoses in the inauguration of a BLISS housing project in Pag-asa, Quezon City	218
Fig. 29.	Perspective view of the Quezon Memorial Project	227

List of Maps

Map 1.	Present-day Metro Manila	4
Map 2.	Manila (Intramuros) and Environs, circa 1650	23
Map 3.	Provincia de Manila, 1899	29
Map 4.	Manila's districts, 1918	31
Map 5.	Rizal province, 1918	32
Map 6.	The towns surrounding Manila, circa 1939	36
Map 7.	Manila and suburbs, 1932	41
Map 8.	The different landed estates surrounding Manila, 1935	47
Map 9.	Quezon City and its surrounding towns, 1939	77
Map 10.	Key places in Quezon City's prewar geobody	79
Map 11.	Route of the 1948 parade to celebrate Quezon's birth anniversary	104
Map 12.	City of Greater Manila under Japanese occupation	108
Map 13.	Proposed territorial jurisdiction for the Quezon City–Novaliches site by the Committee on Capital City Site	121
Map 14.	MWD general map, 1930s	123
Map 15.	Important roads in postwar Quezon City	129
Map 16.	Key places in Quezon City's early postwar geobody	134
Map 17.	Caloocan's partition into two noncontiguous territories	136
Map 18.	Operations of the Malaria Control Field Laboratory Unit in Quezon City, 1948	139
Map 19.	Important housing developments and landmarks in postwar Quezon City	159
Map 20.	Manufacturing employment in Greater Manila, 1960	177
Map 21.	Geographical origins of Manila-bound migrants	188
Map 22.	Squatter colonies in greater Manila, May 1963	196
Map 23.	Location of squatter and slum dwellers, 1968	197
Map 24.	City of Manila and vicinity, 1955	199
Map 25.	Quezon City's barrios, 1970	206

List of Tables

Table 1. Haciendas in Provincia de Tondo and the respective religious orders in charge by the eighteenth century — 24

Table 2. Population of the pueblos of Provincia de Tondo, circa 1840s — 28

Table 3. Population data in Manila and adjacent municipalities, 1903, 1918, and 1939 — 38

Table 4. List of land estates (as of 1935) that would eventually be absorbed, either partially or wholly, by Quezon City — 48

Table 5. Taxable urban lands and improvements within the jurisdiction of Quezon City that were taken from various Rizal towns, 1939 — 78

Table 6. Taxable rural lands and improvements within the jurisdiction of Quezon City that were taken from various Rizal towns, 1939 — 78

Table 7. Population per district, City of (Greater) Manila, August 1942 — 109

Table 8. Ratings by Committee on Capital City Site for the top six sites — 119

Table 9. Quezon City's population per barrio, 1948 — 122

Table 10. Number of taxable and tax-exempt parcels and their values in selected Quezon City areas, July 1955 — 136

Table 11. Number of family dwelling units constructed in PHC and the PHHC's first ten projects, 1956 and 1962 — 160

Table 12. Number of family dwelling units and benefited families in the PHHC's fourteen housing projects, 1963 — 164

Table 13. Rents, incomes, and occupancy limits, PHHC, June 1953 — 167

Table 14. Construction costs (in pesos) per dwelling unit in the PHHC's LCH projects, and inflation-adjusted prices (1965) — 168

Table 15. Number and value of private building construction in selected Philippines cities, 1955 to 1959 — 174

Table 16.	Workers in Quezon City ten years old and over according to industry, 1970	178
Table 17.	Number of households with specific appliances in Quezon City, 1970	178
Table 18.	Population of Quezon City's districts according to sex, circa 1970	185
Table 19.	Mother tongue spoken, and number of speakers according to sex in Quezon City, 1970	189
Table 20.	Population by sex and place of birth in Quezon City, 1970	189
Table 21.	Asking price, distance from Manila, and amount of one-way bus fare to Manila of selected residential lots for sale in Quezon City, 30–31 August 1958	194
Table 22.	Slum colonies and squatter population of Metro Manila, 1982	228
Table 23.	Number of sites and targeted families of priority projects for ZIP per city/municipality, 1978	230
Table 24.	Partial list of novitiates, seminaries, and church headquarters in Quezon City, as of 1986	240

Acknowledgments

THE PUBLICATION OF THIS BOOK is financially supported by the President's Discretionary Budget of Kyoto University for Young Scholar's Research Results, the International Program of Collaborative Research at the Center for Southeast Asian Studies (IPCR-CSEAS) at Kyoto University, and Asian Studies Fund at Kyoto University.

This book is based on my dissertation, which I defended at Kyoto University's Graduate School of Asian and African Area Studies. Completing my doctoral thesis would not have been possible without the guidance of my advisers, Shimizu Hiromu and Caroline Hau. I cannot thank them enough for their mentorship and friendship.

I am also grateful to the people and institutions that helped me in the journey from dissertation writing to book publication: Karina Bolasco, Paolo Tiausas, Nikki Solinap, and the entire team of the Ateneo de Manila University Press; Julius Bautista and Narumi Shitara of the Center for Southeast Asian Studies at Kyoto University; Reiko Nakamura of Kyoto University Press; the Japan Society for the Promotion of Science; Ateneo de Manila University's Faculty Development program; Christi Anne-Castro, Nayiri Mullinix, and the Center for Southeast Asian Studies at the University of Michigan Ann Arbor; Eileen Shen and the editorial staff of the Journal of Southeast Asian Studies; and Ramil Vinarao of Arkpages for preparing the digitized maps.

I am thankful for the librarians and archivists of the following: Ateneo de Manila's Rizal Library (especially Dhea Santos and Bhal Rabe) and University Archives at the UP Diliman Library System, the Filipinas Heritage Library, the Bentley Historical Library and Hatcher Graduate Library at the University of Michigan Ann Arbor, the CSEAS Library at Kyoto University, the Sophia University Central Library, the Quezon City Public Library, and the Caloocan City Public Library, especially Cora Noble.

A lot of people have helped me one way or another in writing this book: my parents and siblings, Chiaki Abe, Jun Aguilar, Clark Alejandrino, Chester Arcilla, Ram Balubal, Momok Barbaza, the Berjamin family, Karl Cheng Chua, Kaloy Cunanan, Francis Gealogo, Loh Kah Seng, Nancy Kwak, Mario Lopez, JPaul Manzanilla, Mike Montesano, Aaron Moralina, Mhel Natividad, Leo

Nery, Zenta Nishio, Andre Ortega, Susie Protschky, Jordan Sand, Tin Sendin, Sydie Soliveres, Angelli Tugado, Tom van de Berg, and the Kadamay organizers and residents of Sitio San Roque in North Triangle.

Para kina Desiree, Cecilia, at Josefina: araw-araw kong gustong umuwi sa bahay natin sa Quezon City.

Abbreviations

ACC	American Chamber of Commerce
ACCJ	*American Chamber of Commerce Journal*
AFP	Armed Forces of the Philippines
AHC	American Historical Collection, Rizal Library, Ateneo de Manila University, Quezon City
BHL	Bentley Historical Library, University of Michigan, Ann Arbor, MI, USA
BOR	Board of Regents, University of the Philippines
BPW	Bureau of Public Works
BT	*Bulletin Today*
CA	Commonwealth Act
CCP	Cultural Center of the Philippines
CIA	Central Intelligence Agency, USA
CPP	Communist Party of the Philippines (Marxist–Leninist–Maoist), est. 1968
CR	*Congressional Record*
DS	*The Diliman Star*
EDSA	Epifanio de los Santos Avenue, Metro Manila
EO	Executive Order
EQP	Elpidio Quirino Papers, Filipinas Heritage Library, Ayala Museum, Makati City
FMP	Frank Murphy Papers, Bentley Historical Library, University of Michigan, Ann Arbor, MI, USA
FQS	First Quarter Storm
GMA	greater Manila area
GSIS	Government Service Insurance System
HMB	Hukbong Mapagpalaya ng Bayan
HUKBALAHAP	Hukbong Bayan Laban sa Hapon

IPC	Institute of Philippine Culture, Ateneo de Manila University, Quezon City
ISI	import-substitution industrialization
JBVP	Jorge B. Vargas Papers, Jorge B. Vargas Museum and Filipiniana Resource Center
JRHP	Joseph Ralston Hayden Papers, Bentley Historical Library, University of Michigan, Ann Arbor, MI, USA
LCH	low-cost housing
LP	Liberal Party
MARP	Manuel A. Roxas Papers, University of the Philippines-Diliman Main Library, Quezon City
MDB	*Manila Daily Bulletin*
MERALCO	Manila Electric Railroad and Light Company, present-day Manila Electric Company
METROCOM	Metropolitan Command, Philippine Constabulary
MFC	Marcelino Foronda Collection, Center for Southeast Asian Studies Library, Kyoto University, Kyoto, Japan
MGC	Mauro Garcia Collection, Sophia University Library, Sophia University, Tokyo, Japan
MHS	Ministry of Human Settlements
MLQP	Manuel L. Quezon Papers, National Library of the Philippines, Manila
MLQP (BHL)	Manuel L. Quezon Papers, Bentley Historical Library, University of Michigan, Ann Arbor, MI, USA
MMA	Meralco Museum and Archives, Pasig City
MMC	Metropolitan Manila Commission
MRO	Malacañang Records Office
MT	*The Manila Times*
MWD	Metropolitan Water District
NCR	National Capital Region
NDC	National Development Company
NDF	National Democratic Front
NGC	National Government Center
NGO	nongovernmental organization
NMPC	National Media Production Center
NHA	National Housing Authority

NHC	National Housing Commission
NICA	National Intelligence Coordinating Agency
NLP	National Library of the Philippines
NP	Nacionalista Party
NPA	New People's Army
NPC	National Planning Commission
OG	*Official Gazette*
PC	Philippine Constabulary
PD	Presidential Decree
PFP	*Philippines Free Press*
PG	*Philippine Graphic*
PHC	People's Homesite Corporation, est. 1938
PHHC	People's Homesite and Housing Corporation, est. 1947
Philamlife	Philippine American Life Insurance Company
PKP	Partido Komunista ng Pilipinas/Communist Party of the Philippines (Marxist–Leninist), est. 1930
PML	Presidential Museum and Library
PNB	Philippine National Bank
PRP	Philippine Radical Papers, Multimedia Services, University of the Philippines-Diliman Main Library, Quezon City
PSHS	Philippine Science High School, Quezon City
PWDC	US Philippine War Damage Commission
QI	Quezon Institute, Quezon City
QMC	Quezon Memorial Circle, Quezon City
RA	Republic Act
SC	Supreme Court of the Philippines
SONA	state of the nation address
SURP	School of Urban and Regional Planning, University of the Philippines-Diliman
UN	United Nations
UNDP	United Nations Development Programme
UP	University of the Philippines
USAID	United States Agency for International Development
USC	University Student Council, University of the Philippines
UST	University of Santo Tomas, Manila
ZIP	Zonal Improvement Program

INTRODUCTION

The Contours of a
Capital at the Margins

FROM 1948 TO 1976, Quezon City was the Philippines's capital city. Such stature fulfilled the original vision behind it as a city that would replace Manila. Realizing that vision entailed the complete remapping of the towns along Manila's northeast border zone from which Quezon City emerged in 1939 and expanded in the next few decades. For a quarter of a century, Quezon City was the nominal seat of power, yet during that period its level of prestige or dominance never matched that of Manila. In 1976 this disparity reached its logical conclusion when Manila regained its pre-eminent position. Thus, one could argue that Quezon City was a failed project.

More lamentable than this apparent failure is that Quezon City's reign as capital remains a forgotten chapter to this day. Its status as the former capital city has no political or cultural value as the average Filipino is most probably unaware of this historical fact. More importantly, Quezon City, which is now part of Metro Manila, holds but little geographic significance for those living outside the metropolis, let alone outside the country. It is a city rarely viewed and understood on its own terms.

For much of the twentieth century, to see Quezon City was to behold it starting from a specific point of entry: Welcome Rotonda. The monument not only literally welcomes people from Manila entering Quezon City but also memorializes this city's former status as the national capital. A Manila-based worker going home to their Quezon City residence or a university student living in downtown commuting to Diliman often passes through this gateway to take Quezon Avenue, the main artery connecting the two cities. This thoroughfare terminates at another roundabout, Elliptical Road, which encircles the perimeter of Quezon Memorial Circle, whose centerpiece is the 66-meter Quezon Memorial Shrine, built in honor of the city's founder,

2   A CAPITAL CITY AT THE MARGINS

President Manuel Quezon. The Elliptical Road is the heart of the city, as it is the location of the city hall and is the most prominent corner of the Diliman quadrangle, a diagonal convergence of four major avenues: North, Timog (South), East, and West Avenues. As such, Diliman is Quezon City's de facto central district; it is the site not only of the city's civic core but also of its oldest and most prominent housing projects. Continuing Quezon Avenue's northeast track past Elliptical Road, one reaches Commonwealth Avenue, reportedly the widest thoroughfare in the country. This highway is the major point of access to two important spaces in the city: the main campus of the country's premier state university, University of the Philippines's (UP) expansive Diliman campus; and Batasang Pambansa in Batasan Hills, formerly Constitution Hill, which houses the country's lower house of Congress. Further up north along Commonwealth Avenue is the vastness of Novaliches, the city's northern frontier adjoining the provinces of Bulacan and Rizal.

At present, however, at a time of intense metropolitan growth, Quezon City is understood less from Manila's standpoint than from the perspective of a much bigger Metro Manila, a polycentric conurbation consisting of sixteen cities and one municipality. Today's Quezon City is often approached from the south: a person coming from the Ninoy Aquino International Airport in Pasay City or from the glitzy business districts in Makati City or Taguig City usually enters Quezon City by passing by another historical monument, the Our Lady of EDSA Shrine. Standing at Quezon City's southernmost point, this Marian image commemorates the 1986 uprising known as the EDSA People Power Revolution that ousted President Ferdinand Marcos, the same president who removed Quezon City's status as capital in 1976. It towers over Metro Manila's most important highway, the circumferential Epifanio de los Santos Avenue (EDSA), the site of People Power. Further along EDSA into the heart of Quezon City, one finds key spaces that have shaped the city. Facing each other in opposite sides of this highway just a kilometer from Our Lady of EDSA are Camp Aguinaldo and Camp Crame, the national headquarters of the Armed Forces of the Philippines and the Philippine National Police, respectively. A stone's throw away from these camps is Araneta Center in Cubao, the city's first commercial district, which has been a shopping and entertainment haven since the 1950s. A few kilometers further north, EDSA bisects the Diliman quadrangle and reveals SM City North EDSA and Trinoma, models of the contemporary (post-Cubao) malling experience. Nearing EDSA's northwestern terminus, one reaches a major Quezon City intersection, the Balintawak Cloverleaf or the Balintawak Interchange, which links the city and the metropolis to the North Luzon Expressway, Metro Manila's passageway to the northern provinces.

The two monuments that greet Quezon City's visitors coming from the city of Manila and the rest of Metro Manila—Welcome Rotonda and the Our

Lady of EDSA Shrine—serve as spatiotemporal signposts of this city's historical geography. They not only mark Quezon City's geographic edges but also signify key moments of its transformation through time, specifically Quezon City's designation as capital city and the end of Marcos's dictatorial regime. At the same time, Quezon City's territory also includes Novaliches's expanse, defined by its long northern border lines that separate it from neighboring provinces. The nebulous, permeable frontier-like conditions in this part of the city, which coincidentally lacks notable border markers, tell a different time-space narrative from the ones that Welcome Rotonda and Our Lady of EDSA offer, one characterized by urban intrusion, rural pushback, and liminality. Despite their contrasts, these stories from the border zones give new angles with which to analyze an oft-neglected city.

Why Quezon City?
THIS BOOK NARRATES the origins of Quezon City and its short-lived status as capital by charting its historical geography. It traces the emergence and evolution of this city's territory from its founding in 1939 as a planned city to its designation as the nation's capital in 1948 and finally to the loss of that status and the aftermath during the tumultuous Marcos era (1965–1986). In the process, the most significant factors behind these processes are identified and assessed based on their impact on the city's stakeholders.

This work does not merely narrate events that happened within Quezon City's spatial limits. First, it focuses on sociospatial dynamics. It traces spatial changes in this city in relation to the simultaneous changes in its sociopolitical context and shows how the sociopolitical is also contingent upon space. It is an exposition of the transformations in Quezon City's morphology from its origins in the parcelized friar estates in Manila's suburbs during the real estate boom of the American colonial period and its founding as a planned city in the Commonwealth era to its elevation to capital city for the fledgling nation-state and its eventual demotion to a component city of a metropolitan region under Marcos's authoritarian regime. Moreover, this work's analysis is not confined to Quezon City's juridical boundaries. Similar to the relationship between society and space described above, it reads Quezon City's historical geography as a product of the dialectics between urban and rural. Thus, one of its core arguments is that one cannot fully understand this city's development without looking at its unique position as a border zone between urban Manila and the rural provinces.

At present, Quezon City is part of Metro Manila that is, without a doubt, the economic and political center of the Philippines. Also known as the National Capital Region, Metro Manila is composed of sixteen cities and one municipality (Pateros), covering an area of 613.9 square kilometers (map 1). In 2015 it posted a population of 12.8 million people.[1]

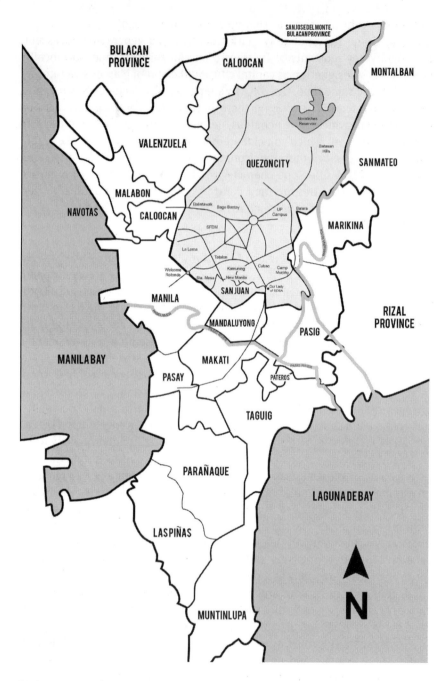

MAP 1. Present-day Metro Manila

THE CONTOURS OF A CAPITAL AT THE MARGINS   5

Metro Manila is no monolith. Within it are competing, though at times cooperating, local units. Economic and political power is dispersed among the component cities, although a few stand out.[2] The city of Manila, for example, exerts much political influence because of its status as national capital. At the same time, Makati City boasts of having the central business district (CBD), but is not without competition from the business districts of Ortigas in Pasig City and Bonifacio Global City in Taguig City. Quezon City enjoys a large population and territory, huge revenues, and is home to the state university's main campus and the lower house of Congress. It seems to wield considerable political and economic power, so much so that its local officials constantly craft proposals to move the capital again from Manila to Quezon City, only for each one to end in futility.[3]

Those proposals are, of course, based on Quezon City's history as the former capital. That designation was the idea right from the start when Quezon City was established in 1939. Arguably, it stands as a project of state planning unparalleled in Philippine history; not even Manila could compare to the extent and deliberate manner in which Quezon City developed. Commonwealth President Manuel Quezon was the main visionary behind it. His ostensible main objectives were a) to provide Manila's working populace a site for affordable housing and b) give the University of the Philippines (UP) a scholarly atmosphere that would eliminate the distractions of urban life. He also wanted to make the city the nation's political center, a status it attained in 1948, four years after his death and two years after the country gained sovereignty as a nation-state. For a significant part of the twentieth century, it was the spatial representation of official nationalism. However, on both objectives—as a city of mass housing and a secluded university town—Quezon City was weighed and found wanting.

The main objective of this book is to offer an explanation to Quezon City's apparent failure as capital city. It argues that the city's unique position as an urban-rural buffer zone separating Manila from its immediate hinterland was one important factor behind the unsuccessful experiment. For a quarter of a century, it was the nominal center, yet its historical geography as Manila's periphery held it back from becoming the predominant urban core of a growing metropolis. On the one hand, the book recognizes Quezon City's position as a center. Not only was Quezon City the post-World War II capital; it was also a center for education and health services, a model city for housing projects, and a sporting and entertainment mecca. On the other hand, it remained peripheral to Manila throughout the twentieth century. As post-World War II administrations failed to develop the new capital, government agencies stayed in the old capital, while vast areas in Quezon City continued to be vacant, thereby attracting migrant-settlers from nearby provinces and evicted slum dwellers from Manila and giving the city a peri-urban character.[4] Simultaneously central and marginal, Quezon City existed as a paradox throughout its short-lived stint as the Philippine capital.

The Spatial Turn and Southeast Asian Cities

THE SO-CALLED "spatial turn" in the social sciences and the humanities has become more prominent in recent years. This shift is not simply an incorporation of geographical analysis in studies, but a change in paradigm. It involves a growing recognition of space as not simply a "container" of human activity, but more importantly a force in itself. It is an acknowledgement that "social identities are frequently forged in conflicts over the boundaries, ownership and meaning of places."[5] A big factor behind this shift is the corpus of works from radical geographers, such as Henri Lefebvre, David Harvey, Doreen Massey, and Edward Soja.[6] Although there are points of divergence that differentiate these scholars, certain fundamental similarities bind them together. One is their criticism of the dichotomy that relegates space to the realm of the static vis-à-vis time, which represents the dynamic. As the "realm of stasis," this view regards the spatial as containing "no true temporality and thus no possibility of politics."[7] Another is their regard for space—without fetishizing it as an analytic concept separate from time—as a significant factor in understanding class analysis and class conflict.[8] For instance, Massey's regard for space as a product of embedded social practices entails a commitment to anti-essentialism for it foregrounds the existence of multiplicity and heterogeneity in space, which can be conceived of as a simultaneity of stories-so-far.[9]

In this sense, the term "sociospatial" is redundant. As much as the social cannot exist outside of space, space is an empty signifier without the social. Yet its use as a conceptual tool remains imperative if only to point to the bias of most historians toward the temporal and their neglect for the spatial. In using this term, this book builds upon Massey's theorization of the "sea-change" in the social sciences in recent years:

> Increasingly the spaces through which we live our lives, and through which the world—and cities—come to be organized are understood as being social products, and social products formed out of the relations which exist between people, agencies, institutions, and so forth. . . . *spatial configurations produce effects*. That is, the way in which society (more specifically the city) is organized spatially can have an impact on how that society/city works.[10]

Urban history has been at the forefront of this spatial turn,[11] thereby enhancing our understanding of cities and urban dynamics. This book applies the same line of analysis on Quezon City. In doing so, it stresses two intertwined, salient details about Quezon City's space: the city's political status as a planned capital and its socioeconomic position as a suburb of Manila. Charting the evolution of its morphology is impossible without taking these factors into account. Furthermore, this book situates this city within the broader framework of urban change at the regional level. Each chapter concludes with insights that link Quezon City's history with contemporaneous developments in Southeast Asia.

The need to situate Quezon City within Southeast Asia is to address the tendency in historiography to depict it as a derivative of planned capital cities, in the mold of Canberra, Brasilia, and Washington, DC. Unfortunately, in the process, analysts de-emphasize its embeddedness in other important regional processes, such as decolonization, the Cold War, postwar authoritarianism, and the ongoing trends of urbanization and the emergence of megacities.[12] Of course, one cannot deny that Quezon City emerged as a planned capital city. However, this specific feature can yield more insights if set against Southeast Asia's long tradition of creating such political centers.

Planned capital cities are not a new phenomenon and can be understood as a distinct urban morphological category in the typology of capital cities.[13] Since the emergence of ancient civilizations, state formation has inevitably involved the selection and planning of sites for the purpose of holding the administrative apparatus of the state. Various considerations influence the selection and planning of capital cities such as the site's prestige and secure location.

Having planned capitals often means that there is a preexisting capital city while the "planning" process is going on. As such, the idea of "planning capital cities" is inexorably tied to the act of "moving capital cities" from the old to the new.[14] At the same time, moving the capital is almost always due to tectonic shifts in the political landscape, a result of changes not just in the ruling regime, but in the nature of the state itself. The crises of the twentieth century brought forth many such examples. The crumbling of European empires, the end of the Second World War, and the onset of decolonization led a considerable number of countries to relocate their capital cities, many of them newly independent nation-states. The move from Manila to Quezon City fits this description.[15]

Another important aspect of planned capital cities is the artificiality of their morphology, as evidenced by their carefully designed boundaries, districts, and street layout. This artificiality stands in contrast to the "natural growth" of unplanned cities, although such an assertion does not attribute an essentialist "natural-ness" to unplanned ones. This dichotomy has been analyzed extensively in the case of Southeast Asia. For example, T. G. McGee and Robert Reed have pointed to the contrast between the sacred inland city and market port city as urban ideal types in premodern Southeast

Asia. Whereas coastal, market-oriented cities typify the "natural," random, and unplanned growth of an urban area, as in Phnom Penh and Mandalay, inland, sacred cities, like Angkor Thom and Pagan, exhibit state centralization as seen in the symmetrical and radial city layout that imitates official cosmography.[16] Similarly, Ross King gives this dichotomy a modern-day reading in his study on Putrajaya and Kuala Lumpur.[17] The distinction is also apparent in the Philippines, as seen in the contrast between "Manila's *laissez-faire* development" (with the exception of Intramuros and parts of Ermita and Malate) and the rational planning of Quezon City, "the only place [in Metro Manila] to possess substantial symmetry in its road layout."[18]

As the space of planned cities is malleable for politicians and planners, the inevitable result is that their morphologies are oriented toward the perpetuation of the dominant ideology and the control of the ruling elite, though such an assertion also does not mean that unplanned cities are bereft of ideology. In today's era of the nation-state, official nationalism is the predominant ideology informing the morphology of planned capitals. Indeed, the artificiality of planned capitals makes them compatible with the imagined nature of the nation,[19] as exemplified by Quezon City—albeit a problematic compatibility since official nationalism is predicated on the notion of the nation as primordial.

President Quezon saw in Quezon City the spatial manifestation of the Philippine nation that emerged from the late-nineteenth-century *ilustrado* tradition. Quezon came from this tradition, which traced its origins to the Propaganda Movement advanced by young upper- and middle-class males in Europe, such as José Rizal and Marcelo H. del Pilar.[20] Ilustrado nationalism's anticolonial thrust, however, gave way to early-twentieth-century Filipino official nationalism. American colonialism cultivated this new variant of nationalism by coopting the second generation of ilustrados, represented by the likes of Quezon and Sergio Osmeña, and turning them into colonial state officials within a decade after the US replaced Spain as colonial masters. Rather than confront US colonialism, this blunted nationalism became preoccupied with state formation and its trappings precisely because its chief advocates were the principal agents of the state.[21] The concern for creating a new capital city was one example.

In this regard, by analyzing the rationales and debates behind the selection and planning of Quezon City, one can understand how Filipino elites projected their ideas of nationhood and sovereignty onto space.[22] As a planned capital, symbolic architecture and civic spaces dominate its landscape: from the spacious, symmetrical quadrangle that defines the city center to the wide boulevards that intensify the visual appeal of modernist government structures. In the middle of the centrally placed Quezon Memorial Circle (QMC) is the Quezon Memorial Shrine, which consists of three 66-meter pylons, each with a statue of an angel on top. The three angels each hold a garland of *sampaguita* (by tradition, the national flower) and represent the three major island groups in the Philippines (Luzon, Visayas, and Mindanao). At the base of the shrine are bas reliefs that depict various historical events in the conventional nationalist narrative of Philippine history and episodes in Quezon's life story, suggesting that the former president's career was the realization of the nation's teleological destiny.

Evidently, planned capital cities symbolize the ascendancy of the "new" vis-à-vis the old capital, which stands for the *ancien régime* that is about to be replaced. The "newness" of planned capital cities becomes even more apparent due to the usual consideration of planners to build upon sparsely settled sites, and thus in places with minimal cultural and economic significance, so as to build from scratch and to minimize complications like residential dislocations and the need to expropriate land. Such is the logic behind the construction of Brasilia in 1960 to replace Rio de Janeiro. In Quezon City's case, however, its site had a significant cultural and economic value prior to its selection as capital. The territories that comprised it were landed estates controlled by powerful clans, personalities, and institutions. In this regard, Quezon City was quite unique compared with other planned cities.

One must also note that many planned capitals emerged in the context of a twentieth-century reaction to the excesses and defects of nineteenth-century industrial cities, which sought to build utopias that tried to combine the best of the urban and rural worlds.[23] Thus, planned capital cities tend to blur the spatial distinction between urban and rural. Their existence adds complexity to the already complicated spatiality of urbanization in the age of urban sprawl. In Southeast Asia, the phenomenon— of vague boundaries separating urban from rural—has been observed by McGee and Ginsburg as early as the 1970s and is not limited to planned capitals. Consequently, Southeast Asian urbanists have developed the concept of "desakota" to comprehend the reality of large cities in which the urban and rural coexist.[24] Looking at the case of Malaysia, McGee argues that new frameworks are needed to make sense of the rural-urban continuum debate, especially in relation to the reality of migration.[25] Similar to desakota, peri-urban is another concept that urban scholars use to comprehend the rural–urban overlaps that result from the rapid expansion of cities. Yap Kioe Sheng defines peri-urbanization as "a piecemeal transformation of rural areas on a city's outskirts into areas with a more urban character."[26] Oftentimes, peri-urban zones attract not just income-poor migrants from the provinces but also evicted settlers in the more central districts, who take advantage of "the lack of planning which leaves land without public access vacant for extended periods of time."[27] Meanwhile, Rimmer and Dick categorize Quezon City as a post-suburban city in the post-Second World War era, characterized by the decentralization of work, the prominence of shopping and recreation, and the rise of the automobile age—a definition that problematizes the applicability of the term "suburban" in non-Western contexts. Based on their analysis, Quezon City falls into the same category as Kebayoran, Petaling Jaya, Toa Payoh, Shah Alam, and Makati.[28] Some scholars even contend that the urban-rural dichotomy seen in the West did not exist in Asia because "there was very much less of an urban-rural split or conflict in Asia" and that cities and villages "were not necessarily seen as antithetical, or even as separate parts of a dichotomy."[29]

In the Philippines, the history of Quezon City presents an instructive example with which to analyze the blurry boundaries between the urban and rural. It exhibited traits of the typical Westernized and middle-class suburb, thanks in large part to its American and US-trained planners, administrators, and property owners. Yet at the same time, it also showed peri-urban qualities, as seen in its vast cogon-covered lots accommodating makeshift shelters for both city-oriented workers and part-time farmers in the city fringes. To a large extent it acted as an interface between city and countryside just outside Manila's boundaries, as though it were a border itself. In contrast to earlier studies that focus on Quezon City's centrality (as national capital) and its center (as symbolized by its imposing civic architecture and symmetrical layout), this work probes Quezon City's peripheral status (as an urban-rural buffer zone) and its geographical peripheries (especially its border zones). It pays minimal attention to the city's spaces of grandeur and instead brings to the fore communities along the boundary lines that separate it from urban Manila and its expansive frontier in which the city seemingly seamlessly blends with the countryside. Such an approach is not specific to Quezon City but a timely analytic shift at a time when scholars, not to mention policy makers, find it more difficult than ever to spatially delimit "the city" or "the urban" due to the increasingly blurry boundaries between city and countryside.

The interchangeable terms "border" and "boundary" literally mean a cartographic line that separates two distinct territories.[30] Nonetheless, these terms also have a more figurative meaning as contact points, "a meeting place of conjoinment where persons and ideas come together; where people and places meet, abut, mingle and neighbour."[31] Expounding further, radical historians and geographers have imbued political and economic value on the seemingly neutral features that define the contours of any city. As Massey points out: "All attempts to institute horizons, to establish boundaries, to secure the identity of places, can in this sense therefore be seen to be *attempts to stabilize the meaning of particular envelopes of space-time. . . .* For such attempts at the stabilization of meaning are constantly the site of social contest, battles over the power to label space-time, to impose the meaning to be attributed to a space, for however long or short a span of time."[32] Although this book still deploys the literal meanings of "border" and "boundary," its analysis is anchored on the more complex understanding of the terms, as articulated by Massey.

A city's borders do not simply delineate its territorial limits. Whereas the urbanized center, as the main locus of the city's economic infrastructures and political symbolisms, defines the city and makes it recognizable to both residents and non-residents, borders provide a haven of sorts to elements of the urban underside. While boundaries separate contiguous towns from one another, they also create corridors of activity that are radically different from those in the center, straddling both sides of the border. The fringe often attracts illicit economic activities such as prostitution and gambling, or is designated to accommodate undesirable spaces, like cemeteries and slaughterhouses. As early as the 1960s scholars have noted the importance of these marginal zones in cities.[33] However, the edge of the city remains neglected in favor of the center, with only a few works paying attention to the former.[34] Although the urban social underside has been foregrounded in a number of studies, the urban geographical underside remains understudied.

Based on the above discussion, it is not enough to look at the linear edges of a city to understand its geographical underside; border zones need to be made prominent in the analysis. This book uses the terms "border areas," "border zones," and "fringe belts," to denote the city's peripheries that straddle both sides of the boundary. This work uses these phrases based on a fusion of Charles Abrams's definition of "buffer zone"—a "strip established to separate and protect one type of land use from another; for example, as a screen to objectionable noise, smoke, and visual aspects of an industrial zone adjacent to a residential area"[35]—and the notion of borderland from geography, defined as the "transition zone within which the boundary lies."[36] The use of these terms coincides with Mike Davis's characterization of "urban edge" as the "societal impact zone where the centrifugal forces of the city collide with the implosion of the countryside."[37] However, although these phrases convey a sense of being amorphous, making borders seem artificial, one must be reminded that these cartographic lines are still real, especially in legal terms. One important implication of this point is that the peripheral-underside character is different in the two sides of the border: those outside the border serve as sites for activities that are prohibited in, but demanded by, the city. This book highlights this duality of the city border: its rigidity gives the border area a legal character that treats it as no different from the city center and sets it apart from surrounding towns;

12 A CAPITAL CITY AT THE MARGINS

yet its fluidity and flexibility provide the border area linkages with the surrounding towns that the city center cannot enjoy as much.

On the one hand, borders are artificial and arbitrary. These lines do not exist in the real world. How they appear on a map are usually based on legal and cartographic definitions, sometimes in complete disregard for natural boundaries (e.g., rivers, cliffs, etc.), with straight lines as the perfect example of geopolitical expediency. As such, borders "are not solid lines, but porous thresholds."[38] People and products constantly cross boundaries. The artificiality of borders also manifests in how national politicians can alter them, or even "erase" a city altogether, for military and ideological considerations. Quezon City's experience from 1939 to 1949, as it went through a war, foreign occupation, re-occupation, and selection as national capital, reveals details about such cartographic flexibility.

On the other hand, borders do have real-life consequences and are potentially disruptive. Ironically, the arbitrariness of borders exposes the reality of power relations that define space. Not everyone can define borders, and they have to be policed for them to be "real." Because they influence wages, rent, product flows, etc., borders are essential in rationalizing and reinforcing the city's material conditions. The history of Quezon City cannot be divorced from the long history of Manila's changing border zones. At the turn of the twentieth century, the edges of Manila, a sizeable portion of which are now parts of Quezon City, were contact points of hostility from the time of the Philippine revolution against Spanish colonialism to the Philippine-American War. In the decades that followed these border zones were turned into privatized, subdivided, consumer-friendly real estate developments that catered to citizens who could afford the democracy of the free market. The emergence of Quezon City in such a context spurred speculative investments in areas just outside its boundaries. A 1971 magazine article shows the realness of city boundaries and its effect on everyday living:

> SINCE the line that divides Manila and Quezon City is a matter largely of interest only to cartographers and map fondlers, or their unlikely cousins the city mayors, census enumerators and tax collectors, one tends to be diffident over such boundaries that define a city's real estate. Unless these divisions, like the Wall that divides West and East Berlin, touch and affect his way of life.

> As in a way it does now the Manila resident and the Quezon City commuter.

> You know you are leaving Manila and entering Quezon City, not merely on reading helpful guideposts like the "Welcome" sign at the España rotunda and the marker in Santa Mesa, but by the recession and finally disappearance of garbage that back in Manila was all over. What before was a vague, ill-defined feeling over the vast difference between Manila and Quezon City assumes something more precise and

THE CONTOURS OF A CAPITAL AT THE MARGINS   13

immediate: Quezon City has no garbage problem. As a Quezon City resident, you feel relieved even if you live only a hundred meters from the Manila–Quezon City boundary, to know that your environment is better.[39]

One of this book's main arguments is that a key factor behind Quezon City's failure as a capital city was its position of marginality vis-à-vis Manila, acting as a border zone between city and countryside, a place for urban-rural encounters. Ideally capital cities are not ordinary urban settlements, but act as the geographical showcase of a province, region, or of a nation. Quezon City's founders and administrators tried to create such an ideal image in the city by emphasizing its civic architecture, expert-led urban planning, and potential as a commercial hub. The city's identity was anchored in two critical state-led initiatives: the construction of low-cost housing projects for the ordinary working class and the creation of the expansive Diliman campus for UP, the premiere state university. However, Quezon City's position as a buffer between Manila and the provinces of Rizal and Bulacan blunted the official vision for the city as a citadel for democracy and a home for the ordinary *tao* (common citizen). Its position as Manila's periphery made it the logical location for establishments that catered to Manila's demand for vices and illicit activities.[40] Quezon City's early history was, in fact, a history of cockpits and cabarets; its vast territory and status as capital made it possible to manipulate its borders as a way of earning quick profits through land speculation. Moreover, because not everyone could take part in the middle-class lifestyle that Quezon City offered, income-poor households subverted the neat symmetry of the city by building slum communities even in areas earmarked for civic development.[41] Many of these informal settlements are populated by migrants from the provinces, further underlining the city's peri-urban character, "blunting rather than sharpening the distinction between rural and urban."[42] Moreover, many of the problems faced by the immediate hinterlands, such as peasant revolts, agrarian disputes, even outbreaks of disease, posed challenges to the capital city.

Notwithstanding its grandiose plans and civic architecture and its reputation as a gleaming, clean city, Quezon City was merely a nominal capital, as confirmed by its loss of such status in 1976. As Salvador Lopez put it, Quezon City was but a Cinderella capital.[43] Although fairy godmother Manuel Quezon gave her fancy clothes via the magic wand of presidential prerogative, it did not take long for the magic to wear off. In contrast, Makati, located southeast of Manila, became a postwar boom town despite the lack of state-directed planning. The disparity between Quezon City and Makati becomes more striking if both are seen as projects of modernization and national development for the young nation-state. The divergent paths the two took are evident. Makati emerged as a successful private-led

14   A CAPITAL CITY AT THE MARGINS

business district and upper-class residential enclave under the direction of one family, the Ayalas—of course, not without the attendant discontent among the marginalized. State-planned Quezon City pales in comparison. Although its spaces nurtured the social reproduction of the middle and upper classes, it also gave birth to sizable urban poor communities, evincing government neglect. State failure also came in the form of the non-implementation of the city's master plan, which led to its anarchic development. The last two chapters of this book elucidate on this matter by discussing the intraurban dynamics that link Quezon City with Manila, Makati, and the rest of the emerging metropolis. In a sense, this work narrates, from Quezon City's standpoint, the development of the conurbation around Manila into present-day Metro Manila.[44]

The City in Philippine Scholarship

REGRETTABLY studies about Philippine cities have been remiss in accounting for the importance of space. In contrast, changes through time are given precedence.

To begin with, much of the existing works on the history of Quezon City are not really scholarly, but of a commemorative kind, celebratory rather than critical. Examples of these works are those written by Manuel Duldulao and Celso Carunungan. However, this does not mean that relevant scholarly literature for the study of Quezon City's history is non-existent. Donovan Storey's essay "Whose Model City? Poverty, Prosperity and the Battle over 'Progress' in Quezon City," and Edson Cabalfin's essay provide a more sober analysis of the city.[45] Still, the challenge of filling in the void of critical studies on Quezon City's history remains and needs to be linked to earlier studies on Philippine urban history.

Given the dearth of scholarly analyses on Quezon City, it becomes imperative that this study look at writings about other urban localities to serve as sources of relevant frameworks. One may begin the search with Ma. Luisa Camagay's review essay, which clarifies the analytical value of cities in Philippine history.[46] Camagay points out that the writing of urban history is related to the shift in Philippine historiography that began in the 1960s. This shift is marked by the change in concern from national and political topics to social and local. Hence, most of the standard works on urban history are also social histories. For example, Manuel Caoili combines concepts from public administration and social history to come up with the standard text on the history of Metro Manila.[47] The topics of urban expansion, the emergence of slums, and suburbanization, as well as the interaction that connect these forces, are tackled in a number of publications.[48] Quite expectedly, Manila has been the focus of urban historiography, and its position as primate city—including the attendant debates regarding the generative or parasitical relationship between the capital and the peripheries—and its cultural resonance as a "storied" place may help explain this historiographical dominance.[49] Nonetheless, if urban historians are serious about sustaining this subfield, they need to address the disparity by adding more to the scant literature on the history of cities outside Metro Manila.[50]

Works on urban history and urban studies in the Philippines are on an upswing in recent years. Twenty-first-century Philippine urban historiography has become more theoretically sophisticated and attuned to the theoretical concerns of other nations, especially in relation to Southeast Asia and even Asia in general. Since the 1950s, scholars have theorized the similarities and differences of the so-called Asian city.[51] Of course, social history continues to be an overarching theme, but in recent years, new frontiers have opened up, such as the history of health and medicine.[52] The regional-comparative approach is not surprising given that in Southeast Asia works on urban history and urban studies have become more prominent.[53] Still, works on urban history that focus on space remain scarce.[54] In this regard, this book aims to contribute to this literature by positioning itself not just within Philippine urban historiography, but also within the ever-expanding terrain of comparative Southeast Asian studies, with an eye for spatial analysis in particular.

Sources and Structure

THIS BOOK RELIES PRIMARILY on documentary analysis as the main methodology. The most important archival materials it uses are the various personal papers of key personalities involved in Quezon City's history. Examples of these are the Manuel L. Quezon Papers, Elpidio Quirino Papers, Joseph Ralston Hayden Papers, and Manuel A. Roxas Papers, among others. Most of the materials listed below are accessible in libraries located in Metro Manila, such as the Rizal Library, Ateneo de Manila (especially the American Historical Collection and the Filipiniana Section), the UP Diliman Library System (especially the Main Library and the library of the School of Urban and Regional Planning or SURP), the Filipinas Heritage Library, and the National Library of the Philippines (NLP). Other important libraries visited are the Center for Southeast Asian Studies Library in Kyoto University, the Sophia University Library in Tokyo, and the Bentley Historical Library and Hatcher Graduate Library, both in the University of Michigan, Ann Arbor.

One important component of the methodology is to collect primary sources relating to the conceptualization and establishment of Quezon City as a chartered territory and to the geographical evolution of the city. As such, government documents comprise a significant portion of the primary sources used in this work. This set of documents includes Quezon City's city charters and the corresponding amendments that have formed its legal basis from

16   A CAPITAL CITY AT THE MARGINS

1939 onwards, the final report of the Committee on Capital City Site, which paved the way for Quezon City's official designation as capital city in 1949, and its master plan.[55] Another important source of information is the official annual reports of two important bodies that oversaw the day-to-day affairs of the city in the postwar years: the Office of the City Mayor and the People's Homesite and Housing Corporation (PHHC). The PHHC also has an unpublished reference manual that contains data about the early decades of Quezon City and its low-cost housing projects.[56] Important statistics and details are found in the various nationwide censuses, starting from 1903 to 1980.[57]

However, government documents only present one side of the story. In fact, focusing on official documents will limit a researcher to questions of government rather than allow one to look at the bigger picture of governance. Urban governance encompasses a wider scope that includes non-governing elites, civil society, nongovernmental institutions, and the like.[58] Indeed, this work minimizes discussions about administrative changes in the local government in favor of giving more space to the actions of activists, slum dwellers, and nongovernmental organizations and how they interacted with the state. Hence, it also looks into the personal correspondences and papers that uncover the personal motives and underlying interests of non-state actors involved in the emergence of Quezon City. While secondary sources point to the significance of civic virtue and urban renewal in the planning of Quezon City, this state-centric analysis should be problematized. By looking into the urban biographies of middle-class and lower-class residents, one can see that tensions arose from conflicting definitions of the ideal city. This book also consults a number of contemporary periodicals such as the *American Chamber of Commerce Journal* (*ACCJ*), *The Diliman Star* (*DS*), the *Philippines Free Press* (*PFP*), and the *Manila Times* (*MT*), as well as published works of well-known contemporary commentators and materials related to the history of key Quezon City-based institutions, such as the University of the Philippines.[59]

Published secondary sources about the founding of Quezon City's and the story of its founder are aplenty. A number of books have published the correspondences, memoirs, and speeches of Manuel L. Quezon, the central figure in the history of the city.[60] Moreover, a handful of biographies, ranging from the hagiographic to the critical, has been written about him, and I use these materials to establish the link between Quezon's personal "urban experiences" and the urban concepts that he introduced when the city was still at a planning stage. One must also include the published memoirs and biographies of personalities who were instrumental in the early decades of Quezon City's history.[61]

Chapter 1 historicizes the process of Manila's urban expansion, with an emphasis on the period between the late nineteenth century and the early twentieth century. It begins with how Spanish colonialism gave the archipelago an urban tradition, with Manila as the undisputed primate city and existing as a walled city to maintain the demarcation between the colonizers in Intramuros and the indios and the Chinese in the Extramuros. This sociospatial order, however, crumbled down in the face of rapid urbanization in the nineteenth century and the onset of American colonialism. The suburbanization that began in the late Spanish period continued under the new colonial regime. In fact, it crystallized into three suburban zones in prewar Manila. However, these zones started out as spaces for guerrilla bands and friar estates. Domestication and democratization were thus needed to prepare the suburbs for the act of consumption, in the form of middle- and upper-class real estate developments and subdivisions. In time, the native elites themselves would appropriate the suburban lifestyle. This scenario sets the stage for the emergence of Quezon City.

Chapter 2 narrates the intertwined urban biographies of Quezon City and Manuel Quezon (from his hometown Tayabas to major "urban stops" in Manila, Washington, DC, and Quezon City). As such, this chapter is not just a narration of how Quezon City came to be, but an exposition on how Quezon's postcolonial imaginings, shaped by his trans-urban political career, helped form the Philippines's future capital city. Quezon City, when it was established in 1939 as a future capital city that would simultaneously provide low-cost housing and a suitable university site, was also a product of the twin process of democratization and domestication. This chapter looks into what I call Manuel Quezon's urban biography, to see how the *provinciano* (someone from the provinces) from Tayabas developed a unique urban consciousness as he moved from Manila to the world cities of St Petersburg, Washington DC, Kyoto, and back to suburban Pasay and Marikina. This chapter argues that these experiences, as well as his authoritarian control over city politics during the Commonwealth period, were crucial in how Quezon determined Quezon City's foundations. But to what extent was Quezon City Quezon's city? This chapter reimagines Quezon's ideal city by factoring in the actions of ordinary residents and Manila's suburban underside.

The third chapter looks at the impact of two "wars," the Second World War and the Cold War, on Quezon City. By focusing on two key documents, the Report of the Committee on Capital City Site and the 1949 Quezon City Master Plan, it dissects how Filipino elite politicians chose Quezon City as the capital and planned it for that purpose. In both crucial acts, the political elite tried to make sense of urban planning in the wake of a destructive war and amid the uncertainty of a peasant rebellion just outside the borders of the newly designated capital city, in stark contrast to Quezon's prewar optimism. The pivotal 1940s also reveal other details about Quezon City's

18   A CAPITAL CITY AT THE MARGINS

borders. It was pivotal in the sense that the city boundaries experienced massive changes throughout the decade, from the Japanese occupation to the administration of President Elpidio Quirino. These changes highlight the dual character of city borders as being simultaneously rigid and porous.

Read against the context of the Cold War, the issue of housing and its role in foregrounding the idealized vision of Quezon City as the home of the ordinary tao are the focal points of chapter 4. This chapter views housing as a fundamentally ideological issue as it fragmented the capital city into differentiated spaces of consumption. The state led the way in constructing low-cost housing projects, albeit in an inadequate manner. Its shortcomings had to be filled in in some way. Private capital took advantage of the huge demand in the housing market, with the emergence of Philamlife Homes, touted as the first gated community in the country, as one of its accomplishments. This development, however, meant the social and geographical exclusion of the masses, who had to get by through informal means of finding shelter amid the pressure of urban living.

Chapter 5 narrates the critical events in Quezon City during the Marcos era, especially in light of the president's decision in 1976 to transfer the capital back to Manila, a decision that was rather fitting. In the early years of Quezon City and when President Quezon proposed the transfer of UP from Manila to Diliman, Marcos was one of the UP student leaders who rallied against Quezon's move. As though "returning the favor" to the president he so admired, it was Marcos who decided to transfer the capital from Quezon City to Manila in 1976, at a time when the conjugal dictatorship of Ferdinand and Imelda was on an urban fantasy overdrive in terms of recreating Manila as "the city of man." This chapter juxtaposes the Marcoses' nativist urbanism with the "realisation of a (sub)urban campus as revolutionary space"[62] in the barricaded UP Diliman Campus in 1971 and the culture of subversion in Quezon City's anonymous suburban spaces. These subversive acts in Quezon City's suburbs culminated in the 1986 EDSA People Power, which turned the tables not only on the Marcos regime but also on the sociospatial dynamics of city-based displays of dissent.

The book concludes by reiterating the important points tackled and reflecting on Quezon City's position within post-authoritarian Metro Manila in light of what it has experienced in its first half-century. It also situates Quezon City against the backdrop of an urbanizing Southeast Asia to see how its experiences can help in understanding the current situation of similar cities in the region.

CHAPTER ONE

From Cattle Rustlers to Cabaret Dancers

QUEZON CITY EMERGED in Manila's northeastern peripheries in 1939. Prior to its birth, the spaces that would constitute it experienced the suburbanization that accompanied Manila's urban boom from the nineteenth century to the 1930s just before the outbreak of the Pacific War in the Philippines. Manila's suburbs stood as a geographical manifestation of a confluence of factors: economic growth under the late Spanish period, American-style urbanism, and the consumerism of the native elite. Thus, Manila's fringes were spaces for the colonial elite.

However, this border zone also coddled Manila's underside during, and even prior to, this period. Charting the historical geography of Manila's urbanization reveals the presence of criminal and marginalized elements in the city fringes. This social underside made its presence felt in the *arrabales* (suburbs) surrounding Intramuros in the nineteenth century as well as in the three distinct suburban zones that began to form outside Manila's juridical borders in the early twentieth century. Moreover, the composition of this social underside demonstrates the dualism of these spaces. Whereas cattle rustlers and bandits betray the rural character of Manila's peripheries, the emergence of cabaret dancers and street gangs in these same spaces points to the effects of urbanization.

Historicizing Manila's suburbanization, therefore, needs to go beyond the usual factors of "flight from blight" and elite consumption. It must also uncover the ideological underpinnings of the process to surface the roles played by the non-elite operating at the margins. Indeed, the American colonial elite perceived suburbanization as a movement away from Spain's autocratic legacy toward the freedom of movement and consumption that American-style urbanism offered. For them, this process was the

19

20   A CAPITAL CITY AT THE MARGINS

transformation of areas that were once friar/feudal estates, battlegrounds of revolution and war, and "brigand" hotbeds into neatly organized residential subdivisions. But at the same time, the suburban underside took this transition as an opportunity to further socioeconomic and political objectives, away from the peering eyes of Manila-based authorities.

Early Philippine Urbanism

THE SIXTEENTH CENTURY saw Southeast Asia developing a robust urban tradition. Replacing the declining inland sacred centers of Pagan and Angkor were the maritime trading ports of Phnom Penh, Palembang, and Malacca. Before the onset of Western colonialism in the region, signaled by the Portuguese occupation of Malacca in 1511, Southeast Asia was a sea of cities in an age of commerce.[1]

However, unlike its neighbors, the Philippines had no precolonial, indigenous urban tradition. No large settlements divorced from agricultural production existed in this archipelago prior to Spanish conquest. The basic sociopolitical unit was the *barangay*, which had about thirty to one hundred families. Maynila was the largest barangay, which at the eve of colonialism had around two thousand inhabitants, including a number of Chinese and Japanese merchants. Cebu, in the Visayan groups of islands, was also an important trade center and thus possessed a relatively large population. However, none of these settlements could be classified a city in terms of size or politico-economic power.[2]

The first Philippine cities emerged due to Spanish colonialism, modulated by the colonial experience in Latin America, especially Mexico. The Spaniards altered the settlement patterns of the islands' native communities via the *reducción* system. As part of the intertwined projects of colonialism and Christian evangelization and with the friars at the forefront, the reducción system consolidated into permanent and accessible settlements, many of which depended on swidden agriculture and thus had to live in dispersed and impermanent abodes in the mountainous interiors.[3] For this purpose the colonizers created *pueblos* (towns) using a distinct spatial pattern, the so-called plaza complex, as set forth in King Philip II's promulgation for the establishment of cities throughout the Spanish empire.[4]

Manila was Spain's centerpiece in this colonial urban experiment. After two failed attempts at building the colonial capital in Cebu and Panay in the Visayas from 1565 to 1570, Miguel López de Legazpi, the first Spanish governor-general, moved to a larger settlement in the northern island of Luzon, the existence of which he learned from the Visayans. In 1570 the Spaniards landed at Maynila, then under Rajah Sulayman. After winning several battles against the indigenous communities of Maynila and adjacent Tondo, Legazpi reestablished and renamed Manila in June 1571. Henceforth, Manila,

FROM CATTLE RUSTLERS TO CABARET DANCERS   21

which the colonizers designated as a Spanish *ciudad* (city), stood as the Philippine capital and remained so throughout the Spanish, American, and Japanese colonial periods until Quezon City replaced it in 1948, two years after Filipinos gained sovereignty as a nation-state.[5]

Legazpi's choice of Manila as capital hinged mainly on its strategic location. Surrounding it was a sizeable and arable hinterland that could feed a large metropolis. At a time when water-based transport was the most efficient mode of mobility, Manila's access to bodies of water made it desirable. To its west lies Manila Bay, providing the city with a natural harbor suitable for trade, especially with the lucrative China market. The Pasig River, which connects Manila Bay to the lake of Laguna de Bai, bisects it crosswise. Inland estuaries, called *esteros*, give Manila an intracity network for conveying passengers and freight.[6]

For defense purposes the Spaniards built walls around Manila. Thus, as a geographical designation, Manila referred to the walled-in area, a definition that lasted from the late sixteenth century to the late nineteenth century. It also came to be known as Intramuros, or "inside the walls." Spanish urban planning, as set out in Philip II's decrees, gave the walled city a plaza-centric layout with gridiron streets.[7] Manila's morphology "vividly reflect[ed] the Spanish concepts of ideal urban form."[8] The thick and towering walls (4.5 kilometers long, covering Manila's entire pentagonal perimeter) also maintained racial segregation, making Manila an exclusively Spanish city and shielding the colonizers from what they perceived to be public health risks. By the eighteenth century Manila was "totally enclosed" from its *arrabales* (suburbs) or Extramuros. Of course, the walls were also permeable as the colonizers were dependent on the services rendered by the natives and Chinese living outside Intramuros.[9]

As capital, Manila was the colonial nerve center for political, economic, and religious affairs. It was the location of the governor-general's palace, the main port for the Manila galleon trade, the residence of the colony's sole archbishop, and the head churches of the major religious orders that proselytized in the colony, namely the Augustinians, Dominicans, Franciscans, Jesuits, and Recollects. Its undisputed position as the foremost city in the colony made it Southeast Asia's first primate city.[10]

Like Batavia, Malacca, and other colonial cities in the region, Manila was an entrepôt linked to smaller trading posts and acted as a beachhead for Europeans to profit from preexisting trade routes that flowed through it.[11] This specific type of urbanization was the consequence of what David Smith and Roger Nemeth described as "pin-prick colonialism." Rather than create an extensive colonial apparatus, as in colonial Latin America, the Spaniards intensified their economic control over a specific colonial center (i.e., Manila). While provinces languished due to state neglect, Manila grew

22   A CAPITAL CITY AT THE MARGINS

as a crucial node for the trans-Pacific Manila–Acapulco galleon trade, which carried the lucrative silk-for-silver exchange between the Chinese and Mexico-based Europeans and laid the foundation for a world economy. The fortunes of Manila's residents—whether native, Chinese, or European—rested on the success or failure of each arriving galleon. Although a cosmopolitan city, connected as it was to Asian, American, and European urban centers, Manila was constrained by Spanish mercantilist policies, much like its walls that controlled the traffic of people and products in and out of the city.[12]

Outside Manila, Extramuros was not just an area for non-European settlements. Its arrabales sustained the economic, political, and religious activities in Intramuros by providing the walled city with the necessary raw materials and manpower. The most populated arrabal was Tondo, located north of the Pasig River. Other arrabales on this side of the Pasig were San Nicolas, Santa Cruz, Sampaloc, San Miguel, Quiapo, and Binondo. Three arrabales occupied the other side of the river: Paco, Ermita, and Malate (map 2).[13] Moreover, a significant community of Chinese (almost all of them males) resided in the Parian, which was a de facto ghetto just outside the eastern walls of Intramuros. Spanish authorities eventually allowed Chinese residents who converted to Catholicism, many of whom married indigenous women, to reside outside Parian. Under the Dominicans the Catholic Chinese, and eventually their Chinese mestizo descendants, built a community in Binondo.[14]

Beyond the arrabales lay a wide expanse of Tagalog rural towns that were part of the province of Morong, which would be renamed Provincia de Tondo and include the capital and its suburbs. To the north were the pueblos of Navotas, Tambobong, and Caloocan. To the east were San Francisco del Monte, San Juan del Monte, San Felipe Neri, and Pasig, and further to the northeast were Novaliches, Montalban, and San Mateo. Down south were Pasay and San Pedro Macati. Spanish conquest was inextricably connected to the evangelization of religious orders, and at the get-go missionaries established their presence in these areas and consolidated them into parishes, which became the nucleus of modern-day towns. The Augustinians were the first ones to do so. They began proselytizing in Tondo in 1572 and expanded eastward to San Felipe Neri in present-day Mandaluyong. Next were the Franciscans, who did the same in Sampaloc, San Francisco del Monte, and then southward to the lakeside towns of Laguna. The Jesuits arrived in the islands in 1581 and evangelized in the Marikina Valley, in present-day Marikina, Taytay, Antipolo, San Mateo, and Tanay.[15]

The missionaries altered the geography and political economy of these areas, as was the case for almost the whole colony. They facilitated the reducción system and introduced new agricultural methods that

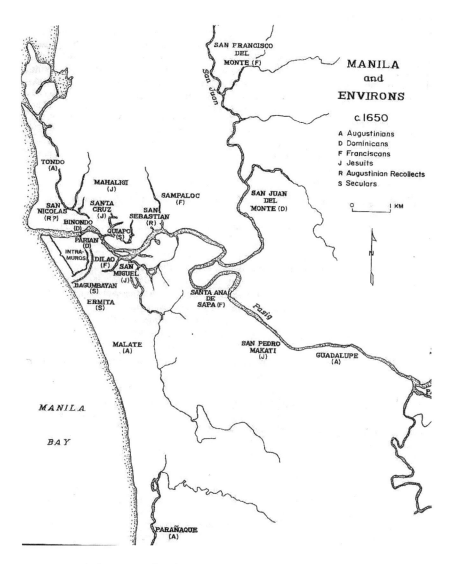

MAP 2. Manila (Intramuros) and Environs, circa 1650
SOURCE: Reed, *Colonial Manila*, 54

encouraged permanent settlements. As primary agents in the establishment of pueblos, they were instrumental in changing land rights in the colony. Most important, they amassed landholdings in their respective mission areas through various means. These estates gave the friars much economic and political power that sometimes provoked Church-state tensions, as some government officials attempted to limit the expansion of such landholdings. Because friars were often the real power holders in local politics,

24   A CAPITAL CITY AT THE MARGINS

they were in a position to accumulate land, even those that the Crown had designated as communal. In many cases they obtained properties through legal means, such as purchasing them from locals. One example is the Mariquina estate, which the Jesuits bought from the native *principalía* (political and economic elite).[16] However, in other cases, "purchases" were actually legalized land grabbing that dispossessed peasants or a result of a de facto foreclosure of mortgaged property, like in two cases involving Augustinian haciendas: one is the case of Sebastián Pérez de Acuña's estate, which the order bought in 1633 and added to their Mandaloya estate; the other is the 5,184-hectare Hacienda de Tala, which was an *estancia* that was previously owned by a certain General Miguel Martínez, who went bankrupt in 1714.[17] Religious orders also obtained land through royal land grants, as in 1590 when Governor-General Santiago de Vera donated a 250-hectare site six kilometers northeast of Manila to the Franciscans, which was eventually named San Francisco del Monte and became the location of their convent.[18]

By the eighteenth century, the orders had consolidated these land-holdings into haciendas (table 1). The religious orders then profited from their estates by leasing parts of them to farmer-cultivators engaged in planting wet-rice, tobacco, sugarcane, and fruits (e.g., cacao, coconut) and raising livestock.[19] Friar haciendas defined the political geography not just

TABLE 1. Haciendas in Provincia de Tondo and the respective religious orders in charge by the eighteenth century

Hacienda	Religious Order
Hacienda of San Mateo	Augustinian
Hacienda of Navotas	Dominican
Hacienda of Mayjaligue	Jesuit
Hacienda of Marikina	Jesuit
Hacienda of Santa Ana	Jesuit
Hacienda of Mandaluyong	Augustinian
Hacienda of Macati	Jesuit
Hacienda of Pasay	Augustinian
Hacienda of Angono	(lay)
Hacienda of Jalajala	(lay)
Hacienda of Maysapang	Augustinian
Hacienda of Muntinlupa	Augustinian

SOURCE: Roth, *The Friar Estates of the Philippines*, 66; see also Pablo Fernandez, *History of the Church in the Philippines (1521–1898)* (Metro Manila: National Book Store, 1979), 267–72

of Morong/Provincia de Tondo, but also its neighboring Tagalog provinces, such as Bulacan, Cavite, and Laguna.

However, as the friars consolidated and expanded their landholdings, abuses against native peasants increased, leading to internecine revolts in some cases. The earliest of such rebellions occurred in 1603.[20] The most notable happened between February and October 1745, due to drastic changes in property rights and land usurpation. Although the Augustinian-owned Meysapan estate in present-day Biñan, Laguna, was the flashpoint of this rebellion, collective action against the orders soon spread into areas nearer to Manila due to a series of Real Audiencia decisions that were unfavorable to tenants, specifically in San Mateo.[21] While Manila officials crushed the revolt, these same friar lands would give birth to another but much larger uprising a century and a half later.

Between the sixteenth and early nineteenth centuries, Manila domi-nated its suburbs. The suburbs derived their identities from the primate city, as encapsulated by the phrase *"Manila y sus arrabales"* (Manila and its suburbs). The British interlude (1762–1764) signaled the end of an epoch for Spanish Manila,[22] albeit not enough to disturb this urban order. Arguably, Spain's expulsion of the Jesuits from their colonies in 1768 had a more lasting impact on the geography of Manila and its surrounding areas than the British occupation. As a result of the expulsion, the colonial govern-ment confiscated and distributed Jesuit properties to the other orders and nonreligious stakeholders. For instance, the king sold to a mestizo Hacienda de Maysilo, which straddled Tambobong and Caloocan, while Navarrese Don Pedro Galarraga, the Marques de Villamediana, bought from the Crown neighboring Hacienda de Piedad.[23]

The early history of urbanism in Manila and its suburbs and surrounding towns reflected the colonial dominance of religious authorities. In Intramuros the state and the Church were partners in defining the city's morphology; outside the walls, religious authorities, acting as landlords and town administrators, were even more influential. However, massive economic changes in the nineteenth century began to undermine Church supremacy, as urbanization started to spread in the arrabales and beyond. These changes would reverse the core-periphery dynamics between Manila and its suburbs.

Rapid Urbanization in the Nineteenth Century

IN 1830 the colonial government opened the port of Manila to international trade, which ended centuries of Spanish mercantilist control over the capital, notwithstanding de facto liberalized trade taking place in the city as early as the 1790s. A confluence of factors caused this policy shift: the momentum of eighteenth-century Bourbon reforms, the successful Latin

26   A CAPITAL CITY AT THE MARGINS

American anticolonial revolutions, and the end of the Manila–Acapulco galleon trade in 1815. French, American, Dutch, and most especially British capital entered Manila, bringing along merchants, goods, innovations, and ideas. Simultaneously, the city supplied Western countries with cash crops, especially sugar, tobacco, and abaca, sourced from different provinces. It consequently experienced a profound transformation. One important change was its rapid urbanization that enveloped the erstwhile sleepy suburbs. By the late nineteenth century, Manila was bursting at its seams, as its population swelled to almost two hundred thousand due to both natural growth and migration. At this juncture the walled city was no longer the focal point, but the arrabal of Binondo.[24]

Binondo was the epicenter of Manila's nineteenth-century commercial growth, the undisputed central business district. It was the location of the customs house, which was formerly in Intramuros. It thus became the hub for many foreign merchant houses that took part in the cash-crop trade. Their Binondo offices and warehouses attracted other tertiary services. Furthermore, this arrabal was the center of operations for many of the Chinese mestizos, as well as the main recipient of the waves of Chinese migrants, with both groups playing big roles in the new trade regime. Manila's economic pulse was most perceptible at Escolta, Binondo's main thoroughfare. The arrabales of San Nicolas, Quiapo, and the southern tip of Santa Cruz prospered due to their proximity to Binondo.[25]

A new urban morphology reflected these changes. The wealth that Binondo's merchant class generated was in full display in the lavish architecture of its residential and commercial structures. To protect Binondo's prime real estate from a perennial urban risk, authorities drew a *corta fuego* or "fireline"—demarcated by Calle Azcarraga, which marked the boundary between Binondo and Tondo—that divided the northern bank into two zones: the inner one was exclusively for houses built of strong materials, the other was where houses made of nipa and bamboo, which authorities considered fire hazards, could be built.[26] Urban mobility slowly shifted from water-based to land-based transport, in the form of *carruajes* (four-wheeled carriages), *carromatas* (two-wheeled carriages), and the horse-drawn streetcar known as the *tranvia*. Not surprisingly, the tranvia's main terminal was in Binondo at Plaza San Gabriel. Increased vehicular traffic also meant corresponding changes in transport infrastructure, as seen in the expansion of the road network and in bridge construction.[27]

The shift to land transport aided the rise of affluent residential areas in the arrabales, such as Quiapo and San Miguel, and even the town of Santa Ana. Many of the suburban houses featured *bahay-na-bato* architecture, a type of design associated with the gentry.[28] Of course, not all arrabales exhibited a gentrified character. Majority of the arrabales' residents

FROM CATTLE RUSTLERS TO CABARET DANCERS   27

were from the middle- and lower-income classes. Fisherfolk populated Tondo's coastline, while hundreds of peasant families resided in Sampaloc. Nonetheless, urbanization reached the underside of Manila society. Tondo's working class (women included) formed the core of Manila's nascent proletariat that provided Binondo with manual labor. The shift to land-based mobility affected the city's occupation structure, as laborers from nearby rural towns sought nonfarm jobs in the transport sector.[29]

While the central arrabales were rapidly growing and the peripheries were becoming suburban enclaves, Intramuros was slowly declining. Because of the altered economy due to the opening of selected Philippine ports to international trade, the Spanish government slowly lost control over the colonial economy. Henceforth, it was the Spanish private sector, the wealthy natives, and foreign interests—all of them based in the arrabales—who dictated the economic direction of the colony. The walled city's eroding economic importance had geographical ramifications. Intramuros suffered from an exodus of wealthy residents, especially Spanish officials, merchants, and their families, with many resettling in Quiapo, San Miguel, and Santa Ana. Consequently, non-Spaniards began buying houses in the Walled City. The ethnic segregation between a European walled city and an Asian suburb thus no longer held true at this point.[30] Nothing exemplifies this transformation better than Governor-General Rafaél Echagüe's decision in 1863 to move Palacio del Gobernador (Governor's Palace) in Intramuros to Malacañang, his erstwhile summer resort in San Miguel. The phrase "Manila y sus arrabales" therefore lost its currency; toward the end of the century and of Spanish colonial rule itself, "Manila" would become synonymous to the entire urban agglomeration and not just Intramuros. At the start of the twentieth century, Intramuros was a "lifeless capital," according to British observer John Foreman.[31]

Geographical transformations were also apparent in areas outside the arrabales. The pueblos of Provincia de Tondo became one of the most populous provinces in the colony in the early nineteenth century. Its twenty-seven pueblos were home to 215,640 inhabitants (table 2). Political boundaries changed drastically with the creation of Provincia de Manila (map 3). This new entity encompassed Manila and its suburbs alongside neighboring towns that were once under Morong: Caloocan, Las Piñas, Malibay, Marikina, Montalban, Muntinlupa, Navotas, Novaliches, Pateros, Pasig, Parañaque, Pandacan, Pineda, Santa Ana, San Pedro Macati, San Juan del Monte, San Mateo, San Felipe Neri, Taguig, and Tambobong.[32] Foreign capital had an influence on the geography of this area, as one by one non-Spanish interests began buying properties in these distant locations.[33] As the arrabales underwent suburbanization, Provincia de Manila's component towns became not just the capital's periphery but also a convenient location for the city's "socially undesirable" necessities, such as cemeteries. For instance, in 1843 the Chinese Cemetery was built in La Loma, Caloocan, upon the governor-general's orders following a disastrous cholera outbreak in Manila. When another cholera epidemic hit Manila in 1882, a new cemetery was constructed adjacent to the Chinese Cemetery, the La Loma Cemetery.[34] The 1843 decree selected La Loma, situated just outside the capital's northern borders, because of its elevation and hilly topography, which would supposedly allow winds to blow disease-carrying miasma away from the city.[35]

In 1896, the Katipunan-led Philippine Revolution against Spain, broke out in the provinces of Central and Southern Luzon, including Provincia de Manila. The Katipunan, founded by Andrés Bonifacio in Tondo in 1892, enjoyed popular support especially from provinces that had vast friar haciendas, the most visible symbol of colonial oppression. As such, armed revolt spread like wildfire through the pueblos and provinces surrounding Manila, including areas that would become part of Quezon City. The first cry of the revolution took place in Caloocan, referred to as the Cry of Balintawak or Cry of Pugad Lawin. Tala and Diliman had Katipunan chapters. Local lore has it that nearby Bago Bantay (literally "new sentinel") got its name because it served as the

TABLE 2. Population of the pueblos of Provincia de Tondo, circa 1840s

Pueblo	Population
Tondo	17,490
Binondo and San Jose	20,875
Tambobong and Navotas	32,223
Caloacan [Caloocan]	6,122
Santa Cruz	9,759
Quiapo	5,025
Sampaloc	6,870
Mariquina	7,495
San Matheo [San Mateo]	5,505
Antipolo	2,600
Taytay	5,810
Cainta	2,330
Pasig	16,440
San Miguel	3,305
Paco	6,500
Hermita [Ermita]	9,305
Malate and Pasay	9,970
Parañaque and Malibay	10,980
Santa Ana	6,995
Macati	3,715
Pateros	5,950
Taguiig [Taguig]	8,418
Bosoboso	615
Laspiñas [Las Piñas]	3,385
Pandacan	4,622
Muntinlupa	2,210
Payatas	435
Total	215,640*

SOURCE: Jean Mallat, *The Philippines: History, Geography, Customs, Agriculture, Industry and Commerce,* trans. Pura Santillan-Castrence (Manila: National Historical Institute, 1983), 117–18

* However, Mallat's computation of the total is wrong. The correct figure is 214,949.

MAP 3. Provincia de Manila, 1899 (take note of Morong Province to its right)
SOURCE: José Algué, *Atlas de Filipinas: Colección de 30 Mapas* (Washington, DC: Government Printing Office, 1900), Appendix Map No. 9

revolutionaries' favored lookout place to spot incoming Spanish forces from Manila. Significant armed encounters happened here, as well as in Novaliches, San Francisco del Monte, and Pasong Tamo, while Katipuneros encamped in Balara in the early phase of the revolution. These places were also strategic gateways to the mountainous areas of San Mateo and Montalban, both of which had served as havens for anti-Spanish *tulisanes* (bandits) in the past.[36] When the tide turned against the Spaniards, revolutionaries swept through the towns of Provincia de Manila. Despite being engulfed by the flames of revolt, the walled city remained unscathed. To protect Intramuros, in 1898 Governor-General Fernando Primo de Rivera ordered the construction of a protective ring of fifteen military blockhouses in the outlying barrios of Manila's arrabales, especially in Sampaloc.[37] These spaces just outside Manila were strategic

30   A CAPITAL CITY AT THE MARGINS

as these were at a distance from state forces based in the capital, but near enough to conduct military operations to disrupt the city.

Two years after the revolution began, the US would be involved in the hostilities due to its war with Spain. However, following a mock battle between the two Western forces, and to the revolutionaries' dismay, Spain surrendered Manila to the Americans, despite the earlier declaration of Philippine independence on 12 June under President Emilio Aguinaldo's leadership. The turnover happened on 13 August 1898, marking the beginning of decades of US control over the city. Given Manila's status, Aguinaldo's revolutionary government had to choose a different site for its capital: Malolos, Bulacan. On 10 December, Spain sold the islands to the US under the Treaty of Paris. Although the Philippine-American War started in the outskirts of Manila on 4 February 1899, with major battles happening in nearby towns, including areas now part of Quezon City, Americans maintained control over the capital city of their new colony.[38]

Manila and American Urbanism

AMERICAN-COLONIAL MANILA began under a military government in 1898 and reverted to civilian rule in 1901 under the Municipal Board and Mayor Arsenio Cruz Herrera, marking the first time a Filipino occupied the city's highest position.[39] However, despite a Filipino governing as mayor, Americans still called the shots in the capital and were the main driving force in Manila's urbanization in the early colonial years.

US colonialism amplified rather than altered late-Spanish Manila's urban patterns. The economic dominance of the northern arrabales, led by Binondo, continued. The city's role as a source of cash crops remained, with the increased trade volume between US and its colony the only substantial change. Expectedly, American merchants and colonial officials were first attracted to Binondo's commercial areas.[40] The American colonial government also institutionalized Intramuros's decline through the 1901 charter of Manila (Act 183), which turned the Walled City into just one of the twelve city districts, alongside its former arrabales. It "made official what had long been tacit: that the City of Manila was not Intramuros alone but also all the arrabales."[41] Within Manila's newly legislated geobody the Walled City no longer held an exalted position.[42]

The 1901 charter gave Manila new borderlines, a by-product of the revolutionary period (map 4). In delineating the city boundary along Sampaloc the Americans drew a straight line from one end to another that corresponded to Primo de Rivera's defensive line of blockhouses used by both Spain and the US against Filipino revolutionaries, a cartographic detail that present-day Manila still exhibits. In effect Sampaloc lost San Francisco del Monte, Tatalon, and Diliman, places which comprised a huge chunk of its

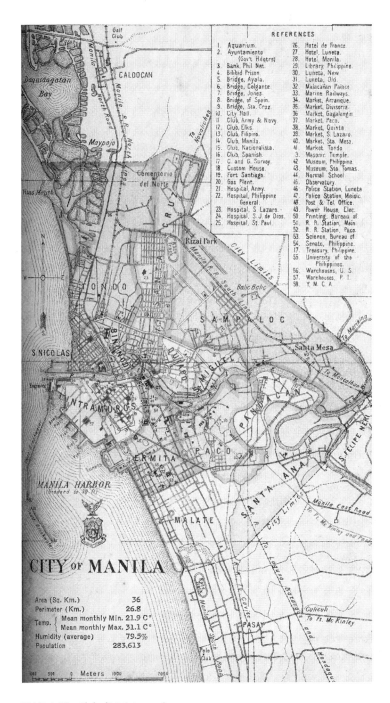

MAP 4. Manila's districts, 1918

SOURCE: Census Office of the Philippine Islands, *Census of the Philippine Islands, 1918*, vol. 1, 146

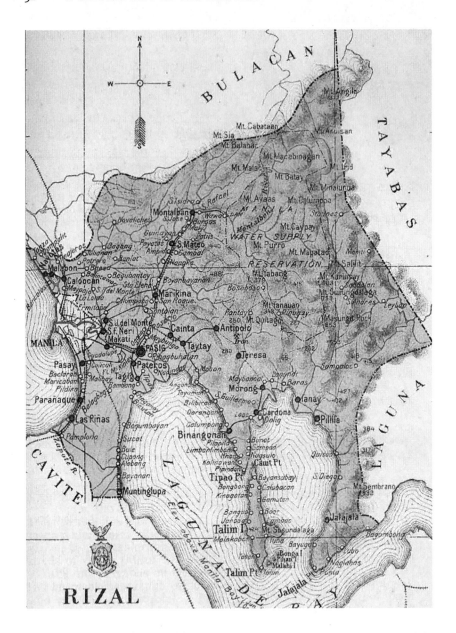

MAP 5. Rizal province, 1918

SOURCE: Census Office of the Philippine Islands, *Census of the Philippine Islands 1918*, vol. 1, 240

FROM CATTLE RUSTLERS TO CABARET DANCERS 33

former territory.[43] A few months prior to the enactment of the charter, the colonial government separated the capital city from Provincia de Manila, whose territory reverted more or less to the previous geographical scope of Morong. That same year the province was named Rizal (map 5) in honor of the country's foremost nationalist, José Rizal, who was executed by the Spaniards in 1896.

Although many Americans initially resided in Intramuros, they eventually moved to the suburbs. The factors behind this exodus were similar to what was observed in the late nineteenth century: the Americans' perception of urban decline in the Walled City and the appeal of the suburbs. Consequently, human activity in Intramuros during the American colonial period was limited to religious, educational, and administrative purposes: "Extramural development left the Walled City to the friars, to students and to a few aristocratic families clinging to the past. Slowly, it became a city of dormitories and boarding houses."[44] Even the Spaniards who remained in Manila after 1898 preferred living outside the Walled City.

Intramuros's deterioration led a number of American and Filipino officials to call for the demolition of its walls and moat. Although a complete demolition never happened due to the intervention of Americans interested in preserving built heritage,[45] city officials tore down portions of the wall to create larger entrance and exit gates and converted the moat into a park. For them, the walls and the moat hindered Manila's development and had to give way to improve traffic conditions and avoid health hazards arising from stagnant water. Hence, one must also see the potency of these acts of physical engineering as instruments of social engineering. Intramuros reordered signified the Americans supplanting the old order. They had rendered obsolete and reduced into mere curiosities this tangible reminder of Spanish rule that was once a boundary separating the colonizer from the colonized. The breaches in the walls showed who the new masters were.[46]

The Americans' perception of urban decay was not limited to Intramuros but applied to the city in general. It moved them to envision a new Manila, whose vitality Spanish autocracy had supposedly drained for three centuries. To make Manila a fitting capital city, they turned to urban planning. In 1905 famed American architect Daniel Burnham completed the blueprint for this "imperial makeover." Anchored in the City Beautiful tradition from the US, the Burnham plan used neoclassical architecture to define not just the aesthetics but also the ideology and pragmatism of American urbanism, as it aimed to convey a democratic order under a benevolent colonial rule to appease Filipinos. The extensive use of public parks and open spaces signified this notion of democratization through urban design.[47]

Aside from the Burnham plan, Americans brought other important urban innovations into Manila. They introduced, for example, motorized urban transportation. The arrival of the electric streetcar and the automobile in the first decade of the twentieth century led to further transformations, such as in the altered street system of the city and the expansion of suburbanization. The electric streetcar replaced the horse-drawn tranvia and was under the management of the Manila Electric Railroad and Light Company (Meralco). Its routes extended to Manila's neighboring towns like Pasay and San Juan, encouraging many to live outside the city. Its competitive fares and geographical reach made the Meralco streetcar, which was also called tranvia, a hit with the masses. Though not as popularly consumed as the electric streetcar, automobiles also had the same effect on suburbanization. In the 1930s, taxis and buses roamed the city streets. Improved land transport benefited both Americans and well-to-do Filipinos who chose to live in the peripheries, either because of affordable rents or their desire to escape the bustle in the downtown, while maintaining access to the central districts.[48]

If transport motorization was a pull factor in suburbanization, the high rents and real estate values in downtown Manila provided the push factor.[49] If in 1901 the lots around Plaza Goiti, Meralco's transport hub in Santa Cruz, were worth PHP 50 per square meter, two decades later, the going rate was PHP 500 at the minimum.[50] By the late 1930s, even the once idyllic suburbs were prime real estate. In 1938 the value of commercial land in Binondo and Santa Cruz was PHP 21,725,760 and PHP 14,544,320, respectively, while their urban residential land was only worth PHP 1,488,640 and PHP 5,370,460. In contrast, Ermita's commercial land was worth PHP 800,130, whereas its urban residential land was valued at PHP 7,472,500. Similarly, Malate's commercial land was valued at PHP 318,180, paling in comparison with that of its urban residential land, PHP 8,875,610.[51] Rapid urban growth in the central districts also meant traffic jams and noise pollution—sources of nuisance for American and Filipino middle classes and elites—that only worsened through the decades.[52]

Another explanation for the suburban push was the perceived urban blight in Manila, not just in Intramuros but also in the business districts. Americans often complained about the downtown area's overcrowded conditions from the early colonial period up to the eve of the Pacific War.[53] Personifying this biased perception were Manila's squatters and slum dwellers.[54]

During the Spanish colonial period, ordinances to regulate urban space forced Manila's poor households to cluster in specific areas in the arrabales, thereby creating what were arguably the first slums in the history of the city, such as those in Tondo. Most notable of these ordinances was the corta fuego, which pushed "fire-hazard" nipa huts, the traditional domicile of income-poor families, away from the downtown. The jobs generated by trade also attracted rural migrants to settle in makeshift and illegal settlements in Tondo's swampy areas.[55] In the American colonial period, the state did not

FROM CATTLE RUSTLERS TO CABARET DANCERS   35

only maintain this "rationalization" of urban space, but also further marginalized the urban poor. A huge contributor to their plight under US colonialism was the tagging of slums as disease-dealing places. Colonial anxiety toward disease made the indigent neighborhoods, which were often flooded, densely packed, poorly lit, and without adequate basic utilities, a convenient scapegoat. Authorities blamed slums during epidemics, even resorting to the burning down of whole communities to supposedly contain the disease.[56]

Manila's informal settlements were not just marginalized spaces; they were the unwanted twin of the city's gentrified suburbs. These two modes of urban living grew together and, in fact, depended on each other. Ostensibly, Manila's underbelly was an affront to the elite and the embodiment of their fears, given that such settlements sprouted in the once-prosperous districts like Intramuros and Santa Cruz.[57] Journalist Leon Ty vividly described the squalor and indignity that informal settlers endured: "Not the rice-fields of Central Luzon. But the slums of Manila, are the hardest on the tenants . . . veritable coops and dog-houses, dark and dank *accesorias* where a goodly portion of the city's Great Unwashed live, suffer and die." At the same time, Manila's urban growth was predicated upon the slums ensuring the social reproduction of cheap labor for the ports, warehouses, and the informal economy. In the slums of Intramuros, monthly rent for a room without light (water was free of charge) was PHP 12, although one could have rooms for two or even three times less than that rate in other parts of Manila.[58]

Slums were all over the city, from proletarian Tondo to gentrified Ermita.[59] Governors-general in the 1920s and 1930s and the Filipino-led Commonwealth government saw the seriousness of the issue and implemented relevant programs. They established housing committees and constructed "model houses" for low-income families.[60] However, these solutions, as exemplified by the *barrio obreros* (laborers' villages) in Avenida de Rizal (Rizal Avenue), Santa Cruz, and in Barrio Vitas, Tondo, failed miserably owing to the lack of institutional support to aid slum dwellers in securing ownership of their houses and lots.[61] In the flagship Barrio Obrero project in Tondo, occupants refused to pay the PHP 3.12 monthly rent when the city government declined their request to make the said rate inclusive of their water bill. Furthermore, even after the completion of the installments to acquire the house, occupants still had to pay a monthly PHP 1 rental for the lot. It did not help that the Municipal Board felt that the housing project was eating up a big chunk of the city budget.[62]

Prewar Manila's Three Suburban Zones

ALTHOUGH THE INNOVATIONS, ideologies, and biases that undergirded Manila's suburbanization were colonial in provenance, middle- and upper-class Filipinos were the main consumers of the lifestyle it engendered. They were

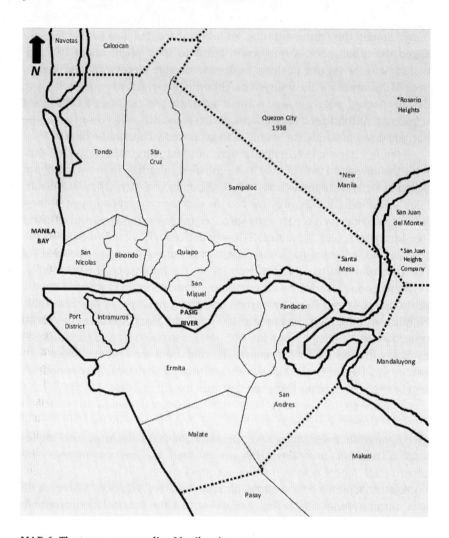

MAP 6. The towns surrounding Manila, circa 1939

as important as the colonizers in remaking the suburban towns surrounding Manila during the prewar period. This peripheral zone sustained the capital in two ways: as spaces of production (e.g., supplying Manila with essential produce, especially fruits and vegetables)[63] and as spaces of consumption (e.g., residential areas that maintained demand for Manila's consumer goods). The succeeding paragraphs elaborate on the latter.

Three zones defined the spatial extent of prewar Manila's suburbs (map 6). One was to the south and covered towns like Pasay and Makati (formerly San Pedro Macati). Another was to the east and included Mandaluyong (formerly San Felipe Neri), San Juan, and Pasig. A third one was the sprawl to the north, encompassing Caloocan, Navotas, and Malabon (formerly Tambobong), an economic powerhouse in the late nineteenth century known for its industries (e.g., textile mills, aquaculture, and cigar factories), transportation facilities, and proximity to Manila.[64]

Suburbanization south of Manila was an offshoot of the elite residential boom that began in Ermita, Paco, and Malate as early as 1905, with Americans leading the way. Coastal Ermita and Malate became the site of many upper-class homes, usually built along Manila Bay. Hence, the south bank developed a reputation as a "respectable" residential area. Contemporary accounts described Ermita as "occupied largely by Americans and the well-to-do classes," and to a lesser extent the same was true for Malate at the start of the century.[65] The Burnham plan also favored the said districts, especially Ermita, and thus reinforced the American character of these areas.[66] Although Burnham's vision for Ermita was never fully implemented, the presence of important government buildings (many in neoclassical style), such as the Department of Agriculture and Department of Finance buildings, the headquarters of the Philippine Post Office, and the UP campus, made this district the spatial embodiment of democracy for Manila Americans.[67] Although not along the coast of Manila Bay, Paco was another location of suburban development south of the Pasig River. Beginning in 1903, Paco's western side that was adjacent to Ermita developed into a residential subdivision under entrepreneur H. M. Jones. However, the subdivision, with lots selling for PHP 2 per square meter, catered more to the middle class.[68] As more Americans resided in these three districts, their real estate values soared.[69] This trend continued into the late 1930s, and its momentum carried it further southward to Pasay's beachfront.[70] By 1939 Pasay had more Americans than the entire downtown area (table 3).

A significant number of Americans also chose to reside in the eastern suburbs such as Sampaloc and Santa Ana. In particular, Santa Mesa, a barrio in Sampaloc, became "a favorite residence spot for many of the American and foreign residents."[71] In the "eastern peripheries" certain perceptions about the relationship between health and geography aided the creation of middle- and upper-class residential subdivisions, perceptions that friars of the early Spanish colonial period also had.[72] The hilly topography, cool microclimate, and efficient drainage supposedly made the eastern suburbs a salubrious site and ideal for residential developments that catered to health-conscious households. Similar to its regard to the southern suburbs, the Burnham plan paid special attention to the eastern peripheries and put premium on its real estate value.[73]

Outside Manila, the eastern towns of San Juan del Monte and Mandaluyong exhibited the same sociospatial dynamic: their physical geography attracted elite suburban residential investments. These towns became the site of

Table 3. Population data in Manila and adjacent municipalities, 1903, 1918, and 1939

District	1903			1918			1939		
	Total	Filipino	American	Total	Filipino	American	Total	Filipino	American
Binondo	16,657	9,069	354	15,696	9,407	46	20,281	8,107	13
Ermita	12,246	10,549	747	14,371	11,785	1,170	18,554	15,809	869
Intramuros	11,460	8,296	1,046	13,027	11,872	165	21,352	19,836	102
Malate	8,855	8,414	233	14,663	13,608	535	54,487	50,524	1,049
Paco	6,691	6,232	142	14,277	13,501	163	30,830	29,076	169
Pandacan	2,990	2,935	3	5,215	5,155	5	11,242	11,097	7
Quiapo	11,139	10,307	210	14,128	12,570	51	21,377	18,871	80
Sampaloc	18,772	17,670	225	35,346	33,913	250	111,995	108,013	334
San Nicolas	29,055	21,346	286	25,972	20,823	29	35,330	24,585	7
Santa Ana	3,255	3,171	10	5,950	5,774	46	25,100	24,397	202
Sta. Cruz	35,030	30,313	498	46,518	43,106	221	94,884	83,997	191
Tondo	39,043	37,926	123	71,905	70,361	97	160,958	155,624	59
Vessels	15,901	15,396	171	4,289	3,781	102	4,387	3,791	49
Total (Manila)	219,928	190,437	4,300	285,306	259,437	2,916	623,492	564,388	3,191

Caloocan	6,291	6,167	57	19,551	19,418	37	38,792	37,873	100
Makati	2,700	2,694	2	12,612	12,312	172	33,945	32,943	73
Malabon	20,136	19,942	5	21,695	21,590	1	33,268	32,935	16
Mandaluyong	4,349	4,330	3	5,806	5,777	1	18,192	17,903	45
Navotas	11,688	11,597	0	13,454	13,400	2	20,861	20,692	0
Novaliches[a]	1,556	1,556	0	-	-	-	-	-	-
Pasay	6,542	6,393	58	18,697	18,263	163	54,954	51,876	1,017
San Juan	1,455	1,422	24	6,172	6,140	6	18,811	17,716	277

Sources: US Bureau of the Census, *Census of the Philippines. 1903*, vol. II, 130, 262–263, 293–294; Philippine Islands Census Office, *Census of the Philippine Islands*, vol. II, 99, 106, 353, 377; Philippine Commission of the Census, *Census of the Philippines, 1939*, vol. I, part 3, 3–4

[a] Previously a pueblo in Bulacan province, Novaliches (including Hacienda de Tala and Piedad, as well as parts of Hacienda de Malinta) became part of Rizal province at the start of American colonial rule (Veneracion, *Kasaysayan ng Bulakan*, 20, 136). Franco-Calairo and Calairo state that it was a separate pueblo beginning in 1855, but did not indicate when that status ended (*Ang Kasaysayan ng Novaliches*, 35). But clearly, sometime between the 1903 and 1918 censuses, Novaliches became part of Caloocan.

middle-class and upper-class real estate developments, such as the Del Monte Subdivision in San Francisco del Monte, New Manila, Santa Mesa Heights, San Juan Heights, San Juan Heights Addition (later on known as simply Addition Hills), Cubao Heights, and Rosario Heights.[74] The marketing ploy of these subdivisions emphasized the elite character and purported healthful living conditions of the area. For example, the developers of Addition Hills boasted that in 1936 they had already sold 206,142 square meters of real estate to Americans and foreigners and that more "prominent people" bought houses in this subdivision. The advertising taglines for Addition Hills conveyed packaged salubrity: "Away from the heat, noise, congestion, and floods of the City."[75] Gregorio Araneta, Inc. declared that the chief advantage of its flagship subdivision, Santa Mesa Heights, was that it was "OUTSIDE MANILA YET WITHIN ITS RADIUS."[76] Upon closer analysis, this pattern of suburbanization shows how the interaction between perception of geography and market forces perpetuated social inequality. As elites set their eyes on more physically desirable land, the increased demand drove prices further up, leaving the poor to divide among themselves marginal urban spaces.

In contrast to the suburbanization east and south of Manila, the residential boom in Caloocan, Navotas, and Malabon catered more to low-income households. While Pasay's rise was linked to gentrified Ermita and Malate, the urban sprawl at the opposite end of the capital was tied to the population growth of Tondo, Manila's working-class district. The juxtaposition between the north and south districts was not lost among the Americans and became a usual feature in American travel writings.[77]

The impact of suburbanization manifested in various aspects of prewar urban life in Manila. Aside from demographic growth, economic indicators evinced this phenomenon. By the end of the 1930s in the towns of Rizal province, "real estate values have risen in value and provided an ideal and sufficient space for Manila's expanding population."[78] Gradually, important institutions—schools, social clubs, and the like—began relocating outside Manila, and companies extended their services to the neighboring towns.[79] Perhaps the most important among these services was transportation, for it was both a reflection and an enabler of suburbanization that allowed the middle and upper classes to minimize the "friction of space."[80] Especially in the southern and eastern suburbs, the electric streetcar and the automobile helped create a crabgrass frontier similar to that of contemporaneous US suburbs.[81] The suburban push of the early twentieth century was the result of a geographically expanding Manila (map 7), an irreversible turn to which politicians had to respond.

MAP 7. Manila and suburbs, 1932; note the formation of zones of growth outside Manila's borders

SOURCE: John Bach, "Manila and Suburbs," 1932 (Manila: John Bach, 1932), JRHP Box 26, Folder 18

42   A CAPITAL CITY AT THE MARGINS

The Emergence of a De Facto Greater Manila

AS SUBURBANIZATION TRESPASSED the political boundaries of Manila's adjacent towns and stepped into Pasay, San Juan, among others, it became more
evident that the capital had outgrown its borders—borders that were only a
few decades old. A "greater Manila" was emerging.[82]

American governors-general from the 1920s to the 1930s saw the need
to expand Manila's territory. In 1920 Governor-General Francis Burton
Harrison asked the legislature

> to enlarge the boundaries of the City of Manila, so that the existing provincial popu-
> lation along the city borders may be granted the privileges and advantages of Manila
> government, and also so that the people of Manila may be at once relieved of the
> perennial problems caused by the existence on the City limits of certain centers of
> low life and disorder.[83]

Despite being a critic of Harrison, Governor-General Leonard Wood
echoed his predecessor's sentiments. Wood even specified Pasay as an area
for annexation to maintain law and order in the capital.[84] Similarly, Eugene
A. Gilmore and Dwight F. Davis urged legislators to respond to this issue.
Gilmore identified possible models in contemporary developments in metropolitan administration in the US and other countries, while Davis suggested
that the Burnham plan be implemented in the capital's satellite towns.[85]

The insistent calls of governors-general betrayed the consistent inaction of the legislature and city government on this matter. Despite the
proactive response of some Filipino officials, most of them were not as
enthusiastic. Responding to calls for extending Manila's city limits, Mayor
Ramón Fernandez asserted in 1920 that the proposal had to wait because
the city still had vacant areas that needed to be populated first.[86] In 1935
Philippine officials, led by a committee that Gilmore formed to draft a bill
to extend Manila's boundaries, discussed a possible merger to fuse certain
towns in Rizal province with Manila. The proposal included Caloocan, San
Juan, Mandaluyong, Makati, Parañaque, and portions of Las Piñas and Pasay.
The bill passed the Senate but floundered in the Lower House.[87]

The legislators' indifference, if not outright hostility,[88] to the idea of a
greater Manila was understandable because residents of the affected towns
detested it. Strong opposition came especially from the business sector,
both American and Filipino. The American Chamber of Commerce (ACC)
asserted that only the people of the affected towns had the right to bolt
out of Rizal province, implying that state-directed annexation was inher-
ently undemocratic.[89]

The government floated another similar proposal in 1937, but the reaction among suburban residents was no different. That year Manila's officials

and President Quezon agreed on the move to place under Manila's jurisdiction certain parts of Rizal province, such as Caloocan, San Juan del Monte, Rosario Heights, Mandaluyong, Makati, and San Francisco del Monte, among others. Alpheus Williams, Quezon's technical assistant, drafted a bill creating a "Greater Manila" in the following year. The bill sought to enlarge Manila's land territory fivefold to include Pasay, Makati, San Juan, Mandaluyong, San Francisco del Monte, Navotas and Malabon, and parts of Caloocan, Pasig, Parañaque, Taguig, and Pateros. Most of the affected real estate developers and brokers protested, including the ACC.[90] Supported by their respective mayors and by the provincial board, Rizal citizens resisted the plan. For instance, "97 per cent of the residents in Caloocan" were against the merger. Their opposition was due to the projected increase in taxes, a sentiment shared by people in Pasay, Mandaluyong, and San Juan. The Pasay Municipal Council even passed a resolution against the annexation plan. The council reminded Quezon that a few years ago he opposed the Laurel bill that sought the fusion of Manila and Pasay, as he "declared that the plan would overburden the Pasay residents financially." The San Juan municipal council argued in a resolution: "The people of Manila are paying 1½ per cent a year for realty tax while San Juan residents pay only 7/8 of 1 per cent per annum. If San Juan is not favored by nature and circumstances to be a business place, the people shall, in the event of annexation, pay 100 per cent more for realty tax." San Juan residents also feared that being part of a large city would place them at the mercy of an unwieldy bureaucracy unlike in a small town where governance was presumably more personal and efficient. What these local officials wanted was greater autonomy for their towns and not a "greater Manila."[91]

Another obstacle to realizing "greater Manila" was the influence of oppositionist politicians. The capital and the suburbs, especially Caloocan, were bailiwicks of Partido Democrata, which often clashed with the dominant Partido Nacionalista.[92] The most renowned Democrata figure, Juan Sumulong, was a Rizal native who represented his province in the legislature and a staunch critic of Quezon, the topmost Nacionalista.

One major reason why Rizal politicians fought annexation was that any major realignments in the provincial geobody would have diminished their political power. The province had had a history of territorial loss in the early twentieth century, beginning in 1903 when Philippine Commission Act No. 942 reduced the number of its municipalities from thirty-two to fifteen. Commerce and Agriculture Secretary Eulogio Rodriguez and his son, Rizal Governor Eulogio Rodriguez, Jr., feared that Manila's expansion into the populous and prosperous suburban towns would have reduced Rizal to a second-class province. Moreover, the towns in question were vast sources of tax revenue and election votes.[93] Santiago Artiaga, Manila's city engineer

44   A CAPITAL CITY AT THE MARGINS

in the 1930s, estimated that Manila's annexation of suburban towns would have translated to an additional Assemblyman for Manila in Congress and a loss of two for Rizal province.[94]

The Rodriguezes tried to strike a compromise with Quezon to push through with the merger but with Manila becoming part of Rizal.[95] The compromise, however, never materialized. As the next chapter will tackle, Quezon was rather stubborn in his objective to remap Manila and its adjacent towns.

Domesticating and Democratizing the Suburbs

THE SUBURBS' GROWTH was so tremendous that it had serious political ramifications. However, suburbanization was also a process that required decades of gestation. Real estate expert P. D. Carman had an interesting hypothesis about this so-called delay in suburban development despite American presence in Manila as early as 1898:

> It will be remembered that as late as 1904 there had still been more or less guerrilla warfare in the provinces. *Tulisanes*, or robber bands, were quite prevalent and there was consequently a feeling of insecurity which had its effect in preventing Manila's population from spreading out very far away from the protection afforded in the City.[96]

Based on Carman's analysis and as the succeeding paragraphs will show, for the colonial elite, suburbanization in Manila was a twin process of domestication and democratization. At the beginning of American colonial rule, the territories surrounding Manila were hostile spaces for the new colonizers. In fact, the spark that ignited the Philippine–American War, Private William Grayson's shooting of a Filipino sentry, happened at the outskirts of Manila in Santa Mesa while both were patrolling their own side of the border that was agreed upon by the two forces. The war's first armed encounters took place in the adjacent and nearby municipalities: Caloocan (especially La Loma), San Juan, San Francisco del Monte, Balintawak, Ugong, Novaliches, and San Mateo. And even after Filipino revolutionaries shifted to guerrilla warfare on 13 November 1899, places like Diliman, Novaliches, and San Francisco del Monte, barrios that were gateways to the Sierra Madre mountains, still saw sporadic attacks from Filipino revolutionaries.[97]

Despite the proclamation of the formal end of hostilities in 1902, much of the suburbs remained *terra incognita* for the colonizers due to the presence of guerrillas, many of them dismissed as *ladrones* (robbers). One of the most well-known guerrillas was Macario Sakay, who continued to fight Americans after 1902. What sustained his struggle for years was the support from townsfolk in areas where he operated, particularly the towns of Rizal province. Philippine Constabulary (PC) Chief Harry Bandholtz

FROM CATTLE RUSTLERS TO CABARET DANCERS   45

acknowledged that Sakay had "too many warm sympathizers in Rizal."[98] Meanwhile, *remontados*, or dissident natives who resisted colonialism by retreating to the uplands, roamed the mountainous areas near Manila, such as Novaliches, San Mateo, and Montalban, places that were known for harboring such elusive figures during the Spanish colonial period. One of Bonifacio's close associates during the Revolution was a remontado named Laóng, who was "said to have 'attracted, catechized, and initiated out-of-hand' many peasants in the fields surrounding Balintawak."[99]

Understandably, Manila Americans felt threatened, as though the capital was an island in an ocean of revolt. The city's porous borders alarmed them considerably because of "numerous" raids by ladrones (or probably guerrillas dismissed as ladrones), who were "able to defy the law officers of the city of Manila simply by crossing over the city limits." The colonial government even considered bringing adjacent towns within Manila's police jurisdiction to address this problem.[100] Suburbanization was therefore impossible without the Americans' "domestication" of these hostile spaces surrounding Manila through anti-guerrilla campaigns aided by Filipino elites.

After domestication comes democratization, which meant for the colonial elite the rule of the "jungle" being subsumed under the modernizing ways of the state. As late as 1937 around 2,650 remontados resided in Rizal province, 602 of which lived in Montalban.[101] Aside from the "savage" ladrones and remontados, Americans also had to contend with Spanish colonialism's feudal remnants, the friar haciendas. These estates were a sensitive political matter because they were an important factor behind the revolutionary fervor that Americans had to extinguish.

> The location of many friar estates in the environs of the capital city of Manila and in close proximity to the sources of liberal and revolutionary ideologies emanating from it was a major reason for the significant role the estates assumed in the revolts against Spain in 1896 and 1898. Had they been situated in some outlying provinces, their position in Philippine history would have probably been quite different—curiosities rather than symbols (and the reality) of monastic power.[102]

Resolving the friar lands issue was thus a priority for the colonial state at the outset. William Howard Taft, the first American civilian governor-general, led the way in finding legal remedies to this tough balancing act. On the one hand, he did not want to antagonize Filipino elites who demanded the expropriation of these estates. On the other hand, he could not undermine the Treaty of Paris, which recognized the property rights of the Catholic Church after the US's purchase of the archipelago. After three years of investigations, dialogues with the Vatican, and negotiations

46   A CAPITAL CITY AT THE MARGINS

with the orders regarding the valuation of the estates, the colonial state passed the Friar Lands Act in 1902. The law sought to democratize access to land (i.e., giving the Church just compensation for haciendas that the state would purchase), then subdividing these estates and distributing parcels to rightful occupants and tenant-farmers who would pay the government in installments at an affordable rate.[103]

However, Taft's initiative "was not a lasting success"[104] for various reasons. First, not all friar estates were part of the purchase because the religious orders wanted to retain some of their properties while the government's meager budget limited them to buy only those perceived to be sites of agrarian unrest. Furthermore, the scope of the purchase was already severely constrained even prior to the negotiations because the friars had begun selling their haciendas to corporate entities that they actually controlled or influenced.[105] For example, on 6 February 1893 the Augustinians formed La Compañía Agricola de Ultramar in Madrid. That same year they sold the San Francisco de Malabon (Cavite), Tala, Malinta, and Piedad estates to the company. The Dominicans employed a similar tactic in 1900 by selling their landholdings to the Philippine Sugar Estates Development Company, a corporation in which they were major stock-holders. Through legal proceedings, they also managed to retain control of the Hacienda de San Juan del Monte, which they sold to Eusebio Orense and Florencio Gonzalez in 1919 for PHP 0.30 per square meter (for a total of PHP 360,000). Orense and Gonzalez eventually struck a profitable deal with the San Juan Heights Development Company, which bought the property for PHP 0.50 per square meter. American businessmen led by H. W. Elser founded the company, which developed residential subdivisions outside Manila: San Juan Heights, Rosario Heights, Cubao Heights, and Addition Hills.[106] Moreover, friars tended to underreport the acreage of their landholdings and sell the difference to a third party, such as what the Augustinians did with Hacienda de Mandaloya. As for the peasant-beneficiaries of the friar land redistribution, many of them could not settle their financial obliga-tions due to various factors, mainly the lack of extension services. The patchy record of the Friar Lands Act was evident in the areas surrounding Manila where the peasants' plight remained unchanged.[107] Most important, the main intention behind the Friar Lands Act was not social justice nor emancipation for landless tenants but to extinguish anticolonial revolts. Thus, it was no coincidence that many among the principalía who fought the Americans became landlords or estate administrators afterwards, such as Mariano Trias, Arturo Dancel, and Aguinaldo.

Many of these affected haciendas comprise Quezon City's present-day territory (map 8). On the surface these spaces evoked the success of land redistribution under the Americans because none of them were under friar

FROM CATTLE RUSTLERS TO CABARET DANCERS 47

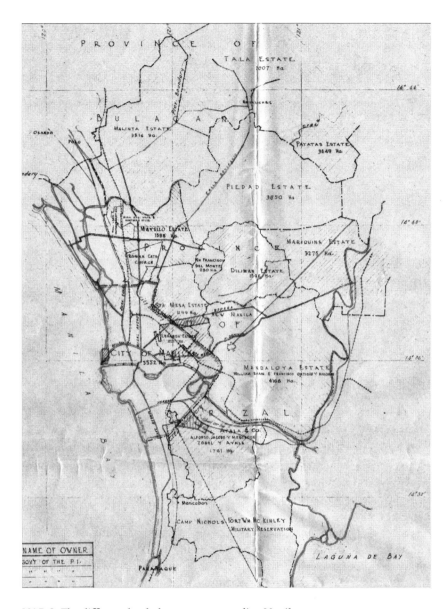

MAP 8. The different landed estates surrounding Manila, 1935

SOURCE: "Map of the City of Manila and Surroundings Showing the Different Estates and Reservations, June 6, 1935," JRHP Box 15, Folder 16

48   A CAPITAL CITY AT THE MARGINS

ownership by the 1930s (table 4). However, upon deeper analysis, they revealed the bankruptcy of colonial land reform, which was undermined by moneyed interests, both Filipino and American.

TABLE 4. List of land estates (as of 1935) that would eventually be absorbed, either partially or wholly, by Quezon City

Name of Estate	Area (has.)	Landowner (1935)
Tala	7,007	Philippine government
Malinta	3,516	Philippine government
Piedad	3,850	Philippine government
Payatas	3,649	Philippine government
San Francisco del Monte	230	San Francisco del Monte, Inc.
Maysilo	1,588	Heirs of Gonzalo Tuason y Patiño
Santa Mesa	1,199	Heirs of Mariano Tuason y de la Paz, et al
Diliman	1,596	Heirs of Mariano Tuason y de la Paz, et al
Mariquina	3,275	Heirs of Mariano Tuason y de la Paz, et al
Mandaloya	4,168	William Shaw and Francisco Ortigas y Barcinas

SOURCE: Based on "Map of the City of Manila and Surroundings Showing the Different Estates and Reservations, June 6, 1935," JRHP Box 15, Folder 16

Hacienda de Mandaloya exemplified elite circumvention of land redistribution. At the start of US colonialism, the Augustinian-controlled Sociedad Agricola de Ultramar owned the estate. Perhaps due to its ostensibly corporate character, the hacienda evaded state purchase. Then, in 1918 prominent Filipino lawyer Francisco Ortigas bought it "for a song— eleven centavos a square metre." He established Ortigas and Company to manage the property and gave shares to close associates, including Quezon and Vicente Madrigal.[108] Ortigas had an unfair advantage in acquiring the estate because in 1904 colonial officials designated his law firm, Del Pan, Ortigas & Fisher, as "special attorneys for the Government to investigate and report on all questions of title arising in connection with the Government's purchase of the Friar Lands." He had also represented the Augustinians in a case prior to this purchase.[109]

The San Francisco del Monte Estate's case mirrored that of Mandaloya. Evading state expropriation, the hacienda became a private corporation under the name of San Francisco del Monte Subdivision. A certain John Gordon purchased it from the Franciscans in 1924 and turned it into a middle-class residential area. The first subdivided lots were sold in

December 1925.[110] The subdivision attracted buyers so quickly that by the 1930s its residents were clamoring for the separation of San Francisco del Monte from San Juan as an independent municipality. They petitioned the Rizal governor, citing San Francisco del Monte's population growth, occupied as it was by "Beautiful residential homes owned by Manila government officials and businessmen."[111]

Rather than tenant-farmers, the colonial elite benefited the most from changes in land ownership in the suburbs. One by one, politicians and prominent personalities bought houses and lots in these areas, further reinforcing the elite character of the said places. The Hacienda de Magdalena, which straddled San Juan and Marikina and is more popularly known as New Manila in present-day Quezon City, exhibited this trend. The estate was incorporated on 28 March 1922, with Doña Magdalena Ysmael Hemady, K. H. Hemady, Felipe Ysmael, Halim Ysmael, and Sidney C. Schwartzkopf as the directors. The Ysmaels (Ismail) and Hemadys "trace their roots to Lebanon," with the former a prominent family connected to the American pharmaceutical company Winthrop-Stearns in the Philippines.[112] The estate catered mainly to upper-class buyers, and therefore was not as populated as the other suburban estates. Maur Aquino Lichauco, daughter of prominent politician Benigno Aquino Sr., reminisced about her family's prewar residence in Broadway Avenue in Magdalena Estate and the exclusivity of that place: "I think there were only about five or six houses. And our nearest neighbor then was Felix Manalo, and then after Felix Manalo it was already Doña Magdalena Hemady's house. She was actually the owner of that subdivision. And I remember my father and Doña Magdalena, they're very good friends."[113] The Aquinos' neighbors belonged to society's upper crust. One of them was Doña Narcisa "Sisang" de Leon, who would establish LVN Films, one of the most successful movie studios in Philippine history. Manalo, founder of the influential Iglesia ni Cristo church, even had a stable of horses in his New Manila home.[114] When Governor-General Frank Murphy had to vacate Malacañang in 1935 to give way to incoming Commonwealth President Manuel Quezon, the Hemadys offered him "without cost [an] entire block about six acres in New Manila" in a site that he could select for his new official residence as US High Commissioner.[115]

Of course, not all estates escaped state expropriation. Nonetheless, those landholdings that the government secured were not entirely free from anomalies. Hacienda de Piedad, which straddled the area roughly between Novaliches and Diliman, illustrated this point. This estate was once owned by the Augustinians, who sold it to the Compañía Agricola de Ultramar on 7 February 1893.[116] The state purchased and subdivided it for redistribution through lease agreements. However, one of the lessees, Arturo Dancel, obtained 1,452 acres, which violated the Friar Lands Act provision regarding

50   A CAPITAL CITY AT THE MARGINS

maximum acreage allowed for lessees. Dancel, a former revolutionary leader, a delegate in Aguinaldo's revolutionary congress, and member of the pro-US Partido Federal, eventually became Rizal governor.[117] In neighboring Hacienda de Payatas, which occupies the northeastern parts of present-day Quezon City, foreigners rather than ordinary natives profited from the land. For much of the American period, the land was owned by the Payatas Estate Company, a Japanese-managed business that had poor relations with its tenants. The situation was so appalling that Montalban, San Mateo, and Marikina residents organized themselves to help tenants and requested the government to purchase the land from the company. The municipal governments of Montalban and San Mateo endorsed their petition.[118]

Likewise, in neighboring Hacienda de Tala in present-day Novaliches, American Frank Carpenter, who served as executive secretary of the colonial government in the early 1900s, governor of the Department of Mindanao and Sulu (1915–1920), and co-proponent of the government-led inquiry on friar estates, leased 2,010.12 hectares of land on 20 April 1908 from the Philippine government. The lease agreement went against the spirit of the Friar Lands Act, which sought to redistribute the said properties to the natives who occupied and tilled the land. Its questionable terms prompted critics to ask: "Were the friar lands bought in order to make landlords of American officials in the Philippines or home owners of the Filipinos?"[119] The property, which eventually became known as the Carpenter Estate, soon appreciated in value because of its location and contiguity. Here, Carpenter built a 25,000-peso home, cattle sheds, and a large mango farm of five thousand trees. The purported 1908 lease agreement, however, was belied by a 1924 Bureau of Lands document stipulating that the estate was "sold by the Bureau of Lands to Governor Carpenter for a total consideration of P67,368.00" in installments that would end on 1 July 1930. This document, which was prepared in light of plans to construct a government asylum in Novaliches, recommended that the state repurchase the Carpenter Estate for PHP 175,000.[120]

Perhaps the most notable among the estates around Manila was the Hacienda de Diliman. Diliman was not a friar hacienda; thus, the Friar Lands Act did not apply to it. Yet the feudal nature of the estate made it a representation of the undemocratic order in the suburbs. In 1794 the Spanish colonial government gave Diliman as a *mayorazgo* (entailed estate) to Binondo-based Chinese mestizo Antonio Tuason for his contribution to the Spanish cause against the British occupation forces in the 1760s. Tuason also profited handsomely from the galleon trade that some historians consider him the richest individual in the late-eighteenth-century Philippines.[121] By the mid-nineteenth century, the land grant had become the "fabulous

FROM CATTLE RUSTLERS TO CABARET DANCERS   51

Teresa de la Paz Estate, the biggest private hacienda in the Philippines next to those of the religious orders."[122] It consisted of two different haciendas: the Mariquina and Santa Mesa-Diliman haciendas. In the late nineteenth century these haciendas produced vegetables that ended up in Manila markets. According to a long-time Diliman resident in the 1950s the Tuasons occasionally exacted a rent of one peseta (20 centavos) from each tenant in the 1880s. Those who had no money could pay in kind, such as eggs or firewood.[123] However, Dutch scholar Gerret Pieter Rouffaer had a rather gloomy description of Diliman when he toured in and around Manila in 1911, and then decided to explore areas beyond San Juan:

> then the great emptiness starts, all of this within the old "encomienda" of the Tuasón family that extends all the way to San Mateo. Under the Spaniards and until 1900 it was completely exempt from taxes and therefore remained largely uncultivated. Now it should yield 80,000 pesos for the Internal Revenue.[124]

The last part of Rouffaer's description points to the sheer economic value the hacienda had attained in the early twentieth century. By the 1920s factions of the Tuason family had become embroiled in a legal scramble over the estate, whose worth had shot up to millions of pesos. Santa Mesa-Diliman and Mariquina were worth PHP 3,550,646 and PHP 1,507,140, respectively. The land value had appreciated immensely because the Tuasons leased portions of the estate to real estate companies like Gregorio Araneta, Inc., developers of Santa Mesa Heights,[125] a subdivision "built over with homes, American homes, chiefly."[126] Against the backdrop of suburban growth, the "feudal" character of the estate stood in stark contrast. Ex-Justice Fred C. Fisher remarked on the Tuasons' courtroom battle over Hacienda de Diliman: "It takes us back to a vanished age. It deals with a pernicious legal institution which was the outgrowth of feudalism and absolute monarchy of the Middle Ages."[127] Nonetheless, the Tuasons eventually allowed the state to purchase and subject the hacienda to redistribution, a move that proved foundational to Quezon City's emergence and will be discussed in the succeeding chapter.

The main beneficiaries of the implementation of the Friar Lands Act in Manila's suburbs were the colonial elite. Landowners and real estate companies capitalized on their access to prime land by turning them into residential subdivisions. In addition, the proximity of these estates to Manila increased the value of the resultant real estate developments, which catered to middle- and upper-class households, whether Filipino or American. Hence, we have Addition Hills urging potential buyers to "Buy at the Edge of the City" and profit from Manila's growth by taking advantage of the subdivision's feature: "greatest height, internal and surrounding

52   A CAPITAL CITY AT THE MARGINS

development and the most reasonable prices on the MANILA BOUNDARY LINE!" (fig. 1).[128]

From the elites' viewpoint, this process represented democratization: friar/feudal lands repurposed for the sake of private consumption. It was democratization in the liberal sense, similar to how Americans imposed eligibility requirements for political participation among Filipinos based on the colonizers' definition of "citizen": democracy in the suburbs meant the freedom to purchase a comfortable lifestyle, a freedom enjoyed only by those who could afford it. Furthermore, it replicated the prevailing discourse in the US that conflated political freedom with the sovereignty of the market and private enterprise and, conversely, authoritarianism with extensive state intervention in the economy. The US—a burgeoning "consumers' republic"—redefined American citizenship, while simultaneously expanding its reach beyond its Pacific coastline into its tropical colony.[129] The effect on the Philippine economy was the reorientation of millions of potential new consumers toward the US market, a process facilitated by free trade between the two countries starting in 1909. As the Philippines supplied the US with much needed cash crops like sugar and abaca, the metropole was the colony's source of luxury goods, such as domestic appliances and automobiles, that sustained the suburban lifestyle of prewar Manila.[130] As an extension of the Manila market, the suburbs were crucial spaces of consumption.

The development of middle- and upper-class enclaves in the former friar/feudal estates reveals another important point about American colonialism. The cases above demonstrate how the Friar Lands Act never attained its purported land-to-the-tiller objective. Perhaps the clearest piece of evidence to prove this failure was the 1935 Sakdal uprising.

Sakdal was a Luzon-based peasant movement founded in 1930 that campaigned against colonialism and rural inequality. It rose in revolt against the government on 2 May 1935, just days before the ratification of the newly drafted 1935 Constitution for the would-be Philippine Commonwealth.[131] Although the 1935 uprising was limited to several towns in Bulacan and Laguna and was easily suppressed, it was a traumatic episode that had long-term repercussions and affected Manila and the suburbs. After the uprising Laguna-based Sakdalistas retreated to Montalban, while Sakdal leaders and members were still active in the towns surrounding Manila, especially in Mandaluyong, San Juan, Caloocan, Malabon, Navotas, Pasig, and Pasay.[132] More importantly Sakdalistas remained agitated about agrarian issues even after the 1935 uprising, leading to intermittent disturbances in the suburbs.[133] Agrarian disputes flared even among those who were not formal Sakdal members. For example, in 1938 the police discovered that "disgruntled farmers of San Juan del Monte and Mandaluyong" planned "to

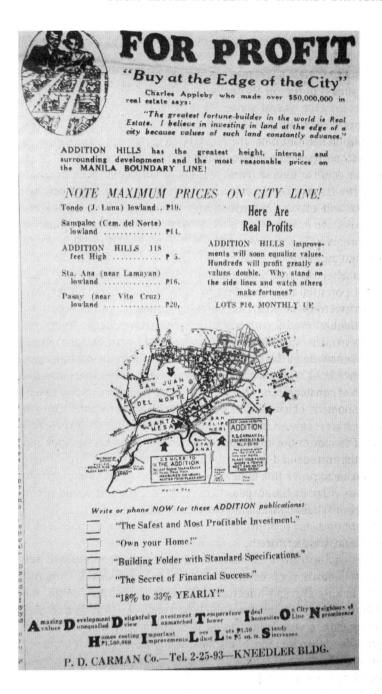

Fig. 1. An Addition Hills advertisement, 1931

Source: "For Profit," Addition Hills advertisement, *The Philippines Herald*, 12 Jan. 1931, p. 2, JRHP Box 12, Folder 18

54   A CAPITAL CITY AT THE MARGINS

rise in revolt on the night of January 5." The revolt, however, was aborted.[134] Sakdalistas also attempted to blow up the Novaliches reservoir, but failed to do so.[135] Thus, there was a creeping fear among Manila residents and officials about a repeat of the revolt just outside Manila that could break out anytime soon. The fear was so serious that Manila Mayor Juan Posadas Jr and the PC devised a detailed plan to defend the capital in case of another Sakdal uprising. In the said plan, the crucial defensive points were located at the suburbs, specifically at the major approaches to the city.[136]

The Sakdal specter coupled with the suburban boom made agrarian unrest a salient issue in Manila and its neighboring towns. Places like Baclaran in Pasay, Malabon, Makati, and Mandaluyong, where lands were still "undisposed" and mired in controversy, became flashpoints of conflict.[137] The urban-rural overlap that characterized the suburbs turned into a vise that increasingly tightened its grip on lowly peasants. Seeing that suburban real estate values rose rapidly, landowners demanded higher rents from tenant-farmers or sold their property to earn a quick buck. Either way, tenant-farmers were at the losing end, stoking further agitation. According to Governor-General Harrison, "agrarian disputes which occur from time to time in the vicinity of Manila" were compounded by the fact that many tenants were "unaware of the increase in recent years in the capital value of the lands they hold."[138] As rents skyrocketed and as landowners saw the profitability in urban development, evictions of hard-up farmers increased. This volatile situation alarmed the Commonwealth government.[139] In 1936 President Quezon recommended "legislation to provide for the expropriation of those portions of the large estates which are urban in character and occupied by the houses of tenants."[140] The legislature moved accordingly and passed an appropriate bill, allocating one million pesos to expropriate identified urban sites in friar lands.[141] This move by Quezon would prove crucial to the birth of Quezon City three years after.

The Suburban Underside

THE AGRARIAN SITUATION in the suburbs in the 1930s demonstrated the heterogeneous landscape of the places that would eventually comprise Quezon City in 1939. Lying just outside the boundaries of the capital, the suburbs exhibited the simultaneity of the urban and rural. And as one goes beyond the surface to reveal the underside, this simultaneity becomes starker.

The presence of remontados, ladrones, Sakdalistas, and dispossessed peasants in the suburbs evoked the persistent rurality just outside prewar Manila. Such was more apparent in places that were farther away from the capital, like Novaliches, which even had a 788-hectare leper colony called Tala Leprosarium,[142] a clear piece of evidence of its isolation. Meanwhile, Hacienda de Tala was "infested by cattle thieves and robbers,"[143] problems

FROM CATTLE RUSTLERS TO CABARET DANCERS   55

that festered Rizal province up to the 1930s.[144] According to one account, "Diliman was the most notorious lair of cattle rustlers. *Krus na Ligas* was runner up."[145] However, it was also during this period that Manila's urbanization began to affect the geography of criminality in the border towns by giving it an urban tinge.

America's "imperial makeover" for Manila was not limited to sanitation and urban planning; a moral prophylaxis also took over the city. This moral crusade targeted vices that had been rampant in the city since the Spanish colonial period. Two of these vices were prostitution and gambling.

Frowned upon but recognized as part of daily life, prostitution became legal toward the end of the Spanish regime. Brothels clustered in the backstreets of Manila's business districts. But when venereal diseases spread in the city, ambivalence turned to hypocrisy as the male-dominated Spanish government cast its gaze on women prostitutes, or *mujeres publicas* (literally, public women).[146] Meanwhile, colonial Manila also served as a haven for cockfighting, enjoyed not just by enthusiasts but even more so by the state and businessmen. Each arrabal had one cockpit, and Thursday and Sunday were designated cockfight days.[147] Though looked down upon by educated natives and Spanish civil officials, cockfighting remained an important form of entertainment for Manileños and a constant contributor to the coffers of the state, which farmed out cockpit contracts beginning in 1861. The government monopoly over cockpit contracts translated to annual revenues of 100,000–200,000 pesos in the last two decades of the nineteenth century.[148]

Two important factors were behind Manila's moral cleansing under US colonialism. One was the Americans' aim to depict Spanish colonialism as autocratic and responsible for these social ills. For instance, Americans emphasized how Spanish overlords perpetrated cockfighting as a vice among Filipinos.[149] The other factor was the upsurge of social reform movements in the US that were byproducts of America's rapid urbanization, from the Progressive Movement, which sought municipal reforms, to antivice crusades such as the Temperance Movement. This trend spilled over into the colony, exemplified by the American protestant missionaries founding the Moral Progress League in the Philippines.[150]

The resulting moral crusade tagged cockpits and cabarets, widely believed to be prostitution fronts, as two of the biggest threats to American-colonial Manila. However it was an uphill battle for the moralists. Cockfighting, the so-called "national sport" of the Philippines,[151] remained immensely popular, while cabarets benefited from the Americans' unofficial policy of toleration of prostitution and the so-called "*querida* system," especially within the military, to maintain colonial rule.[152]

Cabarets, or dance halls, were "a distinctly American addition to Manila's nightlife."[153] A customer would pay a *bailarina*, or taxi dancer, an amount (around twenty centavos, or ten cents, during the 1930s) that allowed him to dance with her for a certain amount of time. If a client, whether American or Filipino, wanted a bailarina to sit and drink with him, he had to pay her the equivalent amount of the dances foregone. In the early American period, most cabaret customers were American soldiers and sailors,[154] but eventually middle- and upper-class Filipinos became frequent patrons too, especially among college students and government employees. Oftentimes, flirting and amorous relationships between dancers and customers occurred. This set-up in cabarets made them a convenient front for prostitution.[155]

Aware of the underground economy in cabarets, moralists denounced cabarets as "a real menace to the health and morals of the city."[156] Unfortunately, the resulting discourse emphasized the perversion of young men's morals rather than the structural oppression of women and how cabarets became "the main cause of the ruin of many girls."[157] Public discussions translated into protests. Public outrage forced the local government to conduct raids and eventually ban them in Manila. In a few instances the municipal board considered bringing dance halls back, only to cave in to "flood of protests" each time.[158]

In effect, notwithstanding the new colonizers' zeal, all they could do was to sweep the dirt under the couch (i.e., forcing cabarets and cockpits to move outside Manila's borders). Cabarets simply transferred to the suburbs near city boundaries to make them accessible to Manila-based patrons. Cockpit operators and gambling syndicates, who were also hounded by authorities, employed the same strategy.[159] For Manila officials, city boundaries acted as a protective shield that kept these unwanted activities away. Ordinances even stipulated the minimum distance from the city borders from which cabarets could operate outside the city.[160] To some extent, this perception toward city borders was true. For example, when the town of Santa Ana was incorporated into Manila's territory at the start of the US colonial period, cockpits in the area had to close down immediately.[161] Because of the moralist rigidity of prohibiting cabarets in Manila, the city was "virtually an island surrounded by the very class of so-called entertainment places which are so rigidly,—at least technically rigidly—barred from the city."[162] This peculiar geography of vice in Manila and its suburbs was explained by a *Bulletin* editorial thus:

That is the natural consequence of the make-believe morality which is satisfied with theoretical regulations but which in reality plays into the hands of those who find the poor police forces of suburban municipalities their best allies and who make the city boundary line with its theoretical rigid regulation to a standing joke, a profitable one to themselves.[163]

FROM CATTLE RUSTLERS TO CABARET DANCERS   57

However, for cabaret and cockpit owners, the same boundaries gave them legal shelter from moral zealots and law enforcers. Their establishments flourished in the suburbs. By the 1920s, big suburban cabarets had become so well-established that they gained a "certain legitimacy" that set them apart from roadside brothels.[164] Just before the outbreak of the Pacific War, at least fourteen cabarets operated in Manila and its surrounding towns. The largest was Makati's Santa Ana Cabaret. Other well-known cabarets were Maypajo and Lerma Cabaret in Caloocan and Whoopee Cabaret in Pasay.[165] One tourist guidebook stated that the major cabarets could "all be visited in one evening,"[166] a piece of evidence pointing to the clustering of these establishments. It even listed a cockpit and a cabaret under a directed tour.[167]

As a result, the areas surrounding Manila gained a reputation for vice and lawlessness.[168] Pasay, reputedly "one of the rottenest in the Philippines," was called "Manila's Sodom and Gomorrha."[169] Manila's municipal board admitted: "The district just beyond the city limits, at several points, is infested with clusters of gambling joints, cockpits, and dance halls of a low order, in some of which prostitution is practiced or fostered."[170] The clustering of cockpits, cabarets, and other places of vice magnified the marginality of the border zones. It exerted a gravitational pull on other nefarious activities, such as robbery, theft, and other petty crimes perpetrated by Chinese *tongs* (criminal groups) and gangs, who included cabarets as part of their respective turfs. Such was the case of Maypajo, Caloocan, in the 1930s.[171]

La Loma in Caloocan stands as an illustrative example of how social and geographical marginalization coincided in a particular space and how socially reprehensible activities existed in spatial clusters. During the Spanish colonial period, La Loma's peripheral character was already apparent. By the 1870s it was the location of two cemeteries, including the Chinese Cemetery. It was also the site of a hospital for the Chinese, who were economically visible and looked down upon by Filipino society. The Chinese presence in La Loma was also visible in the fact that Chinese pork vendors were the main buyers of hogs from the La Loma stockyards, which supplied a significant amount of meat to the city. In 1901, a certain Don Juancho Mapa, along with Pedro Casimiro and Manuel Guison, renovated and expanded a small cockpit, which became known as the La Loma Cockpit and turned into one of the most important sources of income in the area.[172] La Loma also had its own cabaret. Eventually the place gained notoriety for illegal gambling and prostitution, "the Hell's Kitchen of Manila and the rendezvous of gangsters."[173] In the 1930s the notorious Liberty gang operated in La Loma and targeted American cabaret customers.[174] By this decade, La Loma had "two cemeteries, two cabarets, and one cockpit, let alone the

58   A CAPITAL CITY AT THE MARGINS

hundreds of other establishments illicitly run to cater to human concupis-
cence."[175] According to a *Philippines Free Press* article:

> La Loma, of Caloocan, possesses a Yoshiwara of prostitution, a district capping all
> the others in corruption. Next to the cemetery, it desecrates the memory of the dead,
> and adjoining the city boundary line, it insults the morals of the living. . . . On pay
> day carromatas and PU [public utility] cars galore may be found near the military
> barracks, all anxious to conduct their fares to that center of filth and corruption—
> La Loma.[176]

Various factors sustained this sociospatial structure at the fringes of
Manila. First, the profitability of vices discouraged local governments from
enforcing laws because they also benefited from these activities.[177] In the
suburban towns cockpits, cabarets, and other similar establishments contributed generously to municipal coffers.[178] Politicians themselves frequented
cockfights and cabarets and/or derived funding from the cockpit "trusts."
Many of them were thus compromised to begin with, including the police
force. Quezon frequented the cabarets, as well as Governor General Harrison
and Justice George Malcolm.[179] A lot of politicians were cockfighting aficionados, but even for those who were non-enthusiasts the cockpit was a source
of political capital. The crowds the cockpits drew made them appealing to
politicians as places for political gatherings. This attribute of cockpits as strategic political spaces also held true for cabarets, though limited to the middle
and upper classes.[180] Last, because cockpits and cabarets operated outside
city limits, mobility was an important factor. Transport motorization linked
Manila-based patrons of cockpits and cabarets to their suburban locations.[181]
Almost all major cabarets and cockpits were found near streetcar terminals,
while automobility later on became a boon to cabaret clients.[182]

The presence of cockpits and cabarets in Manila's outskirts had serious
implications on proposals to extend the city's boundaries. When officials
deliberated the 1937 annexation plan, they recognized that: "Should the city
boundary be extended all the suburban roadhouses may have to be padlocked,
as the city of Manila has an ordinance prohibiting maintenance of such places
within city limits. This might force women of ill-repute to ply their trade clan-
destinely within city limits, making the vice problem more serious than at
present."[183] Indeed, one of the main reasons given for the annexation plan was
that the local governments in the towns surrounding Manila proved inefficient
in responding to the vice problem in their territories.[184]

* * *

MANILA'S BORDERS AND BORDER ZONES underwent massive changes from
the mid-nineteenth century to the 1930s. In the mid-nineteenth century

Manila was still Intramuros, delineated by thick walls that had separated the Spanish city from its arrabales since the sixteenth century. However, as international trade transformed the city and its arrabales, the walls became increasingly suffocating, leading Manila's elite to seek the expanse and energy of Extramuros. Such was the genesis of Manila's suburbanization. As new colonial masters, the Americans legislated the marginalization of the erstwhile center when they gave Manila a much larger territory to include the arrabales. In the 1920s, riding on the suburban momentum, real estate developers and investors, in collusion with the state and friar landlords who managed to skirt attempts at agrarian reform, began pouring significant capital into Manila's border zones. This move furthered the suburban push. The consequent geographic shift was so dramatic that a succession of proposals to create a "greater Manila" hounded politicians until the 1930s.

Nevertheless, these proposals failed in the face of opposition coming mainly from the suburban towns themselves. Newly built subdivisions in Pasay, San Juan del Monte, and Mandaluyong served as new homes for wealthy households whose livelihoods remained in the capital. The increased population and commercial activity, magnified by the proximity of Manila, meant a rise in real estate values, tax base, and potential voters—crucial factors for Rizal's political and economic elite. It was no surprise therefore that the same elite groups, in tandem with ordinary residents, were the first ones to denounce any move toward their towns' annexation by Manila, notwithstanding the fact that their suburban prosperity was predicated on their geographical position along the fringes of the capital.

Manila's case typifies the suburbanization process of Southeast Asia's urban centers in the late-colonial period. Prewar Singapore saw the hardening of boundaries between suburbanites and the working class, as well as the increasing appreciation for elevated terrain at peripheral areas away from the downtown. In Rangoon the railway divided the city between its urban core and suburbs, which was also divided into three zones that were, in contrast to Manila, defined along racial and class lines.[185] All three cities were colonial ports that experienced rapid growth from the nineteenth to the early twentieth century due to their important roles in international trade.

Not all spaces outside Manila were elite suburbs, however. In the early twentieth century the fringes of the capital cultivated an ecology of actors and activities that subverted the urban order. At the turn of the century, these spaces harbored revolutionary forces that attempted to seize the colonial capital. Because haciendas and other massive landholdings dominated the suburbs, landless and restless peasants formed a significant portion of the population. Clearly, rural unrest was an issue not alien to urban Manila; actually, it hit too close to home. In addition, vice, gangs, and crimes—Manila's urban excesses—thrived at the city's edges. As a result, the Manila's border zones became a contact point between urban and rural sources of subversion.

For landless peasants, living just outside Manila's borders was a curse because of the tremendous economic pressure it exerted on them. For income-poor urbanites, the same borders offered either a passageway to the city's job opportunities and cheap informal housing or, for the deviant ones, an escape route to avoid authorities in Manila. It is this volatile heterogeneous geography of Manila's border zones that provides the context for Quezon City's founding.

CHAPTER TWO

Quezon's City

A DE FACTO GREATER MANILA had emerged by the 1930s due to the suburbanization of the towns surrounding the capital. Real estate developments that sprouted in Manila's peripheries symbolized the democratization and domestication of these erstwhile feudal spaces. Private consumption altered the landscape of these areas that once served as havens for both anticolonial struggles and friar estates. This suburban surge compelled politicians to attempt at redrawing Manila's boundaries to include adjacent municipalities, although they failed due to the opposition of real estate companies and the local officials of the affected towns.

Manuel Quezon, elected president of the Commonwealth government, which was inaugurated in 1935, backed the proposal to expand Manila. His support revealed his interest in the developments in greater Manila and in other urban issues. Sadly, Quezon's biographers have neglected this dimension of his administration. In contrast, they have always been drawn to Quezon's rural policies, and justifiably so: his flagship "social justice" program responded to the agrarian unrest at the time. It was a crucial state intervention in a predominantly agricultural country. The unfortunate result of this historiographical slant, however, is the lack of scholarly attention to a significant part of Philippine history that had repercussions for the would-be independent nation-state: the establishment of Quezon City in 1939.

Although Quezon failed to remap Manila, he succeeded in making something bigger, literally and figuratively: conjuring a purpose-built city, thereby altering the boundaries of the de facto greater Manila. Quezon City grew, as it were, out of Manila's volatile but valuable (economically and politically) border zones. Quezon envisioned it as the future capital to replace Manila. It signified a potential spatial inversion of what was central

61

62   A CAPITAL CITY AT THE MARGINS

and peripheral in the burgeoning metropolis. Its emergence was not just a product of Quezon's urban housekeeping; it helped solidify his rule. Its establishment was a patent example of his authoritarianism, hidden under the narratives of official nationalism and social justice.

Spatializing Official Nationalism

QUEZON CITY WAS FOUNDED during the Commonwealth era. This period represented the culmination of the efforts of the Filipino political elite to negotiate with legislators in Washington for a law setting a definite date for the transfer of sovereignty to the Philippines. Starting in 1919, Filipino politicians regularly sent representatives to the US on independence missions. The sending of independence missions ended when the Quezon-led 1934 mission secured the passage of the Tydings–McDuffie Act, which established the Commonwealth government in 1935 and guaranteed Philippine independence after ten years. The Commonwealth served as a transitional period for Filipinos to assume full domestic autonomy under US sovereignty on the path to complete independence afterwards. In a landslide victory, Quezon was elected the first Commonwealth president.[1]

The Commonwealth period was no mere administrative transition; it was the pinnacle of official Filipino nationalism, which the US colonial state cultivated for decades. Elite Filipino politicians, scholar-bureaucrats, and intellectuals led the way in harnessing a brand of civic nationalism that was acceptable to both the colonizers and the Filipino electorate. This paradox manifested in the establishment of state institutions that defined official Filipino culture in the early decades of American rule.[2] The Commonwealth government took this development to a higher level as it founded more institutions that aimed at defining a national consciousness: from linguistic nationalism, as embodied by the Institute of National Language, to economic nationalism, as defined by the National Economic Council and the state-supported National Economic Protectionism Association.[3]

State-sanctioned civic nationalism had a spatial dimension to it. Throughout the colonial period, the question of a capital city preoccupied Filipino elites. Although the Burnham plan seemed to have ensured Manila's status as capital city for decades to come, the Filipino elites' vision of a Philippine nation led them to question and eventually disregard the said colonial master plan. Save for a few government buildings and the Luneta, Burnham's vision languished at the blueprint stage.

Implementing the Burnham plan fell on the shoulders of the consulting architect, a government position created in 1905 following the abolition of the Bureau of Architecture. The first consulting architect, William Parsons, gradually but meticulously executed Burnham's plan.[4] Although several aspects of the plan came to fruition under Parsons's watch, he doubted the feasibility of sustaining it for a rapidly growing Manila. Filipino architects were just as skeptical. In 1928 acting consulting architect Juan Arellano informed Quezon of his misgivings about the plan. Contrary to Burnham's vision, Arellano advocated putting up the government center at Marikina rather than Ermita. Nonetheless, Arellano remained an adherent of City Beautiful, the same planning paradigm Burnham had for Manila.[5]

Manila's urban problems, already apparent and alarming by the 1930s, discouraged Filipino politicians from investing in Burnham's proposed government center in the capital city. Poor sanitation, perennial flooding, and traffic jams were just a few of these problems. Most pressing of all was the housing crisis: thousands of Manila residents lived in congested informal settlements with inadequate basic services.

Given Manila's situation and the lukewarm bureaucratic support for the Burnham plan, it was no surprise that Quezon did not adhere to the original vision for a government complex. Although the Commonwealth government allocated money for the plan's implementation, exemplified by Commonwealth Act (CA) 457, the government seemed to be always considering moving the civic center elsewhere.[6] Although this law recognized the importance of creating a national government center based on the Burnham plan, it also stipulated that the said complex could be built "on a site to be selected by the President of the Philippines within a radius of thirty kilometres from the Rizal Monument in the said city."[7] Furthermore, Quezon stressed the need to focus on improving existing government buildings rather than constructing new ones, thus making it "unnecessary to undertake the construction of the proposed capitol group of buildings for some years or until such time as the Government's finances warrant the large investment required."[8]

And yet a few years later, Quezon would command the state's vast resources to build a new capital city outside Manila. CA 457 gave him the legal excuse to circumvent the Burnham plan and pursue his desire to create a greater Manila area.[9] Intent on articulating an alternative urbanism to Burnham's ideas, Quezon surely had his own notions of city living and of an ideal capital city. As such, one has to analyze the gradual formation of his urban vision, as reflected in his lived experience and investments in cities and suburbs, in and outside the Philippines, to historicize Quezon's dream city: Quezon City.

"From Nipa Hut to Malacañang": Manuel Quezon's Urban Biography

A NEGLECTED ASPECT of Quezon's life is the numerous times he moved his place of residence. The locations of his different domiciles are not trivial details; they allow us to trace the trajectory of his changing urbanism and hypothesize which spaces mattered to him. The shifts from rural Baler to cosmopolitan Washington, DC, from bustling Manila to suburban Marikina,

64   A CAPITAL CITY AT THE MARGINS

provide the framework to construct his urban biography. Charles Abrams defines "urban personality" as that "quality or collection of qualities which makes the urban person what he is, as distinct from other persons from other environments," a notion premised on the idea that "the urban environment affects personality."[10] Building upon this definition, this book proposes the concept of urban biography to denote the totality of a person's lived experience in a city/cities and how it forms his/her notion of urbanism and urbanity. On the one hand, there exists a variety of economic, social, political formations and perspectives across cities. On the other hand, cities are products of a cross-pollination of these formations and perspectives, defying "geographical destiny" and fragmenting the urban geobody. Thus, I posit that one's knowledge of and immersion in a specific city or set of cities gives him/her a distinct appreciation for urban living that is altered every so often by residence, travel, investments, and access to information.

Quezon was born in 1878 in the isolated town of Baler in the subprovince of Principe, present-day Aurora province. Baler was a rural town throughout the Spanish colonial period largely due to its location in the Sierra Madre mountain range. Balereños were mostly farmers who depended on rice and corn for their livelihood and subsistence. Quezon's early years reflected Baler's rurality and isolation: he grew up in a landed family of local elites and valued the sense of community, reciprocity, and the town's deeply religious Catholic culture.[11] Quezon's wife, Aurora, was not just a girl from his hometown; "the little poor girl of Baler"[12] and Manuel were cousins. Marriages between close relatives were common among Tagalog provincial elites,[13] including those in Baler and neighboring Sariaya and Tayabas.

Quezon the provinciano was a second-generation ilustrado. What differentiated this generation of well-off intellectuals from the likes of Rizal and del Pilar was the nature of their "secular pilgrimage," a term Benedict Anderson used to describe the collective sojourns of the colonized to the colonial capital and the metropole.[14] The second generation was less cosmopolitan than their predecessors who moved to and from European, Asian, and American cities. Nevertheless, second-generation ilustrados did have their own secular pilgrimage, with Washington, DC, (not Spain) as their Mecca. As the Americans increasingly opened the colonial government and bureaucracy to elite Filipinos, more aspiring and educated Filipino youths from the provinces moved to Manila, the center of political power. Such was the case even in the socioeconomic sphere, as Manila's urbanization attracted professionals (lawyers, doctors, pharmacists, etc.) to settle in the capital.[15] Just like many of his contemporary ilustrados, Quezon's secular pilgrimage began with his move to Manila to finish his studies.

Quezon began his sojourn as a student-pilgrim in Manila in the 1890s. He finished his Bachelor of Arts in Colegio de San Juan de Letran and took his law degree in the University of Santo Tomas (UST). It was in these schools that Quezon met fellow student-pilgrims who would occupy positions of power in the colonial government. This informal network based on school ties included close friends Ortigas, Vicente Madrigal, future Philippine president Sergio Osmeña, and eventual nemesis Juan Sumulong.[16] Spending his formative years as an intellectual in Manila, Quezon developed early on an urbanity that would clash with his life as an *insurrecto* (rebel) when he decided to join the revolutionary forces during the Philippine-American War. His nascent urban sensibilities surfaced in an otherwise minor incident while in battle: "It was Christmas (1899) and even then I already had a very pronounced inclination for the frailties of the so-called civilized, modern man. Indeed, my prolonged nomad life as an insurrecto was beginning to weigh heavily upon my nerves."[17] He succumbed to those frailties and temporarily left his guerrilla base in Bataan to spend the holidays in Manila.

Whereas the allure of city life managed to draw Quezon out of a guerrilla base for a few days, the temptation of transnational cosmopolitanism forever changed the trajectory of his life. After his surrender to American authorities, he resumed his studies, passed the bar, and became a prominent lawyer in Tayabas. His success catapulted him to political office, from local fiscal to the National Assembly in 1907. One must note that the establishment of the Assembly was a watershed in colonial politics. It opened new political possibilities under the colonial regime and signaled key shifts in the politics of patronage between the colonizers and the native elite. From dangling appointive bureaucratic positions, the Americans now relied on the elections in selecting Filipinos they would groom for political prominence. From favoring Manila-based elites, the Americans began to accommodate more provincial politicians to consolidate colonialism throughout the archipelago. From the pro-American Partido Federal, the Americans directed their attention to the Partido Nacionalista, notwithstanding its ostensible platform of "immediate independence."[18]

As Majority Floor Leader and Nacionalista stalwart in the National Assembly, Quezon exerted considerable political influence. However, he cemented his dominance not so much in parliamentary parleys in Manila but rather in his stints abroad. And it was a path Quezon deliberately chose. He informed Osmeña, then Speaker of the Assembly, of his desire to attend the International Congress on Navigation in St. Petersburg, Russia, in 1908. According to Quezon: "My purpose in mind was to have my first glimpse of the outside world . . . prepare me for the next post . . . that of Resident Commissioner to the United States."[19] During the American colonial period, resident commissioners represented the Philippines before the US House of Representatives as nonvoting members.

66   A CAPITAL CITY AT THE MARGINS

Quezon's critics regarded his trip to Russia as an expensive 34,000-peso junket, especially since he never made it to the congress and ended up going to other European and American cities: "Quezon's liberally funded grand tour of the capital cities and fleshpots of Europe culminated in an extended visit to Washington and the eastern United States, which convinced him that he should seek his political destiny on a state larger than that afforded by Manila."[20] Quezon viewed it as an educational journey. He recalled how he met Alexander Kerensky and "observe[d] the extreme poverty and ignorance of the masses of the Russian people while their grand dukes were swimming in luxury."[21]

Shortly after this trip, Osmeña appointed Quezon resident commissioner to the US.[22] Thus, he had to move to Washington, DC, to attend congressional sessions. Interestingly, he was in the US capital at the time when the US Congress was investigating the friar lands controversy, which revealed his complicity: he was the Assembly majority floor leader when it approved the bill authorizing the sale of friar lands in large tracts. Clearly, Quezon could not escape from Manila's political specters despite being in Capitol Hill.[23] Nonetheless, his eight-year stint in the US capital shaped his career. Not only did he gain English proficiency and learn "the techniques of Washington society and politics"[24] by the time he returned to the country in 1916, he had also gained a reputation as the Filipinos' primary advocate for independence by securing the Jones Law, the first US law that assured Philippine independence albeit without a specific time table. Such was an ironic outcome, considering that contemporary commentators interpreted Quezon's appointment as Osmeña's maneuver to render the former invisible in Manila politics and establish himself as the undisputed leader of Filipino politicians.[25]

Quezon's post in Washington, DC, however, failed to uproot him from his rural origins or turn him into a full-fledged urbane cosmopolitan. His desire to "return to the land" remained, as he reminisced about his experience as resident commissioner:

> I love that job [as resident commissioner]. It has, for me, some memories which have now become sentiments only. I am attached to it, and I would have liked to finish my public career holding that post . . . . But ever since I started this social program in my own farm, I have lost even the desire to become Resident Commissioner. There is nothing more delightful to me than to go to my little farm, which is not producing anything. I just love to be there.[26]

Nevertheless, Quezon's desire to see the world continued. His participation in the independence missions allowed him to visit various US cities. He headed the first mission, which arrived in Washington, DC, in January

QUEZON'S CITY 67

1919 and went to major cities (e.g., New York, Philadelphia, Boston) to promote the agenda of Philippine independence. Afterwards he was a regular US visitor, holding conferences with American politicians in the US capital and joining "publicity tours" that brought him to Midwestern cities like Denver, Kansas City, and Salt Lake City. Quezon had at least eight US trips in connection to the independence campaign, which ended with the 1934 mission that secured the Tydings–McDuffie Act.[27]

Quezon's activities in US cities were not exclusively political in nature. In December 1927, he entered a sanitarium in Monrovia, California, as he was suffering from tuberculosis. From late 1930 up to early 1931, he once again stayed in California due to his health condition. Three years later, he entered Johns Hopkins Hospital in Baltimore to consult doctors about his bladder-stone. Also, his trips were not limited to the US. For example, after an official visit to the US, Quezon proceeded to Europe, where he and Osmeña visited Bern and Geneva. Quezon's "mixed mission" in 1933 went to Paris before sailing for Washington, DC.[28]

The end of the independence missions marked a geographical shift in Quezon's urban biography. From 1908 to 1934, his US sojourns defined his experience of living abroad. However, with the establishment of the Commonwealth and his election as president, his destinations diversified. Less than a year after the passage of the Tydings–McDuffie Act, he visited Surabaya in September 1934 and talked with Indonesian nationalists about the possibility of independence from the Dutch. He then proceeded to Batavia and got the attention of the local press,[29] perhaps due to how Dutch officials regarded him as a dangerous political figure, "a more subversive character than Marx, Lenin, Trotsky, and Stalin rolled into one."[30] In 1937 he visited Mexico, Cuba, France, and Germany to observe the social conditions in those countries.[31] In Mexico, Pres. Lázaro Cárdenas's policy of expropriating haciendas for redistribution to peasants impressed him so that a few months later he asked the Philippine legislature to use the coconut excise tax for purchasing landed estates and reselling them in small lots to rightful occupants.[32] Although he continued to visit US cities, he made it a point to observe Asian cities along the way. In his 1937 trip to Washington, DC, he turned his transit points in Shanghai and Tokyo into occasions to enhance diplomatic relations by meeting with local officials. In his 1938 trip to Japan, which Quezon said was a personal vacation, he visited Tokyo, Nagoya, Kobe, Hakone, Nagasaki, and Kyoto (fig. 2).[33]

A man of the world, Quezon nurtured an urbanity he was glad to show off to the public. When he learned how to drive a car, Quezon boasted to his colleagues in the Senate about it. Automobility became an indelible part of his life: "And when the automobile was first introduced into the Philippines, his home was his car, his housekeeper, his chauffeur, Aquilino."[34] He was

FIG. 2. Manuel Quezon (seated, fourth from left) at Kiya-machi, Kyoto, accompanied by Tomás Morató (standing, second from left), 1938
SOURCE: Enosawa, *Manuel L. Quezon*

often seen taking his car to go to his preferred place of entertainment in the city, the cabaret, especially the Santa Ana Cabaret in Makati. From his "unpretentious Ford"[35] in the 1920s, his love affair with automobility reached its apex when he assumed the presidency: Quezon became the owner of "a big, handsome limousine" registered under plate number 1.[36]

One must remember that, until he became resident commissioner, Quezon "was a man without a home of his own,"[37] probably a result of the peripatetic nature of his early career, which was always in a state of flux. After leaving Baler for Manila he either lived with his relatives or lodged with his friends in the capital, such as the Buencamino brothers, who rented a house in Santa Mesa. His transient lifestyle continued when he was resident commissioner and even after returning to Manila following the passage of the Jones Law in 1916.[38] He only had his own permanent residence after his marriage to Aurora in 1918. They lived in an upscale part of suburban Pasay where many of their neighbors were Americans.[39] Their Pasay home was "an elaborately furnished, fashionable and exquisitely wrought architectural creation, rising imposingly in an equally splendid location at Roberts Street, Pasay, Rizal" (fig. 3).[40] It was a bahay na bato but with stylistic modifications, many of them, like the gabled windows,

FIG. 3. The Quezons' Pasay residence
SOURCE: Filemon Poblador, ed., *Quezon Memorial Book* (Manila: Quezon Memorial Committee, 1952), 6

American-inspired.[41] Near his Pasay home, Manuel Quezon also had a "cute, elaborately furnished little bungalow where [he] and his cronies entertained special guests, mostly female, in complete privacy."[42]

Despite Manuel being a globe-trotter and having a bright career in Manila, the suburban (and one could argue, bordering on the rural) lifestyle defined the Quezon household. The Quezons wanted a more relaxed neighborhood, one that was not in the middle of the hustle and bustle of city life: "They had been away from home for years, surrounded by friends and environs speaking the dialect the Manila way, yet, inspite of all that, they remained provinciano throughout, and they are proud of it."[43] Manuel's close friend Victor Buencamino, a wealthy Manileño and Cornell-educated *pensionado*, described him: "You'd think Quezon was a little-time *provinciano* [someone from the province] just out of Baler when he was with us on Manga avenue [in Santa Mesa, Manila]. He liked to be completely casual. He moved about the house in *chinelas*, sometimes just in underwear. No gourmet, he liked the old Filipino common dishes: sinigang, adobo, sinañgag, and tinapa in the morning."[44] Manuel also confessed that he planned to devote his time to fishing upon retiring as president.[45] Quezon never reached retirement because of the Second World War and died in office while in exile in the US. However, approximating a retirement home was the Quezons' vacation house in Marikina. In December 1940 they

70   A CAPITAL CITY AT THE MARGINS

moved to this house, "a country home situated on the cliffs overlooking the Mariquina river with mango, papaya, banana and orange trees, and a poultry yard."[46] Quezon stayed at his Marikina home when he became ill from 1940 to 1941 presumably because he felt that the rural atmosphere in Marikina helped in his recovery.[47]

Manuel's position straddling between the urban and the rural was also seen in Aurora, who was "at home both in a nipa hut and in her stately and historic mansion."[48] The *provinciana* Aurora considered herself a laborer despite coming from a prominent family in Baler.[49] She was just as well-educated and culturally refined as her husband—"an ardent student of Japanese culture"[50] who even built a Japanese tea house in the Malacañang grounds and in their Pasay residence—yet preferred the rustic environment of the suburbs, especially that of their Marikina home. When Manuel bought the Marikina property as a gift to Aurora in 1926, he knew she would like it for she "never really became a city woman and was happiest when in the country."[51] When Manuel became president, he had a hard time convincing Aurora to leave their Pasay home for Malacañang.[52]

However, one must not romanticize the Quezons' suburban lifestyle. At a time when living in Manila's suburbs was a distinct part of elite consumption, the Quezons' preference for the rustic-but-accessible came with a hefty price tag—not to mention a political price tag in the form of the attendant compromises in and consequences of property accumulation. Traditional politicians throughout Philippine history have always regarded land ownership as an important (if not the ultimate) status symbol. Aside from the political and economic power that land confers, it also serves as a representation of the elites' personal, and supposedly apolitical, lives. Memoirs of prominent personalities, Quezon included, often devote much attention to how their domiciles, gardens, and farms gave them spaces of respite from their public lives. For the Quezons, however, these supposed spaces of respite turned into problematic places in 1929, when his political opponents used the couple's suburban properties to launch an attack against Manuel.

Around mid-1929, at the height of the long-standing feud between Aguinaldo and Manuel Quezon,[53] the former publicized details about Quezon's questionable properties (fig. 4). Aguinaldo's press release, published by the major dailies, enumerated these properties:

1.   2,700,000 square meters of Dominican friar lands in San Felipe Neri [Mandaluyong] which are now being sold in lots.
2.   His residence in Pasay, valued at PHP 100,000.00.
3.   The residence and grounds of Justice Johnson which he has recently bought for PHP 75,000.00 cash.
4.   A house bought in San Juan del Monte, valued at PHP 40,000.00.

FIG. 4. Editorial cartoon depicting Aguinaldo's search for Quezon's alleged properties

SOURCE: "It's Time to Retire: Quezon-Aguinaldo Fight Getting Tiresome," *Philippine Graphic*, 7 Aug. 1929: 20–21; image in p. 20

5. Fishponds in Pampanga, valued at PHP 60,000.00.
6. Coconut hacienda (about 25,000 trees) and cattle ranch in Tayabas.
7. One third share in the Balintawak Estate, worth PHP 3,000,000.00, where there is talk of building the new capitol.
8. Large tracts of land in Baler and in Infante [Infanta], Tayabas, which the projected railroad will traverse
9. Shares worth PHP 50,000.00 in the lumber mill at Calauag, and numerous shares in other companies.[54]

A week after publishing Aguinaldo's tirade, the *Manila Times* printed Quezon's rebuttal.[55] On the one hand, Quezon denied all allegations regarding his supposed rural properties: the hacienda and a ranch in Tayabas and the property in Infanta. He also clarified that the land in Baler had been his before he entered politics. Regarding the Calauag lumber mill shares, he clarified that even if the book value of his shares was PHP 50,000, he only paid PHP 35,000 for it because of the lien on the shares.[56] As to the Pampanga fishponds, he actually owned two but at a cost of PHP 23,000. On the other hand, Quezon partly admitted to owning the urban and suburban properties in Aguinaldo's list.

Quezon said that his Mandaluyong property was the "most valuable"[57] that he possessed and that his earnings from it had enabled him to acquire other properties. He explained that he owned two million square meters in the Mandaloya Estate, representing one-eleventh of the business, which he bought from Mr. Whitaker and Francisco Ortigas, the owners of the said estate, on 16 July 1920 for PHP 100,000. Quezon also mentioned that he got the PHP 100,000 as a loan from the Philippine National Bank (PNB) that he had already settled. He then went on to boast about the profitability of the said business, which for instance sold the Magdalena Estate for PHP 1.2 million with a PHP 100,000 profit. From 1920 to 1929 Quezon earned more than PHP 168,000 from this property. He also claimed that the Mandaloya Estate appreciated in value because of the rise of the San Juan Heights near it.[58]

As for the other properties, Quezon clarified that his Pasay house and lot cost PHP 50,000 at the time of construction.[59] He stated that he acquired his San Juan house from real estate magnate C. M. Hoskins for PHP 33,000. As to the house he got from Justice Johnson, he corrected this accusation by saying that he bought it from Johnson's son-in-law for PHP 75,000. Quezon explained that he accumulated these properties through the profits he earned from the Mandaloya Estate and loans from banks and friends, which meant that he had outstanding debts amounting to more than PHP 150,000.

As if to lay down all his cards, Quezon disclosed other transactions and properties that Aguinaldo failed to mention. Transactions included a house and lot that he bought and resold for a PHP 10,000 profit and the purchase and resale of 1,600 shares in the *Manila Times* and of a small sum in *La Vanguardia* for a profit of PHP 24,000. He also revealed that he owned a lot in Sariaya, a gift from the Rodriguez family; a lot in San Juan del Monte, which Quezon fondly called "Dalagang Bukid" and given to him by certain Manila residents in appreciation for his efforts in the passage of the Jones Law; and another lot adjacent to the house he bought from Hoskins, which he purchased from Antonio Brias for PHP 12,000.[60]

Quezon admitted that he acquired shares in the Balintawak Estate in 1921, but clarified that the estate was capitalized at PHP 360,100 and that his shares represented only a tenth of this value (PHP 35,650). His partners in the ownership of this property were Sen. Vicente Singson Encarnacion, the president of the said estate, Dr. Baldomero Roxas, and Vicente Arias. An intriguing claim, however, is his denial that the estate would be the site of the future capital city; as the discussion below will show, Balintawak would actually become part of Quezon City, the Philippine capital in the postwar era.[61]

Responding to Aguinaldo's accusations, Quezon bragged: "The only thing that my business transactions show is that not only have I been lucky in some of them, but also in all modesty, I may say, that I am not entirely lacking in business foresight."[62] Based on all these urban and suburban properties that Quezon himself admitted to owning, he did demonstrate his keen business foresight. However, Quezon was no real estate speculator; he never speculated on his purchases, but rather engineered, using his political position, an assured handsome return on investment.[63] As majority floor leader in the National Assembly in the early phase of American rule, he ensured the conversion of former friar lands into corporatized estates for private consumption.[64] Eventually, he involved himself in the operations and ownership of a number of these estates, such as the Mandaloya Estate, Balintawak Estate, and the Magdalena Estate. When the Commonwealth government began to map out the areas that would form a new city outside Manila, it became clearer that Quezon's suburban investments would be affected. And with the president declaring his intention to designate this new city as capital, real estate values in neighboring San Juan, Mandaluyong, Caloocan, and Marikina—places that Quezon had invested in from the 1920s to the 1930s—increased almost overnight. In this sense, one has to approach the early history of Quezon City from the perspective of a business transaction with one party dominating the deal.

The Official Narrative of Quezon City's Nativity

TO A LARGE EXTENT, Quezon City was the product of the "imagination" of just one man: Manuel Quezon. And just like most momentous undertakings, its creation also had its own official narrative.

The oft-repeated story of Quezon City's founding credits Alejandro Roces, Sr.,[65] as the influence behind Quezon's vision: "It was his [Roces's] conception of a model workers' community which fired the enthusiasm of President Quezon, who thereupon gave Don Alejandro practically a free hand to carry the project through to completion."[66] As the narrative goes, Quezon talked about his dream city with Alejandro and son Ramon while having breakfast. His dream city was one where the common tao could grow "roots" and "wings."[67] The elder Roces then suggested to Quezon to purchase a sizeable tract of land for this purpose.[68]

Quezon ordered Ramon to identify lands near Manila that could be expropriated, subdivided, and then sold at affordable prices. Ramon sought the help of friend and former classmate Bobby Tuason, who then talked to his aunt Doña Teresa Tuason, owner of Hacienda de Diliman. The Philippine government already had a previous commitment to Teresa Tuason when it expropriated part of her land for road projects. What followed was a Malacañang meeting that involved Secretary of Finance Manuel Roxas, Secretary of Justice and PNB Chair Jose Abad Santos, PNB President Vicente Carmona, and Alejandro Roces. The problem, however, was that the government had no available funds except for a PHP 3 million fund under the National Development Company (NDC).[69]

To mobilize the said funds, Quezon called for the creation of a new government-owned and controlled corporation. Organized on 14 October 1938, the People's Homesite Corporation (PHC) served as the state vehicle for the realization of Quezon's vision and had an initial capitalization of PHP 2 million for this purpose.[70] Four days later, the PHC board was completed. Alejandro Roces was elected chair, while Jose Paez, president and general manager of the Manila Railroad Company, became vice chair. Ramon Roces was named manager. Other board members were Ambrosio Magsaysay, Vicente Fragante, and Dr. Eugenio Hernando. The PHC immediately acquired Hacienda de Diliman at a cost of five centavos per square meter.[71] Afterwards, the PHC conducted topographical surveys to prepare the land for subdivision into residential lots for sale at affordable rates.[72]

The city that Quezon envisioned appeared to be the culminating project of the decades-long struggle to democratize Manila's suburbs. To create it, the government acquired land from eight haciendas. The centerpiece was Diliman (15,732,189 square meters), while the others were the Tuason-owned Santa Mesa Estate (8,617,883 square meters), Mandaloya (7,813,602 square meters), Magdalena (7,644,823 square meters), Piedad (7,438,369 square meters), Maysilo (2,667,269 square meters), and San Francisco del Monte (2,575,388 square meters). The ostensible beneficiaries were the working class, who had been suffering from a shortage of decent and affordable housing in Manila. Quezon's planned city would be a place where they "could live like men and not like hogs."[73] He declared: "Social welfare can only be built on decent homes."[74] He believed that affordable housing necessitated state intervention to offset the effects of market forces because:

> The theory, and it is a reasonable one, is that there are many thousands of families in Manila who have the ambition to own modest homes of their own and who have saved methodically to realize their dream or are willing enough to work hard to see their ambition fulfilled. Under present circumstances, however, when speculation on land has made the price of desirable lots in Manila and in the suburbs prohibitive to them, this ambition cannot materialize and they are forced to stay in Manila's congested areas as rent payers.[75]

Quezon promised that the state would give residents financial support, apart from basic services like utilities and transportation facilities.[76] With optimism bordering on arrogance, he vowed: "It is the intention of the government to keep the model city a residential area of homeowners and not rent-payers. There is no field for land speculators in the model city. Buyers of lots will be required to construct a home within two years to hasten the development of the city."[77] Upon the opening of applications for homesite lots in December 1938, it received four thousand applications.

Riding on Quezon's democratization narrative, supporters of his project believed that the new city would lead owners of nearby subdivisions to bring their prices down to remain competitive.[78]

Quezon's stated goal of creating low-cost housing projects out of state-purchased estates coincided with another major goal of his: transferring the UP campus outside Manila. As with the housing situation, urban congestion was a pressing concern for the country's state university. More important, he wanted the students to be "brought under a more strict and wholesome supervision and control, and [that] the proper spirit and atmosphere may be created on the University campus."[79]

Years before the planning of Quezon's dream city, university and government officials had already proposed relocating UP from Ermita to a less urbanized location. For example, the revised Burnham plan envisioned a new campus at the "heights behind Manila."[80] In 1921 University President Guy Potter Benton thought of transferring the campus, and the following year he suggested a "100-hectare site in San Juan, Rizal, but the plan fizzled out."[81] Quezon even considered moving it to Tagaytay, Cavite. Although his idea was not realized, Quezon was insistent on relocation. In August 1937 he met with his cabinet and UP officials to discuss the issue and enumerated possible sites: Baguio, Los Baños or Camp Eldrige, Alabang, Tagaytay, Novaliches, and Marikina.[82] Afterwards, university officials, via Assemblyman and UP regent Manuel Roxas, contacted Purdue University President Charles Edward Elliot and Dean Paul C. Packer of Iowa University to study the relocation proposal.[83]

Elliot and Packer arrived in the country in October 1938 and in January 1939 submitted their report endorsing the relocation to the UP Board of Regents (BOR).[84] Although they saw the disadvantages of moving the campus (increased commuting time for students; possible decrease in enrolment; halt in the development of the Manila campus; and the lack of public services in the new site), they believed the following advantages outweighed the potential drawbacks:

First, it provides an opportunity not only to design a [physical] plant especially adapted to the present needs of the University but makes available sufficient land to safeguard its future requirements.

Second, it will have enough large territory to afford adequate recreational opportunities for the students.

Third, with the proposed boulevard development completed, it will be more easily accessible for the students from the metropolitan district of Manila than the present site.

Fourth, it insures an area against the ever pressing needs of other governmental functions which impinge upon the site now occupied.

76   A CAPITAL CITY AT THE MARGINS

Fifth, it would provide an opportunity for faculty members to establish homes in a controlled area.

Sixth, it is possible to provide a better total University student and faculty living environment than in the present location.[85]

As to the specific location of the new campus, they suggested a location in Marikina about five miles from downtown Manila.[86] They also recommended that the architect who would draft the plans for the new site "be sent to the United States for the purpose of studying the general plans of and methods of administering the physical plants of leading American Colleges and Universities."[87] The BOR selected the said site: a 1,500-hectare area straddling the Mariquina and Diliman estates.[88]

To facilitate the necessary legislation, Quezon urged the National Assembly to enact UP's relocation during the 1939 session. On 8 June 1939 the legislature passed CA 442, empowering the BOR with a budget of PHP 17,500,000 to transfer UP to a site outside Manila.[89]

With the legal infrastructure in place for the PHC homesite and the new UP campus, the two institutions became the main anchors for Quezon's envisioned city. Giving this city its legal existence was thus made a lot easier. More importantly, the conjoining of public and affordable housing and education evoked the moral-political discourse of citizenship that undergirded the new city. This discourse, which traces its roots to Western antiquity—demonstrated by how the Latin word *civitas* gave rise to the words "city," "citizen," and "civics"—held Quezon City (and by extension, Quezon) as a paternal figure. Quezon City would offer shelter and education to those who showed worthiness (those who could pass screenings/examinations and pay mortgages/tuition) in exchange for their participation as educated and productive citizens. It was unmistakably a space for the social reproduction of the ideal Philippine nation.

On 18 September 1939 Quezon asked the National Assembly to create a new city in the area to be occupied by the new UP campus and the PHC homesite. He also suggested that all officials of this proposed city be his appointees. On 12 October, less than a month later, the legislature complied: CA 502 created Quezon City and served as its charter. Moreover, it enjoined state officials to plan the city's development as the future capital.[90]

Based on its charter, one could characterize Quezon City as an "invented" or an "imagined city" since it was founded not on a single preexisting settlement but by carving out barrios from various Rizal towns to create a new city that corresponded with the estates the PHC acquired (map 9). Quezon City's initial territory covered 7,355 hectares, one third of which was government-owned, and included the following barrios: Bago Bantay, Balintawak, La Loma, Santol, and Masambong, which were taken

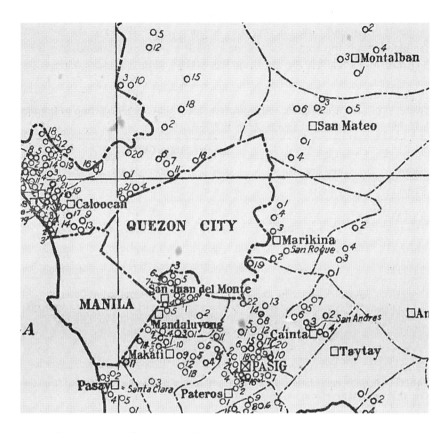

Map 9. Quezon City and its surrounding towns, 1939

N.B. The squares indicate the town/city name, while circles represent barrios.

Source: Commission of the Census, *Census of the Philippines: 1939*, vol. I, part IV, Rizal-2

from Caloocan; Cubao, Diliman, and San Francisco del Monte, which were taken from San Juan; Jesus de la Peña and Tañong, including the new UP site, which were taken from Marikina; and Ugong Norte, which was taken from Pasig.[91] The demographic impact on the affected towns was significant because the barrios Quezon City absorbed were some of the fastest-growing settlements in their original towns. In 1903 the combined population of these barrios was 3,062. In 1918 it increased to 8,789 and then ballooned to 39,013 in 1939.[92]

In its emergence as a new political unit, Quezon City "carefully picked out, piece by piece, from the best parts of several towns."[93] This point can be quantified by the real estate value of the territories lost by the said Rizal towns to Quezon City. Although Caloocan yielded the most number of barrios, in terms of the real estate values of excised properties, San Juan had it worse. It had to

78   A CAPITAL CITY AT THE MARGINS

let go of urban and rural tax revenues amounting to PHP 10,256,270 per year, far higher than the totals for Caloocan (PHP 2,918,430), Mandaluyong (PHP 293,460), Marikina (PHP 837,560), and Pasig (PHP 139,360) (tables 5 and 6).

TABLE 5. Taxable urban lands and improvements within the jurisdiction of Quezon City that were taken from various Rizal towns, 1939

| Town | Land Area (sq m) | Assessed Value (PHP) | | Total |
		Land	Improvements	Assessed Value
Calooocan	6,311,562	1,665,400	800,170	2,465,570
Mandaluyong	102,527	38,050	90,840	129,890
Marikina	268,205	138,810	216,450	355,260
Pasig	3,262	2,470	8,840	11,310
San Juan	17,560,935	6,997,110	2,782,790	9,779,900

SOURCE: Hip. Salvador, Report to His Excellency, the President of the Philippines, Covering Complete Segregation of Real Properties Belonging to Quezon City, 22 Dec. 1939, Appendix A, unpublished report, 1–5, MLQP Series VIII, Box 73, Folder Name: Quezon City, 4–5

TABLE 6. Taxable rural lands and improvements within the jurisdiction of Quezon City that were taken from various Rizal towns, 1939

| Town | Land Area (sq m) | Assessed Value (PHP) | | Total |
		Land	Improvements	Assessed Value
Calooocan	12,585,270	444,720	8,140	452,860
Mandaluyong	1,948,234	163,550	20	163,570
Marikina	10,600,092	482,300	-	482,300
Pasig	4,571,987	124,980	3,070	128,050
San Juan	6,472,312	297,250	179,120	476,370

SOURCE: Hip. Salvador, Report to His Excellency, Appendix A, 1–5

However, it did not take long for the government to revise Quezon City's borders. CA 659, enacted on 21 June 1941, returned the area of Wack Wack Golf and Country Club to Mandaluyong, and the barrios of Jesus de la Peña and lower Barangka to Marikina. However, the same law took the area of Camp Crame away from San Juan and gave it to Quezon City.

In its early years Quezon City was predominantly rural. Tables 5 and 6 show that in 1939 its total taxable urban land area was 24,246,491 square

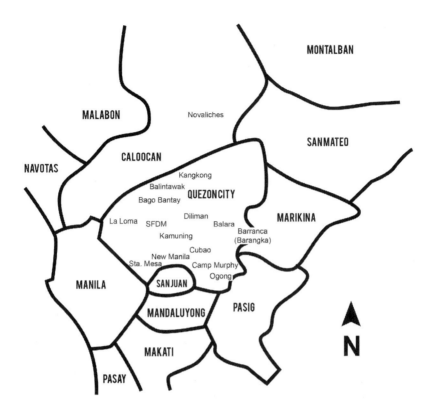

MAP 10. Key places in Quezon City's prewar geobody

meters, much lower than its 36,177,895 square meters of taxable rural land. It was a "dream city out of a wilderness," situated at a "highly malarious location."[94] Despite having populous barrios incorporated in its geobody (map 10), Quezon City's rurality surfaced in other aspects. For example, 1939 census records revealed that Quezon City had 964 farms, totaling 2,123.21 hectares, in contrast to Manila's thoroughly urban geography that had no farms.[95]

Quezon, of course, did not want rural wilderness as the predominant image of the city that bore his name. Moreover, he was unequivocal and persistent in his aim to make Quezon City the capital someday. Hence, it had to conjure images of grandeur and national unity, with an expansive layout complemented by magnificent public edifices. As such, Quezon gave much importance to Quezon City's urban planning. He involved himself in the planning process, from the initial studies to the on-the-spot decisions.[96]

Quezon looked toward the US for planning ideas. In 1938 he instructed Roxas "to make a study of parks, recreational and health facilities in the United States and Europe."[97] In a year's time Roxas visited numerous cities, including major ones along the US Atlantic and Pacific coasts (e.g., New York, San Francisco), European capitals (Paris and Amsterdam), and even Asian cities (e.g., Tokyo, Shanghai). Upon his arrival in Manila, just days after the passage of Quezon City's charter, he recommended to Quezon that the government consult an American expert on park planning.[98] Quezon heeded Roxas's advice, although he was already making his own plans for the new city independent of Roxas's report. On 12 May 1939 he cabled Osmeña, who was then visiting various US and European cities, to convince former consulting architect William Parsons to return to the Philippines and advise the government "on plans for capitol buildings and university buildings at [the] new site."[99] After securing Parsons's positive response, Osmeña sent Quezon his report on his observations and studies abroad. Quezon then inquired the US Department of Interior about the possibility of getting an adviser on the construction of national parks. US authorities recommended Louis Croft, a suggestion that Quezon took. Quezon asked Croft to make a stopover in Japan on his way to the Philippines to study park systems in the said country. Lastly, Quezon requested architect Harry T. Frost, a partner in the US architectural firm Bennett & Frost, which had been involved in significant urban improvements in Washington, DC, and Chicago, to help in planning the new city. Frost agreed to do so in March 1940.[100]

As the Commonwealth government's architectural adviser, Frost directed Quezon City's urban plan, which was approved in 1941. He got help from Arellano and former Bureau of Public Works (BPW) Director Alpheus Williams. Parsons played a crucial role in the initial planning phase; unfortunately, his involvement ended abruptly when he died in December 1939.[101] The 1941 Frost plan (fig. 5) featured wide avenues, large open spaces, and rotundas for major intersections. It also built upon Croft's plan for the major thoroughfares in Manila and nearby towns. At the heart of the city was the 400-hectare Diliman quadrangle formed by four avenues—North, West, South and East—and designed to be the future location of national government buildings. At one of the corners of the quadrangle was the main rotunda, a 25-hectare elliptical site.[102]

Security was one important reason why Diliman became the site of the proposed government complex. Its inland location, in contrast to coastal Ermita, would minimize vulnerability to naval bombardment.[103] Not surprisingly, Quezon City's territory included spaces devoted to protecting the state. Before the city's establishment, the Philippine Army found a new home in a 25-hectare land (which eventually expanded to 100 hectares) donated by the Mandaloya Estate. Construction of the new general headquarters, named Camp Murphy in honor of then-Governor-General Frank Murphy, began in 1934. When Quezon City was founded, Camp Murphy was included in its territory. Near Camp Murphy, along the Quezon City-Mandaluyong border,

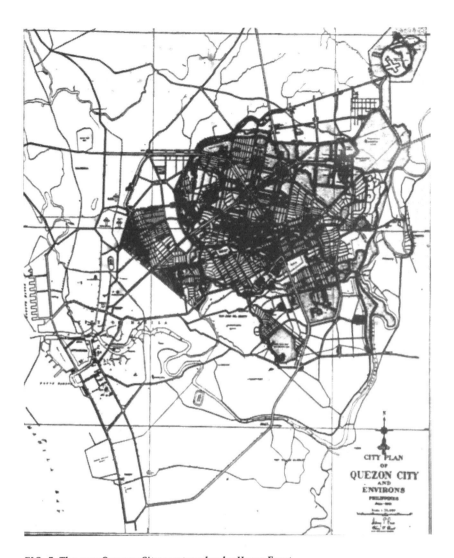

FIG. 5. The 1941 Quezon City master plan by Harry Frost

SOURCE: "Frost Speaks Frankly, Clearly in Describing Plan for Dream Cities, Telling How to Prevent Slums," *MDB* 29 July 1941: 8

was the headquarters of the Philippine Constabulary (PC), Camp General Rafael Crame, which fell under Quezon City's jurisdiction in 1941. The Frost plan also allotted space for the proposed transfer of the Philippine Military Academy (PMA) from Baguio to Quezon City, as suggested by General Douglas MacArthur, military advisor to the Commonwealth Government and field marshal of the Philippine Army.[104] Government celebrations helped articulate Quezon City's position as a space to secure the state. When the cornerstone

FIG. 6. Laying of the cornerstone in Diliman, 15 November 1940
SOURCE: Poblador, *Quezon Memorial Book*, 16

for the capitol was laid down on 15 November 1940 at the Diliman quadrangle to commemorate the Commonwealth's fifth anniversary (fig. 6), the government conducted a military parade. As a "show of military might," the state sought to demonstrate that it was strong enough to withstand the global armed conflicts happening at the time.[105] This event also marked the first time that Quezon delivered his annual state of the nation address (SONA) in Quezon City rather than in Manila, where he had been doing so since 1935.[106]

If the 1940 military parade was the presumptive nation-state's attempt to display its readiness to join the international community of nations, a 1941 international exposition in Quezon City could be read as its civilian equivalent. To celebrate the Commonwealth's sixth anniversary, the government organized the Philippine Exposition of 1941.[107] Here was a soon-to-be independent country—just three decades removed from the humiliating 1904 exposition in St. Louis, Missouri, in which Americans displayed Igorot people as "exhibits," an event forever etched in Quezon's mind—presenting itself as a worthy member of the global community.[108] The exposition grounds covered seventy-five hectares in a site near the Diliman quadrangle. The official narrative woven into this event, which was scheduled to open on 15 November, can be read from one of its advertisements (fig. 7):

> In a world caught in a vast whirlpool of turmoil and war, the Philippines is the one place, outside of the American continent, where one can witness and enjoy orderly progress, peaceful and contented living and unhampered pursuit of happiness.[109]

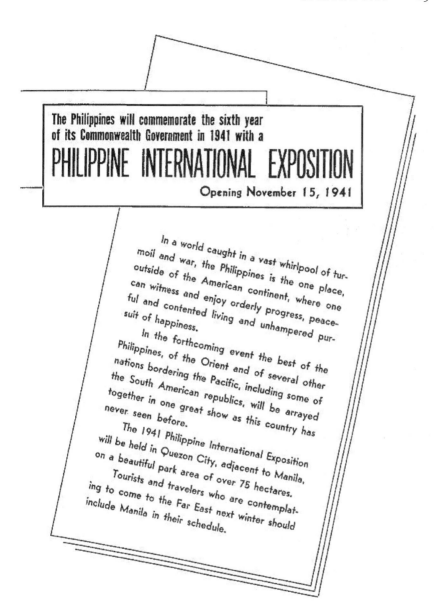

FIG. 7. An advertisement of the 1941 Philippine International Exposition
SOURCE: *ACCJ* Nov. 1940: 15

The exposition, far from conveying a sense of arrogant optimism (as expositions at the time usually did), revealed the anxiety of the presumptive nation-state: it proffered the idea of Quezon City as a haven of peace amid worldwide chaos. At the time of Quezon City's founding, Nazi Germany

FIG. 8. Artwork for Merrit's article comparing Quezon City and Washington, DC
SOURCE: Merrit, "A Tale of Two Cities," 6

was occupying various parts of Europe, while Japan was doing the same in East Asia. Due to these escalating armed conflicts, the government eventually restricted the exposition to local participants.[110]

After the main features of Quezon City's layout were completed, the contrast between the presumptive and current Philippine capital cities became more apparent. According to the American Chamber of Commerce: "In a city so badly equipped with wide streets as is Manila, the contrast with Quezon City in this respect is unbelievable. It is safe to say that no matter how much development should take place in the new city in years to come, there can scarcely be any traffic congestion."[111] The seemingly minor issue of road planning was actually a significant part of Quezon City's early history for it revealed the concept of civic virtue in the plan, similar to the McMillan Plan for Washington, DC. Such was no coincidence because the American and US-trained architects behind Quezon City also imbibed the "behavioralist" school of thought behind the modern plan of Washington, DC. This notion of urban space as an influence in the behavior of citizens had already been seen in Burnham's City Beautiful design and remained in the ideas of Parsons and his fellow planners. Quezon, who was most familiar with Washington, DC's urban plan, saw it fit to apply the same urban ideology in his dream city. This point was evident in how civic virtue became the underlying ideology in the founding of Quezon City: an ideal city to mold ideal citizens. All these details led many to draw parallelisms between Washington, DC, and Quezon City.[112]

QUEZON'S CITY   85

The parallelisms between Quezon City and Washington, DC, go beyond skin-deep similarities; their congruence more substantial than the formulaic "two modern dream cities, one carved out of an Occidental swamp, the other built in an Oriental wilderness" (fig. 8).[113] First, both cases exhibit "shifts" in the urban mentalité of the colonized. The two cities heralded the end of colonialism and were named after the founding fathers of their respective nations. Second, and countering the first one, historians criticize the baroque (i.e., despotic) character of their morphologies, reflected in extravagant thoroughfares and space wastage, that seemed evocative of colonialism.[114] This ironic twist is understandably present in Quezon City because its aesthetics and architectures drew inspiration from Washington, DC, the capital of the Philippines's former colonial master.[115] Last, and notwithstanding contradictions and narcissism—the two cities were so named even before their namesakes died; Washington, DC, was named after George Washington in 1791, eight years before he died, while Quezon City got its name in 1939—both cities were conjured for the explicit purpose of constructing an "imagined community."[116]

Quezon City's Working-Class Mirage

CONSTRUCTING AN IMAGINED COMMUNITY through official nationalism cannot go far if it does not strike a chord with ordinary citizens. In this regard, Quezon proved his ability as a statesman by conjuring a successful narrative for Quezon City that linked it to not only official nationalism but also his slogan of "social justice." As the supposed home for the homeless working class, the city engendered a mass appeal.

In the 1930s, Manila's housing crisis worsened. Although there were other state efforts that addressed this matter, Quezon projected Quezon City to be the grandest testament of his administration's desire "to relieve Manila of a part of its congested population." This city would "offer to government officials, especially the small salaried employees and laborers, for sale or rent, lots where they can build, or have the Government build, their homes."[117]

Through consistent messages in his other pronouncements, Quezon cultivated Quezon City's mass-oriented reputation, as seen in this anecdote:

Once he [Quezon] overheard that some clerks were underpaid and consequently lived a most uncomfortable and miserable lives [sic]. He, therefore, decided to look into the matter, personally visiting the homes of the employees concerned to ascertain the actual conditions in which they were. Finding that the reports were true, he ordered the establishment of a colony for lowly paid employees in Quezon City to be sold to them at cost and on the installment basis.[118]

Furthermore, Quezon's emphasis on how Quezon City enabled beneficiaries to "live in healthful surroundings with modern facilities and conveniences"[119] indicated that he wanted it not to be a mere low-cost housing program but "a model workers' community."[120]

Government statistics regarding Quezon City's first year seemed to validate Quezon's vision:

> [The PHC] has invested P1,472,112.94, as follows: P787,021.35 for the purchase of Diliman Estate in Quezon City, and P685,091.59 for development and improvement. The corporation has practically completed its subdivision and survey of the south development project at Diliman Estate. A total of 5,450 lots ranging in area from 180 to 1,800 square meters have been surveyed, and 3,643 lots are now available for sale at prices ranging from P1.00 to P10.00 per square meter. Thirty-seven and a half kilometers of asphalted first-class roads have been laid out. The corporation has completed the construction of 37 model houses ranging in prices from P1,400 to P4,600 and 310 small houses in the workers' section at an estimated cost of P650 each.[121]

Going beyond the numbers, however, one discovers that the government actually had a hard time achieving the goal Quezon set for Quezon City. Swamped with thousands of homesite applications, the PHC could only process them months after the city's establishment.[122] But more significant than logistical difficulties were the inherent and irreconcilable contradictions within Quezon City.

Right from the start, the government wanted to make the homesite project economically viable (i.e., profitable): "The government in creating the People's Homesite Corporation has no intention of getting into a project of free housing. The sole object of the state is to help the hard-working and thrifty realize their desire to own their own homes."[123] For Quezon, it had to be "developed on a business basis," so "that the Government will not only recover its investment, but may reap a reasonable profit."[124] As such, after the PHC acquired the lots from the Tuasons at PHP 0.05 per square meter, it initially pegged the minimum selling price at PHP 0.50 per square meter—a 500 percent mark-up. The price range then increased, between PHP 2.50 and PHP 7 per square meter, when the PHC began the auction of lots in 1940. The "profit margin," according to the government, was necessary to develop the physical infrastructure in the site.[125] In effect, the city had no place for lower-class (and probably many middle-class) households, who could have not afforded the prices but badly needed decent shelter.

Whereas Quezon City gave the middle class a golden opportunity to own houses and lots, the working class found it difficult, if not impossible, to do the same. At a time when the daily minimum wage was PHP 1, the floor price of PHP 2.50 per square meter was simply out of reach for them. This, despite Quezon's "notoriously fiery" "defense of the laboring class."[126]

It's A New City
But Already Enchanting...

QUEZON CITY

Because there's "The Aristocratic Suburb," NEW MANILA, with its beautiful modern homes, parks, clean, well-lighted asphalted modern homes, and streets, with fruit trees and plants. There are also the ESPAÑA SUBDIVISION, CAMP MURPHY SUBDIVISION, UNIVERSITY SUBDIVISION and SAN JUAN SUBDIVISION all enhancing the beauty of the new city . . . that's one of the reasons why many INVESTORS and HOME-LOVERS are now buying lots in our above-mentioned subdivisions.

ACT RIGHT NOW. NO ADVANCE PAYMENT. You can take possession of the lot you want immediately after paying the first monthly installment. CASH, 20% DISCOUNT.

. . . . and you a

FREE Life Insurance Policy

General Agents:

Juan. Ysmael & Co., Inc.

348 Echague, Manila, Tel. 3-21-44 or 2-23-40—Sundays and after 6 p. m. Tel. 6-87-26 - 20 Broadway, New Manila

FIG. 9. An advertisement of Juan Ysmael & Co's New Manila subdivision

SOURCE: Juan Ysmael & Co., Inc., "Quezon City," *Khaki and Red*, Oct. 1939: 12

To make matters worse, the power of the landlords in Quezon City remained largely intact despite state expropriation of their estates. Just a year prior to the city's founding, sixty Diliman tenants took to Malacañang to protest how the Tuason family took their property through illegal means. Many of them were unaware that the family actually owned the land they had been occupying for generations.[127] Of course, landlord dominance operated mainly through legal frameworks, and in Quezon City's case the real estate market provided such a mechanism. Outside the government homesite in Diliman, landlords-turned-subdivision-magnates reigned supreme. Rather than bring their prices down to compete with PHC, they maintained their rates that catered to middle- and upper-class customers. Furthermore, Quezon City's founding and its status as a future capital city increased the values of the preexisting suburban residential developments nearby. The Juan Ysmael Company even used Quezon City's establishment to promote its properties in Magdalena Estate among middle- and upper-class customers (fig. 9). It branded its New Manila subdivision as "the aristocratic suburb,"[128]

88 A CAPITAL CITY AT THE MARGINS

selling lots at PHP 2 to PHP 5 per square meter. These rates, which were similar to those offered in the PHC Diliman homesite, were way higher than the real estate taxes (PHP 0.02 per square meter) that the Magdalena Estate owners had been paying the government for decades.[129] New Manila's Broadway Avenue was known to many as "Millionaire's Row," while its nearby streets also featured "lines of mansions, giving one the feeling of being in another world and in another era."[130]

Other examples similar to New Manila were the San Juan Heights Co., which claimed that it "blazed" the "trails to Quezon City,"[131] and Santa Mesa Heights, the so-called "Gateway to Quezon City" (fig. 10). A section of Santa Mesa Heights, divided into 1,400-square-meter lots, was known as the "mansion site." Its residents included the who's who of Philippine society: Sen. Claro M. Recto, future senator Gil Puyat, Sec. Eulogio Rodriguez Sr., and Gov. Eulogio Rodriguez Jr., among others. By 31 March 1941 Santa Mesa Heights had sold 900,359 square meters of land, aided in no small way by its donation of land to the government for the construction of wide and asphalted boulevards and the UP's impending transfer to Diliman. The developer of Santa Mesa Heights, Gregorio Araneta Inc., was owned by the Araneta family, whose wealth originated from their sugar landholdings in Negros in the Visayas. The presence of sugar interests in Quezon's dream city was not surprising given his close ties with this important power bloc.[132]

Interestingly, the developer of Santa Mesa Heights credited its "phenomenal growth" to its "location, elevation, beautiful topography and nearness to Manila."[133] The emphasis on Quezon City's elevation to present it as a salubrious location echoed how elite subdivisions in the "eastern peripheries" developed in the 1920s and 1930s. In fact, the state-run Santol Tuberculosis Sanatorium, eventually renamed Quezon Institute (QI), was established in an area that was later on included in Quezon City precisely because of the terrain, microclimate, and vegetation that doctors believed were beneficial for tuberculars.[134]

The issue of accessibility attenuated the class divide in housing. Because Quezon City was "essentially a Manila suburb,"[135] most residents worked in Manila. And given its distance from Manila's downtown, communication and transportation proved critical. Fittingly, one of the first businesses established in the new city was a taxicab company, Acro Taxicab Co. Moreover, the biggest company in prewar Quezon City was the Halili Transit Company, which offered bus and taxi services.[136] Unfortunately, these transport modes were not affordable to minimum wage earners. Although Quezon tried to improve accessibility between the two cities by ordering the Luzon Bus Lines to serve Kamuning residents, who had no markets in their vicinity, inadequate public transportation characterized Quezon City's early history.[137]

Due to the abovementioned factors the state failed in its objective of mass housing in Quezon City. Instead, most of the first beneficiaries

FIG. 10. An advertisement of Gregorio Araneta, Inc.'s Santa Mesa Heights subdivision

SOURCE: *MDB* 15 Nov. 1940: 6

90   A CAPITAL CITY AT THE MARGINS

of Quezon's vision were middle-class households, such as in the case of Kamuning, the first residential community the PHC established. Kamuning's middle-class character contradicted Quezon City's working-class narrative. In the early 1940s Kamuning had the "beginnings of a suburbia: scattered houses amidst trees[,] cogon grass, rice-fields, and rolling hills which were mostly sparsely green with vegetation, being mostly adobe."[138] Its residents even petitioned the PHC to change the name of their area—from the original Barrio Obrero to Kamuning (a fragrant flowering tree/plant, *Murraya paniculata*, that grew in the area)—because they were not *obreros* (laborers); majority of them were government employees and white-collar professionals.[139] Furthermore, the demand for housing by middle-class families emboldened speculators, a development that Quezon denounced.[140] His crusade against speculation was, of course, questionable in light of how his suburban properties increased in value due to Quezon City's establishment. Meanwhile, Manila's working-class population got nowhere fast. As a contemporary observer put it, Quezon City would "nuzzle against Manila's slummy shoulders" but informal settlements would stay put for so long as factories remained in Manila.[141] Thus, the housing crisis lingered.

One cannot deny the opportunity Quezon City afforded to achieve equitable housing. To a large extent it marked a departure from Manila's free-market housing regime to state-directed homesites. Frost even praised the Commonwealth government for its "foresight . . . in acquiring large tracts of land such that over one-third of all the property in what is now Quezon City is public domain."[142] However, and as the subsequent chapters will reiterate, the new city did not just fail in its promise—it practically negated that promise. The PHC, and by extension Quezon City, "reflected none of the working-class bias ascribed to Diliman. Aiming more at the general welfare, the PHC charter was, at its sharpest, 'middle-class' in orientation."[143]

Building Façades

QUEZON'S DOUBLE-SPEAK in promoting Quezon City as a model working-class community would make more sense if read alongside his more important objective of centralizing political power. The very name of the city spoke of how he instrumentalized it for personal and political gain. Initially, the new city was named Balintawak City.[144] According to most narratives, Alejandro Roces was the one who suggested "Quezon City." Quezon supposedly retorted: "Why can't you wait until I'm dead before you name anything after me?"[145] When the bill to establish Quezon City reached Quezon for his final approval, he quibbled again over the city's name. However, legislators, especially Assemblymen Ramon Mitra and Narciso Ramos, prevailed upon him, and he relented (or allowed himself to be persuaded).[146]

Vanity gave Quezon City its name,[147] but the city itself was no mere vanity project; it was a reflection of how Quezon's urban policy served his dictatorial tendencies. His authoritarianism is fairly well established in scholarship. Aruna Gopinath called Quezonian rule a "tutelary democracy," while Theodore Friend highlighted its "maldistribution of political power." Others, like Alfred McCoy and Donovan Storey, have linked this matter with Quezon City's establishment.[148]

Quezon City's founding cannot be understood apart from Quezon's vast powers as chief executive over the legislature.[149] In this asymmetrical relationship, the National Assembly "worked closely with Quezon in passing Quezon-sponsored bills."[150] Quezon City's charter was just one among many examples of this dynamic. Simultaneous with the legislative process of founding Quezon City, Quezon co-opted the assembly to amend the 1935 Constitution and insert provisions that favored him, such as revisions in presidential term limits and the shift from a unicameral to a bicameral legislature. In the dealings involved in UP's relocation, he mobilized state funds toward "bending lesser masters to his personal will."[151] He slashed UP's budget when its leadership opposed him; otherwise, appropriations were easy to be had. Indeed, the relocation happened alongside a significant hike in UP's budget.[152] This, despite the fact that the power of the purse technically belonged to the legislature. It was a clear manifestation of Quezon's Commonwealth legacy: the creation of a strong presidency armed with budget prerogative.

Quezon's use of the national budget as political leverage gains more significance in light of the fact that the state had huge sums of money at its disposal due to the financial intricacies of the Commonwealth government. To lighten the effects of the end of free trade between the US and the Philippines due to the Tydings–McDuffie Act, the US regularly remitted to the Commonwealth government the tariffs on coconut oil imported from the Philippines. Quezon tapped this vast revenue stream to finance a wave of construction projects that focused on "large government buildings and of wide avenues in Manila, including the great Circumferential Road."[153] It was also the source of the PHP 2 million allocation in 1938 for the purchase of large landed estates and the PHP 8.5 million budget for UP's relocation.[154]

Quezon's authoritarianism also manifested in how he handled UP's relocation. His desire to move UP to "a more appropriate site away from the noise of the city which detracts from the serene life of the scholar"[155] was not shared by many student leaders, faculty, and alumni. Protests thus erupted in the campus.[156] Leading the students was UP Student Council (USC) President Roberto S. Benedicto. On 25 February 1938 Quezon held a dialogue with him and more than twenty students to discuss the relocation issue. In that meeting Quezon blasted the opponents of the campus transfer.

He told the students that they were "incompetent to intelligently partake in the discussions." He added: "even the professors can not threaten me if they ever attempted to resign. I'll accept the resignation of every professor and Dean, including the President. I can run this university without a single man of those now constituting the faculty. If necessary, I shall bring professors from every nation of the world." Prodded to explain his stance, Benedicto stated that the impending transfer was an issue of "social justice" because it would make life difficult for UP's Manila-based students, most especially working students, who would have to spend more on room and board.[157] Quezon's response revealed not only his arrogance, but also one of his ulterior motives in pushing for relocation:

> Benedicto — "Manila is a city where the student is in direct touch with the struggles of life and it offers the best opportunity for the student to fit himself for life's battle."
>
> Pres. — "It is precisely because the University is in Manila that I think it should be transferred to another place, away from this city."[158]

These lines, which ended Benedicto and Quezon's heated discussion, uncover the politics behind the latter's urban design for Manila and Quezon City. For Quezon, Manila had become a raucous space; its poverty and radical politics were "polluting" the minds of UP students, who by then formed a significant political force that often questioned government policies. Distant Diliman was thus a spatial remedy to keep students away from "radical elements" and lessen the political noise in Manila. Quezon might have also conceived of Diliman as a self-contained "pastoral campus" in an expanse of greenery, as was the case for many of the prestigious US universities at the time,[159] leading him to think that this location was ideal if UP sought to establish a world-class reputation. Quezon's reaction to the opposition, however, revealed his main consideration. He was "tired of seeing the U.P. students making demonstrations or approving resolutions on public or political questions." As he declared: "There will be no politics in the U.P."[160] Ironically, this episode of student activism demonstrated the university's politicization stemming from state repression. After the dialogue the state clamped down on the students. UP President Jorge Bocobo forbade demonstrations inside the campus, while Manila Mayor Juan Posadas prohibited them from organizing meetings within the city.[161]

The issue of UP's relocation showed that reworking urban space and politics can centralize power. Another example demonstrating this point is the growth of chartered cities during Quezon's administration. Quezon City's founding happened in a period when the national government was in a frenzy of establishing chartered cities. Before the Commonwealth, Manila and Baguio were the only chartered cities. However, under Quezon's

QUEZON'S CITY   93

government, the National Assembly granted charters to ten cities in a span of six years: Bacolod, Dansalan (present-day Marawi), Cavite, Cebu, Davao, Iloilo, San Pablo, Zamboanga, Tagaytay, and Quezon City.[162] The charters of these cities, which were the most populous and economically important cities in the country, shared an important similarity with that of Manila: the chief executive, via the secretary of the interior, dominated municipal affairs unlike in ordinary municipalities. One important reason behind this set-up was that the president had the prerogative of appointing and removing the mayor (even if appointees were non-residents of the said cities, as in the case of Quezon City Mayor Tomás Morató, a Tayabas resident) of chartered cities in contrast to the elective mayoralty position in most towns. This arrangement bypassed the provincial government, led by an elected governor, to the detriment of local autonomy.[163] As such, the Rizal provincial government could not intervene in Quezon City's affairs even if the city was part of the province. Quezon himself "frankly recognized that the new city charters mark[ed] no progress in the direction of democracy"[164]

The Commonwealth government quashed moves to reverse this trend. When the Municipal Board of Manila demanded that the position of mayor be made an elective one, Quezon insisted that it remain appointive, and the proposal fizzled out.[165] In justifying the control of the national government over chartered cities to the detriment of the residents' right to vote, Quezon cited the case of Washington, DC.[166] Manuel Duldulao believes that Quezon's preference for appointed city mayors was a practice he learned from his trips in Latin American countries, most of which were ruled by authoritarian caudillos then.[167] However, the Latin American experience was superfluous for Quezon given his urban biography; his knowledge of local politics in Manila and Washington, DC, was certainly enough to convince him that control over urban centers would be in his interest. In a 1937 speech, Quezon deflected criticisms against the political structure of chartered cities by referring to his personal observations of urban governance in Western cities he had visited:

> The idea of an appointive mayor is not a Filipino creation. It originated in America. There is the city of Washington, governed by a board appointed by the President. In France, prefects are appointed. . . . In America elective city officials have resulted in corruption, and inefficiency, so that in great cities there developed a strong feeling for the city management form of government.[168]

Quezon's push to establish Quezon City was also timely because it happened when Rizal province, a traditionally oppositionist province, was dominated by Eulogio Rodriguez Sr., "the grand old man of Rizal" and Quezon's secretary of agriculture and commerce. Although Rodriguez was a Democrata, he became Quezon's ally during the Commonwealth period. Since then, Rodriguez and fellow Democrata Juan Sumulong, Quezon's constant scourge and a veteran Rizal province politician,[169] became rivals in exerting their influence on provincial politics. Rodriguez overshadowed his competition throughout that decade, as his anointed ones consistently won the local elections. Meanwhile, in his capacity as secretary of agriculture and commerce, he oversaw the government's purchase of the Tuasons' lands that were included in the Diliman homesite.[170]

If chartered cities were by design controlled by the executive branch, Quezon City's dependence on Quezon was much higher. To put it simply: "There is no Democratic nonsense in the charter of Quezon City."[171] While city councils in other chartered cities were elective,[172] Quezon City's was simply based on Quezon's design. Quezon acted as city mayor from 12 October to 4 November 1939, pending the resignation from another position of his intended appointee and close friend Morató, who was then mayor of Calauag, Tayabas, and given the initial appointment of Quezon City chief of police.[173] Other Quezon cronies comprised the city government, whose "roster of officials reads like an all-star selection"[174] because many of them already held high government positions. These Quezon appointees were known as the *Casiana* cronies, named after Quezon's yacht, where these personalities often met to unwind. Two days before the enactment of the Quezon City charter, Quezon announced the appointments aboard the *Casiana*. He appointed BPW Director Vicente Fragante as vice mayor and city engineer. The councilors were Alejandro Roces, Paez, and Director of Health Eusebio Aguilar, who was also named city health officer. Alpheus Williams and Pio Pedrosa were appointed city secretary and treasurer, respectively. Jacob Rosenthal, a Jewish American businessman in Manila, was city assessor. Well-known educator Conrado Benitez was barrio lieutenant.[175] Quezon included in the city government cronies from his home province of Tayabas: Morató, City Engineer Manuel Diaz, and Justice of the Peace Perfecto R. Palacio.[176] Palacio praised the city's administrative structure by boasting: "Politics has nothing to do with the workings of the city government, nor does it have any influence in the appointment of officials therein."[177] Palacio's musings about the so-called absence of politics in the city government echoed the president's remarks about Diliman as an appropriate apolitical site for UP—evidently, a biased statement for he was, after all, a Quezon City official and a Quezon crony.

Cronyism begets corruption, as Quezon City's early history demonstrated. In 1940 the US State Department investigated the city's expenditures and discovered huge anomalous outlays. It concluded that the "profit motive" underpinned these questionable allocations:

QUEZON'S CITY   95

Without going into detail as to how profit is obtained by the politicians and their friends concerned, it may be stated that the chief methods are reportedly as follows:

(a) the land which now forms Quezon City was purchased for a few centavos a square meter by certain politicians and their friends who had prior knowledge of the Government's intention to create the city, and this land has not greatly increased in value;

(b) the People's Homesite Corporation was created to administer the development of the city, and its membership involves some of the same people involved in the land purchase; and

(c) the Santa Clara Lumber Company, whose personnel is identified with members of the Homesite Corporation, obtains any contract on any public project in Quezon City it desires. (The activities of Santa Clara Lumber Company are within the law as, when it submits a bid, the bid is lower than the bid of competitors, in fact unprofitably low. However, after the Homesite Corporation has awarded the contract, it alters the plans of the project, thereby freeing the Santa Clara Lumber Company from the necessity of confining itself to its original estimates.)[178]

Regarding the third item in the report, one must note that Ramon Roces served as president of the Santa Clara Lumber Company. Manuel Diaz, city engineer of Quezon City, was also affiliated with the said company. During the prewar period the company obtained contracts for some of the major structures in Quezon City, such as the QI and UP buildings in Diliman.[179] Snagging such deals in prewar Quezon City was a lucrative source of income because the city was engaged in a state-directed construction spree. From January to June 1941, Quezon City posted the highest value of new construction among all chartered cities except for Manila, totaling PHP 612,800, far exceeding those of the second- and third-highest cities, Davao (PHP 263,710) and Cebu (PHP 254,198).[180] The potential profits from this building binge was perhaps what Fidel Segundo, then chief of staff for intelligence, operations, and training of the Philippine Army, implied in his diary entry regarding the proposed transfer of the PMA to Quezon City:

Pres Q. [Quezon] wants the Acad. [PMA] to be in Quezon City and he uses MacA [MacArthur] to be tool for the proposition. Mil. [Military] expert style. The plan is this. The three million pesos must go to Quezon City by hook or by crook. To justify reduction of Mil. budget it must appear that no such reduction is being made as the supposed reduction is going to the building of a Mil. Acad. But that academy must be built in Q.C. [Quezon City]. Thus two purposes are accomplished. After this money is already spent in Q.C. it will be found without doubt that the selection was poor so that the Mil. Acad. will be moved somewhere again but the Quezon City shall have been built up. MacA is surely acting as a tool and nothing else.[181]

When Quezon died in 1944, he left an estate worth PHP 309,641. The estate included Quezon's insurance policies valued at PHP 30,000 and personal belongings worth PHP 30,000. The rest of his properties were real estate, "distributed in various parcels of land in Baguio valued at PHP 69,800; Pampanga, PHP 69,540.77; Rizal and Quezon Cities, PHP 78,301; Tayabas, PHP 27,000; and Manila, PHP 5,000."[182] At the same time, Aurora was no penniless housewife. She made quite a big investment in Quezon City based on Harrison's recollection: "In Quezon City she owned a grocery store and a drugstore; just before the invasion she had paid 20,000 pesos for beginning construction of the first cinema there; she owned also apartments and two houses in Quezon City."[183] Clearly, a big chunk of the Quezons' wealth came from their suburban properties. Analyzing the allegations of corruption in prewar Quezon City, McCoy stops short of stating that Manuel used Quezon City to accumulate ill-gotten wealth due to the lack of direct evidence.[184] Still, the pieces of circumstantial evidence are simply too difficult to ignore, enough to cast a shadow of doubt upon Quezon's integrity as a public official.

At the same time, it is also plausible that Quezon, like many other Filipino politicians and entrepreneurs past and present, thought that patriotism went hand-in-hand with individual gains. For these elites, like those in other countries, building the nation while profiting from it in the process created not a conflict of interest but a welcome coincidence. Of course, such an interpretation was not something that the marginalized could have made, let alone enjoyed.

Voices from the Margins

THOUGH A PRODUCT of Quezon's political cunning, Quezon City's inherent contradictions made it vulnerable to resistance from various stakeholders, including informal settlers, society's underside, and even mainstream politicians. Despite Quezon's influence over the state apparatus, there were still officials who opposed how he managed the new city.

Foremost of these politicians came from municipalities whose territories were affected by the delineation of Quezon City's territory. Their opposition was tempered, however, by the presence of Quezon's allies in the provincial government: the Rodriguezes. Nevertheless, there were unrelenting critics like Sumulong, whose opposition to Quezon translated into his criticism of Quezon City. He accused Quezon of misusing the proceeds of the coconut oil excise tax, evidenced by the millions spent on Quezon City.[185] He opposed the purchase of Hacienda de Diliman and labelled Quezon City as a city for the privileged class, a project for "enriching the hacienda owners in Marikina, Caloocan, and Sta. Mesa at the public expense."[186] He pointed out how the owners of Mandaloya Estate and Magdalena Estate—whose capital was furnished by the PNB—stood to benefit from infrastructural improvements paid for by the government.[87]

Opposition to Quezon City at the grassroots level also made itself felt. As the government set out to build the infrastructure for the city, it encountered dissent from the residents themselves. For example in 1940, right-of-way problems emerged in Kangkong, a place near Balintawak, when the government wanted to build a 50-meter boulevard there (fig. 11). Kangkong residents demanded compensation worth PHP 1 to PHP 1.50 per square meter, but the government would only give them 20 centavos. The government justified the small amount by saying,

> Their properties consisted mostly of second-growth bushes and bamboo groves of little value, with a few guava trees planted by nature and one or two santol trees here and there. In fact their land has been assessed at five centavos per square meter, and no improvements were mentioned in the assessments except the nipa houses.[88]

FIG. 11. Artwork depicting residents opposing road construction in Kangkong
SOURCE: Capellan, "Kangkong," 3

The government asserted that residents were lucky to get 20 centavos per square meter. They felt insulted and became furious. They pooled all their land titles, got a lawyer, and took the case to court. However, the court upheld the government's price. It maintained that Quezon City should become the new owner of the expropriated land and ordered the local government to deposit the sum needed to cover the cost of the land for the new boulevard. One of the contractors in the Kangkong road construction went to the site, but an old man with a long bolo, reminiscent of Bonifacio, "charged at the workers. Swearing, cursing, and shouting at the top of his voice, he ran toward them. The laborers fled in panic, leaving their tools." The author remembered the cry of Balintawak and mused: "Was this the second 'cry'?"[189]

The allusion to the Cry of Balintawak, although done to mock Kangkong residents, points to another important facet of Quezon City's sociopolitical geography: it encompassed sites with deep connections to anticolonial resistance: Balintawak, Pugad Lawin, Balara, Banlat, Krus na Ligas, Pasong Tamo, and Kangkong.[190] It is not far-fetched to think that Quezon intended the inclusion of these sites to confer upon Quezon City huge historical capital. Ironically, the embers of peasant resistance in these places presented another source of conflict that subverted the state narrative, a topic tackled in the next chapter.

The subversion of the state narrative in Quezon City also came from another self-contradiction in the city's space: the persistence of a suburban underside in the purported model city. Although residents believed their new city was safe, they also acknowledged that its territory used to be "the haunting grounds of thieves, robbers, gangsters, opium dealers, gamblers, and white slave-traffickers."[191] City regulations also hinted at the persistence of rural crimes. A 1940 ordinance mandating the registration of the offspring of large cattle[192] suggested the continued prevalence of cattle rustling in Quezon City. However, the most vivid demonstration of the city's underworld was the persistence of cabarets and cockpits.

At the time of Quezon City's founding, Manila's local government took pride in the fact that, although vice and prostitution continued to be present in the capital, it had achieved satisfactory results in stamping out illegal gambling and illicit "recreational clubs."[193] Through ordinances and law enforcement, Manila officials worked toward "cleaning" the city's image. Just like in Manila's case, one way for politicians to create a positive image for Quezon City was to prohibit cabarets and cockpits. For its advocates, this city was a space of moral cleanliness:

> Quezon City—the heart, the mind, the soul—is clean. Is it not far from the unceasing noise, the rattle of class-wars, that inhibit rest? Is it not away from nightclubs, cockpits, and gambling houses, and brothels that deaden the nerves, devastate the brain, wreck and rot the physique, drive away the soul?[194]

But there's the rub: prior to Quezon City's founding, a number of cabarets and cockpits had been built in areas just outside Manila's borders that eventually became part of the city. These border areas included Galas and La Loma, which at the time had at least three cabarets combined and were known to be frequented by "underworld characters."[195] Thus, "cleaning" Quezon City proved to be problematic.

In the beginning, the authorities were strict. Quezon City's police force set their sights on La Loma and raided houses suspected of being prostitution dens. It also conducted anti-gambling operations in other parts of the city, such as in Santolan and España Extension. On 20 November 1939, the city council passed an ordinance banning dancing schools and cabarets and gave cabarets until 18 January 1940 to leave.[196]

However, inconsistencies soon plagued law enforcement in Quezon City. To drive away cockpits and cabarets the city government hiked license fees to the PHP 2,500–PHP 5,000 range. Although some cabarets folded up due to this move,[197] it was not enough to remove them all because many cabaret and cockpit operators were willing to pay these amounts. Moreover, the city government eventually moved the 18 January 1940 ultimatum to 1 July for unstated reasons.[198] The convergence of interests of cabaret and cockpit operators and of politicians seen in Manila's suburbs held true for Quezon City. For instance, the transfer of the political jurisdiction over La Loma from Caloocan to Quezon City meant that the annual PHP 20,000 tax revenue generated by cockpits and cabarets there was also transferred to the new city. Eventually Quezon had to respect the reality on the ground by allowing existing cockpits in Quezon City to continue operating, while prohibiting the construction of new ones.[199]

The issue of cabarets in Quezon City gained salience in UP's relocation. One oft-repeated reason that government and university officials gave for the transfer was that urban distractions had diluted the spirit of scholarship in the old campus, and that cabarets were a major source of temptation for students.[200] Diliman's rurality, national and university officials thought, would preserve an academic atmosphere. Critics, however, did not buy this logic. Students opposed to the transfer argued that moving to a different place could never "guarantee that cinema houses, dance halls, and houses of prostitution will not follow the university to its new site."[201] They also noted that the new location in the suburban peripheries would make students, especially those who drove their own cars, vulnerable to the temptation of cabarets in the area. In opposing the bill that would enact UP's transfer, Leyte Assemblyman Tomas Oppus specifically mentioned that the cabarets in San Juan and La Loma were too near the new university site.[202] A *Philippine Graphic* article (fig. 12) gave a more detailed exposition on this matter:

When 15,000 families and 6,000 college students move in, how many cabarets will there be in Mariquina, which is only three kilometers, as a college boy's coupe runs, from university town? And will Mariquina cabarets be able to afford to open only over weekends?

The San Juan cabaret is only six kilometers away from the proposed site of the University. That's no farther than the Caloocan cabarets are from the present U.P. campus. And the proposed U.P. campus is only two kilometers away from Camp Murphy, where there are a lot of dashing army men to make the co-ed's heart go pit-a-pat and where, a report has it, there is at least one whorehouse.[203]

FIG. 12. Cartoon depicting a UP student surprised by his sudden proximity to cabarets

SOURCE: "Preview of a University Town," 4

* * *

WHEN QUEZON CITY WAS FOUNDED, its territory was no tabula rasa. Its space was largely defined by its position as part of Manila's border zone. Similar to its neighboring suburban towns, it exhibited sociospatial dualities: the coexistence of elite residential subdivisions and Manila's underside; and the overlapping of urban expansion and surrounding rural areas. It would be therefore incomplete to simply say that Quezon City mirrored unto space the official nationalism of the Commonwealth period. Its dualities undermined the narrative of "model city" and "future capital" its creators conferred upon it. Moreover, these dualities also reflected in the character of its chief architect. Not only was Quezon's urban biography straddling between city and countryside, his politics (and that of his fellow political elites) exhibited the synchronicity of nation-building and corruption that was apparent in Quezon City's beginnings. Not merely eponymous, Quezon City was Quezon's city.

From the start Quezon City was simultaneously progressive and conservative. The idea of transforming and subdividing landed estates into plots for working-class homes turned into a profit-generating machine for private interests and politicians. UP's relocation, couched in the rhetoric of cultivating a scholarly atmosphere to benefit the youth, was in reality the state's surveillance mechanism so that students might "be more closely supervised, not only in their studies, but also in their daily lives."[204] The city sought to give a preview of a postcolonial urban order, yet it was planned based on paradigms of colonial vintage. Quezon's social justice slogan gave his ideal city a veneer of democracy, obscuring how it served his personal objectives. Quezon City was promoted as the cradle for the essence of the Filipino nation, the common tao, but it could not hide its authoritarian roots, its middle-class slant, and its militarist, masculinist paternalism.

In many ways, Quezon City was ahead of its time in Southeast Asia. When it was founded, colonial administrators were still the ones steering the direction of urban development in the region, with Thailand as the notable exception. Because of the extensive domestic autonomy Filipino politicians enjoyed under the Commonwealth, they had the liberty not just to design what they thought were ideal cities but to anticipate in spatial terms the contours of the would-be nation-state. Unfortunately, this moment of anticipation took the form of a future capital city used for cronyism and corruption.

Quezon City thus illustrates what one historian has argued regarding Quezon in terms of the "glaring contrast between what he said he desired and what he did."[205] By looking at his urban biography, one can trace not just the development of his urban ideals, but more importantly the trail of his urban and suburban investments, which tell a tale that runs counter to Quezon City's official narrative. And since he was not alone in this endeavor, interrogating the city's official narrative entails a reassessment of the national(ist) elite, whose names have been bestowed upon the city's districts and thoroughfares.

Unfortunately, past and present historical works on Quezon City replicate Quezon's narrative for the city. The same themes and tropes used in the Commonwealth period appear in retrospective accounts that should have been more critical with the benefit of hindsight. The reason for this historiographical anomaly probably has a spatial dimension as well. Because these works emphasize the politicians, the planning process, and the structures of power in Quezon City's history, the resulting narrative relies heavily on official storylines and sources.

To counteract this tendency, historical analysis has to move the point of emphasis away from the center. By looking at Quezon City's own fringe areas, we see the conflicts and contradictions that undermined the narratives set for it by the powers that be. On the one hand, La Loma and Galas, areas that bordered Manila, gave shelter to society's underside. In this regard, Quezon City was no model city but Manila's rug, under which the unwanted elements in the old capital city—cabarets, cockpits, and criminal elements—could be swept. On the other hand, Kangkong was at the opposite border zone, sharing spaces with the rural barrios of Rizal province. The resistance of disgruntled farmers there against Quezon City's "development aggression" revealed how Quezon's urban project encroached upon the countryside. As the subsequent chapters will show, to interrogate preconceived notions about Quezon City and bring to the surface the stories of its marginalized sectors, one has to move away from its center in Diliman—which also had its own share of conflicts and contradictions—and analyze the sociospatial dynamics of the city's own peripheries.

CHAPTER THREE

Spectral Spaces
beyond Balete Drive

QUEZON CITY PROBABLY FIRST ENTERED POPULAR IMAGINATION through a postwar urban legend, Balete Drive's White Lady. The White Lady is a female ghostly figure who is said to haunt the street of Balete Drive in upscale New Manila (map 11). Although variations of the myth exist, certain elements recur: donning an immaculate white dress, the White Lady came from a wealthy family; she died at the hands of the Japanese during the Second World War; she often appears to taxi drivers, hailing them somewhere in the outskirts of Manila and then asking to be brought to Balete Drive, only to suddenly disappear by the time the car arrives at the destination.[1] Tales about her circulated so widely in the 1950s and 1960s that male drivers "deliberately avoided passing through Balete Street at night for fear of a strange encounter with her."[2] The Quezon City government and its police force even conducted a two-week surveillance in that street in December 1953 in response to widespread rumors.[3]

At many levels, Balete Drive's White Lady fittingly represents Quezon City's early postwar history. The liminality of the urban-rural interface is apparent,[4] both in the myth (Manila as familiar city versus Quezon City as mysterious suburbs) and its oral transmission as myth (modern, urban elements transmitted through the traditional platform of folklore). The brutality of the Japanese occupation and ferocity of Manila's unhampered expansion persistently reappear in spectral form to haunt a city deceived by its own suburban serenity.

Such violence stands in stark contrast to how one Quezon City historian described the first fifteen years of the city (1939–1954) as a dreary and "passive" period.[5] Perhaps this description referred to the city's predominantly rural appearance during this era. In terms of sociopolitical events,

103

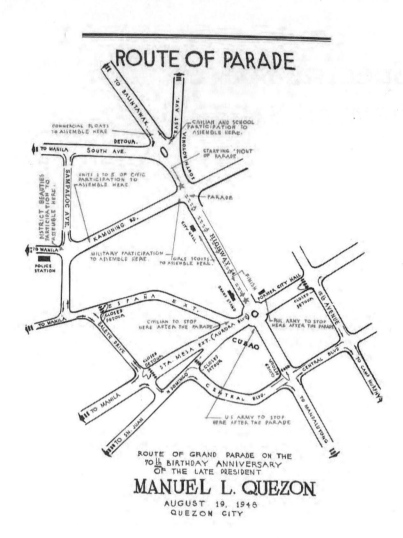

MAP 11. Route of the 1948 parade to celebrate Quezon's birth anniversary

NB. Take note of the key city streets, including Balete Drive

SOURCE: Capital City Planning Commission, *Souvenir Program, 70th Birthday Anniversary Celebration in Honor of the Late President Manuel L. Quezon* (Manila: Benipayo Press, 1948), back cover.

however, this phase in Quezon City's history was far from unexciting, especially the 1940s. This was a time of turmoil, tectonic shifts, and trauma. The Second World War defined the first half of this decade, while the latter half witnessed massive changes in the city's geography. The 1940s was nothing less than pivotal for Quezon City.

Historians of Quezon City often highlight two events in the 1940s: the formal selection of the city as the new capital to replace Manila (1948) and the completion of its new master plan (1949). This chapter discusses the same events but from a different perspective. Rather than focus on the political decisions of national officials and the modernist architectural designs and urban plans, it looks at the geographical peripheries of the city: its boundaries and border zones. Although it narrates events during the Japanese occupation, it focuses not on the battles that occurred in Quezon City but on how wartime conditions affected the stature of the city as a future capital city sitting on Manila's border zones. This chapter shows the oxymoronic character of municipal borders, how they are simultaneously permeable and rigid and how this simultaneity helps define not just the city's territory but more importantly its political-economic realities and ideological underpinnings.

The Japanese Interregnum

FOLLOWING THE ATTACK on Pearl Harbor on 8 December 1941, Quezon called for daily emergency cabinet meetings in his Marikina rest house (fig. 13), which was just outside Quezon City. On 18 December, this house was the silent witness to his last cabinet meeting, which had constituted itself as the Council of War.[6] With Japanese occupation imminent, he left for Corregidor Island six days later en route to the US. However, before leaving, he ordered

FIG. 13. Quezon meets his cabinet at his Marikina home before the Japanese invasion; note that this property is now part of Quezon City

SOURCE: Poblador, *Quezon Memorial Book*, 28

the creation of the City of Greater Manila upon Executive Secretary Jorge Vargas's advice. Through Executive Order 400 issued on 1 January 1942, Quezon formed a new urban entity that encompassed Manila and the suburban towns surrounding it: Caloocan, Pasay, San Juan, Mandaluyong, Makati, Parañaque, and Quezon City. He also divided Quezon City into two: Diliman and San Francisco, and assigned Dr. Florencio Cruz and Gregorio Felipe to govern the two areas, respectively.[7]

Creating the City of Greater Manila was strategic for two reasons. First, with the suburbs' inclusion, these important and populous towns could be spared from the ravages of war if the government declared the capital an "open city."[8] Second, with Vargas's appointment as Greater Manila mayor, under international law the occupation forces could not arrest him. The plan seemed most logical. On 26 December, MacArthur declared Greater Manila an "open city" and commanded the Philippine government and all Philippine combatants to withdraw from its environs. The local government would continue to function with police powers only for the protection of life and property. In effect, US and Filipino forces would not put up any resistance against the invasion. They essentially surrendered Manila to the Japanese.[9]

However, the Japanese occupation forces had different ideas about the capital city. They disregarded the "open city" declaration and attacked parts of Greater Manila.[10] For them, "open city" meant that Greater Manila had become a space for pacification and flushing out of resistance to prepare the capital city for colonial administration. Meanwhile, thousands of Manila residents moved to safer areas surrounding the capital due to constant Japanese bombardment, an exodus that began even before MacArthur's declaration. Many of them felt evacuating to Quezon City was the safe thing to do.[11] Journalist Leon Ty reported that the "flow of the evacuees was in the direction of less populated sections in Sampaloc, Gagalañgin, La Loma, Quezon City, and San Francisco del Monte. Most of the towns in the nearby provinces were thickly populated within a week."[12] Faustino Aguilar related that his Quezon City house became the refuge of sixty-four people when the war broke out.[13] Manila's border towns served as sanctuaries, albeit illusory: Ty related that one of his neighbors took his family and fled the capital to move to "some nice place in Quezon City where there isn't much chance of being bombed or strafed by machine-gun bullets,"[14] only to return to Manila after witnessing a dogfight between two planes just above their temporary abode. Other parts of Quezon City that endured attacks and bombings were San Jose (near Novaliches) and Baesa.[15]

After consolidating control over Greater Manila, the Japanese discarded the newly established municipal boundaries and appointed their own set of city officials. They replaced Mayor Vargas with Leon G. Guinto, who had to work with Japanese advisers in running the city. Meanwhile, the Japanese arrested

SPECTRAL SPACES BEYOND BALETE DRIVE   107

Morató and other local officials sometime in July 1942, believing that there were many hidden firearms in Quezon City and that Morató had something to do with it.[16] Greater Manila's reorganization under the Japanese served not only administrative purposes but also their anti-American, "Asianist" propaganda. As part of their campaign to erase all vestiges of American influence in the country, they redrew the boundaries of Greater Manila. First, they divided it into twelve districts, six of which were the formerly separate towns of Caloocan, Pasay, San Juan, Mandaluyong, Makati, and Parañaque. The Japanese also divided the territory of the former City of Manila into four districts. The last two districts came from the splitting of Quezon City into two along Circumferential Road No. 4. West of the Circumferential Road became the district of Balintawak, which included the barrios of San Francisco del Monte, Galas, and La Loma. The opposite side became the district of Diliman, which encompassed the barrios of Diliman, Cubao, and the UP campus (map 12).[17] The Japanese retained Cruz and Felipe as district chiefs for Diliman and Balintawak, respectively.[18] Within districts were district and neighborhood associations that were expected to instill discipline among Filipinos, an administrative apparatus that colonial officials linked to the prehispanic concept of barangay (see chapter 1, p. 20). Five to fifteen families comprised a neighborhood association, while five to fifteen neighborhood associations formed a district association. Each household had to place a *monpai* (a wooden plate that contains basic demographic information about the household) in a conspicuous place near the entrance of the house.[19]

The new place names that the Japanese used in Greater Manila evoked their agenda of removing vestiges of Western dominance and introducing "new schemes . . . which are more suited to Oriental ideology and idiosyncrasies."[20] The four districts that emerged from the former territory of Manila were rebaptized "Bagumbuhay" (new life), "Bagumpanahon" (new era), "Bagungdiwa" (new spirit), and "Bagumbayan" (new town).[21] The new colonizers picked Bagumbayan, Rizal's execution site in Manila, in recognition of his heroism, while the three other place names stood for the supposed positive transformations in Philippine society under the Japanese. While Diliman did not have much significance apart from being the name of the former hacienda, Balintawak's historical importance provided the reason for its selection. The rationale behind the retention of Balintawak revealed the emphasis the Japanese put in memorializing anti-Western resistance:

> "Balintawak" is the name of the place in Caloocan where in 1896 Andres Bonifacio, . leading the Katipunan organization, raised the famous "Cry of Balintawak," and started the Philippine Revolution against Spain, resulting in the overthrow of Spanish sovereignty in the Philippines. The memory of this name will always be sacred to Filipinos.[22]

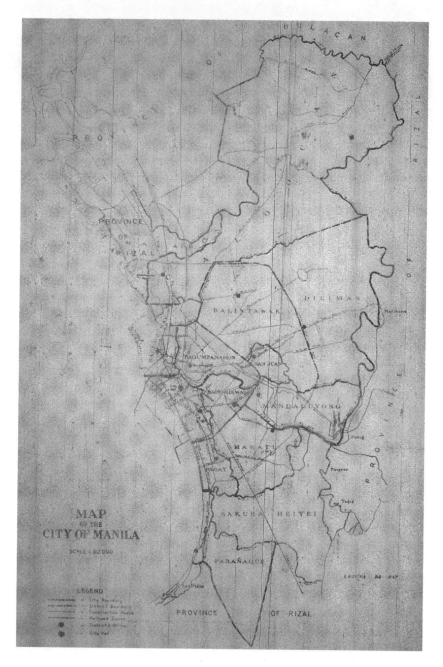

MAP 12. City of Greater Manila under Japanese occupation
SOURCE: Office of the Mayor, *City Gazette* 2(4), 16 Feb. 1943, back cover

SPECTRAL SPACES BEYOND BALETE DRIVE   109

Manila-based Filipino politicians echoed these historicist notions. Guinto claimed that the changes in Greater Manila resulting from Japanese occupation signaled a positive shift in the residents' urbanity, a shift away from the decadence of consumption that they learned from the Americans (and, one might surmise, a shift toward the discipline of both acquiescence to the Japanese and production for the colonial project). He welcomed the erasure of urban "self-centered individualism" that US colonialism purportedly nourished:

> As we became more urbanized, we disdained neighborliness because that might mean undue interference with our predatory activities. What neighbors we were willing to accept as neighbors were those who had expensive cars like ours, those for whom we could throw surprise parties in the hope of improving our social and political preferments, those, in short, who had a peculiar genius for living by the sweat of other people's brows.[23]

Urban changes in Greater Manila were not merely in the realm of the ideological. For one, the city suffered a demographic collapse during the occupation (table 7). However, Quezon City, or at least the areas it previously covered, was a puzzling exception. Diliman and Balintawak's

TABLE 7. Population per district, City of (Greater) Manila, August 1942

District	Area (sq. km.)	Population	Density (population/sq.km)
Bagumbayan	8.1	93,783	11,578.15
Bagungdiwa	7.3	71,205	9,754.11
Bagumpanahon	11.9	238,609	20,051.18
Bagumbuhay	8.7	214,182	24,618.62
Balintawak	30.4	41,157	1,353.85
Diliman	45.9	5,889	128.30
San Juan	3.6	25,546	7,096.11
Caloocan	107.4	48,135	448.18
Mandaluyong	16.5	25,450	1,542.42
Makati	17.1	31,248	1,827.37
Pasay	5.5	57,952	10,536.73
Parañaque	19.4	20,467	1,055

SOURCE: Office of the Mayor, *City Gazette: Published Fortnightly by the Office of the Mayor of the City of Manila*, vol. 1, no. 4, November 16, 1942 (Manila: Office of the Mayor, 1942), 33–35

110   A CAPITAL CITY AT THE MARGINS

combined populations in 1942 (47,046) posted an increase from Quezon City's 1939 population (39,013), an anomaly that was probably due to the exodus of Manila residents. Even more baffling was its residents' seeming financial stability: PHC's housing beneficiaries in Kamuning continued to pay their amortization during the war. In fact, the majority would finish their amortization (264 out of 410 purchasers) and lots (1,128 out of 1,600 purchasers) by the end of the war.[24]

This wartime anomaly does not negate the chaos and suffering in the country, including Quezon City, because of the occupation. Security was poor, and cases of thefts—including in La Loma Cemetery—increased in various places.[25] Poor transport and communication facilities between the city and the countryside made food scarce for city residents. Intraurban movement was difficult due to the lack of transit facilities[26] and the fact that the occupation army confiscated most motor vehicles. Residents in the suburbs had to rely on either the charcoal-fed skeletal city bus service or carromatas. The bus service only had two lines, both of which linked the suburbs to the city center with a common terminus in Plaza Santa Cruz. One of those routes serviced the western areas of Quezon City in Broadway, New Manila, via San Juan and Santa Mesa.[27] Two lines were added eventually, but at the request of the Army: the Sta. Cruz-Las Piñas and the Sta. Cruz-Quezon Institute lines. Urban-suburban transport in the Quezon City area was so badly needed that the city government handled numerous petitions for the extension of the Sta. Cruz-Quezon Institute line up to Kamuning.[28]

The urban-to-rural migration that war induced put an end to prewar suburban dynamics. Bereft of urban activity, the suburbs served the needs of the Japanese. For example, Balintawak became ideologically and logistically important for the colonizers. As the location of the Bonifacio monument, it was the site for ceremonial paeans to Bonifacio by the puppet Philippine government, acts of nationalism that the Japanese sanctioned. At the same time, Balintawak was the checkpoint of the Japanese to regulate the flow of persons and products going in and out of northern Greater Manila, and to intercept guerrillas and contraband goods. The Jesuits' Sacred Heart Novitiate in Novaliches was occupied by the Japanese army, similar to how other religious establishments were converted into camps.[29] Closer to Manila, the Christ the King Seminary along España Extension (present-day E. Rodriguez Avenue) served as the headquarters of the Kalipunang Makabayan ng mga Pilipino (Makapili), a group of civilian collaborators.[30] At the same time, the Japanese army converted the QI into an army hospital.[31]

Diliman's vacant lots caught the attention of the colonizers for various reasons. The Japanese Army and Navy occupied parts of Diliman and, in doing so, removed or destroyed boundary markers for the subdivided lots. The colonizers tried to turn the area into a site for its food production campaign, especially for the establishment of farms that would absorb city-released war prisoners. Diliman also served as the pilot location for the Japanese-sponsored community-farming project and a city nursery.[32] Since the district became the base for agronomists conducting surveys for the food-sufficiency campaign, it offered work opportunities, albeit low-paying and menial ones, to the hundreds of unemployed in the city. The work involved gathering *walis-walisan*, or yellow barleria (*Sida rhombifolia Linn*), a medicinal plant that grew abundantly in the area.[33] Japanese forces also occupied the two three-story concrete buildings in the UP Diliman campus, the College of Liberal Arts (present-day Benitez Hall of the College of Education) and the College of Law and Business Administration (present-day Malcolm Hall of the College of Law).[34] These two structures were the only major establishments that had been completed in the new campus before the outbreak of hostilities.

The effects of the war on Quezon City also manifested in the visible Jewish presence in the city. Adjoining Quezon's Marikina home was a 14-acre lot, which he turned over to Jewish refugees from Germany before the war. They used it free of charge for ten years. Moreover, on 30 December 1939, the Quezon City government issued a building permit to Alex Frieder, chair of the local Jewish Refugee Committee, for the construction of the two-story Home for Refugees in Cubao on the Magdalena Estate. During the war, Magdalena Estate Inc. continued to run its real estate business, and many of those who transacted with it were European Jews.[35] That the company had Jewish connections was perhaps one of the reasons why the Japanese harassed its owners, the Hemadys, who were subjected to a "gruelling investigation which went on for several weeks [. . .] due to a report from an unknown source that the corporation was actively financing some guerrilla organizations."[36]

Although the Japanese had to back away from the Hemadys due to lack of evidence, this episode pointed to the colonizers' growing concern for guerrilla activity in the urban areas. A son of one of the Hemadys' employees related:

> One could also sense the increase in the number of *guerrilleros* thriving in the city and the escalation of their activities. The son of Mr. Hemady's gardener, who worked part-time in the office [Magdalena Estate, Inc.], told me that he recognized some of the businessmen and clients appearing in the corporation as active guerrillas. He himself was inducted as a member of Major Anderson's special guerrilla unit and told of how his outfit kidnapped certain Japanese officers in Marikina and tortured them to death in reprisal for what the enemy did in that area during a *zona*.[37]

Zona referred to the Japanese soldiers' system of herding of males in a community to execute those who were believed to be members or supporters of the anti-Japanese guerrilla movement. Places in Quezon City, like Masambong and San Francisco del Monte, endured this wartime atrocity.[38] But at the same time, such incidents pointed to the reality that, once again, Manila's peripheries were hotbeds of resistance. Guerrillas were active in areas like Santa Mesa, Caloocan, Malabon, San Juan, Mandaluyong, San Mateo, Montalban, and Navotas.[39] Three guerrilla groups operated in Novaliches, Caloocan, including the Hukbong Bayan Laban sa Hapon [People's Army against the Japanese] (Hukbalahap), more popularly known as the Huks and composed mainly of peasants in Central and Southern Luzon. At the same time, many suburban residents served as spies for guerrillas. Unfortunately, regular guerrilla activities in the area led the Japanese to conduct harsher surveillance methods against civilians. Novaliches's distance from Manila also made it a haven for anticolonial writers living in a time of intense censorship and colonial propaganda. According to Teodoro Agoncillo: "The meetings of writers in some faraway place, such as the woods of Novaliches, a few miles north of Manila, were occasions for frank and honest exposition of views on the paramount subject of the Japanese occupation."[40]

The agrarian unrest that constantly disturbed the suburbs in the prewar era reared its ugly head again during the occupation, notwithstanding the altered sociopolitical alignments caused by the war. With the onset of Japanese rule, the former Sakdal movement, now known as Partido Ganap, cast its lot with the new colonizers. Ganapistas regarded the occupation as an opportunity to redress past structural injustices committed against them, albeit in ways that compromised the well-being of other ordinary Filipinos. Moreover, they tried to appropriate the discourse of the Philippine Revolution in ways that tried to remake prewar social relations and align it with the Japanese ideology of co-prosperity. Such was the case in an incident narrated by PHC employee and Quezon City resident Faustino Aguilar to former Quezon City Mayor Morató:

> Ang nangyayari'y bunga ng aking pagiging kawani sa ating Pamahalaan at tiyak na may kinalaman sa "People's Homesite Corp." Maáalala po ninyo na isang nagngangalang Gaudencio Bautista, kilalang "ganap" na nakatira sa isang nayon sa lungsod Quezon, ay nagmanibala sa mga dating nangakatira sa lupain ng mga Tuazon na binibili ng pamahalaan at ginawang bagong lunsod upang magsikilos sila at nang mabawi ang pag-aari sa nasabing lupain, sa matwid na ang mga Tuazon ay walang kakará-karapatan sa pagbibili, sapagka't hindi sila ang mga may-ari at wala namang katibayang hawak, sa tinurang lupain.[41]

> (The present situation is due to my being a government employee and certainly has to do with the PHC. If you can recall, a certain Gaudencio Bautista, a known Ganap member who lives in a barrio in Quezon City, incited former occupants of the Tuason estate, which was bought by the government and turned into a new city, to mobilize

SPECTRAL SPACES BEYOND BALETE DRIVE   113

for the purpose of reclaiming their ownership of the said lands, on the basis that the Tuasons do not have the right to sell the estate because they are not the true owners and do not have proof of ownership.)

The effect of the war on Quezon City is perhaps most vividly captured by Pacita Pestaño-Jacinto's bittersweet 4 August 1942 entry in her published diary:

> Oscar [Pestaño-Jacinto's husband] has just come back from Quezon City. We used to drive there in the old days, top down and doing sixty, till the small hours of the morning like two romantic ghosts under blue moonlight, dreaming dreams. It used to be such a lovely, clean-looking place. But Oscar says it has changed quite a lot. He says that the Quezon Institute, one of the largest and loveliest hospitals in the Islands, has been taken over by the Japanese. It used to be a landmark built on high ground, its simple garden so well cared for. Now there is dirty khaki linen hanging everywhere, along the verandahs, draped under windows, even on the lovely shrubs. And what makes it truly unlovely is the sight of naked figures adorned with G-strings, squatting on the porch rails or walking among the *canna* flowers, like stunted ugly dwarfs.[42]

The abovementioned changes, however, never became permanent due to the quick end of the Japanese occupation. Resurgent US and Philippine armed forces, in tandem with numerous guerrilla units, began winning a series of key battles against the Japanese in October 1944. By February 1945 they were in a position to reoccupy Manila. However, it took a destructive month-long battle before the Japanese finally left Manila, leaving the city in ruins and the most devastated city after the war, second only to Warsaw.[43]

Up from the Ashes

THE US REOCCUPATION of the Philippines signaled the end of the war, while Filipinos struggled to bring back normalcy. It reinstalled the Commonwealth government, with Osmeña as president. He had his hands full as he tried to juggle the problems of reconstruction, especially devastated Manila, the cases of Filipinos who collaborated with the Japanese, and preparing the country for its independence in 1946. All these were too much for him to handle; no wonder that in the 1946 presidential elections he lost to Manuel Roxas despite being the incumbent.

However, the onset of the postwar period did nothing to alter the basic social structures of Philippine society.[44] In the economic sphere, the US–Philippines free trade relations that defined the colonial period resumed after Philippine independence. In the political sphere, Manila and Washington, DC, maintained the so-called "special relations" between the two countries. Although the previously dominant Partido Nacionalista split into two in the 1946 presidential elections—the "liberal" wing led by

114   A CAPITAL CITY AT THE MARGINS

Roxas formed the Liberal Party (LP), while those who sided with Osmeña remained with the Nacionalista Party (NP)—no significant differences distinguished one from the other with regard to their approach to US–Philippines relations.[45] The postwar period saw the continued influence of American institutions over almost all aspects of governance. US rehabilitation agencies were everywhere in the country and gained strategic positions in Philippine political, economic, social, and military affairs. As late as 1947, these agencies and their personnel were numerous, "far exceeding the American establishment here before the war."[46] Their presence in Quezon City was palpable: from the setting up of the Joint US Military Advisory Group (JUSMAG) headquarters in Camp Murphy to the malaria control units the US Public Health Service deployed in 1948.[47]

Under this neocolonial regime, colonial urban and suburban patterns persisted into the era of independence. Manila's position as the country's primate city remained secure. On the surface, disruptions were apparent, especially in terms of the physical destruction of Manila's architecture and urban design and the ensuing housing shortage, but Filipino politicians would turn to established colonial networks and adopted colonial notions, albeit reformulated, to address immediate postwar problems.

For Filipino politicians, the destruction caused by the war was a "blessing in disguise" as it allowed them to "remodel our cities" without the restrictions and limitations present under normal circumstances.[48] The end of the war seemed to have presented much more: an opportunity for the Filipinos to "reinvent themselves" and "reinterpret their identity" through the architecture and urban plan of its capital.[49] However, in the end what happened was a continuation of an urbanism defined by US-derived concepts and designs.

Although Filipino politicians had groomed Quezon City to be the future capital city, the war's aftermath made them think twice. Quezon was already dead, and not all officials were sure that pursuing the prewar plan was feasible. The war had destroyed Manila and rendered it practically incapable of serving as the capital, but Filipino politicians could not immediately take this opportunity to develop Quezon City as Manila's replacement because of the lack of funds. Quezon City was not as devastated as Manila, yet its urban development was stalled because postwar rehabilitation was a more pressing matter for the cash-strapped government. Moreover, the war had also taken its toll on the city's physical infrastructure, which was felt in the decline in city services and security, as well as environmental problems.[50] As will be discussed later in this chapter, despite available funding from the US Philippine War Damage Commission (PWDC), the US agency that disbursed war-damage payments to legitimate claimants, the "grandiose plans" had to be set aside.[51]

SPECTRAL SPACES BEYOND BALETE DRIVE   115

However, by the time the Philippines attained formal independence on 4 July 1946, Quezon City, which at this point was still part of the City of Greater Manila, had already achieved fiscal self-sufficiency to sustain its daily operations. At the end of fiscal year 1945–46, it posted a budget surplus of PHP 109,526. Although it received financial aid from the national government worth PHP 60,000 during that same fiscal year, the surplus was enough to convince Congressman Ignacio Santos Diaz to push for the city's "reinstatement" as a political unit separate from Manila.[52] On 10 October 1946, Quezon City regained its status as a separate city by virtue of Republic Act (RA) 54, which repealed Quezon's 1942 Executive Order that created the City of Greater Manila.[53] By the end of fiscal year 1947, its general funds totaled PHP 564,513.33, while it had other funds worth PHP 173,959.73. City officials kept expenditures (PHP 412,724.82 of the general fund and PHP 83,597.66 of other funds) within the budget to maintain a surplus.[54]

Although the Quezon City government did not get as much funds as Manila from the PWDC, it indirectly benefited from the said commission. The PWDC funded UP's reconstruction efforts in Diliman because the damage sustained by the Ermita campus rendered it unusable. The prewar plan of relocating to Quezon City thus became all the more imperative and timely.[55]

UP received PHP 13 million from PWDC, the single largest allocation to a government entity. From this amount, it earmarked PHP 10 million for the building program in Diliman, especially for the library, College of Liberal Arts, College of Engineering, the Conservatory of Music, and student halls. After its first year as a fully operational campus in Diliman, around 75 percent of building construction had been financed by the PWDC (fig. 14).[56]

Aside from financial help, UP also obtained infrastructural support from the US. The US Army Signal Corps, which used the Diliman campus as its head-quarters during the reoccupation period, had a lease agreement with UP that it could use the place rent-free until June 1948 provided that all the structures and physical improvements in the area would be turned over to UP for free upon the expiration of the lease. On 6 December 1948 the army handed over around "200 buildings of various sizes and constructions like the gymnasium, and the swimming pools, which, with proper care, will be serviceable to the U.P. for the next few years."[57] The quonsets and *sawali* (interwoven splits of bamboo) structures that the US Army left behind became makeshift classrooms, laboratories, dormitories, offices, and residential houses for the faculty.[58] These structures were the enduring symbols of UP Diliman's early years. They were significant additions to the campus, as the two prewar buildings in the Diliman campus sustained damage during the war.[59]

When President Roxas delivered a speech during UP's commencement exercises in 1948, he likened the country's future with the university's bright prospects in Diliman.[60] The transfer happened in a one-month span

The administrative offices will be housed in this building which stands at the entrance of the Quezon City campus. Symbolic statue, "Oblation", is in front of the building.

FIG. 14. Construction of UP Diliman's main administration building, Quezon Hall; take note of the signage that reads: "REHABILITATION PROJECT AIDED BY THE UNITED STATES OF AMERICA THROUGH THE UNITED STATES–PHILIPPINES WAR DAMAGE COMMISSION"

SOURCE: B. M. Gonzalez, *Thirty-seventh Annual Report of the President of the University of the Philippines to the Board of Regents for the Academic Year June 1, 1949 – May 31, 1950* (Quezon City: UP, 1951), 30

between 16 December 1948 and 11 January 1949, the same month that UP and the Philippine government executed the deed of sale of the Diliman property (eight parcels, with an aggregate area of 533 hectares) for a pro-forma cost of PHP 1.[61] On 12 January 1949 UP formally started academic operations and held classes in its new campus, "from *barong-barong* to palace."[62] The first set of faculty and employees who resided in Diliman from the late 1940s to the early 1950s referred to themselves as "pioneers."[63]

Despite the UP community's optimism amid an uphill reconstruction program,[64] not everyone saw things positively. While most of the faculty and students finally gave their support to the relocation, parents and alumni continued to oppose it. University President Bienvenido Gonzalez took note of the "strenuous opposition [to the transfer], often punctuated by

FIG. 15. Laying of the cornerstone of UP Diliman's Gonzalez Hall
SOURCE: Gonzalez, *Thirty-sixth Annual Report*, frontispiece

vicious personal attacks."[65] However, the antagonism caused by the Diliman question quickly dissipated. When the Oblation statue was transferred to Diliman in February 1949 the UP Alumni Association sponsored a motorcade for the ceremonial relocation of UP's foremost symbol. Afterwards UP held a ceremonial laying of the cornerstone of the new library building, sponsored by Aurora Quezon and PWDC chairperson Dr. Frank A. Waring (fig. 15).[66]

The Diliman campus, as Quezon envisioned, was isolated from urban Manila.[67] With its vast but quite inaccessible site, UP earned the moniker "Diliman Republic."[68] At the surface level, this label denoted the self-contained character of the university, which could offer the community all of its basic necessities through its on-campus facilities and services.[69] Beyond self-sustainability, however, this moniker, which had become well known by the 1950s, evoked autonomy and academic asceticism as though UP was a self-contained space. It conjured images of elitism and "isolation from the vulgar world of Philippine politics, the mundane concerns of the larger population, the conflicts of Philippine society—the thousand and one issues that occupied lesser mortals."[70] Rey Casambre, who grew up on campus in the 1950s and 1960s, reminisced about his initial thoughts about the unique space of UP Diliman prior to his involvement in radical politics:

118   A CAPITAL CITY AT THE MARGINS

Academic freedom and the need to be objective appeared to be the rationale for insulating the university from the distractions and disruptions of society, so much the better to diagnose it with a disinterested eye and arrive at correct and effective prescriptions. UP Diliman seemed to have all the qualities of an ivory tower par excellence. Its geographic location, idyllic setting and pleasant climate served this purpose perfectly. Indeed, from the vantage point of our home on M. Viola, on the northwestern corner of the now much-expanded campus, it was a daily luxury to view from a distance the entire metropolis shrouded in thin smog in the early morning, watch the sun sink slowly and disappear behind Manila Bay and Corregidor or the Bataan mountains before dusk set in, then enjoy the glimmering city lights till bedtime. In all these—so distant from the madding crowd—there is not one image, no trace nor hint of poverty or injustice, oppression or exploitation.[71]

But as the subsequent chapters will show, UP's insularity would actually be a factor in turning it into a university fully embedded in the culture and politics of its immediate community and of Philippine society.

Designating and Designing the New Capital City

MANILA'S WARTIME DESTRUCTION gave Filipino politicians another reason to ponder upon the question of moving the capital city to an alternative location. Although Quezon made public declarations about his desire to make Quezon City the capital city upon the attainment of independence, such pronouncements lacked an enabling law. As such, legislators pushed for bills to this effect in several instances during the early postwar years. Nueva Vizcaya Rep. Leon C. Cabarroguis filed a bill in 1945 to combine Manila and Quezon City into one city to be known as Rizal City. Two years later, he refiled a similar measure but wanted the merger to be called "Quezon City" and operate under Manila's charter.[72] Nevertheless, not all Filipino officials thought Quezon City was the rightful heir to Manila, evinced by the failure of these bills to become laws.

In his first SONA, President Manuel Roxas identified neither Manila nor Quezon City as capital city. Instead, he asked Congress to appropriate PHP 50,000 for Quezon's state funeral and temporary mausoleum. In addition, he proposed the construction of a monument to recognize the "historical relationship" between the US and the Philippines, "in recognition of the greatness of mind and heart of the American people who have done and are continuing to do so much to make our national existence possible." Roxas wanted these two memorials—one recalling a deceased leader, the other celebrating an about-to-be-terminated colonial relationship—at the center of the newly born nation: "These two great memorials should be so situated that they will be focal points of the capital city of the Philippines." Afterwards, he vowed to work with Congress to come up with a "definition of our capital city-planning proposals."[73]

SPECTRAL SPACES BEYOND BALETE DRIVE   119

On 23 July 1946, acting on his SONA promise, Roxas promulgated Administrative Order No. 5, creating a Capitol Site Selection Committee to identify the most suitable site for the new capitol.[74] The committee eventually became known as the Committee on Capital City Site, headed by Sen. Melecio Arranz as chair and Jose Paez as vice-chair. Its thirteen members formed five subcommittees to tackle specific issues: public works development, administrative coordination, strategic considerations, general sanitation, and scenic resources. It also conducted a public hearing on 27 January 1947 to increase participation from various sectors.[75]

The committee focused on sixteen proposed sites: Bataan, Quezon City, north Novaliches, north Montalban, San Mateo, Antipolo, Nagcarlan–Liliw, Sto. Tomas–Tanauan, Canlubang, Tagaytay, Baguio, Iloilo, San Pablo, Los Baños, Sibul, and Fort McKinley.[76] Using the five aspects tackled by the subcommittees as the criteria for judging, the committee formulated a rating system to rank all sites: 30 percent for general sanitation, 25 percent for public works and development, 20 percent for strategic consideration, 15 percent for scenic resources, and 10 percent for administrative coordination (table 8).[77]

TABLE 8. Ratings by Committee on Capital City Site for the top six sites

Proposed Site	Sanitation Works	Public Considerations	Strategic	Scenic	Administration	Average
1. Ipo–Novaliches	45	92	80	80	70	71.5
2. Baguio	50	76	90	66	75	69.4
3. Quezon City–Novaliches	54	86	50	72	80	68.3
4. Antipolo–Teresa	25	92	95	61	60	64.6
5. Nagcarlan–Lilio	40	76	75	80	65	62.5
6. Tagaytay	25	52	60	70	60	49.9

SOURCE: Committee on the Capital City Site, Report of Committee on the Capital City Site, 10

Based on the said criteria, the committee enumerated the advantages of combining the Quezon City and Novaliches sites into one: their proximity to Manila compared with other sites, accessibility to other important areas in the country, Quezon City's existing charter, public works facilities, geologic features, large area of government-owned land, healthfulness due

120   A CAPITAL CITY AT THE MARGINS

to elevation, and historical background. On the flipside, the committee also saw their weaknesses: defense liability because of the low elevation of certain areas and proximity to Manila, worsening traffic and congestion in Manila that spilled over into Quezon City, and that it was not as salubrious as Baguio, Tagaytay, or Antipolo.[78]

Given the results, the committee recommended the selection of the Ipo–Novaliches site merged with that of the Quezon City–Novaliches site. In effect, the committee practically picked Quezon City as the capital city. Interestingly, selecting Quezon City as the new capital city was rather expedient since it would make the necessary legislation easier compared with picking a different site among those shortlisted. As noted by Roxas's executive secretary, pursuant to Act No. 1841 of 1908, which was based on the recommendations of the Burnham plan, "the President without congressional approval [could] select any site for the capital city for the construction of the National Capital if it is not more than 30 kilometers from the Rizal monument of the City of Manila."[79] Thus, to avoid legal complications (i.e., repealing or amending Act 1841) and to abide by the selection process that the committee set for itself, Quezon City had to radically expand its existing territory to incorporate Novaliches and Ipo's foothills (map 13), a move designed to expand the city's high-altitude areas. Such a consideration was deemed so important that the committee made a specific recommendation about the future transfer of administrative buildings: "The Capitol Building, the Executive Mansion, and the executive offices will be located on rolling ground with an elevation of approximately three hundred feet above sea level."[80] In summary,

> the Committee concludes that the area now covered by Quezon City extending Northward along the Marikina River to the upper limits of the Novaliches reservoir watershed; thence West to the boundary line of the provinces of Rizal and Bulacan; and down to meet the boundary line again of Quezon City, comprising an approximate total area of SIXTEEN THOUSAND TWO HUNDRED (16,200) more or less, one-fourth of which is owned by the Government, is the best under the circumstances as the capital city of the Republic in the opinion of the Committee.[81]

Novaliches's inclusion in Quezon City was crucial. Not only did it give the city a large area for future expansion, it altered the social geography of the future capital and the towns surrounding it. It offered Quezon City immediate access to key resources, with water and natural resources topping the list of assets it added to the city.

Although Quezon City was far from crowded in the late 1940s, its population was increasing at an exponential rate: from 47,046 in 1942 to 107,977 in just six years, a staggering 21 percent annual growth rate (table 9). Having a larger territory for the eventual capital city was thus a prudent move. Furthermore, the annexed area of Novaliches was sparsely populated.

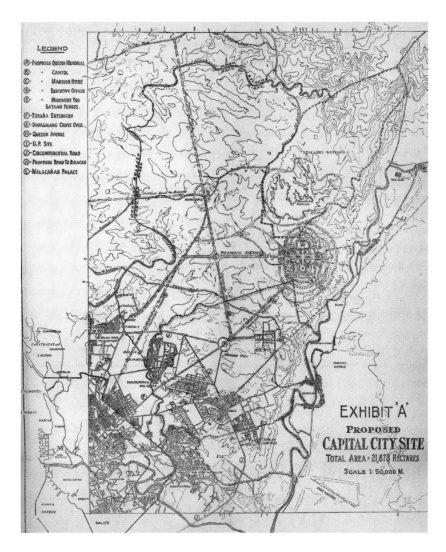

MAP 13. Proposed territorial jurisdiction for the Quezon City–Novaliches site by the Committee on Capital City Site

SOURCE: Committee on the Capital City Site, Report of Committee on the Capital City Site, 22a

Whereas suburbanization had encompassed the older parts of Quezon City, rurality lingered in the barrios of Novaliches:

> It had no electricity, no municipal water supply, no modern means of transportation except for one bus line that serviced the area, no hospital, no high school, no asphalted roads, no fire department, no post-office, no bank, no cinema house—none of the modern conveniences of urban living.[82]

But more than getting space for future growth, the addition of Novaliches had an impact on the geography of health in Quezon City. As stated in the report, the committee considered Novaliches's rolling hills spaces of salubrity. Moreover, Novaliches was the site of significant medical institutions, namely the Tala Leprosarium and the Tala Institute of Malariology.[83] Most important, the Novaliches watershed (also known as the La Mesa watershed) made Quezon City the center of water resources in the greater Manila area.

As with any other urban settlement, securing a reliable source of potable water was a key consideration in planning a city as big as Quezon City. An important component in the initial planning of the Hacienda de Diliman after PHC purchased it in 1938 was the extension of the Metropolitan Waterworks Department (MWD) system to the site to ensure the viability of what was projected to be a huge urban settlement. Established in 1919, the MWD provided water and sewerage services to Manila and its suburbs. Its coverage area stretched from as far north as Montalban to as far south as Parañaque, including places that would comprise Quezon City.[84] Its main source of water was the Angat River Dam in Bulacan, while the reservoir and filtration plants were located in Novaliches and nearby Balara, respectively (map 14). In 1929 the MWD constructed the La Mesa Dam in Novaliches to store the runoff of the 2,570-hectare Novaliches watershed. This structure formed the Novaliches Reservoir, which in the immediate postwar period had a 9-billion gallon capacity and 6 billion gallons of usable capacity. In 1935 the MWD inaugurated its Balara Filter

TABLE 9. Quezon City's population per barrio, 1948

Barrio	Population
Bagumbayan	1,182
Balara	1,214
Balintawak	3,103
Baranca	291
Barilan	1,239
Cruz na Ligas	584
Cubao	11,899
Culiat	1,546
Galas	8,069
Kamuning	9,477
La Loma	25,483
Malamig	394
Malitlit	1,675
Masambong	1,117
Murphy	8,622
Pansol	2,144
San Francisco del Monte	9,321
San José	5,613
Santol	11,726
Sapang Camias	348
Tatalong and Matalahib	2,630
Ugong Norte	300
Total	107,977

SOURCE: Bureau of the Census and Statistics, *1948 Census of the Philippines* (Manila: Bureau of Printing, 1951), 213

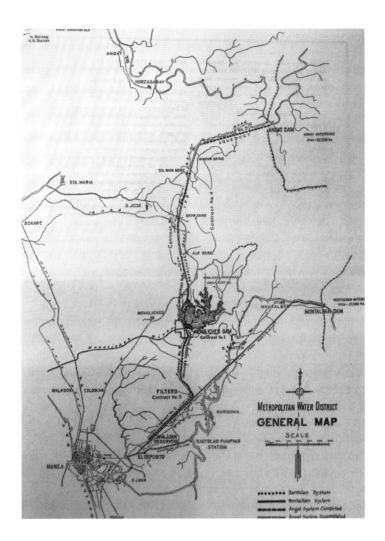

MAP 14. MWD general map, 1930s
SOURCE: MWD, *Manila's Water Supply*, FMP Box 52, Folder 3

Plant, which treated water from Novaliches before it reached consumers.[85] In effect, Novaliches's inclusion in Quezon City's territory made the new capital city the waterworks capital of a would-be Metro Manila, the "Life-giver of Manila and Neighboring Provinces."[86] Furthermore, from these hydrographic features sprung forth several health and recreational resorts, like the Balara Filters Park and the La Mesa Dam Park, which made Quezon City a tourist destination. By the 1950s the Balara Filters was drawing summer crowds to its swimming pools, picnic gardens, and an architecturally exquisite pavilion. In 1951 alone, it had more than a hundred thousand visitors.[87]

124   A CAPITAL CITY AT THE MARGINS

In concluding its report, the Committee on Capital City Site recommended the following: a) to redraw Quezon City's boundaries; b) to declare all public lands in the city unavailable for sale, lease, or homestead; and to reacquire by eminent domain those sold before the war; c) to expropriate undeveloped private estates in the city for public use and to subdivide the remainder for lease to avoid speculation; d) and to develop the city by constructing wide avenues, subdividing expropriated areas for lease or sale to the public, creating a Capital City Planning Commission, maintaining the new UP campus site, issuing a bond worth PHP 20 million to finance city development, and making the appropriate legislations.[88]

After the committee submitted its report to Roxas in April 1947, the president focused on two important next steps: encourage Congress to enact the committee's recommendations and craft a new master plan for Quezon City. For the first objective, he used his 1948 SONA as an opportunity to publicly seek the help of legislators to pass the necessary bill.[89] For the second one, Roxas commissioned a number of architects and engineers to go to the US and "observe modern methods of developing the capital."[90] This group, the Engineering and Architectural Mission of the Philippines, visited various cities in the Americas from September 1947 to January 1948. Its itinerary included San Francisco, Berkeley, Los Angeles, Pasadena, Beverly Hills, Hollywood, Lincoln (Nebraska), Chicago, Urbana, Detroit, Bloomfield Hills, New York, Boston, Cambridge, Washington, DC, Knoxville, Miami, Havana, San Juan (Puerto Rico), Caracas, Rio de Janeiro, São Paolo, Montevideo, Buenos Aires, Santiago de Chile, Lima, Quito, Bogota, Panama City, and Mexico City.[91]

Roxas, however, died on 15 April 1948 while his desired law and master plan were still in the pipeline. His vice president and successor, Elpidio Quirino, took over. On 17 July 1948 Quirino signed RA 333, which declared Quezon City as the capital city.[92] This declaration gained much publicity in a grand parade to celebrate Quezon's seventieth birth anniversary on 19 August. It was a fitting gift to the city's main visionary (see map 11).

Like Quezon City's original 1939 charter (CA 502), RA 333 called for the state to purchase land within the city boundaries (at prices not more than the assessed value as of 1 January 1946) or through expropriation of private estates for eventual resale to the public. It stipulated that the resale value would be the purchase cost plus six percent on cash basis. For those who would pay on installment basis, an added 4 percent would be charged.[93]

One of the major provisions of RA 333, as recommended by the Committee on Capital City Site, was the creation of the Capital City Planning Commission to prepare a master plan. Juan Arellano, who also helped the Frost team craft the 1941 plan, headed this commission. Other members were Ponciano A. Bernardo, Manuel Mañosa, Jose Paez, Salvador

FIG. 16. Quirino inspecting the 1949 Master Plan

SOURCE: Quezon City, *Laying of the Cornerstone of the Capitol Building Souvenir Program* (n.p.: n.p., 1949), 25

Araneta, Pio Joven, and Ernesto D. Rufino.[94] Cesar Concio, an architect who joined Roxas's Engineering and Architectural Mission, served as executive secretary.[95]

The commission submitted Quezon City's master plan to Quirino on 18 March 1949 (fig. 16). It believed that the plan would enable the country "to build a great, modern and beautiful city" in the new capital, the "citadel of democracy in the Orient" (fig. 17).[96] In line with this idea, Constitution Hill, the proposed new site of the Philippine Congress, was designed to be the "most important and imposing center of the City."[97] Constitution Hill, eight kilometers northeast of Diliman quadrangle, was to be connected to the heart of the city by an expansive highway, Commonwealth Avenue. The committee sought to have the government buildings in Constitution Hill (fig. 18), along with the Executive Center, built within the first two years of the plan's implementation.[98]

While the stated purpose of creating Constitution Hill was to construct a grandiose civic center for the new nation-state, the implied objective in the master plan was the isolation of the central administrative apparatus from society at large. As keenly observed by a team of UN housing experts in 1959:

The Philippine legislators who accepted the idea of the new administrative centre with its official model town, and the architects who drew up the plans, obviously had the patterns of Washington, Canberra, or New Delhi in mind. Like their counterparts in the U.S., Australia and India, they propose isolating the heart of governmental activities from the homes of the people by vast expanses of monumental roads, public open spaces, official and semi-official institutions emplaced in large parks, and by the palatial houses and gardens of the more opulent dignitaries and the foreign legations.[99]

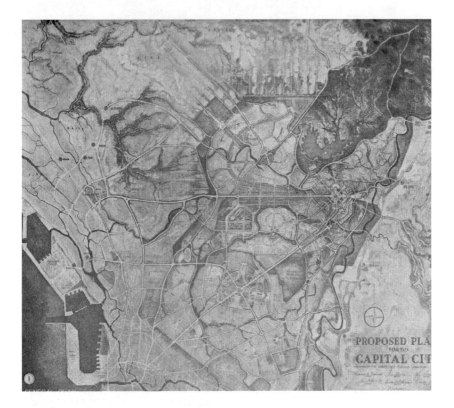

FIG. 17. Quezon City's general design based on the 1949 master plan
SOURCE: Capital City Planning Commission, *The Master Plan*, frontispiece

It was as if the heart of government was bordered not by a defined line, such as a cartographic boundary or a thick wall, but by an amorphous expanse of manicured greenery and fine marble.

With the necessary legislation and the master plan complete, the only thing left to do was Quezon City's inauguration as the national capital of the Philippines. On 22 October 1949, at the grounds of the proposed Constitution Hill, the formal declaration was made. City Mayor Nicanor

Roxas, Quirino's assistant executive secretary and interior undersecretary, led the ceremonies.[100]

FIG. 18. An artist's depiction of the proposed Constitution Hill; note the mountains of San Mateo and Montalban in the background
SOURCE: Capital City Planning Commission, *The Master Plan for the New Capital City*, 11

Colonial Specters

QUEZON CITY WAS THE SUPPOSED SHOWCASE CITY of an independent Philippines, and yet its selection as national capital and its master plan were firmly rooted in American notions of urbanism. From ideas about health in relation to geography to design and architecture, colonial legacies formed a significant part of this young postcolonial capital city.

The notion that certain geographical features made some places more salubrious than others, an idea Filipinos got from the Americans (see chapter 1, p. 37), was evident in the decision-making process of the Committee on Capital City Site. In selecting Quezon City as the new capital, the committee believed its territory had to be expanded so as to include Ipo's foothills and Novaliches's rolling grounds. The reason for this recommendation was not just for Quezon City to have a larger area for future development and population growth, but also in consideration of the benefits of elevated terrain: "with high and covered ground to make up for the deficiencies of the original Quezon City in these respects consisting as it does of relatively low ground, with poor soil, dearth of vegetation and lack of natural protection for military defense."[101] For the committee, "healthfulness due to its elevation" was one of Quezon City's advantages. In contrast, it noted its vast areas of low-lying ground as a drawback; as such, compared with high-altitude Baguio, Tagaytay, and Antipolo, the city was not as salubrious.[102] Apparently, Filipino officials still subscribed to the notion of topographical elevation as a marker of the healthfulness of a place, a legacy of American colonial rule.[103] Such a belief had penetrated popular consciousness that a 1953 Quezon City souvenir program linked the city's "delightful climate, fresh air, glorious warm sunny days for sun bathing, cool and invigorating nights for refreshing sleep" with its reputation as a "sanctuary of rest and cure."[104]

The persistence of this colonial notion of health as a function of geography was once again turned into an opportunity for elite consumption. With its "salubrious" topography, parts of Novaliches became the getaway for the wealthy in Quezon City. For example, Quirino's lavish retirement residence in Novaliches was built on a 12-hectare property, which he named Hilltop. The land used to be owned by Dr. Nicanor Jacinto, who initially

> offered it to [Quirino] to show his family's appreciation for Quirino's help when they were trying to develop their steel mill. Quirino insisted on paying a price based on real estate values prevailing at the time. The property was still a wilderness, but Quirino liked the view it commanded, which included the large lake of La Mesa Dam.[105]

Quirino's rest house was located in an area in Novaliches where other upper-class households bought their own piece of salubrious paradise. They even had their own club, the Capitol Site Club, complete with a set of officers and board of directors.[106] Quirino acquired the said property shortly after the Second World War. Around 1950 the construction of his Arellano-designed residence began. He spent around PHP 44,000 for what he planned as his retirement home and began living there in 1954 following his defeat in the 1953 presidential elections. His Novaliches home also featured a farm stead that was devoted to raising cattle.[107] It was here where he suffered a fatal heart attack on 29 February 1956.[108]

Colonial expertise also played a role in the drafting of a new urban plan for Quezon City. Louis Croft, Roxas's Adviser on Land Planning, was influential in the postwar rebuilding of Quezon City as adviser of the Committee on Capital City Site.[109] Even before the creation of this committee, Croft, who was also part of Frost's team for Quezon City's prewar master plan, was already at the helm of things. He was President Osmeña's special adviser on land planning, and in February 1945—at a time when Manila was just recovering from the trauma and devastation due to the Battle for Manila, and Croft just got released from the UST internment camp—Osmeña tasked him to prepare plans for the reconstruction of destroyed towns and cities. In 1946 Osmeña appointed him to the National Urban Planning

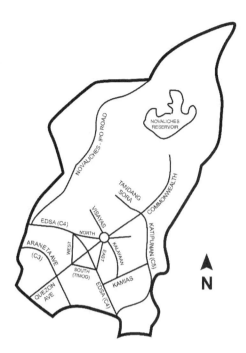

MAP 15. Important roads in postwar Quezon City; note that Araneta Avenue forms part of the Circumferential Road 3 (C3), EDSA is part of C4, and that Katipunan is part of C5

Commission.[110] It is thus not surprising that for the Committee on Capital City Site, Washington, D.C. stood as a "model of farsighted city planning and engineering."[111]

Croft left his imprint not only in Quezon City but in the emerging greater Manila area. In 1945 he planned the overall layout of the major thoroughfares for Manila and its surrounding cities. Building upon the existing road network, he envisioned a much larger metropolis that would be connected to the urban core via new roads. Two north–south routes, five concentric circumferential roads (C1 to C5), and seven radial roads comprised Croft's design, which had Intramuros as the epicenter (map 15). The blueprint was ready and partially built in the prewar period but was only completed in the postwar years. Eventually, Circumferential Road No. 4 (C4), denoted in the Croft plan as the Makati Freeway, became the most important thoroughfare for the growing metropolis. It connected Manila's most important satellite towns, from Caloocan and Quezon City in the north down to the towns of San Juan, Mandaluyong, and Makati, with Pasay as its southern terminus.[112] It was initially called 19 de Junio, in reference to Rizal's birthdate, and renamed Highway 54. In 1959 it was baptized Epifanio de los Santos Avenue

130   A CAPITAL CITY AT THE MARGINS

(EDSA), in honor of the prewar politician and historian from Rizal province.[113] Throughout the postwar period, EDSA served as the main conduit of product and passenger flows coming in and going out of the metropolis. Furthermore, it induced sprawl in the conurbation surrounding Manila.

Even if Filipino architects were the main actors involved in designing Quezon City, American notions of ordered space and urban aesthetics still defined the 1949 master plan. They were led by Arellano, who was one of the architects under Frost who drafted Quezon City's prewar master plan and a former pensionado.[114] The architects who designed the major structures in early postwar Quezon City were also of the same mold as Arellano. Many of them obtained graduate degrees in the US and developed aesthetics that were heavily influenced by American trends. They formed an elite corps of design technocrats, as it were, working at the national level.

Concio was one of these design technocrats. He finished his undergraduate degrees in Civil Engineering in UP in 1928 and Architecture in Mapua in 1932. He became a pensionado in 1938 and obtained a Master in Architecture from the Massachusetts Institute of Technology (MIT) in 1940, with a graduate thesis, "A Design for the University of the Philippines at Diliman, Quezon City," that earned him the highest honor. For his thesis he visited various university campuses aside from his own: Harvard, Yale, Princeton, Columbia, University of William and Mary in Virginia, Cranbrook Academy of Art in Bloomfield Hills, Michigan, etc. He became UP's university architect starting in 1947 and the executive secretary of the Capital City Planning Commission from 1948 to 1950.[115] His most famous project is Quezon Hall, UP Diliman's main administration building (see fig. 14).

Gines Rivera and Carlos Arguelles also belonged to this corps of design technocrats of the early postwar period. Gines Rivera gained fame for creating the master plan for the transfer of the Ateneo de Manila campus to its current Loyola Heights campus in Quezon City.[116] Carlos Arguelles, son of famous prewar architect Tomas Arguelles, graduated from UST's architecture program and pursued further studies to earn an architecture degree in MIT. He became Rivera's associate upon his return to the country in 1949.[117]

Many of these design technocrats participated in the 1947 Engineering and Architectural Mission. Given that the principal cities the mission visited were US cities, it comes as no surprise that Quezon City's 1949 master plan was reminiscent of Washington, D.C. While Filipino architects turned to modernism as a way to move away from colonial architecture, paradoxically this shift became another way for Western aesthetics to persist in the design of Philippine cities for modernism itself was largely a Western product.[118]

As a result, Quezon City mirrored the experience of other postcolonial Southeast Asian cities that had to confront the imperfect legacies of

SPECTRAL SPACES BEYOND BALETE DRIVE   131

colonial town planning and urban institutions. Even the development of de facto segregated elite housing communities based on the colonial elites' perceived relationship between healthfulness and geography was seen in cities like Yogyakarta.[119]

The American imprint on Quezon City's political structure was visible as well because Quirino's vision for it was no different from Quezon's. Presidential appointees comprised the city government: from the mayor down to the councilors and other administrative officials. In fact, Quirino wanted a commission form of government, which would have made the local government even more dependent on the national government and much closer to the US model. He wanted "to make Quezon City similar in many respects to Washington, D.C., which is free from politics, and has a continuity of policy."[120] The proposal, however, never came to fruition.

The US also exerted influence over the new capital through financial means. After all, economic pressure was its chief means of ensuring that the Philippines's postwar order remained congruent to its political-economic interests. The US did so by tying its funding for war damage reparations to the Philippines to the enactment of a free trade agreement between the two countries, more popularly known as the 1946 Bell Trade Act. The Bell Trade Act had provisions for parity rights that would guarantee Americans the same economic rights that Filipinos had in the Philippines, and vice versa. However, given the parity rights provisions, the said agreement could not be enacted into law in the Philippines without amending the Constitution.[121] In essence, the US used the threat of financial ruin to force a charter amendment that perpetuated colonial economic relations between the two countries.

The blackmail worked. The Bell Trade Act effectively revived the prewar trade regime in which the Philippines supplied the US with cash crops (with sugar as the most important) and in turn received manufactured goods. Filipino elites were the main beneficiaries in both transactions: first, as landlords and exporters of cash crops, they enjoyed windfall profits from the trade regime, especially the sugar barons; and second, they then used their earnings to purchase the latest US-made luxury items, in the form of cars, furniture, and high-end appliances. The splurge occasioned by renewed free trade reached catastrophic levels that in 1949 the state had to control the spending of foreign currency, a significant policy shift that the next chapter will discuss. And although these Filipino elites were geographically dispersed throughout the archipelago, they redirected a significant part of their profits to Manila and its suburbs. The Negros-based Aranetas, a clan which built its fortunes on sugar but eventually invested in suburban real estate and commercial development in prewar and postwar Quezon City, exemplify this point.[122]

132   A CAPITAL CITY AT THE MARGINS

Just like in other divisions of the Philippine government at the time, the main hurdle that Quezon City's planners and administrators faced was the issue of funding. Money was of utmost concern because the construction of government buildings in a new site required a huge capital outlay. The Quirino administration had to rely on external sources to fund the implementation of Quezon City's 1949 master plan. After funding Manila's reconstruction efforts, the PWDC had enough capital that Quirino could tap. Funneling PWDC's money to Quezon City was quite expedient since those funds, amounting to around PHP 50 million, would have reverted to the US if the Philippine government could not appropriate them for specific budget items by 1950.[123] In 1948 the PWDC set aside USD 12.5 million (or PHP 25 million) for the construction of government buildings in Quezon City. However, Quirino was hesitant, afraid that the proposed buildings would not be completed within the short time that the PWDC prescribed. The planning, acquisition of land, and actual construction of buildings and highways had to be completed by 30 June 1950; otherwise, the PWDC would discontinue funding. Notwithstanding Arellano's appeal to Quirino that he reconsider his position,[124] the president decided to realign part of the USD 12.5-million allocation to more important budget items. Part of that sum went to the reconstruction of state buildings in Manila, including the restoration of prewar neoclassic structures.[125] More commendable was his decision to divert USD 6.5 million (PHP 13 million) to the reconstruction of destroyed primary schools in remote villages.[126]

In its assessment, the PWDC lamented: the "lack of complementary funds on the part of the Philippine Government would preclude construction of the capital for many years."[127] As a result, the implementation of Quezon City's 1949 master plan had limited funding, a dilemma it had to wrestle with for the succeeding decades.

Colonial continuity was also apparent in UP Diliman. Perhaps one of the most enduring legacies of US Army presence in Diliman was the persistence of military designations of specific areas; "hence, the residential districts are known as Areas 1, 2, 3, 5, 9, and 17."[128] In fact, these place names are still in use to this day. Elmer Ordoñez, a product of the early postwar UP, decried the neocolonial character of his alma mater in the 1950s, as embodied by the quonset huts left by the American armed forces and the new school buildings that were built using the war damage payments from PWDC, whose headquarters were also in Diliman.[129] Despite the fact that the US Army had officially relinquished control of the campus to UP on 6 December 1948, it still "retained a small portion of the area for temporary accommodation of the families and dependents of diplomatic officials who evacuated from China because of the critical situation there."[130] For Ordoñez,

IF UP during the colonial period produced efficient articulators of colonial ideology, the university after the war produced cold warriors or anticommunist and neocolonial intellectuals and professionals. The US funding agencies and foundations saw to that.[131]

More pressing than colonial aesthetics was the persistence of colonial-era problems regarding land ownership in various parts of Quezon City. One must note that neither Quezon City's founding nor the Second World War put an end to the city's agrarian disputes. For example, in May 1949 more than five hundred tenants in the 14-hectare Santa Mesa Subdivision, formerly part of the Tuason estate, protested before the Department of Justice against what they saw as corruption of the Rural Progress Administration (RPA) and the "Ang Buhay" [Life] cooperative. The Roxas administration, through the RPA, purchased the property in question and subdivided the land to allow tenants to purchase lots on an installment basis under the administration of Ang Buhay. The tenants complained about the increasing amounts of amortization, which they attributed to the bloated salaries of Ang Buhay's officials in connivance with RPA. As a result, prices of some lots had shot up to around PHP 25 to PHP 35 per square meter, too expensive for ordinary tenants.[132]

Borders as Faultlines

DESPITE THE VARIOUS DILEMMAS, the national and Quezon City governments were in a celebratory mood after the official designation of the city as the new capital. In 1949 the city government constructed a two-column arch at the junction of España Boulevard and Quezon Avenue, the main artery linking Diliman to the downtown, to mark the boundary between Manila and Quezon City. The said arch still stands to this day. Its circular base forms a roundabout for vehicles entering and leaving the two cities. On top of the arch are the huge letters of "WELCOME," greeting those entering Quezon City from Manila.[133]

This monument, popularly known as Welcome Rotonda, seems to stand for the relaxed nature of borders as mute markers that aid in the neat delineation of two territories. Such is, however, far from the historical truth. As Quezon City underwent a series of changes to its borders from 1948 to 1956 (map 16), conflicts arose from competing stakeholders. Redrawing Quezon City's boundary lines was an unwelcome change for many.

To begin with, the decision to make Quezon City the capital was not an easy one. Even after the committee made the choice in 1947, "leading members of Congress" remained unconvinced about the wisdom behind it.[134] These legislators proposed transferring government buildings to Intramuros instead. Senators even asked Croft to draft a report on the feasibility of

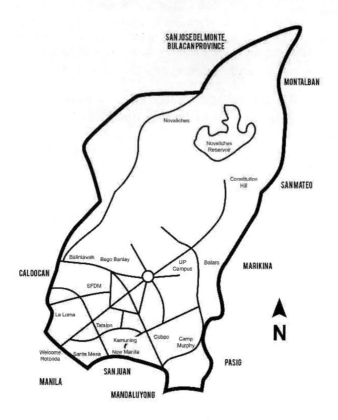

MAP 16. Key places in Quezon City's early postwar geobody

retaining Manila as capital. And in the Senate Committee on City Governments, which was tasked to deliberate on the bill to declare Quezon City the capital, only one senator (Salipada Pendatun) favored adopting the 1947 decision of the Committee on Capital City Site. The other four senators in the committee wanted to retain Manila due to financial considerations.[135]

Even within LP, then the administration party which dominated both houses of Congress, most questioned the idea of selecting Quezon City as the national capital. Seeing this situation, Quirino intervened by calling for a caucus of LP legislators in Malacañang on 22 June 1948. The result was a "long-drawn-out meeting, which started with a heated exchange of arguments" to discuss the issue of selecting the capital city, which was "the most controversial and urgent objective" of this four-hour caucus.[136] The exchange was so fiery that party-mates accused each other of corruption and profiting from the city.

Although Quirino's intervention helped in eventually getting unanimous approval for his desired piece of legislation, behind the scenes the contested bill had to undergo a "tedious deliberation."[137] On 25 June 1948 the Senate debates on this matter were so lengthy that the session ended at 2:30 the morning after. NP Senators Ramon Diokno and Tomas Cabili rallied the opposition and vowed to keep the capital in Manila. Meanwhile, at the House of Representatives, the debates centered on the possibility of real estate speculation that could arise from declaring Quezon City the capital city.[138] In contrast to the Quezon-dominated legislature that founded Quezon City in 1939, the so-called "cold war" between Congress and Quirino was on full display as Malacañang struggled with its legislative agenda.[139]

When RA 333 was finally passed, it did not only declare Quezon City as the new capital city but also enlarged the territory of the city to 156.60 square kilometers. Much of Quezon City's new territory came from the Novaliches district of Caloocan, as endorsed by the Committee on Capital City Site. Baesa, Talipapa, San Bartolome, Pasong Tamo, Novaliches Poblacion, Banlat, Kabuyao, Pugad Lawin, Bagbag, Pasong Putik—with a combined area of 80 square kilometers—were parts of Novaliches that were transferred to Quezon City.

Quezon City's annexation of Novaliches hurt Caloocan in many ways. One, it caused Caloocan to be divided into two noncontiguous territories: South Caloocan, which bordered Manila's northern boundaries, and North Caloocan, which was composed of parts of Novaliches that remained with Caloocan (map 17). Second, it meant the loss of a substantial voting population and potential revenue. Although Novaliches's value in terms of real estate taxes paled in comparison to Quezon City's more urbanized areas (table 10), its impact on Caloocan, which was still a municipality then, was significant.

Understandably, Caloocan's local politicians were some of the most vocal opponents of Quezon City's expansion. One of the most prominent among them was Macario B. Asistio, the longest-tenured Caloocan mayor (1952–1971), who continued to speak against Novaliches's annexation for years after its completion. For Asistio, the boundary changes were detrimental to his town. As such, he tried to negotiate with Caloocan's next-door neighbor:

> This boundary has been so arbitrarily laid out that our rural barrios consisting of an area twice as large as the poblacion and Grace Park has no outlet to the main highway (Bonifacio Road, Quirino–Novaliches Highway). These areas at present have no water supply, no electricity and no good roads. Some barrios even have no roads to speak of, at all. It would be very impractical, not to say foolish, to build roads that end a few kilometers from the logical outlet, as would happen if we now open thoroughfares in these barrios. This portion of Caloocan is our only hope for eventual expansion, but this can not be done unless our boundaries are extended up to the said highways. I have tried since 1954 to secure this relocation of boundaries, with no results except for some empty promises.[140]

136   A CAPITAL CITY AT THE MARGINS

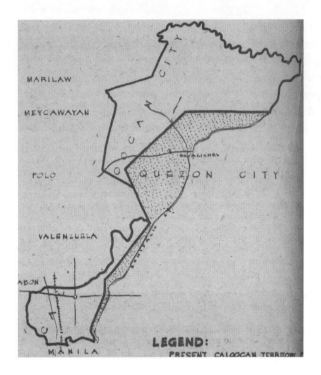

MAP 17. Caloocan's partition into two noncontiguous territories
SOURCE: Quijano de Manila, "Caloocan," 48

TABLE 10. Number of taxable and tax-exempt parcels and their values in selected Quezon City areas, July 1955

District	Taxable Parcels	Valuation (PHP)	Exempt Parcels	Valuation (PHP)
S.F. del Monte	14,687	92,721,490	1,126	9,568,040
Cubao	11,479	93,976,050	815	14,788,150
Diliman	11,587	72,126,600	490	8,334,530
University	1,923	11,460,139	576	21,369,290
Novaliches	7,084	14,986,470	136	2,475,490

SOURCE: Luna, *Quezon City Directory*, 20

Asistio regarded the boundary dispute not as a mere local concern because it involved the rivalry between the two biggest political parties: the NP and LP. Asistio, a Nacionalista, insinuated that LP machinations led to Caloocan's pitiful situation. The splitting of Caloocan into two discontiguous territories happened during the administration of President Quirino, the LP's leader, and at a time when Caloocan was under an LP mayor, Jesus Basa:

> As soon as he assumed office that year [1947], the Liberal [Party] Mayor gave away that portion of Caloocan, consisting of 7,100 hectares to Quezon City, and in that thoughtless, vindictive gesture, isolated almost three-fourths of our remaining territory from access to roads, electricity, water supply and civilization.[141]

Moreover, rumors circulated that the reason Caloocan surrendered territory to Quezon City was because the LP lost in that town in the 1949 elections.[142]

In this struggle against "geographical schizophrenia,"[143] Asistio rallied his hometown to "make representations with proper authorities to get back a portion of what was formerly a part of Caloocan"[144] and make the town's territory a single contiguous landmass again. He referred to Caloocan's northern fragment as "our promised land, our Mindanao."[145] National and Quezon City officials were not as convinced, however.

Caloocan was not the only one affected by Quezon City's expansion. Toward the end of May 1949, Rizal Rep. Lorenzo Sumulong, son of Juan Sumulong, succeeded in passing a law to reduce Quezon City's area by 301 hectares—from 15,660 hectares to 15,359 hectares. The younger Sumulong worked toward this reduction due to complaints from his constituents that Quezon City took lands from Montalban, San Mateo, and Marikina that were not suited for urban residential purposes, including vegetable farms, rice fields and communal areas east of the Marikina River. He stressed that "without these lands, San Mateo, which was losing 105 hectares of rice lands, and Montalban, losing 120 hectares of communal lands, would suffer such deprivation that they would not be able to meet the expenses of their governments."[146] Sumulong's legislative measure became RA 537, which repealed RA 333 and became the new city charter. In its southern borders Quezon City encountered problems with its boundaries with San Juan, which manifested in border disputes and major discrepancies in the maps used by the two local governments. These discrepancies arose "not only due to conflicting claims but also to the lack of adequate surveys."[147]

Although Quezon City looked like the neighborhood bully as it snatched territories of adjacent towns, its geographical expansion had serious drawbacks. Its newfound territory in Novaliches gave it additional problems. Expansion created new battlefronts: one in terms of public health, another involved literal armed encounters.

Quezon City's addition of Novaliches into its geobody meant the disturbance of swamps and marshlands, a sure-fire recipe for malarial outbreaks, similar to what have been documented in other cities.[148] In fact, Manila's

138   A CAPITAL CITY AT THE MARGINS

bout with this disease at the turn of the twentieth century has been linked
by historians to the simultaneous closing of its frontier lands. In Quezon
City's case, it was more alarming given that any outbreak could compromise
the very reason the city was founded and expanded:

> The northern part of the city has been selected as the site for the proposed capitol.
> At present, it consists of undeveloped cogonal land, traversed by the Novaliches and
> Marikina rivers and their tributaries, with prolific breeding of the malaria-vector
> species. That section of the city is actually malarious. Malaria was so markedly prevalent
> from 1927 to 1929 in La Mesa, South and North Portal areas (1, 2, 3), which are located in
> the capitol site, that laborers and their families residing there for the Angat–Novaliches
> Water Projects of the Metropolitan Water District were seriously affected. The labor
> force had to be replenished continuously to finish the projects. At that time, it was not
> uncommon for transients in the region to contract malaria within a short time.[149]

Even prior to the war, the seriousness of the issue forced the Department
of Health to conduct malaria surveys in Quezon City from 1938 to 1941, with the
aid of UP and the city government. On 11 December 1939 the city council passed
Ordinance No. 17, appropriating PHP 5,500 for malaria control. After the war,
the Department of Health's Malaria Control Unit conducted another survey in
1948, occasioned by Novaliches's annexation (map 18). That same year the US
Public Health Service also deployed malaria control units in the city.[150]

But more serious than the problem of malaria was the issue of insurgency. In the immediate postwar period the countryside surrounding Manila
and its suburbs was ablaze due to the struggle of the Huks against the
government. The Huks, who started out as a group of anti-Japanese peasant
guerrillas, were now fighting the Philippine state as a result of decades of
marginalization and discontent. The harassment from Filipino elites and the
US military that they endured toward the end and after the Second World
War catalyzed their insurgency, which began in 1948.[151] The Huk rebellion's
epicenter was Central Luzon, while the Southern Tagalog region was also
a significant battleground. And due to Quezon City's expanded boundaries, the capital city did not only share a border with the Southern Luzon
province of Rizal; it also became adjacent to the Central Luzon province
of Bulacan. In effect the new capital city became the geographical cushion
separating Manila from these hotbeds of dissent. It was a reality not lost
on President Roxas, who, as early as 1946, discussed the matter with the
mayors of towns bordering Laguna and Bulacan. Fittingly, this dialogue with
town mayors happened on the occasion of Quezon City's reinstatement as a
separate city in October 1946 via RA54. The mayors were part of an official
delegation to witness Roxas's signing of this law.[152]

Still, the cushion provided little comfort for Manila because Quezon City's
recently added territories in Novaliches were Huk targets. The rebels directed

SPECTRAL SPACES BEYOND BALETE DRIVE 139

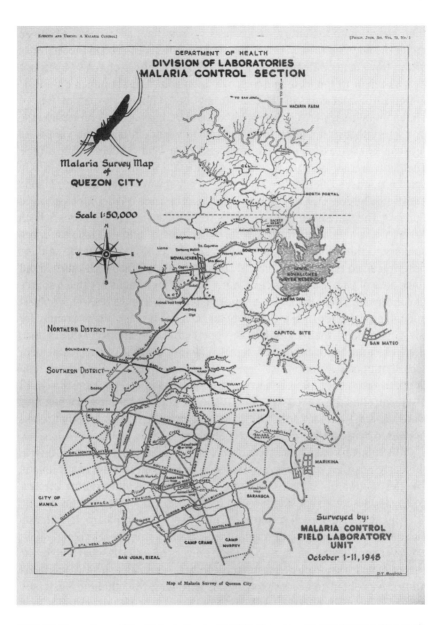

MAP 18. Operations of the Malaria Control Field Laboratory Unit in Quezon City, 1948
SOURCE: Ejercito and Urbino, "A Malaria Survey and Control," facing p. 249

their attention to the entire waterworks system that had become subsumed under the new capital city. Huk activities were often reported in the vicinities of the Novaliches watershed area and the Balara Filters of MWD,[153] perhaps in an attempt to replicate and improve upon what the Katipunan did in the El Deposito waterworks in San Juan during the Philippine Revolution (i.e., to disrupt Manila's water supply).[154] Military and PC intelligence entertained the possibility that a Huk force from Montalban would enter Manila via Balara or Novaliches to assassinate national leaders or launch a large-scale attack. Their intelligence reports recommended installing military checkpoints in various points in Quezon City, such as on the highways from Balara to Manila and from Quezon City to Caloocan, and another one at the intersection at Cubao.[155] The state even went so far as to turn Payatas, which borders both Novaliches and Bulacan, into a virtual buffer zone by offering "land to retired soldiers so they would live there and resist the Huks; however, the soldiers never received titles to the land."[156] The nation-state's model city turned out to be a royal pain as the source of water for the metropolis became a source of concern for state officials. It did not help that the said sites were too vast and underpopulated, making security an even harder task. Unfortunately for the government, their intelligence reports proved quite accurate. In 1950 the Huks attacked a PC detachment in Balara—in what is now, coincidentally, Katipunan Avenue—just beside the UP campus, "sending dorm residents to take cover in basements and the law building."[157] Aware that Huks often patrolled the campus at night, UP police kept off the streets when they were sighted. Even former UP President Francisco Nemenzo avers that rebels flocked to Krus na Ligas during such patrols.[158]

UP Diliman's neighbor Ateneo de Manila relocated to Quezon City in the early postwar years and also faced difficulties in its new environment. The destruction of its Padre Faura and Intramuros facilities during the war compelled Jesuits to consider moving its flagship school. Ateneo's president, Fr. William Masterson, SJ, wanted to purchase a site in Balara, less than a kilometer away south of UP campus and overlooking the Marikina Valley. However, not everyone agreed. Many university officials questioned the choice, which they called "Masterson's folly,"[159] and sarcastically queried if Ateneo was about to accept monkeys as enrollees. Nonetheless, Masterson mustered enough political will and funds to execute his vision. On 8 December 1951, the school held a ceremony to bless the first set of completed buildings in Balara, which was still overwhelmingly rural.[160] Jesuit Fr Alberto Ampil, who was an Ateneo student at the time of the transfer, recalled:

> But we were excited: we were studying among the carabaos and the tiririt ng maya [chirping of the *maya* birds], next to the ricefields by the banks of the Marikina River.

> This was wilderness. Talahib! [Cogon!] In January of 1951, civilization ended at the edge of Bellarmine Hall....
>
> In fact, coming to Loyola at that time was an adventure because you felt like you were always going on a class excursion to the countryside. Every so often, you would see a carabao plodding along on Bellarmine field with a farmer prodding him on with a stick. In fact, there was a father minister of the Jesuit Residence, I think it was Fr Matty Fullam who, so they say, used to shoot BB pellets at the carabaos left to graze on campus![161]

The drastic change in scenery for Ateneans manifested in the cartoons of their student publication, *The Guidon*. The cartoons, which tried to poke fun at the rurality of their new campus, belied the provincial attitude of some well-off students. One showed two students in campus shocked by a tribal spear coming out of nowhere and hitting the trunk of a nearby tree (fig. 19). Appearing on the same page as the previous one, another *Guidon* cartoon had an Atenean who did not know his way around campus asking what seemed to be a Japanese straggler still surviving in the woods: "Excuse me, sir ... Could you direct me to the administration building?"

The rechristening of Ateneo's site as Loyola Heights, in reference to the birthplace of Jesuit founder St. Ignatius of Loyola, thus signaled a significant renaming. Balara's perceived savagery had to give way to Ateneo's

FIG. 19. Editorial cartoon showing the "savagery" of Balara; the caption reads: "Even our cartoons are better since we moved to Loyola Heights"

SOURCE: *The Guidon*, 22 Jan. 1952, p. 5

civilizational might; a native toponym replaced by one with Spanish and American inflections. From that point onward, Ateneo strove to refashion the imagery that Loyola Heights evoked, from frontier landscape to an exalted place of learning atop Quezon City's southeastern hills.

In the same way that state authorities worried about Quezon City's rural peripheries because of the ongoing rebellion, they were also wary of the city's more urbanized areas just outside Manila due to possible infiltration by other subversive elements. In the early postwar years the border zone between the two cities revealed the capital city's underside:

> in the morning and late in the afternoon daily cannot escape seeing dozens of pigs, dogs, chickens, rats, hundreds of lizards and cockroaches, and millions of flies, fighting among themselves over unsightly and obnoxious objects that pile up high around a stone marker at the Quezon City–Manila boundary.[162]

At the same time, Quezon City's rural spaces attracted lawless elements operating in Manila. In 1948 a police raid of a hideout of cattle thieves in Culiat revealed important geographical details about Manila's crime scene:

> The hangout had been in use by fugitives from justice since prewar days but it was only after liberation [from the Japanese] that field telephones, looted from army depots in Quezon City, were installed at strategic points to give the alarm at the approach of suspicious strangers, particularly peace officers. . . . The place had been a haven of safety for fugitives from the law not only from Manila and Quezon City but also from Bulacan, Rizal City [Pasay City] and other places.[163]

Postwar Quezon City's reputation for having poor security[164] was in fact one of the reasons why parents of UP students opposed the relocation to Diliman. President Quirino even acknowledged it in a 11 March 1953 speech before UP students, noting that the parents' "uproarious opposition" was because "this site was then absolutely insecure due to the presence of kidnappers, murderers, holduppers, and all kinds of wrongdoings."[165]

Whereas Quezon City's borders with provinces in Central and Southern Luzon made it a viable gateway for Huks to enter Manila, its border zones next to Manila and Caloocan, which had a large population of Chinese and Chinese-Filipinos, caused the city to be tagged as a potential haven for Chinese Communists. In the early postwar period, the Chinese and Chinese Filipinos, who were initially based in Binondo, San Nicolas, and Santa Cruz, began to settle in areas north of Manila, such as in Grace Park in Caloocan and La Loma and San Francisco del Monte in Quezon City.[166] However, as a result of Mao Zedong's victories against the Kuomintang and the subsequent establishment of the People's Republic of China, Filipino authorities grew more suspicious of the "Chinese" living in and near Manila, regardless

SPECTRAL SPACES BEYOND BALETE DRIVE   143

of nationality and length of residence in the country and despite the fact that many of them fought alongside Filipinos and Americans against the Japanese.[167] Intelligence officers monitored Chinese factories in the Manila–Caloocan–Quezon City border zone due to suspicions that Chinese Communists and business fronts used these places for their meetings and to facilitate the entry of illegal migrants from the mainland. They shadowed individuals with reported links to mainland Communists, many of them residing in the "tri-city" zone. They even alleged that certain Chinese schools in the area spread Communist propaganda.[168]

Aside from subversion, Quezon City's geographical dilemmas in the early postwar era included corruption. Quick money-making schemes capitalized on its status as capital city and sudden territorial expansion. Although C. M. Hoskins was rather bearish in his estimation of speculative activity as a result of legislations affecting Quezon City—according to him, "Speculators were not too active in the Diliman–Novaliches area in spite of the Capital designation, preferring to await the announcement of more definite plans"[169]—one cannot deny that quite a handful profited handsomely through unfair means. Perhaps the most controversial of these cases of fraudulent speculation was the one involving the chair of the Committee on Capital City Site, Senator Melecio Arranz.

In 1948 Arranz came under fire because of allegations that he used his position in the Committee on Capital City Site to reap financial benefits. Between May and June 1948 the *Philippines Free Press* published a two-part exposé revealing Arranz's properties in the site that eventually became part of the capital city, including a hacienda which he, Senate President Jose Avelino, and Benigno Aquino co-owned. He deflected the allegation and even stated that no one in the committee purchased property in the soon-to-be capital.[170] Fellow lawmakers also slammed the senator, most especially Rep. Jose Topacio Nueno. During the heated debates in the four-hour LP caucus on 22 June 1948 to discuss the bill that eventually became RA 333, Nueno "asked pointblank Senator Melecio Arranz if it was true that he owned 120 hectares of land somewhere in the proposed national capital site."[171] Nueno continued his barrage against the senator a few days after in a congressional session,[172] and mainstream media picked up the story. The 3 July 1948 *Philippines Free Press* editorial about Arranz is worth quoting at length:

> Many may believe that the Quezon–Novaliches site is the most suitable for the future Philippine capital. Few will not question the propriety of Sen. Melecio Arranz's sitting as chairman of the committee, which chose the site. A judge disqualifies himself from trying a case in which he is financially interested—properly so. Senator Arranz, on the other hand, according to Ex-Senator Hernaez, did not even

inform the committee of his holdings—considerable—in or near the area when the Quezon–Novaliches site was proposed.

> Later, asked by Congressman Nueno to point out his property on the map, Arranz simply walked out of the room. Arranz has declared that, to avoid speculation, private estates within the site would be expropriated and subdivided by the government. At the same time, as Nueno pointed out, the boundary of the site was so drawn as to exclude (intentionally or unintentionally?) the property of Arranz from expropriation. Surely the senator should have disqualified himself from the deliberations of the committee, knowing what he owns and where it is—in the name of propriety. Propriety: the invisible line dividing the legally permissible from the morally questionable.[173]

Nueno called this border zone around Quezon City in which Arranz's lands were situated the "Arranz Corridor,"[174] a strategic zone that was not subject to expropriation but would inevitably rise in value due to its proximity to the new capital. Arranz reportedly lashed back at Nueno's accusation by saying: "I'm willing to give to the government all my lands there! I can sell them at cost to anybody interested!"[175]

Most probably, the property in question was Arranz's vast landownings in the former Hacienda de Tala, located in North Caloocan just outside Quezon City's borders. Seven years after Quezon City became the capital, Arranz sold his Tala property to prominent businessman Alfonso Sycip—1,119,111 square meters for PHP 335,868—without much media fanfare.[176] Ironically, Arranz, "who is in business when he is not in politics"[177] according to Lewis Gleeck, praised the work of the Committee on Capital City Site members, who "served in a purely technical capacity without any financial interest and with the welfare of the country solely at heart."[178]

Arranz's situation was no isolated case. Early postwar Quezon City dealt with politicians and businessmen profiting from quick but questionable transactions. Another example was Francisco C. de la Rama, the infamous wartime collaborator who made millions from his shady "buy-and-sell" business during the occupation period and then turned himself into a real estate magnate.[179] During the war he bought 1,120,000 square meters of property in Novaliches from a certain Ciriaco Olavides. This property, which was the same controversial piece of land in the former Tala Estate linked to Frank Carpenter (see chapter 1, p. 50), was highly profitable because of its nearly 20,000 ilang-ilang (Cananga odorata) trees, whose flowers were highly sought after in the international market for their aromatic oil. De la Rama was imprisoned after the war due to charges of collaboration, but resumed his business activities after getting a conditional clemency from Quirino. His return to his real estate empire coincided with the then ongoing legislative process to designate and delineate the new capital city:

SPECTRAL SPACES BEYOND BALETE DRIVE   145

Early during the post-war period following my release from prison, I started lobbying for the approval of a resolution to transfer the capital of the Philippines to Quezon City, where the Ilang-Ilang Estate which I owned was located. Powerful government officials at the time, seeing the advantages of such a move, helped me and in due course the resolution was approved. Immediately the value of my property in Novaliches—together with all the surrounding estates—skyrocketted [sic] as I expected and assured me of millions in profit.[180]

De la Rama role in Quezon City's selection as capital was most likely overstated, but the effect of this choice on his properties was most certainly not.[181] The act of choosing capital cities and conjuring their boundaries might be geographically arbitrary, but clearly the economic gains for those who stand to benefit from these acts are as real as it gets.[182]

Cross-border Vices

BORDER MANIPULATION was indeed profitable, but not only in terms of gaining money from abrupt surges in real estate values. The flow of vices, especially prostitution in cabarets and gambling in cockpits, over Quezon City's boundaries was another source of huge revenues in the early postwar period.

During the Japanese occupation, Manila's municipal officials still held a prejudiced view toward cabarets and cockpits. Although in the then-enlarged territory of Greater Manila cabarets and cockpits were allowed to operate, EO 95 prohibited the establishment of these businesses within a radius of two hundred meters from any city hall or municipal building. Cockfights were allowed but only on Sundays and legal holidays, or for a period not exceeding three days during the town fiesta.[183] The Japanese, however, seemed oblivious to the fact that guerrillas often used cockpits for their secret meetings.[184]

In the immediate postwar years, cabarets and cockpits remained important places of entertainment in Manila and its suburbs, even as the occupation period caused major disruptions in the conduct of these businesses in Quezon City. Quite incongruously, Roxas delivered a speech before a Liberal Party convention bewailing the huge problem of homelessness in the city at the Santa Ana Cabaret in 1946, just a few months before the presidential elections.[185] Only several years removed from a devastating war, Manila had fourteen dance halls but no cockpits; Quezon City had one dance hall and one cockpit.[186] A few years later, the new capital city would gradually bring back these establishments that made it infamous in the prewar era. Slowly but steadily, cabarets began to post profits. From January 1947 to August 1950, the La Loma Cabaret, for example, earned PHP 59,160.40 from gate admissions (PHP 0.10 each), PHP 5,339.90 from restaurant sales, PHP 47,459.10 from bar sales.[187]

The war failed to end not just the profitability of cabarets, but also the existence of petty crimes in areas where these establishments were located. Right after the war, gangs continued to dominate the streets of La Loma, for instance.[188]

City ordinances tried to regulate city spaces in relation to cabarets and cockpits, but lacked legal teeth to mitigate their activities. For example, Ordinance No. 2393, approved on 1 March 1955, banned such places of amusement only within a measly 500-meter radius from any public building, school, hospital, or church, yet simultaneously exempting those establishments that had been operating prior to the war.[189] Eventually, cabarets and cockpits, and other similar places of amusement reclaimed their position as significant contributors to the coffers of municipal governments.[190] Expenditure data in 1965 confirm that these establishments continued to generate demand in postwar Manila and its suburbs, including Quezon City. Total expenditures for recreation reached PHP 53,595,000, and out of this total, entrance fees for "cockfights and races" amounted to PHP 1,250,000. This amount did not include purchases of "fighting cocks and feeds" (PHP 3,602,000) nor "losses at cockfights, races, mahjong, sweepstakes, etc." (PHP 3,148,000). Meanwhile, spending on "dances, night clubs, cabarets" amounted to PHP 1,341,000. In comparison, total family expenditures for May amounted to PHP 3,059,652,000.[191] Once again, some local officials saw the political necessity of supporting these vices. In Quezon City it came to a point where, in 1951, two city councilors, Adolfo Eufemio and Ponciano S. Reyes, were recalled from their appointments for pushing for ordinances in support of more legalized cockfights in the city, among other cases of administrative misconduct.[192]

The climax of cockfighting's postwar ascendancy in Quezon City happened in the 1950s. It was a remarkable turn of events from a geographical standpoint. If before, Quezon City's cockpits had to settle in Manila's border zones, now cockfighting was enshrined at the literal center of the nation's new capital city. Fully aware that many of the wealthiest businessmen and politicians in the nascent metropolis were cockfighting enthusiasts and that catering to their favorite pastime would be one lucrative endeavor, J. Amado "Amading" Araneta began a venture to take advantage of this situation. Amading, a member of the wealthy Araneta clan, was a well-known cockfighting aficionado. He had his own private cockpit, and was once reported to have made the largest wager on a fight in Philippine history. In the 1950s he proposed the creation of a one-million-peso international cockpit stadium in Quezon City, which was planned to be 5,200 square meters big and with the capacity of ten thousand people (fig. 20).[193] This proposal became reality with the construction of a coliseum based on a different architectural plan. The Araneta Coliseum, which opened in 1960 and was hailed then as "the largest domed coliseum in the world,"[194] made the nation's capital city the cockfighting capital of the country as well.

FIG. 20. An early design for J. Amado Araneta's proposed International Cockfighting Stadium

SOURCE: Quirino, "Cockfighting Becomes Big Business," 21

Araneta Coliseum soon became the mecca of cockfighting events, attracting aficionados not only in the country but from all over the world. Since 1963 it had been the venue of the summer Cockfight Annual, considered the peak of the cockfight season. In May 1969 it hosted the International Cockfight Derby, the first time an international cockfight event was held in the country and then "the biggest event in native cocker history." This "sabong a la mode" featured 65 bouts and drew a crowd of 8,000.[195]

Araneta Coliseum's impact on Quezon City did not end there. It became Quezon City's undisputed commercial epicenter, a place not just for cockfights but for other important events, like political gatherings. The NP used it as the venue of their party convention to choose their candidates for the 1961 national elections. Benigno "Ninoy" Aquino Jr. recalled that event: "Wine, women and money flowed at the Araneta Coliseum, which was used politically for the first time."[196] The complex that surrounded it, the Araneta Center, served as Quezon City's economic hub for the latter half of the twentieth century.[197]

* * *

POSTWAR URBAN RECONSTRUCTION in Southeast Asia happened alongside decolonization. Hence, the process of restoring cities was tied to the modernist projects of ascendant native elites who wanted to articulate their nationalist visions through architecture and urban planning. City (re)building was nation building. Still, Southeast Asian nations had a hard time shaking off colonial legacies in its "modern cult centres."[198] The revival of Rangoon in the 1950s under U Nu following the civil war saw the continuation of its export-dependent economy and colonial-inspired architecture. And despite Sukarno's desire for a postcolonial Jakarta, its design betrayed its orientation, albeit ambivalent, toward Western modernity.[199]

148   A CAPITAL CITY AT THE MARGINS

Quezon City's rise as the new capital in 1948 must be viewed against this regional context characterized by colonial specters haunting cities in the middle of decolonization.

However, Quezon City was unique in the region in that it was the only instance of a capital city being transferred to a different site during the era of decolonization. Moreover, it was the first planned capital in the region since the time of the sacred cities of Pagan and Angkor. Its geography, although thoroughly secular, was nonetheless similar to these ancient urban centers in that its layout was imposed from above. Such was in contrast to how Manila's boundaries in the early twentieth century responded to the exigencies of everyday economic and social activities, such as in how state authorities had to redraw Manila's territory to include the arrabales, an acknowledgement of the realities on the ground.

Quezon City's borders were an artificial by-product of the largely unilateral actions of the political elite. Municipal boundaries are imaginary as they exist primarily as cartographic elements that conveniently demarcate one political unit from another. As two-dimensional lines, these borders are easily permeable and cannot prevent the constant flow of people and goods from one town to another. However, this does not mean that boundaries are intangible signifiers of political fantasy. Borders, depending on the strictness and leniency of actual enforcement, can become rigid walls mainly because of their legal weight. One important implication of this point is that the peripheral-underside character is different in the two sides of the border: those outside the border serve as sites for activities that are prohibited in, but demanded by, the city in question.

The artificiality of municipal borders was clearly demonstrated in how Quezon hastily remapped Manila and its suburbs to conjure a greater Manila for strategic reasons at the outbreak of war, in how the Japanese simply disregarded Quezon's cartographic maneuver, and in how the Committee on Capital City Site could initiate the territorial expansion of the new capital to favor certain personal interests. Yet, the conflicts and contradictions that erupted during this period of turmoil also showed the very real repercussions of mapping changes. Redrawn boundaries could mean windfall profits from speculation, an economic slowdown for an area suddenly cut off from its municipal center, or increased vulnerability to attacks by insurgents based in towns nearby. In this sense, borders assume a spectral quality that allows it to become simultaneously real and imagined.

On the one hand, our appreciation of space oftentimes can become too rigid, in map-like discipline. From this standpoint, geographical space cannot be destroyed nor created, nor can two entities exist simultaneously in a given space (much like Walter Benjamin's idea of "homogeneous, empty time")[200]; hence, competition over it is a zero-sum game. Caloocan and San

Mateo's geographical quandary resulting from Quezon City's expansion exemplify how this perspective toward space could play out in the real world. On the other hand, various instances show the porosity of delineated spaces, making them subject to negotiations and prone to compromise especially when profits—potential or unrealized—are involved. Quezon City's shady dalliance with cabarets and cockpits demonstrates this point. Its early postwar history thus highlights the duality of the border: its rigidity evokes the assurance of uniformity for the entire territory that it covers, so spaces near the border are treated no differently from spaces at the center (e.g., Novaliches and La Loma, despite their peripheral location, enjoy a legal standing that is the same as Diliman's or anywhere else in Quezon City); yet its fluidity provides border zones linkages with the spaces outside, thus setting distinctions and gradations along a center—periphery continuum (e.g., Novaliches is part of a rural border zone alongside San Mateo and Montalban; La Loma forms an urbanized border zone together with Tondo and Caloocan; while Diliman acts as a sociocivic center; therefore, these three areas are fundamentally different spaces within Quezon City).[201] The fundamental question therefore in understanding the historical geography of a city through its borders is not the degree of a specific border's porosity or rigidity but rather how agents in the city (elites, politicians, entrepreneurs, workers, hooligans, informal settlers, etc.) could manipulate the innate duality of boundaries to attain their respective objectives.

CHAPTER FOUR

Jeprox Ambiguity

"ARCHITECTURE OR REVOLUTION."[1] Famed architect and urban planner Le Corbusier posed this Hamletian dilemma as he tried to make sense of urbanism and housing during the Cold War. Despite his conclusion that the proper use of architecture could prevent violent uprisings, his either-or premise seems to be the cynical flipside of the City Beautiful ideology that Burnham, Parsons, and Arellano tried to implement in Philippine cities: if well-planned architecture and cities could help engender ideal citizens, the reverse also held true—a deficient built environment could create destructive individuals. With decolonization in full swing and social unrest happening on a global scale, Le Corbusier tried to see in the built environment a way to stem this tide of rebellion before it grew into a wave of revolution.

As if responding to Le Corbusier's challenge, Quezon City started its postcolonial era with a series of low-cost housing projects aimed at Manila's working class. This state-led undertaking was not just a focal point of the new capital; the projects became synonymous with the city itself. However, its imprint on the Filipinos' collective memory seems more of a critique of the country's most ambitious plan to craft citizenship through city living. Quezon City's projects penetrated the colloquial lexicon in the form of the pejorative word *jeprox* (or *jeproks*). A play on the word "projects," jeprox signified the postwar, middle-class consumer-citizen, especially its "drug-addled, post-hippie, martial law-era generation,"[2] an epithet that could "mean anything from hippie to mod to reb to flamboyant."[3] The jeprox always found him/herself in an ambivalent state: derided by the lower classes for being self-centered and materialistic yet also treated as declasse by the upper classes for being an upstart or social climber.[4]

151

152   A CAPITAL CITY AT THE MARGINS

In many respects, the rise of the jeprox was indicative of the hardening internal social borders dividing Quezon City in the 1950s and 1960s.

This chapter assays the housing situation in Quezon City during the Cold War. During this time, many Third World nations pursued "modernization" after undergoing decolonization. Whether defined in terms of the supposed linear "stages-of-growth" progression under capitalism or of the inevitable historical march toward socialism, modernization in the postwar period was the common goal that impelled newly independent nation-states to initiate structural economic changes. The Philippines was no exception. In light of this, this chapter pays attention to the relationship between urban housing and the postwar economic transformation of the country—a change characterized by massive rural-to-urban migration, the attempt of the nation-state to industrialize, and the further development of a greater Manila area (GMA)—as it played out in Quezon City. It argues that the issue of housing in the 1950s and early 1960s, specifically the failure of the state to effectively respond to it for the benefit of the lower classes, was at the root of the city's fragmentation despite the intention of planners and administrators to have a cohesive urban network in the new capital city, as stipulated in the 1949 master plan. An inefficient bureaucracy, lack of state financial support, and a weak domestic economy spelled doom for low-cost housing for the masses. In contrast to the success of residential developments for the middle- and upper-classes in Quezon City, which gave the city a suburban character, the desperate urban poor (many of them rural migrants) had to make do with informal settlements, which highlighted the peri-urban heterogeneity of the capital.

Housing and the Cold War

THE HUK INSURGENCY defined the Cold War period in the Philippines. It also bore striking similarities with contemporaneous peasant uprisings in Southeast Asia. The salience of the agrarian issue, the intervention of Western powers, and the influence of communism—three key factors in then ongoing peasant revolts in Malaya and Indochina—were present in the Huk rebellion.

Although the Huk rebellion was a rural uprising, it also had a clear urban dimension, with Quezon City as an important locus. Because Quezon City acted as the geographical buffer zone between Manila and the provinces, it was an important flashpoint in the insurgency. Moreover, it was a crucial battleground between radicals and the state's anti-insurgency apparatus. As the succeeding paragraphs demonstrate, key places in the city became spaces of contestation and surveillance.

Although UP began as a bastion of colonial tutelage, it eventually developed an activist tradition, as seen in the protests against the Diliman relocation (see chapter 2). After the war, this tradition grew more visible and radical due to the presence of the Partido Komunista ng Pilipinas (Communist Party of the Philippines, PKP) cadres in the university, despite the party's weak urban strategy. The prewar PKP lacked effective tactics on how to tap the revolutionary potential of city spaces (such as neighborhoods, slum communities, and schools) aside from the factory, the Communists' eminent domain. Moreover, the leadership shifted its strategy of expanding its mass base just before the war. From an organization dominated by Manila-based laborers, it later focused on peasants in Central and Southern Luzon. At this point, the PKP and the Huks had formed an enduring alliance.[5] And even after the war when the PKP formed underground cells in UP, it "never seriously implemented this strategy" because of its skepticism toward the students' petty-bourgeois orientation.[6]

Nonetheless, postwar UP "was an old haunt for a good number of Party members and sympathizers."[7] This group included a wide range of academics from different units in the university with varying degrees of affinity to the PKP: from mathematics professor Vishnu Gokhale, who influenced would-be PKP officials Jose and Jesus Lava, to UP chief librarian Gabriel Bernardo, who hid subversive documents on behalf of PKP leader Vicente Lava, eldest of the Lava siblings, and managed a book store in prewar Manila that featured Marxist classics. Many UP students and faculty supported the movement, espoused Communism, and even became Huk rebels. In response the government conducted "witch-hunts" in the campus against those suspected of being Huk sympathizers or PKP members, echoing McCarthyist tactics employed in US universities. The Committee on Anti-Filipino Activities of the House of Representatives investigated professors accused of having communist leanings, especially those from the Philosophy Department. Students responded with demonstrations, such as the 500-strong protest in 1961. Campus spaces thus became sites of conflict. One of the most controversial of these conflicts was the uproar caused by the successful campaign of Fr. John P. Delaney, an English Jesuit priest whom activists accused of instigating the so-called witch-hunts, to have a Catholic chapel built inside the campus, the Chapel of the Holy Sacrifice.[8]

UP Diliman's spaces and structures reflected the different dimensions of the postwar Philippines. If the quonset huts left by the US Army represented UP's neocolonial character and the Chapel of the Holy Sacrifice, the Cold War atmosphere, another architectural feature in Diliman symbolized the country's entry into the nuclear age: the imposing nuclear reactor of the Philippine Atomic Energy Commission found at the northern edge of the campus. Towering over the grounds of the said commission, which was established in 1958, was an 85-foot egg-shaped reactor. A grant under a 1955 agreement between the US and the Philippines funded its construction.

154   A CAPITAL CITY AT THE MARGINS

The said agreement built upon US President Dwight Eisenhower's Atoms-for-Peace program, an integral part of his containment strategy against the Soviet Union.[9]

Outside the UP campus, spaces dedicated to combat subversion and secure the state took root in Quezon City. Although the city was a favored place for PKP clandestine meetings and safe houses,[10] as the national capital, Quezon City became the nerve center of the government's anti-insurgency campaign. Just a few kilometers south of UP Diliman were Camp Crame and Camp Murphy, the headquarters of the PC and the Armed Forces of the Philippines (AFP), respectively. Also located near UP is Heroes' Hill, the site of the PWDC Housing Project. This housing project, which was directed by the government-owned People's Homesite and Housing Corporation (PHHC), was "built primarily to billet officials of the U.S. government agencies directly assisting the country." Eventually, the PWDC site housed the personnel of the Joint US Military Advisory Group (JUSMAG), the main conduit of the US to aid the Philippine Army's anti-insurgency campaign. The JUSMAG also served as a front for Central Intelligence Agency (CIA) agents to operate in the country, the most notable among them being Col. Edward Lansdale. Lansdale worked closely with Ramon Magsaysay, especially in the anti-insurgency campaigns when the latter served as secretary of national defense (1950–1953) and president of the republic (1953–1957). In fiscal year 1955–1956, the AFP leased thirty-five dwelling units in the PWDC to JUSMAG personnel.[11] Lansdale described the JUSMAG compound in 1950:

> JUSMAG added a touch of suburbia to the peaceful picture. It was located just outside the city proper in a housing development for upper-middle-class families. The housing tract itself had several score of homes built at the end of World War II to a uniform design, frame two-story buildings and one-story bungalows set in wide lawns along winding roads. A dozen or so houses at one end were surrounded by a wire fence topped by a strand of barbed wire. This segregated area was the JUSMAG compound where the American officers lived. Close by were the JUSMAG headquarters offices, which made use of the building that had housed the land development company.[12]

Lansdale eventually convinced newly appointed Defense Secretary Magsaysay to leave his residence in Singalong, Manila and move to the JUSMAG compound along with his family for security reasons. Lansdale's and Magsaysay's presence in the JUSMAG compound, which was in a residential area and not in a military camp, made the place a target for Huk trigger squads.[13] Nevertheless, Quezon City remained a critical space for US interests. In fact, two places in the city were actually American territory by virtue of the 1947 Military Bases Agreement between the US and the Philippines: the Bago Bantay Transmitter Area and the US Armed Forces Cemetery No. 2 in San Francisco del Monte.[14]

Quezon City's role during the Cold War goes beyond the presence of urban-based sympathizers, Communists, or anti-insurgency agents in the city. Because many of the armed encounters happened in provinces that lay just outside the Manila area, the city was directly affected by the armed conflict. The previous chapter has already tackled Huk activities in Novaliches, especially in the watershed area, and the 1950 attack in Balara near UP Diliman. In 1948 a PC battalion was stationed at the Araneta subdivisions just outside Manila to counter possible Huk activities. And in the summer of 1951, Major Napoleon Valeriano's infamous anti-Huk unit stationed itself in the UP Diliman campus in a strategic move to launch offensives in Central Luzon.[15]

Security became an even more pressing issue because of the rampant petty crimes and troubles at the community level, influenced in no small part by the rapid population increase in greater Manila. The ubiquity of pieces of broken glass on top of the perimeter walls of residential homes spoke of how middle-class insecurity translated into bordered and barbed spaces.[16] Quezon City and national officials responded with various measures to assuage insecure residents and denizens. In light of the turn-over of the UP Diliman campus in 1948, Mayor Ponciano Bernardo and the PC promised university officials that they would maintain peace and order in the area. President Quirino ordered the BPW to finish the access roads leading to the campus and encouraged transportation companies to offer students special rates, especially those who commuted between Manila and Diliman. For added security, the military installed checkpoints along Quezon Avenue.[17]

Perhaps the event that brought home the reality of the Huk rebellion in the lives of Quezon City residents was an incident that took place not in the city but miles away from the metropolis. On 28 April 1949 Mayor Bernardo and Aurora Quezon, along with other companions, were killed by Huk members in an ambush in Bongabon, Nueva Ecija, while they were on their way to Baler.[18]

A few days after the ambush, Assistant Executive Secretary Nicanor Roxas was sworn into office as acting mayor. Under the new mayor, Quezon City's anti-Huk measures continued. He launched the Barangay Organization as a way to combat dissidents at the community level. Ignacio Santos Diaz, who replaced Roxas as mayor on 4 January 1950, sustained the emphasis on security. The Quezon City police increased its manpower from 125 policemen in 1947 to 323 in 1950. It divided the city's territory into four police precincts and strengthened barangay units to help maintain peace and order. Barangay officials appealed to lot owners "to rid their vacant surroundings and lots of tall shrubs, grass and other potential hiding places of bad elements" and facilitated the installation of more electric street lights. Under Diaz the Huk issue became more pronounced as the 1951 national elections drew nearer. Just before the said elections, the atmosphere in Quezon City was jittery because of the news that the Huks would use the city as their jump-off point toward Manila. The police issued a general alert to all precincts and established checkpoints at all strategic points along entrances to the city, while military officials reassured Quezon City residents of their safety.[19] Although the Huks launched no major offensive against Manila during the said election period, the paranoia of that time was almost palpable throughout the metropolis.

The most important effect of the Huk rebellion on early-postwar Quezon City, however, is far from being a bloody episode. It is characterized by violence but of a socioeconomic nature. The effect of the insurgency on the housing situation of the new capital city was no less than profound.

The destruction caused by the Second World War alone created a huge housing crisis in Manila and its environs. Afterwards, the subsequent rebellion in Central and Southern Luzon led to a massive rural-to-urban migration, thus worsening the situation. Migrants came from provinces like Pampanga and Tarlac, where the insurgency was most severe.[20]

This pattern of migration got a boost from the country's adoption of an import-substitution industrialization (ISI) policy in the 1950s.[21] Industrialization, which was part of the overall modernization agenda of the newly independent nation-state, initially stemmed from a foreign currency crisis in 1949. The need to conserve foreign currency, a situation that resulted from the rampant importation of luxury goods made affordable to elite Filipinos by the continuation of free trade (see chapter 3. p. 131), led to the allocation of foreign reserves for capital goods that were used to expand the manufacturing base of the country in the emerging metropolis. Although both push (i.e., rural unrest) and pull (i.e., ISI policy) factors sustained migration, the pull factor did not generate enough jobs for low-income households who comprised the overwhelming majority of migrants. One could characterize this state of affairs as "over-urbanization and under-industrialization."[22] Various features of the ISI policy led to this situation, including import-dependent import substitution, the tendency of state policies to encourage capital-intensive rather than labor-intensive businesses—leading to the slow growth of industrial employment—and the antidevelopmental effects of rent-seeking behaviors that Philippine-style ISI engendered.[23] As will be discussed later in this chapter, most of the new businesses established in Quezon City during the postwar decades were service-oriented rather than of the labor-intensive manufacturing type.

Due to these factors, thousands of income-poor families found themselves without adequate shelter in a city with an inadequate infrastructure. Prices of urban and suburban real estate "zoomed to fantastic heights since liberation." Speculators and real estate companies amassed fortunes, abetted by the lack of state intervention, to the detriment of ordinary people.[24] This combination resulted in an acute housing shortage, not just in Manila but also in its surrounding areas. In the cities and towns of greater Manila the urban poor built makeshift shelters in dangerous, marginal areas, such as along esteros.[25] The sordid appearance of these informal structures prompted many government officials to drive them away from cities. However, Sulu Rep. S. Ombra Amilbangsa reminded his colleagues in Congress about the whole picture with regard to the prevalence of informal settlements in Manila, as he sought to have a one-year moratorium on the evictions in government-owned lands:

> It should be remembered that those people did not enter those public places by the force of their own will under ordinary circumstances. In the period of stress during the enemy occupation, the Government took the initiative to invite them to occupy vacant lots in cities and towns for the furtherance of the food production campaign. [...] On that score, they are not squatters in the full sense of the word.[26]

The root causes of the housing crisis amplified the Cold War politics in the urban areas. Postwar housing expert Charles Abrams put it succinctly: "There is no more fertile ground for revolutionary propaganda than the beleaguered cities of the underdeveloped nations."[27] As rural migrants tried to leave behind places of insurgency in the countryside, they were inadvertently creating new spaces of discontent and potential rebellion in the cities. Military intelligence were especially wary of concentrations of squatters in the northern fringes of Manila because of their capacity to harbor Huk elements. For example, security officials red-flagged Grace Park in Caloocan, which bordered Quezon City's western side, for having a significant presence of squatters from Pampanga, a hotbed of Huk resistance. Security officials surmised that Huks could seek refuge with their relatives living in this slum community and take advantage of this situation. They had the same observations for informal settlements in Tondo, such as in Fugoso, Bangkusay, Balut, and Palomar.[28]

Rep. Jose Corpuz, chair of the House Committee on Agrarian Social Welfare, summarized the importance of the housing issue in relation to the anti-insurgency campaign. In a 1953 committee report he prepared for a house bill calling for the expropriation of landed estates in Manila, he cautioned his fellow lawmakers:

> It has been pointed out very often that the failure of the government to expropriate big landed estates in the agricultural sections of the country for sale to individuals has been responsible in a large measure for agrarian unrest in this country; this has given an opportunity for the spread of Communism. In the City of Manila, there are

158   A CAPITAL CITY AT THE MARGINS

various haciendas owned by a few families, on which tenants have held leases for
decades . . . .

This state of things in the City of Manila has created a very explosive situation
which may at any time give rise to bloodshed when court orders for the demolition
of homes are enforced in ejectment proceedings. At the same time, this situation
foments the spread of Communistic tendencies.[29]

It is apparent that the state viewed urban housing not only as a matter
of providing basic social services but also as an ideological battleground.
The unfortunate consequence of this paradigm was that the state, through
the PHHC and in coordination with US aid agencies, looked at housing less
as a basic need than as a strategic area to lessen people's vulnerability to
communist propaganda.[30]

City of Projects

THE STATE'S VIEW toward urban housing as fundamentally ideological was not
unique to the country. For Americans, the underlying strategy in both the US
and in Cold War fronts where they intervened was "combatting Communism
with homeownership."[31] Homeownership as a goal fit the narrative of abun-
dance that defined American consumer citizenship and stood in contrast to
austerity and the consumers' supposed lack of choices under socialism.[32]
Containment of potential sources of radicalism also factored in the decision
of Singapore's ruling party, the People's Action Party, to invest in high-rise
estates as the main anchor for its housing program starting in the 1960s.[33]

The primary state response to the housing crisis in greater Manila
was a series of low-cost housing (LCH) projects that targeted the lower
and lower-middle classes. This move was nothing new because before the
war the PHC had already been performing this task. Furthermore, Quezon's
decision to build Quezon City was integral to his "social justice" program,
which aimed at extinguishing rural discontent. In a sense, the ideologically
driven urban housing campaign of postwar governments simply continued
Quezon's idea. However, what changed in the postwar period was the
organizational structure behind state-funded urban housing projects. On
4 October 1947 President Roxas issued EO 93 to merge two prewar agencies—the PHC and the National Housing Commission (NHC)—and establish
the People's Homesite and Housing Corporation. After its founding, direct
supervision over the PHHC changed several times, from the Government
Enterprises Council (beginning on 4 October 1947) to the Department of
Economic Coordination (beginning 25 May 1950) to the Office of Economic
Coordination (beginning 22 December 1950).[34]

Just like that of its predecessors, the PHHC's mandate involved acquiring
land for residential subdivision and resale to middle- and low-income

JEPROX AMBIGUITY 159

MAP 19. Important housing developments and landmarks in postwar Quezon City

families at affordable terms.[35] Although the PHHC's operations covered the entire country, its earliest and most well-known housing projects were in Quezon City (map 19). Of its first ten projects, including PHC's prewar Kamuning project and the PWDC housing project, nine were in Quezon City (table 11). In sum, Quezon City enjoyed 95 percent of housing construction under the PHHC.[36] The impact of the PHHC's LCH projects on Quezon City's landscape cannot be overstated.

LCH Project 1 is also known as Roxas District, located south of the Diliman quadrangle and named after the former president. Construction started in 1949, and it was the PHHC's first project after the PHC and NHC merger. LCH Projects 2, 3, and 4 are in the Quirino District, which is to the east of the Diliman quadrangle and just a few kilometers away from the UP campus. Project 4 is the PHHC's biggest project and is divided into two areas: Project 4-A and Project 4-B. Project 5 is in Pandacan, Manila, and is called the Bagong

TABLE 11. Number of family dwelling units constructed in PHC and the PHHC's first ten projects, 1956 and 1962

Fiscal Year	Name	1956	1962
1940–41	Kamuning Housing Project	439	
1946–47	PWDC Housing Project	55	
1949–51	Low-Cost Housing (LCH) Project No. 1	1014	1113
1951–52	Low-Cost Housing (LCH) Project No. 2	1103	1104
1952–53	Low-Cost Housing (LCH) Project No. 3	1220	1212
1953–54	Low-Cost Housing (LCH) Project No. 4	3039	3039
1953–55	Low-Cost Housing (LCH) Project No. 5	480	578
1954–	Low-Cost Housing (LCH) Project No. 6	1230	1289
1954–	Low-Cost Housing (LCH) Project No. 7	1006	
1955–	Low-Cost Housing (LCH) Project No. 8	808	

SOURCE: PHHC, *Annual Report, 1955–1956*, 7; PHHC, *Annual Report, 1961–1962*, 9–10

NOTE: Projects 6, 7, and 8 were completed in 1959, Josefina B. Ramos, "The Punta Multi-Story Tenement Project: An Experiment in High-Rise Public Housing in the Philippines," in National Economic Development Authority, Housing in the Philippines: Preparatory Materials for the Conference on Housing, 16 Apr. 1973 (unpublished manuscript, copy available at the Rizal Library, Ateneo de Manila University), 19.1. The blank items are left blank in the original source.

Barangay Housing Project. Project 6 is in Bagong Pag-asa, Quezon City, while Project 7, is referred to as the South Bago Bantay Housing Project. However, the funding for Project 7 came not from the PHHC's general budget but from foreign aid. Nonetheless, the PHHC was responsible for building the structures for the project, and it eventually took over the daily operations. Adjacent to this site was a project that the PHHC itself financed. Because it was also part of Bago Bantay, the PHHC referred to it as Project X-7. Project 8 is the last of the PHHC LCH projects in Quezon City. Compared to those found in other projects, houses in Project 8 had the largest floor area, and lots were much bigger.[37]

JEPROX AMBIGUITY   161

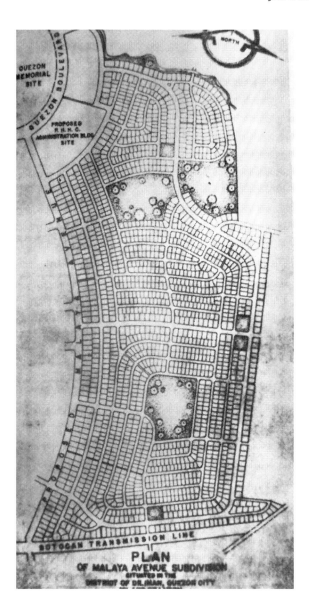

FIG. 21. Street layout of the proposed Malaya Subdivision
SOURCE: PHHC, *Annual Report, 1955–1956*, 87

The PHHC was also instrumental in the establishment of non-LCH sites, such as the UP Teachers Village. UP Teachers Village began with the PHHC's proposed Malaya Subdivision in 1955 (fig. 21). The PHHC planned to subdivide the land, which was adjacent to the proposed Malaya Avenue (present-day Kalayaan Avenue), into 1,787 lots. It allocated the northern third of the area (400 lots) to UP faculty and employees, the central third (750 lots) to Manila public school teachers, and the southern third (637 lots) to Central Bank employees. UP then created an ad hoc committee on university housing to oversee the establishment of Teachers Village in the area that the PHHC allotted to it.[38]

The PHHC's stated goal in creating LCH projects was to turn housing beneficiaries into full-fledged homeowners through affordable installment schemes. To subsidize housing costs, the PHHC relied largely on state funding, although it also found other means of sustaining itself. For instance, in 1947 the PHHC built a 260,000-peso factory along Quezon Avenue to manufacture its own concrete hollow blocks that were used in the construction of dwelling units in Quezon City projects. Although it encountered opposition from private manufacturers of concrete blocks, the move allowed the PHHC to defray operating costs.[39] The most significant item that helped the PHHC financially came in the form of external aid, especially from US agencies. The participation of these agencies in the PHHC projects deserves further scrutiny because it demonstrated how the US deemed the housing situation in the Philippines as a critical issue. As argued by Nancy Kwak, the pouring of financial aid into Philippine housing projects was deeply connected to US strategic interests during the Cold War period.[40]

To understand US intervention in urban housing in the Philippines, one has to begin with the Economic Cooperation Administration (ECA), an aid-giving agency that implemented the Marshall Plan, the main strategic initiative of the US to form a postwar world order congruent to its interests. ECA's ideological underpinnings was no secret. In a primer on ECA prepared by the Philippine Council for United States Aid (PHILCUSA), which Quirino established in 1950 to serve as the Philippines's conduit through which US aid flowed into the country, the Cold War politics behind this ostensible act of altruism was put in unequivocal terms. The primer situated ECA in a postwar landscape with competing forces, in which "communism asserted itself, threatening to engulf the whole world into more turmoil." Theferore, ECA emerged to "meet this global challenge, the United States offered its technical and material resources to aid the tottering economies of those nations whose seemingly inexorable downfall was abetted by their political instabilities."[41]

Then in 1951, the US Congress passed the Mutual Security Act, a global aid program that effectively replaced the Marshall Plan and abolished the ECA. Similarly, this new program targeted income-poor countries in hopes that aid would contain the spread of communism. It resulted in the creation of the Mutual Security Agency (MSA). And in 1953 MSA was replaced by the Foreign Operations Administration (FOA), another short-lived agency that facilitated aid and technical assistance until 1954.[42]

The first time American aid was used for urban housing in the Philippines was in 1951. This financial help enabled the PHHC procure foreign-made building materials for the construction of Project 3, which targeted 1,220 low- and middle-income families. For this project, US aid amounted to $559,000, while the Philippines allocated a counterpart fund of PHP 2.638 million. Years after Project 3's construction, FOA and PHILCUSA funded a resettlement project for 994 income-poor squatter families, transferring them from Manila to a site in Bago Bantay, Quezon City. The 39-hectare site, which had 994 house lots measuring 200 square meters each, became Project 7. This project targeted informal settlers, and applicants were screened by the Slum Clearance Committee under the Office of the President.[43] US aid authorities described the relocation as a project "by the Philippine government with United States assistance to resettle homeless squatters, many of whom were subject to Communist propaganda, and to alleviate unsanitary conditions in the city of Manila."[44]

US housing expertise came alongside financial aid. Right after the war, American consultants began to exert their influence over Philippine housing policies. In 1945 President Osmeña asked Louis H. Pink, Special Insurance Adviser to the President, for his suggestions regarding the housing situation of the Philippines, especially for low-income households. Pink praised the PHC's prewar efforts in helping establish Quezon City, although he also criticized the agency because it "showed little imagination or community planning." Pink submitted his recommendations to Osmeña, and these were followed up by a more detailed report from two American consultants: N. J. Demerath, a sociologist working for the National Housing Agency in Washington, DC, and Richard N. Kuhlman, an architect from Texas. The two reports called for, among other suggestions, more funding for housing, the selection of a competent housing administrator, and the procurement of more US housing experts by the Philippine government.[45] In 1946, upon Osmeña's request and in coordination with Louis Croft and the office of the US High Commissioner, a three-man federal housing commission from the US came to the Philippines to study the housing problem. The mission, headed by Earl Gouger, director of the program division of the US Federal Housing Administration, submitted its report in June 1946. That same year the Economic Survey Mission to the Philippines, also known as the Bell Mission, arrived in the country to study the entire postwar economy. Although its scope of study was much broader than Gouger's, it also made recommendations regarding urban housing albeit in a less comprehensive manner. Both reports noted the inadequate housing provisions for the low-income classes and called for greater government investments in urban housing to remedy the said problem.[46]

The said missions were followed by a housing study conducted by G. F. Cordner, a housing specialist from the MSA. Aside from serving as a

164   A CAPITAL CITY AT THE MARGINS

consultant on the site plan and house constructions in Project 3, Cordner also published a comprehensive analysis of the Philippine housing situation. In this report, he recommended, among other things, an increase in state appropriations for the PHHC to increase its capacity to purchase lands outside Manila for future housing sites. Finally, in 1968 Bernard Wagner submitted a comprehensive housing report.[47] Wagner's consultancy work for the Philippine government was made possible by the United States Agency for International Development (USAID), which was formed in 1961.

United Nations (UN) housing experts also helped the PHHC, but not in a manner that was as extensive as that of the US. In early September 1956 UN Technical Assistance Administration (UNTAA, now defunct) low-cost housing expert George F. Middleton was detailed to the PHHC to help in its research and experiments on housing and construction. Three years later, Charles Abrams and Otto Koenigsberger, UN advisers on housing in the Philippines, completed their report on the housing situation in the country. The sending of UN housing experts to work with the PHHC continued up to the 1960s.[48]

Unfortunately, despite the help of American and UN experts and aid, the housing situation floundered. Notwithstanding the high occupation rates of the completed dwelling units, as seen in official statistics for fiscal year 1962–1963 (table 12), these figures did not reflect the beneficiaries' ability to regularly pay the PHHC until they finally owned their houses and lots. In this regard, the PHHC's success rate varied across the different projects. For instance, as of 1962, 80 percent of the dwelling units in Project 1 had already been completely sold to the tenants, while in Project 2 it was only 54 percent (596 out of 1,104 units).

The case was even more complex in Projects 3 and 7. Because external aid funded these projects, certain conditions that the aid agencies

TABLE 12. Number of family dwelling units and benefited families in the PHHC's fourteen housing projects, 1963

Project	No. of Units	No. of Benefited Families
Project 1	1014	1013
Project 2	1104	1095
Project 3	1220	1212
Project 4-A	1611	1597
Project 4-B	1428	1407
Project 6	1301	1299
Project X-7	30	30
Project 8	301	301
Project 9	63	63
Project 11	195	166
Project 12	275	216
Project 13	234	194
Project 14	59	4
Vitas Housing Project	162	162
Total	8957*	8759

SOURCE: PHHC, *Annual Report, 1962–1963*, 23

* However, the computation of the total is wrong. The correct figure is 8,997.

imposed had to be met before individual sales of houses and lots could be consummated. Unlike in the preceding housing projects, the PHHC removed the "sale-after five-years tenancy" clause in the lease contract for Project 3 houses. Essentially, this change translated into a "rent only" policy, which the MSA, PHILCUSA, and the PHHC believed would eliminate speculation, or the tendency of many beneficiaries "to sell out [their houses purchased from the PHHC] and return to substandard housing." To address this matter, the PHHC imposed a five-year "cooling-off" period in the hopes that families would "become so attached to their dwelling, their neighbors and their community that they [would] not be interested in selling."[49]

This concern about speculation was due to the perception that there were those who took advantage of the subsidized nature of LCH projects, which brought house and lot prices below market levels. The projects were thus vulnerable to profiteering by those who would purchase subsidized houses and lots only to sell them at market-level prices later on. Cordner pointed to Kamuning's case, where the PHC built and sold 439 housing units, yet only a few of the original beneficiaries had remained by the 1950s.[50]

Cordner's argument is not so convincing, however, in light of the experiences of Kamuning residents themselves. Since 1948 Kamuning residents had been imploring Malacañang to reduce lot prices in their area. The Bagong Buhay Confederation, an organization consisting of eight associations in Kamuning, with a total of around 900 member families, represented the residents in this objective.[51] President Quirino endorsed the petition to the PHHC General Manager Fragante: "Mr. Fragante, please consider this petition seriously. I am not in favor of the government making any profit for the service of distributing the lots to the people we are seeking to help and serve."[52] However, the PHHC failed to act on this matter.[53] On 18 April 1949 Kamuning residents sent another petition to Quirino, but this time residents in prime corner lots asked for a reduction of the price range for lots in their area, from PHP 6–11 to PHP 2–5. Once again, despite Quirino's endorsement, the price reduction never happened, leading the residents to reiterate their demand to the president on 31 October 1951:

> During the time when the present petitioners occupied the said government lots sometime in the latter part of 1947 and the early part of 1948, there were lots immediately adjacent to these government lots, just across the creek at Kamuning, Quezon City, being sold by a commercial real estate company for as low as P6.50 and it is believed unjust, if not anomalous, for the government to sell these lots higher than this price of the commercial real estate company then.[54]

Apparently, the PHHC had been selling lots at prices higher, not lower, than the market value.

166   A CAPITAL CITY AT THE MARGINS

The petitioners also noted that before the war, the said lots were priced at PHP 1 per square meter in the interior streets and PHP 2.50 for those along Kamuning Road. Given that these prices already factored in the improvements done to the said property, the residents reasoned that the PHHC's final selling price could not exceed PHP 5 per square meter even if it wanted a 100-percent profit margin. They added that the PHHC had not made any improvements to the said property since 1941.[55]

With the PHHC seemingly inutile, Quirino moved to reduce the price ranges of fourth- and fifth-class lots, from PHP 5.01–7.00 per square meter to PHP 4.66–5.00 and from PHP 3.00–5.00 to PHP 2.19–4.65, respectively. However, the original price ranges for the first-, second-, and third-class lots remained. As a result, on 1 October 1953 the Bagong Buhay Confederation sent another petition to Quirino to address this specific concern aside from presenting other demands, such as removing the PHHC's down-payment policy for occupied lots and the condonation of all interest charged for delayed payments for all petitioners.[56] Despite the confederation's passing of a resolution "expressing profound gratitude"[57] to Quirino—perhaps an act made in light of the then upcoming 1953 presidential elections—the chief executive's failure to get a government corporation to follow his recommendations (assuming of course that such was Quirino's genuine position on the issue) only exposed the hollowness of the state's housing policy. By the 1970s, the residents of Kamuning, Quezon City's original "barrio obrero" belonged "to the dizzy heights of the economic ladder"—a statement that sounds more like an indictment of the state's failure to effect social equity through urban housing.[58]

Kamuning's case illustrated how the PHHC "operate[d] like a private corporation."[59] Unlike most state agencies, the PHHC paid national and local taxes and was thus overly concerned about its financial stability. Congress eventually exempted it from doing so (RA 3463), but only in 1962 at a time when the agency was already neck-deep in crisis.[60] With limited state funding, the PHHC struggled to maintain its viability either by getting loans (which by 1953 had ballooned to PHP 18.3 million) or by trying "to recoup operating capital by selling subdivision lots in the Diliman Estate to individuals of higher income, at a profit, and to make a small profit on the rents charged for its leased dwellings and stores."[61] The obvious outcome was that the PHHC's houses became unaffordable to its intended beneficiaries. As table 13 shows, the most affordable housing units were priced at PHP 20 per month and targeted households within the income range of PHP 120–224 per month. In this situation, rent accounted for as much as 17 percent of the household income. Worse, such financial requirements effectively disenfranchised low-wage earners who comprised the majority of the urban population. The PHHC admitted that given its limited state subsidy and the country's tax system, the stringent regulations on the planning and construction of housing units, and the added responsibility of constructing national and city roads,[62] it could only do so much with regard to fulfilling its mandate:

TABLE 13. Rents, incomes, and occupancy limits, PHHC, June 1953

Unit Type	Upon Admission			For Continued Occupancy
	Monthly Rent	No. of Persons	Income (Pesos)	
	(Pesos)	Min. – Max.	Min. – Max.	No. of Persons
33-R1 mid	20	4 – 7	120 – 224	9
33-R1 end	24	4 – 7	120 – 224	9
33-R2 mid	24	4 – 7	120 – 224	9
33-R2 end	28	4 – 7	120 – 224	9
36-R1 mid	24	5 – 8	160 – 256	10
36-R1 end	28	5 – 8	160 – 256	10
36-R2 mid	28	5 – 8	160 – 256	10
36-R2 end	32	5 – 8	160 – 256	10
36-T	36	5 – 8	180 – 288	10
40-R1 mid	28	6 – 9	180 – 288	11
40-R1 end	32	6 – 9	180 – 288	11
40-R2 mid	32	6 – 9	180 – 288	11
40-R2 end	36	6 – 9	180 – 288	11
40-T	40	6 – 9	250 – 300	11
50-T	50	7 – 11	301 – 410	13

Explanation of symbols: The 33s, 36s and 40s have 2 bedrooms each; the 50s have 3 bedrooms. R1 is a one-story row house and R2 a row house of two stories. T is one half of a twin house all of which are one story. Continued Occupancy limits provide for increase in family size after admission.

SOURCE: Cordner, *Housing*, 16–17

168   A CAPITAL CITY AT THE MARGINS

In its true concept, public housing should serve families who cannot afford decent dwellings, and therefore should charge lower rents than private housing. Most countries accomplish this by subsidizing public housing[.] Unfortunately, however, public housing in the Philippines, unlike those in foreign countries, is financed and treated like private housing and consequently must operate in general principles like one.[63]

The lack of state subsidies forced the PHHC to maintain its profited-oriented business model, which was already in place in PHC's prewar operations (see chapter 2). As an agency catering to low-income consumers, it was bound to experience deficits that the government should have shouldered. Yet the PHHC "veered toward operations that either paid their way or were more profitable. It bought more land, subdivided, improved, and sold it."[64] For instance, if the PHHC bought land for PHP 1.50 per square meter, it would then sell them to tenants for PHP 10. In late 1950s Quezon City it resold its acquired lands to buyers at PHP 8–20 per square meter.

TABLE 14. Construction costs (in pesos) per dwelling unit in the PHHC's LCH projects, and inflation-adjusted prices (1965)

Name of Project	Construction Cost	Consumer Price Index Increase	1965 Projected Cost
Project No. 1	5,417	19%	6,466
Project No. 2	4,000	26%	5,040
Project No. 3	4,800	30%	6,240
Project No. 4a and 4b	4,740	30%	6,162
Project No. 5	4,370	27%	5,550
Project No. 6a and 6b	6,900	26%	8,694
Project No. 7a and 7b	5,460	26%	6,880
Project No. 8a and 8b	14,400	26%	18,144

SOURCE: Ramos, "The Punta Multi-Story Tenement Project," 19.1

According to its own estimates, a private contractor would resell the same land at PHP 15 to PHP 30 per square meter. As a result, the PHHC failed to serve the needs of low-income families. Rather than buying what it should, it purchased only what it could and then sold them at prices its intended beneficiaries could ill afford.[65]

Lot prices were one issue, houses were another. Construction costs of LCH houses ranged from PHP 4,000 to PHP 6,900 per unit, except for Project 8, where units cost the government an average of PHP 14,400 (table 14). Given that Project 8's lot prices were also the highest, one can argue that the PHHC's last housing project in Quezon City was the also the finale in the agency's abdication of its mandate to provide low-cost housing.

The PHHC's failure is vividly demonstrated in this ironic anecdote gathered by a UN housing advisory team about a PHHC employee residing in an LCH project in Quezon City:

> We asked a PHHC male stenographer earning P260 per month who had bought a PHHC house in Quezon City for P6,000 what his budget was for a family of 7. Though paying only 6% interest on his GSIS [Government Service Insurance System] mortgage, his income would have to be a minimum of P360 monthly to pay the interest and amortization on his P6,000 house. He is able to pay the charges only by subletting a room and supplementing his income with a P50 contribution from his parents.[66]

As early as the 1950s, the PHHC had come under fire because of the institutional barriers that hindered many low-income families from owning homes. According to a real estate developer, the agency sold lots "in excess of the price charged until recently to the high-income, well-to-do families in the exclusive Forbes Park Subdivision in Makati."[67] Critics blasted the PHHC for creating "low-cost housing for the rich."[68]

Despite its so-called business model, the PHHC declined beginning in the 1960s due to a confluence of factors. For one, it got involved in a conflict with the Government Service Insurance System (GSIS) over who should retain the properties mortgaged by the PHHC to the GSIS (due to the PHHC's huge debts to GSIS). The tussle led to the mismanagement and poor infrastructure in Project 4.[69] Second, the PHHC suffered from a shaky leadership. For fiscal year 1962–1963 it had a succession of three general managers.[70] Scandal after scandal rocked the agency, often implicating its top brass and even reaching Malacañang—for instance, in 1957 Manila Mayor Arsenio Lacson accused Pres. Carlos P. Garcia of using his power to acquire a PHHC lot worth PHP 57,343.[71] Anomalies, which involved nepotism, shady deals and questionable purchases, the creation of redundant high-salaried positions, and irregularities in lot distribution, forced the Senate to conduct inquiries and Malacañang to penalize erring the PHHC officials.[72] The PHHC's unnecessary operating costs and bloated bureaucracy pushed it to verge of bankruptcy by 1960. Perhaps the only positive thing about all these shortcomings was that the PHHC admitted its faults.[73]

The PHHC aggravated rather than mitigated the housing crisis. During the first eight months of President Diosdado Macapagal's administration (1961–1965), the PHHC managed to build only fifty-six low-cost housing units. Then in fiscal year 1961–1962 it suspended its construction operations; thus, no additional dwelling units for lease were made available that year. The general picture of the PHHC's incompetence was much worse. A government report revealed that from 1947 to 1962 the agency built only 12,000 dwelling units in 17 projects and none from 1963 to 1968.[74] Architect Paulo Alcazaren recalled the problems his family faced in their Project 4 residence:

> Life on Salalilla Street in Project 4 was difficult because the roads were unpaved and remained so until the mid-1960s. Despite its elevation, the township flooded each rainy season. The roads were dusty in summer and muddy during the wet season. As the Project filled up, the drainage got more inadequate, exacerbated by a general lack of maintenance of the canals. The stench from the canal behind us grew each year.[75]

The Role of Private Capital

THE DIRE STATE of public housing was apparent in the fact that in 1960 private financing funded 79 percent of all housing constructions in the country.[76] Private capital in housing even pervaded Quezon City despite the city's image as a monumental state project. It was no marginal presence and was in fact met with state approval.[77]

The importance of private capital to Quezon City's postwar development was evident early on. In 1950 Juan Arellano, as chair of the Capital City Planning Commission, recommended to Quirino the participation of private enterprises in the housing efforts in Quezon City. He believed that the commission "should give priority to the acquisition of land intended for commercial and industrial sections, leaving the development of real estate and sub-divisions to private entities for a while."[78] He noted that a system of insurance on long-term loans could facilitate the inflow of private capital. For UP President Bienvenido Gonzalez, the "principle of leaving the development of home sites at the Capital City to private enterprise is sound and commendable and should in time be feasible and practicable."[79] Apparently, Quezon City's planners and movers encouraged private investments in the city.

The function of the "government as an enabler of the private sector"[80] in housing manifested in the PHHC's support for private developers in Quezon City. The PHHC encouraged private housing projects by selling its properties in the city to interested developers. In 1952 it sold around fourteen hectares of its land in West Triangle along Quezon Avenue to M. Morelos and Sons, Inc., at a rate of PHP 3 per square meter. This site became the Morelos Housing Project, which sold the subdivided lots at PHP 14–18 per square meter and aimed at "upper moderate income families."[81] The PHHC's anomalous sale alarmed President Magsaysay, prompting him to form a fact-finding committee in 1954 to investigate it. This committee concluded that the contract was questionable.[82] Unfortunately, extant sources yield no details about the outcome of the investigation. Nonetheless, this part of West Triangle eventually became notable for its streets named after popular newspapers (e.g., Examiner, Chronicle, Bulletin, etc.) and for its

FIG. 22. The Santa Catalina Site of Gregorio Araneta, Inc.
SOURCE: *Sunday Times Magazine* 12 Feb. 1956: 21

prominent residents, such as *Manila Times* journalist and future senator Benigno Aquino, Jr. and future president Corazon Cojuangco Aquino. The two began living as a married couple in their Times Street residence in 1961. Both came from landed and politically powerful families—the Aquinos and Cojuangcos—that had dominated (and continue to do so) Central Luzon as caciques. Notably, Corazon Aquino was a granddaughter of Juan Sumulong,

172   A CAPITAL CITY AT THE MARGINS

the vocal Quezon oppositionist who criticized Quezon City's founding in 1939.[83]

Private developers who had been carving out prime real estate in Quezon City before the war continued to do so in the postwar decades. Gregorio Araneta, Inc., the developer of Santa Mesa Heights, expanded its operations in the city. It built more middle-class subdivisions in the vicinity of Santa Mesa, like the Santa Catalina Site (fig. 22) and Manresa Site. Meanwhile, New Manila remained an elite enclave, its streets— Broadway, Balete, Gilmore, Hemady (previously Pacific)—synonymous to suburban glamour. Broadway even earned its reputation as a "Senator's row": Senators Lorenzo Tañada, Eulogio Rodriguez, Soc Rodrigo, Emmanuel Pelaez, Oscar Ledesma, Jose Roy, and Magnolia Antonino were neighbors, while Senators Jose Diokno, Cipriano Primcias, and Quintin Paredes lived nearby. Other prominent New Manila residents of the postwar period were Supreme Court Justice Cecilia Muñoz Palma and Henry Belden, president of the Atlantic Gulf and Pacific Co.[84]

Private capital enabled the "suburban exodus" of middle-class Chinese and Chinese Filipinos in the 1960s and 1970s, as they moved out of Binondo toward the towns outside Manila, including Quezon City. By 1970, Quezon City's Chinese population was 4,541.[85] Long marginalized by the Philippine state, they had to turn to private housing since they could not be accommodated in the PHHC's LCH projects. Furthermore, as Chinese Filipinos shifted to light manufacturing, the only sector open to them after the 1954 Retail Trade Nationalization Act (RA 1180) banned them from retail trade, many had to move to the suburbs so that they could live nearer their work places.[86] In Quezon City they settled mainly in the barangays of Doña Imelda, Sienna, Saint Peter, Talayan, Damar, Maharlika, Doña Josefa, which are all found in the southwestern section of the capital, just outside Manila's northern boundary. Thus, Quezon City "can be considered an extension zone for activities of the inhabitants of Binondo."[87]

In Quezon City's southwestern section, middle-class Chinese-Filipino residents clustered in private subdivisions like Damar Village and Grace Village. Damar Village began as a housing project of the San Miguel Corporation for its employees. The company purchased the land in the 1950s at PHP 2 per square meter. Gradually, the village "attracted more and more Chinese as it was well located according to the rules of geomancy and was also close to the business area and the pier."[88] Whereas Damar developed out of a corporate housing project, Grace Village emerged as a result of the relocation to the area of Grace Christian School, a Chinese-Filipino school formerly based in Nagtahan, Manila. Both the school and the village were under the management of Marsch Estate, a Chinese-Filipino land developer. Given the economic nature of this suburban exodus, it differentiated

JEPROX AMBIGUITY   173

Chinese Filipinos between the supposed déclassé who remained in Binondo and the more socially mobile ones who found new homes in the suburbs.[89]

The pattern seen in Grace Village, in which a relocated school became the nucleus for the growth of a new residential area, was replicated in other parts of Quezon City. Exemplifying this trend were St. Theresa's College and St. Mary's College.[90] The transfer of Ateneo de Manila and Maryknoll (present-day Miriam College) was especially notable. On 7 December 1951, Ateneo purchased from Emerito Ramos and the Philippine Building Corporation a 1.3 million square-meter property in the southeastern fringes of the city. This property was originally sold to the Philippine Building Corporation on 1 July 1949 by the Tuason clan, which still owned a vast tract of land in the city notwithstanding the government's purchase of their Diliman estate in 1938. To gather sufficient funds for the purchase, Ateneo sold its Intramuros property (worth PHP 400,000) and a huge chunk of its Balintawak property (worth PHP 240,000). The relocation began in 1951 (see chapter 3, p. 140), and by 1952 the college and high school departments had moved to the new site, now referred to as the Loyola Heights.[91] On 6 June 1952 Ateneo, then an all-boys school, sold the northern portion of its land to all-girls Catholic school Maryknoll, which also decided to transfer its campus to Quezon City from its old site in Malabon. Meanwhile, the Tuasons developed the part of their estate that was adjacent to Ateneo and Miriam into a residential village, La Vista Subdivision. As expected, La Vista attracted potential homeowners among the parents of Ateneo and Miriam students who wished to gain accessibility to the new campuses.[92] Other private upper-class subdivisions that opened in Loyola Heights to cater to this clientele were Loyola Grand Villas, Varsity Hills, and Xavierville Subdivision, which touted itself as the "Ideal Catholic Community." One must note that Ramos was the general manager of Xavierville Estate, which managed the Xavierville Subdivision, and an authorized agent of Varsity Hills.[93]

Along with schools came religious orders and organizations. One by one, Catholic denominations began to establish their foothold in Quezon City. One example was the Dominicans who relocated the historic Santo Domingo Church, and its famous image of the Our Lady of La Naval, to a lot in Quezon City just outside the border of Manila (less than a kilometer from Welcome Rotonda) that they purchased on 9 April 1950. On 10 October 1954 the Archbishop of Manila blessed the new church.[94] Just as the Ateneo relocation coincided with the Jesuits' move to Loyola Heights, the same was true with St. Theresa's and the Missionary Sisters of the Immaculate Heart of Mary.

From the 1950s to the 1960s Quezon City experienced a construction boom, thanks in large part to private investments in housing (table 15). These investments triggered a multiplier effect, generating further construction

A CAPITAL CITY AT THE MARGINS

Table 15. Number and value of private building construction in selected Philippines cities, 1955 to 1959

	1955 Number	1955 Value	1956 Number	1956 Value	1957 Number	1957 Value	1958 Number	1958 Value	1959 Number	1959 Value
Baguio City	319	3,455,950	206	3,213,050	222	3,085,565	309	3,692,850	305	3,119,710
Cebu City	414	3,163,337	899	5,963,070	767	4,513,873	664	4,478,525	323	2,856,636
Quezon City	2,980	27,228,352	3,918	22,108,515	3,941	37,747,620	3,287	40,584,479	3,082	33,600,867
Pasay City	273	3,546,800	381	6,409,200	350	6,509,050	275	5,950,850	296	6,941,000
Total (Phils)	7,822	57,939,858	12,701	78,118,680	12,334	104,922,958	11,018	104,275,447	10,198	106,720,646

Source: Bureau of the Census and Statistics, *Journal of Philippine Statistics*, vol. 13, nos. 4–6, 56

FIG. 23. An advertisement of Araneta Center's Farmer's Market

NOTE: The text in the ad can be translated thus: Largest. Cleanest. Low prices. Attractive. Parking is not a problem. "We are here to serve you!"

SOURCE: "The Coliseum Farmer's Market & Shopping Center," *The Weekly Nation*, 5 Jan. 1970: 22–23.

activity in the form of new commercial establishments, schools, hospitals, and other service-oriented businesses.

Such was the case in the Aranetas' construction of the Araneta Center in Cubao (fig. 23). Revolving around the Araneta Coliseum, the Araneta Center became the city's premier shopping district by the 1960s. It was especially popular for its wet market, restaurants, cinemas (New Frontier Cinema and Nation Cinerama as two of the most notable ones), and even a skating rink. It featured shoe retailers that sold Marikina-made footwear, then a booming industry aided by the government's ISI policy and led by popular shoe brands like Gregg's and Ang Tibay. Araneta Center's Aurora Arcade blossomed along Aurora Boulevard.[95] In 1967 Henry Sy's emerging retail enterprise, SM, which

176   A CAPITAL CITY AT THE MARGINS

began as a shoe store (Shoemart, hence SM) in Manila, built its first shopping mall in Quezon City inside the Araneta Center, SM Cubao. In 1975 Tony Tan Caktiong opened an ice cream parlor in Cubao and named it Jollibee, which is now a billion-peso enterprise.[96] If before, "Manila blurred one's existence in Quezon City"[97] because the former continued to define the social lives of those who lived in the new capital, Cubao gave middle- and upper-class city residents accessible recreational spaces and made them less dependent on Manila for their leisure and entertainment.[98] The Quezon City government was understandably proud of having a space of consumerist modernity within its own territory:

> Cubao, which is Quezon City's most developed district, is the nerve center of activity. It is a city within a city, blinking in the evening with huge neon lights and throbbing at daytime with traffic and shopping chores. Nine first class theaters and the world's largest dome coliseum are located in the area, thus making it the entertainment center. Banks stand almost door to door along both sides of Aurora Boulevard, which cuts through Cubao, from Manila.[99]

The entertainment and broadcast industries saw the benefits in investing in Quezon City. By the 1960s, the city was home to the country's major film outfits and television and radio stations. It was the "Hollywood of the Philippines"—sans the glitz and the glamor. The two largest movie studios in the postwar Philippines, Sampagita Pictures and LVN Pictures, had been in the city early on and until now notwithstanding their status as defunct businesses. Sampagita is in New Manila while LVN is in Cubao. Lesser-known studios like Lebran, Palaris Films, and Royal Production also found a home in the city.[100] These motion picture enterprises clustered in Quezon City due to the area's unique suburban geography that combined picturesque rurality and urban convenience, making film production more feasible:

> Because of its versatility, long mileage of accessible roads and ever-changing panorama, Quezon City provides a matchless variety of scenic locations and offers endless quest of scenes yet to be discovered. Nature has so endowed Quezon City with her bounties of limitless space, adequate facilities and magnificent outdoor scenes.[101]

Broadcasting companies followed suit. Before the Aranetas purchased the land of the Araneta Center in Cubao, the Radio Corporation of America owned the site.[102] The radio station DZBB moved to Quezon City in 1959 and from its new headquarters launched its own television station in 1961, which is now known as GMA. In 1966 ABS-CBN, the country's first television network owned by the powerful Lopez clan, transferred its operations to the present-day Broadcast Center at Bohol Avenue (now Sgt. Esguerra Avenue) in Diliman.[103]

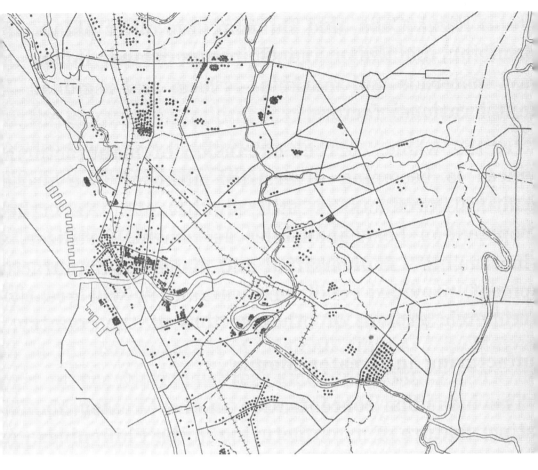

MAP 20. Manufacturing employment in Greater Manila, 1960
SOURCE: Luna, "Manufacturing in the Philippines," 404

Quezon City also had spaces devoted to manufacturing. Some of the earliest manufacturers to establish themselves in the city were the Ysmael Steel Factory, Pepsi Cola Bottling Company, Genuino Ice Plant, Mayon Motor Works, Mission Beverages, Mercado Body Builders, and Halili Enterprises, which focused on transportation services.[104] In the early 1960s, of the 129,704 workers in the manufacturing sector in Greater Manila, 13.08 percent were in Quezon City. For comparison, Manila had 50.30 percent, while Caloocan had 8.64 percent. Quezon City's manufacturing base focused on textiles, fabricated metals, apparel, and beverages. Although Quezon City's most iconic industries, like the Ysmael factory and the Pepsi bottling plant, were

TABLE 16. Workers in Quezon City ten years old and over according to industry, 1970

Industry	Male	Female	Both Sexes
All Industries	152,730	108,459	261,189
Agriculture, Hunting, Forestry, and Fishing	4,792	856	5,648
Mining and Quarrying	337	92	429
Manufacturing	27,534	14,294	41,828
Electricity, Gas, Water, and Sanitary Services	1,539	70	1,609
Construction	17,368	146	17,514
Commerce	18,192	13,924	32,116
Transport, Communication, and Storage	21,845	1,041	22,886
Services	56,798	76,832	133,630
Industry Not Adequately Described	4,325	1,204	5,529

Source: NCSO, *1970 Census of Population*, 25

located in upscale New Manila,[105] most of the factories in the city clustered in the northwestern portion, which is accessible to the North Harbor in Manila and near Caloocan (map 20).[106]

Still, Quezon City's economy in the brief period of ISI was not dominated by manufacturing and thus differed from those of its neighboring towns like Caloocan, Makati, Mandaluyong, Marikina, and Pasig.[107] It was the services sector that defined Quezon City's non-residential spaces, its dominance influencing the city's demography. Compared with nearby cities and towns, Quezon City had a large proportion of middle-class professionals employed in the retailing, entertainment, and academic industries (table 16). In the 1970 census, 51 percent of its population with gainful employment worked in the services sector, while it was only 32 percent for Caloocan and 39 percent for the entire Rizal province. The manufacturing sector, however, tells a different story: 16 percent for Quezon City, 25 percent for Caloocan, and 24 percent for the whole province. Moreover, the services and amenities provided by

TABLE 17. Number of households with specific appliances in Quezon City, 1970

Appliance	WITH	WITHOUT
Radio	89,743	29,044
Television Set	53,286	65,501
Refrigerator	49,423	69,364
Total Number of Households: 118,787		

SOURCE: NCSO, *1970 Census of Population*, 495

these industries (e.g., shopping, restaurants, movies, TV and radio programs, private education) were the same consumer items that defined the middle-class lifestyle in Quezon City (table 17).[108]

At the national level, private capital in housing had become so intensive in the 1960s that by 1970, "the great bulk of housing construction—approximately 80 to 90 per cent—has been carried out by the private sector."[109] The same held true at the local level, including Quezon City. Such a high proportion of private capital relative to overall housing investments not only exposed the government's weakness in providing social services, it also had disastrous effects on the democratization of city space. One of these effects was the disenfranchisement of less affluent residents not only via the mechanisms of the market but even through foul means. Typifying what David Harvey calls "accumulation by dispossession,"[110] original landowners in Barrio San Jose in La Loma experienced harassment through "means of force, violence and intimidation" from the Gregorio Araneta, Inc., when the company attempted to subdivide their lands.[111] The affected residents took their case to court against the company and its partner J. M. Tuason and Co., Inc. However, the court dismissed the complaint against the two companies, a decision the Supreme Court upheld on 15 March 1953. In the following month, the Supreme Court denied the residents' motion for reconsideration. Nonetheless, they filed another complaint for declaratory relief, as tenants in San Jose were already facing eviction.[112] As the next chapter will show, this case would not be the last time that the Aranetas and Tuasons would be involved in land disputes with the urban poor.

Urban dispossession does not always involve coercion; oftentimes, the market serves as the mechanism for property accumulation in the cities.[113] In the case of postwar Quezon City, the presence of private corporate investments produced a crowding-out effect. Rather than ensure that government-owned land benefited low-income families, underfunded state agencies like the PHHC opted to deal with corporations that could pay top dollar for these properties. The PHHC's above-mentioned contract with the Morelos Corporation was a case in point. Another similar example was ABS-CBN's acquisition of a 44,000-square meter lot in Diliman. The company bought the property from the PHHC, a transaction that gave the Macapagal administration a reason to prosecute the Lopezes for allegedly acquiring it through corrupt means. A case was filed, but it got dismissed. But whether or not there was corruption involved, the fact remains that a large private company, owned by one of the most powerful families in the country, obtained a large property in Diliman, which was meant to be a space for the common tao.[114]

The crowding out effect also took the form of private enterprises cornering capital from state-managed funds. One such case was a shady GSIS

180   A CAPITAL CITY AT THE MARGINS

loan extended to Xavierville Real Estate, Inc., owned and managed by Emerito
Ramos, in 1957. The real estate company borrowed PHP 2.5 million from GSIS
to pay financial obligations and increase its working capital. However, the
property it offered as collateral was undeveloped land and had been previously used as security for other loans. This transaction led to a Senate
investigation in 1958, which revealed how the complicity of GSIS officials in
favoring certain individuals imperiled the insurance system of government
employees.[115] It was all the more scandalous considering that Xavierville is
now one of the most exclusive gated communities in the metropolis.

Domesticity, Gated and Gendered

AN IMPORTANT MANIFESTATION of private housing in Quezon City was the
existence of gated communities of the middle and upper classes. Walled-in
communities as a marker of class difference is nothing new in Philippine
history. Arguably, the example of Intramuros has had a profound influence
on how elites from the Spanish colonial period to the present imagine
their ideal urban sociospatial arrangement, one that demonstrates and
fortifies their dominance. In the present-day Philippines, most Manila-
based elites reside in such enclaves like those in Makati—Forbes Park,
Dasmariñas Village, Legazpi Village, Urdaneta Village, Magallanes Village—
that are largely patterned after elite residential spaces in the US, similar
to how other gated communities in other parts of the globe mimicked the
American model.[116] What makes Quezon City historically significant in this
regard is that it prefigured the "Makati model." Prior to Forbes Park's forti-
fication and the rise of Dasmariñas, Quezon City already had its own gated
community: the housing project of the Philippine American Life Insurance
Company (Philamlife) at the northwestern tip of the Diliman quadrangle.
This housing project is not any ordinary residential area; it brands itself as
the country's first gated community.[117]

Philamlife is an insurance company that was established using American
capital. Alabama-native Earl Carroll, the "colossus of Philippine insurance"
was the main figure behind the company.[118] With the Philippines in dire
need of capital for postwar reconstruction, Carroll led the way in establishing Philamlife in 1947 and became its first president. The profiles of two
major figures in the company reveal Philamlife's political significance. Paul
V. McNutt, the last US high commissioner to the Philippines and the first
US ambassador to the country, served as the chairman of the board. One of
Philamlife's founders, Cornelius Vander Starr, was a known operative of the
Office of Strategic Services, the precursor of today's CIA.[119]

At a time when the common tao lacked access to capital, Philamlife
provided urban residents with loans that allowed them to purchase houses,
many of them built in Quezon City. However, the company's role went

FIG. 24. A two-bedroom bungalow in Philamlife Homes
SOURCE: Lindeman, *The Philippine American Life Insurance Company*, 45

beyond providing housing loans or personal insurance. Philamlife claimed that its clientele covered all sectors: from professionals to taxi drivers, urban laborers and rural farmers.[120]

On 22 October 1952, President Quirino conferred with the PHHC officials, Secretary of Labor Jose Figueras, and Carroll and Ramon V. del Rosario of Philamlife to discuss the company's plan for a Quezon City housing project. In the following year, the company bought from the PHHC a 43-hectare property (at a rate of PHP 3 per square meter) at the northern tip of the West Triangle for a housing project on the condition that a ceiling of 5 percent be set for the company's return on investment. This site became the location of the PHP 10 million Philamlife Homes Project. The company completed the project in three phases, corresponding to the development of three parcels of land. The development of the last of these parcels began on 7 February 1955 with a timetable of thirty months. By 30 June 1956, Philamlife had finished 347 houses, 337 of which were occupied.[121]

The Philamlife Homes project was designed to accommodate 600 two- or three-room bungalows in 400-square meter lots (fig. 24).[122] Similar to what the PHHC did in Project 3, the developers imposed a "cooling-off period" on its houses to prevent speculation. However, the prices of the standard houses, PHP 13,000–17,000, even if payable in monthly installments through a 20-year period,[123] were beyond the reach of ordinary workers. Right from the start Philamlife's housing project targeted the so-called "forgotten man" in Philippine housing: "the middle-income fellow." Specifically, it aimed at those

182   A CAPITAL CITY AT THE MARGINS

Manila-based white-collar workers earning between 500 and 1,000 pesos who, according to the company, felt the crunch of the housing shortage.[124]

Touting itself as the first gated community in the country, Philamlife Homes definitely had security as the primary consideration behind this suburban innovation of enclosing the perimeter of a residential area with guarded walls. Moreover, these walls cannot be understood apart from the Quezon City's postwar context, defined by the ongoing Huk rebellion and the city's frontier-like conditions. Furthermore, Cold War politics figured in how certain sectors regarded Philamlife Homes as an effective way to prevent the issue of housing from being hijacked by the left:

> This [example set by Philamlife] must be encouraged for unless private capital is mustered and channeled to mass housing, the government will find itself alone facing a tremendous task under the critical scrutiny of a restless people, who are fast becoming adherents of the doctrine that housing, like the government railroad and water system, is not only too big for private business, but, like education and national defense, is also an obligation of the government.[125]

As a walled community, Philamlife Homes had to have a semblance of self-sufficiency. The company gave the housing project its own shopping center, church, clinic, playgrounds for children, and community center. Carroll even worked with the Benitezes of the Philippine Women's University to have a school built for the subdivision under the direction of the said university. The school, the Jose Abad Santos Memorial School, opened in 1956 in a site within the subdivision. It then transferred to a four-hectare campus beside Philamlife Homes.[126]

In conceptualizing Philamlife Homes, Carroll "wanted to build an American-inspired community patterned after the manner by which houses and neighborhoods [were] built in the United States,"[127] which at the time experienced its postwar suburban boom, the "age of the subdivision."[128] The houses built for Philamlife Homes were "single-detached bungalows with very low or no fences and spacious fronts and backyards" with individual garages.[129] To replicate US models in his project, Carroll turned to Manila's design technocracy (see chapter 3). He picked Carlos Arguelles as the lead architect of Philamlife Homes. Arguelles, who earned his architecture degree from the UST, finished his graduate studies in MIT.[130] Aside from his MIT training, his knowledge of American architecture and housing trends was bolstered by a US trip that Carroll funded so that he could visit "projects in New York, Philadelphia, New Jersey, and other states on the East Coast, paying particular attention to the low-cost housing projects developed for World War II veterans."[131] Angel Nakpil, a Harvard-educated architect, helped Arguelles. The two gave the subdivision the amenities of suburban living: a clubhouse, basketball and tennis courts, and a swimming pool.[132] The success of Philamlife Homes distinguished Arguelles as a prominent architect: "Philamlife Homes has become the template used by countless developers ever since. Arguelles designed the bungalows in variants to suit middle-class Filipino lifestyles that had maids, a central toilet and bath facility and a modern garage."[133]

More than just creating a residential area, Carroll's vision projected a "model community," as if repeating Quezon's vision for the city. For this purpose, Philamlife screened potential homeowners and filtered out

> obvious disqualifications: The community would want no wife-beaters, no drunks, no deadbeats, no obviously antisocial characters. On the positive side, it would want dignified, stable, friendly, and considerate people. But a community composed entirely of people with all the accepted virtues and none of the current vices could be a fairly dull place. Company officials have set up a "rating" system from which they intend to select their new home owners on an objective basis.[134]

Based on this purported objective rating system, the company envisioned its ideal homeowner:

> If the presently contemplated rating system is used, the most highly qualified prospective home owner will be between 25 and 35, married, with three dependents, and will have been steadily employed for the last five years by a reliable and reputable employer. His income will be about P800 (a much higher income will be as much of a disqualification as a much lower one); he will have a savings account or other liquid assets equal to three months income, insurance equal to two years salary, and debts amounting to less than six months income. He will have been paying about P150 monthly for rent for decent quarters in a good neighborhood. He will be a good insurance risk. And, of course, his habits will be temperate, his reputation good, and his morals unquestioned.
>
> In other words, he will be a middle-income man, very probably on the way up. He will be more settled, more thrifty, and generally more promising than most. And the company prayerfully expects that he will be a good citizen in his (and its) community.[135]

Indeed, Philamlife Homes became the model for the other Quezon City subdivisions in the following decades. Elite residential areas like Greenmeadows and Corinthian Gardens anchored themselves on the idea of spatial exclusivity enforced by perimeter walls and roving private security guards. Subdivisions like White Plains and Blue Ridge, "named after famous planned communities in eastern United States . . . provided suburban refuge to the middle and upper class escaping the declining quality of urban life of central Manila."[136] No wonder the city was one of the preferred places of residence of postwar politicians.[137]

184   A CAPITAL CITY AT THE MARGINS

The geographical significance of Philamlife Homes to the general trend of suburbanization is somehow matched by its contributions to the social transformations also taking place in the nascent metropolis. This subdivision was home to future intellectuals of different shades, a new generation of Manila-based personalities who would become prominent during the Marcos era (1965–1986): martial law architect Juan Ponce Enrile, technocrat and Prime Minister Cesar Virata, media man and eventual founder of the Kapisanan ng mga Brodkaster sa Pilipinas Emil Jurado, and even student leader-turned-communist rebel Edgar Jopson.[138] Meanwhile, by the 1960s the erstwhile open spaces surrounding Camp Crame and Camp Murphy had been turned into residential enclaves favored by soldiers and constabulary officials based in these camps, best exemplified by Corinthian Gardens.[139] If these elite spaces are read alongside the private subdivisions and government housing projects discussed above, the overall picture that emerges for postwar Quezon City is one of a vast, gentrified residential suburb:

> It is generally observed that the bulk of Manila's professionals, businessmen, industrialists, public officials and employees, educators, and a good share of its students, live in Quezon City. This fact has led to the inference that people in this part of suburbia are fairly well-off, independent minded, and informed about public affairs. One consequence of this phenomenon, so the popular logic goes, is that they are in a position to evaluate candidates for public office more or less critically. The presence of laborers, unemployed migrants from the provinces, as well as squatters and slum dwellers, does not dilute the generally high social quality of the population. Radio, newspapers, and the grapevine from nearby Manila give these lower classes a relatively better access to goings on in the national government.[140]

Furthermore, Quezon City's atmosphere of domesticity gave it a certain level of femininity that becomes more apparent if compared with the masculine images of Manila and Makati, spaces that dominated the public sphere, especially in terms of politics (Manila) and business (Makati). Interestingly, postwar Quezon City's sex ratio did have a feminine slant (table 18). In 1939 the city's male and female populations were 20,656 and 18,357, respectively. By the 1960s the sex ratio had been reversed.[141]

The feminization of Quezon City's demography coincided with the shift in internal migration patterns in the country. Before the war, rural-to-urban migrants, many of them becoming household servants and unskilled, low-wage workers in greater Manila, were mostly males from Luzon provinces.[142] After the war, Visayan females replaced this group as the largest category of migrants (map 21). For instance, in the 1960s Leyte and Samar were the biggest migrant-sending provinces. Morris Juppenlatz attributed this point to the income-poor status of these two provinces, which were

TABLE 18. Population of Quezon City's districts according to sex, circa 1970

District	Male	Female	Total
Barrio			
Bago Bantay	31,244	33,303	64,547
Bago Bantay Proper	5,693	6,243	11,936
Bagong Pag-asa	6,607	7,088	13,695
Doña Alicia	2,437	2,502	4,939
Ramon Magsaysay	6,413	6,488	12,901
Santo Cristo	3,300	3,276	6,576
Vasra	6,794	7,706	14,500
Balintawak	23,413	23,600	47,013
Apolonio Samson	5,431	5,406	10,837
Baesa	5,043	5,142	10,185
Balingasa	3,520	3,324	6,844
Balon-Bato	4,589	4,564	9,153
Unang Sigaw	4,830	5,164	9,994
Capitol	2,756	2,692	5,448
Central	17,967	20,522	38,489
Central Proper	11,304	13,349	24,653
Piñahan	6,663	7,173	13,836
Cubao	32,777	36,375	69,152
Cubao Proper	24,590	27,073	51,663
Horseshoe	486	543	1,029
Pinagkaisahan	3,176	3,584	6,760
Silangan	2,895	3,392	6,287
Valencia	1,630	1,783	3,413
Diliman	10,469	10,944	21,413
Balara	3,232	3,622	6,854
Cruz na Ligas	3,742	3,732	7,474
Loyola Heights	797	839	1,636
Pansol	2,698	2,751	5,449
Galas	14,061	15,926	29,987
Aurora	2,765	3,330	6,095
Galas Proper	11,296	12,596	23,892

Kamuning	15,524	17,430	32,954
Kamuning Proper	13,615	15,448	29,063
Obrero	1,909	1,982	3,891
La Loma	17,953	20,058	38,011
Murphy	24,859	26,173	51,032
Bagumbayan	670	638	1,308
Libis	3,662	3,836	7,498
Murphy Proper	1,507	1,144	2,651
San Roque	7,920	8,223	16,143
Socorro	10,793	12,039	22,832
Ugong Norte	307	293	600
New Manila	7,746	9,582	17,328
Mariana	4,378	5,747	10,125
New Manila Proper	3,368	3,835	7,203
Novaliches	10,948	11,155	22,103
Gulod	2,733	2,836	5,569
Kaligayahan (Binugsok)	790	728	1,518
Nagkaisang Nayon	3,666	3,693	7,359
Novaliches Proper	1,157	1,241	2,398
Pasong Putik	778	708	1,486
San Agustin	705	744	1,449
Santa Monica	1,119	1,205	2,324
Quadrangle	7,033	8,541	15,574
Quadrangle Proper	800	780	1,580
South Triangle	3,050	3,429	6,479
West Triangle	3,183	4,332	7,515
Quirino	35,547	39,854	75,401
Duyan-Duyan	1,466	1,617	3,083
Escopa	2,904	2,836	5,740
Maria Clara	3,484	4,224	7,7708
Quirino	27,693	31,177	58,870
Roxas	12,548	14,971	27,519
Roxas Proper	10,609	12,893	23,502
Santa Cruz	1,939	2,078	4,017

San Bartolome	7,044	6,762	13,806
Bagbag	1,467	1,472	2,939
San Bartolome	1,592	1,523	3,105
Santa Lucia	2,173	2,102	4,275
Sauyo	1,812	1,675	3,487
San Francisco del Monte	28,476	30,325	58,801
Bungad	956	958	1,914
Camayan	5,350	5,871	11,221
Del Monte	4,588	4,853	9,441
Mariblo	1,125	1,317	2,442
Paltok	9,443	10,052	19,495
San Antonio	7,014	7,274	14,288
San Jose	19,784	23,877	43,661
Manreza	3,052	3,959	7,011
Masambong	4,033	4,450	8,483
San Jose	2,851	3,202	6,053
San Jose Proper	9,848	12,266	22,114
Santol	5,186	5,303	10,489
Santa Mesa Heights	11,904	14,353	26,257
Malamig	5,572	7,235	12,807
Matalahib	2,397	2,915	5,312
Talayan	506	735	1,241
Tatalon	3,429	3,468	6,897
Tandang Sora	21,578	23,889	45,467
Bahay Toro	14,208	16,621	30,829
Culiat	1,958	1,891	3,849
Pasong Tamo	1,072	1,055	2,127
Talipapa	2,735	2,751	5,486
Tandang Sora	1,605	1,571	3,176
Total	358,817	395,635	754,452

SOURCE: NCSO, *1970 Census of Population and Housing: Rizal*, 1–2

(and still are) perennially hit by typhoons.¹⁴³ Although Quezon City did not have a lot of industrial establishments that created demand for low-wage workers from the countryside, its booming residential spaces required the same cheap labor for the social reproduction of middle- and upper-class

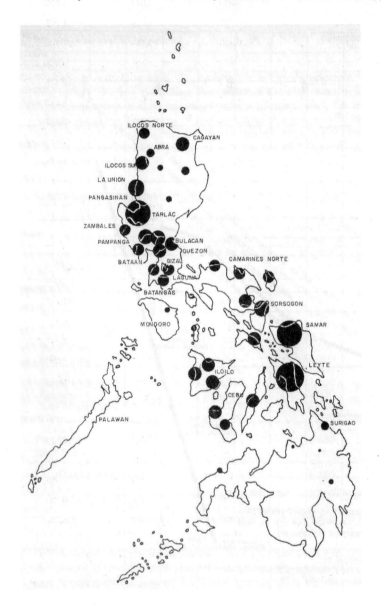

MAP 21. Geographical origins of Manila-bound migrants

SOURCE: Juppenlatz, *Cities in Transformation*, 102

TABLE 19. Mother tongue spoken, and number of speakers according to sex in Quezon City, 1970

Language	Male Speakers	Female Speakers	Total
Tagalog	258,764	269,361	528,125
Iloco	28,950	35,492	64,442
Bicol	14,975	17,831	32,806
Samar-Leyte	10,964	17,311	28,275
Hiligaynon	9,424	14,012	23,436
Cebuano	7,674	11,578	19,432
Pangasinan	9,042	9,765	18,807
Pampango	8,662	9,387	18,049
Chinese	3,012	2,464	5,476
English	2,453	2,196	4,649
All Others	4,863	6,022	10,885
Not Stated	34	36	70

SOURCE: NCSO, *1970 Census of Population: Rizal*, 325

TABLE 20. Population by sex and place of birth in Quezon City, 1970

Place of Birth	Male	Female	Both Sexes
Quezon City	143,259	137,468	280,727
Other Municipality, Same Province	7,359	7,606	14,965
Other Province	204,831	248,584	453,415
Other Country	2,910	1,882	4,792
Not Stated	458	95	553
Total	358,817	395,635	754,452

SOURCE: Based on NCSO, *1970 Census of Population: Rizal*, 387

households. Visayan migrant women, working seven days a week as stay-at-home *yayas* (nannies) and *katulong/kasambahay* (household helpers), gave well-to-do nuclear families the flexibility to balance the time they could allot for home and work—a phenomenon that persists to this day. Language heterogeneity in 1970s Quezon City also lends credence to this dynamic (tables 19 and 20).

190   A CAPITAL CITY AT THE MARGINS

Further analysis of table 18 appears to validate this point: the feminine slant was most prominent in upscale suburban and middle-class urban areas. In New Manila, the female population was 23 percent higher than the male population, and in neighboring San Jose the gap was 20 percent. In the neighborhood of West Triangle, the location of Philamlife Homes and the Morelos Housing Project, the disparity was 36 percent. This gender imbalance held true for Santa Mesa Heights (20 percent), yet within its territory, the urban poor community of Tatalon had an almost balanced sex ratio. Tatalon's case mirrored those of other urban-poor districts and communities like Bago Bantay (6 percent) and Escopa (-2 percent). Quezon City's rural areas also showed a low degree of gender discrepancy, as seen in Novaliches (1 percent) and San Bartolome (-4 percent). Although additional data are needed for corroboration, these figures are enough to hypothesize that the presence of female migrant helpers was a significant factor behind Quezon City's feminized demography.

It is such a grave social and historiographical injustice that documentary sources are silent about female migrant household helpers, considering that they are the backbone of postwar and contemporary suburban life. In the early 1950s, Diliman households even employed an average of two helpers,[144] a luxury that rested on the migrants' dirt-cheap labor, lack of workers' rights and benefits, and desperation to escape rural poverty. Erlinda Enriquez Panlilio recalls her family's yaya in 1950s Kamuning:

> Nila was a semi-literate, young peasant woman from the province of Aklan, who served as *yaya* [maid] for my brother and me. She was as brown as the earth of the fields she had worked in, where she had helped her parents with the *palay* [rice] harvest. She had only reached grade three [in primary school] when she came to Manila to work for us.[145]

Further research, especially one that combines historical and ethnographic methods, is needed to determine whether Nila's experience was typical or if the employment of household helpers was correlated with the increasing shift from extended to nuclear families in postwar suburbs. These historiographical questions would inevitably touch on gender issues: for instance, did Quezon City's domesticity engender heteronormativity (much like in Carroll's statements about his ideal Philamlife Homes household) or a form of suburban matriarchy, "in which the mother is the kingpin in the family . . . [and] the father more like a dormitory occupant and less a headman, parent, and peace officer."[146] Whether suburbanization in greater Manila created liberal feminism, founded on the enhanced responsibility of women as homemakers and citizen-consumers, or reinforced patriarchy through the predominance of the nuclear family[147] should also be part of the agenda of

Philippine urban historians and sociologists. What is certain is that "gender has been deeply influential in the production of 'the geographical.'"[148]

The Masses at the City Margins

THE SUCCESS of private residential developments in Quezon City and the inaccessibility of LCH projects to low-income families gave the capital city a middle-class character. As analyzed by Manuel Caoili, the 258 percent increase in the city's population from 1948 to 1960 was due to the "movement of Manila's middle- and upper-income families into government housing projects and private subdivisions in the city, following the transfer of schools, national government offices and factories into the new national capital."[149] Quezon City's apparent gentrification had its garden city advocates. The most vocal of them came from those who envisioned the application of the garden city concept on the city, an early-twentieth-century urban planning concept that was presented as a remedy to the ills of the Victorian-era industrial town.[150] Quezon City seemed perfect for garden-city advocates because of its large untouched areas and the lack of industrial sites in contrast to the other towns of greater Manila. The community paper *Diliman Star* became their mouthpiece.[151]

Quezon City's gentrified character, although dominant, was far from being unchallenged. Although Philamlife Homes and other similar developments represented the seeming success of an Americanized middle-/upper-class modernity, it was actually being confronted by its dialectical opposite within the city itself. The city's huge number of low-income and informal settlers constantly unsettled their well-to-do "neighbors." Unfortunately, many of them had to live in Quezon City against their wishes; a significant number of the city's urban poor were forcibly relocated from Manila as a result of anti-slum drives in the 1950s and 1960s.

The wave of slum clearance operations in early postwar Manila can be attributed to the bias of city officials against informal settlers. Mayors and councilors regarded them as a menace that had to be eradicated. In many cases they chose Quezon City as a relocation site for those evicted.[152] Beginning in 1951 Manila Mayor Arsenio Lacson forced squatters living in the Port Area, Nagtahan, Intramuros, and Malate to move to Quezon City. The national government's Social Welfare Administration (SWA) then facilitated their transfer to Bago Bantay, located a few kilometers north of the Diliman quadrangle (fig. 25). The resettlement was conducted in a most inhumane way:

> The families and the remnants of materials from their shacks were transported by trucks, made available by the City of Manila, to the demarcated lots on the site; there the families were dumped. No provision had been made to assist the families in the

FIG. 25. Slums in Bago Bantay, 1952
SOURCE: Tutay, "Squatter Trouble," 7

erection of their shelters; nor roads had been constructed; no water, drainage, or any community rehabilitation facilities had been provided. By 1955, a total of 1,333 families had been relocated on the site, which meant that the relocation site was nearly filled, as it was planned originally to relocate 1,380 families.[153]

Only after complaints by the resettled families did the SWA begin fixing the basic utilities in the area. However, problems regarding slum clearance did not stop as Quezon City hosted other slum resettlements in the 1950s. In 1953, the PHHC and the Slum Clearance Committee moved squatter families evicted from a private property in Quezon City to a relocation site in Bagong Pag-asa, which had 652 lots and was adjacent to Bago Bantay. Another site was established in North Bago Bantay. At the beginning of fiscal year 1955–1956, the PHHC resettled about 1,510 families from slum areas in Manila to these two resettlement sites. In the following fiscal year, the Slum Clearance Committee recorded almost 6,000 families resettled in sites in and outside Quezon City.[154] Other PHHC resettlement sites were a 91.3-hectare portion of the Novaliches Subdivision (1955), the Gabriel Estate (1956), which was southwest of the Novaliches Watershed in Quezon City, the Kamarin Site (1956) in Caloocan, just outside Quezon City, and the Sapang Palay site (1960) in San Jose del Monte, Bulacan, which was the largest and most famous of these sites. The "exodus" of slum families from Manila continued in the 1960s. From December 1963 to March 1964, following the demolition of informal communities in Intramuros and North Harbor, many of the affected families moved to the existing squatter colonies in Quezon City, especially in the East and North Triangles. Even the PHHC sites were not exempt from having their own share of informal settlers. To encourage these informal settlers to relocate, the PHHC compensated them for the cost of the improvements they made in the lots they occupied. In the fiscal year 1956–1957, compensations of this nature totaled PHP 30,203.92.[155]

At the end of fiscal year 1961–62, the PHHC's Tenancy Division received 14,561 applications for dwelling accommodations, a fact that, the PHHC itself acknowledged, pointed to greater Manila's acute housing shortage.[156] Although state-supported resettlements seemed to evince government action on urban problems, the nature of these relocations showed state failure. Because many of the slum dwellers chose to live in congested areas in the city center due to their accessibility to places of work and potential income, the act of relocating them to relatively distant places in Quezon City exerted a pressure on their meager incomes (whether in the form of higher transport costs or a shift to lower-paying jobs in the vicinity). Furthermore, basic services were often inadequate in the PHHC resettlement sites like Bago Bantay and Kamarin. Although Kamarin 1 had 3,489 lots and Kamarin 2 offered 1,657 lots with an average of 377 square meters, most of the awardees disliked the area because of "the lack of water and light facilities, undeveloped subdivision roads which become mud pool during the rainy season and the lack of transportation facilities."[157]

The issue of transportation was crucial because of its direct impact on household finances. While areas in Quezon City farther up north offered rent cheaper than in the downtown, living in such locations meant a 300 percent increase in travel costs. Conversely, while living in areas nearer to Manila made daily travel more affordable, it also meant higher rents (table 21).

Inadequate transport facilities in postwar greater Manila worsened the situation of income-poor households. Although transport companies, such as the Metropolitan Transportation Service (METRAN) and the Halili Bus Company, allowed Quezon City residents to travel to Manila and back, only middle-class passengers could afford their fares. There were even bus operators who overcharged hapless passengers shuttling between the two cities.[158] Meanwhile, jeepneys—a cheap transport mode that operated as minibuses built using the chassis of American jeeps left behind after the war—were mainly confined to the more urbanized sections of Manila. Moreover, options were severely limited, even for the middle classes. For example, the Royal Bus Company, the only firm licensed to operate in Roxas District (Project 1) in the 1950s, provided such poor service that not enough buses were available during rush hours. In terms of infrastructure, as late as 1960, Quezon City only had eighteen national highways with a total length of 378.32 kilometers.

194   A CAPITAL CITY AT THE MARGINS

TABLE 21. Asking price, distance from Manila, and amount of one-way bus fare to Manila of selected residential lots for sale in Quezon City, 30–31 August 1958

Area (sq. m)	Price per sq. m.	Total Price	Distance from Manila	One-Way Bus Fare
1. 630	21.00	13,290.00	9	0.10
2. 460	18.00	8,280.00	10	0.10
3. 420	25.00	10,500.00	8	0.10
4. 315	–	4,500.00	8	0.10
5. 934	7.00	6,538.00	25	0.30[a]
6. 34,225	14.00	479,150.00	30	0.30[b]
7. 198	14.00	2,772.00	30	0.30[b]
8. 1,539	26.00	40,014.00	7	0.10
9. 1,300	14.00	18,200.00	7	0.15
10. 456	21.00	9,576.00	9	0.10
11. 1,500	27.00	40,500.00	7	0.10
12. 1,200	28.00	33,600.00	7	0.10
13. 784	31.00	24,304.00	7	0.10
14. 620	21.00	13,020.00	7	0.10
15. 2,000	32.00	64,000.00	8	0.10
16. 404	13.50	5,454.00	7	0.10
17. 500	18.00	9,000.00	8	0.10
18. 701	25.00	17,525.00	7	0.10
19. 300	25.00	7,500.00	7	0.10
20. 690	35.00	24,150.00	7	0.10
21. 1,528	22.00	33,616.00	7	0.10
22. 440	15.00	6,600.00	14	0.15

NOTES:

[a] Bus transportation at present available but inadequate

[b] No bus transportation at present

SOURCE: Abrams and Koenigsberger, "A Housing Program for the Philippine Islands," 69

In comparison, Davao City had 27 highways (577.92 km), while Zamboanga City had 49 (1,074.22 km). As late as 1969, less than eight kilometers of national roads and none of the city roads in Quezon City were cemented.[159]

The lack of services for the resettled households was just one aspect behind the failure of resettlement projects in Quezon City. The most important issue that the state could not address was employment: the relocation areas in Quezon City were simply too far from the usual sources of livelihood for the urban poor. As a result, many of those relocated left the sites and defiantly returned to Manila.[160] In Bagong Pag-asa, despite efforts in 1954 to issue contracts of sale of the occupied land to the affected families, the PHHC found out that "many, if not most, of the relocated squatters immediately sold their 'rights' to the lots and went back to squatting in Manila, enriched by the experience."[161] In Gabriel Estate, with no adequate government support for the families, only a few of the original families remained. The PHHC and SWA discovered the same thing in the Bago Bantay resettlement sites in the late 1950s and in Bagong Pag-asa as well.[162] Aprodicio Laquian narrates: "Ten years after the move, most of the original tenants were not in Bago Bantay anymore. Many of them sold the 'rights' to their lots. They simply pocketed the money, went back to Manila, and squatted again, richer by the experience."[163] This pattern of eviction, relocation, and return to Manila among informal settlers revealed the holes not only in the capital city's projection of a well-planned suburbia, but also in the intercity dynamics of the emerging metropolis. In the first place, the reason why Manila kept on demolishing slums and transferring their inhabitants to Quezon City was that it wanted to create an image of modernity for the old capital.[164]

Despite this "merry-go-round ejection squatting affair,"[165] the urban poor populations of Quezon City and the other towns surrounding Manila continued to increase (maps 22 and 23). In his study on urban informality in Manila, Morris Juppenlatz calculated that urban squatters constantly grew at around 15 percent annually from 1946 to 1963. In 1946 the absolute figure was 23,000 persons, while in 1956 it grew to 98,000, then reaching 282,730 in 1963. In 1963 Quezon City had at squatter population of at least 14,200, or 5 percent of the squatter population in greater Manila.[166] It was on its way to becoming the nation's biggest "slurb."[167]

However, to focus on state failure in understanding the "slum question" might prevent us from seeing the issue from another important angle: that of the perspective of slum dwellers themselves. To begin with, informal communities are not negative externalities but are significant contributors to the economy, whether in the formal and informal circuits. Then, as now, they provided a crucial source of labor made cheaper by the "depressed" costs of their household expenses, a direct result of their not having to invest in formal housing. Only by beginning with this premise can we appreciate the slum dwellers' historical agency.

Quezon City's informal settlers in the early postwar decades came from different walks of life. For example, most of the Bago Bantay settlers were Pampanga refugees who sought a new life in Manila and its suburbs (fig. 26).[168] Sitio San Roque in the North Triangle, just across EDSA from

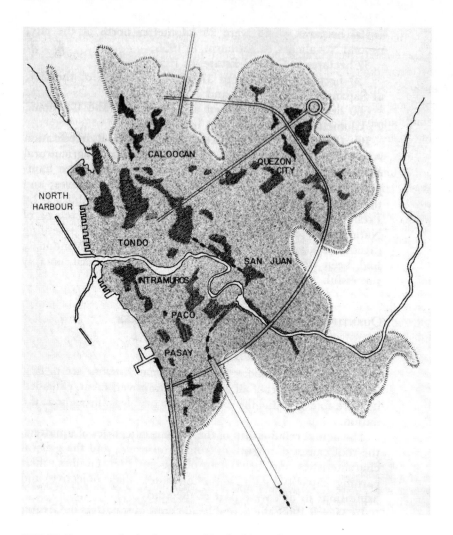

MAP 22. Squatter colonies in greater Manila, May 1963
SOURCE: Juppenlatz, *Cities in Transformation*, 98

Philamlife Homes, was a relocation site for Huk rebels who had surrendered to the government.[169] There were also "builder squatters," slum dwellers "who worked on the many construction projects in the city, built shanties for their families, and then stayed put even after the construction work was done."[170] The provision in the 1949 Quezon City master plan for public housing to be given to the estimated ten thousand laborers needed for the construction of national buildings in Quezon City was honored more in the breach than in the observance. Apparently, those who built the city could not find decent shelter in it. Such was also the case with the residents

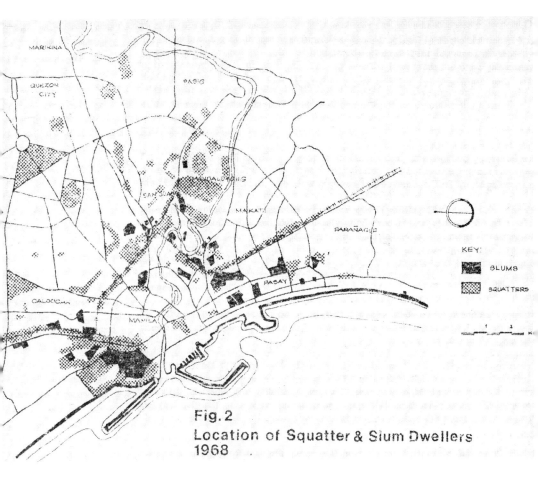

MAP 23. Location of squatter and slum dwellers, 1968

SOURCE: Institute of Planning, University of the Philippines, *A Planning Strategy for Metropolitan Manila, A.D. 2000: A Policy Study in Environmental Planning* (Quezon City: Institute of Planning, UP, 1968), 10–11

of Escopa, the area immediately north of Camp Murphy that was owned by a Japanese national before the war and then expropriated by the Quirino administration in 1948. Originally called ISCOPA as a crude acronym for the 1st Company of the Philippine Army, which occupied the area following its expropriation, Escopa became property of the Department of Social Welfare in 1953 and attracted illegal settlers soon after. Many of them were laborers involved in the PHHC's construction projects. Escopa itself was within the territory of Project 4. In 1975 Escopa housed 1,246 squatter families.[171] The commonality that bound these different groups together was the fact that they could not afford decent housing in the city, even in the PHHC's LCH

FIG. 26. A vibrant street scene in Bago Bantay

SOURCE: Maramag, "The City Can Use Its Squatter Areas," 10

projects. Many also turned to illegal housing because of the complexities and added costs of securing building permits from local authorities.[172]

A marginalized sector, Quezon City's urban poor occupied the city's marginal spaces. Oftentimes, these marginal spaces took the form of river and estero banks. The presence of slum dwellers along these waterways only magnified their marginality, especially during floods. In 1959, Quezon City squatter families who were affected by a disastrous flood were relocated to Sapang Palay. A more catastrophic flood on 28 May 1960 uncovered the plight of the city's informal communities, as it hit Quezon City the hardest.[173] According to media reports, "nearly all the casualties were poor people who had to live as squatters on the banks of creeks and dry river beds because there was no other place for them to build their shanties."[174] Floods affected middle-class households, like those living in Roxas District, but the situation of the city's slum dwellers, like those in Tatalon and communities along the Dario River, was much worse.[175]

Quezon City slum dwellers also occupied parts of the city that were designated as civic centers and meant to convey urban grandeur but remained bereft of activity, like the Constitution Hill, the Quezon Memorial Circle (QMC), the Diliman quadrangle, and the UP campus (map 24).[176] This

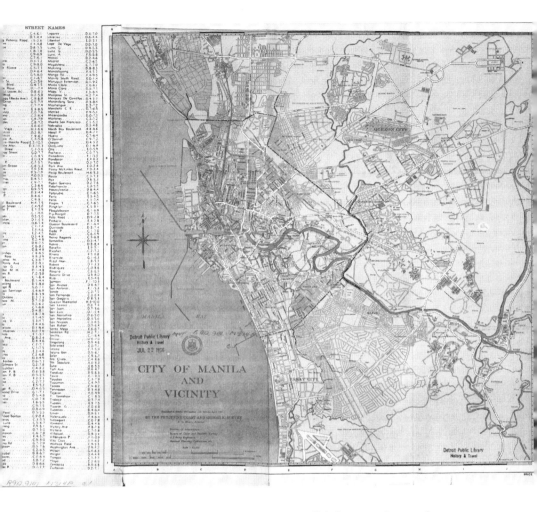

MAP 24. City of Manila and vicinity, 1955; note Manila's dense road network in contrast to Quezon City's vast open spaces, especially near the Diliman quadrangle and QMC, found in the upper right corner of the map

SOURCE: Philippine Coast and Geodetic Survey, "City of Manila and Vicinity, 1955" (Manila: Philippine Coast and Geodetic Survey, 1955); map courtesy of the Stephen S. Clark Library, Hatcher Graduate Library, University of Michigan, Ann Arbor, MI

development was a grave sin from the perspective of the city's planners who envisioned "a city without blighted areas."[177] The state responded in May 1968 with a massive slum clearance in the QMC. Many of those evicted ended up in Sapang Palay, Carmona in Cavite, and San Pedro Tunasan in Laguna.[178] However, from the perspective of the informal settlers, occupying these pockets of vacant land was an assertion of their place in the city.

200   A CAPITAL CITY AT THE MARGINS

Even the PHHC's LCH projects harbored slums. The story of Alfonso Perlas, a slum dweller in Project 8, is instructive. His family dismantled their hut in Marikina and rebuilt it in Project 8. They rented a 600-square meter lot for PHP 100 a month. However, their hut eventually became too small for them, and they had to find a new place. They did so in another area in Quezon City: 4,000 square meters for a PHP 100 monthly rent. Perlas liked the new place because he found it peaceful, unlike his former house in Pasig, where he could hear his neighbors quarrel: "You'd get roused from your sleep because the rooms were adjacent, the houses close together. Here it's spacious, so it's peaceful." [179]

A similar peripatetic narrative characterized the life of Teresa Cardenas, whose family's first home was in Tandang Sora, Quezon City: "Our walls were made of lawanit (woodboard) which we bought piece by piece when we had the money. It kept out the rain. We were so poor then that our roof was made of grass." [180] To occupy the land Cardenas's family paid PHP 15 annually. In 1959 the lot owner asked them to move out so that he could build a subdivision on his property. They transferred to Teresa's grandmother's residence in Kamuning. Shortly after, the family moved in to a neighboring lot. However, seven years later, the lot's owner asked the settlers to vacate it because he wanted to build an apartment there. [181]

Despite the difference in tone, the two anecdotes illustrate the precarity of postwar Quezon City's urban poor. As the years passed, their numbers multiplied, a demographic transformation with huge implications for Quezon City's politics. For instance, illegal settlers in an area in the East Triangle organized themselves into a group called Piñahan Homeowners' Association and successfully persuaded President Ramon Magsaysay to subdivide the land they occupied and resell the lots to them, despite the land being earmarked for government buildings. Although only a small fraction of the lots were awarded to the settlers, as most of them ended up with outsiders who had the money and influence, their action demonstrated the urban poor's capacity to exercise agency. In fact, the Magsaysay and Macapagal administrations ordered investigations to look into how settlers got the raw end of the deal. [182]

The urban poor's political power got a further boost from a law passed in 1959, RA 2259. This law stipulated that local officials in chartered cities should be elected rather than appointed. [183] As such, as slum dwellers increased in chartered cities, so did their capacity to influence not just local but also national politics, given the clout of chartered cities. In Quezon City one of the effects of the RA 2259 was the formation of the Quezon City Citizens League. On the surface, it was a civic organization established by officials of the city's various middle- and upper-class homeowners associations. Its objective was to push for good governance at the city level and combat patronage politics. It did so through campaigns and by fielding in their own candidates in the local elections.[184] However, the league was a reaction of the middle class to what they perceived was the urban poor's increased political power under RA 2259. It grew out of a fear that the significant number of low-income households in Quezon City would lead to, from the league members' perspective, less than ideal electoral results.[185]

When the Citizens League succeeded in having six of its candidates elected to the city council in November 1959, there were those who lauded the outcome. Quezon City voters were intelligent, they claimed.[186] However, for all the pretense of enlightenment—and ilustrado posturing—of the Citizens League, it could not hide its elitist arrogance. Its middle-class orientation showed in how league members mapped out Quezon City's electorate using the subscriber list of electric company Meralco and determined that the "overwhelming majority of Quezon City residents had incomes well above most other communities in the country." Based on this piece of information—and in an ironic display of ignorance and illogic—they "inferred that the city people generally had a high level of education and were probably far better informed than most Filipinos about public affairs."[187] The elitism was more patent in how the League geographically differentiated the electorate:

> Knowing conditions in the various areas and districts of the city, the League planners made a rough classification based on income, information and "intelligence." The idea was to design the most suitable campaign techniques for each broad class. Three were identified: (1) Areas where people were "intelligent", very well informed, or had the highest incomes—Sta. Mesa Heights, Heroes Hills, Phil-Am Life, Horseshoe Drive, U.P. Diliman; (2) Areas where people were "intelligent", informed, and had average incomes—the government housing projects; and (3) areas of the lower and lowest income people, which included squatter and slum dwellers.[188]

Although the Citizens League sparked similar political movements in Pasay and Makati and continued their participation in the succeeding elections, traditional politics stumped their sophomore attempt. It lost its bid for the mayoralty position and a number of slots in the Quezon City council. Meanwhile, the campaign of the Citizens League in Pasay proved futile against the machinations of traditional politicians. Backed by patron–client ties with the city's urban poor, Quezon City Mayor Norberto Amoranto remained safe in his post for more than two decades.[189]

Electoral clout, of course, does not mean that the informal settlers ruled Quezon City. On the contrary, rather than become a haven for the common tao, Quezon City grew into a space dominated by gated communities and middle-class enclaves. The working-class mirage that it projected in the Commonwealth era persisted in the postwar period.

Other continuities characterized postwar Quezon City. As if maintaining a heritage of rebelliousness, it became a hotbed of radicalism during the Cold War era. As such, security became the topmost concern for national and city administrators even as they were responding to a different, but related, social crisis: the issue of urban housing. Continuity was also apparent in how Quezon City's development remained tied to the US: if Quezon City's public spending hinged upon the coconut oil excise tax from the US, in the postwar era it was dependent upon US aid. Most remarkable is the colonial–postcolonial continuity of socioeconomic structures. Unequal land distribution seemed to have defied not just temporal but also spatial boundaries. In the early decades of the postcolonial period, the unequal distribution of land in the countryside, which fueled the Huk insurgency as early as the prewar era, was more or less replicated in Manila, Quezon City, and the other suburban towns in the postwar period. Filipino politicians themselves recognized the seriousness of this situation and the urgency of coming up with a remedy. Rep. Corpuz stated it in unequivocal terms:

> Presently, most of the residential lands in the City of Manila and in Quezon City are owned by a few moneyed people who sell or lease their lands at exorbitant prices. Hence, it is proposed to break up these big landholdings to enable the poor people of the above-mentioned cities to have a land of their own at low cost on which to build their homes, thereby solving the housing problems in these two cities.[190]

* * *

PRACTICALLY ALL SOUTHEAST ASIAN CITIES, especially capitals, were preoccupied with the issue of housing during the postwar period. State responses and results differed, however. While the Singaporean state managed to consolidate its control over housing through multistory public flats, Kuala Lumpur and Jakarta still saw the persistence and sprawling of single-dwelling kampongs in the city's margins. Despites these divergences, the idea of forging citizenship—and thereby reinforcing state legitimacy— through housing was common among the cities in the region,[191] including Quezon City. Whether the state attained the desired outcome was, of course, not uniform.

Postcolonial Quezon City did replicate some of the hallmarks of American suburbanization. Traditionally, suburbanization had been to a "large extent a class-based process," one that was "steered by housing choices of the middle classes."[192] Quezon City was a space founded on the idea of democratization via consumption, which eventually gave way to the exacerbation of inequality through market and state mechanisms.[193] It had urban plans drawn by experts, many of them US-trained, but these blueprints neglected social planning, as admitted by the city vice mayor in

1971.[194] However, the overall result was not geographical homogeneity often associated with suburbia,[195] but a patchy peri-urban settlement of upper-class "stateside" enclaves, public-funded low-cost housing for the middle classes, and scattered informal settlements of rural migrants and evicted slum dwellers. Furthermore, state policies (especially by the PHHC), market mechanisms (resulting in the crowding-out effect), and the unequal distribution of basic services in the city (particularly in slum resettlement areas) prevented low-income families from gaining access to specific spaces in the city and, consequently, from enjoying productive lives. Meanwhile, the upper class, represented by the Tuasons, Aranetas, and Lopezes, capitalized on Quezon City's spaces to further accumulate wealth. Interestingly, the said families built their fortunes in the lucrative sugar industry in the Visayas, especially the Aranetas and Lopezes, and then reinvested in urban-based enterprises and properties,[196] a trend that was already apparent as early as the 1930s (see chapter 1). As landlord power defines rural geography to generate surplus profit, its consumption patterns in the cities remakes urban morphology. Hence, Quezon City's actual spatial division of wealth was far from the original social justice vision that underlined its creation.

Once again, the disparity between objective and outcome hounded Quezon City. The PHHC's projects benefited not those who badly needed housing but those who had the means to get by. It was a classic case of "middle-class [perhaps even upper-class] 'poaching'" of public housing.[197] As a result, the supposedly working-class projects cradled an inverted, ambivalent identity, the jeprox. The jeprox personified the ambiguity of Quezon City, straddling between urbanity and rurality, between being a periphery and being a capital city. As Cebu-born Paulo Alcazaren confesses, "I was born in a fishing village, but it was my life in the Projects that has set the direction of my professional life."[198] More important, jeprox ambiguity found itself denigrating the urban poor and yet indignant of how the ruling class monopolized space and power. This struggle of the jeprox and Quezon City to definitively locate their position within society would get even tougher as the country entered the Marcos era. It was the "long 1970s," a decade which Nick Joaquin tagged as "the Jeproks Era."[199]

CHAPTER FIVE

The Submissive
and Subversive Suburbs

FERDINAND MARCOS'S PRESIDENCY was a definitive period in Philippine history. His extended stay in Malacañang (1965–1986) was a tumultuous era. His increasing arrogation of political power, the cases of corruption in his administration, and his subservience to US interests led to a wave of opposition from various fronts. Aside from his opponents among traditional politicians and business interests, his vocal critics came from the labor unions, the urban poor, and academia. Youth activist groups, such as the national-democratic (natdem) organizations Samahang Demokratiko ng Kabataan (SDK) and Kabataang Makabayan (KM), gained prominence as they staged rallies in Manila left and right, especially in the wave of demonstrations that occurred in the first three months of 1970, known as the First Quarter Storm (FQS).[1] Simultaneously, Marcos had to contend with large-scale rebellions in the countryside, namely, that of the Moro secessionists under the Moro National Liberation Front (MNLF) and the re-established (1968) Communist Party of the Philippines (CPP) and its armed wing, the New People's Army (NPA), which was operating virtually throughout the country.[2]

Amid this state of political instability, Marcos imposed drastic, draconian measures in the metropolitan area to maintain control. The regime rationalized these actions by pointing to perennial problems such as flooding, security, and housing. The Marcos era was thus a period that fundamentally transformed Quezon City and the entire greater Manila.

This chapter details the Marcos-era sociospatial changes within Quezon City (map 25) and in the city's relations with the wider metropolis. It begins by analyzing the ironic outcome of student radicalism in UP's new campus; rather than serve as a university town devoid of politics, Diliman's ecology aided the formation of a barricaded commune of anti-Marcos youth activists.

205

206 A CAPITAL CITY AT THE MARGINS

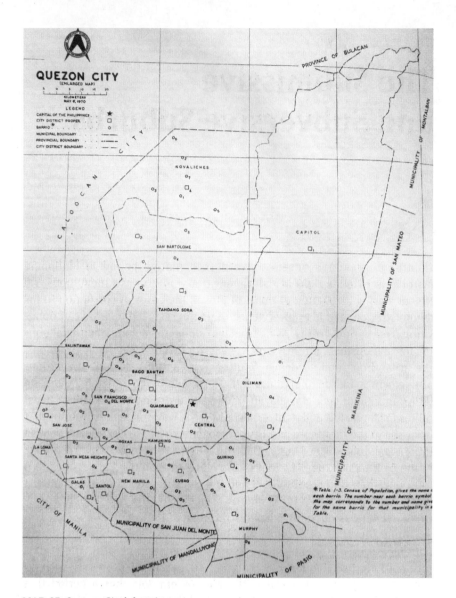

MAP 25. Quezon City's barrios, 1970

SOURCE: National Census and Statistics Office, *1970 Census of Population and Housing: Rizal*, xx

Next, it shows the interlinked urban realities of the 1970s: the metropolitanization of greater Manila, Quezon City's lost status as capital city under the regime, and the city's emergence as the country's biggest home of informal settlements. Finally, the chapter assesses Quezon City's liminality in relation to its supportive and subversive roles vis-à-vis the Marcos dictatorship.

Barricading UP's "Sylvan Enclave"[3]

"THE CAMPUS ATMOSPHERE will be truly academic. There will be no unnecessary disturbances to the scholastic tranquility of the University."[4] Such was the description of university officials of UP's Diliman campus following the 1948 relocation. Right from the start, a major reason behind President Quezon's decision to push for the transfer was to insulate students from Manila politics and subject them to more stringent supervision in a controlled environment.

Diliman was the ideal location because it was distant, figuratively and literally, from Manila. At the time of the relocation, it still lacked access roads and transportation services that would have made it more accessible to downtown Manila. Despite eventual improvements in infrastructure, commuting between Manila and Diliman remained difficult, even up to the 1970s. UP faculty and personnel who wanted to avoid it had to settle with temporary in-campus residential quarters.[5] UP journalism professor Luis Teodoro described 1960s Diliman thus:

> The roads to UP were in fact all deserted by 5 p.m., except for an occasional JD bus or two, and the rare automobile owned by one of the UP's similarly rare rich boy or girl. Going to UP was, to many Manilans, a major undertaking similar to going to Antipolo to look at the as yet uncontaminated falls, or to Pansol in Laguna for the hot springs.
>
> One couldn't help this impression, the bus trip to Diliman from Quiapo, which then took all of 20 minutes, consisting of going through a traffic-free Quezon Avenue, and whizzing through its tree-lined portions after the bus had crossed EDSA (then known simply as Highway 54), and then going down a University Avenue still choked with trees, into a campus where ancient acacia trees formed over the narrow streets green canopies through which little sunlight passed.[6]

Although the new campus seemed surrounded by an impenetrable border, the intended insulation of UP students from Manila's "distractions" did not happen. UP Diliman's radical tradition since the time of the Huk rebellion spoke of the students' engagement with society rather than their isolation from it. Arguably, and ironically, it was Diliman's position within Quezon City that made UP a bastion of radicalism once again during the Marcos era.

To begin with, Quezon City's numerous slum areas constantly provided students not just a visible reminder of state abandonment of the urban poor, but also spaces for consciousness-raising, solidarity, and mobilization with the marginalized. Slum areas were not just near Diliman; a significant number were actually living on campus. UP's first informal settlement developed in the vicinity of its Arboretum in the early 1960s.[7] There were also slums near Quezon City's secondary schools, which jumpstarted

208   A CAPITAL CITY AT THE MARGINS

radicalization quite early for would-be activists. A perfect example was Jan Quimpo, one of the Quimpo siblings, who were well known within activist circles.[8] In 1970, amid widespread anti-Marcos demonstrations in Manila, Jan entered the Philippine Science High School (PSHS), a prestigious public secondary school located in North Triangle near the QMC.[9] The campus was surrounded by informal settlements of (peri)urban-poor families, living in the marginality of the city—countryside interface. Jan's brother Nathan described the sociospatial duality of poverty in Quezon City in his recollection of how it affected the then-high school student:

> Jan was happy visiting and spending time with the squatter families who lived on the future site of the PSHS in North Triangle, the area bounded by EDSA (then still Highway 54), Quezon Avenue, and North Avenue. These families eked out a living quarrying blocks from soft volcanic deposits called adobe, which was ubiquitous in the area. They lived in jerry-built shacks with cast-off corrugated sheets for roofing.
>
> Jan wanted to learn about living with the poor in the countryside by spending time with these people. He took me to the place once, and yes, it looked like a provincial area, a place overrun with cogon grass, with the dwellings still sparse, small vegetable plots near the shacks, and ponds where rainwater filled the quarries . . . This patch of North Triangle (where a huge mall was later to sprout) was Jan's "little Isabela" in the city. He described the people as really no different from poor families in the countryside.[10]

The plight of urban poor communities in other parts of Quezon City that were rather distant from Diliman also affected youth activists. The destruction of shanties in the Araneta—Tuason lot in Tatalon along Araneta Avenue, for example, was one of the issues raised in the People's March of March 1970, one of the protests of the FQS.[11]

Aside from immersing themselves among the city's urban poor, Quezon City students became sensitive to issues about oil prices and the situation of jeepney drivers. They saw the relevance of this issue because many of them were residents of or dormers in Manila and thus had to take the daily commute. As such, the series of strikes that jeepney drivers conducted to protest the oil price hikes directly affected these students.[12]

The most notable of these jeepney strikes was spearheaded by the drivers' organization Pangkalahatang Sanggunian [General Council of] Manila and Suburbs Drivers Association and lasted from the 6th to the 14th of January 1971. One of the highlights of the strike was the mobilization on 13 January. Jeepney drivers from outside Manila gathered first at Welcome Rotonda and then marched to Plaza Miranda, a public plaza fronting Quiapo Church that was often used for political gatherings. Even Quezon City Mayor Amoranto planned to lead a march of city residents to the Pandacan Oil Depot, only to be dissuaded by Manila Mayor Antonio

Villegas. Unfortunately, the protestors at Plaza Miranda met a terrible fate, as three thousand troopers of the infamous antiriot squad Metropolitan Command (Metrocom) violently dispersed them. The dispersal was dubbed "Black Wednesday."[13] However, the most significant result of this eight-day confrontation was the decision of UP activists to put up barricades in the Diliman campus. This episode is known as the Diliman Commune.[14]

On 1 February 1971, as a reaction to the jeepney strike and the consequent state repression, more agitated UP students joined the protests against the oil price hike by boycotting classes and blocking traffic on campus. USC Chairperson Ericson Baculinao led these students. When campus security forces intervened, the blockade turned into a barricade. Violence erupted when UP professor Inocente Campos, a known Marcos loyalist, became the target of student protestors after showing his displeasure with the traffic disruption. They threw pillboxes (a colloquial for grenade-like improvised explosives) at his car and hit the left rear tire. In retaliation, he drew his gun and fired at them. One of them, Pastor Mesina Jr., was critically wounded and would die three days later at the hospital. After the shooting incident, the police came and chased students into the campus. Yet, for a week, the latter stood their ground and held the state forces at bay by putting up more barricades before the police or the Metrocom could reach the campus.

As the students were now in control of the campus (fig. 27), they organized themselves and "reorganized" the school to maximize and protect

FIG. 27. Metrocom officers in front of Quezon Hall during the Diliman Commune
SOURCE: "Siege at Diliman," *Graphic* 17 Feb. 1971

their gains. With the 1871 Paris Commune serving as their inspiration,[15] the self-styled communards renamed university buildings to mark the end of the *ancien régime*: the Faculty Center became Sison Hall, named after CPP founder Jose Maria Sison; Palma Hall became Dante Hall, in honor of Kumander Dante, the nom de guerre of NPA founder Bernabe Buscayno; the main library, Gonzalez Hall, became Amado Guerrero Hall, taken from Sison's nom de guerre. The communards replaced traditional academic instruction with activist pedagogy and published propaganda materials in the university press. They also played the Internationale, revolutionary songs, and a looped recording of Marcos in bed with mistress Dovie Beams over the university radio station.[16] The barricades thus functioned as a bastion for revolutionary knowledge and re-education. They redefined the autonomy that the university supposedly enjoyed; rather than employing the myopic notion of academic freedom as freedom from political interference, the communards realigned autonomy toward a more progressive sense, that of asserting independence from the state to politicize education and re-learn the idea of learning as something that could not be insulated from society. In a way, the Commune repudiated Diliman's original purpose. The communards announced its break from UP's purported reactionary pedagogical heritage thus: "A University which before was the center of colonial education has now become a consolidated center of national democratic activism."[17] In effect, UP Diliman became a city within a city.

While the Commune controlled the campus, UP President Salvador Lopez maintained contact with Baculinao and the commune leadership, and also negotiated with the Metrocom and the Quezon City police, led by Tomas Karingal, to dissuade them from entering the campus. In the end, Lopez, with the help of some faculty, persuaded students to dismantle the barricades. The Commune ended on 9 February.

Although the Commune lasted only nine days, it created a ripple effect in the metropolis "during the second wave of confrontation not only in UP but in Greater Manila as well."[18] Such is evidenced by UP's next-door neighbor Ateneo de Manila, which also exhibited student radicalism and employed the barricade strategy shortly after the Diliman Commune's conclusion.

In contrast to UP, Filipinos do not normally associate radicalism with Ateneo. This view is understandable given the elite composition of its studentry and the anticommunist reputation of the Jesuits who run the school. One must also note the sociospatial character of Ateneo. Similar to UP, the Ateneo campus was in an isolated part of the metropolis. However, "the fenced expanse of the Ateneo" made it "another campus, another time unto itself."[19] Inside Ateneo's gated perimeter one found a "country-club atmosphere."[20] Still, these sociospatial barriers were no match for two external forces that managed to breach them. One such external force was

THE SUBMISSIVE AND SUBVERSIVE SUBURBS   211

state repression. The Ateneo campus was also subjected to harassment by the state, as exemplified by the Metrocom raid in the afternoon of 13 January 1971, just a few weeks before the start of the Diliman Commune. Four Ateneans were arrested, prompting the Ateneo student council to condemn the raid as a "flagrant violation of the time-honored autonomy of the university."[21] The other external force was student radicalism, which strengthened as state repression intensified. In response to the Metrocom raid, Ateneo and Maryknoll students mobilized in front of Camp Crame to denounce the PC and demand Marcos's impeachment.[22]

It is thus no surprise that Ateneans put up their own barricades to replicate the Diliman Commune. The catalyst and the display of dissent were the same: students staged along Katipunan Avenue sympathy protests for the striking jeepney drivers and built barricades in front of Ateneo's main gate. The Ateneo protests also faced repression. The police dispersed the mobilization and beat up a number of rallyists. However, whereas Lopez tried his best to get along well with UP communards, Ateneo officials threatened the students involved with sanctions. Ateneo President Jose Cruz, SJ, a confidant of President Marcos, made it clear that he would not tolerate their actions.[23] Nonetheless, Atenean activists did not cower. In the 1971 student council elections held that same month, Alex Aquino, a radical student who participated in the FQS, won the elections over the so-called moderates, with much support from the Ateneo chapters of SDK and KM.[24]

While the politics of Ateneo's student activism had its unique issues that distinguished it from that of UP and other Manila schools (e.g., the Filipinization of the administration, faculty, and the curriculum), the rhetoric of breaking the barriers that separated the university from the rest of society held true in the Jesuit-run school. Such was apparent in the document that encapsulated Ateneo's radical era, the Down from the Hill Manifesto. This 1968 manifesto, whose title was derived from a line in the school's alma mater song, was written by a group of Atenean student writers, led by Emmanuel Lacaba and Alfredo Navarro Salanga. It enjoined Ateneans to support the Filipinization movement and leave the comforts of their gated existence and "lofty perches in the hills of Loyola Heights" to be in solidarity with the rest of Filipino society and "respond to the changing social realities of the country."[25] Moreover, it inverted the metaphorical imagery that Ateneans had for their elevated, literally and figuratively, campus; Balara, with its inaccessibility and purported savagery (see chapter 3, p. 141), turned into Loyola Heights, which should be criticized for its sociospatial exclusivity. "Down from the Hill" was thus a clarion to erase the borders of such exclusivity, an exhortation to Ateneans to be in solidarity with the marginalized.

Even before the Commune, many Ateneans, as well as Maryknoll students, had already been participating in mass mobilizations notwithstanding the

212   A CAPITAL CITY AT THE MARGINS

elitist reputation of their schools. They made their presence felt in the FQS, such as in the Second People's March against Poverty of 17 March 1970, in which they joined hands with fellow student-activists in schools from different parts of the metropolis.[26] Most of the FQS mobilizations happened in downtown Manila where a string of colleges and universities—fondly called the university belt—surrounded important government buildings, including Malacañang. This setting gave geographic primacy to places like Mendiola and Plaza Miranda in the radical student movement.[27] Against this context, the Diliman and Ateneo barricades gain additional historical significance for establishing Quezon City as an important *site* (and not just *source*) of student activism next to Manila.

The Diliman Commune opened the eyes of youth activists not just to the efficacy of militant action and the reality of fascist repression but also to the details of spatial politics:

> Ang teritoryo ng UP sa Diliman ay maraming kagalingan kaysa ibang lugar para sa pagtatatag ng isang malayang purok sa estilo ng isang komyun. Ito ay may malawak na kapaligirang pangharap na bakante sa mga kabahayan, samantalang ang kanyang likuran ay may mga base ng populasyon na maaaring pagtaguan sa panahon ng pananalakay mula sa labas. Sa gitnang bahagi ng kampus ay may matataas na gusali na nagsisilbing taliba upang matanawan ang mga paglusob. Kaya't sa kanyang kabuuan, ang pangyayaring ito ay mabuti sa mga rebolusyonaryong mga mag-aaral upang makapagtayo ng isang baseng pangkultura.[28]
>
> (UP's Diliman campus has a lot of advantages compared to other places for the establishment of a free zone similar to that of a commune. It has a vast front yard that has no structures, while the back side has a residential population base that can serve as places to hide in when there are attacks from outside. In the middle of the campus are tall buildings that serve as watchtowers to provide a lookout for attacks. Therefore, in sum, this event [the Diliman Commune] is beneficial for revolutionary students who want to build a cultural base.)

The Commune was therefore a learning experience for would-be "urban guerrillas [or] city partisans."[29] It allowed them to see how the specific geography and built environment of an urban/suburban setting could give rise to a space of progressivism. It was a reminder that any attempt to remake society is always an act *in space*, that revolutionary action necessitates revolutionary place-making, and that recreating spaces goes beyond the renaming of places and involves the reorientation of their functions and the remapping of their features.[30] The lessons that UP activists learned from the Diliman Commune came in handy in the years to come, as barricades resurfaced every now and then during the dark years of the Marcos era.[31]

In Hedman and Sidel's assessment, the Diliman campus "not only emerged as the first such enclave for a new radical politics of the early

THE SUBMISSIVE AND SUBVERSIVE SUBURBS   213

mid-1960s, but also as the premier site for the realisation of a (sub)urban campus as revolutionary space."[32] Quite paradoxically, UP's geographical isolation and status as an autonomous space made the barricades possible. On the one hand, in a city as busy as Manila, communards would have found it too difficult to barricade streets and sustain a self-contained enclave for days.[33] On the other hand, UP's status as the state university enabled communards and Lopez to assert their freedom from police interference— it was (and still is), after all, the Diliman Republic. One must note that a year before the commune happened, Lopez and Mayor Amoranto signed an agreement that prohibited the Quezon City police force from entering the campus without a written request from the university president.[34] Clearly, one cannot divorce the Diliman Commune, along with the other urban-based radical actions from the 1960s to Marcos's downfall, from the spatial politics of the metropolis. Hedman and Sidel are worth quoting at length:

> Such displays of "revolutionary fervor" could not but underscore the ambiguous position many U.P. students occupied in the city. They typically enjoyed full student privileges at this elite university located on what remained a suburban campus enclave in relative insulation from everyday life in the metropolis. Many students, perhaps especially those provincial high-school graduates of "middle-class and even working-class and peasant origins" and those commuting from modest boarding houses from as far afield as Quiapo, also experienced the growing social stratification and mounting political contestation of the city beyond the university. The rise and fall of the "Diliman Commune", whilst swift, served as a dramatic subversion of the spatial hierarchy of the city by the "communards" and their fellow activists.[35]

Nativist Urbanism and Other Metropolitan Musings

MOST OF THE TIME, standing on the other side of the numerous barricades put up throughout the tumultuous Marcos years were the forces of the PC's Metropolitan Command. The frequent encounters between activists and the Metrocom were no coincidence; Marcos created this police force precisely in response to the geographical expansion of radicalism in the metropolis. In fact, the establishment of this PC unit was just one aspect of his larger design to recreate greater Manila to further his authoritarian rule.

Upon the recommendation of US military and police advisers, Marcos established the Metrocom through an EO in 1967 "as a modern crowd control unit."[36] It was the result of the continuous training of the police force with American advisers within the Cold War context of the back-and-forth transfer of counter-insurgency knowledge in the CIA's Southeast Asian arena. USAID provided the necessary financial support by funding Metrocom's computerized identification systems.[37] In his EO, Marcos gave the PC "police jurisdiction over the Greater Manila Area" for the first time in history.[38] Metrocom's initial organization was a force of about three hundred officers and men that operated in Manila, Quezon City, Caloocan City, Pasay City, and in the municipalities of Las Piñas, Makati, Malabon, Mandaluyong, Navotas, Marikina, Parañaque, Pasig, and San Juan.

Although Metrocom's main mandate was to combat criminality, its importance to the regime lay in suppressing urban-based protests. Its "first big success" was the "bloody suppression" of the demonstrations held on the occasion of Marcos's taking of his oath of office for his second term on 30 December 1969.[39] With the onset of the FQS in the following month, January 1970, it was the state's primary instrument in clamping down on mobilizations through violent dispersals.

Metrocom's founding was a watershed in the history of metropolitan administration in the Philippines if read against the context of police inefficiency in chartered cities during the early postwar period. The problems of an outdated organization structure and inadequate training and equipment were worsened by the fact that both the city mayor and the president, through the PC, exercised administrative control over the police force. In effect, the chief of police of a chartered city served two masters.[40] By creating Metrocom, Marcos removed a serious weakness of the state, but at the expense of democratic control over the police force. Furthermore, to tighten his grip over the metropolis, in 1974 he reorganized the PC's administrative structure in greater Manila by creating the Metropolitan Police Force (Metropol),[41] which "amplified his control over Manila's police" as it "coordinate[d] policing among the four cities and nine municipalities of metropolitan Manila. . . . By early 1971, Metropol had a twenty-four-hour communications capacity covering the four provinces, 113 municipalities, and six million people within a forty-mile radius of Manila."[42]

Based on these moves, security had become a metropolitan issue, or, at least, Marcos wanted to make it appear so. Indeed, part of his rationalization for declaring martial law in 1972 was the spate of violence that occurred not just in Manila but also in the wider metropolis, including Quezon City. Before his declaration, a series of bombings targeted important establishments, including the 17 August incidents at the Philippine Long Distance Telephone Company exchange at East Avenue and the Philippine Sugar Institute building at North Avenue; a water main on Aurora Boulevard and Madison Avenue on 19 August; and the Constitutional Convention area at the Quezon City Hall on 18 September.[43]

The issue of security in greater Manila revealed a larger predicament: the absence of a metro-wide political structure. Starting from the granting of independence in 1946 up to 1972, cooperation among local governments to address supralocal concerns had been tenuous. The same was true about the relationship between these local governments and the national government.[44] The lack of inter-municipal coordination reflected in almost all aspects of governance, from security to urban planning. To an extent, the national government induced this metropolitan anarchy. For example, with regard to urban planning, although President Quirino consolidated authority over planning matters in the National Planning Commission (NPC), an agency under the Office of the President, the Local Autonomy Act of 1959 (RA 2264) "empowered local municipal boards and city councils to adopt their own subdivision and zoning regulations. Although the NPC might be consulted, it reserved to local interests (in the case of Metropolitan Manila each of its eight constituent parts) the final decision on master plans prepared by the national government."[45]

Despite clamor from various sectors for the merger of cities and towns in greater Manila, this consolidation never happened under the postwar regimes prior to Marcos. While President Magsaysay supposedly supported the merger of Quezon City, Manila, and Pasay, this idea died with him when he passed away in 1957. In President Garcia's succeeding term, cooperation among the mayors remained problematic, not to mention their diverging opinions about the possibility of a merger. Manila Mayor Arsenio Lacson supported the idea, arguing that many of Manila's problems go beyond the city borders. Quezon City Mayor Norberto Amoranto opposed it but without elaborating on his position. Pasay City Mayor Pablo Cuneta did not comment on the issue, although reports had it that he opposed the merger.[46]

The succeeding years showed no progress. The local governments either ignored or fought one another, resulting in the inefficient delivery of basic services.[47] Metropolitan Manila existed as a de facto urban reality, yet its emergence prior to the Marcos years was mainly informed "by the imperatives of electoral and/or business cycles rather than by any discernible overarching vision for urban renewal and/or sustainable development."[48] Only with Marcos's martial law declaration on 23 September 1972 did things change drastically in the politics of greater Manila.[49] Such was in keeping with Marcos's vision of martial law as heralding a fundamental transformation of the country, which he dubbed the New Society.

One of Marcos's priorities for this New Society was greater Manila's reorganization. This objective coincided with his desire to address another perennial metrowide problem: flooding. Just a few months after declaring martial law, he created the Inter-Agency Committee on Metropolitan Manila (IACMM) to study metropolitan consolidation. This committee divided its work into seven panels, each focusing on a particular aspect of governance. One panel dealt with flooding, the Panel on Flood Control and Damage. The geographic scope of its study corresponded with that of another Marcos-created council, the Metropolitan Manila Flood Control and Drainage Council (MMFCDC), which he created just a few weeks after declaring martial law.

The MMFCDC covered seventeen cities and towns in greater Manila.[50] When the IACMM was formed, Marcos instructed its members to focus on a much smaller area—the four cities of Manila, Quezon, Caloocan, and Pasay, and the municipalities of Makati, Mandaluyong, and San Juan—presumably because these cities and towns were the most populous in the GMA. But in the course of its deliberations, the committee recommended the inclusion of Las Piñas, Parañaque, Malabon, Navotas, Pasig, Pateros, Marikina, Muntinlupa, Taguig, and Valenzuela, for a total of seventeen cities and municipalities. The rationale was that these localities comprised the jurisdiction of both the Metrocom and the Panel on Flood Control and Drainage.[51]

With Marcos's monopoly over power and funding coming from the World Bank, everything went smoothly for his plan of metropolitan consolidation. The IACMM released its report in January 1973, less than three months after convening. Among its recommendations was the creation of a juridical metropolitan entity to monitor greater Manila's problems. Via a supposed referendum on 27 February 1975, residents in greater Manila voted in favor of consolidating the four cities and thirteen municipalities—with the same geographical scope as that of the MMFCDC, the IACMM, and the Metrocom—into an integrated unit based on guidelines to be set by the president. Finally, on 7 November 1975, Marcos created the Metropolitan Manila Commission (MMC), the juridical entity encompassing Manila and its suburbs.[52]

The president appointed his wife, Imelda, as MMC governor, making her one of the most powerful officials during martial law, if not the "de facto vice president."[53] As governor, she exercised power over Metro Manila's 4.5 million inhabitants. Assisting her in this regard was former Quezon City Vice Mayor Ismael Mathay, Jr.[54] Some, like Stephen Seagrave, believed her appointment was Ferdinand's way of appeasing Imelda following her frustrations with the internal conflict within the president's inner circle in the early years of martial law. Others, such as Gerardo Sicat, saw it as the president's "political penance" to Imelda after his love affair with actress Dovie Beams became publicized toward the end of his first term.[55] Regardless of the reason, this move made Imelda the administrator of the country's most populous and urbanized political unit. Metro Manila served as a convenient training ground for her as a potential successor to the president. With all the economic resources and political capital under her command, she secured her position within the regime independent of her being the president's wife.

Imelda's control over urban affairs expanded with another appointment, that of minister of human settlements. Her role as MMC governor was even subsumed to this higher administrative position. As head of the Ministry of Human Settlements (MHS), which the president created in 1978, Imelda promoted the concept of "human settlements," which the United Nations Development Programme (UNDP) espoused.[56]

THE SUBMISSIVE AND SUBVERSIVE SUBURBS   217

One objective behind the establishment of the MHS was to address the problem of coordinating numerous agencies dealing with housing, an administrative conundrum that was already evident before martial law. For example, in Marcos's first term as president, in the Sapang Palay relocation program, "no less than 19 public and private agencies were involved."[57] Because the National Housing Authority (NHA), which was created during the early years of martial law to replace the moribund PHHC, was already handling housing issues at the time the MHS was established, the older agency was subsumed under the new one. The MHS was also given a corporate arm to implement its projects, the Human Settlements Development Corporation, capitalized at a staggering amount of half a billion pesos in 1978. Two years later, that amount increased fivefold.[58] Indeed, as MHS minister, Imelda centralized administrative control over housing. Unfortunately, this development had serious repercussions.

One negative effect of centralization under MHS was its increasing interference in the affairs of other agencies due to the open-ended definition of its mandate. Cabinet members feared the MHS for being a "super-ministry," performing "like a second government, trying to access resources from these other ministries, and getting them to do the work her ministry was defined to do."[59] Imelda's arrogation of power put her in a collision course with the president's top-level technocrats, including Finance Minister and eventual Prime Minister Cesar Virata, who did not support the creation of the MHS.[60] In a speech before the Interim Batasang Pambansa, the president's rubber stamp legislature, she divulged that certain people in government felt the MHS was too powerful, and then went on to enumerate what she thought were the eleven basic needs of a human settlement: water; power; food; clothing; economic base; medical services; education, culture, and technology; ecological balance; sports and recreation; shelter; and mobility. Imelda essentially confirmed her critics' fears: "The goal, therefore, of the Ministry of Human Settlements is to make all these eleven basic needs for human settlements available in varying levels and degrees for all towns and cities of the Philippines."[61]

Another repercussion of MHS's growing power was the instrumentalization of housing for the Marcoses' gain. The MHS turned into an agency for the dispensation of "super patronage."[62] For instance, the condominiums built under Imelda's Bagong Lipunan Sites and Services (BLISS) housing projects in Quezon City became a platform for her to return favors to friends and allies (fig. 28).[63] In a BLISS project in the UP Diliman campus, "the housing awards were given mainly to outsiders instead of those within the university who needed housing—faculty members and administrative workers."[64] Worse, this specific housing project happened under an anomalous usufruct agreement so brazen that even university administrators complained about

FIG. 28. The Marcoses in the inauguration of a BLISS housing project in Pag-asa, Quezon City

SOURCE: Juanico, *Metro Manila*, 3

this virtual "land grab." However, mismanagement, mounting expenditures, and Imelda's penchant for rushing projects hampered BLISS. By the mid-1980s, BLISS and the entire housing industry teetered on the brink of a collapse, compounded by the 1983 financial crisis. In the end it failed to address the housing needs of low-income households.[65]

Most tragic was MHS's transformation into an agency that facilitated more evictions rather than mass housing. Imelda, in Orwellian fashion, used the MHS to launch "state-sponsored assaults on urban spaces associated with the collective experiences and memories of the metropolitan *masa* [masses]."[66] She gained notoriety for building walls that covered Metro Manila's slums to prevent them from interrupting the gaze of foreign VIPs whenever they visited the country. Her claim that she was beautifying the metropolis rationalized the oppression of the urban poor.[67] In this regard, Metro Manila's urban space mirrored the antidevelopmental logic of the Marcos regime, which also felt pressure from the World Bank to implement massive resettlement programs.[68] The ideological value of urban space—as marker of the Marcoses' magnificence or as object of the foreign gaze—superseded its use value as a place to provide shelter for those who could not afford housing via the formal market.

MMC's founding and Imelda's tenure in MHS revealed the importance of urban centers to the Marcoses' "conjugal dictatorship."[69] Both agencies

THE SUBMISSIVE AND SUBVERSIVE SUBURBS   219

demonstrated how a city could be turned into a repressive state apparatus. Still, a richer understanding of the value of cities to the dictatorship is predicated on an analysis of the Marcoses' view of urbanism. Analyzing this facet of the dictatorship shows how cities can become an ideological state apparatus as well.[70]

To analyze the Marcoses' peculiar view of urbanism, one has to begin with the nativist-nationalism that permeated their ideology and projection of power. They were preoccupied with finding and presenting the purportedly unadulterated "Filipino soul,"[71] an exercise in essentialism that they also used to gain political capital. The Marcoses' "palingenetic" myth making involved an imagined "Great Malayan culture."[72] In the process, they tapped indigenous concepts, precolonial history, and nationalism to legitimize the regime. Such was apparent in the various endeavors through which they tried to impress their legacy on Philippine culture, exemplified by the *Tadhana* [Destiny] history project, the "discovery" of the "Stone-Age" Tasaday, the proposal to rename the Philippines "Maharlika," among others. They even presented themselves as personifications of the mythical Malakas and Maganda.[73] The sheer number of notable structures built under the Marcos era was enough to define a Marcosian architecture, one of the dominant motifs of which is the *bahay kubo* (nipa hut). Through this appropriation of an indigenous built form, Marcosian architecture conveyed a sense of "purity" from colonial designs, evoking a sort of cultural rebirth.[74]

These cultural endeavors were not only ideologically motivated but also congruent with the dictatorship's development strategy, which regarded tourism as an important revenue generator. Under martial law, tourism was the third highest foreign-exchange earner for the country. Moreover, it helped sanitize the Marcoses' image among foreigners and dignitaries. Toward these ends, in 1973 the regime created the Ministry of Tourism, marking the first time in Philippine history that this aspect of governance attained cabinet-level importance.[75] In 1976 this ministry entered in an agreement with UP to establish the Asian Institute of Tourism (AIT). Adjoining the institute's main hall was the AIT House, a building that functioned as a hotel and conference site with amenities similar to those of five-star hotels.[76] Standing as a tangible representation of state intervention in university affairs, AIT became the object of derision of students and faculty critical of the regime. They denounced its vocational nature and turned it into the "whipping boy on campus." Paradoxically, the AIT occupied the peripheries of the Diliman campus, yet it held a prominent position within UP during the Marcos era:

> Its physical structures also presented a glaring contrast to most of the old, poorly maintained buildings and facilities on campus, and this fact aroused mixed

220 A CAPITAL CITY AT THE MARGINS

sentiments of envy and disdain from many of the University constituency, even as they ventured to enjoy its carpeted and air-conditioned comforts.[77]

The Marcoses' nativist-nationalism also figured in their interpretation and management of urban space. In their sociospatial imaginary, Manila held an exalted place. Throughout the Marcos era, the presidential couple paid special attention to Manila's cultural capital. The Marcoses conducted a comprehensive restoration of Intramuros's walls, renovated the Rizal Park, the Paco Park, and the Quiapo Mosque, restored the prewar Metropolitan Theater, and celebrated the discovery of pre-Spanish relics in Santa Ana.[78] Towering above all these was the Cultural Center of the Philippines (CCP), the centerpiece of the Marcoses' nativist-nationalist urban complex.

The CCP came into existence as a result of EO 30 of 1966. Imelda hailed it as the "sanctuary of the Filipino soul" and echoed her husband's vision: "In the words of the President, the Cultural Center should be a place where the Filipino can discover the soul of his people, and relate the saga of his race to the vast human experience that begins in the past and advances into the limitless future."[79] The CCP complex was the articulation of the Marcoses' palingenesis through state architecture. It was such a huge undertaking that its construction and development lasted at about the same length of time as the Marcos regime itself, consuming a gigantic amount of public funds and foreign loans in the process. At present, it occupies an area of 77 hectares that straddles the Manila–Pasay border and is complemented by a reclaimed 240-hectare beach front along Manila Bay. Some of the most important buildings in the complex are the Folk Arts Theater, the Philippine International Center for Trade and Exhibits, the Philippine International Convention Center, the Tahanang Filipino (also known as the Coconut Palace), the Manila Film Center, and the flagship CCP Theater of Performing Arts.[80]

All these projects, from the renovation of important historical sites to the CCP complex, were part of a coherent design, that of turning Manila into a "City of Man."[81] As MMC governor, Imelda articulated her "City of Man" vision in light of the urban excesses of the metropolis that had led to pollution, traffic congestion, inadequate housing, and urban decay.[82] She wanted to reverse this trend by pointing to Manila's glorious past that citizens had to recover. In sum, she conveyed a tripartite spatio-temporal narrative of Manila's development: starting with unspoiled, historic Manila; next, Metropolitan Manila's present state of urban degeneration; and hopefully ending with a bright future as Manila becomes the City of Man:

> We must put an end to this blight, to this inhuman evisceration of a Manila which was once known as "The City of our Affections." We remember, historically, a city that was the seat of a national civilization, radiant with her own personality. She

THE SUBMISSIVE AND SUBVERSIVE SUBURBS   221

was not created to pander only to economic need but to realize social ideals and exalt cultural values.

We must, therefore, renew and recreate this city, bestow it and revive it with our love.[83]

Ostensibly, Imelda called for a reversal of the rapid pace of urbanization and a repudiation of the economic pragmatism underlying metropolitan growth. A year after she delivered this speech, she was already singing a different tune. She talked about the plans of the national government regarding

a blueprint for Metro Manila which cuts through the Sierra Madres to Infanta in Quezon Province, at the rim of the Pacific Ocean. The national plan will have a Metro Manila bordered by the Pacific Ocean and the China Sea. Two air and sea ports within the region will be on call for the convenience and facilitation of our country's international commerce. In this way is Manila truly joined to the rest of the country, while she reaches out to the rest of the world.[84]

Even more tragic than this equivocation was Imelda's monumental corruption and criminal recklessness (exemplified by the senseless deaths in the Manila Film Center tragedy) that characterized her and her husband's edifice complex.[85] If one juxtaposes her urban visions (if not hallucinations) vis-à-vis urban realities, Imelda's Manila was no "city of man" but a "third world city in first world drag."[86]

Razing Cogon for a Forsaken Capital

IN CONTRAST TO how the Marcoses packaged Manila as the undisputed locus of national culture, Quezon City was marginalized in their urban imaginary. It seemed as if they felt that the capital city lacked the cultural and historical capital that would have given it an international brand like Manila and merited it to be an integral space in their nativist-nationalist agenda. In addition, the city was bogged down by a lot of problems that it would have embodied the image of decaying Metropolitan Manila in Imelda's tripartite City of Man narrative. Although it still played a role in the Marcoses' metropolitan makeover, its place in the overall scheme of things was dwarfed by that of the city of Manila.

Before martial law, it was already apparent that Quezon City acted more as the northern gateway, and not the center, of Metro Manila. Cubao, as the transportation hub due to its position as the northernmost urbanized segment of the metropolis, connected Metro Manila to provinces up north. Then, as now, its bus terminals along EDSA served passengers bound for destinations as far as Baguio, Cagayan, and the Ilocos region. A few

222   A CAPITAL CITY AT THE MARGINS

kilometers north of Cubao was the Balintawak Market, which was built in 1966 and eventually became the largest wet market and foremost distribution hub for meat and produce in Metro Manila. That same year Marcos called for the construction of the Balintawak Interchange, more popularly known as the Balintawak Cloverleaf, at the EDSA–North Luzon Expressway intersection, thereby solidifying the area's position as the main urban-rural node of northern Metro Manila.[87]

Interestingly, one of Quezon City's roles in the Marcoses' design for Metro Manila was related to health. The capital city became the regime's favored location for a series of state-built specialized "designer hospitals," such as the National Kidney and Transplant Institute, Philippine Heart Center, Lung Center of the Philippines, and Philippine Children's Hospital—institutions standing near each other at the northeastern edge of the Diliman quadrangle. The reason behind this clustering is unclear based on available sources, but the convenience of having swathes of vacant government-owned land in that part of the city was a possible factor and something that Manila lacked. Imelda treated these hospitals as her projects and was there to attend their inauguration ceremonies.[88] In 1976 Imelda also led the launching of the Philippine Medical Center, slated to be built on the UP Diliman campus and envisioned to "link with present and projected specialty hospitals like the Philippine Heart Center, the National Lung Center, the Cancer Center and other specialized service hospitals."[89] The said medical center was never built, however.

Unfortunately, this building spree occluded Imelda's twisted notion of health care. Rather than devote state resources to address diseases that plagued ordinary Filipinos, such as tuberculosis, she favored boutique hospitals that operated under the logic of medical tourism. Worse, financing these supposedly modern medical centers caused further fiscal instability: funding came from foreign loans and the GSIS, thus putting pressure on precious government resources. Quezon City did not develop into a medical mecca; rather, it served as a mere appendage to the Marcoses' edifice complex.[90]

The contrast between Manila and Quezon City was more apparent in Imelda's decision to repackage a 1961 plan to build a Philippine–American Cultural Center in a 10-hectare lot in Quezon City, a move that led to CCP's establishment. She liked the initial concept but not the chosen site: "when I looked at the property I found that it was full of squatters. I was not going to begin the Center by driving away squatters. So I looked around for another place: that site off Roxas Boulevard. What I found was water; what we did was reclaim it."[91]

Imelda's reason for rejecting Quezon City as the site of an important cultural center revealed an important factor behind the city's marginalized position during the Marcos era: the "squatter problem." In his 1969 SONA,

THE SUBMISSIVE AND SUBVERSIVE SUBURBS   223

President Marcos admitted that housing remained a "serious national problem." He then blamed past presidents for neglecting this issue and drew attention to resettlement projects under his administration, including those involving informal settlers in Quezon City.[92]

Since Quezon City lacked the labor-intensive businesses that were more common in Manila and Caloocan, most of its slums were not "internally generated." The existence of slums in the capital city in the 1950s and early 1960s, as detailed in the previous chapter, resulted from forced relocations of Manila's informal settlers. Yet by the time Marcos was president, the number of informal settlements in Quezon City was increasing at a consistent rate. Ironically, its status as capital city made it a perfect location not just for informal settlers, but also professional squatters who profited handsomely from the desperation of those who could not afford formal housing. Speculators bought land in the city and held on to these properties, hedging on their expectation of a bustling capital city. However, because of the interminable construction of government buildings and facilities in Quezon City, many of these sites allowed informal settlers to occupy idle portions of their lands to generate revenue in the meantime. Simultaneously, other enterprising urban poor households felt justified in inhabiting unused government land in the capital.[93]

But why was Quezon City's development as national capital so slow? Despite provisions for constructing a government complex in the 1949 master plan, the national government lacked the will and the capital to execute it. President Quirino's decision not to use PWDC funding (see chapter 3, p. 132) left his administration and the succeeding ones with minimal financial resources for the construction of wide avenues and stately buildings. In effect, Quezon City's position as capital remained nominal for the most part. That the NPC still had to pass a resolution endorsing the transfer of the capital to Quezon City[94] despite the existence of a law (RA 333) guaranteeing it betrayed the uncertainty of implementation. It took until February 1955 for the Office of the President to finally authorize the construction of national buildings in Quezon City. President Magsaysay allocated PHP 2 million for this endeavor in that year and an annual PHP 10 million henceforth for four years until its completion.[95] However, the plans and models just for the proposed legislative center in Constitution Hill—based on an extravagant Brasilia-inspired design that drew criticisms—already demanded an estimated PHP 30 million. Its construction began in 1958 but halted in August 1960 due to insufficient funds. The result was the eventual abandonment of the whole project.[96]

Moreover, only a few national government agencies grabbed the opportunity to relocate to Quezon City. Perhaps the most notable of them was the Department of Agriculture and Natural Resources (DANR), which, along

224   A CAPITAL CITY AT THE MARGINS

with other affiliated units, moved into an area near the QMC that DANR Secretary Salvador Araneta picked.[97] Needless to say, Magsaysay's projected timeline was never met. In the succeeding administrations the development of Quezon City's civic center received less attention from Malacañang, save for the procurement of a few lots allotted for national government buildings, forcing the local government to fend off for itself. In 1964 the Quezon City government created its own Planning Board, which turned out to be ineffective because it lacked funds and expertise.[98]

Quezon City was the seat of government only nominally, for most national government offices stayed put in the old capital. Before martial law, it was nowhere near realizing the original vision for it. The planned government district to surround the QMC stood practically vacant, save for a few government agencies,[99] including the city hall, the PHHC, and DANR. A 1973 Japanese urban transport study remarked, "the vast space of land contains only scattered government offices and school buildings and the remaining parts are still unoccupied."[100]

In 1973 UP President Lopez described the capital city's vacuousness that bordered on the eerie:

> it is a sad experience to ride around the Elliptical Road in front of Quezon City Hall, along the grand curving axis of Commonwealth Avenue towards the site of the national capitol. The first sight that greets the eye is the broad expanse of untended lawn around the Quezon monument, the only central park of a capital city in the civilized world I know that is surrounded by a wired fence in order to prevent people from entering and enjoying it—a park completely untended, unlighted, undeveloped, abandoned to the weeds, where the only visible improvement is a psychedelic multi-colored fountain that sometimes works.[101]

Constitution Hill, intended to be Quezon City's focal point based on the 1949 master plan, suffered a fate similar to that of QMC. Initially, President Quirino succeeded in overseeing the government's acquisition of 136 hectares of land in the city from private donors as part of executing the plan for Constitution Hill. This area became known as the National Government Center (NGC). However, after the donation, further acquisition of land for the NGC failed because of financial and infrastructural woes, not to mention the opposition of those who resisted the very idea of transferring the capital city. Although the 1960s saw attempts to develop the NGC as a civic center, these moves were but *ningas-cogon* (flash in the pan; literally, burning cogon) actions. In 1963 steel girders were built in the area in preparation for a 13-story legislative building, but further construction stalled afterwards. These skeletal structures remained unfinished and was left to rust.[102] Towering over cogon overgrowth, they stood as monuments to the capital's state of perpetual incompleteness:

THE SUBMISSIVE AND SUBVERSIVE SUBURBS   225

The gradual migration of national government offices to Quezon City, the official capital, merely symbolizes the expansion of Manila in which remain the offices of the President, the Congress, the Supreme Court, and many national agencies. The rusting steel girders of the once-proposed capitol in Quezon City, on the edge of the northern Marikina Valley, symbolize the continuing political lure of the core city—as well as the irresoluteness of Filipino leaders in planning for the metropolis.[103]

In the early 1960s, the NGC began to attract low-income families in search of shelter in the suburbs. These families included workers employed in the NGC construction projects and victims of demolitions in Manila who were supposed to have been relocated to Bulacan. The settlers believed that since the area was state-owned, they had the right to occupy the land.[104] A codified set of regulations for the use of spaces in the capital city[105] failed to stem the tide of migrant-settlers. The presence of these informal settlements provided another reason for officials to defer the transfer of government agencies and activities to Quezon City, similar to how Imelda nixed the planned Philippine–American Cultural Center in favor of the CCP Complex.

In effect, despite the official declaration of Quezon City as capital in 1948, Manila remained the de facto center of power throughout the postwar decades. Although it lost its allure as a residential area for the wealthy, Manila retained its political importance. For one, Malacañang stayed in its original San Miguel site. Consequently, anti-government protests continued to gravitate toward Mendiola. Meanwhile, Plaza Miranda, "where Manila's pulse beats strongest," maintained its position as the mecca of political gatherings where politicians come face to face with the common tao.[106] Writing in 1971, Carmen Guerrero Nakpil remarked that when Quezon City replaced Manila as the capital, it "was then actually little more than a blueprint and is now no better than a satellite city."[107] As late as the 1970s, many Filipinos were not even aware that Quezon City was the actual capital city.[108]

If Quezon City could not lay claim as the country's political center, neither could it pretend to be the economic hub despite its official status as a fully urbanized city, defined in 1970 as having a minimum density of 1,000 persons per square kilometer.[109] Compared with Quezon City, Makati had a better chance of replacing Manila as the nation's capital because by the martial law period it had overtaken Manila in terms of commercial significance. This shift was primarily due to the efforts of the Ayala Corporation to consolidate its landholdings and wealth in Makati. The spaces that this company set aside for urban development eventually became the hub of the country's largest businesses, while its plush residential communities served as residences of the country's richest families and individuals (see chapter 4). Similar to Quezon City, Makati was once a friar hacienda that turned into a Manila suburb by the early twentieth century. However,

226   A CAPITAL CITY AT THE MARGINS

whereas Makati could be regarded as the product of the seeming efficiency of private capital in remaking urban spaces, Quezon City represented the rotten fruit of inept state-directed city planning. None of this, however, is to gloss over the dispossession and inequality that came with Makati's "well-organized" urban growth.[110]

Movie actor Ronald Remy Kookooritchkin, who became Quezon City vice mayor in the 1970s, lamented his city's failure to live up to Quezon's dream:

> Have we anything to visit except possibly the Araneta complex? As the epitome of culture? Aside from the Pangkat Kawayan [bamboo ensemble], have we developed a cultural heritage? And as the moving spirit of the country? Have we not even been overshadowed by a town called Makati? Why therefore did we fail in this dream? What did we do wrong? What had we failed to do?[111]

While Kookooritchkin pinned the blame on decades of inaction and indifference of the city government, he pinned his hopes on Marcos's martial law to reverse the situation, so that "[t]his dream of Quezon merged in the pursuit of the New Society."[112] It was, however, a pipe dream dashed when Quezon City's sordid tale reached its logical conclusion on 24 June 1976, with Marcos decreeing the restoration of Manila's status as capital. The rationale behind this decision took on a familiar refrain from the Marcoses' idealization of Manila, the spatial incarnation of their "City of Man":

> WHEREAS, Manila has always been, to the Filipino people and in the eye of the world, the premier city of the Philippines, it being the center of trade, commerce, education and culture;
>
> WHEREAS, Manila from time immemorial has been the seat of the national government of the Philippines;
>
> WHEREAS, Manila has now become a popular site of international meetings and conferences;
>
> WHEREAS, the City of Manila has modern transportation, communication and accommodation facilities and all the other physical attributes of a modern city.[113]

Two years after this move, President Marcos ordered another transfer. On 31 March 1978 he ordered that Quezon's remains be moved from the Manila North Cemetery to the newly completed Quezon Memorial Monument within QMC, a shrine that also stood as a testament to the snail's pace development of the city, which the public also criticized (fig. 29).[114] On the one hand, it was Marcos's act of paying respects to the Filipino politician he emulated. On the other hand, it was payback time: Quezon finally returned to his dream city, which sadly for him was capital city no more, thanks to Marcos. For Marcos it was probably poetic justice because he was "one of the rebel student

FIG. 29. Perspective view of the Quezon Memorial Project; note, however, that the proposed buildings surrounding the Quezon Memorial Shrine were never built

SOURCE: Poblador, *Quezon Memorial Book*, 163

leaders" in UP at the time when students virulently opposed Quezon's decision to transfer the campus from Manila to Diliman.[115]

Two months after the transfer of Quezon's remains, the Batasang Pambansa [National Legislature] building, finally completed, opened to the public. Atop Constitution Hill (present-day Batasan Hills), this new structure housed the legislature of the martial law regime as stipulated in the recently promulgated 1973 Constitution.[116] While this act seemed to be Marcos's way of giving Quezon City a space of power, it was but a hollow gesture, as hollow as the façade of parliamentarism that this new institution embodied. Much like Quezon City's erstwhile status as capital, the power of the Batasang Pambansa in an authoritarian regime was nothing more than nominal.

The Squatter Capital of the Philippines

ALTHOUGH MARCOS caused Quezon City's dethronement, under his regime the city became capital yet again but for an entirely different, and rather dubious, reason. During the Marcos era, the city had the largest population of informal settlers, making it the unofficial squatter capital of the country.

In 1968, three years into Marcos's first term as president, Manila had the biggest concentration of slum dwellers and squatters (80,436 individuals), and Quezon City was a distant second (32,747 individuals).[117] However, by 1972, the year Marcos declared martial law, Quezon City had overtaken

228   A CAPITAL CITY AT THE MARGINS

Manila in terms of its number of squatter families, with 30,046 families as against Manila's 27,108 and thereby accounting for a fourth of Metro Manila's total.[118] With its vast open spaces attracting households desperate for their own space in the metropolis,[119] Quezon City had replaced Manila as the squatter capital, an unwelcome distinction it held throughout and even after the Marcos regime (table 22).

TABLE 22. Slum colonies and squatter population of Metro Manila per city/municipality, 1982

City/Municipality	No. of colonies	Squatter families	Population individuals	Total city/municipal population	Percent squatter of total pop'n
Quezon City	142	61,984	371,904	1,296,099	29
Manila	83	90,916	545,496	1,732,044	32
Pasay City	36	12,817	76,902	294,709	26
Makati	22	13,602	81,612	545,823	15
Pasig	19	6,283	37,898	309,337	12
Marikina	17	6,414	32,484	204,995	16
Muntinlupa	17	6,599	39,594	116,754	34
Parañaque	17	6,030	36,180	156,955	23
Caloocan City	12	21,680	130,080	492,549	26
Malabon	11	8,148	48,883	240,919	20
Mandaluyong	10	10,595	63,570	288,570	22
Navotas	10	9,338	56,020	129,314	43
Las Piñas	8	4,932	29,592	98,655	30
San Juan	7	3,662	21,972	176,802	12
Valenzuela	4	3,510	21,060	160,841	13
Taguig	no data	8,269	49,614	134,238	37
Pateros	no data	491	2,946	45,277	7
Total	415	274,270*	1,645,815*	6,423,884*	26

NOTE: This table shows Quezon City having the largest number of slum colonies, despite placing only second to Manila in terms of the number of squatter families and individuals. The fluctuations in the ranks of Manila and Quezon City throughout the Marcos period, and until today, are due to the lack of standard definitions for "slums" and "squatters."

SOURCE: Pilar Ramos-Jimenez, Ma. Elena Chiong-Javier, and Judy Carol C. Sevilla, *Philippine Urban Situation Analysis* (Manila: UNICEF Manila, 1986), 12, as cited in *Business Day*, 16 July 1982

* However, the computation made by Ramos-Jimenez et al for the totals for squatter families, population (individuals), and total city/municipality population are erroneous. The correct figures are 275,270, 1,645,807, and 6,423,881, respectively.

Marcos's economic policies were a crucial factor behind the increase in the number of informal settlers in Quezon City and Metro Manila in general. Due to mounting trade deficits beginning in the late 1960s, the regime found itself in a balance-of-payment crisis in 1970. Henceforth, the economy was kept afloat by debt-driven growth. The remedial policies that he implemented, based on conditions the International Monetary Fund (IMF) imposed in exchange for stand-by credit (e.g., peso devaluation, promotion of "nontraditional" exports, increased borrowing), only made things worse and even contributed to another balance-of-payment crisis in 1983. Marcos doubled down on his IMF-sanctioned contractionary measures that led to further catastrophe. Prices skyrocketed, and local businesses crumbled. The economic slump hit the ordinary Filipino the hardest, as unemployment rates rose and real wages fell.[120] Amid this situation, the ranks of the urban poor grew. In the twilight years of the Marcos era, Quezon City did not only have the highest housing backlog (more than 76,000 units) among all Philippine towns and cities, including Manila (less than 52,000 units), but also the highest number of squatter families (30,046) in Metro Manila.[121] And as if to bring the irony closer to home, what should have been the government center in Constitution Hill hosted one of the densest squatter communities in the country.

Expectedly, the state's drive to solve the "slum problem" gave due emphasis on Quezon City. Such was the case in Marcos's main slum improvement strategy in Metro Manila, the Zonal Improvement Program (ZIP). A World Bank-funded joint venture of the NHA, the Quezon City government, and the United Nations Environmental Programme, ZIP sought to upgrade 236 slum communities, covering 173,572 families and an aggregate area of 638 hectares. ZIP implemented its pilot project in Escopa in 1977, which involved 1,246 households. One of its main accomplishments was expropriating an adjacent 4.50-hectare site to reduce Escopa's density.[122] In the following year, the NHA listed its ZIP priority sites per city/municipality in Metro Manila (table 23). Quezon City led Metro Manila in both the number of sites and number of targeted families.

ZIP's success, however, was limited. The inadequate involvement, even noncooperation, of local governments and the MMC in ZIP projects caused difficulties and delay in the turnover of sites and led to the high cost of land acquisition, which made some sites unaffordable to beneficiaries.[123] Despite these slum improvement schemes, the number of informal communities in Metro Manila continued to increase in the 1980s (see table 23). This, despite the Marcoses' highly repressive policy of slum eviction.

Imelda's term as MHS minister and MMC governor was defined in large part by her confrontations with Metro Manila's slum communities. Her bias against informal communities intensified as she implemented the

230 A CAPITAL CITY AT THE MARGINS

TABLE 23. Number of sites and targeted families of priority projects for ZIP per city/municipality, 1978

City/Municipality	Number of Sites	Number of Families
Manila	37	27,509
Caloocan	8	20,420
Navotas	10	3,931
Malabon	9	2,945
Quezon City	62	35,163
Marikina	8	2,126
Pasig	10	6,250
Mandaluyong	10	7,772
San Juan	3	3,300
Makati	10	2,541
Pasay	18	26,900
Parañaque	4	4,232
Las Piñas	5	969
Muntinlupa	8	2,860

SOURCE: Based on tabulated data from Gaudencio V. Tobias, *Priority Projects of the National Housing Authority* (Makati: Technology Resource Center, 1978), 21–27

metro-wide flood-control program that her husband initiated in 1972. The framework behind this disaster-mitigation program regarded estero-dwelling slum communities as a hindrance to state objectives rather than as victims of structural inequalities, let alone agents of change. Consequently, state response, at both the national and local levels, consisted of slum clearance and finding ways to deter illegal construction along the banks of rivers and esteros.[124] Under Imelda, who worked with Metro Manila's local governments and the NHA chief, former Metrocom commanding general (1968–1969) Gaudencio Tobias, more demolitions took place, cloaked under so-called beautification efforts. The state then transferred evicted households to faraway relocation sites, such as in Dasmariñas, Cavite, located 28 kilometers away from Manila, thus making it harder for them to find viable sources of livelihood. While the flood-control program stipulated that the government had to find a relocation site for evicted slum dwellers, it said nothing about how to sustain the relocation sites or to address the roots of why slum communities existed along waterways in the first place.[125] Local governments took the cue from the MMC governor and conducted their own evictions. For

THE SUBMISSIVE AND SUBVERSIVE SUBURBS   231

example, after a typhoon hit Metro Manila in May 1976, the Quezon City local government evicted some "1,500 squatter families living along creeks, rivers, and other waterways . . . relocated temporarily on a government property in the outskirts of the city upon the approval of [the NHA]."[126]

The same inhumane logic operated in how the state responded to slums that were not living along waterways. In a violent demolition at Constitution Hill in 1978 to clear space for the Batasang Pambansa, nine infants died. On 6 March 1985 policemen used assault rifles against helpless squatters in Barangay Payatas in a violent demolition that left 2,000 squatter families homeless. Needless to say, the relocation sites under the Marcos regime gave no thought to the basic needs of evictees, as exemplified by the mosquito-infested rice fields of a site in Barrio Capri, Novaliches.[127] Perhaps state actions emboldened the private sector to also do the same thing, as illustrated by the violent demolition of informal settlers in Bagumbayan, a riverine Quezon City barrio.[128] Arguably, the greatest tragedy in the treatment of slum dwellers lay in the fact that they were far from being parasitical or a source of hazard to the city, as the powers that be pigeonholed them: "One may even assert that the massive construction projects launched by the Marcos government and the companies owned by Marcos' cronies during this period *required the existence of these urban slums* as a source of cheap labor."[129] And yet, the state would rather depict them as freeloaders, a stereotype captured in Imelda's famous quip: "Why do I build a Heart Center or a Convention City instead of urban mass housing? I believe we just can't do that. I don't believe in building houses for anyone because I don't want our people to be mendicant."[130]

Despite all that, Marcos's authoritarianism had its limits. The dictatorship sought popular legitimacy and depended to an extent on populist platitudes. Hence, the regime could not simply evict all informal communities even if it wanted to, as attested by its adoption of slum upgrading schemes though ZIP. Since the early postwar period, political observers and politicians had regarded informal settlements as an important electoral bailiwick. This political reality was something that Marcos had to contend with despite his authoritarian grip on political power.[131] In certain significant cases, the regime had to give a certain leeway to local powerholders as seen in the case of Payatas, which came under the de facto rule of squatting syndicates empowered by Marcos. Syndicate leaders in turn "formed urban poor settlers into homeowners' associations and linked the associations to corporations . . . [and] created alliances with other groups present in Payatas, including those formed from World War II veterans and their descendants" (see chapter 3, p. 140).[132]

Still, the urban poor's political clout did not rest solely on patron–client ties; progressive and radical politics did mold many slum communities in

232   A CAPITAL CITY AT THE MARGINS

Quezon City. Even prior to martial law, communist organizers found a ready audience in the slums of Manila and Quezon City, with one recalling "how receptive the slum dwellers were to his message of armed revolution."[133] Authoritarian tactics failed to silence the urban poor during martial law, and instead produced the opposite effect: urban poor communities organized themselves and created alliances with the religious, students, and other sectors. Rather than be cowed by repression, many informal communities in Quezon City took this as an opportunity to consolidate their ranks and strengthen their unity. Having the largest concentration of slum communities in the city (and possibly in the entire country), NGC in Constitution Hill became a hub of organized urban poor organizations. Notwithstanding the presence of squatter syndicates in the NGC that engaged in patron–client relations with oligarchic elements, the community also gave birth to progressive people's organizations.[134]

Organized urban poor groups in Quezon City were found in both large communities, like Tatalon, and smaller settlements, like Hillcrest in Cubao. In both sites, residents banked on their unity and alliances with external groups to resist attempts at demolition. Because state forces attacked their right to the city, they often resorted to barricades as a preferred mode of defense, like in the cases of Bagumbayan and Ugong Norte—fringe areas of Quezon City near the Pasig border—in 1974.[135] In April 1983 the women of Samahang Maralita para sa Makatao at Makatarungang Paninirahan [Association of the Urban Poor for Humane and Just Housing], or SAMA-SAMA, the largest and most organized group in the NGC,

> placed their bodies in the paths of Quezon City bulldozers attempting to demolish homes in an area of Commonwealth. Some of the women were shot, but they decided, even though most had children, to return to the barricades and risk their lives for rights to the land.[136]

Quezon City's slums produced a cadre of future activists who fought the regime. One of them was Crispin Beltran, an Albay native and former Huk guerrilla who moved to the city after the war to find a job. Initially, he stayed in Tondo but moved to NGC in 1975, where the Beltran family had stayed since.[137]

Furthermore, the pre-Martial Law dynamics between Quezon City's slums and students, as exemplified above by Jan Quimpo's case, strengthened after 1972. The issues of the urban poor continued to radicalize the youth. Jan and Nathan's younger brother Jun was one of those politicized because of his engagement with Quezon City's informal communities. As a UP student, he joined the Constitution Hills Committee, a student organization that extended basic necessities to the urban poor of Constitution Hill.

THE SUBMISSIVE AND SUBVERSIVE SUBURBS   233

When Jun became part of the organization's core group, he immersed himself in the underground network of activists who organized the settlers.[138] From Constitution Hill, Jun moved to another urban poor community to become a full-time organizer. He chose Tatalon, "a sprawling urban poor community in Quezon City known for its violent resistance to the government's shanty-town demolition teams."[139] The issue of land tenure in Constitution Hill and other Metro Manila slums also radicalized Ateneans in the same manner that the Constitution Hill and the urban poor communities surrounding Loyola Heights helped form progressivism among the student members of the Young Christian Community in the 1970s.[140]

Meanwhile, the informal and low-income communities within and surrounding the UP Diliman campus grew in number and became more organized during martial law. More important, they remained critical spaces for the "social reproduction" of student activism. Author Jose "Butch" Dalisay's "sociospatial imagination" (to appropriate C. Wright Mills's phrase) of home at the time of his incarceration during martial law is illuminating: "Home to me then was a community of squatter shanties in Old Balara, a stone's throw from the university where I had spent much of that freshman year studying Mao instead of math."[141] Inside the campus, the highest concentration of informal settlers was along the adjacent streets of Ricarte, Palaris, and Dagohoy, collectively known by the acronym Ripada. In 1983 UP President Edgardo Angara ordered a census of all illegal settlers on campus. The census revealed that 1,988 squatter families lived in UP, two-thirds of which resided in Ripada. That same year, Angara issued a memorandum to facilitate the relocation of Ripada settlers to Caloocan. In response, the affected families set up barricades and succeeded against the attempts of university authorities at demolishing their houses in January and February 1985. However, UP officials, in coordination with the NHA and Metrocom, eventually prevailed, and by 8 February 1985, more than thirty houses had been dismantled.[142]

Clearly, a mutualism developed between slum communities and students in Quezon City. As slum dwellers radicalized the students, the students also aided the slum dwellers in their organizing efforts. The links between youth radicalism and the urban poor situation were apparent to a senior MHS official:

> Moreover, large slum and squatter communities mushroomed not only in Manila and suburbs but in many other cities of the country. The socio-economic implications of the housing situation caught the attention not only of the government but more so of the students and intellectuals. Together, these groups in the early 1970s constituted a militant force pressing government to improve the living conditions of the people.[143]

234   A CAPITAL CITY AT THE MARGINS

In a sense, Quezon City did become the working-class model community, although not in the way that Quezon intended it to be. Rather than a sanitized space to inculcate middle-class aspirations among the proletariat and precariat, it evolved into a place of politicization for both the workers and the other sectors who worked with them toward a more just society.

Oases of Dissent and Democracy

THE PRESENCE OF SLUMS, however, failed to remove Quezon City's suburban reputation from popular consciousness. For writer Sarah Lumba, who grew up in Marikina in the late 1970s, Quezon City was orderly, too orderly in fact:

> It didn't help, I suppose, that most of my classmates lived in Quezon City. Their neighborhoods—at least those that I frequented—all seemed to have a uniformed look. Gated subdivisions like Philamlife usually had wide roads and white bungalows with well-trimmed bermuda grass on the front lawn. The homes in Projects 1 to 6, which were meant for civil servants and ordinary wage earners, all had cement asbestos sheets on roofs, and *gumamela* [hibiscus] and *caimito* [star apple] trees whose branches hung halfway across the gridded roads were on their front yards. What you saw street after street was predictable, even boring, but they were easy on the eyes and perhaps easier for the mind to label and judge.[144]

The city, in contrast to Marikina, "seemed to be the epitome of modernity" for Lumba. Marikina at the time exuded rurality, but one which Marcosian brutality turned into a dumping ground for hogtied victims of torture and summary executions: "During martial law, Marikina became synonymous with the term 'salvaging.'"[145]

Compared with "lawless" Marikina, Quezon City was regimented. And yet it was this suburban order that made it an ideal locus for the social reproduction of the dictatorial regime. Its middle-class households and the lifestyles they engendered, not to mention conservative aspirations and values, were viable bases of support for the regime. Its noise-free, gated subdivisions helped ensure that the affluent segments in society would remain politically quiet. Such was the suggestive take of former Marcos media czar Primitivo Mijares on the rise to power of Minister of Public Information Francisco Tatad, "who used to ride the bus during his brief career as a working newspaperman but who now has a mansion at the exclusive Quezon City millionaires' enclave known as La Vista."[146] Meanwhile, in New Manila, "the old rich have congregated."[147] Similarly, Philamlife Homes had its own "contribution" to the social reproduction of the dictatorship. A good number of Marcos's trusted administrators once resided in this gated community: Defense Minister Enrile, Prime Minister Virata, Central Bank Governor Gregorio Licaros, and Minister of Agrarian Reform Conrado Estrella, among others.[148] Enrile and Virata, both key players of the martial law regime, were even neighbors in

THE SUBMISSIVE AND SUBVERSIVE SUBURBS   235

Philamlife Homes when both were still young married adults.[149] Marcos's trusted generals had their own luxurious urban enclave within Quezon City just outside Camp Aguinaldo (named after Emilio Aguinaldo, replacing the original name, Camp Murphy), the Corinthian Gardens, which, according to scholar Donovan Storey, was even "more exclusive" than Makati's famed Forbes Park.[150]

However, while it would be expedient to describe Philamlife Homes as a manifestation of Quezon City's position as a conservative suburbia, one should also note that this place was the same environment that helped shape Edgar Jopson's consciousness as a student activist. This disjuncture was no anomaly; after all, geography is not destiny. Although Quezon City was a space of conformity to authority, it also had pockets of counter-culture during martial law. Nonetheless, its oases of dissent and democracy were markedly different from those in Manila, further highlighting the distinction between the two cities.

For much of the postwar period, Quezon City had been (and still is) a heterogeneous space, and Marcos-era Cubao was a microcosm of that heterogeneity. On the one hand, Cubao bred consumerist conformity. Developed by the Aranetas, a clan that was simultaneously linked and opposed to the Marcoses through marriage ties and electoral rivalries, it was the city's commercial and entertainment center. It was an "urban escape hatch," a place of leisure "affording escape from the sameness, tedium, or funlessness" of suburban living.[151] Mimicking Makati, Cubao represented middle-class aspirations and the economic dominance of the elite. At the same time, akin to the bread-and-circus strategy of Roman emperors, Marcos utilized its potential to pacify the populace when in October 1975 his government supported the historic boxing match between Muhammad Ali and Joe Frazier at the Araneta Coliseum. Dubbed "Thrilla in Manila," the much-hyped bout enhanced the regime's popularity. Three years after this fight, the Araneta Coliseum co-hosted the FIBA Basketball World Cup—a significant event in a country where basketball is the most popular sport.[152]

On the other hand, Cubao signified a new form of dissent. From feminist groups protesting against beauty pageants to labor groups establishing networks with traditional politicians, Quezon City's commercial hub attracted various underrepresented sectors who mobilized their ranks for progressive causes. For example, it was at the Araneta Coliseum where the Kilusang Mayo Uno (May First Movement) was founded in 1980, with the choice of the venue indicating the new labor confederation's alliance with opposition politician Gerardo "Gerry" Roxas. Labor Day celebrations were again held there the following year. And it was at the Araneta Coliseum that labor leader Felixberto Olalia delivered a speech calling for a general strike to denounce Marcos's anti-worker policies.[153]

236   A CAPITAL CITY AT THE MARGINS

Another notable articulator of Cubao's position as a space for dissent, but in a rather nontraditional manner, was Tony Perez. In the 1980s Perez established his place in the Philippine literary scene by publishing a series of novels and stories that were set in Cubao. His writings showed the quotidian and fantasy worlds of the

> new urban sub-middle class composing the labor forces at the lower tiers of the service industries of the metropolis. In his Cubao series, Perez's abiding interest lies in how individual persons experientially renew themselves out of the demeaning and crushing conditions of their daily grind as small-time or casual service providers.[154]

For example, the plot of his novella *Cubao 1980* revolves around the "redemption" of the narrator, Tom, "from the demeaning, petty living he makes as a call boy [male prostitute] on the proliferating seedy inner fringes of Cubao."[155] Despite its reputation as a modern commercial center, by the 1970s Cubao was already showing signs of urban blight.[156] Its innermost nooks harbored spaces for the world's oldest profession. As Nick Joaquin described it: "The night spots in the Cubao area still have the every-hour-on-the-hour floor show and the nudes on parade travel the tables."[157] That Cubao became Quezon City's most prominent red-light district was no surprise because it was sandwiched between two masculine spaces: to its south, the martial masculinity of Camp Aguinaldo and Camp Crame; to the north, libidinal manhood contained in UP and Ateneo, which remained an exclusively male school until 1976. After all, male students and soldiers had always been the traditional clientele of Manila's brothels since colonial times (see chapters 1 and 2).

Unmistakably counter-culture, Perez's works tackled homosexuality in the city amid the masculinist atmosphere of martial law and the Marcoses' attempt to "normalize" the traditional, nuclear family.[158] Perez believed Cubao to be the historic birthplace of the Philippine gender revolution, as emblazoned in the title of his 1992 book, *Cubao 1980 at Iba Pang mga Katha: Unang Sigaw ng Gay Liberation Movement sa Pilipinas* (Cubao 1980 and Other Writings: The First Cry of the Gay Liberation Movement in the Philippines).[159] Alluding to the first cry of the Katipunan when they began their anticolonial revolution in 1896, Perez consecrated Cubao as a revolutionary space akin to Balintawak or Pugad Lawin. J. Neil Garcia, however, notes the paradox in Perez's text for being "appallingly homophobic" in its didacticism, yet it "does contain [the] most disturbingly lurid descriptions of male-to-male sex." In a sense, the book advocates "a kind of half-hearted if disingenuous 'liberation' after all."[160]

In her analysis of Perez's works on Cubao, Neferti Tadiar notes that he "fashions unremarkable characters"[161] in stark contrast to those that inhabit

THE SUBMISSIVE AND SUBVERSIVE SUBURBS   237

fictional Manila in the works of literary giant Nick Joaquin and the movies of Lino Brocka and Ishmael Bernal.[162] Perhaps, the setting of Cubao is part of the reason behind this contrast. Whereas Edgardo Reyes, and Brocka in the film adaptation, gives grit and grime to his characters in *Maynila: Sa Mga Kuko ng Liwanag* (Manila: In the Claws of Neon Lights) by situating them in the streets of Binondo, those in Perez's stories seem to fade into the suburban anonymity of Quezon City's generic-looking streets.

In the few literary works that mention Quezon City in passing, the image of the city is often one of opulence set against Manila's proletarian attributes. F. Sionil Jose's *Sin*, *The Feet of Juan Bacnang*, and *Ermita*, Liwayway Arceo's *Canal de la Reina*, and Rosario de Guzman-Lingat's *Ano Ngayon, Ricky?* (What Now, Ricky?) depict the city as an elite space. In Jose's works, which chronicle the experiences of the Filipino elite across generations, the city is booty, apportioned for Quezon's trusted cronies. In *Ano Ngayon, Ricky?*, a bildungsroman novel revolving around the radicalization and disillusionment of Tondo-born Ricky set against the context of the FQS, the city is a place of guarded mansions, swimming pools, and private cars.[163] The description of the Quezon City residence of Professor Alba, initially Ricky's mentor who turned out to be a manipulative character, is worth quoting at length:

> MAGANDA ANG BAHAY na nakatirik sa isang malaking sukat ng lupang malapit sa hanggahan ng Maynila at Quezon City. May security guard na nagbukas ng pinto ng bakuran at sumaludo sa kanila nang makilala ang abogadong kanyang kasama. Malawak ang hardin at sadya ang pagkakaayos. May mga ilaw na kinulayang nagsabit sa mga punongkahoy. Sa tagiliran ng bahay, kumikislap ang tubig ng isang swimming pool. Ang mga halakhak at kalansing ng kristal ay sumasabay sa magandang tugtuging nagmumula sa loob ng bahay.[164]

> (The house situated in an expansive lot near the boundary between Manila and Quezon City was beautiful. A security guard opened the gate entrance and saluted before them upon recognizing the lawyer. The garden was big and manicured. There were colored lights hanging from the trees. At the side of the house, the water of the swimming pool sparkled. The laughter and clink of crystal accompanied the lovely music that emanated from inside the house.)

Arceo turns to this trope in describing the Quezon City abode of character Gracia in *Canal de la Reina*, set in pre-martial law Manila. The narrator begins the description with the living room—"Ang salas na maliit ngunit may mamahaling-anyong tahanan" (small living room but in an expensive-looking house)—that had a thick, sliding glass door, a black piano, an oil painting of Gracia. The house was not gated, but it had a garage, as well as carpets, a telephone, and an air conditioner. Arceo thus paints a contrast between Gracia's space of comfort and the main setting of the novel: Canal

238   A CAPITAL CITY AT THE MARGINS

de la Reina, a populated and polluted estero in Tondo.[165] The same distinction appears in F. Sionil Jose's dichotomization of well-known schools in the metropolis in *The Feet of Juan Bacnang*: a contrast between the university belt's raucous streets, rowdy and bloody demonstrations, and scattering of slums, on one side; and the "antiseptic confines" of Ateneo and UP Diliman, whose students had "bodyguards the whole day."[166]

This Manila–Quezon City dichotomy in literature conveyed an actual sociospatial distinction between the two, notwithstanding the heterogeneous reality of these two spaces. It was a distinction between urban decay and the new suburbia. It was a distinction between the rowdy, shirtless *tambays* and the prim-and-proper urban professionals.[167] It was a distinction that even had a life-or-death implication for a number of anti-Marcos activists. On 27 September 1984 when a massive student rally occupied Welcome Rotonda,[168] the police dispersed it with gunshots. Student protestors scampered away, although rally marshals tried to guide their fellow students in finding a safe place. The problem, however, was that the activists were dispersed in the Quezon City side of the Rotonda. One of them, Susan Quimpo, recalls her predicament that day: "Had this been Malacañang or the University Belt area in Manila, I would have known how best to escape. But I was unfamiliar with the streets of Quezon City, and apparently, so were the rally marshals."[169] As such, the marshals instructed fellow rallyists to proceed to Santo Domingo Church. This church was a logical place to seek refuge because it was under the Dominicans, who supported the anti-dictatorship movement.[170] Unfortunately, cops blocked the thoroughfares leading to the church, forcing student-protestors to take their chances in the side streets and back alleys of Quezon City to make their way across the boundary and into Manila.[171]

Although Susan Quimpo explains that it was the activists' unfamiliarity with Quezon City's streets that endangered them, another possible factor was the physical appearance of these streets. The Manila side of the border (Sampaloc) had more back alleys, itinerant vendors, passers-by that could have enabled dispersed protestors to blend in the crowd because parts of the city retained (and still does up to this day) the early modern city planning that made it quite similar to pre-Haussmann Paris which had an array of narrow streets.[172] The opposite was the case in the Quezon City side (Santa Mesa Heights), which had wider streets, gated houses, and a substantially lower "street population." The above-mentioned extract from de Guzman-Lingat's novel eloquently articulates this stark juxtaposition. One might suspect that even if the activists were familiar with the streets in this part of Quezon City, they would have still stuck out like a sore thumb in the area and would have been effortlessly cornered by the police. The "emptiness" of that side of Quezon City, where residences were tightly

THE SUBMISSIVE AND SUBVERSIVE SUBURBS   239

guarded spaces with clear demarcations between public and private, made hiding for dispersed activists difficult.

But while the generic appearance of Quezon City's streets (with UP's urban planners going as far as saying the city lacked a visual identity and interesting dimensions)[173] made them inhospitable for dispersed rally- ists, this same feature turned the city into a strategic place for the covert activities of anti-Marcos forces. The anonymity of Quezon City's expansive residential areas and their relative distance from Manila could probably explain why it was the activists' preferred location for establishing their organizations' headquarters. For example, KM's national headquarters was along Quezon Avenue, while its regional headquarters was in Kamias corner Anonas. Other natdem groups established their safe houses, also known as UG (underground) houses, in other locations in the city.[174] The inconspic- uousness of Quezon City's residential spaces was just one among various reasons for this spatial clustering. Other important factors were the prox- imity of the schools and universities, especially UP, that were instrumental in providing membership and leadership to these groups and the relatively low rents in the city compared with those in Manila. The irony here, of course, was that UP's relocation in Diliman was precisely intended to insu- late it from such radicalizing elements.

For these same reasons legal organizations and NGOs set up shop in Quezon City, as well as opposition forces that were not aligned with the natdem movement.[175] After conducting a series of arson attacks on hotels and business establishments in Metro Manila in 1979, members of the Light- a-Fire Movement (LAFM), an underground anti-Marcos group aligned with social democrats, found refuge in the Good Shepherd Convent in Quezon City to avoid arrest. Good Shepherd sisters were in fact supporters of the movement and even helped the movement in preparing their leaflets.[176]

That Church people took care of LAFM members was no coincidence and no isolated incident. The presence of major religious organizations and their headquarters and convents in Quezon City made them a crucial partner of anti-Marcos groups, including urban poor groups, labor unions, student activists, and other people's organizations.[177] Quezon City's distance from Manila made it an ideal location for convents, seminaries, and novitiates (table 24). Its "inspiring atmosphere, soul-stirring tranquility, and ideal retreat that is within the orb of modern living but far from the madding crowd . . . [were] requisites that are so conducive to religious training."[178] New Manila, for instance, housed a number of religious spaces: the Christ the King Seminary, the CICM headquarters and chapel for its Belgian Fathers, and the Carmelite Convent on Gilmore Street. St. Theresa's College was also known for its activist-nuns who ran the school.[179] In contrast to the friars' dominance over the early-twentieth-century estates that would

240   A CAPITAL CITY AT THE MARGINS

TABLE 24. Partial list of novitiates, seminaries, and church headquarters in Quezon City, as of 1986

Classification	Religious Affiliation
Novitiates/Convents	
St. Paul's Novitiate	[undetermined]
Carmelite Convent	Roman Catholic
St. Joseph's Novitiate (Aurora Boulevard)	Roman Catholic
St. Joseph's Novitiate (España Extension)	Roman Catholic
Real Monasterio de Sta. Clara	Roman Catholic
Holy Ghost Convent	Roman Catholic
Good Shepherd Convent	Roman Catholic
Pink Sisters Convent	Roman Catholic
Seminaries	
Christ the King Mission Seminary	Roman Catholic
San Jose Seminary	Roman Catholic
Sacred Heart Seminary	Roman Catholic
St. Andrew's Theological Seminary	Episcopalian
Jesuit Novitiate Seminary	Roman Catholic
Theological Schools	
Loyola School of Theology	Roman Catholic
Maryhill School of Theology	Roman Catholic
Headquarters	
Churh of Jesus Christ and the Latter-Day Saints	Mormon
Iglesia ni Cristo Central Temple	Iglesia ni Cristo
National Council of Churches in the Philippines	Ecumenical-Protestant
United Church of Christ in the Philippines	Evangelical

SOURCES: Sarte and Agbayani, *Quezon City*, 11; Apilado, "The United Church of Christ," 335–58; Reyes, "The St. Andrew's Theological Seminary," 359–68

eventually comprise Quezon City, the religious spaces in the latter half of the century were less homogeneous and hegemonic. Its city spaces even embraced non-Christian denominations.[180]

During martial law, Quezon City was home to a number of non-Catholic Christian denominations, many of them with progressive leanings. One of these churches was the United Church of Christ in the Philippines (UCCP), which had its headquarters in West Triangle along EDSA. In 1974 the UCCP began to publicly oppose the abuses of the regime, one of the first churches

THE SUBMISSIVE AND SUBVERSIVE SUBURBS   241

to do so. In its public statements, it declared its stance "against the perpet-uation of one-man rule" and for the "immediate restoration of all civil and political liberties of all citizens."[181] UCCP's next-door neighbor, the National Council of Churches in the Philippines (NCCP), an ecumenical council of various Protestant churches, was another notable religious organization that fought the regime. One of NCCP's members was the Episcopal Church in the Philippines, whose headquarters was moved from Manila to Quezon City in 1947 with the opening of St. Andrew's Theological Seminary in Cathedral Heights along E. Rodriguez Avenue. The dean and faculty members of the seminary joined anti-Marcos rallies. Historian William Henry Scott, its most renowned faculty, was even incarcerated for some time due to allegations of being a subversive.[182]

Since many of these religious organizations had their own missionary arms, many of these religious groups had a special concern for "ethnic minorities." Once again, the Episcopal Church supported the struggles of the indigenous peoples, as radicalized priests came into contact with oppressed groups in faraway provinces.[183] The Catholic clergy also did their part, such as in the 1975 peace pact that the Episcopal Commission on Tribal Filipinos of the Catholic Bishops Conference of the Philippines helped organize at the St. Bridget's School in Quezon City. This event promoted the campaign of Kalinga leader Macli-ing Dulag against the Chico River Dam project pushed by the Marcos regime in the Cordillera region.[184] Meanwhile, the Catholic S.V.D. clergy backed the struggle of the Tinguians of eastern Abra in northern Luzon. Conrado Balweg, a Tinguian, entered the S.V.D. Christ the King Seminary in Quezon City, with the hopes of becoming a priest[185]; eventually, he joined the NPA and led the armed revolt against Marcos in the Cordilleras.

Although there were religious and Church officials (both Catholic and non-Catholic) who curried favor with the regime, many of them felt the oppression of the dictatorship. This was especially true for Church groups that had strong ties with marginalized sectors, such as the Association of Major Religious Superiors of the Philippines, which actively supported the fight of Tatalon's urban poor. Local Catholic parishes in Quezon City also helped in the local campaigns of their parishoners, as seen in the case of priests involved in the struggle of SAMA-SAMA for the right to housing in NGC. It is quite telling that in Robert Youngblood's list of twen-ty-two military raids on church establishments from 1972 to 1984, eleven happened in Metro Manila, nine of which were in Quezon City: St. Joseph's College (October 1973), Our Lady of Holy Angels Seminary (October 1973), Trinity College (October 1973), NCCP Headquarters (October 1973), Sacred Heart Novitiate (June 1974), Loyola House of Studies (April 1978), San Jose Seminary (April 1978). The remaining two in Metro Manila were offices of

Church publications in Manila. As a result of these raids the traditionally conservative leadership of the Catholic and Protestant Churches began to be more critical of the regime.[186]

One of the most important places in the anti-Marcos struggle, the Catholic Santo Domingo Church, was the location of Senator Benigno "Ninoy" Aquino Jr's wake after his assassination on 21 August 1983. The wake not only drew thousands of mourners but also provided a venue for Manila Archbishop Jaime Cardinal Sin to decry the atmosphere of tyranny in the country.[187] Thus, Quezon City's distinct space in the anti-Marcos narrative became more pronounced.

Aquino's death sparked widespread protests and noise barrages in Quezon City, Manila, and nearby towns, and an epic funeral procession where tens of thousands of mourners joined. Other demonstrations followed in the wake of the assassination. However, the nature of these protests were substantially different from those that defined the FQS and the early martial law years. In the post-1983 protests the so-called "middle forces" became more prominent. They were the middle and upper classes of Metro Manila "who looked to big business (the so called Makati crowd) and the Catholic Church (in which Cardinal Sin played a leading role) in their moralist anti-dictatorship stance."[188] Many of them did not identify with the radical left, although in the broad coalition of Justice for Aquino, Justice for All there was significant participation from the natdem forces, while Marxist thought also spread among anti-Marcos church forces. Class politics was also conspicuously less pronounced. The difference was spatially visible: the epicenter of these protests were in Quezon City, namely, the Aquinos' residence in Times Street, West Triangle, and the Santo Domingo Church along Quezon Avenue.[189]

The growing discontent toward Marcos intensified after the assassination, as Quezon City occupied a more prominent position in the anti-Marcos movement. In the 8 March 1984 Lakbayan march of 70,000 protestors from Central and Southern Luzon, those who came from the northern provinces marched through important places in the city: the UP campus, Katipunan Road, Aurora Boulevard, E. Rodriguez Avenue, and then stopping at the Christ the King Seminary for a lunch break before proceeding to Manila.[190] Quezon City played a leading role in the commemoration of Ninoy's first death anniversary. Jaime Cardinal Sin held mass at the Santo Domingo Church before a huge crowd that marched toward Rizal Park afterwards. According to a *Bulletin Today* report:

> The marchers from Quezon City were the most numerous. The Quezon City marchers were so many that while the lead group was entering the Rizal Park, the tail end

THE SUBMISSIVE AND SUBVERSIVE SUBURBS   243

of the march had just crossed the Quezon City-Manila boundary at the Welcome Rotonda.

The distance between Quezon City's Welcome Rotonda and Rizal Park is 5.5 kilometers.[191]

In May 1984 the Batasang Pambansa elections were held, in which opposition candidates gained a significant number of seats. The elections revealed that cities had become the bailiwick of anti-Marcos forces. Oppositionists prevailed in urban areas, especially in Metro Manila, where they won fifteen of the twenty-one seats partly because they were able to mobilize election inspectors and thus minimized electoral fraud and violence.[192] Incidents of vote buying and violence still occurred, and the Marcoses tried to flex their muscle in the national capital. As MMC governor, Imelda "became chief spokesperson for 'Operation Zero'—any barangay which reported zero votes for the opposition would be given cash awards."[193] However, a more fatal blow to the regime came two years later, when Marcos called for a snap presidential election on 7 February 1986 to salvage whatever shred of legitimacy he had left. He had previously used such snap elections to manufacture popular mandate; but this time around, the situation was different because of his opponent: Ninoy's widow, Cory Aquino.[194]

Cory claimed that she reached her decision to run for president on 8 December 1985 after a retreat at the Pink Sisters' Convent at New Manila.[195] Seemingly inconsequential, this detail once again points to the role of religious spaces in the city as places of refuge during the Marcos era. Subsequent episodes bolster this assertion. Although Quezon City was tagged as a hot spot for potential violence during the snap elections, the Santo Domingo Church drew huge crowds and became a sort of agora in the days following the polls.[196] When computer workers and tabulators of the Commission on Elections (Comelec) staged a walk-out on 9 February 1986 to protest the apparent cheating in the tallying of votes for the snap elections, Church leaders went out of their way to protect them. Fearing for the security of the thirty-five Comelec workers after they issued a press statement about their actions, Cardinal Sin decided to temporarily house them in Ateneo's Loyola House of Studies and then in the nearby Cenacle Retreat House.[197] Consequently, the role played by Quezon City's churches, convents, and seminaries was crucial in creating the now dominant narrative of Marcos's downfall as a "miraculous revolution."[198]

That "miraculous revolution" broke out a few weeks after the walk out. The final straw was when AFP Vice Chief of Staff Fidel Ramos and Enrile publicly withdrew their support for Marcos on 22 February 1986. Fearing a reprisal from the president, the two and their trusted soldiers holed up inside Camp Aguinaldo. Aware of the ongoing situation, Archibishop Jaime

244   A CAPITAL CITY AT THE MARGINS

Cardinal Sin, in a message aired via radio broadcast, urged people to gather at EDSA outside Camp Aguinaldo to protect Ramos and Enrile.[199] People Power was launched.

One could argue that EDSA People Power was the apex of a new strand of anti-Marcos activities, both overt and covert, that seemed to have gravitated toward Quezon City beginning in the 1980s. It featured, for example, an image of the Lady of the Holy Rosary of La Naval de Manila, carted by the Dominicans to EDSA from Santo Domingo Church,[200] rather than the usual banners and placards of Mendiola and Plaza Miranda. And of course, People Power was a "Quezon City protest," in that it literally took place in the Quezon City section of EDSA. Following Sin's announcement, crowds filled the highway especially in the segment between the Ortigas intersection and Cubao, although other nearly violent encounters happened in areas such as at the corner of Timog Avenue and Quezon Avenue, as well as in Libis, where two battalions of loyalist soldiers faced the barricades of thousands of pro-Cory supporters.[201]

At the same time, EDSA People Power was a "Quezon City protest" because of the "absence" of class politics. This classless-ness manifested in how EDSA People Power fused together the wide spectrum of anti-Marcos forces: from professionals and students to priests and the urban poor. As Florentino Hornedo put it: it was "spontaneous and drew its participants from across social lines. It was popular and unstructured." People Power was a "nonconfrontational third party, a go-between"[202] The 1986 uprising thus differed from the usual anti-Marcos Mendiola or Plaza Miranda affair. Violence did punctuate EDSA People Power at times, with the most notable fatalities being those of loyalist soldiers killed in their futile attempt to prevent rebel forces from taking over the broadcasting stations of Channel 4 and Channel 9, both in Quezon City.[203] Yet the Filipinos memorialize the event as a "bloodless revolution"; with the emphasis on its peacefulness as a clear counterpoint to the rallies of militant groups or the armed struggle waged in the countryside. In more ways than one, EDSA People Power was a "rebellion that defied the rules."[204] Delia Aguilar's feminist analysis of the event highlights how it "served to diversify the class entities engaged in the field of struggle, germinating multifarious cause-oriented groups within which incubated a revitalized focus on women's issues."[205] People Power had different slogans and a different crowd:

> People Power shattered the myth of the silent majority. What was more incredible was that it flushed the country's affluent citizens out of their homes, mobilizing them in a scope never seen before. The human shield at Camp Crame and Camp Aguinaldo consisted not only of workers and the urban poor but also of the upper classes from prominent businessmen, professionals, artists and fashion designers, to even the well-heeled friends of the Marcos regime.[206]

THE SUBMISSIVE AND SUBVERSIVE SUBURBS   245

Or as more succinctly, albeit whimsically, put by one of those who trooped to EDSA, "It was like one big homecoming of the Ateneo, Assumption, La Salle."[207]

This statement directs us to the paradox of EDSA People Power's purported classlessness as a distinctly middle-class claim. The shift of anti-Marcos mass mobilizations away from Manila toward Quezon City, culminating in EDSA, was not merely a geographical one, a shift in the "spaces of resistance,"[208] but a pivot away from the class politics that characterized the rallies in Plaza Miranda and Mendiola. Of course, this does not mean that all participants in the EDSA uprising were from the middle class. For instance, significant segments came from the urban poor, including organized groups from Tatalon and Constitution Hill.[209] Nonetheless, People Power saw a revamp of the guiding narrative of the rebellion: from a peasant–workers alliance working with the progressive middle classes versus imperialism, feudalism, and bureaucrat capitalism to a moralist conflict that was more palatable to and in keeping with the interests of the middle class, that of democracy-loving Filipinos vs. the corrupt Marcos dictatorship.[210] A newspaper reporter's juxtaposition of the two cities during the final days of People Power is telling: "While Quezon City seems to be the country's liberated area, in Manila the situation is still under the control of the Marcos loyalists."[211]

The significance of EDSA People Power thus goes beyond the toppling of Marcos. It marked the transformation of EDSA as a new site of protest, a "middle-class alternative" to the usual spaces of protest in Manila. With the building of the EDSA Shrine, the Catholic hierarchy has effectively cemented EDSA's status as a "classless" site.[212] It is a claim to being neutral, civil, and moderate (evinced by the usual conflation of the terms middle class, moderates, and, civil society), tenuous as it is, that seeks to establish moral authority by its middle-ground position between dictatorship and communism, between conservatism and radicalism. It is a discourse that perfectly fits into Quezon City's official narrative, as it was imagined by Quezon in 1939.

* * *

THE 1970S saw the instrumentalization of Southeast Asian capitals by authoritarian regimes. In the name of strengthening the nation-state, militarist Rangoon, New Order Jakarta, Lee Kuan Yew's Singapore, Mahathir Mohammad's Kuala Lumpur, and autoritarian Bangkok were refashioned to glorify the ruling regimes and stifle dissent. The centralization of power in cities meant the disenfranchisement of the poor, leading to the rapid increase of the urban poor in many of these cities, as exemplified by

246   A CAPITAL CITY AT THE MARGINS

Bangkok's *khlongs* (canals) and Jakarta's kampongs. Still, these conditions did not prevent uprisings and revolts from challenging (and in some cases toppling) the powers that be.[213] The same was true for Quezon City under the Marcos regime.

The Marcos era caused major inversions in Quezon City's sociospatial order. The 1971 Diliman Commune symbolized the inversion of the Diliman campus: what was intended to be an isolated university town turned out to be a politicized space fully immersed in its surroundings. Rather than a mere city of letters that was autonomous from municipal or city authorities, Diliman emerged as a place of progressive enlightenment premised on actual involvement with marginalized sectors and communities in a periurban ecology.

Outside UP, martial law caused other role reversals in the city. Consumerist Cubao morphed into a venue of deviance. The church was no longer an institution of landlords but an organization with members that went against the dictatorship. Constitution Hill, which urban plans exalted as a grandiose civic center, became one of the largest urban poor communities in the country. In this regard, the entire city was inverted: from capital city to squatter capital.

Quezon City thus became a space of contradictions. It was a middleclass space that was complicit in martial law's oppression, yet it was also the subversive suburbia. Interestingly, Quezon City's history of suburban seclusion influenced how the city played a role in the anti-Marcos struggle. For example, the presence of convents and seminaries in the city was due to its being distant, literally and figuratively, from hyper-urban Manila; yet, these were the same religious spaces that became the pockets of resistance that forced the dictator out of Malacañang. Hegemonic masculine spaces dominated Quezon City yet it also harbored areas like Cubao, which incubated LGBT liberation, and EDSA, which allowed a "cross-class urban women's movement" to emerge.[214] Although urbanization and metropolitanization made Quezon City deeply connected to Manila, the politics of the Marcos era seemed to have made the boundaries separating the two capital cities even clearer.

Bar none, the greatest inversion in this period was Quezon City's revenge against Marcos. As if holding a grudge against the dictator for his decision to remove its status as capital city, Quezon City dealt the final blow against the regime in EDSA People Power. The city did not reclaim its preeminent position as a result, but the events in EDSA in February 1986 signaled the beginning of the end of its subordinate status vis-à-vis Manila. Henceforth, Quezon City was no longer peripheral, but a central part of an ever-growing metropolitan region.

CONCLUSION

Past, Imperfect, Tense

"FUTURE PERFECT" was the official slogan of the Quezon City Diamond Jubilee Celebration in 2014. Evidently, city officials did not merely commemorate Quezon City's founding in 1939 but also proclaimed its future as a global city, charting its direction toward eventual perfection. It was as if they were talking in the future perfect tense, totally certain about the eventual completion of an action. For Mayor Herbert Bautista,

> As the birthplace of many important events, endeavors and revolutions that shaped the nation's historical and economic history, Quezon City is indeed a bastion of continued innovation. . . . The 75th-year celebration of cityhood gives us the perfect opportunity to show off what Quezon City has to offer. Thus we came up with a master plan that commemorates its rich past, as well as welcomes its progressive future, which we all excitedly look forward to.[1]

Bautista's vision is but a continuation of renewed metropolitan dreams for Quezon City in the post-authoritarian Philippines. As early as the mayoral term of Brigido "Jun" Simon Jr. (1986–1987, 1988–1992), who took over after Marcos's downfall, city officials were already entertaining ambitions of a "Metro Quezon."[2] Up to this day, proposals to make Quezon City the capital city again recur every so often.[3]

However, by looking at Quezon City's history from its inception to the end of the Marcos era, this book uncovers aspects of its past that interrogate the perfection and certainty that dominant narratives had conferred upon the city from its beginnings to the present and reveal the tensions that such narratives ignore. Indeed, posing the question of uncertainty opens up the possibility of history, as no history could be written if the future were perfect and everything could be anticipated.[4] In many ways, ambiguity and

247

248   A CAPITAL CITY AT THE MARGINS

insecurity characterized Quezon City's formative decades (1939–1986), as it struggled to perform its role as the nation's capital.

The Imperfect Past of a Capital at the Margins

MANILA'S northern and eastern suburban border zones cradled Quezon City in the prewar period. Burdened by the pressure caused by the suburban explosion that began in Extramuros in the nineteenth century and accelerated in the American colonial period, Manila's boundaries always seemed to be about to burst. Although this process of suburbanization involved elements of Manila's underside, exemplified by the existence of vice and petty crime in the border zones, middle- and upper-class consumption was the key driving force. These border zones, once dominated by landed estates, were to be reformed for the domestic reproduction of the well-to-do. Quezon City's founding, despite its founder's social justice rhetoric and the disruptions due to the Second World War, sustained the said class bias and even served as a mechanism for further capital accumulation of the landed and well connected.

Borders were an especially sensitive issue for Quezon City compared with other towns due to its nature as a purpose-built, planned city. Because the city emerged not out of a preexisting settlement but through legislative fiat, its municipal boundaries were artificial and quite arbitrary, in contrast to how Manila's borders reflected socioeconomic realities, as seen in territorial changes in its 1901 charter. This arbitrariness then served the interests of those who used Quezon City to amass wealth, especially after the city was designated as national capital in 1948. Real estate developers snagged prime properties in the city just outside Manila's boundaries and turned them into gentrified subdivisions. Land speculation occurred as though it was endemic to the city landscape. Politicians and entrepreneurs, many of whom had considerable influence over how the city borders were delineated and policed, capitalized on Quezon City's status as capital. Hence, the city was not merely the spatial form of official nationalism but an instrument to further socioeconomic inequality.

This intensification of social asymmetries was magnified along Quezon City's border zones. On the one hand, its southern edges and its peripheries just outside Manila's eastern limits gave rise to some of the most exclusive residential areas, from prewar New Manila to Corinthian Gardens in the 1970s. On the other hand, its border zones abutting northern Manila and Caloocan, best represented by La Loma, stored Manila's necessary undesirables: cockpits, cabarets, and the Chinese. State authorities thus tended to associate these places with criminality. Furthermore, for Manila mayors, Quezon City was a vast space just outside Manila's borders that served as a convenient catch basin for evicted slum dwellers.

However, Quezon City's historical geography was also formed by the clash between the urban and the rural. The urban push coming from Manila demanded from it the social reproduction of a specific type of labor: educated, highly trained white-collar employees who constituted a professional and managerial class for a growing metropolis. This process of social reproduction was (and still is) sustained by Quezon City's public and private housing projects, school campuses, and recreational facilities. Neither an industrial town like Caloocan nor a commercial center like Makati, the postwar capital city had a distinctly middle-class domestic demeanor. Yet the rural also exerted an equal amount of pressure on it. From the Sakdals and dispossessed peasants of the prewar period to the Huks who roamed the expanse of Novaliches in the postwar period, agrarian unrest was the enduring specter that kept Manila and Quezon City's urban elites on their toes. Even the rural hinterland outside Luzon exerted its influence on Quezon City at various levels: from above, capital from Visayan caciques like the Aranetas and Lopezes defined the city's geography, and from below, folkloric creatures and fantastical tales lit the imagination of many middle- and upper-class children who grew up listening to the stories of their Visayan kasambahay.[5]

Therefore, in many ways, Quezon City was Manila's buffer zone, although it was this very liminality that made the postwar capital nothing but a nominal center. Despite its exalted status in the urban hierarchy, it remained peripheral. That churches preferred to build seminaries and convents in this city (even as late as the martial law era) evinced the city's marginal location and idyllic atmosphere in contrast to urban Manila. Of course, Quezon City underwent structural changes, especially after the war, but these were almost imperceptible, drowned by the sound and the fury emanating from neighboring Manila, especially if one looks at how the two cities loomed in the popular imagination. In the 1930s, Manila was Escolta, inebriated by the jazz age, whereas Quezon City was Hacienda de Diliman, enveloped by a deceptive serenity of the swaying of cogon. In the early postwar decades, Manila was Arsenio Lacson and Asiong Salonga,[6] energetic personalities who gave the city a certain edge, whereas Quezon City was the nameless middle-income office employee who worked nine-to-five, Monday to Friday, to pay for his two-bedroom house somewhere in the PHHC's projects. In the 1970s Manila was neon-lit Avenida de Rizal and Plaza Miranda enthralling artists like Nick Joaquin and Lino Brocka, whereas Quezon City was Enrile and Virata playing tennis in the clubhouse of Philamlife Homes. Indeed, one can also make the case that in its early decades Quezon City had no identity to speak of. While Joaquin's and Brocka's works have birthed iconic representations of Manila, no such writer or film maker exists for Quezon City—only passing mentions in the novels of F. Sionil Jose and Rosario de Guzman-Lingat. The nearest approximation would be Tony Perez's writings about Cubao.

250   A CAPITAL CITY AT THE MARGINS

In many ways Quezon City was a space that served the status quo, corroborating what other urban scholars have observed about suburban conservatism. It was a city built on the promise of democratization, but the democracy that the city offered was the escapist freedom of upper- and middle-class consumption that only applied to those who could afford it. It brings to mind Lewis Mumford's idea of the suburb as the "anti-city":

> ultimate outcome of the suburb's alienation from the city . . . with the extension of the democratic ideal through the instrumentalities of manifolding and mass production. In the mass movement into suburban areas a new kind of community was produced, which caricatured both the historic city and the archetypal suburban refuge . . . Thus the ultimate effect of the suburban escape in our time is, ironically, a low-grade uniform environment from which escape is impossible.[7]

Quezon City's residential enclaves performed their roles in creating submissive subjectivities, which proved crucial in propping up the Marcos regime. His generals lived in comfort in Corinthian Gardens. His technocrats, many of them educated in the isolated campuses of UP and Ateneo, settled in a similar fashion, tucked away in other plush subdivisions in the city. Meanwhile, many of those from the middle class were too busy to care, as they had to work hard to pay the housing mortgage in the city's "projects."

Quezon City's role in the political economy of the metropolis was supplemented by its ideological function, characterized by tensions between its progressive underpinnings and reactionary predilections.[8] The ideas of domestication and democratization, which the Americans first articulated and was later on championed by Philippine elites, were evident in the way Quezon City was packaged. Quezon emphasized how his urban brainchild would transform landed estates into housing projects for the common tao and how it would become the capital of a postcolonial nation and a citadel of democracy on this side of the planet, ideas that the 1949 master plan reemphasized. Yet, at the same time, Quezon designed it as an apolitical space, thereby (and paradoxically) contributing to its conservative tendencies. The city's early charters made its local government an appendage of the chief executive, leaving no room for partisan electoral tussles. A college town insulated from the rest of society much like its Ivy League counterparts, Diliman should have been the ideal place for undisturbed learning, with its inaccessible location serving as an impenetrable border to keep distractions (i.e., Manila's politics and poverty) at bay. Its educated and well-to-do population base made Diliman—the heart of Quezon City—undeniably middle class.[9] This middle-class orientation expressed its distinct preference for moral politics over class politics in the Citizens League for Good Government of the 1950s.[10]

PAST, IMPERFECT, TENSE   251

However, despite Quezon City's submissive nature as a suburban city, its assemblage of student activists, slums, and anonymous, secluded places made it a space for anti-authoritarianism. Enrile and Jopson spent their formative years in Philamlife Homes and yet would lead contrasting lives. As Herbert Gans put it, the suburbs "changes some people, but not in uniform ways."[11] A gender dimension also exists in Quezon City's duality, as seen in the clash between the city's heteronormative conservatism and its capacity for transgressive sexuality. Although it was designed to reinforce state control, Quezon City proved instrumental to the politicization of the middle class, especially during the Marcos era. The clustering in one city of academic institutions, NGO headquarters, and progressive churches—all of them institutions that enjoyed varying levels of spatial autonomy—allowed pro-democracy and left-wing ideas to circulate at a time of intense repression. That sense of spatial autonomy also sprang from the atmosphere of anonymity in the city's middle-class residential areas. Quite incongruously, slums became a defining feature of Quezon City, influencing not just its land use policies but the landscape of its social movements. Informal settlers also straddled between submission and subversion, as they tried to move away from patron–client politics of the postwar decades toward progressivism and antiauthoritarianism in the Marcos era.

Ten years after Marcos "demoted" Quezon City by removing its status as capital in 1976, the city got its revenge by serving as the primary locus of his downfall. Today, Quezon City acts as the de facto capital city of the 1986 People Power Revolution, as it is the site of the EDSA Shrine, the People Power Monument, and the Bantayog ng mga Bayani.[12] It was urban poetic justice.

EDSA People Power represents the pinnacle of various sociospatial inversions in Quezon City's historical geography throughout the city's history. One such inversion came from how the dispossessed and the desperate flocked to the suburban fallows of Quezon City and turned it into the squatter capital of the country. Constitution Hill, slated to be the city's sociocivic center, became the vast informal settlement today more popularly known as Batasan Hills. UP also demonstrated a profound sociospatial reversal. Rather than become an insulated university town that served the state in silence, it bred dissent and critical thinking, aided in no small way by Quezon City's urban and peri-urban poor. The wave of social awareness generated by the radical combination of slums and students also infected the middle and upper classes, leading many of them to leave their gated existence and go out in the streets in the heady days of February 1986. In a way, EDSA gave the middle class an avenue to appropriate the radical rhetoric of the Left sans class politics, following their awakening from suburban slumber after Ninoy's assassination in 1983. Unfortunately, in

252   A CAPITAL CITY AT THE MARGINS

this ambivalent space of activism between moderation and militancy, the national-democratic Left was effectively marginalized.[13]

That Cory Aquino, a Quezon City housewife, stood as People Power's preeminent anti-Marcos figure suited the Manila–Quezon City dichotomy perfectly. Cory embodied domesticity, while Marcos was martial masculinity. Of course, such a contrast has important limitations, and one cannot treat this in a Manichean way. For instance, Cory Aquino's standing as an icon of democracy has serious pitfalls; most notably in how she embodied rural caciquism while amassing urban/suburban powers, quite similar to what the Tuasons, Aranetas, and Lopezes wielded in Quezon City.[14] Moreover, classlessness was not a preserve of EDSA's middle class. Marcos also deployed it as a suitable ideology to combat the radicalism of the CPP-NPA and the Moro rebels. Hence, his call for a "revolution from the center."

Despite being a planned city, in a scale unrivalled in the country, Quezon City's presumed picture-perfect morphology could not hide the conflicts and contradictions—not to mention crime and corruption—that belied its supposed stature as a model community. It was thus a capital at the margins, in reference to both its questionable status as the de jure political center and its peripheral status vis-à-vis Manila. Yet, by the end of the Marcos era, it had become the gravitational center of anti-dictatorship forces, monumentalized by the Our Lady of EDSA Shrine. Quezon City's post-authoritarian sociospatial transition demonstrates what Massey argues about space:

> we recognise space as always under construction. Precisely because space on this reading is a product of relations-between, relations which are necessarily embedded material practices which have to be carried out, it is always in the process of being made. It is never finished; never closed. Perhaps we could imagine space as a simultaneity of stories-so-far.[15]

Southeast Asian Connections

THE ANALYTIC SIGNIFICANCE of looking at a capital city's geographical edges to understand its historical geography goes beyond the territorial boundaries of the Philippine nation-state. One could even argue that such a paradigm is even more critical today. The present-day delicate political situation in Southeast Asia's urban centers have led two governments to move their capital cities to peripheral locations. The two new capitals are Malaysia's Putrajaya and Myanmar's Naypyitaw.

In 1999 Malaysia's federal government transferred its administrative offices to the newly created city of Putrajaya from Kuala Lumpur, which had been geographically expanded in the 1990s to cover erstwhile rural areas

PAST, IMPERFECT, TENSE   253

to reflect its rapid growth, as seen in the areas of Petaling Jaya, Klang, and other neighboring towns in Selangor.[16] However, it is also precisely because of this runaway kampong-type of urbanization that the federal government felt that the capital city had to be relocated to the more modern and rationally planned 4,931-hectare site in Putrajaya.[17] Furthermore, one cannot avoid reading this move as a strategy of the United Malays National Organization (UMNO), Malaysia's most dominant political party, to respond to Malaysia's spatial politics: the rural has been UMNO's traditional stronghold while cities (with large concentrations of marginalized Chinese Malaysians), like Kuala Lumpur and Georgetown, Penang, have been consistently anti-establishment.

Naypyitaw is a more recent creation than Putrajaya, although the circumstances of their emergence share a number of commonalities. Yangon (formerly known as Rangoon), the most urbanized and populous city in Myanmar, was the former colonial and postcolonial capital city. In 2006 the national government announced its decision to move the capital to a newly created city in an inaccessible location in the landlocked Pyinmana district. It was a virtual administrative island, with wide, straight highways and no infrastructure to support a resident population.[18]

The commonalities of Putrajaya, Naypyitaw, and Quezon City go beyond their being purpose-built, planned capital cities in Southeast Asia. A more important convergence is their psuedoutopian-authoritarian underpinnings. Putrajaya was the product of the imagination of long-time strongman Mahathir Mohammad and his technocrats and served as the crystallization of the political aspirations of Mahathir and UMNO to conjure a dream city of technocracy and developmental authoritarianism. As the purported urban reflection of the Malaysian nation, Putrajaya emphasizes order and perfection. Its architecture and public art represent the predominant Malay-Islamic character of official Malaysian nationalism, in contrast to the more fragmented urbanism of Kuala Lumpur, where Chinese Malaysians have asserted their right to economic and symbolic spaces.[19] Putrajaya is thus an enclave of Malay-Muslim dominance, away from the contested spaces of Kuala Lumpur. Similarly, in choosing Naypyitaw, Burmese officials have considered essentialist notions of culture, oriented toward a "decolonized" urbanism—including geomancy, thereby making the new capital simultaneously modern and non-modern—although it seems that security is the predominant consideration of Myanmar's military-run government. Naypyitaw's inaccessibility makes it practically impossible for city-based protests to paralyze the state, such as in the historic 8888 Uprising, which was led by Rangoon-based university students. The spatial logics in Putrajaya and Naypyitaw echo Haussmannian tactics in preventing urban uprisings.[20] The similarities between the undemocratic features of Putrajaya and Naypyitaw and Quezon and Marcos's preoccupation with

254   A CAPITAL CITY AT THE MARGINS

metropolitan remapping are thus no coincidence. Nevertheless, the future of Naypyitaw and Putrajaya, as well as that of social movements that challenge the power structures behind these capitals, cannot be ascertained. The long list of failed capitals in world history—Quezon City included—should serve as a lesson for all stakeholders in both capital cities.

However, one must note an important difference between Putrajaya and Naypyitaw. Putrajaya's proximity to Kuala Lumpur, in contrast to other planned cities, enables the expansion of Malaysia's primate city into a bigger urban agglomeration driven by middle-class consumption and suburbanization, like what is now existing in Metro Manila. In this sense, Putrajaya follows Quezon City's historical experience as a key component in postwar metropolitanization, which has paved the way for Southeast Asian megacities.[21]

The emergence of such Southeast Asian megacities makes border zones all the more consequential to our understanding of socioeconomic processes that have global ramifications. Urban centers like Jakarta, Bangkok, Saigon are just a few examples of Southeast Asian urban agglomerations that are constantly and rapidly outgrowing and shedding their territorial boundaries due to capital and demographic flows that are often transnational in character.[22] How are we to analyze the transformations in these conurbations in terms of urban-rural dynamics, metropolitan administration, and political economy without disregarding the narratives of groups that are figuratively and literally in the peripheries? These are crucial transformations given that the reproduction of labor will remain concentrated in these megacities in the foreseeable future.[23]

While these Southeast Asian conurbations are now globally oriented metropolises, urban problems that have plagued them since the twentieth century persist. Housing inequality probably tops that list. For instance, the greater Jakarta region, Jabodetabek (Jakarta, Bogor, Depok, Tanggerang, Bekasi), was supposed to have been the site for *rumah sejahtera* (prosperous housing for the poor); instead, upper-middle-class residences have filled Jakarta's satellite towns.[24] Metropolitan growth also means that these megacities are bigger powder kegs. Coups and opposition politics in Bangkok have toppled a number of administrations; demonstrations in Jakarta put an end to the New Era in 1998; and Kuala Lumpur has teetered at the brink several times, from the 1969 race riots to the more recent Bersih and anti-Najib mobilizations.[25]

The increasing prominence of urban-based protests represents a key spatial shift in the region. From the nineteenth century to the 1970s, rural uprisings were par for the course in Southeast Asia, but in the late- and post-Cold War periods, city-based rebellions and riots have been exerting more pressure on the establishment, even toppling a few regimes in the process. Quezon City's history illustrates this shift: from the colonial to the early postcolonial periods, Quezon City's spaces have cradled a succession of peasant uprisings in the form of the Katipunan, Sakdal revolt, and the Huk rebellion; but by the late twentieth century, its streets have generated city-based uprisings. These displays of dissent are typified by the EDSA People Power and its 2001 reincarnation, both typically led by university students, the religious, and middle-class city dwellers, but also include revolts by the urban poor, as displayed by the Marcos-era resistance of Payatas and Tatalon residents.[26] How should we approach this trend from a spatial point-of-view? Quezon City's history offer clues that could aid in crafting a comparative framework to respond to such a pressing question.

Social Justice and Quezon City

TODAY'S QUEZON CITY conveys a bitter irony given that it was founded on the idea of social justice. It is thus only fitting to conclude this book by assessing the city' past and present based on this original intent. The historical and theoretical explorations of this work are, after all, geared toward contributing to not just scholarly knowledge but more importantly the praxis of contemporary Philippine urban social movements. Such an orientation stems from David Harvey's assertion in *Social Justice and the City* that space, social justice, and urbanism cannot be understood in isolation from each other.[27]

In the first two decades of the twenty-first century, Metro Manila has increasingly become a "decentralized and fragmented urban regime."[28] Within it are competing sites of political, economic, and cultural power, a reflection of the polycentricity that has characterized post-authoritarian Philippines. No city has a monopoly of political capital: Manila has Malacañang and the Supreme Court, the Senate is in Pasay City, and the Lower House is in Quezon City. The "anarchy of families"[29] of the metropolitan economy is reflected in an anarchic urban geography. The postwar central business district that the Ayala patriarchy created in Makati City is now competing with the Ortigas Center, which straddles Pasig City and Mandaluyong City, and the Ty family, which owns Eastwood City in Quezon City. The Ayala model of privatized urban planning of economic centers piloted in Makati is also replicated in the Filinvest Corporate City in Muntinlupa City and more recently in Bonifacio Global City in Taguig City.[30] Simply put, "Metro Manila has no center" because it is the center.[31] This anarchy, however, makes Metro Manila's role as the country's primary node for economic globalization clear.[32] To perform this function, the metropolis depends on the predominance of the neoliberal economic model within its space, which has been the case as early as the 1990s, leading to the creation of "global city imaginaries."[33]

Quezon City is clearly abreast with this intercity "competition" not just within Metro Manila but also in the region. In the present era of neoliberal urbanism, its government officials and business interests have steered the city toward gentrification and large-scale rezoning of urban spaces as it tries to keep pace with other global-oriented Southeast Asian cities. At present, even Southeast Asian "secondary cities" like Surabaya, Georgetown, and Cebu exhibit traits that are indicative of this trend: for instance, the growth of the middle class and the commodification of urban spaces combined under one roof with the rise of "new" shopping malls often referred to as mixed-use developments.[34] This current fad of combining consumption and production spaces oriented toward the middle class is seen in Eastwood City, Ayala Technohub in UP Diliman, and the soon-to-be completed Quezon City Central Business District in North Triangle—all of which are by-products of this wholescale remapping of the city effected by the collusion of state and capital to ensure the city's profitability. These changes are hallmarks of the process of gentrification that is dependent on capitalists investing on what is considered "hip" by the middle class, leading to the displacement of spaces for the lower class.[35]

Unfortunately, the glitzy establishments and green architecture that these new developments boast occlude the war that state and capital are waging against the urban poor, whose labor allow such developments to happen in the first place. Beneath gentrification's veneer are violent demolitions and the widespread dispossession of informal settlers, not to mention the nonphysical violence of anti-labor practices (e.g., subsistence wages, lack of job security, union busting, etc.) that state and capital employ.[36] Quezon City's slums, long "forgotten places"[37] that reproduce the low-wage labor required by capital, are under attack. The dreamy refashioning of the city's terrain and skyline diverts the attention of the middle class away from class-based tensions brewing beneath the surface. Amid the cosmetic changes in the city, for the urban poor in Tatalon, Sitio San Roque, Payatas, and Batasan Hills/NGC, Quezon City is "a changeless land" in terms of structural oppression.[38] A Tatalon resident who participated in the 1986 People Power summed up his dim view of post-authoritarian society thus: "At EDSA rich and poor came together, but now it is as it was before—they can't be bothered with us."[39]

Notwithstanding Quezon City's seeming changelessness, analytic concepts to understand its spaces cannot be perpetually valid; after all, all cities—all spaces for that matter—are sociohistorical constructs that are "always under construction."[40] No longer marginalized, Quezon City is just as significant an urban space as Manila or Makati in the post-authoritarian Philippines. But even as Quezon City transitions from being a failed and forgotten capital to a presumptive global city, the urban poor's plight should force us to acknowledge that all these global city musings would only be illusory if we fail to recognize the significance of analyzing a city's historical geography from the margins.

Notes

Introduction: The Contours of a Capital at the Margins

1   "Philippines Population 2016," *World Population Review*, http://worldpopulationreview.com/countries/philippines-population/, accessed 26 Oct. 2016.

2   Marqueza C. L. Reyes, "Spatial Structure of Metro Manila: Genesis, Growth and Development," *Philippine Planning Journal* 29 (2)–30 (1), 1998: 1–34; Emma Porio, "Shifting Spaces of Power in Metro Manila," *City* 13 (1), 2009: 110–19, esp. 113–18.

3   Daphne J. Magturo, "Quezon City Moves to Replace Manila as Country's Capital," *Philippine Daily Inquirer*, 24 May 2012, http://newsinfo.inquirer.net/199881/quezon-city-moves-to-replace-manila-as-country%E2%80%99s-capital, accessed 2 Oct. 2013.

4   Chester L. Hunt, "The Moth and the Flame: A Look at Manila's Housing Problems," *Philippine Quarterly of Culture and Society* 8 (2–3), 1980: 99–107.

5   Simon Gunn, "The Spatial Turn: Changing Histories of Space and Time," in *Identities in Space: Contested Terrains in the Western City since 1850*, ed. Simon Gunn and Robert J. Morris (Hants, England: Ashgate, 2001), 9.

6   Henri Lefebvre, *The Production of Space* (Oxford: Blackwell, 1991); David Harvey, *Social Justice and the City* (Oxford: Basil Blackwell, 1988); Doreen Massey, *For Space* (London: Sage, 2005); Doreen Massey, "On Space and the City," in *City Worlds*, ed. Doreen Massey, John Allen, and Steve Pile (London and New York: Routledge, 1999); Edward W. Soja, *Postmodern Geographies: The Reassertion of Space in Critical Social Theory* (London: Verso, 1989).

7   Doreen Massey, *Space, Place, and Gender* (Minneapolis: University of Minnesota Press, 1994), 251.

8   For a detailed discussion on the competing thoughts within the Marxist tradition of geography, see Soja, *Postmodern Geographies*, 43–75.

9   Massey, *For Space*, 10–12.

10   Massey, "On Space and the City," 159, 162. Italics in the original.

11   Gunn, "The Spatial Turn," 1.

12   On Southeast Asia's urban upsurge, see Hans-Dieter Evers and Rüdiger Korff, *Southeast Asian Urbanism: The Meaning and Power of Social Space* (Singapore: Institute of

Southeast Asian Studies, 2000), 1; K. C. Ho and Hsin-Huang Michael Hsiao, "Globalization and Asia-Pacific Capital Cities: Primacy and Diversity," in *Capital Cities in Asia-Pacific: Primacy and Diversity*, ed. K. C. Ho and Hsin-Huang Michael Hsiao (Taipei: Center for Asia-Pacific Area Studies, Research Center for Humanities and Social Sciences, Academia Sinica, 2006), 3; Peter J. Rimmer and Howard Dick, *The City in Southeast Asia: Patterns, Processes and Policy* (Singapore: NUS Press, 2009), esp. ch. 3.

13   Arnold Toynbee, *Cities on the Move* (London: Oxford University Press, 1970); Yves Boquet, "From Paris and Beijing to Washington and Brasilia: The Grand Design of Capital Cities and the Early Plans for Quezon City," *Philippine Studies: Historical and Ethnographic Viewpoints* 64 (1), 2016: 43–71.

14   Edward Schatz, "When Capital Cities Move: The Political Geography of Nation and State Building," The Helen Kellogg Institute for International Studies Working Paper #303 (2003), 5, https://kellogg.nd.edu/publications/workingpapers/WPS/303.pdf, accessed 17 Aug. 2014.

15   Toynbee, *Cities on the Move*, 83–84, 139; Boquet, "From Paris and Beijing," 46–49. On the historical trajectory of African capital cities, see G. Hamdan, "Capitals of the New Africa," in *The City in Newly Developing Countries: Readings on Urbanism and Urbanization*, ed. Gerald Breese (Englewood, NJ: Prentice-Hall, 1969).

16   T. G. McGee, *The Southeast Asian City: A Social Geography of the Primate Cities of Southeast Asia* (London: Bell, 1967); Robert Reed, "The Colonial Origins of Manila and Batavia: Desultory Notes on Nascent Metropolitan Primacy and Urban Systems in Southeast Asia," *Asian Studies* 5 (3), 1967: 543–62, esp. 549–53.

17   Ross King, *Kuala Lumpur and Putrajaya: Negotiating Urban Space in Malaysia* (Singapore: NUS Press, 2008).

18   Michael Pinches, "Modernisation and the Quest for Modernity: Architectural Form, Squatter Settlements, and the New Society in Manila," in *Cultural Identity and Urban Change in Southeast Asia: Interpretive Essays*, ed. M. R. Askew and W. S. Logan (Geelong, VIC: Deakin University Press, 1994), 17–18.

19   Benedict Anderson, *Imagined Communities: Reflections on the Origin and Spread of Nationalism* (Pasig City: Anvil, 2003); Ho and Hsiao, "Globalization and Asia-Pacific Capital Cities," 5–6.

20   Anderson, *Imagined Communities*; Michael Charleston B. Chua, "Ang Paghiraya sa Nasyon: Ang mga Pagdiriwang ng Anibersaryo ng Komonwelt ng Pilipinas (1936–1941)" [Imagining the Nation: Celebrations of the Anniversary of the Philippine Commonwealth (1936–1941)], *Social Science Diliman* 4 (1–2), 2007: 91–127, esp. 92–93. Ilustrados, which literally means "enlightened ones," refer to the middle- and upper-class Filipino males who comprised the educated class of the late nineteenth century. On the ilustrados and their role in the Propaganda Movement, see John N. Schumacher, *The Propaganda Movement, 1880–1895: The Creation of a Filipino Consciousness, the Making of the Revolution* (Quezon City: Ateneo de Manila University Press, 1997).

21   Resil B. Mojares, *Brains of the Nation: Pedro Paterno, T. H. Pardo de Tavera, Isabelo de los Reyes and the Production of Modern Knowledge* (Quezon City: Ateneo de Manila University Press, 2006), 493–95. See also Michael Cullinane, *Ilustrado Politics: Filipino Elite Responses to American Rule, 1898–1908* (Quezon City: Ateneo de Manila University Press, 2003).

22   The two most important primary documents needed to accomplish this task are: Committee on Capital City Site, *Report of the Committee on Capital City Site, Manila, April*

7, 1947 (Manila: Committee on Capital City Site); and Capital City Planning Commission, *The Master Plan for the New Capital City* (Manila: Capital City Planning Commission, 1949).

23   Robert Fishman, *Urban Utopias in the Twentieth Century: Ebenezer Howard, Frank Lloyd Wright, and Le Corbusier* (Cambridge: MIT Press, 1977).

24   T. G. McGee defines *desakota* as "regions of an intense mixture of agricultural and nonagricultural activities that often stretch along corridors between large city cores," "The Emergence of *Desakota* Regions in Asia: Expanding a Hypothesis," in *The Extended Metropolis: Settlement Transition in Asia*, ed. Norton Ginsburg, Bruce Koppel, and T. G. McGee (Honolulu: University of Hawai'i Press, 1991), 7. Specifically, McGee classifies Manila as a type-3 desakota, characterized by high density but with slow economic growth, often located close to secondary urban centers and exhibit surplus labor and persistent low productivity in agricultural and nonagricultural activities (ibid., 8–9, 13). For more on desakotas, see Terry McGee, "The Spatiality of Urbanization: The Policy Challenges of Mega-Urban and Desakota Regions of Southeast Asia," UNU-IAS Working Papers No. 161, Apr. 2009, http://archive.ias.unu.edu/resource_centre/161%20Terry%20McGee.pdf, accessed 26 Oct. 2016; Harold Brookfield, Abdul Samad Hadi, and Zaharah Mahmud, *The City in the Village: The In-Situ Urbanization of Villages, Villagers and Their Land around Kuala Lumpur, Malaysia* (Singapore: Oxford University Press, 1991).

25   T. G. McGee, *The Urbanization Process in the Third World: Explorations in Search of a Theory* (London: G. Bell and Sons, 1971), 35. The so-called McGee–Ginsburg thesis calls for a reevaluation of the notion that the urban-rural divide grows as urbanization intensifies (McGee, "The Emergence of *Desakota* Regions," 4–5).

26   Yap Kioe Sheng, "Peri-Urban Transformations in Southeast Asia," in *Routledge Handbook of Urbanization in Southeast Asia*, ed. Rita Padawangi (Abingdon and New York: Routledge, 2019), 31.

27   Ibid., 35.

28   Rimmer and Dick, *The City in Southeast Asia*, 49.

29   Rhoads Murphey, "City and Countryside as Ideological Issues: India and China," *Comparative Studies in Society and History* 14 (3), 1972: 250–67. Quote is on p. 253; cf. McGee, *The Urbanization Process*, 22–31.

30   Alison Mountz, "Border," in *Key Concepts in Political Geography*, ed. Carolyn Gallaher, Carl T. Dahlman, Mary Gilmartin, Alison Mountz, with Peter Shirlow (Los Angeles: Sage, 2009), 198.

31   Ibid., 200.

32   Massey, *Space, Place, and Gender*, 5, italics in orig.

33   J. W. R. Whitehand, "Fringe Belts: A Neglected Aspect of Urban Geography," *Transactions of the Institute of British Geographers* 41 (1967): 223–33.

34   David Thomas, "The Edge of the City," *Transactions of the Institute of British Geographers* 15 (2), 1990: 131–38; Alan Waterhouse, *Boundaries of the City: The Architecture of Western Urbanism* (Toronto: University of Toronto Press, 2015).

35   Charles Abrams, *The Language of Cities: A Glossary of Terms* (New York: The Viking Press, 1971), 348; Whitehand, "Fringe Belts."

36   J. R. V. Prescott, *The Geography of Frontiers and Boundaries* (London: Hutchinson University Library, 1965), 30.

37   Mike Davis, *Planet of Slums* (London: Verso, 2007), 46.

38   Mountz, "Border," 200.

39   Ernesto M. Macatuno, "The Big City," *Sunday Times Magazine*, 15 Aug. 1971: 26–27. Quote is on p. 26.

260   A CAPITAL CITY AT THE MARGINS

40   To an extent, the red-light district in Ermita, Manila, affirms Ernest Burgess's well-known concentric zone model, which holds that places of vice cluster near the center. Nonetheless, the mere presence of red-light districts in Manila's outskirts should be enough reason to be cautious about the applicability of such Western-derived frameworks.

41   In any country, the capital city represents opportunities for monetary gain. Toynbee gives the example of Brazil, where, following the announcement of the decision to build a new capital city, a huge number of poor Brazilians trooped to Brasilia to take advantage of the situation by grabbing the new jobs that the city created (*Cities on the Move*, 226). The book uses the word "slum" to emphasize the income-poor character of informal communities and not as a way to denigrate the individuals that inhabit them or their mode of living.

42   McGee, *The Urbanization Process*, 53.

43   Salvador Lopez, "Quezon City: Cinderella Capital of the Philippines," *Philippine Planning Journal* 4 (2) / 5 (1–2), 1973/1974: 9–13.

44   By definition, conurbation denotes a "large, unplanned aggregation of urban communities" (Abrams, *The Language of Cities*, 72).

45   Manuel Duldulao, *Quezon City* (Makati: Japuzinni, 1995); Celso Almadin Carunungan, *Quezon City: A Saga of Progress* (Quezon City: Cultural and Tourism Affairs Office, Office of the Mayor, 1982); Donovan Storey, "Whose Model City? Poverty, Prosperity and the Battle over 'Progress' in Quezon City," in *Asian Futures, Asian Traditions*, ed. Edwina Palmer (Folkestone, Kent, UK: Global Oriental, 2005)"; Edson Cabalfin, "The Politics of the Nation in the Urban Form of Informal Settlements in Quezon City, Philippines," in *Reading the Architecture of the Underprivileged Classes: A Perspective on the Protests and Upheavals in Our Cities*, ed. Nnamdi Elleh (Surrey, England: Ashgate, 2014).

46   Ma. Luisa T. Camagay, "Ang Papel ng mga Siyudad/Lungsod sa Kasaysayan ng Pilipinas: Isang Paglilinaw" [The Role of Cities in Philippine History: A Clarification], in *The Journal of History: Selected Papers on Cities in Philippine History*, ed. Maria Luisa T. Camagay and Bernardita Reyes Churchill (Quezon City: Philippine National Historical Society, 2000).

47   Manuel Caoili, *The Origins of Metropolitan Manila: A Political and Social Analysis* (Quezon City: University of the Philippines Press, 1999). Similar examples include Robert Reed's two books, *City of Pines: The Origins of Baguio as a Colonial Hill Station and Regional Capital* (Baguio City: A-Seven, 1999) and *Colonial Manila: The Context of Hispanic Urbanism and Process of Morphogenesis* (Berkeley: University of California Press, 1978) and Maria Luisa T. Camagay, *Kasaysayang Panlipunan ng Maynila, 1765–1898* [The Social History of Manila, 1765–1898] (Quezon City: M. L. T. Camagay, 1992).

48   Mary R. Hollnsteiner, "The Urbanization of Metropolitan Manila," in *Changing South-East Asian Cities*, ed. Y. M. Yeung and C. P. Lo (Singapore: Oxford University Press, 1976); D. J. Dwyer, "The Problem of In-migration and Squatter Settlement in Asian Cities: Two Case Studies, Manila and Victoria-Kowloon," in *Changing South-East Asian Cities*, ed. Y. M. Yeung and C. P. Lo (Singapore: Oxford University Press, 1976); Catherine Guéguen, "Moving from Binondo to the 'Chinese Villages' of the Suburbs: A Geographical Study of the Chinese in Metro-Manila," *Journal of Chinese Overseas* 6 (2010): 119–37; Paulo Alcazaren, Luis Ferrer, and Benvenuto Icamina, *Lungsod Iskwater: The Evolution of Informality as a Dominant Pattern in Philippine Cities* (Pasig City: Anvil, 2011); Alvin A. Camba, "Private-led Suburbanization: Capital Accumulation and Real Estate Development in Postwar Greater Manila, 1945–1960," *Philippine Social Science Review* 63 (2), 2011: 1–29.

49   Cristina Evangelista Torres, *The Americanization of Manila, 1898–1921* (Quezon City: University of the Philippines Press, 2010); Camba, "Private-led Suburbanization"; Michael D. Pante, "Peripheral Pockets of Paradise: Perceptions of Health and Geography in Early

Twentieth-Century Manila and Its Environs," *Philippine Studies* 59 (2), 2011: 187–212. Artistic works by the likes of Lino Brocka, Ishmael Bernal, Nick Joaquin, Edgardo Reyes, and many others form the foundation of Manila's status as a "storied" place, an attribute that Quezon City lacks because of its newness. Chapter 5 elaborates on this contrast. On Manila as a primate city, see Michael McPhelin, "Manila: The Primate City," *Philippine Studies* 17 (4), 1969: 781–89.

50   Examples of non-Metro Manila Philippine urban histories are Reed, *City of Pines*; Concepcion G. Briones, *Life in Old Parian* (Cebu City: Cebuano Studies Center, University of San Carlos, 1983); Resil B. Mojares, "'Daybayan': A Cultural History of Space in a Visayan City," *Philippine Quarterly of Culture and Society* 40 (3–4), 2012: 170–86; Danilo Madrid Gerona, *La Ciudad de Nueva Caceres: The Rise of a Sixteenth Century Spanish City* (n.p.: Galleon Publisher, 2014).

51   Norton S. Ginsburg, "The Great City in Southeast Asia," *American Journal of Sociology* 60 (5), 1955: 455–62; Aprodicio A. Laquian, "The Asian City and the Political Process," in *The City as a Centre of Change in Asia*, ed. D. J. Dwyer (Hong Kong: Hong Kong University Press, 1972); Dwyer, "The Problem of In-migration."

52   Ronaldo B. Mactal, *Kalusugang Pampubliko sa Kolonyal na Maynila, 1898–1918: Heograpiya, Medisina, Kasaysayan* [Public Health in Colonial Manila, 1898–1918: Geography, Medicine, History] (Quezon City: University of the Philippines Press, 2009); Pante, "Peripheral Pockets of Paradise."

53   For example, Evers and Korff, *Southeast Asian Urbanism*; Rimmer and Dick, *The City in Southeast Asia*; King, *Kuala Lumpur and Putrajaya*.

54   Cf. Mojares, "'Daybayan.'"

55   Philippine Commonwealth, "Commonwealth Act No. 502: An Act to Create Quezon City," 1939, Chan Robles Virtual Law Library, http://www.chanrobles.com/commonwealthactno502.htm#.UIDpYmcv8sE, accessed 18 Oct. 2012; Committee on Capital City Site, "Report of the Committee on Capital City Site"; Capital City Planning Commission, *The Master Plan for the New Capital City*. Unfortunately, no extant copies of annual city reports of the Quezon City government during the period under study are available in the libraries and archives consulted for this research.

56   People's Homesite and Housing Corporation (PHHC), "Basic Reference Manual, as of December 31, 1968," unpublished document, copy available at the UP Diliman Main Library.

57   For example, US Bureau of the Census, *Census of the Philippines, Taken under the Direction of the Philippine Commission in the Year 1903*, 4 vols. (Washington, DC: United States Bureau of the Census, 1905); Philippine Islands Census Office, *Census of the Philippine Islands Taken under the Direction of the Philippine Legislature in the Year 1918* (Manila: Bureau of Printing, 1920); Philippine Commission of the Census, *Census of the Philippines, 1939*, 3 vols. (Manila: Bureau of Printing, 1940).

58   On urban government vis-à-vis urban governance, see Shane Ewen, *What is Urban History?* (Cambridge: Polity, 2016), 64–70.

59   Isayas Salonga, *Rizal Province Directory*, vol. 1: *History, Government and General Information with the Full Text of the Philippine Independence Law* (Manila: General Printing Press, 1934); Isayas Salonga, *Rizal Province Today: A Souvenir of the Province of Rizal Depicting Its History and Progress* (Manila: Salonga Publishing Company, 1940); A. V. H. Hartendorp, *History of Industry and Trade of the Philippines* (Manila: American Chamber of Commerce, 1958); A. V. H. Hartendorp, *History of Industry and Trade of the Philippines: The Magsaysay Administration* (Manila: Philippine Education Company, 1961); UP, *Resurgence of the University* (Manila: University of the Philippines, 1948); UP,

262 A CAPITAL CITY AT THE MARGINS

University Perspectives: Reports of the President's Ad Hoc Committees (Quezon City: University of the Philippines, 1962–63).

60 Manuel Luis Quezon, *Quezon in His Speeches*, ed. Pedro de la Llana and F. B. Icasiano (Manila: State Publishing, 1937); Sergio R. Mistica, *President Manuel Luis Quezon as I Knew Him: A Character Study from Anecdotes and Other Sources* (n.p.: Capt. S. R. Mistica and F. R. Roman, 1947).

61 Authorized biographies include Isabelo P. Caballero and M. de Gracia Concepcion, *Quezon: The Story of a Nation and Its Foremost Statesman* (Manila: International Publishers, 1935) and G. H. Enosawa, *Manuel L. Quezon: From Nipa House to Malacañan* (Tokyo: Japan Publicity Agency, 1940). Early postwar hagiographies include Sol H. Gwekoh, *Manuel L. Quezon: His Life and Career* (Manila: University Publishing Company, 1948) and Carlos Quirino, *Quezon: Paladin of Philippine Freedom* (Manila: Filipiniana Book Guild, 1971). The more recent and more critical assessments of Quezon's political career include Aruna Gopinath, *Manuel L. Quezon: The Tutelary Democrat* (Quezon City: New Day, 1987); Theodore Friend, *Between Two Empires: Philippines' Ordeal and Development from the Great Depression through the Pacific War, 1929–1946* (Manila: Solidaridad, 1964); Alfred McCoy, "Quezon's Commonwealth: The Emergence of Philippine Authoritarianism," in *Philippine Colonial Democracy*, ed. Ruby Paredes (Quezon City: Ateneo de Manila University Press, 1989); and Storey, "Whose Model City?"

62 Eva-Lotta E. Hedman and John T. Sidel, *Philippine Politics and Society in the Twentieth Century: Colonial Legacies, Post-Colonial Trajectories* (London: Routledge, 2000), 128.

1. From Cattle Rustlers to Cabaret Dancers

1 McGee, *The Southeast Asian City*, 29–51; Anthony Reid, *Southeast Asia in the Age of Commerce, 1450–1680*, vol. 1: *The Lands below the Winds* (New Haven: Yale University Press, 1988).

2 Daniel F. Doeppers, "The Development of Philippine Cities before 1900," *The Journal of Asian Studies* 31 (4), 1972: 769–92, esp. 770–71.

3 Ibid., 774–75.

4 Reed, *Colonial Manila*, 41–43; Donn Vordis Hart, *The Philippine Plaza Complex: A Focal Point in Cultural Change* (New Haven: Southeast Asia Studies, Yale University, 1955).

5 Doeppers, "The Development of Philippine Cities," 772; Reed, *Colonial Manila*.

6 Reed, *Colonial Manila*.

7 The same form was used in the Americas, a way to "see", "patrol" and manage space to prevent indigenous attacks or rebellions. For the full text of Philip II's decree regarding "Prescriptions for the Foundation of Hispanic Colonial Towns," see Gerard Lico and Lorelei D. C. de Viana, *Regulating Colonial Spaces (1565–1944): A Collection of Laws, Decrees, Proclamations, Ordinances, Orders and Directives on Architecture and the Built Environment during the Colonial Eras in the Philippines* (Manila: National Commission for Culture and the Arts, 2017), 21–24.

8 Reed, *Colonial Manila*, 43.

9 Doeppers, "The Development of Philippine Cities," 769, 778–79, 782; Jose Victor Z. Torres, *Ciudad Murada: A Walk through Historic Intramuros* (Manila: Intramuros Administration; Vibal, 2005), 1–6.

10 Ibid., 1–6.

11 Reed, "The Colonial Origins of Manila and Batavia," 553–62.

NOTES   263

12   Raquel A. G. Reyes, "Flaunting It: How the Galleon Trade Made Manila, circa 1571–1800," *Early American Studies: An Interdisciplinary Journal* 15 (4), 2017: 683–713; David A. Smith and Roger J. Nemeth, "Urban Development in Southeast Asia: An Historical Structural Analysis," in *Urbanisation in the Developing World*, ed. David Drakakis-Smith (London: Croom Helm, 1986), 127–31. On colonial Batavia and Malacca, see McGee, *The Southeast Asian City*, 49–51; Barbara Watson Andaya and Leonard Y. Andaya, *A History of Malaysia*, 2nd ed. (Honolulu: University of Hawai'i Press, 2001), 58–65.

13   Isagani Medina, "Beyond Intramuros: The Beginnings of Extramuros de Manila up to the 19th Century—A Historical Overview," in *Manila: Selected Papers of the Annual Conferences of the Manila Studies Association, 1989–1993*, ed. Bernardita Churchill (Quezon City: Manila Studies Association, 1994).

14   Edgar Wickberg, *The Chinese Mestizo in Philippine History* (Manila: Kaisa para sa Kaunlaran, 2001).

15   Nicholas P. Cushner, *Landed Estates in the Colonial Philippines*, Monograph Series no. 20 (New Haven: Yale University, Southeast Asia Studies, 1976), 10.

16   On the impact of the Church on land tenure in the Philippines, see John Leddy Phelan, *The Hispanization of the Philippines: Spanish Aims and Filipino Responses, 1565–1700* (Metro Manila: Cacho Hermanos, 1985), 116–18. The Jesuits' Mariquina estate was also known as Hacienda de Jesús de la Peña, Horacio de la Costa, *The Jesuits in the Philippines, 1581–1768*, reprint ed. (Quezon City: Ateneo de Manila University Press, 2014), 268–69. This book uses "Mariquina" to refer to the estate and "Marikina" to denote the town.

17   Cushner, *Landed Estates*, 12–36. This book uses "Mandaloya" to refer to the Augustinian estate east of Manila and "Mandaluyong" to refer to the town. An estancia is a royal land grant of about 1,700 hectares for cattle grazing. On Hacienda de Tala, see Marshall S. McLennan, *The Central Luzon Plain: Land and Society on the Inland Frontier* (Quezon City: Alemar-Phoenix, 1980), 91–92. For a list of friar estates, their former owners, mode and year of acquisition, and other pertinent details, see Rene R. Escalante, *The American Friar Lands Policy: Its Framers, Context, and Beneficiaries, 1898–1916* (Manila: De La Salle University Press, 2002), 24–29.

18   Erwin Schoenstein, OFM, "San Pedro Bautista in the Philippines," in *400 Years, 1578–1978: Franciscans in the Philippines*, ed. Jesús Galindo (Manila: Franciscans in the Philippines, 1979), 125. In 1613 the Franciscans moved the convent to Sampaloc due to the supposed unsanitary conditions in San Francisco del Monte, although they retained control over the old site until the American colonial period (Martin R. Gaerlan, *Sampaloc's Sacred Ground: The Franciscan Backstory [1613–1918]* [Quezon City: Martin R. Gaerlan and Gaerlan Management Consulting, 2014]), 16. The Franciscan church in San Francisco del Monte is also historic because it was constructed under the direction of San Pedro Bautista (Saint Peter the Baptist), one of the twenty-six martyrs executed in Nagasaki, Japan, on 5 Feb. 1597, upon Toyotomi Hideyoshi's orders, Schoenstein, "San Pedro Bautista in the Philippines," 128–29.

19   Cushner, *Landed Estates*, 12–45.

20   Ibid., 57.

21   Ibid., 59–66; Dennis Morrow Roth, *The Friar Estates of the Philippines* (Albuquerque: University of New Mexico Press, 1977), 100–116; Fernando Palanco Aguado, "The Tagalog Revolts of 1745 according to Spanish Primary Sources," *Philippine Studies* 58 (1–2), 2010: 45–77. The Real Audiencia was the highest court of the Spanish colonial state.

22   Doeppers, "The Development of Philippine Cities," 783.

264   A CAPITAL CITY AT THE MARGINS

23   The two haciendas, though not that fertile, were devoted to planting rice, sugarcane, indigo, coffee, and other crops (Jaime Balcos Veneracion, *Kasaysayan ng Bulakan* [Cologne: Bahay-Saliksikan ng Kasaysayan, 1986], 100; McLennan, *The Central Luzon Plain*, 92–93; Leopoldo R. Serrano, *A Brief History of Caloocan* [Manila: L. R. Serrano, 1960], 2). On the circumstances surrounding the Jesuit expulsion and its repercussions, see De la Costa, *The Jesuits in the Philippines*. By the nineteenth century, a Tuason-owned company owned much of Hacienda de Maysilo (Daniel F. Doeppers, *Feeding Manila in Peace and War, 1850–1945* [Madison: University of Wisconsin Press, 2016], 99).

24   Benito Legarda, Jr., *After the Galleons: Foreign Trade, Economic Change and Entrepreneurship in the Nineteenth-Century Philippines* (Quezon City: Ateneo de Manila University Press, 1999); Doeppers, "The Development of Philippine Cities," 784–88; Daniel F. Doeppers, "Migration to Manila: Changing Gender Representation, Migration Field, and Urban Structure," in *Population and History: The Demographic Origins of the Modern Philippines*, ed. Daniel F. Doeppers and Peter Xenos (Quezon City: Ateneo de Manila University Press, 1998).

25   Wickberg, *The Chinese Mestizo*; Edgar Wickberg, *The Chinese in Philippine Life, 1850–1898* (Quezon City: Ateneo de Manila University Press, 2000); John Foreman, *The Philippine Islands* (Mandaluyong: Cacho Hermanos, 1985), 344; Camagay, *Kasaysayang Panlipunan ng Maynila*, 11–13; Medina, "Beyond Intramuros," 52.

26   Lorelei de Viana, *Three Centuries of Binondo Architecture, 1594–1898: A Socio-Historical Perspective* (Manila: UST Publishing House, 2001); Xavier Huetz de Lemps, "Materiales Ligeros vs. Materiales Fuertes [Light Materials vs Strong Materials]: The Conflict between Nipa Huts and Stone Buildings in 19th-Century Manila," in *The Philippine Revolution and beyond*, vol. 1, ed. Elmer Ordoñez (Manila: Philippine Centennial Commission, 1998); Greg Bankoff, "A Tale of Two Cities: The Pyro-Seismic Morphology of Nineteenth-Century Manila," in *Flammable Cities: Urban Conflagration and the Making of the Modern World*, ed. Greg Bankoff, Uwe Lübken, and Jordan Sand (Madison: University of Wisconsin Press, 2012). For a sample of Manila ordinances pertaining to this morphological segregation, see Lico and de Viana, *Regulating Colonial Spaces*, 32–33; 54–72, 83.

27   US Bureau of the Census, *Census of the Philippines*, vol. 4, 601; John Bowring, *A Visit to the Philippine Islands* (Manila: Filipiniana Book Guild, 1963), 15–16; Foreman, *The Philippine Islands*, 348–49; Camagay, *Kasaysayang Panlipunan ng Maynila*, 16–17.

28   Fernando N. Zialcita and Martin I. Tinio, Jr., *Philippine Ancestral Houses (1810–1930)* (Quezon City: GCF, 1980); Gerard Lico, *Arkitekturang Filipino: A History of Architecture and Urbanism in the Philippines* (Quezon City: University of the Philippines Press, 2008), 158–65.

29   Maria Luisa T. Camagay, *Working Women in Manila in the 19th Century* (Quezon City: University of the Philippines Press; Center for Women's Studies, 1995); Daniel F. Doeppers, "Migrants in Urban Labor Markets: The Social Stratification of Tondo and Sampaloc in the 1890s," in *Population and History: The Demographic Origins of the Modern Philippines*, ed. Daniel F. Doeppers and Peter Xenos (Quezon City: Ateneo de Manila University Press, 1998), 256.

30   Huetz de Lemps, "Materiales Ligeros," 162.

31   Xavier Huetz de Lemps, "Shifts in Meaning of 'Manila' in the Nineteenth Century," in *Old Ties and New Solidarities: Studies on Philippine Communities*, ed. Charles Macdonald and Guillermo Pesigan (Quezon City: Ateneo de Manila University Press, 2000); Foreman, *The Philippine Islands*, 344. Malacañang has been the official residence of the country's head of state ever since.

32 Jaime Escobar y Lozano, *El Indicador del Viajero en las Islas Filipinas* [Guide for Travelers in the Philippine Islands] (Manila: Tipo-Litografía de Chofre y Cia, 1885), 51.

33 Otto van den Muijzenberg, *The Philippines through European Lenses: Late 19th Century Photographs from the Meerkamp van Embden Collection* (Quezon City: Ateneo de Manila University Press, 2008), 55–56.

34 Gaerlan, *Sampaloc's Sacred Ground*, 49.

35 Richard T. Chu and Teresita Ang See, "Toward a History of Chinese Burial Grounds in Manila during the Spanish Colonial Period," *Archipel: Études Interdisciplinaires sur le Monde Insulindien* 92 (2016): 63–90, http://archipel.revues.org/283, accessed 17 Oct. 2017. A cemetery for non-Spanish foreigners (mostly Westerners) was built in San Pedro Macati in the nineteenth century.

36 Manuel Sastrón, *La Insurrección en Filipinas* [The Insurrection in the Philippines], vol. I (Madrid: La Viuda de M. Minuesa de los Ríos, 1897), 197; Rosalina M. Franco-Calairo and Emmanuel Franco Calairo, *Ang Kasaysayan ng Novaliches* [The History of Novaliches] (Quezon City: Rosalina M. Franco-Calairo and Emmanuel Franco Calairo, 1997), 53–65; Veneracion, *Kasaysayan ng Bulakan*, 137; Eladio Neira, *Glimpses into the History of San Juan, MM* (San Juan: Life Today, 1994), 95–99; Z. A. Salazar, *Agosto 29–30, 1896: Ang Pagsalakay ni Bonifacio sa Maynila*, trans. Monico M. Atienza (Quezon City: Miranda Bookstore, 1994), 1–41; Greg Bankoff, *Crime, Society, and the State in the Nineteenth-Century Philippines* (Quezon City: Ateneo de Manila University Press, 1996), 61; Foreman, *The Philippine Islands*, 238; "Historical Data and Cultural Life of Bago-Bantay," 2, HDP: Province of Rizal, Quezon City, History of Barrios (NLP, Manila); Santiago V. Alvarez, *The Katipunan and the Revolution*, trans. Paula Carolina S. Malay (Quezon City: Ateneo de Manila University Press, 1992), 17–27, 145–48, 163–65; Vic Hurley, *Jungle Patrol: The Story of the Philippine Constabulary* (Mandaluyong City: Cacho Hermanos, 1985), 77. Balara's significance to the revolution was such that at the time of Bonifacio's fateful stay in Cavite from December 1896 to May 1897, his companions were referred to as "Balara Men" (Soledad Borromeo-Buehler, *Scripted by Men, Not by Fate: Andres Bonifacio in Cavite. An Analytical Narrative with Commentary on Selected Sources* [Quezon City: University of the Philippines Press, 2017], 8, 21, 149, 169). San Mateo's importance for revolutionaries was due to Mount Tapusi, which they believed was where mythical hero Bernardo Carpio was imprisoned (Reynaldo Clemeña Ileto, *Pasyon and Revolution: Popular Movements in the Philippines, 1840–1910* [Quezon City: Ateneo de Manila University Press, 1979], 99–103). Historians have yet to reach a consensus as to the location, as well as the date, of the first cry of the Revolution, whether it was Balintawak or Pugad Lawin. Both sites were then under Caloocan and are now part of Quezon City. On this historiographical impasse, see Soledad Borromeo-Buehler, *The Cry of Balintawak: A Contrived Controversy* (Quezon City: Ateneo de Manila University Press, 1998). Cf. Serrano, *A Brief History of Caloocan*, 4.

37 Gaerlan, *Sampaloc's Sacred Ground*, 89–90. Aguinaldo referred to these blockhouses as "bahay calapate" (pigeon houses) (Benito J. Legarda, Jr., *The Hills of Sampaloc: The Opening Actions of the Philippine-American War, February 4–5, 1899* [Makati: Bookmark, 2001], 7).

38 Ruby Paredes, "For Want of a City: Manila in the Balance of Resistance and Capitulation," in *The Philippine Revolution and beyond*, vol. 2, ed. Elmer Ordoñez (Manila: Philippine Centennial Commission, 1998), 621; Michael D. Pante, "Prolonged Decline: Intramuros during the American Colonial Period," in *Manila: Selected Papers of the 22nd Annual Manila Studies Conference*, ed. Bernardita Reyes Churchill, Marya Svetlana T. Camacho,

and Lorelei D. C. de Viana (Manila: Manila Studies Association; National Commission for Culture and the Arts, 2014).

39   Municipal Board of Manila, *Report of the Municipal Board of the City of Manila for the Period from August 7, 1901, to June 30, 1902* (Manila: Bureau of Public Printing, 1903), 7.

40   Walter Robb, "The Growth of a City: Manila," *American Chamber of Commerce Journal (ACCJ)* 10 (2), 1930: 9, 11.

41   Nick Joaquin, *Manila, My Manila: A History for the Young* (Manila: The City of Manila, 1990), 137.

42   Pante, "Prolonged Decline."

43   Gaerlan, *Sampaloc's Sacred Ground*, 98–103.

44   Esperanza Bunag Gatbonton, *Intramuros: A Historical Guide* (Manila: Intramuros Administration, 1980), 15.

45   "Demolition of City Walls," *Manila Times (MT)*, 25 June 1903, 1.

46   Pante, "Prolonged Decline"; Lewys Harsant, "Medieval and Modern Manila," *Manila Times Anniversary Issue*, 1911, 37–40.

47   Daniel Burnham, "Report on Proposed Improvements at Manila," in Philippine Commission, *Report of the Philippine Commission to the President, 1905*, part 1, 627–35 (Washington, DC: Government Printing Office, 1905). On the ideological value of American urban planning, see Ian Morley, "Modern Urban Designing in the Philippines, 1898–1916," *Philippine Studies: Historical and Ethnographic Viewpoints* 64 (1), 2016: 3–42. The phrase "imperial makeover" is from Daniel F. Doeppers, "Manila's Imperial Makeover: Security, Health, and Symbolism," in *Colonial Crucible: Empire in the Making of the Modern American State*, ed. Alfred W. McCoy and Francisco A. Scarano (Quezon City: Ateneo de Manila University Press, 2010).

48   Pante, "Peripheral Pockets of Paradise," 202–6. One could also argue that this trend was connected to the tendency among many Manila Americans to maintain a rather insulated lifestyle (Florence Horn, *Orphans of the Pacific: The Philippines* [New York: Reynal and Hitchcock, 1941], 90–91; Gerald E. Wheeler, "The American Minority in the Philippines during the Prewar Commonwealth Period," *Asian Studies* 4 (2), 1966: 362–73, esp. 362.

49   In 1905 American John Bancroft Devins commented, "Rents in Manila are absurdly high, and the food supply is proportionately dear. It costs me about one-third more to live here than it did in Boston." His remarks were an exaggeration, but they revealed that living in Manila was quite expensive (*An Observer in the Philippines: Or, Life in Our New Possessions* [Boston: American Tract Society, 1905], 319).

50   Phil D. Carman, "Real Estate," *ACCJ* 1 (4), 1921: 23.

51   Philippine Commission of the Census, *Census of the Philippines, 1939: Special Bulletin No. 3 (Real Property)* (Manila: Bureau of Printing, 1940), 612–13.

52   "Report of the Mayor of the City of Manila to the Honorable the Secretary of the Interior, Covering the Period from January 1 to June 30, 1939," unpublished report, 17, Manuel L. Quezon Papers (MLQP) Series VIII, Box 47; Robb, "The Growth of a City," 9; Jesus V. Merrit, "The Shame of Manila," *Philippines Free Press (PFP)*, 16 Mar. 1940: 60–61.

53   Joshena Ingersoll, *Golden Years in the Philippines* (Palo Alto, California: Pacific Books, 1971), 33.

54   Although often used interchangeably, the terms "squatter" and "slum dweller" have different meanings. A squatter is one "who settles on the rural or urban land of another without title or right," while a slum is a "building or area that is deteriorated, hazardous, unsanitary, or lacking in standard conveniences" (Abrams, *The Language of Cities*, 285–

86, 294). However, since many of those who live in squalid conditions in the city are illegal settlers, the said terms are often conflated with one another.

55 Huetz de Lemps, "Materiales Ligeros"; Bankoff, "A Tale of Two Cities"; Alcazaren et al., *Lungsod Iskwater*, 4–5.

56 Alcazaren et al., *Lungsod Iskwater*, 5–9; Mactal, *Kalusugang Pampubliko*, 33–40; "Trend of the City's Growth," *MT*, 6 Feb. 1905: 3.

57 Walter Robb, "The Drab amid the Beautiful," *ACCJ* 10 (11), 1930: 8–9; Mactal, *Kalusugang Pampubliko*, 105–31.

58 Leon Ty, "A Real Tenancy Problem," *PFP*, 29 July 1939: 20–23. Quotes are from p. 20. Accesorias were single- or two-story multiunit structures that were often rented out and had commercial establishments at the ground floor and residential spaces at the second floor, similar to the shophouses of urban Southeast Asia (Lico, *Arkitekturang Filipino*, 168–69).

59 Ty, "A Real Tenancy Problem," 21; Merrit, "The Shame of Manila," 61.

60 See the following documents found in the Joseph Ralston Hayden Papers (JRHP) Box 15, Folder 16: Charles H. Forster, "Report of the Committee Appointed by His Excellency the Governor-General by Executive Order No. 450"; Memo of A. D. Williams for Hon. Ramon Torres, Secretary of Labor, 6 July 1935; Memo of Fermin Alvarez for Secretary Torres, 30 Jan. 1935; C. M. Hoskins, "Project for Providing Low-Priced Houses in Manila for those Affected by Slum Clearance"; C. M. Hoskins, "Manila Housing and Slum Clearance as a Whole." See also G. C. Dunham, Memo for Governor-General, 10 Jan. 1935, JRHP Box 15, Folder 17; Ramon Torres, Memorandum for the Governor-General, 15 July 1935, Frank Murphy Papers (FMP) Box 52, Folder 27. On Commonwealth-era programs, see Manuel Quezon, *Message of His Excellency, Manuel Quezon, President of the Philippines, to the 1st National Assembly (Second state of the nation address), 16 Oct 1937*, MLQP Series III, Box 19; Manuel Quezon, *Fourth Annual Report of the President of the Philippines to the President and the Congress of the United States Covering the Period January 1 to June 30, 1939* (Manila: Bureau of Printing, 1940), 8–12; Sergio Osmeña, *The City Hall and a New and Beautiful Manila* (Manila: Bureau of Printing, 1941), 5.

61 Ty, "A Real Tenancy Problem," 22; "The Hard-Working Man Deserves a Home," *Philippine Graphic (PG)*, 3 Nov. 1938: 2–3, 79.

62 "Houses Built for Workmen Create Puzzle," *Manila Daily Bulletin (MDB)*, 26 Mar. 1936, JRHP Box 26, Folder 19; "Board against Mayor's Social Service Plan," *MDB*, 6 Mar. 1937, JRHP Box 26, Folder 20. See also "Tondo Dwellers Sniff at City's Nice New Apartment Houses for P6.70," *MDB*, 15 June 1938, JRHP Box 26, Folder 6.

63 Doeppers describes the prewar suburbs as a "Metropolitan Garden Ring," *Feeding Manila*, 128.

64 Isabelo de los Reyes, *El Folk-lore Filipino*, trans. Salud C. Dizon and Maria Elinora P. Imson (Quezon City: University of the Philippines Press, 1994), 504–39; Doeppers, *Feeding Manila*, 21–29.

65 "Trend of the City's Growth," 3.

66 Burnham, "Report on Proposed Improvements," 631.

67 Walter Robb, "The Growth of Manila: Changing Ermita (Fourth Paper)," *ACCJ* 10(5), 1930: 9, 11, 26–27.

68 Walter Robb, "Why Buy a Home? We May Not Be Here Long," *ACCJ* 7 (8), 1927: 12–13.

69 Ibid., 12; George Nellist, *Men of the Philippines: A Biographical Record of Men of Substantial Achievement in the Philippine Islands* (Manila: Sugar News Co, 1931), 54, 57; American Express, *Manila and the Philippines* (Manila: American Express, [1933?]), 11.

70 Lewis E. Gleeck, Jr., *The Manila Americans (1901–1964)* (Manila: Carmelo & Bauermann, 1977), 21; Robb, "Why Buy a Home?," 12; Phil Carman, "P. D. Carman Describes Remarkable Growth of Manila since American Occupation," *ACCJ* 2(3), 1922: 10–12; Wheeler, "The American Minority," 362. It is interesting to note that prehispanic Malate also served as a summer resort of native chieftains and continued to do so even after the Spanish conquest, see Antonio de Morga, *Sucesos de las Islas Filipinas*, ed. J. S. Cummins (Cambridge: Hakluyt Society, 1971), 286.

71 Ingersoll, *Golden Years*, 34; Manila Merchants Association, *Manila: The Pearl of the Orient: Guide Book to the Intending Visitor* (Manila: Manila Merchants Association, 1908), 35. See also Carman, "Real Estate," 23.

72 Robb "Why Buy a Home?," 12. On this colonial notion that linked geography with health, see Pante, "Peripheral Pockets of Paradise."

73 Joseph Earle Stevens, *The Philippines circa 1900: Yesterdays in the Philippines* (Manila: Filipiniana Book Guild, 1968), 208; Nellist, *Men of the Philippines*, 54, 57; "Enlarging the Boundaries of Manila," *ACCJ* 17 (10), 1937: 39–40; Salonga, *Rizal Province Today*, 16; Burnham, "Report on Proposed Improvements," 633–35.

74 Philippine Commission of the Census, *Census of the Philippines, 1939: Special Bulletin No. 3*, 476–77; Salonga, *Rizal Province Directory*, 137–38; "Gregorio Araneta, Inc.," *The Tribune XIV Anniversary*, 17 June 1939, 117; "San Juan Heights Co., Inc.," *The Tribune XIV Anniversary*, 17 June 1939, 118–19; Santiago Artiaga, *Brief History of San Juan del Monte, Rizal* (n.p.:n.p., n.d.), 27.

75 Pante, "Peripheral Pockets of Paradise," 201.

76 "Gregorio Araneta, Inc.," 117.

77 Harsant, "Medieval and Modern Manila," 40; Robb, "The Growth of a City: Manila," 11; "Trend of the City's Growth," 3.

78 Santiago P. Alalayan, "Economic Social Progress of Rizal Remarkable, Governor Says," *MDB*, 3 Apr. 1939, JRHP Box 26, Folder 17.

79 One example of expanded services was Manila Railroad Company's Express Pick-up and Delivery Service, Manila Railroad Company, "Don't Waste Money: Use Our Free Service," *ACCJ* 7 (7), 1927: 12.

80 Charles Abrams defined this phrase as "the idea that any movement is costly because it is restrained by gravity and physical friction and because it takes time. In order to overcome distance one has to expend time, energy, fuel, endure discomfort and delay, etc." (*The Language of Cities*, 116).

81 Cf. Kenneth T. Jackson, *Crabgrass Frontier: The Suburbanization of the United States* (Oxford: Oxford University Press, 1985), 103–15, 157–71.

82 Robb, "Why Buy a Home?," 12.

83 Francis Burton Harrison, *Eighth Annual Message of Governor-General Francis Burton Harrison to the Fifth Philippine Legislature, Delivered October 16, 1920 at the Opening of the Second Session* (Manila: Bureau of Printing, 1920), 13.

84 Leonard Wood, *Message of Governor-General Leonard Wood to the Seventh Philippine Legislature, Delivered July 16, 1925 at the Opening of the First Session* (Manila: Bureau of Printing, 1925), 11; Leonard Wood, *Message of Governor-General Leonard Wood to the Seventh Philippine Legislature, Delivered July 16, 1926 at the Opening of the Second Session* (Manila: Bureau of Printing, 1926), 12–13.

85 Eugene A. Gilmore, *Mensaje del Gobernador General Interino Eugene A. Gilmore a la Séptima Legislatura Filipina Leído el 16 de Julio de 1927 en la Apertura del Tercer Periodo de Sesiones* (Manila: Bureau of Printing, 1927), 21–25; Dwight F. Davis, *Message of*

Governor-General Dwight F. Davis to the Ninth Philippine Legislature, Delivered July 16, 1931 at the Opening of the First Session (Manila: Bureau of Printing, 1931), 33–34.

86   "'Improve City' Mayor's Plea," *MT*, 15 May 1920: 1.

87   "Enlarging the Boundaries of Manila," 39–40. Fittingly, a street in New Manila in present-day Quezon City, part of the greater Manila Gilmore envisioned, now bears his name.

88   Francis Burton Harrison, *Origins of the Philippine Republic: Extracts from the Diaries and Records of Francis Burton Harrison*, ed. Michael P. Onorato (Ithaca, NY: Cornell University, Southeast Asia Program, 1974), 23.

89   "Expansion," *ACCJ* 7 (9), 1927: 10.

90   "Expansion of City of Manila Agreed upon," *MDB*, 1 Sept. 1937; "Enlarging the Boundaries of Manila," 39–40; "Pasay Annexation to Manila is Fought; Council Passes Resolution," *MDB*, 1 Oct. 1937, JRHP Box 26, Folder 16; "Greater Manila Bill is Drafted," *Tribune*, 3 Mar. 1938, JRHP Box 26, Folder 23; Frank Murphy, "Report of the High Commissioner to the Secretary of War, July 1936" FMP Box 53, Folder 33.

91   "Annexation Is Being Fought," *MDB*, 11 July 1938, JRHP Box 26, Folder 16; "Quezon's Plan Being Opposed," *Tribune*, 15 Sept. 1937, JRHP Box 26, Folder 21; "Pasay Annexation to Manila is Fought; Council Passes Resolution," *MDB*, 1 Oct. 1937, JRHP Box 26, Folder 16. Both quotes are found in "Annexation of Towns Opposed by Residents," *MDB*, 11 July 1938, JRHP Box 26, Folder 16; "Rizal Governor Asks for More Autonomy for Municipalities," *Tribune*, 7 Feb. 1937, JRHP Box 27, Folder 2.

92   Caloocan was under Democrata leadership from 1910 to 1935 (Serrano, *A Brief History of Caloocan*, 7).

93   "Rizal Officials Oppose Manila Expansion Plan," *PG*, 18 Aug. 1938: 33.

94   Harrison, *Origins of the Philippine Republic*, 23.

95   "Rizal Officials Oppose Manila Expansion Plan," 33.

96   Carman, "P. D. Carman Describes Remarkable Growth." On the definition of *tulisan*, see Francis A. Gealogo, "Ang Hermeneutika ng Pakikipagtunggali: Ang Pagpapakahulugan sa Diskurso ng Pakikibakang Panlipunan" [The Hermeneutics of Opposition: Defining the Discourse of Social Struggle], *Philippine Social Sciences Review*, Special Issue: *Ang Kilusang Masa sa Kasaysayang Pilipino, 1900–1992* [Mass Movements in Philippine History, 1900–1992] (Jan.–Dec. 1994): 1–37, esp. 18.

97   Legarda, *The Hills of Sampaloc*; Serrano, *A Brief History of Caloocan*, 5–6; J. M. Thompson, "Report of Col. J. M. Thompson," in *Annual Reports of the War Department for the Fiscal Year Ended June 30, 1901*, part 3 (Washington, DC: Government Printing Office, 1901), 169; John R. M. Taylor, *The Philippine Insurrection against the United States: A Compilation of Documents*, vol. 1 (Pasay City: Eugenio Lopez Foundation, 1971), 194–98, 203–4, 208; John R. M. Taylor, *The Philippine Insurrection against the United States: A Compilation of Documents with Notes and Introduction*, vol. 2: *May 19, 1898 to July 4, 1902* (Pasay City: Eugenio Lopez Foundation, 1971), 325; Neira, *Glimpses into the History of San Juan*, 100; Filemon V. Tutay, "A Squatter for 70 Years," *PFP*, 24 May 1952: 6–7, 63, esp. 7.

98   On ladrones, see Gealogo, "Ang Hermeneutika ng Pakikipagtunggali," 27; Ileto, *Pasyon and Revolution*, 193. One should also note Quezon's crucial role in ending guerrilla resistance in Southern Luzon, resulting from his close collaboration with Bandholtz (Manuel Quezon, *The Good Fight: The Autobiography of Manuel Luis Quezon* [Mandaluyong: Cacho Hermanos, 1985], 88–97; cf. Cullinane, *Ilustrado Politics*).

99   US Philippine Commission, *Report of the United States Philippine Commission to the Secretary of War for the Period from December 1, 1900, to October 15, 1901*, part 2 (Washington, DC: Government Printing Office, 1901), 199; Muijzenberg, *The Philippines*

through European Lenses, 56; Franco-Calairo and Calairo, *Ang Kasaysayan ng Novaliches*, 82; Ileto, *Pasyon and Revolution*, 186; Gealogo, "Ang Hermeneutika ng Pakikipagtunggali," 28–29.

100 "Extend Limits," *MT,* 13 May 1905, 6.

101 Genoroso S. Maceda, "The Remontados of Rizal Province," *Philippine Journal of Science* 64 (1): 313–21; Escalante, *The American Friar Lands Policy*, 49–54.

102 Roth, *The Friar Estates*, 2. Ironically, for the brief period that the Philippine revolutionary government was in power, it failed to remedy the situation. After confiscating the friar haciendas, Aguinaldo's government left the administration of the estates to the *principales* (chiefs; native elite) without removing the tenants' burden of paying rent, which was an important source of funds for the First Philippine Republic (Escalante, *The American Friar Lands Policy*, 57–60).

103 Escalante, *The American Friar Lands Policy*, 93.

104 Roth, *The Friar Estates*, 1.

105 Such a corporate entity was called "*sociedad anonima*" (anonymous company), Veneracion, *Kasaysayan ng Bulakan*, 193.

106 Escalante, *The American Friar Lands Policy*, 55–56; "San Juan Heights Co., Inc.," 136–37.

107 Escalante, *The American Friar Lands Policy*, 112, 117, 135–38; Neira, *Glimpses into the History of San Juan*, 113–15. The friars' strategy of creating corporate entities to mask their control over landholdings prefigure modern-day tactics to evade agrarian reform, typified by sham land-use conversion.

108 Salvador Araneta, *Reflections of a Filipino Exile*, ed. Michael P. Onorato (Fullerton, CA: California State University, 1979), 7–8. Quote is on p. 7. Quezon, Ortigas, and Madrigal began their long-lasting friendship in the early 1890s in the law school of the Dominican-run Colegio de San Juan de Letran, Manila. Ortigas's wife, Julia Vargas Ortigas, served as president of the Philippine Tuberculosis Society, an organization actively supported by Quezon, who was also a tubercular, "Up from Ramshackles to Institute," *The Bulletin of the Quezon Institute* 1 (1), 1939: 93–103.

109 W. L. Goldsborough, "Francisco Ortigas: President of the Code Committee," *Philippine Law Journal* 1 (7), 1915: 327–29. Quote is on p. 328. For more on Ortigas's legal career, see Juan A. Cabildo, "Francisco Ortigas: His Place in Our Contemporary Esteem," *The Herald Mid-Week Magazine*, 3 Oct. 1934: 3, 13, 18, JRHP Box 31, Folder 4.

110 "Enlarging the Boundaries of Manila," 40; Salonga, *Rizal Province Directory*, 140.

111 "New Town in Rizal Planned," *MDB*, 29 Nov. 1937, JRHP Box 27, Folder 2.

112 "Recent Incorporations," *ACCJ* 2 (5), 1922: 35. Quote is from Felice Prudente Sta. Maria, "In the Steps of the Founder: A History of the City of Manuel Luis Quezon," in *Quezon City: The Rise of Asia's City of the Future*, ed. Regina A. Samson and Marily Y. Orosa (Quezon City: Local Government of Quezon City, 2010), 70. Note that map 7 does not include Magdalena Estate.

113 Cynthia Y. Sycip, *Memories of a Hero* (n.p.: n.p., 1984), 23.

114 Ibid., 25. Cf. Nick Joaquin, "Ninoy's Early Years," in *Ninoy Aquino: The Man, the Legend*, ed. Asuncion David Maramba (Mandaluyong: Cacho Hermanos, 1984), 30–31.

115 The Hemadys, Cablegram to Frank Murphy, 11 Mar. 1935, FMP Box 54, Folder 27.

116 Del Pan, Ortigas y Fisher, "Hacienda de Piedad," in Philippine Commission, *Fifth Annual Report of the Philippine Commission, 1904*, part 1 (Washington, DC: Government Printing Office, 1905), 774–75.

NOTES   271

117 Aside from Dancel, Aguinaldo also occupied a considerable size of friar land that went over the acreage limit. However, Escalante gives a different figure for Dancel's leaseholdings (1,397 acres) in Hacienda de Piedad, *The American Friar Lands Policy*, 142.

118 Felipe del Rosario, Letter to Frank Murphy, Aug. 1934, MLQP Series VII, Box 183, Folder Name: Bureau of Lands, 1934; Municipal Secretary of Montalban, Letter to Jorge B. Vargas, 17 Nov. 1919, MLQP, Series VIII, Box 74, Folder Name: Montalban; Resolution by the Municipal Government of San Mateo, Rizal, 13 Nov. 1919, MLQP Series VIII, Box 75, Folder Name: San Mateo. Prior to Quezon City's founding, Hacienda de Payatas occupied areas that were under the political jurisdictions of San Mateo, Montalban, and Marikina.

119 Carpenter was cleared for irregularities in this transaction in a highly irregular manner for he was part of the committee that investigated complaints related to the Friar Lands Act, W. Cameron Forbes, Dean C. Worcester, and Frank W. Carpenter, *The Friar-Land Inquiry* (Manila: Bureau of Printing, 1910), 73, 100. The quoted text is from "The Tala Estate," 20 Apr. 1908, p. 5, unsigned, undated, and unpublished manuscript, MLQP Series VII, Box 182, Folder Name: Bureau of Lands, 1908–11. The said document pegged Carpenter's lease holdings in Tala at 16,740 acres (6,774 hectares), a much larger area than what was officially reported. Nonetheless, a minority report of Democrats in the US Congress regarding land administration in the Philippines "singled out for condemnation the lease of the Tala estate to Executive Secretary Frank Carpenter," Frank Hindman Golay, *Face of Empire: United States–Philippine Relations, 1898–1946* (Quezon City: Ateneo de Manila University Press, 1997), 146.

120 Bureau of Lands, Letter to the Governor-General, undated and unpublished letter, MLQP Series VII, Box 183, Folder Name: Bureau of Lands, 1924. The MLQP has an undated and unsigned document supposedly authored by the US attorney general, the Philippine attorney general, and the Philippine solicitor general that states: "Looking beyond the agreement, we find from the evidence, the creation of an American landlord who is an executive officer of the Philippine government with a private estate being and to be improved out of the Insular Treasury. Comment upon such a transaction is superfluous." "The Opinions of the Attorney General of the United States and of the Attorney General and Solicitor General of the Philippine Islands Do Not Sustain the Sales of the San Jose and Tala Estates," undated and unsigned document, 2, MLQP, Series VII, Box 183, Folder Name: Bureau of Lands, Undated. For a more sympathetic account of Carpenter's career, see Lewis E. Gleeck, Jr., "Achievement and Tragedy: The Life of Frank W. Carpenter," *Bulletin of the American Historical Collection* 19 (1), 1991: 70–78. Gleeck asserts that the accusations against Carpenter were baseless and that the Tala mango farm and cattle-raising business were funded by a PhP50,000 *en gratia* payment from the Philippine Congress at the end of Carpenter's tenure in Mindanao. Gleeck, however, cites no sources for this statement.

121 "Medieval 'Mayorazgo' Precipitates Legal Battle," *ACCJ* 6 (12), 1926: 15–17; "Christian Centuries," *ACCJ* 20 (11), 1940: 7, 12; Doeppers, *Feeding Manila*, 99, 131; Legarda, *After the Galleons*, 315–17.

122 Luciano P. R. Santiago, "The Last Hacendera: Doña Teresa de la Paz, 1841–1890," *Philippine Studies* 46 (3), 1998: 340–60. Quote is on p. 340.

123 Doeppers, *Feeding Manila*, 131; Tutay, "A Squatter for 70 Years," 7.

124 Otto van den Muijzenberg, ed., trans., *Colonial Manila, 1909–1912: Three Dutch Travel Accounts* (Quezon City: Ateneo de Manila University Press, 2016), 118. Rouffaer mistook Diliman for an encomienda, which denotes a group of households for tax-collection purposes.

125 "Medieval 'Mayorazgo,'" 15; Walter Robb, "Santa Mesa Heights" (Growth of Manila Series, 6th Paper), *ACCJ* 10 (7), 1930: 5–7; "Gregorio Araneta, Inc.," 117.

126 "Medieval 'Mayorazgo,'" 17.

127 Ibid., 15.

128 "For Profit," Addition Hills advertisement, *The Philippines Herald*, 12 Jan. 1931, 2, JRHP Box 12, Folder 18.

129 Emily S. Rosenberg, *Spreading the American Dream: American Economic and Cultural Expansion, 1890–1945* (New York: Hill and Wang, 1982); Lizabeth Cohen, *A Consumers' Republic: The Politics of Mass Consumption in Postwar America* (New York: Vintage, 2004), 18–61.

130 Shirley Jenkins, *American Economic Policy toward the Philippines* (Stanford: Stanford University Press, 1954), 32–33; Raquel A. G. Reyes, "Modernizing the Manileña: Technologies of Conspicuous Consumption for the Well-to-do Woman, circa 1880s–1930s," *Modern Asian Studies* 46 (1), 2012: 193–220; Pante, "Peripheral Pockets of Paradise," 202–6.

131 Motoe Terami-Wada, *Sakdalistas' Struggle for Philippine Independence, 1930–1945* (Quezon City: Ateneo de Manila University Press, 2014), 1–10.

132 Ibid., 83–86, 100; Basilio J. Valdes, Confidential Memorandum for the Superintendent, 2 May 1935, JRHP, Box 25, Folder 23; "Rizal Governor Studies Needs of Residents," *MDB*, 17 Jan. 1938, JRHP Box 25, Folder 21; "Sakdalistas are Massing," *MDB*, 4 May 1935, JRHP Box 25, Folder 23; "21 Sakdals in Rizal Nabbed," *MDB*, 25 Dec. 1935, JRHP Box 25, Folder 27; Milagros Guerrero, ed., *Under Stars and Stripes. Kasaysayan: The Story of the Filipino People*, vol. 6 (n.p.: Asia Publishing, 1998), 164.

133 See the following articles found in JRHP Box 25, Folder 27: "Caloocan Soldiers Capture Two More Men," *Tribune*, 20 Oct. 1936; "Sakdal Leaders Flee to Hills When Freed after Their Investigation," *MDB*, 21 Oct. 1936; "P.C. Soldiers Mopping Up in Provinces," 21 Oct. 1936; "Rizal Sakdals Reported Planning New Uprising," *MDB*, 16 Dec. 1936; "Police Alert as Sakdalistas Agitate Anew," *MDB*, 12 Aug. 1937; "Police Mobilized as New Sakdal Uprising Threat is Reported," 12 Oct. 1937; "Rizal Police Watch Sakdals," *MDB*, 21 Jan. 1938; "Rizal Sakdals Plan Uprising," *MDB*, 12 May 1936. See also J. Weldon Jones, Weekly Report—Miscellaneous Topics for Week Ending October 18, 1936, 2, FMP Box 54, Folder 35; J. Weldon Jones, Weekly Report—Miscellaneous Topics for Week Ending October 25, 1936, 3, FMP Box 54, Folder 35.

134 "Rizal Farmers' 'Revolt' Fails to Materialize," *MDB*, 11 Jan. 1938, JRHP Box 13, Folder 6.

135 Doeppers, *Feeding Manila*, 400.

136 The plan was in preparation for an anticipated attack not just from Sakdalistas but also from Communists and their purported allied organizations in and around the city. See Tentative Agreement Reached in the Conference Held in the Office of the Mayor, undated and unpublished document, JRHP Box 26, Folder 18; Plan of Action by the Constabulary, Manila Police and Other Government Entities in Case of an Attack by Communist and Other Seditious Organizations in the City of Manila, undated and unpublished document, JRHP Box 26, Folder 18.

137 "Rizal Governor Asks for More Autonomy for Municipalities," *Tribune*, 7 Feb. 1937, JRHP Box 27, Folder 2. In the case of Malibay in Pasay, occupants of the land came into conflict with Dolores Casals, who insisted that she got the estate from revolutionary general Mariano Trias in exchange for a property in Cavite. Trias's claim to previous ownership was that Church authorities ceded the land to him (Miguel R. Cornejo, *A Plea for Justice by the People of Malibay to His Excellency, the Governor-General of the Philippine Islands*

[Manila: n.p., 1928], 11–21). Copy courtesy of Mauro Garcia Collection (MGC), Sophia University, Tokyo.

138 Harrison, *Eighth Annual Message*, 7.

139 "Up Goes the Price of the Estates," *PFP*, 5 Oct. 1935, 4, 38, JRHP Box 13, Folder 4; "Undisposed Friar Lands," *Tribune*, 17 Feb. 1937, JRHP Box 13, Folder 5; "Baclaran Tenants Being Boycotted," *MDB*, 25 Jan. 1938, JRHP Box 13, Folder 6; "Eviction Case Stirs Tenants," *MDB*, 17 Aug. 1938, JRHP Box 13, Folder 6; "Terms of Scale Now in Hands of Rodriguez," *Tribune*, 22 Jan. 1936, JRHP Box 18, Folder 17.

140 Frank Murphy, "Report of the High Commissioner to the Secretary of War, June 1936," 5, FMP Box 53, Folder 32.

141 Frank Murphy, "Report of the High Commissioner to the Secretary of War, July 1936," FMP Box 53, Folder 33.

142 Franco-Calairo and Calairo, *Ang Kasaysayan ng Novaliches*, 81–84.

143 Marlin E. Olmsted, *Administration of Philippine Lands*, vol. 1 (Washington, DC: Government Printing Office, 1911), 268.

144 "Cattle Rustling," *Tribune*, 29 Mar. 1938, JRHP Box 27, Folder 4. In the annual provincial report of Rizal for 1939–1940, seven cases of "theft of large cattle" were reported. Although the number seemed insignificant, the actual figure is likely much higher than this because the report noted that cattle owners were reluctant to report such incidents for fear of retribution (Province of Rizal, Annual Report for the Fiscal Year of 1939–1940 to the Secretary of the Interior, 10 Jan. 1941, 6, MLQP Series VIII, Box 73, Folder Name: Annual Report for the Fiscal Year of 1939–1940, Rizal). For an analysis of the changing nature of criminality in nineteenth-century Philippines, see Bankoff, *Crime, Society, and the State*, esp. chapters 2 and 3.

145 Fidel L. Ongpauco, "Quezon City: From Cogonland to Metropolis," *Philippine Panorama*, 24 Nov. 1974: 7, 20. Quote is on p. 7. Ongpauco also asserts that the establishment of Camp Murphy and Camp Crame in the city led "Cattle rustlers, brigands, highway robbers" to flee the area (ibid., 20).

146 Camagay, *Working Women*, 99–118; Luis C. Dery, "Prostitution in Colonial Manila," *Philippine Studies* 39 (4), 1991: 475–89, esp. 486. However, the Spanish colonial state eventually saw the practicality of tolerating and regulating prostitution (Bankoff, *Crime, Society, and the State*, 41–44).

147 Camagay, *Kasaysayang Panlipunan ng Maynila*, 140.

148 Wickberg, *The Chinese Mestizo*, 113–14; Bankoff, *Crime, Society, and the State*, 53–55.

149 Frank Charles Laubach, *The People of the Philippines: Their Religious Progress and Preparation for Spiritual Leadership in the Far East* (New York: G. H. Doran, 1925), 402; George A. Malcolm, *The Commonwealth of the Philippines* (New York: Appleton-Century, 1936), 339.

150 Patricio N. Abinales, "Progressive–Machine Conflict in Early-twentieth-century U.S. Politics and Colonial-state Building in the Philippines," in *The American Colonial State in the Philippines: Global Perspectives*, ed. Julian Go and Anne L. Foster (Pasig City: Anvil, 2005), 157; Alfred W. McCoy, *Policing America's Empire: The United States, the Philippines, and the Rise of the Surveillance State* (Quezon City: Ateneo de Manila University Press, 2011), 243; Alfred W. McCoy and Alfredo Roces, *Philippine Cartoons: Political Caricature of the American Era, 1900–1941* (Quezon City: Vera Reyes, 1985), 140.

151 "Councilor Wants National Sport of P.I. Be Recognized," *MT*, 8 Apr. 1926: 1.

152 Caroline S. Hau, Katrina Tuvera, and Isabelita O. Reyes, "Introduction," in *Querida: An Anthology*, ed. Caroline S. Hau, Katrina Tuvera, and Isabelita O. Reyes (Mandaluyong City:

Anvil, 2013), 7–8. Querida means "mistress." On prostitution during the late Spanish and American colonial periods, see Andrew Jimenez Abalahin, "Prostitution Policy and the Project of Modernity: A Comparative Study of Colonial Indonesia and the Philippines, 1850–1940," PhD dissertation, Cornell University, 2003.

153 George A. Malcolm, *American Colonial Careerist: Half a Century of Official Life and Personal Experience in the Philippines and Puerto Rico* (Boston: The Christopher Publishing House, 1957), 199; [Anon.] *'Gateway' to Manila. The Only Complete GUIDE BOOK to the Orient's Most Charming City*, 13th ed., February 1938 (n.p.: n.p., 1938), 48.

154 [Anon.] *'Gateway' to Manila*, 53–54; Mason Lowe, "Joe Goes Ashore," *Philippine Magazine* 35 (3), 1938: 136, 150–51.

155 Ignacio Villamor, *Criminality in the Philippine Islands, 1903–1908* (Manila: Bureau of Printing, 1909), 56; Laubach, *The People of the Philippines*, 406; "Board Scored for Measures to Foster Vices," *MT*, 14 Apr. 1926: 3; "Bounded Morality," JRHP Box 12, Folder 11; "To Study or to Gamble," *PG*, 3 July 1929: 10; Malcolm, *The Commonwealth of the Philippines*, 345; Emanuel A. Baja, *Philippine Police System and Its Problems* (Manila: Pobre's Press, 1933), 455; McCoy, *Policing America's Empire*, 244.

156 Baja, *Philippine Police System*, 450.

157 Villamor, *Criminality in the Philippine Islands*, 74.

158 Ibid., 56; McCoy, *Policing America's Empire*, 244; "Cabaret Ordinance Is Now in Effect," *MT*, 20 July 1926: 2; "Charter Revision Experts Favor City Cockpits," *MT*, 27 Aug. 1926: 1; "Councilor Wants National Sport of P.I. Be Recognized," *MT*, 8 Apr. 1926: 1; "Manila Women Leaders Protest Cabaret Plan," *PG*, 11 Aug. 1938: 28. Quote is from Laubach, *The People of the Philippines*, 406. While section 590 of the revised ordinances of 1917 allowed the maintenance of a public dance hall for so long as the proper licenses were obtained, section 98 prohibited the playing of any musical instrument in saloons, bars, or drinking places—a seemingly ridiculous provision that actually targeted cabarets (George A. Malcolm, ed., *The Charter of the City of Manila and the Revised Ordinances of the City of Manila* [Manila: Bureau of Printing, 1917], 90–91).

159 Baja, *Philippine Police System*, 355, 450; [Anon.] *Gateway to Manila (Shopping in Old Manila): A Complete Practical Guidebook to the Orient's Most Charming City* ([Manila]: n.p., 1934), 35–36; "The First Great American Investment in the Philippines," *MT Anniversary Issue*, 1910: 24–25; Peter Keppy, "Southeast Asia in the Age of Jazz: Locating Popular Culture in the Colonial Philippines and Indonesia," *Journal of Southeast Asian Studies* 44 (3), 2013: 444–64; Torres, *The Americanization of Manila*, 178; McCoy, *Policing America's Empire*, 244; Villamor, *Criminality in the Philippine Islands*, 83; Supreme Court (SC), en banc, "Constancio Joaquin vs. Godofredo B. Herrera, Lope K. Santos and the Provincial Board of Rizal, and Jose Javier," G.R. no. L-11217, 28 Feb. 1918, *The Lawphil Project*, http://www.lawphil.net/judjuris/juri1918/feb1918/gr_l-11217_1918.html, accessed 7 Nov. 2016.

160 In the 1920s it was one kilometer away from the city borders, "Cabarets Slipped over on City," *MT*, 30 Mar. 1926: 1. Eventually, it became half a kilometer, George A. Malcolm, ed., *The Charter of the City of Manila and the Revised Ordinances of the City of Manila* (Manila: Bureau of Printing, 1927), 407.

161 "Santa Ana Cockpits Closed," *MT*, 17 Feb. 1902: 1.

162 "Bounded Morality," *Bulletin*, 15 Oct. 1934, JRHP Box 12, Folder 11.

163 Ibid.

164 McCoy, *Policing America's Empire*, 244.

NOTES   275

165   Philippine Education Company, *Manila City Directory, 1941* (Manila: Philippine Education Company, 1941), 347; Norbert Lyons, "The Scenic Route to Montalban," *ACCJ* 2 (6), 1921: 9–12, esp. 10–11; [Anon.] *'Gateway' to Manila* (1938), 54; Malcolm, *The Commonwealth of the Philippines*, 346; Lowe, "Joe Goes Ashore," 136; Salonga, *Rizal Province Directory*, 115. Gleeck, an expert on the history of the Manila American community, asserts that many Filipino-American mestizas were "the offspring of Canson's Santa Ana bailerinas and American fathers, some of them prominent in the community," *The Manila Americans*, 98.

166   [Anon.] *'Gateway' to Manila* (1938), 54.

167   Ibid., 48.

168   Harrison, *Eighth Annual Message*, 13; D. L. Francisco, "'You Can't Search Me,'" *PFP,* 1 Sept. 1934: 4, JRHP Box 12, Folder 20.

169   "Pasay Placed under Strict Quarantine," *MT,* 18 May 1920: 1.

170   Municipal Board of Manila, *Annual Report of the Municipal Board of the City of Manila for the Fiscal Year 1908* (Manila: Bureau of Printing, 1909), 55.

171   "Bounded Morality"; "Rizal Police Watch Thugs," *MDB,* 7 Mar. 1938, JRHP Box 12, Folder 26; "Opium Smokers Arrested in Spectacular Raid, Chase," *Tribune,* 26 June 1938, JRHP Box 12, Folder 26; Villamor, *Criminality in the Philippine Islands*, 56; Serafin E. Macaraig, *Social Problems* (Manila: Educational Supply Co., 1929), 414–17; McCoy, *Policing America's Empire*, 357; "Are the Suburbs Unsafe for the Gobs?," *PG,* 22 Sept. 1938: 10–11, 78. Maypajo Cockpit in Caloocan was, according to some accounts, the largest in the world, George Hamlin Fitch, *The Critic in the Orient* (San Francisco: Paul Elder and Company, 1913), 61; Lyons, "The Scenic Route to Montalban," 10. There were also cases in which cabaret employees were themselves gangsters, McCoy and Roces, *Philippine Cartoons*, 65.

172   Richard T. Chu, *Chinese and Chinese Mestizos of Manila: Family, Identity, and Culture, 1860s–1930s* (Pasig City: Anvil, 2010), 223–24; Doeppers, *Feeding Manila*, 211; Donald Denise Decaesstecker, *Impoverished Urban Filipino Families* (Manila: UST Press, 1978), 29–31.

173   Malcolm, *American Colonial Careerist*, 199; McCoy, *Policing America's Empire*, 357. A rather anomalous feature of La Loma was the presence of a golf course adjoining the North Cemetery. The members of the club that operated the course, however, decided to move to another location, somewhere in Mandaluyong. The new course opened in 1931 as the Wack Wack Golf and Country Club (Lewis E. Gleeck, Jr., *Bill Shaw, the Man and the Legend: A Life with A.G.&P. and Wack-Wack* [n.p.: William J. Shaw Foundation, 1998], 28).

174   Francisco, "'You Can't Search Me,'" 4; "No Vice in Rizal!," *PFP,* 19 Dec. 1931, JRHP Box 12, Folder 22a; Macaraig, *Social Problems*, 414–17; [Anon.] *'Gateway' to Manila* (1938), 54; Malcolm, *American Colonial Careerist*, 199; Gleeck, *The Manila Americans*, 91; Supreme Court, en banc., "Sy Chiuco vs. Collector of Internal Revenue," G. R. no. L-13387, 28 Mar. 1960, *The Lawphil Project,* http://www.lawphil.net/judjuris/juri1960/mar1960/gr_l-13387_1960. html, accessed 18 May 2015. Other gangs, such as the Magdaragat, also operated in La Loma ("Cop is Assaulted by Magdaragat," *Herald,* 15 May 1931, JRHP Box 12, Folder 18; "Gang Assaults 15 Musicians," *MDB,* 18 May 1931, JRHP Box 12, Folder 18; "Gangs Active without Fear of Policemen," *Tribune,* 15 May 1931, JRHP Box 12, Folder 18). Police officials believed that this gang was formed in reaction to the abusive behavior of drunk Americans in cabarets, especially military men ("Are the Suburbs Unsafe for the Gobs?," 10–11, 78).

175   "The Menace of La Loma," *Tribune,* 10 Sept. 1931, JRHP Box 12, Folder 22a. See also Decaesstecker, *Impoverished Urban Filipino Families*, 28.

176   "The Legacy of Years," *PFP,* 19 Sept. 1931, JRHP Box 12, Folder 22a.

276   A CAPITAL CITY AT THE MARGINS

177   Villamor, *Criminality in the Philippine Islands*, 84; "Councilor Wants National Sport of P.I.
      Be Recognized," 1.
178   Lewis E. Gleeck, Jr., *The American Half-Century (1898–1946)*, rev. ed. (Quezon City: New
      Day, 1998), 262; McCoy, *Policing America's Empire*, 358, 368.
179   McCoy and Roces, *Philippine Cartoons*, 41–42, 151; Francisco, "'You Can't Search Me'"; "Vice
      Trusts Denounced," *MT*, 12 Apr. 1926: 1; "All Dance Halls are Closed Here," 1; McCoy, *Policing
      America's Empire*, 369; "Valdes Orders P.C. Campaign on Gangsters," *Tribune*, 7 Sept. 1938,
      JRHP Box 12, Folder 26; Villamor, *Criminality in the Philippine Islands*, 84; Malcolm,
      American Colonial Careerist, 88; Malcolm, *The Commonwealth of the Philippines*, 346;
      Victor Buencamino, *Memoirs of Victor Buencamino* (Mandaluyong: Jorge B. Vargas
      Filipiniana Foundation, 1977), 220–21; Gleeck, *The American Half-Century*, 206; Gleeck,
      The Manila Americans, 100–101.
180   Trinidad Fernandez Legarda, "The Ladies of Malacañang," *Philippine Magazine* 26 (1),
      1929: 138–40, 162–72, esp. 140.
181   "The First Great American Investment," 25; Lyons, "The Scenic Route to Montalban," 10;
      Fitch, *The Critic in the Orient*, 61; Malcolm, *The Commonwealth of the Philippines*, 340;
      "Are the Suburbs Unsafe for the Gobs?," 78.
182   Torres, *The Americanization of Manila*, 178; "To Study or to Gamble," *PG*, 3 July 1929: 10;
      American Express, *Manila and the Philippines* (Manila: American Express, 1939), 38;
      [Anon.] *Gateway to Manila* (1934), 35–36.
183   "Expansion of City of Manila Agreed upon."
184   "Pasay Annexation to Manila is Fought."
185   McGee, *The Southeast Asian City*, 67–69; Norman Edwards, "The Colonial Suburb: Public
      Space as Private Space," in *Public Space: Design, Use and Management*, ed. Chua Beng
      Huat and Norman Edwards (Singapore: Centre for Advanced Studies, National University
      of Singapore; Singapore University Press, 1992).

2. Quezon's City

1   Bernardita Reyes Churchill, *The Philippine Independence Missions to the United States,
     1919–1934* (Manila: National Historical Institute, 1983).
2   Mojares, *Brains of the Nation*, 493–95.
3   On prewar economic nationalism, see the first two chapters of Yusuke Takagi, *Central
     Banking as State Building: Policymakers and their Nationalism in the Philippines, 1933–
     1964* (Quezon City: Ateneo de Manila University Press, 2016).
4   Lico, *Arkitekturang Filipino*, 256–57; Norma I. Alarcon, *The Imperial Tapestry: American
     Colonial Architecture in the Philippines* (Manila: University of Santo Tomas Publishing
     House, 2008), 71–73; Ian Morley, "The Filipinization of the American City Beautiful, 1916–
     1935," *Journal of Planning History* 20 (10), 2017: 1–30, esp. 2–3.
5   Sta. Maria, "In the Steps of the Founder," 56; Carunungan, *Quezon City*, 51; Juan M. Arellano
     "Landscaping Plans for Manila," *Philippine Magazine* 32 (1), 1935: 28–29; Lico, *Arkitek-
     turang Filipino*, 311–14; Morley, "The Filipinization of the American City Beautiful," 2–3,
     17–19.
6   "Quezon Reveals Serious Plans to Establish New City, Move University of the Philippines
     to Tagaytay," *MDB*, 15 Aug. 1936, JRHP Box 18, Folder 7; The Walking Reporter, "Vote-Getting
     Move to Scrap Burnham Plan Temporarily Is Nipped in Bud," *MDB*, 23 Nov. 1938, JRHP Box
     26, Folder 23.

7   Philippine Commonwealth, Commonwealth Act No. 457 – An Act to Further Section One of Act Numbered Thirty-Five Hundred and Ninety-Seven, as Amended, 8 June 1939, *Chan Robles Virtual Law Library*, http://laws.chanrobles.com/commonwealthacts/2_commonwealthacts.php?id=83, accessed 7 Nov. 2016. See also "Government Center Plan to be Pushed," *Tribune*, 1 Feb. 1938 and "Government Center," *Tribune*, 11 Feb. 1938, JRHP Box 13, Folder 17; "To Start First Unit of Government Center" and "Builders Busy on Beginning of Government's P20,000,000 Plan," *MDB*, 24 Mar. 1939, JRHP Box 13, Folder 18.

8   Manuel L. Quezon, *Messages of the President*, vol. 2, part 1, rev. ed. (Manila: Bureau of Printing, 1938), 222.

9   "Government May Build on Diliman Site," *MDB*, 8 Aug. 1939, JRHP Box 31, Folder 16.

10   Abrams, *The Language of Cities*, 331. Cf. McPhelin, "Manila: The Primate City," 786–87.

11   Quezon, *The Good Fight*, 2–8; Carlos Madrid, *Flames over Baler: The Story of the Siege of Baler, Reconstructed from Original Documentary Sources* (Quezon City: University of the Philippines Press, 2012), 6–12.

12   "Aurora Aragon—The Little Poor Girl of Baler," *PFP*, 22 Feb. 1941: 44–45.

13   Dante C. Simbulan, *The Modern Principalia: The Historical Evolution of the Philippine Ruling Oligarchy* (Quezon City: University of the Philippines Press, 2005), 70; Doeppers, *Feeding Manila*, 361, n. 22; Brian Fegan, "Entrepreneurs in Votes and Violence: Three Generations of a Peasant Political Family," in *An Anarchy of Families: State and Family in the Philippines*, ed. Alfred W. McCoy (Quezon City: Ateneo de Manila University Press, 1994), 55.

14   Anderson based the concept of secular pilgrimage on the experiences of colonial elites who came from various locations in the colony but ended up in common destinations, specifically the colonial capital and the metropole, in their pursuit of socioeconomic mobility (*Imagined Communities*, 114–16). Rizal's *El Filibusterismo* vividly depicted secular pilgrimage through characters like Juanito Pelaez, Tadeo, and Isagani (*El Filibusterismo: Subversion*, trans. Soledad Lacson-Locsin [Makati City: Bookmark, 1996]).

15   Daniel F. Doeppers, *Manila, 1900–1941: Social Change in a Late Colonial Metropolis* (Quezon City: Ateneo de Manila University Press, 1984).

16   "Juan Sumulong is Prominent Rizal Citizen," *MDB*, 22 Apr. 1939, JRHP Box 24, Folder 22; Manuel A. Caoili, "Quezon and His Business Friends: Notes on the Origins of Philippine National Capitalism," Paper/Lecture Delivered for the Andres Soriano Professorial Chair in Business and Public Administration at the College of Public Administration, University of the Philippines-Manila, 15 Jan. 1986, 21 (Unpublished manuscript, copy available at the UP-Diliman Main Library).

17   Quezon, *The Good Fight*, 67.

18   On these crucial political changes, see Cullinane, *Ilustrado Politics*.

19   Quezon, *The Good Fight*, 108–9. Cf. Enosawa, *Manuel L. Quezon*, 42–43.

20   Golay, *Face of Empire*, 165–66. Cf. Caballero and Concepcion, *Quezon*, 95, 103; Enosawa, *Manuel L. Quezon*, 42.

21   Quezon, *The Good Fight*, 109–10.

22   Caballero and Concepcion, *Quezon*, 112; Manuel L. Quezon, *Messages of the President*, vol. 5, part 1 (Manila: Bureau of Printing, 1941), 133.

23   Golay, *Face of Empire*, 166.

24   Caballero and Concepcion, *Quezon*, 125.

25   Ibid., 112; Enosawa, *Manuel L. Quezon*, 51–55. Enosawa argued, however, that Osmeña was initially hesitant in appointing Quezon because it could lead to the latter challenging his authority, *Manuel L. Quezon*, 44.

26 Quezon, *Messages of the President*, vol. 5, part 1, 133.

27 Churchill, *The Philippine Independence Missions*, 13–17, 30, 48–49, 96, 183, 307.

28 Ibid., 108, 190, 247, 286–87, 368–69; Enosawa, *Manuel L. Quezon*, 151; Mistica, *President Manuel Luis Quezon*, 89, 165.

29 Quirino, *Quezon*, 269; Java-Bode, "Quezon at Batavia: Visit to Java of Famous Philippine Politician," *Java-Bode*, 1 Sept. 1934, Document #10, Quezon Papers, Jorge B. Vargas Papers (JBVP), Jorge B. Vargas Museum and Filipiniana Research Center, University of the Philippines-Diliman, Quezon City. Quezon's informal talks with Indonesian nationalists in Surabaya influenced him greatly. During his wartime exile, he toyed with the idea of a regional association in Southeast Asia, especially among "Malay" nations (Friend, *Between Two Empires*, 271).

30 Wilbur Burton, "Indonesia and the Philippines," *Philippine Magazine*, Aug. 1940: 306, 313–16. Quote is on p. 306. Dutch colonial officials had a reason to be concerned with Quezon because Indonesian Marxist revolutionary Tan Malaka befriended him when the latter visited the Philippines from 1925 to 1927 (John Nery, *Revolutionary Spirit: Jose Rizal in Southeast Asia* [Singapore: Institute of Southeast Asian Studies, 2011], 129).

31 Manuel L. Quezon, *Second Annual Report of the President of the Philippines to the President and the Congress of the United States Covering the Period January 1 to December 31, 1937* (Manila: Bureau of Printing, 1938), 34; Jorge B. Vargas, Letter to Manuel L. Quezon, 20 Apr. 1937, MLQP, Bentley Historical Library (BHL) Roll 19, Box 53.

32 Quirino, *Quezon*, 306; Quezon, *Second Annual Report*, 10.

33 Quezon, *The Good Fight*, 173–80; Enosawa, *Manuel L. Quezon*, 150; Paul V. McNutt, *Third Annual Report of the United States High Commissioner to the Philippine Islands to the President and Congress of the United States Covering the Calendar Year 1938 and the First Six Months of 1939* (Washington, DC: Government Printing Office, 1943), 34; Manuel L. Quezon, Conference Given by the President before the Representatives of the Foreign and Local Press Held at Malacañang, 3 Aug. 1938, 11–21, MLQP (BHL), Roll 41, Box 88.

34 Mistica, *President Manuel Luis Quezon*, 146. See also ibid., 13.

35 Buencamino, *Memoirs of Victor Buencamino*, 191.

36 Mistica, *President Manuel Luis Quezon*, 15.

37 Ibid., 146.

38 Cornelia Lichauco Fung, *Beneath the Banyan Tree: My Family Chronicles* (Hong Kong: CBL Fung, 2009), 87.

39 Buencamino, *Memoirs of Victor Buencamino*, 194; "Aurora Aragon," 45; Morton J. Netzorg, *Jock Netzorg: Manila Memories*, ed. Michael P. Onorato (Laguna Beach, CA: Pacific Rim, 1988), 8.

40 Mistica, *President Manuel Luis Quezon*, 146; cf. Quijano de Manila, "Nonong Quezon's Life with Father," in *Quezon: Thoughts and Anecdotes about Him and His Fights*, ed. Juan F. Rivera (Quezon City: Juan F. Rivera, 1979), 125–28.

41 The Quezons' Pasay residence corroborates Kiyoko Yamaguchi's argument that American influence hybridized the aesthetics and lifestyle of the Filipino elite of this era, "The New 'American' House in the Colonial Philippines and the Rise of the Urban Filipino Elite," *Philippine Studies* 54 (3), 2006: 412–51.

42 Buencamino, *Memoirs of Victor Buencamino*, 193.

43 Mistica, *President Manuel Luis Quezon*, 147.

44 Buencamino, *Memoirs of Victor Buencamino*, 194. Italics in the original. Pensionados were Filipino students sent by the colonial government to US universities for studies at the tertiary level on the condition that they would serve the country afterwards. A good

number of pensionados were architects and planners who were key players in Quezon City's development (Morley, "The Filipinization of the American City Beautiful," 3–5).

45   Mistica, *President Manuel Luis Quezon*, 69.

46   Quezon, *The Good Fight*, 193.

47   Mistica, *President Manuel Luis Quezon*, 29.

48   "Aurora Quezon," 45.

49   Ibid., 44.

50   Enosawa, *Manuel L. Quezon*, 176.

51   Quijano de Manila, "Nonong Quezon's Life with Father," 124.

52   Quezon, *The Good Fight*, 183.

53   The Quezon-Aguinaldo feud began in the 1920s, when Aguinaldo supported Governor-General Wood, whom Quezon castigated for supposedly undermining the authority of Filipino politicians. Satoshi Ara, "Emilio Aguinaldo under American and Japanese Rule: Submission for Independence?," *Philippine Studies: Historical and Ethnographic Viewpoints* 63 (2), 2015: 161–92, esp. 167–69.

54   "General Aguinaldo Hurls Vitriolic Attack against Senator Quezon in Heated Statement on Independence," *MT*, 21 July 1929: 1, 5. Extract is found in p. 5. See also "Questions Quezon's Wealth: Aguinaldo Lists Senator's Possessions," *PG*, 24 July 1929: 20.

55   "'Not So Rich as Aguinaldo Declares,' Says Senate President Quezon in Answer to General's Statement," *MT*, 28 July 1929: 1, 4–5.

56   It must be noted that Quezon and Morató were business partners in the Calauag Saw Mill (Tomás Morató, Letter to Manuel L. Quezon, 6 Apr. 1929, MLQP [BHL] Box 61).

57   "'Not So Rich as Aguinaldo Declares,'" 4.

58   Ibid., 4–5.

59   Unverified reports, however, alleged that Quezon's Pasay residence was "a gift from Don Vicente Madrigal for coal contracts for Manila Railroad [MRC]" ("The Whirligig: A Guide Post for Governors General," 3, unpublished and undated document, FMP Box 55, Folder 29A).

60   "'Not So Rich as Aguinaldo Declares,'" 5.

61   Ibid., 4. Singson Encarnacion was a lawyer-politician who came from the prominent Singson family of Vigan, Ilocos Sur. When Madrigal and Ortigas were still planning to purchase the Mandaloya Estate, they encouraged him to join them. However, he declined because he wanted to focus on the Balintawak Estate Corporation. Similarly, this corporation involved the most powerful men in the country, such as Quezon, Osmeña, and Baldomero Roxas, a physician from Lipa, Batangas, and a close friend of Rizal. See Celine Singson Rondain, *Vicente Singson Encarnacion: A Biography* (n.p.:n.p., n.d.), 6–7, 55, copy courtesy of the Filipiniana Section, UP-Diliman Main Library; Takagi, *Central Banking as State Building*, 53–54.

62   "'Not So Rich as Aguinaldo Declares,'" 5.

63   Of course, Quezon had no monopoly over this modus operandi. Osmeña and his scions in Cebu perfected the skill of combining political prowess with business acumen in real property (Resil B. Mojares, "The Dream Goes on and on: Three Generations of the Osmeñas, 1906–1990," in *An Anarchy of Families: State and Family in the Philippines*, ed. Alfred W. McCoy [Quezon City: Ateneo de Manila University Press, 1994], 317–18).

64   Golay, *Face of Empire*, 166.

65   Alejandro Roces was "an imperious and independent" friend of Quezon: Roces owned the TVT (*Tribune–Vanguardia–Taliba*) chain of newspapers, which supported Osmeña, Quezon's rival, and the Hare–Hawes–Cutting Act (HHC), which Quezon opposed. In

response, Quezon convinced his trusted and wealthy friends to purchase Roces's media outfits. In the process Quezon obtained not only an important segment of print media, but also the services of Carlos P. Romulo, one of the most brilliant journalists in the country then, to be his secretary (Friend, *Between Two Empires*, 115).

66 "More about Quezon City," *ACCJ* 20 (1), 1940: 29–30. Quote is on p. 29.

67 Duldulao, *Quezon City*, 35.

68 Ibid., 35–36.

69 Sta. Maria, "In the Steps of the Founder," 68–70.

70 Quezon, *Fourth Annual Report*, 36; Manuel L. Quezon, *Third Annual Report of the President of the Philippines to the President and the Congress of the United States, Covering the Calendar Year Ended December 31, 1938* (Washington, DC: Government Printing Office, 1940), 7. Prior to its incorporation the PHC was initially named Home Owners Suburbs Administration, "New Firm Will Run Model City," *MDB*, 12 Oct. 1938, JRHP Box 31, Folder 8.

71 "Christian Centuries," *ACCJ* 20 (11), 1940: 7, 12; "Model City's Directors Meet," *MDB*, 19 Oct. 1938, JRHP Box 31, Folder 8.

72 Manuel L. Quezon, *Messages of the President*, vol. 4, part 1 (Manila: Bureau of Printing, 1939), 709. For the PHC's by-laws, see PHC, "By-Laws of the People's Homesite Corporation," Manuel A. Roxas Papers (MARP) Series IV, Box 35, Folder Name: People's Homesite and Housing Corporation, undated.

73 Jesus V. Merrit, "A Tale of Two Cities," *PFP*, 22 Feb. 1941: 6, 8. Quote is on p. 6.

74 Quezon, *Messages of the President*, vol. 4, part 1, 708.

75 "The Hard-Working Man Deserves a Home," *PG*, 3 Nov. 1938: 2–3, 79.

76 Quezon, *Messages of the President*, vol. 4, part 1, 709.

77 "The Hard-Working Man," 79.

78 "Four Thousand Apply for Diliman Homesites," *PG*, 1 Dec. 1938: 22; "Model City Plan," *Tribune*, 11 Oct. 1938, JRHP Box 31, Folder 8.

79 Manuel L. Quezon, *Message of His Excellency, Manuel Quezon, President of the Philippines, to the Second National Assembly, Delivered 24 January 1939* (Manila: Bureau of Printing, 1939), 21.

80 Joseph Ralston Hayden, *The Philippines: A Study in National Development* (New York: Macmillan, 1947), 303.

81 Cristino Jamias, *The University of the Philippines: The First Half Century* (Quezon City: UP, 1962), 143–46. Quote is from UP, *Resurgence of the University*, 25.

82 "Quezon Reveals Serious Plans;" "Bocobo Studies Plan to Transfer U.P. Out of City," *MDB*, 31 Aug. 1937, JRHP Box 18, Folder 8. According to one newspaper report, majority of students favored either Alabang or Tagaytay for the relocation (Manuel Vijungco, "Officials Study Transfer of State University Outside of Manila," *MDB*, 2 Sept. 1937, JRHP Box 18, Folder 8).

83 Manuel L. Quezon, Radiogram Message to the Secretary of War, 4 Aug. 1938, MARP Series IV, Box 56, Folder Name: UP Committee on Educational Policy, Mar–Oct 1938; "Advisers for U.P. Chosen," *Tribune*, 23 June 1938; "Educators Accept U.P. Offer," *Tribune*, 1 July 1938; "U.P. Advisers to Study Transfer," *Tribune*, 15 Sept. 1938, JRHP Box 18, Folder 9. Colonial connections led to Roxas's selection of a dean from Iowa University, whose president at the time was former vice governor-general Eugene Gilmore, Julius C. Edelstein, "Roxas Studies University Teaching, Methods in U.S.," *Tribune*, 23 June 1938, JRHP Box 18, Folder 9.

84 "Transfer of U.P. to be Studied by Advisers," *PG*, 22 Sept. 1938: 30; "Take Up Report on U.P. Survey," *MDB*, 6 Jan. 1939, JRHP Box 18, Folder 10.

85 Paul C. Packer and Edward Charles Elliott, Advisers Memoranda for the Committee on Educational Policy of the Regents of the University of the Philippines, October–

NOTES   281

December(?), 1938, Manila, 1–2, unpublished report, JRHP Box 18, Folder 3. Underscoring in original.

86   "U.P. to be Transferred to Spot near Caloocan; Plans are Drawn," *PG*, 6 Oct. 1938: 29. See also Cipriano Cid, "U.P. to Move to New Locale near San Juan," *MDB*, 1 Oct. 1938, JRHP Box 18, Folder 9.

87   Packer and Elliott, Advisers Memoranda, 19.

88   Quezon, *Message to the Second National Assembly, 24 January 1939*, 21; Quezon, *Messages of the President*, vol. 4, part 1, 708; "U.P. Transfer Discussed," *Tribune*, 22 Oct. 1938, JRHP Box 18, Folder 9. The 600-hectare portion of the Mariquina Estate that became part of the new campus was then owned by the PNB (Bonifacio S. Salamanca, "Bocobo Fosters a Vibrant Nationalism [1934–1939]: Reassertion of Filipino Values as an Underlying Concept of Academic Life," in *University of the Philippines: The First 75 Years [1908–1983]*, ed. Oscar M. Alfonso [Quezon City: University of the Philippines Press, 1985], 248).

89   Quezon, *Message to the Second National Assembly, 24 January 1939*, 22–23; Quezon, *Fourth Annual Report to the President and the Congress of the US*, 49.

90   "Locale for U.P. May Embrace Barrio Obrero," *MDB*, 7 Oct. 1938, JRHP Box 18, Folder 9; Quezon, *Messages of the President*, vol. 5, part 1, 361–62. Many secondary accounts state that Quezon allowed the bill to lapse into law without signing it, e.g., Hartendorp, *History of Industry and Trade*, 410–11. However, a contemporary newspaper article contradicts this point, "Quezon City Is Organized," *MDB*, 13 Oct. 1939, 3.

91   Philippine Commission of the Census, *Census of the Philippines, 1939*, vol. 1, part 4-Rizal, 5.

92   Ibid., 4–5.

93   Carunungan, *Quezon City*, 41.

94   Merrit, "A Tale of Two Cities," 8.

95   Philippine Commission of the Census, *Census of the Philippines, 1939*, vol. 1, part 4-Rizal, 1490.

96   Louis P. Croft, "On-the-Spot-Decisions" (Letter to Juan F. Rivera, 5 Aug. 1948), in *Quezon: Thoughts and Anecdotes about Him and His Fights*, ed. Juan F. Rivera (Quezon City: Juan F. Rivera, 1979), 189.

97   Special Mission to the United States, *Report of the Special Mission to the United States, 1938–1939* (Manila: Bureau of Printing, 1939), 5.

98   Ibid., 5–7.

99   Jones, Radiogram Message to the US Secretary of State, 27 July 1939, MLQP (BHL) Roll 19, Box 54.

100   Osmeña, Radiogram Message to Quezon, 25 May 1939, MLQP (BHL) Roll 19, Box 54; Cipriano Cid, "Osmeña Makes Report on His Studies in U.S.," *MDB*, 26 Oct. 1939: 1, 6. On Croft's assignment, see the following in MLQP (BHL) Roll 20, Box 54: Manuel L. Quezon, Radiogram Message to Gruening, Department of Interior, 26 Oct. 1939; Manuel L. Quezon, Radiogram Message to Hampton, Department of Interior, 4 Dec. 1939; Manuel L. Quezon, Radiogram Message to Hampton, Department of Interior, 26 Dec. 1939. On Frost's assignment, see Frost, Radiogram Message to Quezon, 22 Mar. 1940, MLQP (BHL), Roll 20, Box 55.

101   Alcazaren et al., *Lungsod Iskwater*, 59; Lico, *Arkitekturang Filipino*, 355–56; Manuel L. Quezon III, "Prologue," in *Quezon City: The Rise of Asia's City of the Future*, ed. Regina A. Samson and Marily Y. Orosa (Quezon City: Local Government of Quezon City, 2010), 36; "Hope in Municipal Architecture," *ACCJ* 20 (11), 1940: 10; Carunungan, *Quezon City*, 59.

102   Harry T. Frost, "Quezon City: Functional Planning Gets Its Chance," *Philippines* 1 (4), 1940: 16–17; "Hope in Municipal Architecture," 10. The idea of having rotundas, however, was

282 A CAPITAL CITY AT THE MARGINS

not Croft's original idea. As early as 1938 and prior to his involvement in planning Quezon City, Quezon had already broached the concept to the press, "Press Conference Notes, March 3, 1938," 40, MLQP (BHL), Roll 41.

103 Pio Pedrosa, however, stated that defense was a specious motive; for him Quezon's real motivation was to create a capital city along the lines set by Brazil, Australia, and Turkey, "The Beginnings of Quezon City," *Historical Bulletin* 8 (4), 1964: 23–32, esp. 24.

104 Wenceslao Balisi y Lugo, ed., *Quezon City Beautiful: The Year Book and the First National Souvenir of the New Metropolis* (Quezon City: Quezon City Pub. House, 1942), 43, 74–75; "Building for Constabulary," *MDB*, 1 July 1941: 8; Fidel Segundo, Diary of Fidel Segundo, 3 Apr. 1940, *The Philippine Diary Project*. http://philippinediaryproject.com/1940/04/03/wednesday-april-3-1940/, accessed 27 Aug. 2016.

105 Frost, "Quezon City," 16–17; "Hope in Municipal Architecture," 10. Quote is from "Show of Military Might Will Feature Festivities Today," *MDB*, 15 Nov. 1940: 1, 6.

106 Chua, "Ang Paghiraya sa Nasyon," 115.

107 Francis B. Sayre, *Fourth Annual Report of the United States High Commissioner to the Philippine Islands to the President and Congress of the United States Covering the Fiscal Year July 1, 1939 to June 30, 1940* (Washington, DC: Government Printing Office, 1943), 49; Balisi, *Quezon City Beautiful*, 63.

108 "The Philippine Exposition Goes Ahead," *ACCJ* 20, no. 11 (1940): 14–15; Quezon, *The Good Fight*, 120. The Igorots, a group of upland communities in northern Luzon, attracted attention and controversy in the 1904 St. Louis World's Fair because of the G-strings they wore and their practice of eating dog meat, all under the peering gaze of Americans (Jose D. Fermin, *1904 World's Fair: The Filipino Experience* [Quezon City: University of the Philippines Press, 2004]).

109 "The Philippine Exposition Goes Ahead," 14.

110 Sayre, *Fourth Annual Report*, 49. Interestingly, the Magdalena Estate advertised its houses and lots as "war-proof" (Balisi, *Quezon City Beautiful*, 73).

111 "More about Quezon City," 29.

112 Merrit, "A Tale of Two Cities," 6.

113 Ibid., 6.

114 Lewis Mumford, *The City in History* (San Diego: Harcourt, 1989), 404–5; C. M. Harris, "Washington's Gamble, L'Enfant's Dream: Politics, Design, and the Founding of the National Capital," *The William and Mary Quarterly* 56 (3), 1999: 527–64.

115 Lico, *Arkitekturang Filipino*, 353.

116 Anderson, *Imagined Communities*.

117 Manuel L. Quezon, *Message of His Excellency, Manuel Quezon, President of the Philippines, to the 2nd National Assembly (Fifth state of the nation address)* (Manila: Bureau of Printing, 1940), 8.

118 Mistica, *President Manuel Luis Quezon*, 131.

119 Quezon, *Third Annual Report of the President*, 7.

120 Quezon, *The Good Fight*, 172; Hartendorp, *History of Trade and Industry*, 410–11. Quote is from Manuel Quezon, *Sixth State of the Nation Address*, 31 Jan. 1941, 47, MLQP Series III, Box 21.

121 Manuel L. Quezon, *Fifth Annual Report of the President of the Philippines to the President and the Congress of the United States Covering the Period July 1, 1939, to June 30, 1940* (Washington, DC: Government Printing Office, 1941), 22. See also "10,000 Families Benefited by Purchase of Big Estate," *Tribune*, 20 Oct. 1938, and "Rush Transfer of Labor Lots," *MDB*, 20 Oct. 1938, JRHP Box 25, Folder 20.

NOTES 283

122 Quezon, *Sixth State of the Nation Address*, 47; "Home Sites to Be Sold Later," *MDB*, 27 Feb. 1940: 1, 6.

123 "The Hard-Working Man," 79.

124 Manuel L. Quezon, Message to the National Assembly, 1940, 4th draft, 14, unpublished manuscript, MLQP (BHL) Box 89.

125 "The Hard-Working Man," 3; "Diliman Lots Ready to Be Sold," *Philippines Commonweal*, 14 Dec. 1939: 24.

126 Sta. Maria, "In the Steps of the Founder," 65.

127 "60 Diliman Tenants Claim Tuason Estate," *PG*, 27 Oct. 1938: 34; Tutay, "A Squatter for 70 Years," 7.

128 "News of the Week: Quezon City," *PFP*, 21 Oct. 1939: 36–38. Quote is on p. 36.

129 Pedrosa, "The Beginnings of Quezon City," 29.

130 Fernando J. Mañalac, *Manila: Memories of World War II* (Quezon City: Giraffe, 1995), 53.

131 Balisi, *Quezon City Beautiful*, 22.

132 Ibid., 36–37; "Thousands to See Sta. Mesa Heights," *MDB*, 15 Nov. 1940: 3; "Gregorio Araneta, Inc.," 117; Yoshiko Nagano, *State and Finance in the Philippines, 1898–1941: The Mismanagement of an American Colony* (Singapore: NUS Press, 2015), 107; Caoili, "Quezon and His Business Friends," 24. Patriarch Gregorio Araneta lawyered for Quezon and Osmeña in the controversial Board of Control case in 1926, and for Madrigal and Singson Encarnacion when Wood accused the two PNB officials of corruption (Maria Lina A. Santiago, *Araneta: A Love Affair with God and Country* [Quezon City: Sahara Heritage Foundation, 2007], 64).

133 Balisi, *Quezon City Beautiful*, 37.

134 Ibid., 43; "Up from Ramshackles to Institute," 95. See also Pante, "Peripheral Pockets of Paradise," 194. Like Quezon City, QI was named after Quezon at a time when he was still president.

135 "Manila and Quezon City," *ACCJ* 21 (1), 1941: 9, 12, 38. Quote is on p. 9.

136 Ibid., 9; Balisi, *Quezon City Beautiful*, 32–33, 96.

137 Carunungan, *Quezon City*, 68; Rafael L. Peña, "Kamuning: A Revelation in Time," in *Age of Gold: Sacred Heart Parish, Kamuning, Q.C., Golden Jubilee, 1941–1991*, ed. Angelo J. de los Reyes (Quezon City: Sacred Heart Parish, Angelo J. de los Reyes, 1991), 18.

138 Angelo J. de los Reyes and Resty Lumanlan, *Sandiwaan sa Kamuning: A Pastoral Experience* (Quezon City: Resty Lumanlan, 1981), 79.

139 Peña, "Kamuning," 18; Julita P. Arrogante, "Kamuning and Its Beginnings," in *Age of Gold*, 19–20; Carunungan, *Quezon City*, 68. This Barrio Obrero was different from the one in Tondo that was mentioned in chapter 1. In the 1930s the government named a handful of housing projects for laborers "Barrio Obrero" in different parts of the country.

140 Merrit, "A Tale of Two Cities," 8.

141 Balisi, *Quezon City Beautiful*, 33. Nonetheless, there were those who saw the possibility of making Quezon City an industrial town, a "potential Pittsburgh." According to Japanese businessman and Quezon City resident Ikeuchi Kenjiro, there were slums in Brixton Hills in Santa Mesa (Balisi, *Quezon City Beautiful*, 35, 90).

142 "Frost Speaks Frankly, Clearly in Describing Plan for Dream Cities, Telling How to Prevent Slums," *MDB*, 29 July 1941: 1, 8. Quote is on p. 8.

143 Romeo B. Ocampo, "Historical Development of Philippine Housing Policy. Part 1. Prewar Housing Policy," Occasional Paper No. 6, November 1976, College of Public Administration, University of the Philippines, 16–26. Quote is on p. 21.

144 Cipriano Cid, "Quezon Calls Assembly to Meet Monday," *MDB*, 23 Sept. 1939: 1, 3; B. P. Garcia, "Plow through Quezon's Bills on Emergency," *MDB*, 28 Sept. 1939: 1, 6.

145 Sta. Maria, "In the Steps of the Founder."

146 Quezon III, "Prologue," 36. Politicians pandering to Quezon did not stop after Quezon's death. In 1945 Nueva Vizcaya Rep. Leon C. Cabarroguis proposed changing Baguio's name to "Quezon City," *Congressional Record (CR)* I (5), 18 Aug. 1945: 648.

147 Chua, "Ang Paghiraya sa Nasyon," 124.

148 Gopinath, *Manuel L. Quezon*; Friend, *Between Two Empires*, 151; McCoy, "Quezon's Commonwealth"; Storey, "Whose Model City?"

149 Ricardo Jose, "Advocate of Independence: Manuel L. Quezon and the Commonwealth, 1935–1944," in *Philippine Presidents: 100 Years*, ed. Rosario Mendoza Cortes (Quezon City: Philippine Historical Association, New Day, 1999), 109; Gopinath, *Manuel L. Quezon*, 47–62.

150 Jose, "Advocate of Independence," 117.

151 Reuben Ramas Cañete, *Sacrificial Bodies: The Oblation and the Political Aesthetics of Masculine Representations in Philippine Visual Cultures* (Quezon City: University of the Philippines Press, 2012), 96.

152 This incident was not the first time that Quezon used UP's budget as leverage. At the height of the debates about the HHC Act in 1933, Quezon cut UP's budget by one-third when UP President Rafael Palma spoke in favor of the said law. The budget cut led to Palma's resignation. Quezon then ensured that the BOR would select a trusted ally, Jorge Bocobo, as university president (Friend, *Between Two Empires*, 114).

153 Hartendorp, *History of Industry and Trade*, 411.

154 Quezon, *Fourth Annual Report*, 48–50.

155 Manuel L. Quezon, Speech before President Gonzales, Delegates from Other Universities, Members of the Faculty and Student Body, 19 Oct. 1939, 3, MLQP (BHL), Box 88. For a more detailed narrative about UP's relocation to Diliman, see Michael D. Pante, "Far from Isolation: The Spatial Politics of the Relocation of the Main Campus of the University of the Philippines, 1930s–1970s," *Sojourn: Journal of Social Issues in Southeast Asia* 33 (3): 499–535.

156 Quezon, Speech before President Gonzales, 3. See the following newspaper articles in JRHP Box 18, Folder 9: "Plan Poll on U.P. Transfer," *MDB*, 14 Jan. 1938; "Student Demonstration," *Tribune*, 23 Feb. 1938; "U.P. Students Will Demonstrate against Transfer Proposal Today," *MDB*, 24 Feb. 1938. Of course, there were faculty members who were optimistic about Diliman, like the couple Francisco and Paz Marquez Benitez. See Virginia Benitez Licuanan, *Paz Marquez Benitez: One Woman's Life, Letters, and Writings* (Quezon City: Ateneo de Manila University Press, 1995), 145. The Benitez residence, known as the Miranila, remains one of the most notable pieces of architecture in Quezon City. Built in 1929, a decade prior to Quezon City's founding, it featured a Neocastillian style (Lico, *Arkitekturang Filipino*, 328).

157 "As to My Meeting with the Student Council," unpublished transcript, MLQP (BHL) Roll 41. Both quotes are in p. 3.

158 Ibid., 8. For a newspaper report of this meeting between Quezon and student leaders, see "Quezon Stops U.P. Students' Parade, Lectures Leaders on How to Behave," *MDB*, 25 Feb. 1938. Ferdinand E. Marcos, who was then a student in UP, also led in the anti-Quezon and anti-relocation protests (*Presidential Speeches*, vol. 1. [(Manila): Ferdinand E. Marcos, 1978], 421; Priscila S. Manalang, "Remembering UP in the Thirties," in *The University Experience: Essays on the 82nd Anniversary of the University of the Philippines*, ed.

Belinda A. Aquino [Quezon City: University of the Philippines Press, 1991], 34). In tragi-comic fashion, for all his activist rhetoric Benedicto would become a Marcos crony and control the country's lucrative sugar trade during the martial law period (Primitivo Mijares, *The Conjugal Dictatorship of Ferdinand and Imelda Marcos*, rev. ed. [Quezon City: Ateneo de Manila University Press, 2017], 698; Michael S. Billig, *Barons, Brokers, and Buyers: The Institutions and Cultures of Philippine Sugar* [Quezon City: Ateneo de Manila University Press, 2003], 56).

159 David C. Perry and Wim Wiewel, "From Campus to City: The University as Developer," in *The University as Urban Developer: Case Studies and Analysis*, ed. David C. Perry and Wim Wiewel (New York: M. E. Sharpe, 2005).

160 "As to My Meeting," 3–4. On prewar UP's radicalization, see "Communism in University of the Philippines?," *PFP,* 6 Feb. 1932: 47–48.

161 "U.P. Student Leaders in Quandary after Being Rebuked by Quezon," *MDB,* 26 Feb. 1938, JRHP Box 18, Folder 9. For all of Quezon's magniloquence about making UP an apolitical space, in the Commonwealth period it was another Quezon political vehicle. Its BOR was composed of the president's close associates like Vargas, Francisco Ortigas Jr, and Singson Encarnacion. When asked by Paz Marquez Benitez in a private conversation in 1938 about his plans for UP, Quezon replied: "I intend to run it thru the Board of Regents" (Licuanan, *Paz Marquez Benitez,* 136). The predominance of male politicians and businessmen in the BOR persisted until it eroded due to the radicalism in UP in the 1970s, when the studentry and faculty gained representation (Judy Taguiwalo, "Pangkalahatang Welga sa UP, Pebrero 4, 1969: Militante at Matagumpay na Pagsulong sa Demokratisasyon ng Unibersidad" [General Strike in UP, February 4, 1969: The Militant and Successful Progress of Democratization in the University], in *Serve the People: Ang Kasaysayan ng Radikal na Kilusan sa Unibersidad ng Pilipinas* [The History of the Radical Movement in the University of the Philippines], ed. Bienvenido Lumbera, Judy Taguiwalo, Roland Tolentino, Arnold Alamon, and Ramon Guillermo [Quezon City: IBON; Congress of Teachers and Educators for Nationalism and Democracy; Alliance of Concerned Teachers, 2008], 99).

162 Camagay, "Ang Papel ng mga Siyudad," 12–13. On the divergent opinions in the National Assembly regarding chartered cities, see "City Charters Plan Opposed by Assembly," *MDB,* 31 July 1936, and "Assembly Leaders Encouraged by Quezon's Favorable Attitude toward Establishment of Chartered Cities," *MDB,* 26 Aug. 1936, JRHP Box 24, Folder 4.

163 John H. Romani and M. Ladd Thomas, *A Survey of Local Government in the Philippines* (Manila: Institute of Public Administration, University of the Philippines, 1954), 83–85; Hayden, *The Philippines,* 298, 304–9; Golay, *Face of Empire,* 356.

164 Hayden, *The Philippines,* 305.

165 Ibid., 301. Camagay postulates that *lungsod,* the Tagalog word for *city,* entered the vocabulary during Commonwealth period, another piece of evidence that points to the significance of urban politics in Quezon's administration. Camagay, however, does not cite her source for this assertion ("Ang Papel ng mga Siyudad," 9). Nonetheless, Quezon did not approve all measures toward the creation of chartered cities. One notable exception was the move to create a city charter for Lipa, Batangas, which he vetoed in 1938 (Quezon, *Messages of the President,* vol. 4, part 1, 502).

166 Ibid., 306.

167 Duldulao, *Quezon City,* 32.

168 Manuel L. Quezon, "'We Shall Not Permit Injustices,'" in *Quezon in His Speeches,* ed. Pedro de la Llana and F. B. Icasiano (Manila: State Publishing, 1937), 147–48. See also Quezon, *Messages of the President,* vol. 3, part 1, 116.

169 Golay, *Face of Empire*, 244.
170 Benjamin Nadurata, "Supremacy of Rodriguez in Rizal Proven," *MDB*, 14 Nov. 1938, JRHP Box 24, Folder 16; "Juan Sumulong is Prominent Rizal Citizen," *MDB*, 22 Apr. 1939, JRHP Box 24, Folder 22; "10,000 Families Benefited by Purchase of Big Estate," *Tribune*, 20 Oct. 1938, and "Rush Transfer of Labor Lots," *MDB*, 20 Oct. 1938, JRHP Box 25, Folder 20.
171 Hayden, *The Philippines*, 304.
172 Quezon, *Second State of the Nation Address*, 147.
173 Duldulao, *Quezon City*, 40. The position of Quezon City Chief of Police was almost given to a future US president. In early October 1939, Quezon conferred with Gen. Douglas MacArthur regarding key appointments in the city government. MacArthur recommended Dwight Eisenhower, who was then a lieutenant-colonel and MacArthur's senior assistant (Carunungan, *Quezon City*, 54).
174 "Mayor M. L. Quezon Heads New City," *Philippines Commonweal*, 19 Oct. 1939: 3.
175 Carunungan, *Quezon City*, 55; Duldulao, *Quezon City*, 31; Pedrosa, "The Beginnings of Quezon City," 25. For the complete roster and revamps, see Philippine Education Company, *Manila City Directory, 1941* (Manila: Philippine Education Company, 1941), 100.
176 "News of the Week: Quezon City," *PFP*, 21 Oct. 1939: 37. For a more detailed discussion on Quezon's cronyism, see Caoili, "Quezon and His Business Friends."
177 Perfecto R. Palacio, "Quezon City after One and a Half Year," in Balisi, *Quezon City Beautiful*, 28–29. Quote is on p. 28.
178 US State Department, "Impairment of Democracy through Creation of Cities," quoted in McCoy, "Quezon's Commonwealth," 137.
179 Pedrosa, "The Beginnings of Quezon City," 27; Franz Weissblatt, ed. *Who's Who in the Philippines: A Biographical Dictionary of Notable Living Men of the Philippines*, vol. II, *1940–1941* (Manila: Franz Weissblatt, 1940), 156, copy courtesy of MGC; "Santa Clara Lumber Co., Inc.: Then and Now," *The Tribune XIV Anniversary*, 17 June 1939, 138. See also Santa Clara Lumber Company advertisement in *The Bulletin of the Quezon Institute* 1 (1), 1939: xxiv.
180 Bureau of the Census and Statistics, *Journal of Philippine Statistics* 1 (3), 1941: 223.
181 Segundo, Diary of Fidel Segundo, 3 Apr. 1940. The transfer, however, never happened due to the outbreak of war.
182 Gwekoh, *Manuel L. Quezon*, 130.
183 Francis Burton Harrison, Diary of Francis Burton Harrison, 24 Aug. 1942, *The Philippine Diary Project*. https://philippinediaryproject.wordpress.com/1942/08/24/august-24-1942/, accessed 27 Aug. 2016.
184 McCoy, "Quezon's Commonwealth," 137. Cf. Caoili, "Quezon and His Business Friends," 32.
185 Merrit, "A Tale of Two Cities," 8; "Quezon Using Amendments to Cover Failures, Sumulong Says," *MDB*, 11 June 1940, JRHP Box 26, Folder 7. See also Storey, "Whose Model City?," 182.
186 Balisi, *Quezon City Beautiful*, 54. See also Carunungan, *Quezon City*, 46.
187 Balisi, *Quezon City Beautiful*, 22.
188 Amado Garson Capellan, "Kangkong—A Road Builder's Headache," *PFP*, 4 Jan. 1941: 3.
189 Ibid., 3.
190 Crisostomo, *Quezon City*, 1–6; Jose Y. Dalisay Jr., "From Dreams and Green Fields, a City Comes to Life," in *Quezon City at 75: Resurgent & Resilient*, ed. Cynthia Alberto Diaz (Quezon City: Erehwon, Local Government of Quezon City, 2014), 45. Ceres S. C. Alabado's novel, *Kangkong 1896* (Pasay City: Pamana, 1969), gives the area its well-deserved place in revolutionary lore. This work of historical fiction for young adults imparts a keen spatial

NOTES   287

appreciation for the early phase of the revolution as it played out in locations like Balara, Balintawak, and Krus na Ligas in the pre-Quezon City era.

191   Palacio, "Quezon City after One and a Half Year," 29.

192   See SP90 in Quezon City Council, 1940 Quezon City Ordinances (SP19–SP100), n.d. (unpublished and unpaginated compilation available at the Quezon City Public Library).

193   City of Manila, "Report of the Mayor of the City of Manila to the Honorable the Secretary of the Interior Covering the Period from January 1 to June 30, 1939," 2–3, unpublished report, MLQP Series VIII, Box 47.

194   Balisi, *Quezon City Beautiful*, 43.

195   "Cabarets in Quezon City Ordered Closed," *Philippines Commonweal*, 18 Jan. 1940: 12. Quote is from "Quezon City to Get Own Police," *MDB*, 25 Nov. 1939: 3.

196   "Cabarets in Quezon City," 12; D. L. Francisco, "Law Enforcement in Quezon City," *PFP*, 17 Feb. 1940: 20–22; "Three Cabarets Must Move Out of Quezon City," *MDB*, 11 Jan. 1940: 1. See Ordinance No. 6 in Quezon City Council, 1939 Quezon City Ordinances (1–100), n.d. (unpublished and unpaginated compilation available at the Quezon City Public Library).

197   Balisi, *Quezon City Beautiful*, 89.

198   "Cabarets in Quezon City," 12; Francisco, "Law Enforcement in Quezon City," 22; "No Cabarets in Quezon City," *PFP*, 24 Feb. 1940: 35.

199   "Quezon City Loses 'Borrowed' Officers, Finds Itself without Police Force," *MDB*, 24 Nov. 1939: 1; Balisi, *Quezon City Beautiful*, 71.

200   Fernando E. V. Sison and Gregorio San Agustin, Memorandum for the Committee on the Transfer of the University of the Philippines, 25 Mar. 1938, p. 4, MARP Series IV, Box 56, Folder Name: UP Committee on Educational Policy, Mar–Oct 1938; "Preview of a University Town," *PG*, 24 Nov. 1938: 4–5, 54, 58; "Quezon Reveals Serious Plans."

201   "Quezon Stops Students' Parade."

202   "Transfer of U.P. Passes Assembly in Second Reading Despite Objections," *MDB*, 27 Apr. 1939, JRHP Box 18, Folder 10.

203   "Preview of a University Town," 58.

204   Manuel L. Quezon, *Peace and Social and Economic Security of Nations: Speech of His Excellency Manuel L. Quezon, President of the Philippines* (Manila: Bureau of Printing, 1939), 6.

205   Gopinath, *Manuel L. Quezon*, 41.

3. Spectral Spaces beyond Balete Drive

1   Rolando B. Tolentino, *Sipat Kultura: Tungo sa Mapagpalayang Pagbabasa, Pag-aaral at Pagtuturo ng Panitikan* [A Look at Culture: Toward Emancipatory Reading, Studying, and Teaching of Literature] (Quezon City: Ateneo de Manila University Press, 2007), 48–50.

2   Millette T. Ocampo, "Swan Song for Broadway," in *The Manila We Know*, ed. Erlinda Enriquez Panlilio (Mandaluyong City: Anvil, 2017), 121.

3   Ambeth R. Ocampo, *Bonifacio's Bolo* (Pasig City: Anvil, 1995), 221.

4   Tolentino, *Sipat Kultura*, 53–54, 231.

5   Isabelo T. Crisostomo, *Quezon City: Ang Paglikha ng Inyong Lunsod* [The Creation of Your City] (Quezon City: Capitol Publishing, 1971), 23.

6   Mistica, *President Manuel Luis Quezon*, 124; Antonio A. Hidalgo, *The Life, Times and Thoughts of Don Pio Pedrosa* (Quezon City: Milflores, 2000), 47.

288   A CAPITAL CITY AT THE MARGINS

7   See the full text of Quezon's EO in Manuel L. Quezon, EO 400, s. 1942, Creating the City of Greater Manila, 1 Jan. 1942, Malacañang Records Office, http://www.gov.ph/1942/01/01/executive-order-no-400-s-1942/, accessed 8 Sept. 2016.

8   Antonio de las Alas, Diary of Antonio de las Alas, 26 June 1945, *The Philippine Diary Project*, https://philippinediaryproject.wordpress.com/1945/06/27/june-26-1945-tuesday/, accessed 27 Aug. 2016.

9   Teodoro A. Agoncillo, *The Fateful Years: Japan's Adventure in the Philippines, 1941–45*, vol. 1, 2nd ed. (Quezon City: University of the Philippines Press, 2001), 76; Alfredo B. Saulo, *"Let George Do It": A Biography of Jorge B. Vargas* (Quezon City: University of the Philippines Press, 1990), 97–102, 139.

10   Saulo, *"Let George Do It,"* 102; Thelma B. Kintanar, Clemen C. Aquino, Patricia B. Arinto, and Ma. Luisa T. Camagay, *Kuwentong Bayan: Noong Panahon ng Hapon. Everyday Life in a Time of War* (Quezon City: University of the Philippines Press, 2006), 25–27.

11   Adalia Marquez, *Blood on the Rising Sun: A Factual Story of the Japanese Invasion of the Philippines* (New York: DeTanko, 1957), 6; Fe Rodriguez-Arcinas, "A Sociological Analysis of a Specialized Community—Diliman," MA thesis, University of the Philippines-Diliman, 1954, 15–16; Doeppers, *Feeding Manila*, 310.

12   L. O. Ty, "Forced Migration," *PFP*, 20 Dec. 1941: 24–27; Juan Labrador, *A Diary of the Japanese Occupation: December 7, 1941–May 7, 1945* (Manila: Santo Tomas University Press, 1989), 33.

13   Faustino Aguilar, *Nang Magdaan ang Daluyong* [When the Surge Arrived] (Manila: PSP Press, 1945), 9. Aguilar also mentioned that many of those who sought refuge in Quezon City were Chinese ("intsik") (ibid., 39).

14   Ty, "Forced Migration," 25.

15   Ibid., 25; Aguilar, *Nang Magdaan ang Daluyong*, 8, 40, 43; Labrador, *A Diary of the Japanese Occupation*, 124.

16   Office of the Mayor, *City Gazette: Published fortnightly by the Office of the Mayor of the City of Manila*, vol. 1, no. 1, 1 Oct. 1942 (Manila: Office of the Mayor, 1942), 1.

17   Office of the Mayor, *City Gazette: Published Fortnightly by the Office of the Mayor of the City of Manila*, vol. 1, no. 2, 16 Oct 1942 (Manila: Office of the Mayor, 1942), 24–25; Office of the Mayor, *City Gazette: Published Fortnightly by the Office of the Mayor of the City of Manila*, vol. 1, no. 4, 16 Nov. 1942 (Manila: Office of the Mayor, 1942), 34.

18   *City Gazette*, vol. 1, no. 1, 1.

19   *City Gazette*, vol. 1, no. 2, 16.

20   Ibid., 16, 21, 23.

21   Bagumbayan included the former districts of Port Area, Intramuros, Ermita, and Malate; Bagungdiwa, the former districts of Paco, Pandacan, and Santa Ana; Bagumpanahon, the former districts of Sampaloc, Santa Cruz, Quiapo and San Miguel; and, Bagumbuhay, the former districts of Tondo, Binondo, and San Nicolas (*City Gazette*, vol. 1, no. 4, 33).

22   *City Gazette*, vol. 1, no. 2, 25.

23   Leon Guinto, "Regarding the New Filipino," in *City Gazette*, vol. 1, no. 4, 17–22.

24   Gregorio Anonas, Memorandum for His Excellency Re: Resumption of Operation of the National Development Company and Its Subsidiaries, 6 July 1945, p. 15, EQP BiFi, File 003; Faustino Reyes, Excerpt from Memorandum, 2 July 1945, p. 2. This document is Exhibit E of Anonas's previously cited memo.

25   Aguilar, *Nang Magdaan ang Daluyong*, 117; Teodoro A. Agoncillo, *The Fateful Years: Japan's Adventure in the Philippines, 1941–45*, vol. 2, 2d ed (Quezon City: University of the Philippines Press, 2001), 544.

NOTES 289

26 Meralco, Estimate for Reconstruction, 1944, Meralco Museum and Archives (MMA), Pasig City.
27 *City Gazette*, vol. 1, no. 1, 7; Kintanar et al., *Kuwentong Bayan*, 157.
28 Office of the Mayor, *City Gazette: Published Fortnightly by the Office of the Mayor of the City of Manila*, vol. 1, no. 5, 1 Dec. 1942 (Manila: Office of the Mayor, 1942), 49.
29 Forbes J. Monaghan, *Under the Red Sun: A Letter from Manila* (New York: Declan X. McMullen, 1946), 208; Jose Ma. Bonifacio M. Escoda, *Warsaw of Asia: The Rape of Manila* (Quezon City: Giraffe, 2000), 55.
30 Pacita Pestaño-Jacinto, *Living with the Enemy: A Diary of the Japanese Occupation* (Pasig City: Anvil, 1999), 101; Labrador, *A Diary of the Japanese Occupation*, 247; Franco-Calairo and Calairo, *Ang Kasaysayan ng Novaliches*, 99; Terami-Wada, *Sakdalistas' Struggle*, 195.
31 "Historical Data for Quezon City," 5, HDP Quezon City.
32 Anonas, Memorandum for His Excellency, 15–16; *City Gazette*, vol. 1, no. 1, 7; Office of the Mayor, *City Gazette: Published Fortnightly by the Office of the Mayor of the City of Manila*, vol. 1, no. 3, 6 Nov. 1942 (Manila: Office of the Mayor, 1942), 8.
33 Office of the Mayor, *City Gazette: Published Fortnightly by the Office of the Mayor of the City of Manila*, vol. 1, no. 4, 16 Nov. 1942 (Manila: Office of the Mayor, 1942), 24.
34 Guillermo R. Lazaro, "Gonzalez as an Adamant Visionary (1939–43, 1945–51)," in *University of the Philippines: The First 75 Years (1908–1983)*, ed. Oscar M. Alfonso (Quezon City: University of the Philippines Press, 1985), 273.
35 Frank Ephraim, *Escape to Manila: From Nazi Tyranny to Japanese Terror* (Champaign: University of Illinois Press, 2003), 68–71; Quezon, *The Good Fight*, 193; Carunungan, *Quezon City*, 69; Mañalac, *Manila*, 73. Quezon was eventually recognized for his efforts in saving Jewish refugees during the Second World War.
36 Mañalac, *Manila*, 78.
37 Ibid., 75–76.
38 Michael Francis Ramos, "The Beginnings (1950–1974)," in *Lakbay: 40 Years of Cornerstone-Building in Faith*, 8–17 (Quezon City: Resurrection of Our Lord Parish, 2015), 10.
39 Kintanar et al., *Kuwentong Bayan*, 198, 419; Serrano, *A Brief History of Caloocan*, 7; Angeles S. Santos, *Ang Malabon (Katipunan ng Mahahalagang Kasulatan tungkol sa Bayang Malabon, Lalawigan ng Rizal)* [Malabon (A Compilation of Important Writings about the Town of Malabon, Rizal Province)] (Malabon: Dalubhasaang Epifanio de los Santos Press, 1975), 25–29; Antonio M. Molina, *Dusk and Dawn in the Philippines: Memoirs of a Living Witness of World War II* (Quezon City: New Day, 1996), 200; Labrador, *A Diary of the Japanese Occupation*, 163, 199; Agoncillo, *The Fateful Years*, vol. 2, 534, 641.
40 Franco-Calairo and Calairo, *Ang Kasaysayan ng Novaliches*, 99–103; Luis Taruc, *Born of the People* (New York: International Publishers, 1953), 181. Quote is from Agoncillo, *The Fateful Years*, vol. 2, 598.
41 Aguilar, *Nang Magdaan ang Daluyong*, 123–24; cf. Terami-Wada, *Sakdalistas' Struggle*, 174–77.
42 Pestaño-Jacinto, *Living with the Enemy*, 76.
43 Alfonso J. Aluit, *By Sword and Fire: The Destruction of Manila in World War II, 3 February –3 March 1945* (Makati City: Bookmark, 1994).
44 Benedict J. Kerkvliet, "Withdrawal and Resistance: The Political Significance of Food, Agriculture, and How People Lived during the Japanese Occupation in the Philippines," in *Autonomous Histories, Particular Truths: Essays in Honor of John R. W. Smail*, ed. Laurie Sears (Madison, WI: Center for Southeast Asian Studies, University of Wisconsin, 1993).

45 Although Partido Nacionalista and Nacionalista Party (NP) refer to the same party founded in 1907, I use the latter to refer to the postwar incarnation to avoid confusion.

46 Hartendorp, *History of Industry and Trade*, 253.

47 People's Homesite and Housing Corporation (PHHC), *Annual Report for the Fiscal Year 1955–1956* (Manila: PHHC, 1956), 12; Capital City Planning Commission, *The Master Plan for the New Capital City*, AP-24.

48 Elpidio Quirino, *The Quirino Way: Collection of Speeches and Addresses of Elpidio Quirino* (n.p.: Juan Collas, 1955), 246.

49 Lico, *Arkitekturang Filipino*, 375.

50 "Quezon City of Pre-War Grandeur Now Favorite Haunt of Rats, Crooks," *MT*, 21 Mar. 1946: 1.

51 Malcolm, *American Colonial Careerist*, 182.

52 *CR*, I (63), 30 Aug. 1946: 1360.

53 Philippine Congress, Republic Act No. 54: An Act to Repeal Executive Order Numbered Four Hundred Dated January Two Nineteen Hundred and Forty-Two and Executive Order Numbered Fifty-Eight Dated July Twenty-Six, Nineteen Hundred and Forty-Five, 10 Oct. 1946, *Chan Robles Virtual Law Library*, http://laws.chanrobles.com/republicacts/1_republicacts.php?id=54, accessed 3 Nov. 2016; "Drive against Gangsterism Covers Rizal," *MT*, 11 Oct. 1946: 1, 16.

54 Department of Finance, *Annual Report of the Secretary of Finance to the President of the Philippines for the Period from July 1, 1946 to June 30, 1947* (Manila: Bureau of Printing, 1949), 46.

55 UP, *Resurgence of the University*, 10.

56 UP, *Resurgence of the University*, 13–14, 30–31; United States Philippine War Damage Commission (PWDC), *Eighth Semiannual Report of the United States Philippine War Damage Commission, Manila, Philippines, for Period Ending June 30, 1950* (Washington, DC: Government Printing Office, 1950), 37; Lazaro, "Gonzalez as an Adamant Visionary," 287.

57 UP, *Resurgence of the University*, 26.

58 Elmer A. Ordoñez, *Diliman: Homage to the Fifties* (Quezon City: University of the Philippines Press, 2003), 4. For personal recollections of everyday life in Diliman in the 1950s and 1960s see Erlinda Enriquez Panlilio, "UP Beloved," in *The Manila We Knew*, ed. Erlinda Enriquez Panlilio (Pasig City: Anvil, 2006) and the essays in Narita Manuel Gonzalez and Gerardo T. Los Baños, eds., *U.P. Diliman: Home and Campus* (Quezon City: University of the Philippines Press, 2010). Most of these essays, however, overemphasize the idyllic atmosphere of the campus to the point of depicting it as a conflict-free space.

59 Lazaro, "Gonzalez as an Adamant Visionary," 273.

60 Vicente Tirona Paterno, *On My Terms: The Autobiography of Vicente Tirona Paterno* (Pasig City: Anvil, 2014), 35.

61 For a copy of the deed of sale, see Teodoro Evangelista, Deed of Sale, undated and unsigned document, EQP B132F3, File 004. Unfortunately, the sale covered land in Krus na Ligas where a community had long been settled prior to UP's transfer to Diliman. The affected residents repeatedly petitioned the university to remedy the situation. In 1975 UP transferred nine hectares of the Krus na Ligas site to the occupants through the Presidential Assistance for Housing and Resettlement Administration, Jose N. Endriga, "Corpuz and Soriano's Bifocal Administrations (1975–1981)," in *University of the Philippines: The First 75 Years*, ed. Oscar M. Alfonso (Quezon City: University of the Philippines Press, 1985), 531–32. More recently, in 2016, the UP BOR decided to sell lots in Krus na Ligas to bona fide residents. UP BOR, *The University of the Philippines Gazette*, vol. 46, no. 5: *Decisions of the Board of Regents,*

1318th Meeting, 27 May 2016 (Quezon City: Office of the Secretary, UP, 2016), 46–47, http://osu.up.edu.ph/wp-content/uploads/2016/08/1318-GAZETTE.pdf, accessed 28 Aug. 2016.

62   B. M. Gonzalez, *Thirty-sixth Annual Report of the President of the University of the Philippines to the Board of Regents for the Academic Year June 1, 1948–May 31, 1949* (Quezon City: University of the Philippines, 1950), 6. Quote is from UP, *Resurgence of the University*, 29.

63   Shirley S. Arandia, "Recollections of a Pioneer," in *U.P. Diliman: Home and Campus*, ed. Narita Manuel Gonzalez and Gerardo T. Los Baños (Quezon City: University of the Philippines Press, 2010).

64   UP, *Resurgence of the University*, 7–9.

65   Gonzalez, *Thirty-sixth Annual Report*, 6.

66   Ordoñez, *Diliman*, 3–5; Gonzalez, *Thirty-sixth Annual Report*, 6. The said library building is now named after Gonzalez. For a personal account of the transfer, see chapter 3 of Vicente C. Ponce, *Killing the Spider: Memoirs of Engr. Vicente C. Ponce* (Quezon City: E.C. TEC Commercial, 2010). Ponce was an engineering student at the time of relocation and became the engineering inspector and supervisor of construction at the Diliman campus in the 1950s (ibid., 32, 65).

67   Pante, "Far from Isolation."

68   Ramon C. Portugal, "The Diliman 'Republic,'" *Sunday Times Magazine*, 13 Jan. 1952: 12–14. Cf. Elmer A. Ordoñez, *The Other View*, vol. 3. *The Last Posts: The Manila Times (2010–2012)* (Quezon City: University of the Philippines Press, 2013), 300; Ponce, *Killing the Spider*, 131–34.

69   Rey Claro Casambre, "Growing up in the Diliman Republic," in *Serve the People: Ang Kasaysayan ng Radikal na Kilusan sa UP* [The History of the Radical Movement in UP], ed. Bienvenido Lumbera, Judy Taguiwalo, Roland Tolentino, Arnold Alamon, and Ramon Guillermo ([Quezon City]: IBON; Congress of Teachers and Educators for Nationalism and Democracy; Alliance of Concerned Teachers, 2008), 64.

70   Luis V. Teodoro, "UP in the Sixties: Life in the 'Diliman Republic,'" in *The University Experience: Essays on the 82nd Anniversary of the University of the Philippines*, ed. Belinda A. Aquino (Quezon City: University of the Philippines Press, 1991), 58.

71   Casambre, "Growing up in the Diliman Republic," 67. Eventually, Casambre joined the communist movement and still is a consultant to the National Democratic Front.

72   *CR* I (3), 16 Aug. 1945: 632; I (10), 10 June 1946: 190; II (45), 30 Apr. 1947: 648. On Cabarroguis's bills, see *CR* I (5), 18 Aug. 1945: 644; II (6), 4 Feb. 1947: 51.

73   Manuel Roxas, "Message on the State of the Nation to the Second Congress of the Philippines, June 3, 1946," in *Speeches, Addresses and Messages as President of the Philippines*, vol. 1: *Jan. 1946–Feb. 1, 1947*, 71–101 (Manila: Bureau of Printing, 1954), 99.

74   Committee on Capital City Site, "Report of the Committee on Capital City Site," 5.

75   Ibid., 5–8.

76   Ibid., 8.

77   Ibid., 9.

78   Ibid., 13–14.

79   S. V. Esguerra, Memorandum of 19 May 1947, EQP, B4F2, File 003.

80   Committee on Capital City Site, "Report of the Committee on Capital City Site," 18–19.

81   Ibid., 18.

82   Teodora V. Tiglao, *Health Practices in a Rural Community* (Quezon City: Community Development Research Council, University of the Philippines, 1964), 14.

83 Franco-Calairo and Calairo, *Ang Kasaysayan ng Novaliches*, 84, 101; Tiglao, *Health Practices in a Rural Community*, 22–23.

84 MWD, *Manila's Water Supply: Inauguration of Balara Filter Plant, October 24, 1935* (Manila: Bureau of Printing, 1935), 3–9, 22–23; P.W. Mack, Letter of MWD Acting Manager to the Secretary of the Interior, 15 Sept. 1926, unpublished letter, JRHP Box 26, Folder 26; "Rush Projects in Quezon City," *MDB*, 25 Apr. 1940, JRHP Box 31, Folder 10.

85 MWD, *Manila's Water Supply*, 7–13. On the Angat River Dam, see Sayre, *Fourth Annual Report*, 49. On the Balara Filters, see MWD, *Manila's Water Supply*; Black & Veatch International Consulting Engineers, *Master Plan for a Sewerage System for the Manila Metropolitan Area: Final Report* (Manila: Black & Veatch, 1969), 9-4; Francisco R. Coquia, "Development of Water Resources in the Philippines for Municipal-Industrial Uses," in United Nations Bureau of Flood Control, *Proceedings of the Sixth Regional Conference on Water Resources Development in Asia and the Far East*, Water Resources Series No. 28, 218–23 (New York: UN, 1965), 219.

86 Alona H. Sarte and Veronica F. Agbayani, *Quezon City: The Promised City with a Glorious Past, a Tangible Present and a Bright Future* (Manila: Catholic Trade School, 1953), 23.

87 Alexander A. Luna, ed., *Quezon City Directory, 1956–57* (Manila: Metro Publishing, 1956), 18; MWD, *Annual Report of the Metropolitan Water District for the Fiscal Year Ending June 30, 1951* (Manila: Bureau of Printing, 1952), 43; Paulo Alcazaren, "Jeproks: My Life in the Projects," in *The Manila We Know*, ed. Erlinda Enriquez Panlilio (Pasig City: Anvil, 2017), 106.

88 Committee on Capital City Site, "Report of the Committee on Capital City Site," 19–21.

89 Manuel A. Roxas, "Third State of the Nation Address, January 26, 1948: The Nation on the Road to Prosperity," *Official Gazette (OG)*, http://www.gov.ph/1948/01/26/manuel-roxas-the-nation-on-the-road-to-prosperity-third-state-of-the-nation-address-january-26-1948/, accessed 27 Oct. 2015.

90 Quezon City, *The Quezon City of Today* (Quezon City: Quezon City Hall, 1970), 7.

91 Information Sheet on Cesar H. Concio, 1951, 4, unpublished manuscript, JBVP, SG: National Planning Commission, Folder 2.

92 Philippine Congress, Republic Act 333 – An Act to Establish the Capital of the Philippines and the Permanent Seat of the National Government, 17 July 1948, *OG*, https://www.officialgazette.gov.ph/1948/07/17/republic-act-no-333/, accessed 27 Oct. 2015.

93 "Capital Site Bill Approved by President," *MT*, 16 July 1948: 1, 8.

94 Capital City Planning Commission, *The Master Plan for the New Capital City*, 3; "Juan Arellano Named to Head Planning Commission for New Capital Site in Quezon City," *MT*, 24 July 1948: 1, 4.

95 Information Sheet on Cesar H. Concio, 4.

96 Capital City Planning Commission, *The Master Plan for the New Capital City*, 5.

97 Ibid., 10.

98 Ibid., 8.

99 Charles Abrams and Otto Koenigsberger, "A Housing Program for the Philippine Islands," 88, unpublished report prepared for the United Nations Technical Assistance Administration (UNTAA), 14 January 1959, copy courtesy of the SURP Library, UP-Diliman, Quezon City.

100 Quezon City, *Laying of the Cornerstone*.

101 Committee on Capital City Site, "Report of the Committee on Capital City Site," 13.

102 Ibid., 14.

103 Pante, "Peripheral Pockets of Paradise."

NOTES   293

104 Sarte and Agbayani, *Quezon City*, 31.
105 Salvador P. Lopez, *Elpidio Quirino: The Judgment of History* (n.p.: Elpidio Quirino Foundation, 1990), 167.
106 Mamerto S. Miranda, Letter to Elpidio Quirino, 16 July 1951. EQP B56F5, File 034.
107 Pedro S. Sales, Memorandum for the Director of Animal Industry, 14 Aug. 1952, EQP B135F10, File 003; Elpidio Quirino and Pablo M. Sarangaya, Building Contract, unsigned contract, 15 May 1951, EQP B135F10, File 006; Pablo M. Sarangaya, Letter to the Country Gentleman, 8 May 1951, EQP B135F10, File 007.
108 Lopez, *Elpidio Quirino*, 167–69.
109 Committee on Capital City Site, "Report of the Committee on Capital City Site," 5. According to Quezon City resident Juan C. Cruz (most probably a pseudonym), who introduced himself as an "under-cover man for President Quirino," Croft was one of the "active saboteurs inside the government" and even called Quirino "dirty names." Croft supposedly did these things while he was in the Urban Planning Office. Cruz enumerated eleven other names in the Planning Office who were allegedly also anti-Quirino (Juan C. Cruz, Letter to Federico Mangahas, 4 Dec. 1949, EQP B56F5, File 016).
110 Sergio Osmeña, *Ten Months of President Osmeña's Administration: A Review of Work Done under Unprecedented Difficulties* (n.p.: n.p., n.d.), 14, copy available at AHC; Jorge B. Vargas, "City and National–Regional Planning in the Philippines: Its Nature, Problems," 7 Mar. 1953, 1, unpublished manuscript, JBVP, SG: National Planning Commission, Folder 2. According to a newspaper report, Croft strengthened his urban plans with the help of "invaluable suggestions" from "civic-minded Americans and Europeans" who were his fellow internees at the UST internee camp during the war (Renato Arevalo, "Out of the Ruins," *MT*, 10 June 1945: 6).
111 Committee on Capital City Site, "Report of the Committee on Capital City Site," 1.
112 Louis Croft, "General Plan of Major Thoroughfares, Metropolitan Manila: Preliminary Report," Prepared by the President's Office on City Planning, 13 June 1945, 5–10, copy available at AHC.
113 Philippine Congress, Republic Act 2140 – An Act Changing the Name of Highway 54 in the Province of Rizal to Epifanio de los Santos Avenue in Honor of Don Epifanio de los Santos, a Filipino Scholar, Jurist, and Historian, 7 Apr. 1959, *Chan Robles Virtual Law Library*, http://www.chanrobles.com/republicacts/republicactno2140.html#.WBQNVPp96Uk, accessed 29 Oct. 2016.
114 Ordoñez, *Diliman*, 87–88.
115 Information Sheet on Cesar H. Concio, 1–6.
116 Paulo Alcazaren, "Requiem for a Master Architect," *Philippine Star*, 30 Aug. 2008, http://www.philstar.com/modern-living/82437/requiem-master-architect, accessed 3 Sept. 2016.
117 Ibid.
118 Lico, *Arkitekturang Filipino*, 375.
119 Pauline K. M. van Roosmalen, "Netherlands Indies Town Planning: An Agent of Modernization (1905–1957)," in *Cars, Conduits, and Kampongs: The Modernization of the Indonesian City, 1920–1960*, ed. Freek Colombijn and Joost Coté (Leiden: Brill, 2015), 111–12; Farabi Fakih, "Kotabaru and the Housing Estate as Bulwark against the Indigenization of Colonial Java," in *Cars, Conduits, and Kampongs: The Modernization of the Indonesian City, 1920–1960*, ed. Freek Colombijn and Joost Coté (Leiden: Brill, 2015).
120 "Commission Form of Government Planned for Capital; Bill Signed," *MT*, 18 July 1948: 1, 14.
121 Jenkins, *American Economic Policy*, 64–69.
122 Salvador Araneta, *A Molave of His Country* (Malabon: AIA, 1970); Santiago, *Araneta*.

123 "Capital Site Bill Approved by President," 8.

124 Juan Arellano, Letter of Arellano to His Excellency, Elpidio Quirino, 9 Oct. 1948, 1, EQP, B4F2, File 003. However, a newspaper reported that the amount was PHP 21 million, not PHP 25 million, "Capital Site Agreed upon," 14.

125 Lico, *Arkitekturang Filipino*, 367.

126 US Philippine War Damage Commission (US PWDC), *Eighth Semiannual Report of the United States Philippine War Damage Commission, Manila, Philippines, for Period Ending June 30, 1950* (Washington, DC: Government Printing Office, 1950), 30.

127 Ibid., 36.

128 Portugal, "The Diliman 'Republic,'" 13.

129 Ordoñez, *Diliman*, 88. Cf. Hartendorp, *History of Industry and Trade*, 403; Ponce, *Killing the Spider*, 71.

130 Gonzalez, *Thirty-sixth Annual Report*, 5.

131 Ordoñez, *Diliman*, 88.

132 "Ang Ligalig ng mga Taga-Subdivision ng Santamesa" [The Uproar of the Residents of Santa Mesa Subdivision], *Lipang Kalabaw*, 28 May 1949: 7.

133 Luna, *Quezon City Directory*, 18.

134 "Walled City Urged as Capitol Site as Quezon City Draws Opposition," *MT*, 3 June 1948: 1–2.

135 "Discard Antipolo as Capital Site," *MT*, 22 June 1948: 1, 4.

136 "Capital Site Agreed upon," *MT*, 23 June 1948: 1, 14.

137 "Capital Site Bill Approved by President," 1.

138 "Senate Holds up Capital Site," *MT*, 26 June 1948: 1, 14.

139 Ibid., 1.

140 Macario B. Asistio, "Why Caloocan Should Be a City," in *2 Golden Decades: Kalookan, 1951–1970*, ed. Agapito M. Joaquin (n.p.: n.p., 1971), 103–4, copy available at the Caloocan City Library. See also Serrano, *A Brief History of Caloocan*, 8.

141 Macario B. Asistio, "Asistio to Businessman," in *2 Golden Decades*, 210–12. Quote is on pp. 211–12. See also Serrano, *A Brief History of Caloocan*, 7.

142 Quijano de Manila, "Caloocan: The 39th City," *PFP*, 24 Feb. 1962: 46–48, 50, esp. 48.

143 Ibid., 50.

144 Augusto F. Perez, "Office of the City Engineer: Its Organization, Programs, and Accomplishments," in *2 Golden Decades*, 142–149. Quote is on p. 149. See also Macario B. Asistio, "Liham sa mga Taga-Kalookan," in *2 Golden Decades*, 156–160, esp. p. 159.

145 Quijano de Manila, "Caloocan," 50.

146 Carunungan, *Quezon City*, 83.

147 Black & Veatch, *Master Plan for a Sewerage System*, 3–4.

148 See, for example, the interplay among fascist modernity and malarial geographies in Italian cities in Federico Caprotti, *Mussolini's Cities: Internal Colonialism in Italy, 1930–1939* (Youngstown, NY: Cambria, 2007).

149 Antonio Ejercito and Cornelio M. Urbino, "A Malaria Survey and Control in Quezon City," *Philippine Journal of Science* 79 (3), 1950: 249–64. Quote is on pp. 249–50.

150 Ibid., 259–60; Capital City Planning Commission, *The Master Plan for the New Capital City*, AP-24. See Ordinance No. 17 in Quezon City Council, *1939 Quezon City Ordinances*.

151 Benedict Kerkvliet, *The Huk Rebellion: A Study of Peasant Revolt in the Philippines* (Quezon City: New Day, 1979); Vina Lanzona, *Amazons of the Huk Rebellion: Gender, Sex, and Revolution in the Philippines* (Quezon City: Ateneo de Manila University Press, 2009).

152 "Drive against Gangsterism," 1.

NOTES   295

153   Guillermo B. Francisco, Secret Memorandum for the President, 19 Oct. 1950, p. 5, EQP B4F4, File 001; National Intelligence Coordinating Agency (NICA), Spot Intelligence Report No. 26, 1 Dec. 1949, p. 2, EQP B5F9, File 001; A. G. Gabriel, Daily Intelligence Summary, 6 Oct. 1950, p. 5. EQP B6F1, File 003; A. G. Gabriel, Weekly Intelligence Summary No. 42, p. 4, 19 Feb. 1951, EQP B6F4, File 007; A. G. Gabriel, Weekly Intelligence Summary No. 44, 5 Mar. 1951, p. 5, EQP B6F5, File 003. Up to the 1970s clashes between government forces and dissident armed groups (including the HMB and the upstart New People's Army) continued to happen in Novaliches (Ferdinand E. Marcos, Diary of Ferdinand E. Marcos, 9 Feb. 1970, *The Philippine Diary Project*, https://philippinediaryproject.wordpress.com/1970/02/09/february-9-1970-monday/, accessed 27 Aug. 2016).

154   Interestingly, Huk leader Luis Taruc worked for the MWD in the prewar period (Taruc, *Born of the People*, 24–25).

155   NICA, Spot Intelligence Report No. 12, Re: Projected Huk Assassination Plot, 7 Nov. 1949, EQP B5F7, File012, 2–3; Francisco, Secret Memorandum for the President, 2.

156   Phillip C. Parnell, "The Composite State: The Poor and the Nation in Manila," in *Ethnography in Unstable Places: Everyday Lives in Contexts of Dramatic Political Change*, ed. Carol J. Greenhouse, Elizabeth Mertz, and Kay B. Warren (Durham: Duke University Press, 2002), 150.

157   Ordoñez, *Diliman*, 7. See also Arandia, "Recollections of a Pioneer," 269.

158   Ordoñez, *The Other View*, vol. 3, 62–63, 301.

159   Anselmo B. Mercado, "Father Masterson's 'I'mpossible Dream," *Kinaadman* 32, 2010: 1–21, esp. 7.

160   See the special issue of *The Guidon* on the blessing of the new campus on 8 Dec. 1951, copy courtesy of ADMUA.

161   Alberto V. Ampil, "An Interview with Fr Alberto V Ampil, SJ: Ms Chay Florentino-Hofileña, Interviewer," in Ateneo de Manila, *University Traditions: The Social Sciences Interviews*, ed. Ramón Sunico (Quezon City: Ateneo de Manila University, Office for Mission and Identity and Organizational Development, 2010), 10. Most probably, Ampil was referring to January 1952, and not 1951.

162   "There are Strange Goings on in Q.C.," *The Diliman Star* (*DS*), 8 Nov. 1952: 7.

163   Filemon V. Tutay, "Gang Hideout Busted," *PFP*, 21 Aug. 1948: 6–7, 59. Quote is on p. 6.

164   "Quezon City of Pre-War Grandeur," 1; "Drive against Gangsterism," 1, 16.

165   Quirino, *The Quirino Way*, 374.

166   Guéguen, "Moving from Binondo."

167   Caroline S. Hau, *The Chinese Question: Ethnicity, Nation, and Region in and beyond the Philippines* (Quezon City: Ateneo de Manila University Press, 2014), 176–77; cf. Yung Li Yuk-wai, *The Huaqiao Warriors: Chinese Resistance Movement in the Philippines, 1942–45* (Quezon City: Ateneo de Manila University Press, 1996).

168   See the following files in EQP B6F3: A. G. Gabriel, Daily Intelligence Summary No. 346, 12 Jan. 1951, 4, File 001; NICA, Daily Intelligence Summary No. 352, 19 Jan. 1951, 2, File 004; A. G. Gabriel, Weekly Intelligence Summary, No. 38, 22 Jan. 1951, 11–12, File 005. See also A. G. Gabriel, Weekly Intelligence Summary No. 44, 5 Mar. 1951, 7, EQP B6F5, File 003.

169   C. M. Hoskins, "Real Estate," *ACCJ* 24 (8), 1948: 289–90.

170   Teodoro M. Locsin, "One More Racket? The Case of the Capital City Site," *PFP*, 22 May 1948: 2–3, 59; Teodoro M. Locsin, "One More Racket? (continuation)," *PFP*, 19 June 1948: 4–5.

171   "Capital Site Agreed upon," 14.

172   "Senate Holds up Capital Site," 14.

173   "Propriety," *PFP*, 3 July 1948: 10.

174 "Senate Holds up Capital Site," 14.

175 "Capital Site Agreed upon," 14.

176 Antonio Varias, "Real Estate," *ACCJ* 31 (8), 1955: 349. Sycip was chair of the Philippine Chinese General Chamber of Commerce from 1934 to 1935 and 1937 to 1941 (Wong Kwok-Chu, *The Chinese in the Philippine Economy, 1898–1941* [Quezon City: Ateneo de Manila University Press, 1999], 77–78).

177 Gleeck, *The American Half-Century*, 428.

178 Committee on Capital City Site, "Report of the Committee on Capital City Site," 2.

179 Antonio de las Alas, Diary of Antonio de las Alas, 17 May 1945, *The Philippine Diary Project*, https://philippinediaryproject.wordpress.com/1945/05/17/may-17-1945-thursday/, accessed 27 Aug. 2016.

180 F. C. de la Rama, *I Made Millions and Lost Them* (n.p.: Nation-Ad, 1957), 223.

181 However, de la Rama failed to rake in the profits because of complications in the title of the property and the actual administration of the land during and after the war. At the time de la Rama wrote his memoirs, the estate was worth PHP 12 per square meter and PHP 13.44 million in total (ibid., 224–25). According to the 1948 exposé of the *Philippines Free Press*, the hacienda co-owned by Arranz, Avelino, and Aquino mentioned above was purchased from de la Rama, Locsin, "One More Racket? (continuation)," 4.

182 The profitability of moving capital cities was also demonstrated in the case of Trece Martires, the current capital of Cavite province. Local strongman Justiniano Montano lobbied the transfer of Cavite's capital to the said town. The relocation pushed through and led to the increase in the real estate values of his properties in Trece Martires (John Sidel, "Walking in the Shadow of the Big Man: Justiniano Montano and Failed Dynasty Building in Cavite, 1935–1972," in *An Anarchy of Families: State and Family in the Philippines*, ed. Alfred W. McCoy [Quezon City: Ateneo de Manila University Press, 1994], 137).

183 Office of the Mayor [City of Manila], *City Gazette: Published Fortnightly by the Office of the Mayor of the City of Manila*, vol. 1, no. 6, 16 Dec. 1942 (Manila: Office of the Mayor, 1942), 83, 88.

184 Jose A. Quirino, "Cockfighting Becomes Big Business," *PFP*, 4 Aug. 1956: 20–23, esp. 22.

185 Leon O. Ty, "'Many of Our Countrymen are Homeless,'" *PFP*, 18 Sept. 1947: 4–5, 49.

186 Bureau of the Census and Statistics, *Facts and Figures about Economic and Social Conditions of the Philippines, 1946–1947* (Manila: Bureau of Printing, 1948), 100–101. On the postwar resurgence of prostitution in Manila, see Leon Ty, "Another Gardenia for Manila?" *PFP*, 31 Jan. 1948: 8, 41.

187 SC, en banc. "Sy Chiuco vs. Collector of Internal Revenue," G. R. no. L-13387, 28 Mar. 1960, *The Lawphil Project*, http://www.lawphil.net/judjuris/juri1960/mar1960/gr_l-13387_1960.html, accessed 18 May 2015.

188 "Rival Gangsters Stage Gun Duel in Cabaret; 1 Killed, 4 Wounded," *MT*, 16 Apr. 1946: 1.

189 Quezon City Council, 1955 Ordinances, n.d. (unpublished and unpaginated compilation available at the Quezon City Public Library).

190 SC, en banc, "Pedro Casimiro vs. Leon Roque and Ernesto Gonzales," G. R. no. L-7643, 27 Apr. 1956, *The Lawphil Project*, http://www.lawphil.net/judjuris/juri1956/apr1956/gr_l-7643_1956.html, accessed 14 Sept. 2016.

191 Bureau of the Census and Statistics, *Special Release no. 70-B (Region I), Series of 1968, Month of May: Total Family Expenditures by Expenditure Group and Item of Expenditure, Region I: 1965* (Manila: Bureau of the Census and Statistics, 1968), 1, 8.

192 I. Santos Diaz, Memorandum for His Excellency, Pres. Elpidio Quirino, 5 Nov. 1951, 1–2. EQP, B56F5, File 039.

NOTES   297

193   Quirino, "Cockfighting Becomes Big Business," 23. J. Amado Araneta was a friend of de la Rama, who blamed his financial ruin partly to his addiction to gambling (including cockfighting), which Araneta abetted.

194   Quijano de Manila, *Reportage on Lovers: A Medley of Factual Romances, Happy or Tragical, Most of Which Made News* (Pasig City: Anvil, 2009), 49.

195   For a vivid description of the 1969 derby in Araneta Coliseum, see the chapter entitled "May 1969" in Quijano de Manila, *Manila: Sin City? And Other Chronicles* (Metro Manila: National Book Store, 1980), 237–51. Both quotes are on p. 237.

196   Nick Joaquin, *The Aquinos of Tarlac: An Essay on History as Three Generations* (Metro Manila: Solar, 1986), 285.

197   Quirino, "Cockfighting Becomes Big Business."

198   McGee, *The Southeast Asian City*, 76.

199   Laquian, "The Asian City and the Political Process," 44–49; Donald M. Seekins, *State and Society in Modern Rangoon* (Abingdon: Routledge, 2011), 82–84; Abidin Kusno, *Behind the Postcolonial: Architecture, Urban Space and Political Cultures in Indonesia* (London and New York: Routledge, 2000); Freek Colombijn and Joost Coté, "Modernization of the Indonesian City, 1920–1960," in *Cars, Conduits, and Kampongs: The Modernization of the Indonesian City, 1920–1960*, ed. Freek Colombijn and Joost Coté (Leiden: Brill, 2015), 9.

200   Anderson, *Imagined Communities*, 24–25.

201   La Loma's notoriety has parallels in Ho Chi Minh City's outer-city districts, which the Vietnamese press depicted as zones of "social evils," Erik Harms, *Saigon's Edge: On the Margins of Ho Chi Minh City* (Minneapolis: University of Minnesota Press, 2011), 11.

4, *Jeprox* Ambiguity

1   Le Corbusier, *Toward an Architecture*, trans. John Goodman (Los Angeles: Getty Research Institute, 2007), 89. Cf. Fishman, *Urban Utopias in the Twentieth Century*, 187.

2   Eric S. Caruncho, *Punks, Poets, Poseurs: Reportage on Pinoy Rock & Roll* (Pasig City: Anvil, 1996), 130. Juan de la Cruz Band's 1976 rock hit "Laki sa Layaw" (spoiled brat; pampered child) popularized the term *jeprox*.

3   Quijano de Manila, *Language of the Streets and Other Essays* (Metro Manila: National Book Store, 1980), 21.

4   Clearly, the jeprox and Quezon City's projects stood in contrast to the lower-class connotation (even actual ghettoization) of the (housing) projects in the American popular imagination. On the ghettoization of public housing in the US, see Jackson, *Crabgrass Frontier*, 219–30.

5   Jim Richardson, *Komunista: The Genesis of the Philippine Communist Party, 1902–1935* (Quezon City: Ateneo de Manila University Press, 2011), 152, 230–35, 255–57; "Communism in University of the Philippines?," 47–48; Gregorio Santayana [pseud. Jose Lava], "Milestones in the History of the Philippine Communist Party" (1950), 9–11, 31, unpublished manuscript, copy courtesy of the Filipiniana Section, Rizal Library, Ateneo de Manila University.

6   P. N. Abinales, "The Left and the Philippine Student Movement: Random Historical Notes on Party Politics and Sectoral Struggles," *Kasarinlan: Philippine Journal of Third World Studies* 1 (2), 1985: 41–45. Quote is on p. 42.

7   Jose Y. Dalisay, Jr., *The Lavas: A Filipino Family* (Pasig City: Anvil, 1999), 99.

8   Ibid., 99–100; Paterno, *On My Terms*, 25, 32; Ordoñez, *Diliman*, 7–10; Teodoro, "UP in the Sixties," 62; Reynaldo C. Ileto, "The 'Unfinished Revolution' in Philippine Political

Discourse," *Southeast Asian Studies* 31 (1), 1993): 62–82, esp. 64–65; Preciosa de Joya, "Exorcising Communist Specters and Witch Philosophers: The Struggle for Academic Freedom of 1961," *Kritika Kultura* 26 (2016): 4–32, http://journals.ateneo.edu/ojs/kk/article/view/KK2016.02602/2220, accessed 13 Aug. 2016. For analyses of the intra-campus tussles of the 1950s, see Rosario Mendoza Cortes, "Tan's Devoted Presidency (1951–1956): A Campus Shaken by Strife until Redeemed by Sobriety," in *University of the Philippines: The First 75 Years*, ed. Oscar M. Alfonso (Quezon City: University of the Philippines Press, 1985), 324–31, and Milagros C. Guerrero, "Sinco's Clash with Conservatism (1958–1962)," in *University of the Philippines: The First 75 Years*, ed. Oscar M. Alfonso (Quezon City: University of the Philippines Press, 1985), esp. 375–82. For sympathetic accounts about Delaney and his cause, see the various essays in the chapter entitled "Religious Life on Campus," in Gonzalez and Los Baños, *U.P. Diliman*, 89–158; and Oscar L. Evangelista, *Icons and Institutions: Essays on the History of the University of the Philippines, 1952–2000* (Quezon City: University of the Philippines Press, 2008), 1–24.

9   F. M. Serrano, *Atoms-for-Peace in the Philippines: Official Report of the Philippine Delegation to the International Conference on the Peaceful Uses of Atomic Energy* (New York: Philippine Mission to the United Nations, [1955?]); Roland S. B. Escalante, "Symbol of Our Nuclear Era," *PFP*, 28 Sept. 1963: 10–11.

10 Dalisay, Jr., *The Lavas*, 115, 141–42.

11 PHHC, *Annual Report, 1955–1956*, 12, 96.

12 Edward Geary Lansdale, *In the midst of Wars: An American's Mission to Southeast Asia* (New York: Harper & Row, 1972), 18.

13 Ibid., 35–37, 46.

14 Patricia Ann Paez, *The Bases Factor: Realpolitik of RP–US Relations* (Manila: Center for Strategic and International Studies of the Philippines, 1985), 382.

15 Ongpauco, "Quezon City," 20; Ordoñez, *The Other View*, vol. 3, 62, 115, 293–97. Valeriano also worked closely with Lansdale (ibid., 297).

16 McCoy, *Policing America's Empire*, 384; Catuca [pseud.], "The Darker Life," *DS*, 22 Nov. 1952: 3.

17 UP, *Resurgence of the University*, 27; Ordoñez, *Diliman*, 7.

18 Crisostomo, *Quezon City*, 13; Carunungan, *Quezon City*, 80.

19 Carunungan, *Quezon City*, 82, 99–100. Quote is on p. 95.

20 Charles Abrams, *Man's Struggle for Shelter in an Urbanizing World* (Cambridge: MIT Press, 1964), 80–81; Caoili, *The Origins of Metropolitan Manila*, 60.

21 On the ISI experiment in the 1950s, see John H. Power and Gerardo P. Sicat, *The Philippines: Industrialization and Trade Policies* (Paris: Development Centre of the Organization for Economic Co-operation and Development; London: Oxford University Press, 1971); and chapters 4 and 5 of Takagi, *Central Banking as State Building*. See also Alejandro Lichauco, *Nationalist Economics: History Theory and Practice* (Quezon City: Institute for Rural Industrialization, 1988), 138–62; James K. Boyce, *The Political Economy of Growth and Impoverishment in the Marcos Era* (Quezon City: Ateneo de Manila University Press, 1993), 7.

22 For a nuanced take on this phrase, see McPhelin, "Manila: The Primate City," 789.

23 Power and Sicat, *The Philippines*, 102–15; Emmanuel S. de Dios and Paul D. Hutchcroft, "Political Economy," in *The Philippine Economy: Development, Policies, and Challenges*, ed. Arsenio M. Balisacan and Hal Hill (Quezon City: Ateneo de Manila University Press, 2003), 47; Romeo Bautista and Gwendolyn Tecson, "International Dimensions," in *The*

Philippine Economy: Development, Policies, and Challenges, ed. Arsenio M. Balisacan and Hal Hill (Quezon City: Ateneo de Manila University Press, 2003), 154.

24 Ty, "'Many of Our Countrymen are Homeless,'" 4. Lot prices in Manila could fetch prices as high as PhP 100 per square meter, while floor prices were no lower than PHP 15 per square meter (Ibid., 4).

25 Crisostomo, *Quezon City*, 26; G. Viola Fernando, House Bill no. 2798, submitted during the third session of the Second Congress of the Republic of the Philippines, 1953, p. 1, JBVP, SG: National Planning Commission, Folder 2.

26 S. Ombra Amilbangsa, Paulino A. Alonzo, and Gaudencio E. Abordo, House Bill no. 2850, submitted during the third session of the Second Congress of the Republic of the Philippines, 1953, 1. JBVP, SG: National Planning Commission, Folder 2.

27 Abrams, *Man's Struggle for Shelter*, 287. In Indonesia, concerns about slums turning into hotbeds of communism predate the Cold War. As a result of the 1926 uprising by the Partai Komunis Indonesia in Banten, urban planners in Batavia began to contemplate about the susceptibility of kampong dwellers to radical ideologies and the necessary steps to mitigate it (Hans Versnel and Freek Colombijn, "Rückert and Hoesni Thamrin: Bureaucrat and Politician in Colonial Kampung Improvement," in *Cars, Conduits, and Kampongs: The Modernization of the Indonesian City, 1920–1960*, ed. Freek Colombijn and Joost Coté [Leiden: Brill, 2015], 142–43).

28 NICA, Spot Intelligence Report No. 12, 3–5.

29 Jose O. Corpuz, Committee report no. 1833, submitted by the House Committee on Agrarian and Social Welfare, 10 Mar. 1953, ii. JBVP, SG: National Planning Commission, Folder 2.

30 In many ways urban housing worked in the same way as rural resettlements in Mindanao did in the name of counter-insurgency (Alfredo B. Saulo, *Communism in the Philippines: An Introduction*, rev. ed. [Quezon City: Ateneo de Manila University Press, 1990], 48; Morris Juppenlatz, *Cities in Transformation: The Urban Squatter Problem of the Developing World* [St. Lucia: University of Queensland Press, 1970], 97; Faina C. Abaya-Ulindang, *Resettling the Huks in the Land of Promise: The Story of the Economic Development Corps in Mindanao, 1950–1970* [Manila: National Historical Commission of the Philippines, 2017]).

31 Nancy H. Kwak, *A World of Homeowners: American Power and the Politics of Housing Aid* (Chicago: University of Chicago Press, 2015), 46. Interestingly, Sen. Joseph McCarthy, infamous for whipping up anticommunist hysteria in the US, was vice-chairman of a joint housing committee in Congress. McCarthy viewed public housing as "a breeding ground for communists" (ibid., 30).

32 This link was apparent in the rise of suburbia in postwar America. On this matter, see chapter 5 of Cohen, *A Consumers' Republic*.

33 Loh Kah Seng, *Squatters into Citizens: The 1961 Bukit Ho Swee Fire* (Singapore: NUS Press, 2013).

34 PHHC, *Annual Report, 1955–1956*, 6.

35 Ibid., 6; Roman Careaga, "People's Homesite and Housing Corporation: Its Vital Role," *DS*, 22 Nov. 1952: 2, 5, esp. p. 2.

36 Gary S. Makasiar, "Housing Summary," in National Economic Development Authority, Housing in the Philippines: Preparatory Materials for the Conference on Housing, 16 Apr. 1973 (unpublished manuscript, copy available at the Rizal Library, Ateneo de Manila University), 13.

37 PHHC, *Annual Report, 1961–1962* (n.p.: PHHC, [1962?]), 9–10.

38 PHHC, *Annual Report, 1955–1956*, 86; UP, *University Perspectives*, 431–49.

39 "Historical Data for Quezon City," 6; J. S. Furnivall, *Experiment in Independence: The Philippines* (Manila: Solidaridad, 1974), 95. The factory, however, was eventually sold to a private company, who then sold the blocks to the PHHC at retail prices (Abrams, *Man's Struggle for Shelter*, 83).

40 Kwak, *A World of Homeowners*, 46.

41 PHILCUSA, "The Philippines and ECA Assistance: Annual Report of the Philippine Council for United States Aid for the Period Ending June 30, 1952," 1, EQP B22F7, File 002. The establishment of PHILCUSA was a direct result of a bilateral agreement, often referred to as the Quirino–Foster Agreement, between the US and the Philippines regarding US aid (ibid., 12).

42 Ibid., 11; G. Frank Cordner, *Housing: Challenge to the Philippines* (Manila: US Foreign Operations Mission to the Philippines, 1953), 1–2; George E. Taylor, *The Philippines and the United States: Problems of Partnership* (New York: Frederick A. Praeger, 1964), 5–6; Kwak, *A World of Homeowners*, 265.

43 PHILCUSA, Progress Report by Project under the ECA Aid Program to the Philippines as of March 31, 1952, p. 3, EQP B22F6, File 011; Cordner, *Housing*, 7–8, 22–23; PHHC, *Annual Report, 1955–1956*, 42; PHHC, *Annual Report, 1961–1962*, 9–10; SWA, *Annual Report of the Social Welfare Administration for the Fiscal Year 1956–1957* (Manila: SWA, [1958?]), 14.

44 US Congress, *Mutual Security Act of 1958: Hearings before the Committee on Foreign Affairs, House of Representatives, Eighty-Fifth Congress, Second Session*, part 1 (Washington, DC: Government Printing Office, 1958), 874.

45 Luis [Louis] H. Pink, "A Housing Program for the Philippines," *ACCJ* 32 (2), 1946: 6, 21, 24–25, 28; N. J. Demerath and Richard N. Kuhlman, "Toward a Housing Program for the Philippines: A Report to the National Housing Commission," 20 Oct. 1945, 22–24, unpublished report, copy courtesy of the Filipiniana Division, UP-Diliman Main Library. The *ACCJ* misspelled Pink's first name.

46 Osmeña, *Ten Months of President Osmeña's Administration*, 14; Cordner, *Housing*, 1, 44–47. The Bell Mission was led by Daniel W. Bell, President of the American Security and Trust Company, PHILCUSA, "The Philippines and ECA Assistance, 4.

47 Hartendorp, *History of Industry and Trade*, 404; Cordner, *Housing*, 24; Bernard Wagner, *Housing and Urban Development in the Philippines* (Manila: USAID, 1968), 1.

48 PHHC, *Annual Report for the Fiscal Year 1956–1957* (Manila: Bureau of Printing, 1958), 33; Abrams and Koenigsberger, "A Housing Program for the Philippine Islands"; PHHC, *Annual Report, 1962–63* (n.p.: PHHC, [1963?]), 9.

49 Cordner, *Housing*, 25. See also PHHC, *Annual Report, 1961–1962*, 9, 12.

50 Cordner, *Housing*, 25.

51 Gregorio AQ. Limjoco, Resolution expressing profound gratitude to His Excellency, 25 Oct. 1953, p. 1. EQP B114F5, File 015.

52 Gregorio AQ. Limjoco, Letter to Elpidio Quirino, 1 Oct. 1953, 1. EQP B114F5, File 015.

53 Ibid., 1.

54 Kamuning Corner Lots Association, Letter to Elpidio Quirino, 31 Oct. 1951, p. 1. EQP B56F5, File 038.

55 Ibid., 1–2.

56 Limjoco, Letter to Elpidio Quirino, 1–2.

57 Limjoco, Resolution Expressing Profound Gratitude to His Excellency, 1.

58 de los Reyes and Lumanlan, *Sandiwaan sa Kamuning*, 74.

59 Cordner, *Housing*, 17.

60 Ibid., 17; PHHC, *Annual Report, 1961–1962*, 2.

NOTES   301

61   Cordner, *Housing*, 16.

62   PHHC, *Annual Report, 1955–1956*, 11–12.

63   Ibid., 11.

64   Abrams, *Man's Struggle for Shelter*, 83.

65   *CR* III (43), 5 Apr. 1948: 880; Abrams and Koenigsberger, "A Housing Program for the Philippine Islands," 71, 77.

66   Abrams and Koenigsberger, "A Housing Program for the Philippine Islands," 71.

67   Severo Julian, "'Facts and Figures': Support Rogers Exposé of PHHC," *PFP,* 9 Aug. 1952: 40–41. Quote is on p. 40. A group of realtors who formed an advisory committee on urban land and housing held a contrasting view. In their report to Quirino, they observed: "Selling prices of lots sold by the PHHC have been found too low leaving a very substantial margin for speculators, who in many cases, have purchased the best lots with the intention of reselling them." However, such a divergent view is perhaps a product of the realtors underlying interest in maintaining "fair competition" in the urban land market, a bias the realtors themselves recognized (F. Calero, Report of the Advisory Committee on Urban Land and Housing Distribution and the Squatters Problem, 30 Apr. 1951, unpublished report, 32, EQP B132F2, File 001). Furthermore, the same committee lamented that the PHHC's operations were "not being carried out in a truly business-like manner" (ibid., 33).

68   Alberto M. Alfaro, "Low-Cost Housing for the Rich?," *PFP,* 28 Jan. 1956: 20, 45–46.

69   Diosdado Macapagal, *A Stone for the Edifice: Memoirs of a President* (Quezon City: Mac Publishing, 1968); PHHC, *Annual Report, 1961–1962*, 10.

70   PHHC, *Annual Report, 1962–1963*, 8.

71   Amador F. Brioso, Jr., *Arsenio H. Lacson of Manila* (Mandaluyong City: Anvil, 2015), 213.

72   N. G. Rama, "Hasty PHHC Deal Questioned," *PFP,* 2 Aug. 1958: 30–31, 34–35; Napoleon G. Rama, "Stinking Mess in the PHHC," *PFP,* 20 Sept. 1958: 5, 69; Ramiro C. Alvarez, "'Twilight' Scandals at the PHHC," *PFP,* 2 Apr. 1966: 22; SC en banc, Vicente Fragante vs PHHC, G.R. No. L-16020, 30 Jan. 1962, *Chan Robles Virtual Law Library,* http://www.chanrobles.com/scdecisions/jurisprudence1962/jan1962/gr_l-16020_1962.php, accessed 28 Aug. 2016.

73   Abrams, *Man's Struggle for Shelter*, 81–83; Hartendorp, *History of Industry and Trade: The Magsaysay Administration*, 70; Abrams and Koenigsberger, "A Housing Program for the Philippine Islands," 7; PHHC, *Annual Report, 1961–1962*, ii.

74   Malacañang Press Office, *The New Era Starts: The First Year of the Macapagal Administration* (Manila: n.p., [1963?]), 12, 47, 222.

75   Alcazaren, "Jeproks," 103.

76   Aprodicio A. Laquian, *Slums are for People: The Barrio Magsaysay Pilot Project in Philippine Urban Community Development* (Honolulu: East–West Center Press, 1971), 227, 230.

77   Camba, "Private-led Suburbanization."

78   Juan Arellano, Letter to Elpidio Quirino, 5 Jan. 1950, 1. EQP B4F2, File 001.

79   B. M. Gonzalez, Letter to Elpidio Quirino, 17 Mar. 1950, 1. EQP B4F2, File 002.

80   Camba, "Private-led Suburbanization," 11.

81   Sale Agreement between PHHC and Miguel Morelos & Sons, Inc., 3 Dec. 1952, p. 1, EQP B33F5, File 001; PHHC, *Annual Report, 1955–1956*, 96.

82   Office of the President, Official Month in Review: March 1954, *OG* 50 (3), lxv–xcii, http://www.gov.ph/1954/03/01/official-month-in-review-march-1954/, accessed 24 Aug. 2016; Office of the President, Official Month in Review: February 1955, *OG* 51 (2), liii–xci, http://www.gov.ph/1955/02/01/official-month-in-review-february-1955/, accessed 24 Aug. 2016.

83   Isabelo T. Crisostomo, *Cory: Profile of a President* (Quezon City: J. Kriz, 1986), 7.

84 Cristina Pantoja Hidalgo, "Elegy to My Lost Home," in *The Manila We Know*, ed. Erlinda Enriquez Panlilio (Mandaluyong City: Anvil, 2017); Ocampo, "Swan Song for Broadway," 120–22.

85 Guéguen, "Moving from Binondo," 122; National Census and Statistics Office (NCSO), *1970 Census of Population and Housing: Rizal* (Manila: National Census and Statistics Office, [1974?]), 320.

86 Hau, *The Chinese Question*, 30–31; Guéguen, "Moving from Binondo," 122.

87 Guéguen, "Moving from Binondo," 130.

88 Ibid., 132.

89 Ibid., 132; Hau, *The Chinese Question*, 217–18.

90 "Historical Data for Quezon City," 5–6.

91 Roman A. Cruz, Jr., "The Ateneo Story," in Ateneo de Manila University, *Aegis 1959*, 1–138 (Quezon City: Ateneo de Manila University, [1959?]), 68; "Six New Buildings at Balara All Set for Dec. 8th Blessing," *The Guidon*, 27 Nov. 1951: 1; "Loyola's Sons Frolic on New Heights," *The Guidon*, 22 Jan. 1952: 8; "Reconstruction," *The Guidon* 1949 Christmas-Tide News Magazine, 4, copy courtesy of the Ateneo de Manila University Archives. See also the special issue of *The Guidon* on the blessing of the new campus on 8 Dec. 1951, copy courtesy of the Ateneo de Manila University Archives.

92 Supreme Court of the Philippines, first division, "La Vista Association, Inc. vs. Court of Appeals, et al," G.R. no. 95252, 5 Sept. 1997, http://sc.judiciary.gov.ph/jurisprudence/1997/sep1997/95252.htm, accessed 30 Nov. 2015. Cf. Delia D. Aguilar, *Filipino Housewives Speak*, ed. Marjorie Evasco (Manila: Institute of Women's Studies, St. Scholastica's College, 1991), 27. Also, both Ateneo and Maryknoll received war damage payments from the PWDC. The amounts approved for Ateneo and Maryknoll were PHP1,322,199.80 and PHP36,794.16, respectively. For comparative purposes, the corresponding amount earmarked for the Archbishop of Manila was PHP 3,305,033.12 (John A. O'Donnell, Letter to Congressman John W. McCormack, 22 Apr. 1949, 4–5, EQP B21F5, File022).

93 See Xavierville Estate advertisement on p. 5 of the *The Guidon*, 23 Sept. 1952.

94 Rolando V. de la Rosa, *Beginnings of the Filipino Dominicans* (Manila: UST Publishing House, 1990), 196.

95 Alcazaren, "Jeproks," 104; Meliton B. Juanico, *Metro Manila: A Travel and Historical Guide* (Quezon City: M. J. Editorial Consultants, 1983), 183.

96 Ibid., 109; Hedman and Sidel, *Philippine Politics and Society*, 131; James Farrer, "Globalizing Asian Cuisines: From Eating for Strength to Culinary Cosmopolitanism—A Long History of Culinary Globalization," *Education about Asia* 16 (3), 2011: 33–37, esp. 35, http://s3.amazonaws.com/academia.edu.documents/6977629/Farrer_EAA-16-3.pdf?AWSAccessKeyId=AKIAJ56TQJRTWSMTNPEA&Expires=1478267784&Signature=B7yuAPAYbtZRBw7%2BZgLf%2FhdP%2FCs%3D&response-content-disposition=inline%3B%-20filename%3DGlobalizing_Asian_Cuisines_From_Eating_f.pdf, accessed 4 Nov. 2016.

97 Jose V. Abueva, *Quezon City Experiment: The Story behind the Quezon City Citizens League for Good Government and the 1959 Election*, reprint (Manila: Regal Printing, 1963), 3.

98 Hedman and Sidel, *Philippine Politics and Society*, 124; Edward R. Kiunisala, "Politics around Manila," *PFP*, 2 Nov. 1963: 4–5, 62–63, 68, esp. p. 62; Quezon City, *The Quezon City of Today*, 5.

99 Quezon City, *The Quezon City of Today*, 5.

100 "Historical Data for Quezon City," 6; Capital City Planning Commission, *Souvenir Program*, 44.

101 Sarte and Agbayani, *Quezon City*, 39.

NOTES   303

102 Escoda, *Warsaw of Asia*, 54.

103 ABS-CBN emerged from the merger of CBN Channel 9 and ABS Channel 3, both owned by the Lopezes. Eñing Lopez bought the Quezon City site along Bohol Avenue (44,027 square meters) for a "bargain price of P14 per square meter," Raul Rodrigo, *Phoenix: The Saga of the Lopez Family*, vol. 1: *1800–1972* (Manila: Eugenio López Foundation, 2000), 241.

104 "Historical Data for Quezon City," 6; Capital City Planning Commission, *Souvenir Program*, 44–45.

105 Ysmael Steel was owned by Johnny Hashim Ysmael, heir of Magdalena Hemady. A giant robot stood on the front lawn of the steel factory, making for a unique landmark (Alcazaren, "Jeproks," 105; Ocampo, "Swan Song for Broadway," 122).

106 Telesforo Luna, Jr., "Manufacturing in the Philippines," in Robert E. Huke, *Shadows on the Land: An Economic Geography of the Philippines*, 395–421 (Manila: Bookmark, 1963), 403. For this source, Luna defined Greater Manila as a unit composed of Manila, Quezon City, Caloocan City, Pasay City, Navotas, Malabon, San Juan, Mandaluyong, Makati, and Parañaque (ibid., 397). See also Sarte and Agbayani, *Quezon City*, 43.

107 Paul Cardenas, "The Industrialization of Rizal," *Chronicle Magazine*, 29 Dec. 1962: 14–19.

108 Rodriguez-Arcinas, "A Sociological Analysis," 130–37.

109 Department of Public Works, Transportation and Communications (DPWTC), Planning and Project Development Office, *Metro Manila Housing Program* ([Manila]: DPWTC, 1975), 3.

110 David Harvey, "The 'New' Imperialism: Accumulation by Dispossession," *Socialist Register* 40, 2004: 63–87.

111 Jose Alcantara, Elias Benin, and Pascual Pili, Letter to Elpidio Quirino, 1 Oct. 1953, p. 1. EQP B56F5, File 051.

112 Ibid., 1–3. Interestingly, around this time the Tuasons and Aranetas were embroiled in a legal dispute regarding their properties in Quezon City following the death of matriarch Angela S. Tuason. See Frank Brady, *Angela I. Tuason de Perez and Antonio Perez versus Judge Hermogenes Caluag and J. Antonio Araneta, G.R. No. L-6182: Memorandum in Lieu of Oral Argument* (Manila: McCullough Printing, 1952).

113 One can also argue that private capital simply passes the "burden" of employing violence to the state and its repressive apparatuses whenever these acts of accumulation elicit hostile reactions from the dispossessed, a sort of twisted application of the common practice of outsourcing business processes in the post-Fordist age.

114 "Palace Cites Lopez Misuse of Powers," *MT*, 14 Jan. 1963: 1, 7; Malacañang Press Office, *The New Era Starts*, 30; Rodrigo, *Phoenix*, vol. 1, 272–73. At the time the Lopezes' economic and political might rivalled that of President Macapagal, who tried to use the powers of the state to neutralize their clout. Eugenio "Eñing" Lopez owned Meralco, the *Manila Chronicle*, ABS-CBN, and other important companies. His brother Fernando was the Vice President of the Republic (1949–1953, 1965–1972). Theirs was a textbook example of rent-seeking behavior (Alfred W. McCoy, "Rent-Seeking Families and the Philippine State: A History of the Lopez Family," in *An Anarchy of Families: State and Family in the Philippines*, ed. Alfred W. McCoy [Quezon City: Ateneo de Manila University Press, 1994]).

115 Leon Ty, "Scandalous and Shocking," *PFP*, 19 July 1958: 2–3, 32–33.

116 Amante F. Paredes, "The Growing Pains of Suburban Towns," *Chronicle Magazine*, 29 Dec. 1962: 20–22, esp. 21; Lico, *Arkitekturang Filipino*, 387; Samer Bagaeen and Ola Uduku, "Gated Histories: An Introduction to Themes and Concepts," in *Gated Communities: Social Sustainability in Contemporary and Historical Gated Developments*, ed. Samer Bagaeen and Ola Uduku (London: Earthscan, 2010), 2. Ironically, most of these Makati enclaves identify themselves as "villages," a term used to denote small, tightly-knit, rural

304   A CAPITAL CITY AT THE MARGINS

communities. Moreover, one must take note of the colonial origins of these place names; perhaps a reflection of the elite residents' colonial nostalgia. Using current place names as markers of historical memory, Ambeth Ocampo juxtaposes the sociospatial character of Makati and Quezon City: Magallanes, Dasmariñas, Legazpi, and Urdaneta, all important figures in the early Spanish colonial period, are now names of upscale Makati villages while Sikatuna is used for a village in suburban Quezon City ("Bohol and the Blood Compact," *Philippine Daily Inquirer*, 18 Oct. 2013, http://opinion.inquirer.net/63541/bohol-and-the-blood-compact, accessed 14 Sept. 2016). Ocampo refers to Sikatuna Village in Diliman, which is named after a prehispanic Bohol chieftain. Forbes Park is named after American governor-general W. Cameron Forbes.

117   It is perhaps the first of its kind in Southeast Asia, although further research needs to be done to ascertain this point. Although Forbes Park was established earlier (1949) than Philamlife Homes, it was not fully enclosed from outsiders, unlike the walled perimeter of the latter. Up until today, some houses in Forbes Park that are along McKinley Road, a public thoroughfare, are accessible to nonresidents.

118   Ed. C. de Jesus and Carlos Quirino, *Earl Carroll: Colossus of Philippine Insurance* (n.p.: Earl and Rose Carroll, 1980).

119   Ibid., 125; Douglas Waller, *Wild Bill Donovan: The Spymaster Who Created the OSS and Modern American Espionage* (New York: Free Press, 2011), 209–10; John Lindeman, *The Philippine American Life Insurance Company* (Manila: Carmelo & Bauermann, n.d.), ix, 19–23.

120   Isagani V. Tolentino, "Sa Namarco Mayroon, Hulugan pa," *Filipinas: Magasing Tagapamansag ng Katarungang Panlipunan*, 16 Jan. 1958: 8–9, esp. p. 8; Lindeman, *The Philippine American Life Insurance Company*, 24.

121   PHHC, *Annual Report, 1955–1956*, 96; PHHC, *Annual Report, 1956–1957*, 32; Lindeman, *The Philippine American Life Insurance Company*, 36.

122   Lindeman, *The Philippine American Life Insurance Company*, 45; "PhilAm plan materializes," *DS*, 15 Nov. 1952: 1, 12, esp. p. 1.

123   Cordner, *Housing*, 25; Lindeman, *The Philippine American Life Insurance Company*, 51.

124   Lindeman, *The Philippine American Life Insurance Company*, 49–50. Cf. Lico, *Arkitekturang Filipino*, 386.

125   Careaga, "People's Homesite and Housing Corporation," 5.

126   Lico, *Arkitekturang Filipino*, 386; Lindeman, *The Philippine American Life Insurance Company*, 50. The school was named after former Chief Justice Jose Abad Santos, who was martyred during the Japanese occupation and was a family friend of the Benitezes (Licuanan, *Paz Marquez Benitez*, 237).

127   Louie Benedict R. Ignacio, "The Emergence of a Gated Community in the Philippines: The Case of Philam Homes Subdivision, Quezon City, Philippines," MA thesis, Ateneo de Manila University, 2010, 47. See also Lindeman, *The Philippine American Life Insurance Company*, 52.

128   Jackson, *Crabgrass Frontier*, 231–45.

129   Ignacio, "The Emergence of a Gated Community," 49.

130   De Jesus and Quirino, *Earl Carroll*, 158–59.

131   Ibid., 159.

132   Ibid., 159–60.

133   Alcazaren, "Requiem for a Master Architect."

134   Lindeman, *The Philippine American Life Insurance Company*, 51–52.

135   Ibid., 52.

NOTES   305

136   However, these place names "bore no relation or reference to the environmental character of the site they signif[ied]" (Lico, *Arkitekturang Filipino*, 388).

137   Simbulan, *The Modern Principalia*, 130–31, 269.

138   Juan Ponce Enrile, *Juan Ponce Enrile: A Memoir*, ed. Nelson A. Navarro (Quezon City: ABS-CBN Publishing, 2012), 124; Gerardo P. Sicat, *Cesar Virata: Life and Times through Four Decades of Philippine Economic History* (Quezon City: University of the Philippines Press, 2014); Lea Manto-Beltran, "Emil Jurado: A Man of Letters; A Father of Journalists," *The Manila Times*, 20 June 2015, http://www.manilatimes.net/a-man-of-letters-a-father-of-journalists/193533/, accessed 1 Dec. 2015; Lorna Kalaw Tirol, "Edgar Jopson: The 'Magis' Seeker," in *Six Young Filipino Martyrs*, ed. Asuncion David Maramba (Pasig City: Anvil, 1997), 135. Enrile's father, Alfonso Ponce Enrile, was a member of the board of directors of the Philamlife Insurance Company, while Virata's uncle, Leonides S. Virata, was the company president and treasurer, Philippine American Life Insurance Company, *Annual Report, 1952* (n.p.: Philippine American Life Insurance Company, [1952?]), 6–7.

139   Abueva, *Quezon City Experiment*, 2.

140   Ibid., 1.

141   Philippine Commission of the Census, *Census of the Philippines, 1939*, vol. 1, part 4-Rizal, 6–7. See also McGee, *The Urbanization Process*, 108–14.

142   Daniel F. Doeppers, "Migration to Manila: Changing Gender Representation, Migration Field, and Urban Structure," in *Population and History: The Demographic Origins of the Modern Philippines*, ed. Daniel F. Doeppers and Peter Xenos (Quezon City: Ateneo de Manila University Press, 1998), 168.

143   Juppenlatz, *Cities in Transformation*, 103. One must also note that Quezon City's demographic upswing was due mainly not to natural growth but migration. See Department of Public Works and Communications, Institute of Planning, University of the Philippines, and Presidential Advisory Council on Public Works and Community Development, "Physical Planning Strategy for the Philippines: Population Trends and Existing Growth Areas," Dec. 1971 (unpublished manuscript, copy available at the SURP Library, UP-Diliman), III.4–III.71. Prior to this shift in migration patterns, Visayan migrants, specifically from Leyte, were already forming communities in Tatalon as early as the 1930s (Michael Pinches, "The Working Class Experience of Shame, Inequality, and People Power in Tatalon, Manila," in *From Marcos to Aquino: Local Perspectives on Political Transition in the Philippines*, ed. Benedict J. Kerkvliet and Resil B. Mojares [Quezon City: Ateneo de Manila University Press, 1991], 167).

144   Rodriguez-Arcinas, "A Sociological Analysis," 161.

145   Erlinda Enriquez Panlilio, "The Fireflies of Kamuning," in *The Manila We Knew*, ed. Erlinda Enriquez Panlilio (Pasig City: Anvil, 2006), 57.

146   Abrams, *The Language of Cities*, 303.

147   Robyn Dowling, "Suburban Stories, Gendered Lives: Thinking through Difference," in *Cities of Difference*, ed. Ruth Fincher and Jane M. Jacobs (New York and London: Guilford, 1998), 69–71.

148   Massey, *Space, Place, and Gender*, 177. For an account of a Quezon City housewife that deals with, albeit tangentially, the role of the kasambahay in a middle-class household, see Aguilar, *Filipino Housewives Speak*, 30–32. For an account of a Visayan kasambahay who eventually gained middle-class employment, see ibid., 38–52.

149   Caoili, *The Origins of Metropolitan Manila*, 68–69.

306   A CAPITAL CITY AT THE MARGINS

150   Peter Hall, *Cities of Tomorrow: An Intellectual History of Urban Planning and Design in the Twentieth Century*, 3rd ed. (Malden, MA: Blackwell, 2002), 88–93; Lico, *Arkitekturang Filipino*, 383–85.

151   Ordoñez, *Diliman*, 9.

152   Abrams and Koenigsberger, "A Housing Program for the Philippine Islands," 17–18; Alcazaren et al., *Lungsod Iskwater*, 64.

153   Juppenlatz, *Cities in Transformation*, 92.

154   Ibid., 93–95, 126–127; PHHC, *Annual Report, 1955–1956*, 92; SWA, *Annual Report, 1956–1957*, 15, 17.

155   PHHC, *Annual Report, 1955–1956*, 86, 92; PHHC, *Annual Report, 1956–1957*, 31; "Ex-Slum Dwellers' Fiesta," *Sunday Times Magazine*, 2 Mar. 1952: 30; Filemon V. Tutay, "Squatter Trouble," *PFP*, 3 May 1952: 6–7, 27, 50; Esteban F. Paredes, "Squatter Problem of Manila," *PFP*, 1 Dec. 1956: 26–27; Alfredo T. Daguio, "Mass Rescue from the Slums," *The Weekly Nation*, 26 Nov. 1965: 16–17. For more details on Sapang Palay, see Jaime Balcos Veneracion, *Sapang Palay: Hacienda, Urban Resettlement and Core of the City of San Jose del Monte, Bulacan* (Manila: National Commission for Culture and the Arts, 2011), 106.

156   PHHC, *Annual Report, 1961–1962*, 12.

157   PHHC, *Annual Report, 1962–1963*, 11–12. Quote is on p. 12.

158   Abrams and Koenigsberger, "A Housing Program for the Philippine Islands," 87; Office of Public Information, *Blue Book: First Anniversary of the Republic of the Philippines* (Manila: Bureau of Printing, 1947), 92. UP Diliman was served by the JD and MD buses and Halili Transit. In the 1950s, the fare from Quiapo to Diliman was twenty centavos for a 40-minute ride, and ten centavos if coming from Cubao (Evangelista, *Icons and Institutions*, 172; Ordoñez, *Diliman*, 4; Panlilio, "UP Beloved," 73–74). On overcharging, see Irineo A. Mercado, and Jose Sebastian, "It's Not Fair, Say Bus Riders," *PFP*, 11 June 1966: 60–61. However, the government had to sell METRAN in 1947 because of the company's mounting losses due to recurrent strikes starting in 1946, "Strikes," *PFP*, 26 Apr. 1947: 10; "Meralco Men Vote to Call Strike Today," *MT*, 28 Feb. 1946: 1, 8; "Bus Strikers Stage March to Malacañan," *MT*, 1 Mar. 1946: 1, 8.

159   Leon O. Ty, "'Royal Grant' to Royal Buses," *PFP*, 25 Feb. 1956: 10–11, 63; Bureau of the Census and Statistics, *Journal of Philippine Statistics*, vol. 13, nos. 1–3, 65; DPWTC, *The Philippine Highways: A Technical Report* (Manila: DPWTC, 1958), 13; Jose V. Abueva, Sylvia H. Guerrero, and Elsa P. Jurado, "Metro Manila Today and Tomorrow," Final Report Submitted to the First National City Bank by the Institute of Philippine Culture, Ateneo de Manila University, 15 Dec. 1972, 61, copy available at the Rizal Library, Ateneo de Manila University.

160   Leandro A. Villoria, "Manila," in *Rural–Urban Migrants and Metropolitan Development*, ed. Aprodicio A. Laquian (Toronto: INTERMET, 1971), 147.

161   Juppenlatz, *Cities in Transformation*, 93–95.

162   Ibid., 93; Task Force on Human Settlements, Development Academy of the Philippines, *Technical Report: Housing Policy Guidelines for the MBMR* (Quezon City: Development Academy of the Philippines, 1975), 21–22; SWA, *Annual Report, 1956–1957*, 20.

163   Laquian, *Slums are for People*, 23.

164   F. Landa Jocano, *Social Work in the Philippines: A Historical Overview* (Quezon City: New Day, 1980), 130.

165   SWA, *Annual Report, 1956–1957*, 14.

166   In Morris Juppenlatz's table showing the estimated population of slum dwellers and squatters in different parts of the GMA, the figure of 14,200 is given for "Cubao." "Cubao"

here most probably refers to the entire Quezon City as the city nor any of its constituent parts do not appear in the table (*Cities in Transformation*, 97–100).

167 A contraction of the words slum and suburb, "slurb" originates from California, where slums among suburbs "have emerged in residential areas carved out of agricultural land that connect urban centers" (Abrams, *The Language of Cities*, 287).

168 Ileana A. Maramag, "The City Can Use Its Squatter Areas," *Sunday Times Magazine*, 8 Jan. 1956: 9–11, esp. 10.

169 This piece of information is based on personal testimonies of long-time San Roque residents in a KontraKasaysayan focus group discussion that the author attended at UP Diliman on 17 December 2014. The author expresses its gratitude to the FGD organizers, led by KADAMAY, a nationwide alliance of urban poor organizations, and Chester Arcilla and Andre Ortega of KontraKasaysayan.

170 Office of the President, "Squatting and Slum Dwelling in Metropolitan Manila (Special Committee Report)," *Philippine Sociological Review* 16 (1–2), 1968: 92–105. Quote is on p. 95.

171 Quezon City Human Settlements Task Force, "Urban Redevelopment Project: Barrio Escopa, Quezon City, Metropolitan Manila. Background Information," 1976, 1. Copy available at the Hatcher Graduate Library, University of Michigan.

172 Capital City Planning Commission, "The Master Plan for the New Capital City," 27; Maramag, "The City Can Use Its Squatter Areas," 10; F. Calero, Report of the Advisory Committee, 30–31.

173 Juppenlatz, *Cities in Transformation*, 95; Filemon V. Tutay, "Worst Flood in Years," *PFP*, 4 June 1960: 6–7, 42–43, 79; Dwyer, "The Problem of In-migration," 139; Carlos P. Ramos, "Manila's Metropolitan Problem," *Philippine Journal of Public Administration* 5 (2), 1961: 89–117, esp. 93.

174 Leon O. Ty, "'Why Didn't I Also Die?,'" *PFP*, 4 June 1960: 4, 77. Quote is on p. 77.

175 Tutay, "Worst Flood in Years."

176 DPWTC, *Metro Manila Housing Program*, 49; Juppenlatz, *Cities in Transformation*, 107; Daguio, "Mass Rescue from the Slums," 17.

177 Capital City Planning Commission, "The Master Plan for the New Capital City," AP-8.

178 Veneracion, *Sapang Palay*, 106; Villoria, "Manila," 143.

179 William J. Keyes and Maria C. Roldan Burcroff, *Housing the Urban Poor: Nonconventional Approaches to a National Problem* (Quezon City: Ateneo de Manila University Press, 1976), 33.

180 Ibid., 27.

181 Ibid., 28.

182 Alfredo T. Daguio, "What is the Squatter? Animal, Vegetable, Mineral?," *The Weekly Nation*, 3 Dec. 1965: 26–27.

183 Although the act included Quezon City, it did not apply to the cities of Manila, Cavite, Trece Martires, and Tagaytay, Philippine Congress, Republic Act 2259: An Act Making Elective the Offices of Mayor, Vice-Mayor and Councilors in Chartered Cities, Regulating the Election in Such Cities and Fixing the Salaries and Tenure of Such Offices, 19 June 1959, *The Lawphil Project*, http://www.lawphil.net/statutes/repacts/ra1959/ra_2259_1959.html, accessed 10 Sept. 2016.

184 Abueva, *Quezon City Experiment*, 3–10; A. Oliver Flores, "A Political Revolution," *Sunday Times Magazine*, 29 Sept. 1963: 48–53.

185 The elite agenda behind calls for good governance, voters' education, and other similar movements continue to this day and are common in Southeast Asia (Mark R. Thompson,

"Southeast Asia's Subversive Voters: A Philippine Perspective," *Philippine Studies: Historical and Ethnographic Viewpoints* 64 [2], 2016: 265–87).

186 Abueva, *Quezon City Experiment*, 3–10.

187 Ibid., 16–17.

188 Ibid., 17. Cf. Flores, "A Political Revolution," 50.

189 Kiunisala, "Politics around Manila," 62; Edward R. Kiunisala, "The Fight for the Cities," *PFP*, 23 Nov. 1963: 6, 75; Ernesto M. Macatuno, "A Citizens' Movement Tackles the Political Pros," *Sunday Times Magazine*, 26 Sept. 1971: 20–21; Macatuno, "The Big City," 27; Chic Fortich, *Escape! Charito Planas: Her Story* (Quezon City: New Day, 1991), 19.

190 Jose O. Corpuz, Committee report no. 1855, submitted by the House Committee on Agrarian and Social Welfare, 20 Mar. 1953, ii. JBVP, SG: National Planning Commission, Folder 2.

191 Loh, *Squatters into Citizens*; Chua Beng Huat, *Political Legitimacy and Housing: Stakeholding in Singapore* (London and New York: Routledge, 1997). On Indonesia as an example of this point, see Freek Colombijn, "Public Housing in Post-colonial Indonesia: The Revolution of Rising Expectations," *Bijdragen tot de Taal-, Land- en Volkenkunde* 167 (4), 2011: 437–58, esp. p. 444; Abidin Kusno, "Housing the Margin: Perumahan Rakyat and the Future Urban Form of Indonesia," *Indonesia* 94, 2012: 23–56, esp. p. 26.

192 Alan Harding and Talja Blokland, *Urban Theory: A Critical Introduction to Power, Cities and Urbanism in the 21st Century* (Los Angeles: Sage, 2014), 143.

193 Cohen, *A Consumers' Republic*, 194–256.

194 Benjamin V. Afuang, "A Master Plan on Parks," *Sunday Times Magazine*, 29 Aug. 1971: 38–39.

195 Dowling, "Suburban Stories," 69–71.

196 Billig, *Barons, Brokers, and Buyers*, 52.

197 Davis, *Planet of Slums*, 65.

198 Alcazaren, "Jeproks," 109.

199 Quijano de Manila, *Language of the Street*, 21. On the long 1970s, see Vicente L. Rafael, "Contracting Colonialism and the Long 1970s," *Philippine Studies: Historical and Ethnographic Viewpoints* 61 (4), 2013: 477–94.

5. The Submissive and Subvsersive Suburbs

1 The most notable and widely read account of the FQS is Jose F. Lacaba, *Days of Disquiet, Nights of Rage: The First Quarter Storm & Related Events* (Manila: Salinlahi, 1982). Long-time journalist Hermie Rotea's account of the FQS is rather underappreciated, despite its attention to the geographic details of the demonstrations, *Behind the Barricades: I Saw Them Aim and Fire!* (n.p.: Hermie Rotea, 1970). "National-democratic organizations" are a broad range of progressive groups that subscribe to the characterization of Philippine society as semicolonial and semifeudal.

2 In 1968 PKP cadre Jose Ma. Sison established a separate communist party, but this time incorporating Mao Zedong thought. Although this new party also uses "Partido Komunista ng Pilipinas" as its official name, this book follows the convention of using PKP for the old party and the CPP for the new one.

3 The phrase "sylvan enclave" is from Teodoro, "UP in the Sixties," 58.

4 UP, *Resurgence of the University*, 31.

5 Ibid., 27–28.

6 Teodoro, "UP in the Sixties," 58.

NOTES   309

7   Leslie E. Bauzon, "Angara's Toughminded Leadership (1981–19): The Diamond Jubilee Highlighted by Reform of the University System," in *University of the Philippines: The First 75 Years*, ed. Oscar M. Alfonso (Quezon City: University of the Philippines Press, 1985), 581.

8   The Quimpos were a middle-class family of twelve living in Metro Manila. During martial law, seven of the ten siblings either joined the natdem movement and/or went underground. Two of them (Ronald Jan and Ishmael/Jun) were killed under the Marcos regime (Susan F. Quimpo and Nathan Gilbert Quimpo, *Subversive Lives: A Family Memoir of the Marcos Years* [Manila: Anvil, 2012]).

9   Philippine Institute of Architects, *Report on the Quezon Memorial Park and Related Subjects* (Makati: Philippine Institute of Architects, 1969), 1.

10   Quimpo and Quimpo, *Subversive Lives*, 37–38.

11   Lacaba, *Days of Disquiet*, 131.

12   Mila D. Aguilar, "January 13: View of the Impending Avalanche," *Graphic*, 27 Jan. 1971: 4–5. Quote is on p. 5. The price hike was a direct result of the oil shocks of the 1970s, which were also a crucial factor behind the declaration of martial law (Rodrigo, *Phoenix*, vol. 1, 349–63).

13   Edward E. Kiunisala, "Black Wednesday on Plaza Miranda," *PFP*, 23 Jan. 1971: 4, 45.

14   There is a plethora of personal and journalistic accounts of the Diliman Commune, yet there seems to be no secondary work that can be regarded as the definitive assessment of this important event. The closest are the essays of Oscar L. Evangelista, who depicts the Commune as an important episode in Salvador Lopez's term as UP president, and Mong Palatino, a UP student activist during the early 2000s (Oscar L. Evangelista, "Lopez's Beleaguered Tenure [1969–1975]: Barricades on Campus at the Peak of Student Discontent," in *University of the Philippines: The First 75 Years*, ed. Oscar M. Alfonso [Quezon City: University of the Philippines Press, 1985], 459–64; Mong Palatino, "Pagbabalik-tanaw sa Diliman Commune" [Looking back at the Diliman Commune], in *Serve the People: Ang Kasaysayan ng Radikal na Kilusan sa Unibersidad ng Pilipinas* [The History of the Radical Movement in the University of the Philippines], ed. Bienvenido Lumbera, Judy Taguiwalo, Roland Tolentino, Arnold Alamon, and Ramon Guillermo [(Quezon City): IBON; Congress of Teachers and Educators for Nationalism and Democracy; Alliance of Concerned Teachers, 2008]). For first-hand personal accounts, see Ordoñez, *Diliman*, 15–16; Quimpo and Quimpo, *Subversive Lives*, 40–42; Cesar "Sonny" Melencio, *Full Quarter Storms: Memoirs and Writings on the Philippine Left (1970–2010)* (Quezon City: Transform Asia, 2010), 23–27. For articles in mainstream media, see Mila D. Aguilar, "The Liberation of the State University," *Graphic*, 24 Feb. 1971: 6–8; Petronilo Bn. Daroy, "Commune, 'Communists' and Communards," *Graphic*, 24 Feb. 1971: 6–8; Daroy, "Invasion of the Campus," *Graphic*, 3 Mar. 1971: 12–15; Rodolfo G. Tupas, "The Exercise of Restraint," *Sunday Times Magazine*, 7 Mar. 1971: 10–11. For Lopez's point-of-view, see Lisandro E. Claudio, *Liberalism and the Postcolony: Thinking the State in 20th-Century Philippines* (Quezon City: Ateneo de Manila University Press, 2017), 127–28. For a disparaging take on this event, see Enrile, *Juan Ponce Enrile*, 327–330. The narrative of the Diliman Commune in this chapter is a composite account based on these sources and unpublished materials from the PRP.

15   On the Paris Commune as an urban social movement, see David Harvey, *Paris, Capital of Modernity* (New York and London: Routledge, 2006), 305–8.

16   Sterling Seagrave, *The Marcos Dynasty* (New York: Harper & Row, 1988), 225; Hedman and Sidel, *Philippine Politics and Society*, 128, 138.

17 Provisionary Directorate of the Free Community of Diliman, Manifesto from the Barricades, undated and unpublished manifesto, 2, Philippine Radical Papers (PRP), UP-Diliman Main Library, Reel 8, Box 14/23.01.

18 Ericson M. Baculinao and June C. Pagaduan, "'Barricades are Fine': Resolution Endorsing the Barricades as a Form of Protest," 13 Feb. 1971, Arkibong Bayan, The Diliman Commune of 1971, Part II, http://www.arkibongbayan.org/2010/2010-03March28-DilimanCommune2/upsc/IMG_0201.jpg;http://www.arkibongbayan.org/2010/2010-03March28-DilimanCommune2/upsc/IMG_0202.jpg, accessed 16 Dec. 2015.

19 Jose Y. Dalisay Jr, *Killing Time in a Warm Place* (Pasig City: Anvil, 2006), 172–73.

20 Benjamin Pimentel, *Rebolusyon! A Generation of Struggle in the Philippines* (New York: Monthly Review Press, 1991), 44.

21 F. V. Tutay, "Charges and Counter-Charges," *PFP,* 13 Jan. 1971: 11, 30, 38. Quote is on p. 11.

22 Ibid., 38.

23 Stephen Henry S. Totanes, "Student Activism in the Pre-Martial Law Era," in *Down from the Hill: Ateneo de Manila in the First Ten Years under Martial Law, 1972–1982*, ed. Cristina Jayme Montiel and Susan Evangelista (Quezon City: Ateneo de Manila University Press, 2005), 31. The Jesuit order was certainly not monolithic in its relationship with Marcos. Prominent Jesuits publicly condemned the dictatorship, such as Antonio Olaguer and historian Horacio de la Costa (Mark R. Thompson, *The Anti-Marcos Struggle: Personalistic Rule and Democratic Transition in the Philippines* [Quezon City: New Day, 1996], 73, 84). The latter parts of this chapter will demonstrate the Jesuits' role in the anti-Marcos struggle.

24 Totanes, "Student Activism in the Pre-Martial Law Era," 31. Despite Ateneo's reputation as a stronghold of social democrats (socdem), who were often at odds with the national democrats in terms of ideology and strategy, it had its fair share of natdem activists (Meynardo P. Mendoza, "Natdems, Socdems, and the Ateneo," in *Down from the Hill: Ateneo de Manila in the First Ten Years under Martial Law, 1972–1982*, ed. Cristina Jayme Montiel and Susan Evangelista [Quezon City: Ateneo de Manila University Press, 2005]; Susan Evangelista, "The Faculty, Administration, and Social Development Professionals during Martial Law," in *Down from the Hill: Ateneo de Manila in the First Ten Years under Martial Law, 1972–1982*, ed. Cristina Jayme Montiel and Susan Evangelista [Quezon City: Ateneo de Manila University Press, 2005], 150–62).

25 Totanes, "Student Activism in the Pre-Martial Law Era," 9. The full text of the manifesto is appendix A of Cristina Jayme Montiel and Susan Evangelista, eds., *Down from the Hill: Ateneo de Manila in the First Ten Years under Martial Law, 1972–1982* (Quezon City: Ateneo de Manila University Press, 2005), 265–72.

26 Totanes, "Student Activism in the Pre-Martial Law Era," 20.

27 Examples of schools in the university belt are San Beda College, University of the East, and Manuel L. Quezon University. Mendiola is a short thoroughfare that connects one of Malacañang's gates to C. M. Recto Avenue.

28 "Ang Leksiyon ng Pakikibaka," *Bandilang Pula: Pahayagan ng Malayang Purok ng Diliman,* 12 Feb. 1971, 1, 6, Arkibong Bayan, The Diliman Commune of 1971, Part II: "A Up Professor's View and Account of the Diliman Commune," http://www.arkibongbayan.org/2010/2010-03Marchs28-DilimanCommune2/bandilangpula/IMG_0216.jpg, accessed 16 Dec. 2015. Quote is on p. 1.

29 "Ang Depensa ng Diliman," *Bandilang Pula: Pahayagan ng Malayang Purok ng Diliman,* 12 Feb. 1971: 4–5, 8, Arkibong Bayan, The Diliman Commune of 1971, Part II, http://www.arkibongbayan.org/2010/2010-03March28-DilimanCommune2/bandilangpula/

IMG_0219.jpg; http://www.arkibongbayan.org/2010/2010-03March28-DilimanCommune2/bandilangpula/IMG_0220.jpg; http://www.arkibongbayan.org/2010/2010-03March28-DilimanCommune2/bandilangpula/IMG_0223.jpg, accessed 16 Dec. 2015.

30   Unfortunately, remnants of sexism were still present in the Commune. For example, in commending the role of women communards, the USC made a distinction between the primary (and martial) task of defending the barricades vis-à-vis the "auxiliary" tasks of ensuring shelter and food supply, USC, "Resolution Commending the Revolutionary Courage of the Heroic Defenders of the Diliman Commune against the Fascist State and Its Campus Collaborators," 13 Feb 1971, unpublished resolution, 1, PRP Reel 9, Box 18/02.36.

31   UP student activists barricaded strategic parts of the campus in September 1984 and then again in November that same year in protest against tuition increase, Ma. Luisa T. Camagay, "Edgardo J. Angara: Steering the University in the Nation's Transition," in *UP in the Time of People Power (1983–2005): A Centennial Publication*, ed. Ferdinand C. Llanes (Quezon City: University of the Philippines Press, 2009), 17–18; Bauzon, "Angara's Toughminded Leadership," 573–79.

32   Hedman and Sidel, *Philippine Politics and Society*, 128.

33   FQS mobilizations did feature barricades, e.g., Rotea, *Behind the Barricades*; Joaquin, *The Aquinos of Tarlac*, 344–45, but these blockades never lasted for more than a few hours.

34   Taguiwalo, "Pangkalahatang Welga sa UP," 99.

35   Hedman and Sidel, *Philippine Politics and Society*, 129.

36   McCoy, *Policing America's Empire*, 389.

37   Seagrave, *The Marcos Dynasty*, 207–8.

38   McCoy, *Policing America's Empire*, 389.

39   Seagrave, *The Marcos Dynasty*, 220.

40   Romani and Thomas, *A Survey of Local Government*, 109–10.

41   Caoili, *The Origins of Metropolitan Manila*, 148.

42   McCoy, *Policing America's Empire*, 389.

43   Mijares, *The Conjugal Dictatorship*, 85. For the full text of the declaration of martial law, see Ferdinand E. Marcos, Proclamation No. 1081, s. 1972: Proclaiming a State of Martial Law in the Philippines, *OG*, http://www.gov.ph/1972/09/21/proclamation-no-1081/, accessed 11 Sept. 2016.

44   Afuang, "A Master Plan on Parks," 38–39; Dwyer, "The Problem of In-Migration," 139.

45   Dwyer, "The Problem of In-Migration," 140.

46   Hermie Rotea, "Plan for a Greater Manila," *This Week*, 8 Jan. 1961: 10–14.

47   Aprodicio A. Laquian, *The City in Nation-Building: Politics and Administration in Metropolitan Manila* (Manila: School of Public Administration, University of the Philippines, 1966), 47; Sicat, *Cesar Virata*, 471.

48   Hedman and Sidel, *Philippine Politics and Society*, 123.

49   The proclamation document is dated 21 September, but the actual declaration happened on 23 September.

50   Imelda Romualdez Marcos, *Metropolitan Manila and the Magnitude of Its Problems*, ed. Ileana Maramag (Metropolitan Manila: NMPC, 1976), 41.

51   Inter-Agency Committee on Metropolitan Manila (IACMM), *Metropolitan Manila Authority: A Development and Reform Strategy Proposal* (Manila: Government Printing Office, 1973), 11–12; Michael D. Pante, "The Politics of Flood Control and the Making of Metro Manila," *Philippine Studies: Historical and Ethnographic Viewpoints* 64 (3–4), 2016: 555–92.

52   Neferti Xina M. Tadiar, *Fantasy-Production: Sexual Economies and Other Philippine Consequences for the New World Order* (Quezon City: Ateneo de Manila University Press, 2004), 82; Ton van Naerssen, Michel Ligthart, and Flotilda N. Zapanta, "Managing Metropolitan Manila," in *The Dynamics of Metropolitan Management in Southeast Asia,* ed. Jürgen Rüland (Singapore: Institute of Southeast Asian Studies, 1996), 173; Marcos, *Metropolitan Manila and the Magnitude of Its Problems,* 8, 41; Caoili, *The Origins of Metropolitan Manila,* 145–52.

53   Seagrave, *The Marcos Dynasty,* 259.

54   Mijares, *The Conjugal Dictatorship,* 147–48. Before martial law, Mathay, as Quezon City vice mayor, oversaw a number of slum relocations (Afuang, "A Master Plan on Parks," 39).

55   Seagrave, *The Marcos Dynasty,* 259; Sicat, *Cesar Virata,* 415–16. Ferdinand and Beams began their affair when she was in the country in 1968 to shoot the film *Maharlika,* which he partially funded to extol his fallacious heroic exploits during the Second World War. On the Marcos–Beams affair, see ch. 10 of Mijares, *The Conjugal Dictatorship* and Hermie Rotea, *Marcos' Lovey Dovie* (Los Angeles: Liberty, 1983).

56   Imelda Romualdez Marcos, *The Ideas of Imelda Romualdez Marcos,* vol. 2, ed. Ileana Maramag (Metropolitan Manila: NMPC, 1978), 231; Sicat, *Cesar Virata,* 417–18.

57   Office of the President, "Squatting and Slum Dwelling," 104. Cf. Nancy H. Kwak, "Slum Clearance as a Transnational Process in Globalizing Manila," in *Making Cities Global: The Transnational Turn in Urban History,* ed. A. K. Sandoval-Strausz and Nancy H. Kwak (Philadelphia: University of Pennsylvania Press, 2018), 103.

58   Sicat, *Cesar Virata,* 463, 467.

59   Ibid., 418.

60   Ibid., 420–21, 462.

61   Marcos, *The Ideas of Imelda Romualdez Marcos,* vol. 2, 229.

62   Donovan Storey, "Housing the Urban Poor in Metro Manila," *Philippine Studies* 46 (3), 1998: 267–92, esp. 276.

63   Ibid., 276.

64   Sicat, *Cesar Virata,* 468.

65   Ibid., 468; Storey, "Housing the Urban Poor," 275–76; Endriga, "Corpuz and Soriano's Bifocal Administrations," 531; John F. Doherty, *The Philippine Urban Poor,* ed. Belinda A. Aquino, Philippine Studies Occasional Paper No. 8 (Honolulu: Philippine Studies Program, Center for Asian and Pacific Studies, University of Hawai'i, 1985), 25–29.

66   Hedman and Sidel, *Philippine Politics and Society,* 129.

67   Tadiar, *Things Fall Away,* 146–47.

68   Eventually, as will be discussed below, the World Bank would shift its stance from resettlement toward slum upgrading (Kwak, "Slum Clearance as a Transnational Process," 104–6).

69   This phrase is the title of Primitivo Mijares's book, *The Conjugal Dictatorship of Ferdinand and Imelda Marcos.*

70   Louis Althusser, *On the Reproduction of Capitalism: Ideology and Ideological State Apparatuses,* trans. G. M. Goshgarian (London: Verso, 2014).

71   Imelda Romualdez Marcos, *The Ideas of Imelda Romualdez Marcos,* vol. 1 (Metro Manila: NMPC, 1978), 13.

72   I borrow the term "palingenetic" from Gerard Lico, *Edifice Complex: Power, Myth, and Marcos State Architecture* (Quezon City: Ateneo de Manila University Press, 2003), 39.

73   Ibid., 45–47. *Tadhana* was a multivolume book project that portrayed Philippine history as a narrative that links precolonial society with the purported preordained rise of the

Marcoses. The Tasadays were presented by the regime as a hitherto uncontacted ethnic group in Mindanao, a claim eventually exposed as a hoax. Maharlika was a prehispanic term to denote the warrior class in precolonial Luzon. Malakas and Maganda were the first man and woman in a precolonial creation myth. Malakas and Maganda literally mean "strong" and "beautiful," respectively.

74 Ibid., 152–53.

75 A. Lin Neumann, "Tourism Promotion and Prostitution," in *The Philippines Reader: A History of Colonialism, Neocolonialism, Dictatorship, and Resistance*, ed. Daniel B. Schirmer and Stephen Rosskamm Shalom (Cambridge, MA: South End, 1987), 182; Linda K. Richter, *The Politics of Tourism in Asia* (Honolulu: University of Hawai'i Press, 1989), 54–55.

76 Juanico, *Metro Manila*, 177.

77 Endriga, "Corpuz and Soriano's Bifocal Administrations," 518.

78 Lico, *Edifice Complex*, 60, 78; Marcos, *The Ideas of Imelda Romualdez Marcos*, vol. 1, 36–37; Marcos, *The Ideas of Imelda Romualdez Marcos*, vol. 2, 327. Imelda even referred to the Metropolitan Theater as the "ancestral home of the Filipino heritage" (ibid., 328).

79 Marcos, *The Ideas of Imelda Romualdez Marcos*, vol. 1, 16.

80 Lico, *Edifice Complex*, 104.

81 Marcos, *The Ideas of Imelda Romualdez Marcos*, vol. 1, 257.

82 Imelda herself explains the hodge-podge of concepts that comprise her philosophy in Ramona S. Diaz's documentary, *Imelda* (New York: CineDiaz, 2003).

83 Marcos, *The Ideas of Imelda Romualdez Marcos*, vol. 1, 266.

84 Marcos, *The Ideas of Imelda Romualdez Marcos*, vol. 2, 80.

85 I borrow the term "edifice complex" from the title of Lico's book *Edifice Complex: Power, Myth, and Marcos State Architecture*.

86 Bobby Benedicto, "The Queer Afterlife of the Postcolonial City: (Trans)gender Performance and the War of Beautification," *Antipode* 47 (3), 2015: 580–97. Quote is on p. 583.

87 Office of the President, "Official Week in Review: June 16–June 30, 1966," *OG* 62 (31), 1966: cclxi–cclxxvii, http://www.gov.ph/1966/08/01/official-week-in-review-june-16-june-30-1966/, accessed 5 Nov. 2016; Eric Giron, "Urbanization of Suburbia," *Philippine Panorama*, 15 Aug. 1976: 26.

88 Marcos, *The Ideas of Imelda Romualdez Marcos*, vol. 1, 179; Lico, *Arkitekturang Filipino,* 464.

89 Marcos, *The Ideas of Imelda Romualdez Marcos*, vol. 2, 29.

90 Sicat, *Cesar Virata*, 461; Raissa Robles, *Marcos Martial Law: Never Again*, ed. Alan Robles (Quezon City: Filipinos for a Better Philippines, 2016), 162, 172. Filipinos jokingly call this cluster of hospitals "*bopis* complex," Rolando B. Tolentino, *Almanak ng Isang Aktibista* (Quezon City: University of the Philippines Press, 2011), 345. Bopis is a local dish made of pig innards. The humor in this phrase is multilayered, as it also hints at the Marcoses' vampirish nature, like an *aswang* (a malevolent, blood-sucking folkloric creature) feeding off Filipinos' internal organs (i.e., lungs, heart, and kidneys).

91 Quijano de Manila, "A Stage for Greatness," *PFP*, 13 Sept. 1969, quoted in Lico, *Edifice Complex*, 88.

92 Ferdinand E. Marcos, *New Filipinism: The Turning Point* (State of the nation message to the Congress of the Philippines, 27 January 1969) (n.p.: Manila, [1969?]), 92, 95.

93 Erhard Berner, *Defending a Place in the City: Localities and the Struggle for Urban Land in Metro Manila* (Quezon City: Ateneo de Manila University Press, 1997), 13–19; Dwyer, "The Problem of In-Migration," 139.

94 NPC, Minutes of the 41st Meeting, Resolutions Nos. 162 to 166, 28 Nov. 1951, p. 4, EQP B7F8, File 018.

95 Office of the President, Official Month in Review: February 1955.

96 Lico, *Arkitekturang Filipino*, 380–81.

97 Araneta, *Reflections of a Filipino Exile*, 40. The enthusiasm of Secretary Araneta, who belonged to the Araneta clan that was influential in Quezon City's history, in moving to Quezon City was expected given his participation in drafting the 1949 master plan. For his intellectual biography, see chapter 2 of Claudio, *Liberalism and the Postcolony*.

98 Caoili, *The Origins of Metropolitan Manila*, 124–26, 196–97.

99 Abueva, *Quezon City Experiment*, 1; Berner, *Defending a Place in the City*, 14–15.

100 Overseas Technical Cooperation Agency, Government of Japan, *Urban Transport Study in Manila Metropolitan Area* (Manila: Planning and Project Development Office, 1973), 30. Cf. University of the Philippines, Institute of Planning, "Goals and Policies for Quezon City" (Studio Work II, 3rd Trimester, 1972–1973), 31. Copy available at the SURP Library, UP Diliman. See also Alcazaren, "Jeproks," 101.

101 Lopez, "Quezon City," 10.

102 Ibid., 10.

103 Abueva et al., "Metro Manila Today and Tomorrow," 12.

104 Cabalfin, "The Politics of the Nation"; Lou Antolihao, *Culture of Improvisation: Informal Settlements and Slum Upgrading in a Metro Manila Locality* (Quezon City: Institute of Philippine Culture, Ateneo de Manila University, 2004), 26–27; Marcos, *New Filipinism*, 95.

105 Capital City Planning Commission, *Subdivision Regulations of the Capital City* (Manila: Bureau of Printing, 1950).

106 Hedman and Sidel, *Philippine Politics and Society*, 130.

107 Carmen Guerrero Nakpil, *A Question of Identity: Selected Essays* (Manila: Vessel, 1973), 195.

108 Ongpauco, "Quezon City," 7.

109 In 1948 its density was 668.9 persons per square kilometer, but shot up to 2,394.6 by 1960 and then to 4,539.4 in 1970, Bureau of the Census and Statistics, *Philippines 1970 Population. Special Report No. 2: Urban Population* (Manila: Bureau of the Census and Statistics, 1972), 3; Bureau of the Census and Statistics, *Philippines 1970 Population. Special Report No. 3: Population, Land Area, and Density: 1948, 1960 and 1970* (Manila: Bureau of the Census and Statistics, 1972), 31.

110 Simbulan, *The Modern Principalia*, 73–74; Alcazaren, "Jeproks," 106–7; Paredes, "The Growing Pains of Suburban Towns," 20–22; Carmen A. Navarro, "A Sophisticated Suburb in Makati," *Chronicle Magazine*, 29 Dec. 1962: 24–27; Edward R. Kiunisala, "City of Tomorrow," *PFP*, 26 Oct. 1963: 14–15, 103, 106.

111 Ronald (Remy) Kookooritchkin, "Quezon City May Yet Be the Show Place of the Nation," *Examiner*, 12 Oct. 1975: 12–13. Quote is on p. 13.

112 Ibid., 13.

113 Ferdinand E. Marcos, Presidential Decree No. 940, June 24, 1976, Establishing Manila as the Capital of the Philippines and as the Permanent Seat of the National Government, *The Lawphil Project*, http://www.lawphil.net/statutes/presdecs/pd1976/pd_940_1976.html, accessed 14 Jan. 2016.

114 Veltisezar B. Bote, "A Land of Unfinished Memorials," *This Week*, 27 Nov. 1960: 10–13; CL Leones, "The Durable Amoranto," *Philippine Panorama*, 14 Sept. 1975: 7.

115 Marcos, *Presidential Speeches*, vol. 1, 421.

116 Lico, *Arkitekturang Filipino*, 472.

NOTES   315

117   Laquian, *Slums are for People*, 216–17.
118   Task Force on Human Settlements, *Housing Policy Guidelines for the MBMR*, 12.
119   Afuang, "A Master Plan on Parks," 38.
120   Boyce, *The Political Economy of Growth*, 248–59; Robin Broad, *Unequal Alliance: The World Bank, the International Monetary Fund, and the Philippines* (Quezon City: Ateneo de Manila University Press, 1988).
121   DPWTC, *Metro Manila Housing Program*, 23, 31.
122   Quezon City Human Settlements Task Force, "Urban Redevelopment Project: Barrio Escopa," 1976, 2; Ramos-Jimenez et al., *Philippine Urban Situation Analysis*, 54; Kwak, "Slum Clearance as a Transnational Process," 107–6; Julie G. Viloria and David Williams, "Evaluation of Community Upgrading Programs in Metro Manila," in *Shelter Upgrading for the Urban Poor: Evaluation of Third World Experiences*, ed. Reinhard J. Skinner, John L. Taylor, and Emiel A. Wegelin (Manila: Island Publishing, 1987), 26–27.
123   Ramos-Jimenez et al., *Philippine Urban Situation Analysis*, 54; Viloria and Williams, "Evaluation of Community," 32.
124   Marcos, *Metropolitan Manila and the Magnitude of Its Problems*, 47–49; "FM Sets up Waterways Committee," *Bulletin Today* (*BT*), 5 Mar. 1976: 5; "QC Sets aside Temporary Squatter Relocation Site," *BT*, 8 June 1976: 24.
125   Marcos, *The Ideas of Imelda Romualdez Marcos*, vol. 1, 260; Office of the First Lady, *Compassion and Commitment*, ed. Ileana Maramag (Manila: National Media Production Center, 1975), 19; Cicero D. Jurado, Jr., "Estero Dredging for Flood Control," *FOCUS Philippines*, 10 Apr. 1976: 20–21, 24–25; Cicero D. Jurado, Jr., "Relocating the Squatters," *FOCUS Philippines*, 14 Aug. 1976: 10–11, 35.
126   "QC Sets aside," 24.
127   Doherty, *The Philippine Urban Poor*, 13, 17, 31.
128   Tony Antonio, "Barrio Tense, Waits for Demolition Teams," *BT*, 2 Mar. 1976: 1, 8.
129   Ricardo Manapat, *Some Are Smarter than Others: The History of Marcos Crony Capitalism* (New York: Aletheia, 1991), 16–17.
130   Doherty, *The Philippine Urban Poor*, 16.
131   Tutay, "Squatter Trouble," 7; Office of the President, "Squatting and Slum Dwelling," 97; Pinches, "The Working Class Experience of Shame," 170–71.
132   Phillip C. Parnell, "Criminalizing Colonialism: Democracy Meets Law in Manila," in *Crime's Power: Anthropologists and the Ethnography of Crime*, ed. Philip C. Parnell and Stephanie C. Kane (New York: Palgrave Macmillan, 2003), 202.
133   Gregg R. Jones, *Red Revolution: Inside the Philippine Guerrilla Movement* (Boulder, CO: Westview, 1989), 104.
134   Ramos-Jimenez et al., *Philippine Urban Situation Analysis*, 43–44. Cf. Parnell, "The Composite State," 154–70.
135   Melencio, *Full Quarter Storms*, 57. On Tatalon's struggle, see "Mamamayan ng Tatalon, Nagpetisyon!," *Pagsilang: Pahayagan ng Lakas ng Diwang Rebolusyonaryo* 3 (8), Nov. 1974: 1. The struggle of Tatalon residents included famed Sakdalista Salud Algabre, who saw injustice in how the Tuasons held on to the land. According to her: "the reason why I neglected my children is because I helped fight the avidity of the Tuasons in Tatalon" (Thelma B. Kintanar and Carina C. David, "Salud Algabre, Revolutionary," *Review of Women's Studies* 6 [1], 1996: 75–84). Unfortunately, on 23 July 1985 Tatalon suffered a violent reprisal from both state forces and the Aranetas that left two dead and seventeen injured among the residents. According to reports, Marcos's son-in-law (Irene Marcos's

husband) Gregorio Maria "Greggy" Araneta owned the disputed land (Robles, *Marcos Martial Law*, 149). On Hillcrest, see Keyes and Burcroff, *Housing the Urban Poor*, 44–46.

136 Parnell, "The Composite State," 155.

137 Ofel Beltran, "Si Ka Bel ang Aking Ama," in *Ka Bel: Mga Liham*, ed. Kenneth Roland A. Guda (Quezon City: Crispin B. Beltran Resource Center, 2010), 35–37. Beltran served as a partylist representative in the House of Representatives thrice (2001, 2004, and 2007). It was a homecoming of sorts for Beltran, given that the House of Representatives held sessions at the Batasang Pambansa, which is part of the NGC.

138 Quimpo and Quimpo, *Subversive Lives*, 198–199. "Constitution Hill" and "Constitution Hills" were both commonly used in the postwar and Marcos periods to refer to the same place.

139 Ibid., 202; Maria Christina Pargas Bawagan, "Some Trying Times of My Life," in *Tibak Rising: Activism in the Days of Martial Law*, ed. Ferdinand C. Llanes (Mandaluyong City: Anvil, 2012), 13.

140 Ibid., 12–13; Evangelista, "The Faculty," 191.

141 Dalisay, *Killing Time in a Warm Place*, 3.

142 Bauzon, "Angara's Toughminded Leadership," 581–87.

143 Jose L. Merin, "The Political Economy of Housing in the Philippines, 1946–1980," in MHS, *Philippine Shelter System and Human Settlements* (Metro Manila: MHS, 1982), 17–26. Quote is on p. 23.

144 Sarah F. Lumba, "My Marikina," in *The Manila We Know*, ed. Erlinda Enriquez Panlilio (Mandaluyong City: Anvil, 2017), 169–70.

145 Ibid., 171–72. Since martial law, *salvage* has taken on the meaning of a summary execution in Philippine English.

146 Mijares, *The Conjugal Dictatorship*, 507. In contrast, Mijares was a resident of Project 6 (ibid., 71).

147 Aguilar, *Filipino Housewives Speak*, 125.

148 Other Philamlife Homes residents who also became prominent government officials include Executive Secretary Rufino Hechanova, PNB President Placido Mapa Jr, Ambassador Augusto Espiritu, Central Bank Governor Jose Fernandez, and Manila Mayor Antonio Villegas (Enrile, *Juan Ponce Enrile*, 124).

149 Sicat, *Cesar Virata*, 74.

150 Storey, "Housing the Urban Poor," 273. See also Michael Pinches, "Entrepreneurship, Consumption, Ethnicity and National Identity in the Making of the Philippines' New Rich," in *Culture and Privilege in Capitalist Asia*, ed. Michael Pinches (London and New York: Routledge, 1999), 294.

151 Abrams, *The Language of Cities*, 329.

152 Mijares, *The Conjugal Dictatorship*, 710–11. Quezon City's lack of global appeal is evident in how the bout was titled "Thrilla in Manila" despite the fact that it happened outside Manila. This event's legacy is somehow preserved in the form of a Quezon City shopping mall. Named Ali Mall, this establishment was built in 1976 in the Araneta Center after the match. For an interesting description of Ali Mall, see Gina Apostol, "The Unintended," in *Manila Noir*, ed. Jessica Hagedorn (Mandaluyong City: Anvil, 2013), 154: "During the best of times Ali Mall is a decrepit, cramped cement block of shops hosting Rugby glue sniffers, high school truants, and depressed carnival men on break. It was built in 1976, a paean to the Thrilla in Manila, which took place directly across the street at the Araneta Coliseum in Cubao, site of the match that destroyed the career of the heavyweight champion of the world, Joe 'The Gorilla' Frazier, and the source of our modern discomfort perhaps—a sense

of the futility of earthly striving—whenever one thinks about Muhammad Ali. Cubao is the omen of Ali's shambling shadow. Cubao heralds an incommunicable fall."

153 Judy Taguiwalo, "Babaeng 'Makibaka' sa Likod ng Rehas" [Makibaka Woman behind Bars], in *Tibak Rising: Activism in the Days of Martial Law*, ed. Ferdinand C. Llanes (Mandaluyong City: Anvil, 2012), 44; Ferdinand C. Llanes, "Mga Huling Mayo Uno ni Ka Bert Olalia," [Comrade Bert Olalia's Final May Firsts] in *Tibak Rising: Activism in the Days of Martial Law*, ed. Ferdinand C. Llanes (Mandaluyong City: Anvil, 2012), 220–22.

154 Neferti Xina M. Tadiar, *Things Fall Away: Philippine Historical Experience and the Makings of Globalization* (Quezon City: University of the Philippines Press, 2004), 220.

155 Ibid., 229.

156 Lopez, "Quezon City," 10; Emere Distor, "Out of the House: Activism 101," in *Tibak Rising: Activism in the Days of Martial Law*, ed. Ferdinand C. Llanes (Mandaluyong City: Anvil, 2012), 32–33.

157 Quijano de Manila, *Manila: Sin City?*, 265.

158 Rolando B. Tolentino, *Contestable Nation-Space: Cinema, Cultural Politics, and Transnationalism in the Marcos–Brocka Philippines* (Quezon City: University of the Philippines Press, 2014), 95. Depictions of heteronormative suburbia in the global north are but hollow stereotypes nowadays, as shown in Dowling, "Suburban Stories," 69–71.

159 See chapter 3 of J. Neil C. Garcia, *Philippine Gay Culture: Binabae to Bakla, Silahis to MSM*, 2d ed (Quezon City: University of the Philippines Press, 2008).

160 J. Neil C. Garcia, "The City in Philippine Literature," *Likhaan: The Journal of Philippine Contemporary Literature* 8, 2014: 161–84. Quotes are on p. 178.

161 Tadiar, *Things Fall Away*, 225.

162 On Manila's cityscape under Marcos's rule in the films of Bernal and Brocka, who directed the film adaptation of Reyes's *Sa mga Kuko ng Liwanag*, see Tolentino, *Contestable Nation-Space*, 85–120. On Manila as a subject and setting in Philippine literature, see E. San Juan Jr, "Encircle the Cities by the Countryside: The City in Philippine Writing," in *History and Form: Selected Essays*, 150–67 (Quezon City: Ateneo de Manila University Press, 1996).

163 F. Sionil Jose, *Sin: A Novel* (Manila: Solidaridad, 1994); F. Sionil Jose, *The Feet of Juan Bacnang* (Manila: Solidaridad, 2011), 30; F. Sionil Jose, *Ermita: A Filipino Novel* (Manila: Solidaridad, 1988), 40; Liwayway A. Arceo, *Canal de la Reina: Isang Nobela* (Quezon City: Ateneo de Manila University Press, 1985); Rosario de Guzman-Lingat, *Kung Wala na ang Tag-Araw/Ano Ngayon, Ricky? (Dalawang Nobela)* [If Summer is Gone/What Now, Ricky? (Two Novels)] (Quezon City: Ateneo de Manila University Press, 1996), 283, 374.

164 De Guzman-Lingat, *Ano Ngayon, Ricky?*, 414.

165 Arceo, *Canal de la Reina*, 57, 99–101.

166 Jose, *The Feet of Juan Bacnang*, 131.

167 *Tambay* is a colloquial term that came from the phrase "stand by," which in Philippine English took on the meaning of "to loiter." Hence, a tambay is one who is idle and wastes time away.

168 Welcome Rotonda was and still is a favorite rallying point among activists. The conduct of a typical mobilization starts at Welcome Rotonda and ends at the heart of Manila, either at Plaza Miranda or at Mendiola. For examples, see the various essays in Lacaba, *Days of Disquiet*; Melencio, *Full Quarter Storms*, 33; Mendoza, "Natdems, Socdems, and the Ateneo," 140. Leslie Bauzon connects this mobilization with the September 1984 barricades at UP Diliman ("Angara's Toughminded Leadership," 577).

169 Quimpo and Quimpo, *Subversive Lives*, 360.

170 Robert L. Youngblood, *Marcos against the Church: Economic Development and Political Repression in the Philippines* (Quezon City: New Day, 1993), 63.

171 Quimpo and Quimpo, *Subversive Lives*, 361.

172 Cf. Harvey, *Paris*, 113.

173 UP Institute of Planning, "Goals and Policies for Quezon City," 90–91.

174 Lacaba, *Days of Disquiet*, 176; Mendoza, "Natdems, Socdems, and the Ateneo," 131; Melencio, *Full Quarter Storms*, 3, 30, 64, 93. Ironically, these were probably the same reasons why the military and police often chose similar places in Quezon City to conduct torture against perceived enemies of the state (Melencio, *Full Quarter Storms*, 6). For instance, the UG unit that prepared copies of *Liberation*, an English-language newsletter of the underground movement, moved to a safehouse in October 1972, "a kind of way station for comrades coming in from the provinces for consultations," only to find out that the house directly behind it was the residence of a military colonel involved in "sona" operations to flush out "bad elements" in target communities. Later on, the unit transferred to Novaliches (Rolly Peña, "*Liberation*: Early Days," in *Tibak Rising: Activism in the Days of Martial Law*, ed. Ferdinand C. Llanes [Mandaluyong City: Anvil, 2012], 188). For an account about a UG house in Quezon City, see Joey Flora, "Close(t) Encounters inside the CPP," in *Tibak Rising: Activism in the Days of Martial Law*, ed. Ferdinand C. Llanes (Mandaluyong City: Anvil, 2012). Interestingly, Lualhati Abreu mentions that her group's UG house in 1973 was said to be a haunted house along the dreaded Balete Drive (see chapter 3; Lualhati Milan Abreu, *Agaw-Dilim, Agaw-Liwanag* [Quezon City: University of the Philippines Press, 2009], 69–70).

175 Fortich, *Escape!*, 79, 83.

176 The LAFM emerged in 1976 as an anti-Marcos and anticommunist "third force" and was heavily influenced and supported by the Jesuits and lay members of the Partido Demokratikong Sosyalista ng Pilipinas. It also received financial help from wealthy businessmen, like J. Amado Araneta (Eduardo B. Olaguer, *Light a Fire II: Confessions of a Jesuit Terrorist-Son* [Quezon City: Edolaguer Family Publishing, 2005], 155–60). Cf. Thompson, *The Anti-Marcos Struggle*, 84–88.

177 E.g., Parnell, "The Composite State," 154–55.

178 Sarte and Agbayani, *Quezon City*, 28.

179 Ocampo, "Swan Song for Broadway," 118–19; Aguilar, *Filipino Housewives Speak*, 61.

180 In 1971, with funding coming from a donation by the Libyan government, the Islamic Directorate of the Philippines purchased a 4.9-hectare site along Tandang Sora Avenue to create an Islamic center. The site became Salam Mosque Compound (Akiko Watanabe, "Representing Muslimness: Strategic Essentialism in a Land Dispute in Metro Manila," *Philippine Studies* 56 [3], 2008: 285–311, esp. 289).

181 Mariano C. Apilado, "The United Church of Christ in the Philippines: Historical Location, Theological Roots, and Spiritual Commitment," in *Chapters in Philippine Church History*, ed. Anne C. Kwantes (Mandaluyong City: OMF Literature, 2001), 353–54.

182 Rex R. B. Reyes, Jr., "The St. Andrew's Theological Seminary," in *Chapters in Philippine Church History*, ed. Anne C. Kwantes (Mandaluyong City: OMF Literature, 2001), 364–66; Gerard A. Finin, *The Making of the Igorot: Contours of Cordillera Consciousness* (Quezon City: Ateneo de Manila University Press, 2005), 315.

183 Finin, *The Making of the Igorot*, 222.

184 Ma. Ceres P. Doyo, *Macli-ing Dulag: Kalinga Chief, Defender of the Cordillera* (Quezon City: University of the Philippines Press, 2015), 19; Manuel C. Lahoz, *Of Tyrants and Martyrs: A Political Memoir* (Quezon City: University of the Philippines Press, 2017), 179–80.

NOTES   319

185 Lahoz, *Of Tyrants and Martyrs*; Finin, *The Making of the Igorot*, 218; Jose F. Lacaba, "Kasangga o Kabangga?" [Friend or Foe?], *Mr. & Ms.*, 19 Mar. 1985: 14–15. However, it must also be mentioned that the SVD found itself against its workers in a labor strike involving the Arnoldus Woodworks, Inc., a company controlled by the religious group. According to reports, Balweg and de la Torre tried to mediate between the two sides (ibid., 14–15).

186 Youngblood, *Marcos against the Church*, 86, 114–15; Parnell, "Criminalizing Colonialism," 201, 214. Cf. Evangelista, "The Faculty," 192–93, 201.

187 Youngblood, *Marcos against the Church*, 63; Melencio, *Full Quarter Storms*, 88–91.

188 Mark R. Thompson, "The EDSAs: From Cross-class to Class-based," in *Remembering/ Rethinking EDSA*, ed. JPaul S. Manzanilla and Caroline S. Hau (Mandaluyong City: Anvil, 2016), 316.

189 Quimpo and Quimpo, *Subversive Lives*, 335. In contrast to the Marcoses, who were Manila aficionados, the Aquinos were longtime Quezon City residents, especially Ninoy. Although born in Tarlac, he grew up in a suburban home in New Manila and eventually moved to West Triangle.

190 "Triumphant End for Lakbayan," *Malaya*, 8 Mar. 1984, in *Ninoy Aquino: The Man, the Legend*, ed. Asuncion David Maramba (Mandaluyong: Cacho Hermanos, 1984).

191 "Aquino Extolled on Anniversary," *Bulletin Today*, 22 Aug. 1984, in *Ninoy Aquino: The Man, the Legend*, ed. Asuncion David Maramba (Mandaluyong: Cacho Hermanos, 1984), 202.

192 Thompson, *The Anti-Marcos Struggle*, 127–28. Kaa Byington, however, presents a slightly higher figure for the opposition: 16 of 21 Metro Manila seats [*Bantay ng Bayan: Stories from the NAMFREL Crusade (1984–1986)* (Manila: Bookmark, 1988), 59–60].

193 Ibid., 54.

194 Thompson, *The Anti-Marcos Struggle*, 141.

195 Salvador Escalante and J. Augustus Y. De La Paz, *The EDSA Uprising? The Five-Percent Revolution, EDSA in Retrospect* (Quezon City: Truth and Justice Foundation, 2000), 19; Crisostomo, *Cory*, 157.

196 Tessa M. Jazmines, "The Lighter Side of the Polls," *Sunday Times Magazine*, 16 Feb. 1986: 13.

197 Reynaldo Santos Jr, "1986 Comelec Walkout Not about Cory or Marcos," *Rappler*, 25 Feb. 2013, http://www.rappler.com/nation/politics/elections-2013/22582-1986-comelec-walkout-not-about-cory-or-marcos, accessed 4 Sept. 2016.

198 Lisandro E. Claudio, *Taming People's Power: The EDSA Revolutions and Their Contradictions* (Quezon City: Ateneo de Manila University Press, 2013), 36.

199 For a scholarly account of Marcos's downfall, see Gemma Nemenzo Almendral, "The Fall of the Regime," in *Dictatorship and Revolution: Roots of People's Power*, ed. Aurora Javate-de Dios, Petronilo Bn. Daroy, and Lorna Kalaw-Tirol (Metro Manila: Conspectus, 1988).

200 Florentino H. Hornedo, "'People Power' as the Traditional Go-Between," in *Pagmamahal and Pagmumura* [Loving and Cursing]: *Essays* (Quezon City: Office of Research and Publications, Ateneo de Manila University, 1997), 134.

201 Sheila S. Coronel, "A Rebellion that Defied the Rules," *Sunday Times Magazine*, 2 Mar. 1986: 6–9. For a detailed account of the historic four days at EDSA, see Quijano de Manila, *The Quartet of the Tiger Moon: Scenes from the People-Power Apocalypse* (n.p.: Book Stop, 1986).

202 Hornedo, "'People Power' as the Traditional Go-Between," 133, 137. Cf. Caroline S. Hau, *Elites and Ilustrados in Philippine Culture* (Quezon City: Ateneo de Manila University Press, 2017), 172–86. On UP's participation, see Camagay, "Edgardo J. Angara," 24–26. Quezon City's organized urban poor participated in EDSA People Power. SAMA-SAMA members

and Tatalon residents took pride in having played a part in both the snap elections and the EDSA uprising, Ramos-Jimenez et al., *Philippine Urban Situation Analysis*, 43; Parnell, "The Composite State," 155–57; cf. Pinches, "The Working Class Experience of Shame," 170–73.

203 Crisostomo, *Cory*, 1–2.

204 Coronel, "A Rebellion that Defied the Rules," 6–9.

205 Aguilar, *Filipino Housewives Speak*, 11.

206 Thelma Sioson-San Juan, "Is 'Burgis' Power for Real?," *Sunday Times Magazine*, 9 Mar. 1986: 5–7. Quote is on p. 5.

207 Ibid., 5. Like Ateneo, Assumption College (Makati) and De La Salle University (Manila) have a reputation of being elite schools.

208 Porio, "Shifting Spaces," 114–15.

209 Parnell, "Criminalizing Colonialism," 214; Pinches, "The Working Class Experience of Shame," 170–73.

210 The natdem movement marginalized itself from other pro-democracy forces when it decided to boycott the 1986 snap elections, an error it eventually acknowledged.

211 Quijano de Manila, *The Quartet*, 67.

212 Claudio, *Taming People's Power*, 32.

213 See chapters 5 and 6 of Seekins, *State and Society in Modern Rangoon*; Ross King, *Reading Bangkok* (Singapore: NUS Press, 2011), 71–84; Arai Kenichiro, "Jakarta 'Since Yesterday': The Making of the Post-New Order Regime in an Indonesian Metropolis," *Southeast Asian Studies* 4 (3), 2015: 445–86, esp. 448.

214 Aguilar, *Filipino Housewives Speak*, 11.

Conclusion: Past, Imperfect, Tense

1 "Quezon City Rolls out Plans for 'Future Perfect' Diamond Jubilee Celebration," *Philippine Star*, 3 Apr. 2014, http://www.philstar.com/food-and-leisure/2014/04/03/1308011/quezon-city-rolls-out-plans-future-perfect-diamond-jubilee, accessed 15 Mar. 2016.

2 Berner, *Defending a Place in the City*, 11.

3 One interesting example of this undying dream for Quezon City to be capital again is the Quezon City team in the Maharlika Pilipinas Basketball League, a semi-professional league that was established in 2017 with teams based in different parts of the country. Nicknamed "Capitals," Quezon City's team carries a logo that closely resembles that of the Washington Wizards, the National Basketball Association team based in the US capital.

4 I am grateful to Carol Hau for this insight.

5 For a literary exploration on the connection between rural folklore, urban domesticity, and Visayan feminine labor, see Sabina Murray, "Broken Glass," in *Manila Noir*, ed. Jessica Hagedorn (Mandaluyong City: Anvil, 2013).

6 Brioso, *Arsenio H. Lacson*, 71.

7 Mumford, *The City in History* (San Diego: Harcourt, 1989), 486.

8 On the "moral minimalism" of American suburbs, defined by its tendency to avoid social conflicts and confrontations and fostered by the high social status enjoyed by its residents, see M. P. Baumgartner, *The Moral Order of a Suburb* (New York and Oxford: Oxford University Press, 1988), 3, 10–13.

NOTES   321

9   On the laidback, middle-class lifestyle in post-authoritarian Quezon City, see for example the various essays in Alfred A. Yuson, *Confessions of a Q.C. House-husband and Other Privacies* (Pasig: Anvil, 1991).

10   On the divergence between moral and class politics and how it plays out in Metro Manila, see Wataru Kusaka, *Moral Politics in the Philippines: Inequality, Democracy, and the Urban Poor* (Singapore: NUS Press, 2017).

11   Quoted in Abrams, *The Language of Cities*, 331.

12   On the significance of these sites of remembrance, see Claudio, *Taming People's Power*.

13   Indeed, most non-Left accounts of the Marcos period reckon Ninoy's death as the start of anti-Marcos movements after years of cowered silence, a dominant narrative that disregards earlier responses to the dictatorship by the natdems and Moros, among others.

14   Benedict Anderson, "Cacique Democracy in the Philippines," in *The Spectre of Comparisons: Nationalism, Southeast Asia and the World* (London: Verso, 1998). Another example, albeit a less prominent one, of such a clan is the Lichaucos. See Doeppers, *Feeding Manila*, 108.

15   Massey, *For Space*, 9.

16   Brookfield et al., *The City in the Village*, 10–14; Lim Heng Kow, *The Evolution of the Urban System in Malaya* (Kuala Lumpur: Penerbit Universiti Malaya, 1978), 98–106; Jamalunlaili Abdullah, "Economic Growth, Expansion of the Middle Class and the Suburbanization of Kuala Lumpur's Metropolitan Area, Malaysia," in *The Rise of Middle Classes in Southeast Asia*, ed. Takashi Shiraishi and Pasuk Phongpaichit (Kyoto: Kyoto University Press; Trans Pacific Press, 2008).

17   King, *Kuala Lumpur and Putrajaya*, 131. King, however, qualifies this modernity as Arabic-Islamic in character. An instructive official document concerning the planning of Putrajaya is John Jebasingam Issace, "Creating the Essence of Cities: The Planning & Development of Malaysia's New Federal Administrative Capital, Putrajaya," World Bank discussion paper, 2005, esp. pp. 1–3, http://info.worldbank.org/etools/docs/library/235915/S5_p22paper.pdf, accessed 10 Oct. 2013. Take note of the oxymoron in the title of the document. It runs parallel to the paradox of artificial capital cities founded on primordialist nationalism.

18   Maung Aung Myoe, "The Road to Naypyitaw: Making Sense of the Myanmar Government's Decision to Move Its Capital," Asia Research Institute Working Paper Series No. 79, November 2006, esp. pp. 3–4.

19   King, *Kuala Lumpur and Putrajaya*, 131; Muhizam Mustafa, "Public Art in the Federal Territory of Putrajaya: Questions of Value and Role," *Wacana Seni Journal of Arts Discourse* 8, 2009: 69–96, esp. p. 92.

20   Seekins, *State and Society in Modern Rangoon*, 161–65; Maung, "The Road to Naypyitaw," 5–11, 19. Naypyitaw is a precolonial term to denote "royal capital" or "palace site" (ibid., 3). Of course, antidemocratic spatial logic also operates in cities that have grown organically, as seen in the elimination of civic spaces in Suharto-era Jakarta to minimize protests (Mike Douglass, "The Globalization of Capital Cities: Civil Society, the Neoliberal State and the Reconstruction of Urban Space in Asia-Pacific," in *Capital Cities in Asia-Pacific: Primacy and Diversity*, ed. K. C. Ho and Hsin-Huang Michael Hsiao [Taipei: Center for Asia-Pacific Area Studies, Research Center for Humanities and Social Sciences, Academia Sinica, 2006], 32–33). On Haussmannian urbanism, see Harvey, *Paris*, 99–105. Nonetheless, Haussmannian tactics failed to prevent the 1871 uprising that led to the establishment of the Paris Commune.

21   Morshidi Sirat, "Kuala Lumpur: Primacy, Urban System and Rationalizing Capital City Functions," in *Capital Cities in Asia-Pacific: Primacy and Diversity*, ed. K. C. Ho and

Hsin-Huang Michael Hsiao (Taipei: Center for Asia-Pacific Area Studies, Research Center for Humanities and Social Sciences, Academia Sinica, 2006), 77; Hamzah Sendut, "The Structure of Kuala Lumpur, Malaysia's Capital City," in *The City in Newly Developing Countries: Readings on Urbanism and Urbanization*, ed. Gerald Breese (Englewood, NJ: Prentice-Hall, 1969), 472–73; Abdullah, "Economic Growth," 243–54.

22   Chris Baker and Pasuk Phongpaichit, *A History of Thailand*, 3rd ed. (Melbourne: Cambridge University Press, 2014), 161–63, 201–4.

23   Davis, *Planet of Slums*, 9–11.

24   Arai Kenichiro, "Jakarta 'Since Yesterday': The Making of the Post-New Order Regime in an Indonesian Metropolis," *Southeast Asian Studies* 4 (3), 2015: 445–86.

25   For a spatial analysis of protests and riots in Kuala Lumpur, Bangkok, and Jakarta, see King, *Kuala Lumpur and Putrajaya*, 66, 79; King, *Reading Bangkok*; Kusno, *Behind the Postcolonial*, chapter 4.

26   However, dichotomizing urban- and rural-based dissent in Southeast Asia is unsound because in many cases organizational and ideological linkages connect the two. For examples of urban-based uprisings and riots in Southeast Asia, see Baker and Pasuk, *A History of Thailand*, 184–89, 273–78; Andaya and Andaya, *A History of Malaysia*, 297–300.

27   Harvey, *Social Justice and the City*, 17.

28   Boris Michel, "Going Global, Veiling the Poor: Global City Imaginaries in Metro Manila," *Philippine Studies* 58 (3), 2010: 383–406, esp. 391; cf. Porio, "Shifting Spaces."

29   Alfred W. McCoy, ed., *An Anarchy of Families: State and Family in the Philippines* (Quezon City: Ateneo de Manila University Press, 1994).

30   Michel, "Going Global," 389; Reyes, "Spatial Structure of Metro Manila," 24–29.

31   Quote is from Claudio, *Taming People's Power*, 31. But while Metro Manila has no symbolic heart, EDSA serves as its spinal cord, and a fragile one at that. Its fragility causes perennial metropolitan paralysis, whether in terms of mobility, economics, or politics.

32   Gavin Shatkin, "Colonial Capital, Modernist Capital, Global Capital: The Changing Political Symbolism of Urban Space in Metro Manila, the Philippines," *Pacific Affairs* 78 (4), 2005–2006: 577–600, esp. 588–94.

33   Ibid., "Colonial Capital," 591–93; Michel, "Going Global." On neoliberalism and urban development in Metro Manila, see also Gavin Shatkin, "Planning to Forget: Informal Settlements as 'Forgotten Places' in Globalising Metro Manila," *Urban Studies* 41 (12), 2004: 2469–2484, esp. 2475–77.

34   Ho and Hsiao, "Globalization and Asia-Pacific Capital Cities," 4; Douglass, "The Globalization of Capital Cities," 34–37.

35   Harding and Blokland, *Urban Theory*, 146–50.

36   Arnisson Andre C. Ortega, *Neoliberalizing Spaces in the Philippines: Suburbanization, Transnational Migration, and Dispossession* (Quezon City: Ateneo de Manila University Press, 2018), 286–89.

37   Gavin Shatkin, "Planning to Forget: Informal Settlements as 'Forgotten Places' in Globalising Metro Manila," *Urban Studies* 41 (12), 2004: 2469–84.

38   David G. Timberman, *A Changeless Land: Continuity and Change in Philippine Politics* (Makati: Bookmark, 1991). Cf. Parnell, "The Composite State," 160–70.

39   Pinches, "The Working Class Experience of Shame," 186.

40   Massey, *For Space*, 9.

References

Archival Materials and Personal Papers

Ateneo de Manila University Archives (ADMUA)

Bentley Historical Library (BHL), University of Michigan, Ann Arbor, MI
Frank Murphy Papers (FMP)
Joseph Ralston Hayden Papers (JRHP)
Manuel L. Quezon Papers (MLQP-BHL)

Center for Southeast Asian Studies Library, Kyoto University, Kyoto
Marcelino Foronda Collection (MFC)

Filipinas Heritage Library, Makati City
Elpidio Quirino Papers (EQP)

Meralco Head Office, Pasig City
Meralco Museum and Archives (MMA)

National Library of the Philippines, Manila
Historical Data Papers (HDP)
Manuel L. Quezon Papers (MLQP)

Sophia University Library, Sophia University, Tokyo
Mauro Garcia Collection (MGC)

Jorge B. Vargas Museum and Filipiniana Resource Center, University of the Philippines-Diliman,
    Quezon City
Jorge B. Vargas Papers (JBVP)

University of the Philippines-Diliman Main Library, Quezon City
Manuel A. Roxas Papers (MARP)
Philippine Radical Papers (PRP)

324 A CAPITAL CITY AT THE MARGINS

Other Unpublished Materials

Abrams, Charles and Otto Koenigsberger. "A Housing Program for the Philippine Islands." Report prepared for the United Nations Technical Assistance Administration (UNTAA), 14 Jan. 1959. Copy available at the School of Urban and Regional Planning (SURP) Library, UP-Diliman, Quezon City.

Abueva, Jose V., Sylvia H. Guerrero, and Elsa P. Jurado. "Metro Manila Today and Tomorrow." Final Report Submitted to the First National City Bank by the Institute of Philippine Culture, Ateneo de Manila University, 15 Dec. 1972. Copy available at the Rizal Library, Ateneo de Manila University.

Caoili, Manuel A. "Quezon and His Business Friends: Notes on the Origins of Philippine National Capitalism." Paper/Lecture Delivered for the Andres Soriano Professorial Chair in Business and Public Administration at the College of Public Administration, University of the Philippines-Manila, 15 Jan. 1986. Copy available at the UP-Diliman Main Library.

Croft, Louis. "General Plan of Major Thoroughfares, Metropolitan Manila: Preliminary Report." Prepared by the President's Office on City Planning, 13 June 1945. Copy available at the American Historical Collection (AHC), Rizal Library, Ateneo de Manila University.

Demerath, N. J. and Richard N. Kuhlman. "Toward a Housing Program for the Philippines: A Report to the National Housing Commission," 20 Oct. 1945. Copy available at the Filipiniana Division, UP-Diliman Main Library, Quezon City.

Department of Public Works and Communications, Institute of Planning, University of the Philippines, and Presidential Advisory Council on Public Works and Community Development. Physical Planning Strategy for the Philippines: Population Trends and Existing Growth Areas, Dec. 1971. Copy available at the SURP Library, UP-Diliman.

Makasiar, Gary S. "Housing Summary." In National Economic Development Authority, Housing in the Philippines: Preparatory Materials for the Conference on Housing, 16 Apr. 1973. Copy available at the Rizal Library, Ateneo de Manila University.

Ocampo, Romeo B. "Historical Development of Philippine Housing Policy. Part 1. Prewar Housing Policy," Occasional Paper No. 6, November 1976, College of Public Administration, University of the Philippines, 16–26. Copy available at the National College of Public Administration and Governance Library, UP-Diliman.

People's Homesite and Housing Corporation. "Basic Reference Manual, as of December 31, 1968." Copy available at the UP-Diliman Main Library.

Quezon City Council. 1939 Quezon City Ordinances (1–100), n.d. Compilation available at the Quezon City Public Library.

———. 1940 Quezon City Ordinances (SP19–SP100), n.d. Compilation available at the Quezon City Public Library.

———. 1955 Ordinances, n.d. Compilation available at the Quezon City Public Library.

Quezon City Human Settlements Task Force. "Urban Redevelopment Project: Barrio Escopa, Quezon City, Metropolitan Manila. Background Information," 1976. Copy available at the Hatcher Graduate Library, University of Michigan.

Ramos, Josefina B. "The Punta Multi-Story Tenement Project: An Experiment in High-Rise Public Housing in the Philippines." In National Economic Development Authority, Housing in the Philippines: Preparatory Materials for the Conference on Housing, 16 Apr. 1973. Copy available at the Rizal Library, Ateneo de Manila University.

Santayana, Gregorio [pseud. Jose Lava]. "Milestones in the History of the Philippine Communist Party." Copy available at the Filipiniana Section, Rizal Library, Ateneo de Manila University.

University of the Philippines, Institute of Planning. "Goals and Policies for Quezon City." Studio Work II, 3rd Trimester, 1972–1973. Copy available at the SURP Library, UP Diliman.

REFERENCES   325

Published Materials

Abaya-Ulindang, Faina C. *Resettling the Huks in the Land of Promise: The Story of the Economic Development Corps in Mindanao, 1950–1970*. Manila: National Historical Commission of the Philippines, 2017.

Abdullah, Jamalunlaili. "Economic Growth, Expansion of the Middle Class and the Suburbanization of Kuala Lumpur's Metropolitan Area, Malaysia." In *The Rise of Middle Classes in Southeast Asia*, ed. Takashi Shiraishi and Pasuk Phongpaichit, 237–56. Kyoto: Kyoto University Press; Trans Pacific Press, 2008.

Abinales, P. N. "The Left and the Philippine Student Movement: Random Historical Notes on Party Politics and Sectoral Struggles." *Kasarinlan: Philippine Journal of Third World Studies* 1 (2), 1985: 41–45.

———. "Progressive–Machine Conflict in Early-twentieth-century U.S. Politics and Colonial-state Building in the Philippines." In *The American Colonial State in the Philippines: Global Perspectives*, ed. Julian Go and Anne L. Foster, 148–81. Pasig City: Anvil, 2005.

Abrams, Charles. *The Language of Cities: A Glossary of Terms*. New York: The Viking Press, 1971.

———. *Man's Struggle for Shelter in an Urbanizing World*. Cambridge: MIT Press, 1964.

Abreu, Lualhati Milan. *Agaw-Dilim, Agaw-Liwanag*. Quezon City: University of the Philippines Press, 2009.

Abueva, Jose V. *Quezon City Experiment: The Story behind the Quezon City Citizens League for Good Government and the 1959 Election*, reprint. Manila: Regal Printing, 1963.

Afuang, Benjamin V. "A Master Plan on Parks." *Sunday Times Magazine*, 29 Aug. 1971: 38–39.

Agoncillo, Teodoro A. *The Fateful Years: Japan's Adventure in the Philippines, 1941–45, vol. 1*, 2d ed. Quezon City: University of the Philippines Press, 2001.

———. *The Fateful Years: Japan's Adventure in the Philippines, 1941–45, vol. 2*, 2d ed. Quezon City: University of the Philippines Press, 2001.

Aguilar, Delia D. *Filipino Housewives Speak*, ed. Marjorie Evasco. Manila: Institute of Women's Studies, St. Scholastica's College, 1991.

Aguilar, Faustino. *Nang Magdaan ang Daluyong* [When the Surge Arrived]. Manila: PSP Press, 1945.

Aguilar, Mila D. "January 13: View of the Impending Avalanche." *Graphic*, 27 Jan. 1971, 4–5.

———. "The Liberation of the State University." *Graphic*, 24 Feb. 1971, 6–8.

Alabado, Ceres S. C. *Kangkong 1896*. Pasay City: Pamana, 1969.

Alarcon, Norma I. *The Imperial Tapestry: American Colonial Architecture in the Philippines*. Manila: University of Santo Tomas Publishing House, 2008.

Alcazaren, Paulo. "Jeproks: My Life in the Projects." In *The Manila We Know*, ed. Erlinda Enriquez Panlilio, 99–109. Mandaluyong City: Anvil, 2017.

———, Luis Ferrer, and Benvenuto Icamina. *Lungsod Iskwater: The Evolution of Informality as a Dominant Pattern in Philippine Cities*. Mandaluyong City: Anvil, 2011.

Alfaro, Alberto M. "Low-Cost Housing for the Rich?." *Philippines Free Press (PFP)*, 28 Jan. 1956: 20, 45–46.

Algué, José. *Atlas de Filipinas: Colección de 30 Mapas*. Washington, DC: Government Printing Office, 1900.

Almendral, Gemma Nemenzo. "The Fall of the Regime." In *Dictatorship and Revolution: Roots of People's Power*, ed. Aurora Javate-de Dios, Petronilo Bn. Daroy, and Lorna Kalaw-Tirol, 176–220. Metro Manila: Conspectus, 1988.

Althusser, Louis. *On the Reproduction of Capitalism: Ideology and Ideological State Apparatuses*, trans. G. M. Goshgarian. London: Verso, 2014.

Aluit, Alfonso J. *By Sword and Fire: The Destruction of Manila in World War II, 3 February – 3 March 1945*. Makati City: Bookmark, 1994.

Alvarez, Ramiro C. "'Twilight' Scandals at the PHHC." *PFP*, 2 Apr. 1966: 22.

Alvarez, Santiago V. *The Katipunan and the Revolution*, trans. Paula Carolina S. Malay. Quezon City: Ateneo de Manila University Press, 1992.

American Express. *Manila and the Philippines*. Manila: American Express, [1933?].

——. *Manila and the Philippines*. Manila: American Express, 1939.

Ampil, Alberto V. "An Interview with Fr Alberto V Ampil, SJ: Ms Chay Florentino-Hofileña, Interviewer." In *University Traditions: The Social Sciences Interviews*, ed. Ramón Sunico, 3–31. Quezon City: Ateneo de Manila University, Office for Mission and Identity and Organizational Development, 2010.

Andaya, Barbara Watson and Leonard Y. Andaya. *A History of Malaysia*, 2nd ed. Honolulu: University of Hawai'i Press, 2001.

Anderson, Benedict. *Imagined Communities: Reflections on the Origin and Spread of Nationalism*. Pasig City: Anvil, 2003.

——. "Cacique Democracy in the Philippines." In *The Spectre of Comparisons: Nationalism, Southeast Asia and the World*, 192–226. London: Verso, 1998.

[Anon.] *Gateway to Manila (Shopping in Old Manila): A Complete Practical Guidebook to the Orient's Most Charming City*. [Manila]: n.p., 1934.

——. *'Gateway' to Manila. The Only Complete GUIDE BOOK to the Orient's Most Charming City*, 13th ed., February 1938. n.p.: n.p., 1938.

Antolihao, Lou. *Culture of Improvisation: Informal Settlements and Slum Upgrading in a Metro Manila Locality*. Quezon City: Institute of Philippine Culture, Ateneo de Manila University, 2004.

Antonio, Tony. "Barrio Tense, Waits for Demolition Teams." *Bulletin Today*, 2 Mar. 1976: 1, 8.

Apilado, Mariano C. "The United Church of Christ in the Philippines: Historical Location, Theological Roots, and Spiritual Commitment." In *Chapters in Philippine Church History*, ed. Anne C. Kwantes, 335–58. Mandaluyong City: OMF Literature, 2001.

Apostol, Gina. "The Unintended." In *Manila Noir*, ed. Jessica Hagedorn, 152–71. Mandaluyong City: Anvil, 2013.

"Aquino Extolled on Anniversary." *Bulletin Today* 22 Aug. 1984. In *Ninoy Aquino: The Man, the Legend*, ed. Asuncion David Maramba, 202–5. Mandaluyong: Cacho Hermanos, 1984.

Ara, Satoshi. "Emilio Aguinaldo under American and Japanese Rule: Submission for Independence?" *Philippine Studies: Historical and Ethnographic Viewpoints* 63 (2), 2015: 161–92.

Arai, Kenichiro. "Jakarta 'Since Yesterday': The Making of the Post-New Order Regime in an Indonesian Metropolis." *Southeast Asian Studies* 4 (3), 2015: 445–86.

Arandia, Shirley S. "Recollections of a Pioneer." In *U.P. Diliman: Home and Campus*, ed. Narita Manuel Gonzalez and Gerardo T. Los Baños, 268–74. Quezon City: University of the Philippines Press, 2010.

Araneta, Salvador. *A Molave of His Country*. Malabon: AIA, 1970.

——. *Reflections of a Filipino Exile*, ed. Michael P. Onorato. Fullerton, CA: California State University, 1979.

Arceo, Liwayway A. *Canal de la Reina: Isang Nobela*. Quezon City: Ateneo de Manila University Press, 1985.

Arellano, Juan M. "Landscaping Plans for Manila." *Philippine Magazine* 32 (1), 1935: 28–29.

Arevalo, Renato. "Out of the Ruins." *MT*, 10 June 1945: 6.

Arrogante, Julita P. "Kamuning and Its Beginnings." In *Age of Gold: Sacred Heart Parish, Kamuning, Q.C., Golden Jubilee, 1941–1991*, ed. Angelo J. de los Reyes, 19–20. [Quezon City?]: Sacred Heart Parish, Angelo J. de los Reyes, 1991.

Artiaga, Santiago. *Brief History of San Juan del Monte, Rizal*. n.p.: n.p., n.d.

Asistio, Macario B. "Asistio to Businessmen." In *2 Golden Decades: Kalookan, 1951–1970*, ed. Agapito M. Joaquin, 210–12. n.p.: n.p., 1971. Copy available at the Caloocan City Library.

——. "Liham sa mga Taga-Kalookan." In *2 Golden Decades: Kalookan, 1951–1970*, ed. Agapito M. Joaquin, 156–60. n.p.: n.p., 1971. Copy available at the Caloocan City Library.

——. "Why Caloocan Should Be a City." In *2 Golden Decades: Kalookan, 1951–1970*, ed. Agapito M. Joaquin, 102–8. n.p.: n.p., 1971. Copy available at the Caloocan City Library.

REFERENCES   327

Bagaeen, Samer and Ola Uduku. "Gated Histories: An Introduction to Themes and Concepts." In *Gated Communities: Social Sustainability in Contemporary and Historical Gated Developments*, ed. Samer Bagaeen and Ola Uduku, 1–8. London: Earthscan, 2010.

Baja, Emanuel A. *Philippine Police System and Its Problems*. Manila: Pobre's Press, 1933.

Baker, Chris and Pasuk Phongpaichit. *A History of Thailand*, 3rd ed. Melbourne: Cambridge University Press, 2014.

Balisi y Lugo, Wenceslao, ed. *Quezon City Beautiful: The Year Book and the First National Souvenir of the New Metropolis*. Quezon City: Quezon City Pub. House, 1942.

Bankoff, Greg. *Crime, Society, and the State in the Nineteenth-Century Philippines*. Quezon City: Ateneo de Manila University Press, 1996.

———. "A Tale of Two Cities: The Pyro-Seismic Morphology of Nineteenth-Century Manila." In *Flammable Cities: Urban Conflagration and the Making of the Modern World*, ed. Greg Bankoff, Uwe Lübken, and Jordan Sand, 170–89. Madison: University of Wisconsin Press, 2012.

Baumgartner, M. P. *The Moral Order of a Suburb*. New York and Oxford: Oxford University Press, 1988.

Bautista, Romeo and Gwendolyn Tecson. "International Dimensions." In *The Philippine Economy: Development, Policies, and Challenges*, ed. Arsenio M. Balisacan and Hal Hill, 136–71. Quezon City: Ateneo de Manila University Press, 2003.

Bauzon, Leslie E. "Angara's Toughminded Leadership (1981–19): The Diamond Jubilee Highlighted by Reform of the University System." In *University of the Philippines: The First 75 Years (1908–1983)*, ed. Oscar M. Alfonso, 541–89. Quezon City: University of the Philippines Press, 1985.

Bawagan, Maria Christina Pargas. "Some Trying Times of My Life." In *Tibak Rising: Activism in the Days of Martial Law*, ed. Ferdinand C. Llanes, 12–15. Mandaluyong City: Anvil, 2012.

Beltran, Ofel. "Si Ka Bel ang Aking Ama." In *Ka Bel: Mga Liham*, ed. Kenneth Roland A. Guda, 34–41. Quezon City: Crispin B. Beltran Resource Center, 2010.

Benedicto, Bobby. "The Queer Afterlife of the Postcolonial City: (Trans)gender Performance and the War of Beautification," *Antipode* 47 (3), 2015: 580–97.

Berner, Erhard. *Defending a Place in the City: Localities and the Struggle for Urban Land in Metro Manila*. Quezon City: Ateneo de Manila University Press, 1997.

Billig, Michael S. *Barons, Brokers, and Buyers: The Institutions and Cultures of Philippine Sugar*. Quezon City: Ateneo de Manila University Press, 2003.

Black & Veatch International Consulting Engineers. *Master Plan for a Sewerage System for the Manila Metropolitan Area: Final Report*. Manila: Black & Veatch, 1969.

Boquet, Yves. "From Paris and Beijing to Washington and Brasilia: The Grand Design of Capital Cities and the Early Plans for Quezon City." *Philippine Studies: Historical and Ethnographic Viewpoints* 64 (1), 2016: 43–71.

Borromeo-Buehler, Soledad. *The Cry of Balintawak: A Contrived Controversy*. Quezon City: Ateneo de Manila University Press, 1998.

———. *Scripted by Men, Not by Fate: Andres Bonifacio in Cavite. An Analytical Narrative with Commentary on Selected Sources*. Quezon City: University of the Philippines Press, 2017.

Bote, Veltisezar B. "A Land of Unfinished Memorials." *This Week*, 27 Nov. 1960: 10–13.

Bowring, John. *A Visit to the Philippine Islands*. Manila: Filipiniana Book Guild, 1963.

Boyce, James K. *The Political Economy of Growth and Impoverishment in the Marcos Era*. Quezon City: Ateneo de Manila University Press, 1993.

Brady, Frank. *Angela I. Tuason de Perez and Antonio Perez versus Judge Hermogenes Caluag and J. Antonio Araneta, G.R. No. L-6182: Memorandum in Lieu of Oral Argument*. Manila: McCullough Printing, 1952.

Briones, Concepcion G. *Life in Old Parian*. Cebu City: Cebuano Studies Center, University of San Carlos, 1983.

Brioso, Amador F. Jr. *Arsenio H. Lacson of Manila*. Mandaluyong City: Anvil, 2015.

Broad, Robin. *Unequal Alliance: The World Bank, the International Monetary Fund, and the Philippines*. Quezon City: Ateneo de Manila University Press, 1988.

Brookfield, Harold, Abdul Samad Hadi, and Zaharah Mahmud. *The City in the Village: The In-Situ Urbanization of Villages, Villagers and Their Land around Kuala Lumpur, Malaysia*. Singapore: Oxford University Press, 1991.

Buencamino, Victor. *Memoirs of Victor Buencamino*. Mandaluyong: Jorge B. Vargas Filipiniana Foundation, 1977.

Bureau of the Census and Statistics. *1948 Census of the Philippines*. Manila: Bureau of Printing, 1951.

———. *Facts and Figures about Economic and Social Conditions of the Philippines, 1946–1947*. Manila: Bureau of Printing, 1948.

———. *Journal of Philippine Statistics* 1 (3) *September 1941*. Manila: Bureau of the Census and Statistics, 1941.

———. *Journal of Philippine Statistics* 13 (1–3) (Jan–Mar). Manila: Bureau of the Census and Statistics, 1960.

———. *Philippines 1970 Population. Special Report No. 2: Urban Population*. Manila: Bureau of the Census and Statistics, 1972.

———. *Philippines 1970 Population. Special Report No. 3: Population, Land Area, and Density: 1948, 1960 and 1970*. Manila: Bureau of the Census and Statistics, 1972.

———. *Special Release no. 70-B (Region I), Series of 1968, Month of May: Total Family Expenditures by Expenditure Group and Item of Expenditure, Region I: 1965*. Manila: Bureau of the Census and Statistics, 1968.

Burnham, Daniel. "Report on Proposed Improvements at Manila." In Philippine Commission. *Report of the Philippine Commission to the President, 1905*, part 1, 627–635. Washington, DC: Government Printing Office, 1905.

Burton, Wilbur. "Indonesia and the Philippines." *Philippine Magazine*, Aug. 1940: 306, 313–16.

Byington, Kaa. *Bantay ng Bayan: Stories from the NAMFREL Crusade (1984–1986)*. Manila: Bookmark, 1988.

Cabalfin, Edson. "The Politics of the Nation in the Urban Form of Informal Settlements in Quezon City, Philippines." In *Reading the Architecture of the Underprivileged Classes: A Perspective on the Protests and Upheavals in Our Cities*, ed. Nnamdi Elleh, 153–70. Surrey, England: Ashgate, 2014.

Caballero, Isabelo P. and M. de Gracia Concepcion. *Quezon: The Story of a Nation and Its Foremost Statesman*. Manila: International Publishers, 1935.

Camagay, Maria Luisa T. "Edgardo J. Angara: Steering the University in the Nation's Transition." In *UP in the Time of People Power (1983–2005): A Centennial Publication*, ed. Ferdinand C. Llanes, 14–29. Quezon City: University of the Philippines Press, 2009.

———. *Kasaysayang Panlipunan ng Maynila, 1765–1898*. [The Social History of Manila, 1765–1898] Quezon City: M. L. T. Camagay, 1992.

———. "Ang Papel ng mga Siyudad/Lungsod sa Kasaysayan ng Pilipinas: Isang Paglilinaw." [The Role of Cities in Philippine History: A Clarification] In The *Journal of History: Selected Papers on Cities in Philippine History*, ed. Maria Luisa T. Camagay and Bernardita Reyes Churchill, 9–19. Quezon City: Philippine National Historical Society, 2000.

———. *Working Women in Manila in the 19th Century*. Quezon City: University of the Philippines Press; Center for Women's Studies, 1995.

Camba, Alvin A. "Private-led Suburbanization: Capital Accumulation and Real Estate Development in Postwar Greater Manila, 1945–1960." *Philippine Social Science Review* 63 (2), 2011: 1–29.

Cañete, Reuben Ramas. *Sacrificial Bodies: The Oblation and the Political Aesthetics of Masculine Representations in Philippine Visual Cultures*. Quezon City: University of the Philippines Press, 2012.

REFERENCES   329

Caoili, Manuel. *The Origins of Metropolitan Manila: A Political and Social Analysis.* Quezon City: University of the Philippines Press, 1999.
Capellan, Amado Garson. "Kangkong—A Road Builder's Headache." *PFP,* 4 Jan. 1941: 3.
Capital City Planning Commission. *The Master Plan for the New Capital City.* Manila: Capital City Planning Commission, 1949.
——. *Souvenir Program, 70th Birthday Anniversary Celebration in Honor of the Late President Manuel L. Quezon.* Manila: Benipayo Press, 1948.
——. *Subdivision Regulations of the Capital City.* Manila: Bureau of Printing, 1950.
Caprotti, Federico. *Mussolini's Cities: Internal Colonialism in Italy, 1930–1939.* Youngstown, NY: Cambria, 2007.
Cardenas, Paul. "The Industrialization of Rizal." *Chronicle Magazine,* 29 Dec. 1962: 14–19.
Careaga, Roman. "People's Homesite and Housing Corporation: Its Vital Role." *TDS,* 22 Nov. 1952: 2, 5.
Carman, Phil D. "Real Estate." *ACCJ* 1 (4), 1921: 23.
——. "P. D. Carman Describes Remarkable Growth of Manila since American Occupation." *ACCJ* 2 (3), 1922: 10–12.
Caruncho, Eric S. *Punks, Poets, Poseurs: Reportage on Pinoy Rock & Roll.* Pasig City: Anvil, 1996.
Carunungan, Celso Almadin. "A Desperate Move." *The Weekly Nation,* 15 Mar. 1971: 2–3, 37.
——. *Quezon City: A Saga of Progress.* Quezon City: Cultural and Tourism Affairs Office, Office of the Mayor, 1982.
Casambre, Rey Claro. "Growing up in the Diliman Republic." In *Serve the People: Ang Kasaysayan ng Radikal na Kilusan sa UP* [The History of the Radical Movement in UP], ed. Bienvenido Lumbera, Judy Taguiwalo, Roland Tolentino, Arnold Alamon, and Ramon Guillermo, 63–72. [Quezon City]: IBON; Congress of Teachers and Educators for Nationalism and Democracy; Alliance of Concerned Teachers, 2008.
Catuca [pseud.]. "The Darker Life." *The Diliman Star,* 22 Nov. 1952: 3.
Chu, Richard T. *Chinese and Chinese Mestizos of Manila: Family, Identity, and Culture, 1860s–1930s.* Pasig City: Anvil, 2010.
Chua Beng Huat. *Political Legitimacy and Housing: Stakeholding in Singapore.* London and New York: Routledge, 1997.
Chua, Michael Charleston B. "Ang Paghiraya sa Nasyon: Ang mga Pagdiriwang ng Anibersaryo ng Komonwelt ng Pilipinas (1936–1941)" [Imagining the Nation: Celebrations of the Anniversary of the Philippine Commonwealth (1936–1941)]. *Social Science Diliman* 4 (1–2), 2007: 91–127.
Churchill, Bernardita Reyes. *The Philippine Independence Missions to the United States, 1919–1934.* Manila: National Historical Institute, 1983.
Clark, Victor S. "Labor Conditions in the Philippines." *Bulletin of the Bureau of Labor* 58, 1905: 721–905.
Claudio, Lisandro E. *Liberalism and the Postcolony: Thinking the State in 20th-Century Philippines.* Quezon City: Ateneo de Manila University Press, 2017.
——. *Taming People's Power: The EDSA Revolutions and their Contradictions.* Quezon City: Ateneo de Manila University Press, 2013.
Cohen, Lizabeth. *A Consumer's Republic: The Politics of Mass Consumption in Postwar America.* New York: Vintage, 2004.
Colombijn, Freek. "Public Housing in Post-colonial Indonesia: The Revolution of Rising Expectations." *Bijdragen tot de Taal-, Land- en Volkenkunde* 167 (4), 2011: 437–58.
—— and Joost Coté. "Modernization of the Indonesian City, 1920–1960." In *Cars, Conduits, and Kampongs: The Modernization of the Indonesian City, 1920–1960,* ed. Freek Colombijn and Joost Coté, 1–26. Leiden: Brill, 2015.
Committee on Capital City Site. *Report of the Committee on Capital City Site, Manila, April 7, 1947.* Manila: Committee on Capital City Site, 1947.

Coquia, Francisco R. "Development of Water Resources in the Philippines for Municipal-Industrial Uses." In *United Nations Bureau of Flood Control, Proceedings of the Sixth Regional Conference on Water Resources Development in Asia and the Far East*, Water Resources Series No. 28, 218–223. New York: UN, 1965.

Le Corbusier. *Toward an Architecture*, trans. John Goodman. Los Angeles: Getty Research Institute, 2007.

Cordner, G. Frank. *Housing: Challenge to the Philippines*. Manila: US Foreign Operations Mission to the Philippines, 1953.

Cornejo, Miguel R. *A Plea for Justice by the People of Malibay to His Excellency, the Governor-General of the Philippine Islands*. Manila: n.p., 1928. Copy available at the Mauro Garcia Collection (MGC), Sophia University, Tokyo.

Coronel, Sheila S. "A Rebellion that Defied the Rules." *Sunday Times Magazine*, 2 Mar. 1986: 6–9.

Cortes, Rosario Mendoza. "Tan's Devoted Presidency (1951–1956): A Campus Shaken by Strife until Redeemed by Sobriety." In *University of the Philippines: The First 75 Years (1908–1983)*, ed. Oscar M. Alfonso, 295–337. Quezon City: University of the Philippines Press, 1985.

Crisostomo, Isabelo T. *Quezon City: Ang Paglikha ng Inyong Lunsod* [The Creation of Your City]. Quezon City: Capitol Publishing, 1971.

———. *Cory: Profile of a President*. Quezon City: J. Kriz, 1986.

Croft, Louis P. "On-the-Spot-Decisions" (Letter to Juan F. Rivera, 5 Aug. 1948). In *Quezon: Thoughts and Anecdotes about Him and His Fights*, ed. Juan F. Rivera, 189. Quezon City: Juan F. Rivera, 1979.

Cruz, Roman A. Jr. "The Ateneo Story." In Ateneo de Manila University, *Aegis 1959*, 1–138. Quezon City: Ateneo de Manila University, [1959?].

Cullinane, Michael. *Ilustrado Politics: Filipino Elite Responses to American Rule, 1898–1908*. Quezon City: Ateneo de Manila University Press, 2003.

Cushner, Nicholas P. *Landed Estates in the Colonial Philippines*. New Haven: Yale University, Southeast Asia Studies, 1976.

Daguio, Alfredo T. "Mass Rescue from the Slums." *The Weekly Nation*, 26 Nov. 1965: 16–17.

———. "What is the Squatter? Animal, Vegetable, Mineral?" *The Weekly Nation*, 3 Dec. 1965: 26–27.

Dalisay, Jose Y., Jr., "From Dreams and Green Fields, a City Comes to Life." In *Quezon City at 75: Resurgent & Resilient*, ed. Cynthia Alberto Diaz, 23–91. Quezon City: Erehwon, Local Government of Quezon City, 2014.

———. *Killing Time in a Warm Place*. Pasig City: Anvil, 2006.

———. *The Lavas: A Filipino Family*. Pasig City: Anvil, 1999.

Daroy, Petronilo Bn. "Commune, 'Communists' and Communards." *Graphic*, 24 Feb. 1971, 6–8.

———. "Invasion of the Campus." *Graphic*, 3 Mar. 1971, 12–15.

Davis, Dwight F. *Message of Governor-General Dwight F. Davis to the Ninth Philippine Legislature, Delivered July 16, 1931 at the Opening of the First Session*. Manila: Bureau of Printing, 1931.

Davis, Mike. *Planet of Slums*. London: Verso, 2007.

de Dios, Emmanuel S. and Paul D. Hutchcroft. "Political Economy." In *The Philippine Economy: Development, Policies, and Challenges*, ed. Arsenio M. Balisacan and Hal Hill, 45–73. Quezon City: Ateneo de Manila University Press, 2003.

de Guzman-Lingat, Rosario. *Kung Wala na ang Tag-Araw/Ano Ngayon, Ricky? (Dalawang Nobela)*. [If Summer is Gone/What Now, Ricky? (Two Novels)] Quezon City: Ateneo de Manila University Press, 1996.

de Jesus, Ed. C. and Carlos Quirino. *Earl Carroll: Colossus of Philippine Insurance*. n.p.: Earl and Rose Carroll, 1980.

de la Costa, Horacio. *The Jesuits in the Philippines, 1581–1768*, reprint ed. Quezon City: Ateneo de Manila University Press, 2014.

REFERENCES   331

de la Rama, F. C. *I Made Millions and Lost Them*. n.p.: Nation-Ad, 1957.
de la Rosa, Rolando V. *Beginnings of the Filipino Dominicans*. Manila: UST Publishing House, 1990.
de los Reyes, Angelo J. and Resty Lumanlan. *Sandiwaan sa Kamuning: A Pastoral Experience*. Quezon City: Resty Lumanlan, 1981.
de los Reyes, Isabelo. *El Folk-lore Filipino*, trans. Salud C. Dizon and Maria Elinora P. Imson. Quezon City: University of the Philippines Press, 1994.
de Viana, Lorelei. *Three Centuries of Binondo Architecture, 1594–1898: A Socio-historical Perspective*. Manila: UST Publishing House, 2001.
Decaesstecker, Donald Denise. *Impoverished Urban Filipino Families*. Manila: UST Press, 1978.
del Pan, Ortigas y Fisher. "Hacienda de Piedad." In *Philippine Commission, Fifth Annual Report of the Philippine Commission, 1904*, part 1. Washington, DC: Government Printing Office, 1905.
Department of Finance. *Annual Report of the Secretary of Finance to the President of the Philippines for the Period from July 1, 1946 to June 30, 1947*. Manila: Bureau of Printing, 1949.
Department of Public Works and Communications, Bureau of Public Highways. *The Philippine Highways: A Technical Report*. Manila: Department of Public Works and Communications, 1958.
Department of Public Works, Transportation and Communications (DPWTC), Planning and Project Development Office. *Metro Manila Housing Program*. [Manila]: DPWTC, 1975.
Dery, Luis C. "Prostitution in Colonial Manila." *Philippine Studies* 39 (4), 1991: 475–89.
Devins, John Bancroft. *An Observer in the Philippines: Or, Life in Our New Possessions*. Boston: American Tract Society, 1905.
Distor, Emere. "Out of the House: Activism 101." In *Tibak Rising: Activism in the Days of Martial Law*, ed. Ferdinand C. Llanes, 31–34. Mandaluyong City: Anvil, 2012.
Doeppers, Daniel F. "The Development of Philippine Cities before 1900." *The Journal of Asian Studies* 31 (4), 1972: 769–92.
———. *Feeding Manila in Peace and War, 1850–1945*. Madison: University of Wisconsin Press, 2016.
———. *Manila, 1900–1941: Social Change in a Late Colonial Metropolis*. Quezon City: Ateneo de Manila University Press, 1984.
———. "Manila's Imperial Makeover: Security, Health, and Symbolism." In *Colonial Crucible: Empire in the Making of the Modern American State*, ed. Alfred W. McCoy and Francisco A. Scarano, 489–98. Quezon City: Ateneo de Manila University Press, 2010.
———. "Migrants in Urban Labor Markets: The Social Stratification of Tondo and Sampaloc in the 1890's." In *Population and History: The Demographic Origins of the Modern Philippines*, ed. Daniel F. Doeppers and Peter Xenos, 253–63. Quezon City: Ateneo de Manila University Press, 1998.
———. "Migration to Manila: Changing Gender Representation, Migration Field, and Urban Structure." In *Population and History: The Demographic Origins of the Modern Philippines*, ed. Daniel F. Doeppers and Peter Xenos, 139–79. Quezon City: Ateneo de Manila University Press, 1998.
Doherty, John F. *The Philippine Urban Poor*, ed. Belinda A. Aquino, Philippine Studies Occasional Paper No. 8. Honolulu: Philippine Studies Program, Center for Asian and Pacific Studies, University of Hawai'i, 1985.
Douglass, Mike. "The Globalization of Capital Cities: Civil Society, the Neoliberal State and the Reconstruction of Urban Space in Asia-Pacific." In *Capital Cities in Asia-Pacific: Primacy and Diversity*, ed. K. C. Ho and Hsin-Huang Michael Hsiao, 27–46. Taipei: Center for Asia-Pacific Area Studies, Research Center for Humanities and Social Sciences, Academia Sinica, 2006.

Dowling, Robyn. "Suburban Stories, Gendered Lives: Thinking through Difference." In *Cities of Difference*, ed. Ruth Fincher and Jane M. Jacobs, 69–88. New York and London: Guilford, 1998.

Doyo, Ma. Ceres P. *Macli-ing Dulag: Kalinga Chief, Defender of the Cordillera*. Quezon City: University of the Philippines Press, 2015.

Duldulao, Manuel. *Quezon City*. Makati: Japuzinni, 1995.

Dwyer, D. J. "The Problem of In-migration and Squatter Settlement in Asian Cities: Two Case Studies, Manila and Victoria-Kowloon." In *Changing South-East Asian Cities*, ed. Y. M. Yeung and C. P. Lo, 131–41. Singapore: Oxford University Press, 1976.

Edwards, Norman. "The Colonial Suburb: Public Space as Private Space." In *Public Space: Design, Use and Management*, ed. Chua Beng Huat and Norman Edwards, 24–39. Singapore: Centre for Advanced Studies, National University of Singapore; Singapore University Press, 1992.

Ejercito, Antonio and Cornelio M. Urbino. "A Malaria Survey and Control in Quezon City." *Philippine Journal of Science* 79 (3), 1950: 249–64.

Endriga, Jose N. "Corpuz and Soriano's Bifocal Administrations (1975–1981)." In *University of the Philippines: The First 75 Years*, ed. Oscar M. Alfonso, 499–540. Quezon City: University of the Philippines Press, 1985.

Enosawa, G. H. *Manuel L. Quezon: From Nipa House to Malacañan*. Tokyo: Japan Publicity Agency, 1940.

Enrile, Juan Ponce. *Juan Ponce Enrile: A Memoir*, ed. Nelson A. Navarro. Quezon City: ABS-CBN Publishing, 2012.

Ephraim, Frank. *Escape to Manila: From Nazi Tyranny to Japanese Terror*. Champaign: University of Illinois Press, 2003.

Escalante, Rene R. *The American Friar Lands Policy: Its Framers, Context, and Beneficiaries, 1898–1916*. Manila: De La Salle University Press, 2002.

Escalante, Roland S. B. "Symbol of Our Nuclear Era." *PFP*, 28 Sept. 1963: 10–11.

Escalante, Salvador and J. Augustus Y. De La Paz. *The EDSA Uprising? The Five-Percent Revolution, EDSA in Retrospect*. Quezon City: Truth and Justice Foundation, 2000.

Escobar y Lozano, Jaime. *El Indicador del Viajero en las Islas Filipinas* [Guide for Travelers in the Philippine Islands]. Manila: Tipo-Litografía de Chofre y Cia, 1885.

Escoda, Jose Ma. Bonifacio M. *Warsaw of Asia: The Rape of Manila*. Quezon City: Giraffe, 2000.

Evangelista, Oscar L. *Icons and Institutions: Essays on the History of the University of the Philippines, 1952–2000*. Quezon City: University of the Philippines Press, 2008.

———. "Lopez's Beleaguered Tenure (1969–1975): Barricades on Campus at the Peak of Student Discontent." In *University of the Philippines: The First 75 Years (1908–1983)*, ed. Oscar M. Alfonso, 443–98. Quezon City: University of the Philippines Press, 1985.

Evangelista, Susan. "The Faculty, Administration, and Social Development Professionals during Martial Law." In *Down from the Hill: Ateneo de Manila in the First Ten Years under Martial Law, 1972–1982*, ed. Cristina Jayme Montiel and Susan Evangelista, 145–204. Quezon City: Ateneo de Manila University Press, 2005.

Evers, Hans-Dieter and Rüdiger Korff. *Southeast Asian Urbanism: The Meaning and Power of Social Space*. Singapore: Institute of Southeast Asian Studies, 2000.

Ewen, Shane. *What is Urban History?* Cambridge: Polity, 2016.

Fakih, Farabi. "Kotabaru and the Housing Estate as Bulwark against the Indigenization of Colonial Java." In *Cars, Conduits, and Kampongs: The Modernization of the Indonesian City, 1920–1960*, ed. Freek Colombijn and Joost Coté, 152–71. Leiden: Brill, 2015.

Fegan, Brian. "Entrepreneurs in Votes and Violence: Three Generations of a Peasant Political Family." In *An Anarchy of Families: State and Family in the Philippines*, ed. Alfred W. McCoy, 33–107. Quezon City: Ateneo de Manila University Press, 1994.

Fermin, Jose D. *1904 World's Fair: The Filipino Experience*. Quezon City: University of the Philippines Press, 2004.

REFERENCES   333

Fernandez, Pablo. *History of the Church in the Philippines (1521–1898)*. Metro Manila: National Book Store, 1979.

Finin, Gerard A. *The Making of the Igorot: Contours of Cordillera Consciousness*. Quezon City: Ateneo de Manila University Press, 2005.

Fishman, Robert. *Urban Utopias in the Twentieth Century: Ebenezer Howard, Frank Lloyd Wright, and Le Corbusier*. Cambridge: MIT Press, 1977.

Fitch, George Hamlin. *The Critic in the Orient*. San Francisco: Paul Elder and Company, 1913.

Flora, Joey. "Close(t) Encounters inside the CPP." In *Tibak Rising: Activism in the Days of Martial Law*, ed. Ferdinand C. Llanes, 91–97. Mandaluyong City: Anvil, 2012.

Flores, A. Oliver. "A Political Revolution." *Sunday Times Magazine*, 29 Sept. 1963: 48–53.

Forbes, W. Cameron, Dean C. Worcester, and Frank W. Carpenter. *The Friar-Land Inquiry*. Manila: Bureau of Printing, 1910.

Foreman, John. *The Philippine Islands*. Mandaluyong: Cacho Hermanos, 1985.

Fortich, Chic. *Escape! Charito Planas: Her Story*. Quezon City: New Day, 1991.

Francisco, D. L. "Law Enforcement in Quezon City." *PFP*, 17 Feb. 1940: 20–22.

Franco-Calairo, Rosalina M. and Emmanuel Franco Calairo. *Ang Kasaysayan ng Novaliches* [The History of Novaliches]. Quezon City: Rosalina M. Franco-Calairo and Emmanuel Franco Calairo, 1997.

Friend, Theodore. *Between Two Empires: Philippines' Ordeal and Development from the Great Depression through the Pacific War, 1929–1946*. Manila: Solidaridad, [1964?].

Frost, Harry T. "Quezon City: Functional Planning Gets Its Chance." *Philippines* 1 (4), 1940: 16–17.

Fung, Cornelia Lichauco. *Beneath the Banyan Tree: My Family Chronicles*. Hong Kong: CBL Fung, 2009.

Furnivall, J. S. *Experiment in Independence: The Philippines*. Manila: Solidaridad, 1974.

Gaerlan, Martin R. *Sampaloc's Sacred Ground: The Franciscan Backstory (1613–1918), Most Holy Trinity Parish, Balic-Balic, Sampaloc, Manila*. [Quezon City]: Martin R. Gaerlan and Gaerlan Management Consulting, 2014.

Garcia, J. Neil C. "The City in Philippine Literature." *Likhaan: The Journal of Philippine Contemporary Literature* 8, 2014: 161–84.

———. *Philippine Gay Culture: Binabae to Bakla, Silahis to MSM*, 2d ed. Quezon City: University of the Philippines Press, 2008.

Gatbonton, Esperanza Bunag. *Intramuros: A Historical Guide*. Manila: Intramuros Administration, 1980.

Gealogo, Francis A. "Ang Hermeneutika ng Pakikipagtunggali: Ang Pagpapakahulugan sa Diskurso ng Pakikibakang Panlipunan" [The Hermeneutics of Opposition: Defining the Discourse of Social Struggle]. *Philippine Social Sciences Review*, Special Issue: *Ang Kilusang Masa sa Kasaysayang Pilipino, 1900–1992* [Mass Movements in Philippine History, 1900–1992] Jan.–Dec. 1994: 1–37.

Gerona, Danilo Madrid. *La Ciudad de Nueva Caceres: The Rise of a Sixteenth Century Spanish City*. n.p.: Galleon Publisher, 2014.

Gilmore, Eugene A. *Mensaje del Gobernador General Interino Eugene A. Gilmore a la Séptima Legislatura Filipina Leído el 16 de Julio de 1927 en la Apertura del Tercer Periodo de Sesiones* [Message of Acting Governor-General Eugene A. Gilmore to the Seventh Philippine Legislature Read on 16 July 1927 at the Opening of the Third Session]. Manila: Bureau of Printing, 1927.

Ginsburg, Norton S. "The Great City in Southeast Asia." *American Journal of Sociology* 60 (5), 1955: 455–62.

Giron, Eric. "Urbanization of Suburbia." *Philippine Panorama*, 15 Aug. 1976: 26.

Gleeck, Lewis E. Jr. "Achievement and Tragedy: The Life of Frank W. Carpenter." *Bulletin of the American Historical Collection* 19 (1), 1991: 70–78.

———. *The American Half-century (1898–1946)*, rev ed. Quezon City: New Day, 1998.

——. *Bill Shaw, the Man and the Legend: A Life with A.G.&P. and Wack-Wack*. n.p.: William J. Shaw Foundation, 1998.

——. *The Manila Americans (1901–1964)*. Manila: Carmelo & Bauermann, 1977.

Golay, Frank Hindman. *Face of Empire: United States–Philippine Relations, 1898–1946*. Quezon City: Ateneo de Manila University Press, 1997.

Goldsborough, W. L. "Francisco Ortigas: President of the Code Committee." *Philippine Law Journal* 1 (7), 1915: 327–29.

Gonzalez, B. M. *Thirty-sixth Annual Report of the President of the University of the Philippines to the Board of Regents for the Academic Year June 1, 1948 – May 31, 1949*. Quezon City: University of the Philippines, 1950.

Gonzalez, Narita Manuel and Gerardo T. Los Baños, eds. *U.P. Diliman: Home and Campus*. Quezon City: University of the Philippines Press, 2010.

Gopinath, Aruna. *Manuel L. Quezon: The Tutelary Democrat*. Quezon City: New Day, 1987.

Guéguen, Catherine. "Moving from Binondo to the "Chinese Villages" of the Suburbs: A Geographical Study of the Chinese in Metro-Manila." *Journal of Chinese Overseas* 6, 2010: 119–37.

Guerrero, Milagros C. "Sinco's Clash with Conservatism (1958–1962)." In *University of the Philippines: The First 75 Years (1908–1983)*, ed. Oscar M. Alfonso, 339–87. Quezon City: University of the Philippines Press, 1985.

——, ed. *Under Stars and Stripes. Kasaysayan: The Story of the Filipino People*, vol. 6. n.p.: Asia Publishing, 1998.

Guinto, Leon. "Regarding the New Filipino." *City Gazette* 1 (4): 17–22.

Gunn, Simon. "The Spatial Turn: Changing Histories of Space and Time." In *Identities in Space: Contested Terrains in the Western City since 1850*, ed. Simon Gunn and Robert J. Morris, 1–18. Hants, England: Ashgate, 2001.

Gwekoh, S. H. *Manuel L. Quezon: His Life and Career*. Manila: University Publishing Company, 1948.

Hall, Peter. *Cities of Tomorrow: An Intellectual History of Urban Planning and Design in the Twentieth Century*, 3d ed. Malden, MA: Blackwell, 2002.

Hamdan, G. "Capitals of the New Africa." In *The City in Newly Developing Countries: Readings on Urbanism and Urbanization*, ed. Gerald Breese, 146–61. Englewood, NJ: Prentice-Hall, 1969.

Harding, Alan and Talja Blokland. *Urban Theory: A Critical Introduction to Power, Cities and Urbanism in the 21st Century*. Los Angeles: Sage, 2014.

Harms, Erik. *Saigon's Edge: On the Margins of Ho Chi Minh City*. Minneapolis: University of Minnesota Press, 2011.

Harris, C. M. "Washington's Gamble, L'Enfant's Dream: Politics, Design, and the Founding of the National Capital." *The William and Mary Quarterly* 56 (3), 1999: 527–64.

Harrison, Francis Burton. *Eighth Annual Message of Governor-General Francis Burton Harrison to the Fifth Philippine Legislature, Delivered October 16, 1920 at the Opening of the Second Session*. Manila: Bureau of Printing, 1920.

——. *Origins of the Philippine Republic: Extracts from the Diaries and Records of Francis Burton Harrison*, ed. Michael P. Onorato. Ithaca, NY: Cornell University, Southeast Asia Program, 1974.

Harsant, Lewys. "Medieval and Modern Manila." *Manila Times Anniversary Issue*, 1911: 37–40.

Hart, Donn Vordis. *The Philippine Plaza Complex: A Focal Point in Cultural Change*. New Haven: Southeast Asia Studies, Yale University, 1955.

Hartendorp, A. V. H. *History of Industry and Trade of the Philippines*. Manila: American Chamber of Commerce, 1958.

——. *History of Industry and Trade of the Philippines: The Magsaysay Administration*. Manila: Philippine Education Company, 1961.

REFERENCES   335

Harvey, David. "The 'New' Imperialism: Accumulation by Dispossession." *Socialist Register* 40, 2004: 63–87.
———. *Paris, Capital of Modernity.* New York and London: Routledge, 2006.
———. *Social Justice and the City.* Oxford: Basil Blackwell, 1988.
Hau, Caroline S. *The Chinese Question: Ethnicity, Nation, and Region in and beyond the Philippines.* Quezon City: Ateneo de Manila University Press, 2014.
———. *Elites and Ilustrados in Philippine Culture.* Quezon City: Ateneo de Manila University Press, 2017.
———, Katrina Tuvera, and Isabelita O. Reyes. "Introduction," in *Querida: An Anthology*, ed. Caroline S. Hau, Katrina Tuvera, and Isabelita O. Reyes, 1–14. Mandaluyong City: Anvil, 2013.
Hayden, Joseph Ralston. *The Philippines: A Study in National Development.* New York: Macmillan, 1947.
Hedman, Eva-Lotta E. and John T. Sidel. *Philippine Politics and Society in the Twentieth Century: Colonial Legacies, Post-colonial Trajectories.* London: Routledge, 2000.
Hidalgo, Antonio A. *The Life, Times and Thoughts of Don Pio Pedrosa.* Quezon City: Milflores, 2000.
Hidalgo, Cristina Pantoja. "Elegy to My Lost Home." In *The Manila We Know*, ed. Erlinda Enriquez Panlilio, 110–15. Mandaluyong City: Anvil, 2017.
Ho, K. C. and Hsin-Huang Michael Hsiao. "Globalization and Asia-Pacific Capital Cities: Primacy and Diversity." In *Capital Cities in Asia-Pacific: Primacy and Diversity*, ed. K. C. Ho and Hsin-Huang Michael Hsiao, 3–26. Taipei: Center for Asia-Pacific Area Studies, Research Center for Humanities and Social Sciences, Academia Sinica, 2006.
Hollnsteiner, Mary R. "The Urbanization of Metropolitan Manila." In *Changing South-East Asian Cities*, ed. Y. M. Yeung and C. P. Lo, 174–84. Singapore: Oxford University Press, 1976.
Horn, Florence. *Orphans of the Pacific: The Philippines.* New York: Reynal and Hitchcock, 1941.
Hornedo, Florentino H. "'People Power' as the Traditional Go-Between." In *Pagmamahal and Pagmumura* [Loving and Cursing]: *Essays*, 129–39. Quezon City: Office of Research and Publications, Ateneo de Manila University, 1997.
Hoskins, C. M. "Real Estate." *ACCJ* 24 (8), 1948: 289–90.
Huetz de Lemps, Xavier. "Materiales Ligeros vs. Materiales Fuertes [Light Materials vs Strong Materials]: The Conflict between Nipa Huts and Stone Buildings in 19th-Century Manila." In *The Philippine Revolution and Beyond*, vol. 1, ed. Elmer Ordoñez, 160–72. Manila: Philippine Centennial Commission, 1998.
———. "Shifts in Meaning of 'Manila' in the Nineteenth Century." In *Old Ties and New Solidarities: Studies on Philippine Communities*, ed. Charles Macdonald and Guillermo Pesigan, 219–33. Quezon City: Ateneo de Manila University Press, 2000.
Hunt, Chester L. "The Moth and the Flame: A Look at Manila's Housing Problems." *Philippine Quarterly of Culture and Society* 8 (2–3), 1980: 99–107.
Hurley, Vic. *Jungle Patrol: The Story of the Philippine Constabulary.* Mandaluyong City: Cacho Hermanos, 1985.
Ileto, Reynaldo Clemeña. *Pasyon and Revolution: Popular Movements in the Philippines, 1840–1910.* Quezon City: Ateneo de Manila University Press, 1979.
———. "The 'Unfinished Revolution' in Philippine Political Discourse." *Southeast Asian Studies* 31 (1), 1993: 62–82.
Ingersoll, Joshena. *Golden Years in the Philippines.* Palo Alto, California: Pacific Books, 1971.
Institute of Planning, University of the Philippines. *A Planning Strategy for Metropolitan Manila, A.D. 2000: A Policy Study in Environmental Planning.* Quezon City: Institute of Planning, UP, 1968.
Inter-Agency Committee on Metropolitan Manila (IACMM). *Metropolitan Manila Authority: A Development and Reform Strategy Proposal.* Manila: Government Printing Office, 1973.

Jackson, Kenneth T. *Crabgrass Frontier: The Suburbanization of the United States*. Oxford: Oxford University Press, 1985.

Jamias, Cristino. *The University of the Philippines: The First Half Century*. Quezon City: UP, 1962.

Jazmines, Tessa M. "The Lighter Side of the Polls." *Sunday Times Magazine*, 16 Feb. 1986: 13.

Jenkins, Shirley. *American Economic Policy toward the Philippines*. Stanford: Stanford University Press, 1954.

Joaquin, Nick. *Manila, My Manila: A History for the Young*. Manila: The City of Manila, 1990.

———. *The Aquinos of Tarlac: An Essay on History as Three Generations*. Metro Manila: Solar, 1986.

———. "Ninoy's Early Years." In *Ninoy Aquino: The Man, the Legend*, ed. Asuncion David Maramba, 29–41. Mandaluyong: Cacho Hermanos, 1984.

Jocano, F. Landa. *Social Work in the Philippines: A Historical Overview*. Quezon City: New Day, 1980.

Jones, Gregg R. *Red Revolution: Inside the Philippine Guerrilla Movement*. Boulder, CO: Westview, 1989.

Jose, F. Sionil. *Ermita: A Filipino Novel*. Manila: Solidaridad, 1988.

———. *The Feet of Juan Bacnang*. Manila: Solidaridad, 2011.

———. *Sin: A Novel*. Manila: Solidaridad, 1994.

Jose, Ricardo. "Advocate of Independence: Manuel L. Quezon and the Commonwealth, 1935–1944." In *Philippine Presidents: 100 Years*, ed. Rosario Mendoza Cortes, 106–29. Quezon City: Philippine Historical Association, New Day, 1999.

Juan Ysmael & Co. Inc. "Quezon City." *Khaki and Red*, Oct. 1939: 12.

Juanico, Meliton B. *Metro Manila: A Travel and Historical Guide*. Quezon City: M. J. Editorial Consultants, 1983.

Julian, Severo. "'Facts and Figures': Support Rogers Exposé of PHHC." *PFP*, 9 Aug. 1952: 40–41.

Juppenlatz, Morris. *Cities in Transformation: The Urban Squatter Problem of the Developing World*. St. Lucia: University of Queensland Press, 1970.

Jurado, Cicero D., Jr., "Estero Dredging for Flood Control." *FOCUS Philippines*, 10 Apr. 1976: 20–21, 24–25.

———. "Relocating the Squatters." *FOCUS Philippines*, 14 Aug. 1976: 10–11, 35.

Keppy, Peter. "Southeast Asia in the Age of Jazz: Locating Popular Culture in the Colonial Philippines and Indonesia." *Journal of Southeast Asian Studies* 44 (3), 2013: 444–64.

Kerkvliet, Benedict J. *The Huk Rebellion: A Study of Peasant Revolt in the Philippines*. Quezon City: New Day, 1979.

———. "Withdrawal and Resistance: The Political Significance of Food, Agriculture, and How People Lived during the Japanese Occupation in the Philippines." In *Autonomous Histories, Particular Truths: Essays in Honor of John R. W. Smail*, ed. Laurie Sears, 175–93. Madison, WI: Center for Southeast Asian Studies, University of Wisconsin, 1993.

Keyes, William J. and Maria C. Roldan Burcroff. *Housing the Urban Poor: Nonconventional Approaches to a National Problem*. Quezon City: Ateneo de Manila University Press, 1976.

King, Ross. *Kuala Lumpur and Putrajaya: Negotiating Urban Space in Malaysia*. Singapore: NUS Press, 2008.

———. *Reading Bangkok*. Singapore: NUS Press, 2011.

Kintanar, Thelma B. and Carina C. David. "Salud Algabre, Revolutionary." *Review of Women's Studies* 6 (1), 1996: 75–84.

Kintanar, Thelma B., Clemen C. Aquino, Patricia B. Arinto, and Ma. Luisa T. Camagay. *Kuwentong Bayan: Noong Panahon ng Hapon [Everyday Life in a Time of War]*. Quezon City: University of the Philippines Press, 2006.

Kiunisala, Edward R. "Black Wednesday on Plaza Miranda." *PFP*, 23 Jan. 1971: 4, 45.

———. "City of Tomorrow." *PFP*, 26 Oct. 1963: 14–15, 103, 106.

———. "The Fight for the Cities." *PFP*, 23 Nov. 1963: 6, 75.

———. "Politics around Manila." *PFP*, 2 Nov. 1963: 4–5, 62–63, 68.

REFERENCES   337

Kookooritchkin, Ronald (Remy). "Quezon City May Yet Be the Show Place of the Nation." *Examiner,* 12 Oct. 1975: 12–13.
Kusaka, Wataru. *Moral Politics in the Philippines: Inequality, Democracy, and the Urban Poor.* Singapore: NUS Press, 2017.
Kusno, Abidin. *Behind the Postcolonial: Architecture, Urban Space and Political Cultures in Indonesia.* London and New York: Routledge, 2000.
———. "Housing the Margin: Perumahan Rakyat and the Future Urban Form of Indonesia." *Indonesia* 94, 2012: 23–56.
Kwak, Nancy H. *A World of Homeowners: American Power and the Politics of Housing Aid.* Chicago: University of Chicago Press, 2015.
———. "Slum Clearance as a Transnational Process in Globalizing Manila." In *Making Cities Global: The Transnational Turn in Urban History,* ed. A. K. Sandoval-Strausz and Nancy H. Kwak, 98–113. Philadelphia: University of Pennsylvania Press, 2018.
Labrador, Juan. *A Diary of the Japanese Occupation: December 7, 1941 – May 7, 1945.* Manila: Santo Tomas University Press, 1989.
Lacaba, Jose F. *Days of Disquiet, Nights of Rage: The First Quarter Storm & Related Events.* Manila: Salinlahi, 1982.
———. "Kasangga o Kabangga?" [Friend or Foe?] *Mr. & Ms.,* 19 Mar. 1985: 14–15.
Lahoz, Manuel C. *Of Tyrants and Martyrs: A Political Memoir.* Quezon City: University of the Philippines Press, 2017.
Lansdale, Edward Geary. *In the Midst of Wars: An American's Mission to Southeast Asia.* New York: Harper & Row, 1972.
Lanzona, Vina. *Amazons of the Huk Rebellion: Gender, Sex, and Revolution in the Philippines.* Quezon City: Ateneo de Manila University Press, 2009.
Laquian, Aprodicio A. "The Asian City and the Political Process." In *The City as a Centre of Change in Asia,* ed. D. J. Dwyer, 41–55. Hong Kong: Hong Kong University Press, 1972.
———. *The City in Nation-building: Politics and Administration in Metropolitan Manila.* Manila: School of Public Administration, University of the Philippines, 1966.
———. *Slums Are for People: The Barrio Magsaysay Pilot Project in Urban Community Development.* Honolulu: East–West Center Press, 1969.
Laubach, Frank Charles. *The People of the Philippines: Their Religious Progress and Preparation for Spiritual Leadership in the Far East.* New York: G. H. Doran, 1925.
Lazaro, Guillermo R. "Gonzalez as an Adamant Visionary (1939–43, 1945–51)." In *University of the Philippines: The First 75 Years (1908–1983),* ed. Oscar M. Alfonso, 259–93. Quezon City: University of the Philippines Press, 1985.
Lefebvre, Henri. *The Production of Space.* Oxford: Blackwell, 1991.
Legarda, Benito, Jr. *After the Galleons: Foreign Trade, Economic Change and Entrepreneurship in the Nineteenth-century Philippines.* Quezon City: Ateneo de Manila University Press, 1999.
———. *The Hills of Sampaloc: The Opening Actions of the Philippine–American War, February 4–5, 1899.* Makati City: Bookmark, 2001.
Legarda, Trinidad Fernandez. "The Ladies of Malacañang." *Philippine Magazine* 26 (1), 1929: 138–40, 162–72.
Leones, CL. "The Durable Amoranto." *Philippine Panorama,* 14 Sept. 1975: 6–8.
Lichauco, Alejandro. *Nationalist Economics: History Theory and Practice.* Quezon City: Institute for Rural Industrialization, 1988.
Lico, Gerard. *Arkitekturang Filipino: A History of Architecture and Urbanism in the Philippines.* Quezon City: University of the Philippines Press, 2008.
———. *Edifice Complex: Power, Myth, and Marcos State Architecture.* Quezon City: Ateneo de Manila University Press, 2003.
——— and Lorelei D. C. de Viana. *Regulating Colonial Spaces (1565–1944): A Collection of Laws, Decrees, Proclamations, Ordinances, Orders and Directives on Architecture and the Built*

Environment during the Colonial Eras in the Philippines. Manila: National Commission for Culture and the Arts, 2017.

Licuanan, Virginia Benitez. *Paz Marquez Benitez: One Woman's Life, Letters, and Writings.* Quezon City: Ateneo de Manila University Press, 1995.

Lim Heng Kow. *The Evolution of the Urban System in Malaya.* Kuala Lumpur: Penerbit Universiti Malaya, 1978.

Lim, Rodrigo C. *Who's Who in the Philippines.* Manila: Claudio Nera, 1929.

Lindeman, John. *The Philippine American Life Insurance Company.* Manila: Carmelo & Bauermann, n.d.

Llanes, Ferdinand C. "Mga Huling Mayo Uno ni Ka Bert Olalia" [Comrade Bert Olalia's Final May Firsts] in *Tibak Rising: Activism in the Days of Martial Law,* ed. Ferdinand C. Llanes, 220–23. Mandaluyong City: Anvil, 2012.

Locsin, Teodoro M. "One More Racket? The Case of the Capital City Site." *PFP,* 22 May 1948: 2–3, 59.

———. "One More Racket? (continuation)." *PFP,* 19 June 1948: 4–5.

Loh Kah Seng. *Squatters into Citizens: The 1961 Bukit Ho Swee Fire.* Singapore: NUS Press, 2013.

Lopez, Salvador P. *Elpidio Quirino: The Judgment of History.* n.p.: Elpidio Quirino Foundation, 1990.

———. "Quezon City: Cinderella Capital of the Philippines." *Philippine Planning Journal* 4 (2) / 5 (1–2), 1973 / 1974: 9–13.

Lowe, Mason. "Joe Goes Ashore." *Philippine Magazine* 35 (3), 1938: 136, 150–51.

Lumba, Sarah F. "My Marikina." In *The Manila We Know,* ed. Erlinda Enriquez Panlilio, 169–81. Mandaluyong City: Anvil, 2017.

Luna, Alexander A., ed. *Quezon City Directory, 1956–57.* Manila: Metro Publishing, 1956.

Luna, Telesforo Jr. "Manufacturing in the Philippines." In Robert E. Huke, *Shadows on the Land: An Economic Geography of the Philippines,* 395–421. Manila: Bookmark, 1963.

Lyons, Norbert. "The Scenic Route to Montalban." *ACCJ* 2 (6), 1921: 9–12.

Macapagal, Diosdado. *A Stone for the Edifice: Memoirs of a President.* Quezon City: Mac Publishing, 1968.

Macaraig, Serafin E. *Social Problems.* Manila: Educational Supply Co., 1929.

Macatuno, Ernesto M. "The Big City." *Sunday Times Magazine,* 15 Aug. 1971: 26–27.

———. "A Citizens' Movement Tackles the Political Pros." *Sunday Times Magazine,* 26 Sept. 1971: 20–21.

Maceda, Genoroso S. "The Remontados of Rizal Province." *Philippine Journal of Science* 64 (1), 1937: 313–21.

Mactal, Ronaldo B. *Kalusugang Pampubliko sa Kolonyal na Maynila (1898–1918): Heograpiya, Medisina, Kasaysayan* [Public Health in Colonial Manila (1898–1918): Geography, Medicine, History]. Quezon City: University of the Philippines Press, 2009.

Madrid, Carlos. *Flames over Baler: The Story of the Siege of Baler, Reconstructed from Original Documentary Sources.* Quezon City: University of the Philippines Press, 2012.

Malacañang Press Office. *The New Era Starts: The First Year of the Macapagal Administration.* Manila: n.p., [1963?].

Malcolm, George A. *American Colonial Careerist: Half a Century of Official Life and Personal Experience in the Philippines and Puerto Rico.* Boston: The Christopher Publishing House, 1957.

———, ed. *The Charter of the City of Manila and the Revised Ordinances of the City of Manila.* Manila: Bureau of Printing, 1917.

———, ed. *The Charter of the City of Manila and the Revised Ordinances of the City of Manila.* Manila: Bureau of Printing, 1927.

———. *The Commonwealth of the Philippines.* New York: Appleton-Century, 1936.

Mallat, Jean. *The Philippines: History, Geography, Customs, Agriculture, Industry and Commerce,* trans. Pura Santillan-Castrence. Manila: National Historical Institute, 1983.

Manalang, Priscila S. "Remembering UP in the Thirties." In *The University Experience: Essays on the 82nd Anniversary of the University of the Philippines*, ed. Belinda A. Aquino, 30–37. Quezon City: University of the Philippines Press, 1991.

Manapat, Ricardo. *Some Are Smarter than Others: The History of Marcos Crony Capitalism.* New York: Aletheia, 1991.

Manila Merchants Association. *Manila: The Pearl of the Orient: Guide Book to the Intending Visitor.* Manila: Manila Merchants Association, 1908.

Manila Railroad Company. "Don't Waste Money: Use Our Free Service." *ACCJ* 7 (7), 1927: 12.

Mañalac, Fernando J. *Manila: Memories of World War II.* Quezon City: Giraffe, 1995.

Maramag, Ileana. "The City Can Use Its Squatter Areas." *Sunday Times Magazine*, 8 Jan. 1956: 9–11.

Marcos, Ferdinand E. *New Filipinism: The Turning Point* (State of the nation message to the Congress of the Philippines, 27 January 1969. n.p.: Manila, [1969?].

———. *Presidential Speeches*, vol. 1. [Manila]: Ferdinand E. Marcos, 1978.

Marcos, Imelda Romualdez. *The Ideas of Imelda Romualdez Marcos*, vol. 1. Metro Manila: National Media Production Center (NMPC), 1978.

———. *The Ideas of Imelda Romualdez Marcos*, vol. 2, ed. Ileana Maramag. Metro Manila: NMPC, 1978.

———. *Metropolitan Manila and the Magnitude of Its Problems*, ed. Ileana Maramag. Metro Manila: NMPC, 1976.

Marquez, Adalia. *Blood on the Rising Sun: A Factual Story of the Japanese Invasion of the Philippines.* New York: DeTanko, 1957.

Massey, Doreen. *For Space.* London: Sage, 2005.

———. "On Space and the City." In *City Worlds*, ed. Doreen Massey, John Allen, and Steve Pile, 157–71. London and New York: Routledge, 1999.

———. *Space, Place, and Gender.* Minneapolis: University of Minnesota Press, 1994.

McCoy, Alfred W., ed. *An Anarchy of Families: State and Family in the Philippines.* Quezon City: Ateneo de Manila University Press, 1994.

———. *Policing America's Empire: The United States, the Philippines, and the Rise of the Surveillance State.* Quezon City: Ateneo de Manila University Press, 2011.

———. "Quezon's Commonwealth: The Emergence of Philippine Authoritarianism." In *Philippine Colonial Democracy*, ed. Ruby Paredes, 114–60. Quezon City: Ateneo de Manila University Press, 1989.

———. "Rent-Seeking Families and the Philippine State: A History of the Lopez Family." In *An Anarchy of Families: State and Family in the Philippines*, ed. Alfred W. McCoy, 429–536. Quezon City: Ateneo de Manila University Press, 1994.

——— and Alfredo Roces. *Philippine Cartoons: Political Caricature of the American Era, 1900–1941.* Quezon City: Vera Reyes, 1985.

McGee, T. G. "The Emergence of Desakota Regions in Asia: Expanding a Hypothesis." In *The Extended Metropolis: Settlement Transition in Asia*, ed. Norton Ginsburg, Bruce Koppel, and T. G. McGee, 3–25. Honolulu: University of Hawai'i Press, 1991.

———. *The Southeast Asian City: A Social Geography of the Primate Cities of Southeast Asia.* London: Bell, 1967.

———. *The Urbanization Process in the Third World: Explorations in Search of a Theory.* London: G. Bell and Sons, 1971.

McLennan, Marshall S. *The Central Luzon Plain: Land and Society on the Inland Frontier.* Quezon City: Alemar-Phoenix, 1980.

McNutt, Paul V. *Third Annual Report of the United States High Commissioner to the Philippine Islands to the President and Congress of the United States Covering the Calendar Year 1938 and the First Six Months of 1939.* Washington, DC: Government Printing Office, 1943.

McPhelin, Michael. "Manila: The Primate City." *Philippine Studies* 17 (4), 1969: 781–89.

Medina, Isagani. "Beyond Intramuros: The Beginnings of Extramuros de Manila up to the 19th Century—A Historical Overview." In *Manila: Selected Papers of the Annual Conferences of the Manila Studies Association, 1989–1993*, ed. Bernardita Churchill, 50–67. Quezon City: Manila Studies Association, 1994.

Melencio, Cesar "Sonny." *Full Quarter Storms: Memoirs and Writings on the Philippine Left (1970–2010)*. Quezon City: Transform Asia, 2010.

Mendoza, Meynardo P. "Natdems, Socdems, and the Ateneo." In *Down from the Hill: Ateneo de Manila in the First Ten Years under Martial Law, 1972–1982*, ed. Cristina Jayme Montiel and Susan Evangelista, 121–44. Quezon City: Ateneo de Manila University Press, 2005.

Mercado, Anselmo B. "Father Masterson's 'I'mpossible Dream." *Kinaadman* 32 (2010): 1–21.

Mercado, Irineo A. and Jose Sebastian. "It's Not Fair, Say Bus Riders." *PFP,* 11 June 1966: 60–61.

Merin, Jose L. "The Political Economy of Housing in the Philippines, 1946–1980." In Ministry of Human Settlements, *Philippine Shelter System and Human Settlements,* 17–26. Metro Manila: Ministry of Human Settlements, 1982.

Merrit, Jesus V. "The Shame of Manila." *PFP,* 16 Mar. 1940: 60–61.

———. "A Tale of Two Cities." *PFP,* 22 Feb. 1941: 6, 8.

Metropolitan Water District (MWD). *Annual Report of the Metropolitan Water District for the Fiscal Year Ending June 30, 1951*. Manila: Bureau of Printing, 1952.

———. *Manila's Water Supply: Inauguration of Balara Filter Plant, October 24, 1935*. Manila: Bureau of Printing, 1935.

Michel, Boris. "Going Global, Veiling the Poor: Global City Imaginaries in Metro Manila." *Philippine Studies* 58 (3), 2010: 383–406.

Mijares, Primitivo. *The Conjugal Dictatorship of Ferdinand and Imelda Marcos*, rev. ed. Quezon City: Bughaw, an imprint of Ateneo de Manila University Press, 2017.

Mistica, Sergio R. *President Manuel Luis Quezon as I Knew Him: A Character Study from Anecdotes and Other Sources*. n.p.: Capt. S. R. Mistica and F. R. Roman, 1947.

Mojares, Resil B. *Brains of the Nation: Pedro Paterno, T. H. Pardo de Tavera, Isabelo de los Reyes and the Production of Modern Knowledge*. Quezon City: Ateneo de Manila University Press, 2006.

———. "'Daybayan': A Cultural History of Space in a Visayan City." *Philippine Quarterly of Culture and Society* 40 (3–4), 2012: 170–86.

———. "The Dream Goes on and on: Three Generations of the Osmeñas, 1906–1990." In *An Anarchy of Families: State and Family in the Philippines*, ed. Alfred W. McCoy, 311–46. Quezon City: Ateneo de Manila University Press, 1994.

Molina, Antonio M. *Dusk and Dawn in the Philippines: Memoirs of a Living Witness of World War II*. Quezon City: New Day, 1996.

Monaghan, Forbes J. *Under the Red Sun: A Letter from Manila*. New York: Declan X. McMullen, 1946.

Montiel, Cristina Jayme and Susan Evangelista, eds. *Down from the Hill: Ateneo de Manila in the First Ten Years under Martial Law, 1972–1982*. Quezon City: Ateneo de Manila University Press, 2005.

Morga, Antonio de. *Sucesos de las Islas Filipinas* [Events in the Philippine Islands], ed. J. S. Cummins. Cambridge: Hakluyt Society, 1971.

Morley, Ian. "Modern Urban Designing in the Philippines, 1898–1916." *Philippine Studies: Historical and Ethnographic Viewpoints* 64 (1), 2016: 3–42.

———. "The Filipinization of the American City Beautiful, 1916–1935." *Journal of Planning History* 20 (10), 2017: 1–30.

Mountz, Alison. "Border." In *Key Concepts in Political Geography*, ed. Carolyn Gallaher, Carl T. Dahlman, Mary Gilmartin, Alison Mountz, with Peter Shirlow, 198–209. Los Angeles: Sage, 2009.

REFERENCES   341

Muijzenberg, Otto van den. *The Philippines through European Lenses: Late 19th Century Photographs from the Meerkamp van Embden Collection*. Quezon City: Ateneo de Manila University Press, 2008.

———, ed., trans. *Colonial Manila, 1909–1912: Three Dutch Travel Accounts*. Quezon City: Ateneo de Manila University Press, 2016.

Mumford, Lewis. *The City in History*. San Diego: Harcourt, 1989.

Municipal Board of Manila. *Annual Report of the Municipal Board of the City of Manila for the Fiscal Year 1908*. Manila: Bureau of Printing, 1909.

———. *Report of the Municipal Board of the City of Manila for the period from August 7, 1901, to June 30, 1902*. Manila: Bureau of Public Printing, 1903.

Murphey, Rhoads. "City and Countryside as Ideological Issues: India and China." *Comparative Studies in Society and History* 14 (3), 1972: 250–67.

Murray, Sabina. "Broken Glass." In *Manila Noir*, ed. Jessica Hagedorn, 56–68. Mandaluyong City: Anvil, 2013.

Mustafa, Muhizam. "Public Art in the Federal Territory of Putrajaya: Questions of Value and Role." *Wacana Seni Journal of Arts Discourse* 8, 2009: 69–96.

Naerssen, Ton van, Michel Ligthart, and Flotilda N. Zapanta. "Managing Metropolitan Manila." In *The Dynamics of Metropolitan Management in Southeast Asia*, ed. Jürgen Rüland, 168–206. Singapore: Institute of Southeast Asian Studies, 1996.

Nagano, Yoshiko. *State and Finance in the Philippines, 1898–1941: The Mismanagement of an American Colony*. Singapore: NUS Press, 2015.

Nakpil, Carmen Guerrero. *A Question of Identity: Selected Essays*. Manila: Vessel, 1973.

National Census and Statistics Office (NCSO). *1970 Census of Population and Housing: Rizal*. Manila: National Census and Statistics Office, [1974?].

Navarro, Carmen A. "A Sophisticated Suburb in Makati." *Chronicle Magazine*, 29 Dec. 1962: 24–27.

Neira, Eladio. *Glimpses into the History of San Juan, MM*. San Juan: Life Today, 1994.

Nellist, George. *Men of the Philippines: A Biographical Record of Men of Substantial Achievement in the Philippine Islands*. Manila: Sugar News Co., 1931.

Nery, John. *Revolutionary Spirit: Jose Rizal in Southeast Asia*. Singapore: Institute of Southeast Asian Studies, 2011.

Netzorg, Morton J. *Jock Netzorg: Manila Memories*, ed. Michael P. Onorato. Laguna Beach, CA: Pacific Rim, 1988.

Neumann, A. Lin. "Tourism Promotion and Prostitution." In *The Philippines Reader: A History of Colonialism, Neocolonialism, Dictatorship, and Resistance*, ed. Daniel B. Schirmer and Stephen Rosskamm Shalom, 182–87. Cambridge, MA: South End, 1987.

Ocampo, Ambeth R. *Bonifacio's Bolo*. Pasig City: Anvil, 1995.

Ocampo, Millette T. "Swan Song for Broadway." In *The Manila We Know*, ed. Erlinda Enriquez Panlilio, 116–28. Mandaluyong City: Anvil, 2017.

Office of Public Information. *Blue Book: First Anniversary of the Republic of the Philippines*. Manila: Bureau of Printing, 1947.

Office of the First Lady. *Compassion and Commitment*, ed. Ileana Maramag. Manila: NMPC, 1975.

Office of the Mayor [City of Manila]. *City Gazette: Published Fortnightly by the Office of the Mayor of the City of Manila*, vol. 1, no. 1, October 1, 1942. Manila: Office of the Mayor, 1942.

———. *City Gazette: Published Fortnightly by the Office of the Mayor of the City of Manila*, vol. 1, no. 2, October 16, 1942. Manila: Office of the Mayor, 1942.

———. *City Gazette: Published Fortnightly by the Office of the Mayor of the City of Manila*, vol. 1, no. 3, November 6, 1942. Manila: Office of the Mayor, 1942.

———. *City Gazette: Published Fortnightly by the Office of the Mayor of the City of Manila*, vol. 1, no. 4, November 16, 1942. Manila: Office of the Mayor, 1942.

——. *City Gazette: Published Fortnightly by the Office of the Mayor of the City of Manila*, vol. 1, no. 5, *December 1, 1942*. Manila: Office of the Mayor, 1942.

——. *City Gazette: Published Fortnightly by the Office of the Mayor of the City of Manila*, vol. 1, no. 6, *December 16, 1942*. Manila: Office of the Mayor, 1942.

Office of the President. "Squatting and Slum Dwelling in Metropolitan Manila (Special Committee Report)." *Philippine Sociological Review* 16 (1–2), 1968: 92–105.

Olaguer, Eduardo B. *Light a Fire II: Confessions of a Jesuit Terrorist-Son*. Quezon City: Edolaguer Family Publishing, 2005.

Olmsted, Marlin E. *Administration of Philippine Lands*, vol. 1. Washington, DC: Government Printing Office, 1911.

Ongpauco, Fidel L. "Quezon City: From Cogonland to Metropolis." *Philippine Panorama*, 24 Nov. 1974: 7, 20.

Ordoñez, Elmer A. *Diliman: Homage to the Fifties*. Quezon City: University of the Philippines Press, 2003.

——. *The Other View*, vol. 3. *The Last Posts: The Manila Times (2010–2012)*. Quezon City: University of the Philippines Press, 2013.

Ortega, Arnisson Andre C. *Neoliberalizing Spaces in the Philippines: Suburbanization, Transnational Migration, and Dispossession*. Quezon City: Ateneo de Manila University Press, 2018.

Osmeña, Sergio. *The City Hall and a New and Beautiful Manila*. Manila: Bureau of Printing, 1941.

——. *Ten Months of President Osmeña's Administration: A Review of Work Done under Unprecedented Difficulties*. n.p.: n.p., n.d. Copy available at the AHC, Rizal Library, Ateneo de Manila University.

Overseas Technical Cooperation Agency, Government of Japan. *Urban Transport Study in Manila Metropolitan Area*. Manila: Planning and Project Development Office, 1973.

Paez, Patricia Ann. *The Bases Factor: Realpolitik of RP–US Relations*. Manila: Center for Strategic and International Studies of the Philippines, 1985.

Palanco Aguado, Fernando. "The Tagalog Revolts of 1745 according to Spanish Primary Sources." *Philippine Studies* 58 (1–2), 2010: 45–77.

Palatino, Mong. "Pagbabalik-tanaw sa Diliman Commune" [Looking back at the Diliman Commune]. In *Serve the People: Ang Kasaysayan ng Radikal na Kilusan sa Unibersidad ng Pilipinas* [The History of the Radical Movement in the University of the Philippines], ed. Bienvenido Lumbera, Judy Taguiwalo, Roland Tolentino, Arnold Alamon, and Ramon Guillermo, 103–5. [Quezon City]: IBON; Congress of Teachers and Educators for Nationalism and Democracy; Alliance of Concerned Teachers, 2008.

Panlilio, Erlinda Enriquez. "The Fireflies of Kamuning." In *The Manila We Knew*, ed. Erlinda Enriquez Panlilio, 55–61. Pasig City: Anvil, 2006.

——. "UP Beloved." In *The Manila We Knew*, ed. Erlinda Enriquez Panlilio, 70–84. Pasig City: Anvil, 2006.

Pante, Michael D. "Far from Isolation: The Spatial Politics of the Relocation of the Main Campus of the University of the Philippines, 1930s–1970s." *Sojourn: Journal of Social Issues in Southeast Asia* 33 (3), 2018: 499–535.

——. "Peripheral Pockets of Paradise: Perceptions of Health and Geography in Early Twentieth-century Manila and Its Environs." *Philippine Studies* 59 (2), 2011: 187–212.

——. "The Politics of Flood Control and the Making of Metro Manila." *Philippine Studies: Historical and Ethnographic Viewpoints* 64 (3–4), 2016: 555–92.

——. "Prolonged Decline: Intramuros during the American Colonial Period." In *Manila: Selected Papers of the 22nd Annual Manila Studies Conference*, ed. Bernardita Reyes Churchill, Marya Svetlana T. Camacho, and Lorelei D. C. de Viana, 78–108. Manila: Manila Studies Association; National Commission for Culture and the Arts, 2014.

Paredes, Amante F. "The Growing Pains of Suburban Towns." *Chronicle Magazine*, 29 Dec. 1962: 20–22.

Paredes, Esteban F. "Squatter Problem of Manila." *PFP*, 1 Dec. 1956: 26–27.

Paredes, Ruby. "For Want of a City: Manila in the Balance of Resistance and Capitulation." In *The Philippine Revolution and beyond*, vol. 2, ed. Elmer Ordoñez, 620–40. Manila: Philippine Centennial Commission, 1998.

Parnell, Phillip C. "The Composite State: The Poor and the Nation in Manila." In *Ethnography in Unstable Places: Everyday Lives in Contexts of Dramatic Political Change*, ed. Carol J. Greenhouse, Elizabeth Mertz, and Kay B. Warren, 146–77. Durham: Duke University Press, 2002.

———. "Criminalizing Colonialism: Democracy Meets Law in Manila." In *Crime's Power: Anthropologists and the Ethnography of Crime*, ed. Philip C. Parnell and Stephanie C. Kane, 197–220. New York: Palgrave Macmillan, 2003.

Paterno, Vicente Tirona. *On My Terms: The Autobiography of Vicente Tirona Paterno*. Pasig City: Anvil, 2014.

Pedrosa, Pio. "The Beginnings of Quezon City." *Historical Bulletin* 8 (4), 1964: 23–32.

Peña, Rafael L. "Kamuning: A Revelation in Time." In *Age of Gold: Sacred Heart Parish, Kamuning, Q.C., Golden Jubilee, 1941–1991*, ed. Angelo J. de los Reyes, 17–19. [Quezon City?]: Sacred Heart Parish, Angelo J. de los Reyes, 1991.

Peña, Rolly. "*Liberation*: Early Days." In *Tibak Rising: Activism in the Days of Martial Law*, ed. Ferdinand C. Llanes, 186–90. Mandaluyong City: Anvil, 2012.

People's Homesite and Housing Corporation (PHHC). *Annual Report for the Fiscal Year 1955–1956*. Manila: PHHC, [1956?].

———. *Annual Report for the Fiscal Year 1956–1957*. Manila: Bureau of Printing, 1958.

———. *Annual Report, 1961–1962*. n.p.: PHHC, [1962?].

———. *Annual Report, 1962–63*. n.p.: PHHC, [1963?].

Perez, Augusto F. "Office of the City Engineer: Its Organization, Programs, and Accomplishments." in *2 Golden Decades*, 142–49.

Perry, David C. and Wim Wiewel. "From Campus to City: The University as Developer." In *The University as Urban Developer: Case Studies and Analysis*, ed. David C. Perry and Wim Wiewel, 3–21. New York: M. E. Sharpe, 2005.

Pestaño-Jacinto, Pacita. *Living with the Enemy: A Diary of the Japanese Occupation*. Pasig City: Anvil, 1999.

Phelan, John Leddy. *The Hispanization of the Philippines: Spanish Aims and Filipino Responses, 1565–1700*. Metro Manila: Cacho Hermanos, 1985.

Philippine American Life Insurance Company. *Annual Report, 1952*. n.p.: Philippine American Life Insurance Company, [1952?].

Philippine Coast and Geodetic Survey. "City of Manila and Vicinity, 1955." Manila: Philippine Coast and Geodetic Survey, 1955. Map courtesy of the Stephen S. Clark Library, Hatcher Graduate Library, University of Michigan, Ann Arbor, MI.

Philippine Commission of the Census. *Census of the Philippines, 1939*, 3 vols. Manila: Bureau of Printing, 1940.

———. *Census of the Philippines, 1939: Special Bulletin No. 3 (Real Property)*. Manila: Bureau of Printing, 1940.

Philippine Education Company. *Manila City Directory, 1939–1940*. Manila: Philippine Education Company, [1940?].

———. *Manila City Directory, 1941*. Manila: Philippine Education Company, 1941.

Philippine Institute of Architects. *Report on the Quezon Memorial Park and Related Subjects*. Makati: Philippine Institute of Architects, 1969.

Philippine Islands Census Office. *Census of the Philippine Islands Taken under the Direction of the Philippine Legislature in the Year 1918*. Manila: Bureau of Printing, 1920.

Pimentel, Benjamin. *Rebolusyon! A Generation of Struggle in the Philippines.* New York: Monthly Review Press, 1991.

Pinches, Michael. "Entrepreneurship, Consumption, Ethnicity and National Identity in the Making of the Philippines' New Rich." In *Culture and Privilege in Capitalist Asia*, ed. Michael Pinches, 277–303. London and New York: Routledge, 1999.

———. "Modernisation and the Quest for Modernity: Architectural Form, Squatter Settlements, and the New Society in Manila." In *Cultural Identity and Urban Change in Southeast Asia: Interpretive Essays*, ed. M. R. Askew and W. S. Logan, 13–42. Geelong, VIC: Deakin University Press, 1994.

———. "The Working Class Experience of Shame, Inequality, and People Power in Tatalon, Manila." In *From Marcos to Aquino: Local Perspectives on Political Transition in the Philippines*, ed. Benedict J. Kerkvliet and Resil B. Mojares, 166–86. Quezon City: Ateneo de Manila University Press, 1991.

Pink, Luis [Louis] H. "A Housing Program for the Philippines." *ACCJ* 32 (2), 1946: 6, 21, 24–25, 28.

Ponce, Vicente C. *Killing the Spider: Memoirs of Engr. Vicente C. Ponce.* Quezon City: E.C. TEC Commercial, 2010.

Porio, Emma. "Shifting Spaces of Power in Metro Manila." *City* 13 (1), 2009: 110–19.

Portugal, Ramon C. "The Diliman 'Republic.'" *Sunday Times Magazine*, 13 Jan. 1952: 12–14.

Power, John H. and Gerardo P. Sicat. *The Philippines: Industrialization and Trade Policies.* Paris: Development Centre of the Organization for Economic Co-operation and Development; London: Oxford University Press, 1971.

Prescott, J. R. V. *The Geography of Frontiers and Boundaries.* London: Hutchinson University Library, 1965.

Quezon, Manuel. *Fifth Annual Report of the President of the Philippines to the President and the Congress of the United States Covering the Period July 1, 1939, to June 30, 1940.* Washington, DC: Government Printing Office, 1941.

———. *Fourth Annual Report of the President of the Philippines to the President and the Congress of the United States Covering the Period January 1 to June 30, 1939.* Manila: Bureau of Printing, 1940.

———. *The Good Fight: The Autobiography of Manuel Luis Quezon.* Mandaluyong: Cacho Hermanos, 1985.

———. *Message of His Excellency, Manuel Quezon, President of the Philippines, to the 1st National Assembly (Second state of the nation address), 16 Oct. 1937. QP Series III, Box 19.*

———. *Message of His Excellency, Manuel Quezon, President of the Philippines, to the 2nd National Assembly* (Fifth state of the nation address). Manila: Bureau of Printing, 1940.

———. *Message of His Excellency, Manuel Quezon, President of the Philippines, to the Second National Assembly, Delivered 24 January 1939.* Manila: Bureau of Printing, 1939.

———. *Messages of the President*, vol. 2, part 1, rev. ed. Manila: Bureau of Printing, 1938.

———. *Messages of the President*, vol. 4, part 1. Manila: Bureau of Printing, 1939.

———. *Messages of the President*, vol. 5 part 1. Manila: Bureau of Printing, 1941.

———. *Peace and Social and Economic Security of Nations: Speech of His Excellency Manuel L. Quezon, President of the Philippines.* Manila: Bureau of Printing, 1939.

———. *Quezon in His Speeches*, ed. Pedro de la Llana and F. B. Icasiano. Manila: State Publishing, 1937.

———. *Second Annual Report of the President of the Philippines to the President and the Congress of the United States Covering the Period January 1 to December 31, 1937.* Manila: Bureau of Printing, 1938.

———. Sixth State of the Nation Address, 31 Jan. 1941. MLQP Series III, Box 21.

———. *Third Annual Report of the President of the Philippines to the President and the Congress of the United States, Covering the Calendar Year Ended December 31, 1938.* Washington, DC: Government Printing Office, 1940.

———. "'We Shall Not Permit Injustices.'" In *Quezon in His Speeches*, ed. Pedro de la Llana and F. B. Icasiano, 147–48. Manila: State Publishing, 1937.

Quezon III, Manuel L. "Prologue." In *Quezon City: The Rise of Asia's City of the Future*, ed. Regina A. Samson and Marily Y. Orosa, 24–43. Quezon City: Local Government of Quezon City, 2010.

Quezon City. *Laying of the Cornerstone of the Capitol Building Souvenir Program*. n.p.: n.p., 1949.

———. *The Quezon City of Today*. Quezon City: Quezon City Hall, 1970.

Quijano de Manila [pseud. Nick Joaquin]. "Caloocan: The 39th City." *PFP*, 24 Feb. 1962: 46–48, 50.

———. *Language of the Streets and Other Essays*. Metro Manila: National Book Store, 1980.

———. *Manila: Sin City? And Other Chronicles*. Metro Manila: National Book Store, 1980.

———. "Nonong Quezon's Life with Father." In *Quezon: Thoughts and Anecdotes about Him and His Fights*, ed. Juan F. Rivera, 124–34. Quezon City: Juan F. Rivera, 1979.

———. *Reportage on Lovers: A Medley of Factual Romances, Happy or Tragical, Most of Which Made News*. Pasig City: Anvil, 2009.

———. *The Quartet of the Tiger Moon: Scenes from the People-Power Apocalypse*. n.p.: Book Stop, 1986.

Quimpo, Susan F. and Nathan Gilbert Quimpo. *Subversive Lives: A Family Memoir of the Marcos Years*. Manila: Anvil, 2012.

Quirino, Carlos. *Quezon: Paladin of Philippine Freedom*. Manila: Filipiniana Book Guild, 1971.

Quirino, Elpidio. *The Quirino Way: Collection of Speeches and Addresses of Elpidio Quirino*. n.p.: Juan Collas, 1955.

Quirino, Jose A. "Cockfighting Becomes Big Business." *PFP*, 4 Aug. 1956: 20–23.

Rafael, Vicente L. "*Contracting Colonialism* and the Long 1970s." *Philippine Studies: Historical and Ethnographic Viewpoints* 61 (4), 2013: 477–94.

Rama, Napoleon G. "Hasty PHHC Deal Questioned." *PFP*, 2 Aug. 1958: 30–31, 34–35.

———. "Stinking Mess in the PHHC." *PFP*, 30 Sept. 1958: 5–6, 69.

Ramos, Carlos P. "Manila's Metropolitan Problem." *Philippine Journal of Public Administration* 5 (2), 1961: 89–117.

Ramos, Michael Francis. "The Beginnings (1950–1974)." In *Lakbay: 40 Years of Cornerstone-Building in Faith*, 8–17. Quezon City: Resurrection of our Lord Parish, 2015.

Ramos-Jimenez, Pilar, Ma. Elena Chiong-Javier, and Judy Carol C. Sevilla. *Philippine Urban Situation Analysis*. Manila: UNICEF Manila, 1986.

Reed, Robert. *City of Pines: The Origins of Baguio as a Colonial Hill Station and Regional Capital*. Baguio City: A-Seven, 1999.

———. *Colonial Manila: The Context of Hispanic Urbanism and Process of Morphogenesis*. Berkeley: University of California Press, 1978.

———. "The Colonial Origins of Manila and Batavia: Desultory Notes on Nascent Metropolitan Primacy and Urban Systems in Southeast Asia." *Asian Studies* 5 (3), 1967: 543–62.

Reid, Anthony. *Southeast Asia in the Age of Commerce, 1450–1680*, vol. 1: *The Lands below the Winds*. New Haven: Yale University Press, 1988.

Reyes, Marqueza C. L. "Spatial Structure of Metro Manila: Genesis, Growth and Development." *Philippine Planning Journal* 29 (2)–30 (1), 1998: 1–34.

Reyes, Raquel A. G. "Flaunting It: How the Galleon Trade Made Manila, circa 1571–1800." *Early American Studies: An Interdisciplinary Journal* 15 (4), 2017: 683–713.

———. "Modernizing the Manileña: Technologies of Conspicuous Consumption for the Well-to-do Woman, circa 1880s–1930s." *Modern Asian Studies* 46 (1), 2012: 193–220.

Reyes, Rex R. B., Jr., "The St. Andrew's Theological Seminary." In *Chapters in Philippine Church History*, ed. Anne C. Kwantes, 359–68. Mandaluyong City: OMF Literature, 2001.

Richardson, Jim. *Komunista: The Genesis of the Philippine Communist Party, 1902–1935*. Quezon City: Ateneo de Manila University Press, 2011.

Richter, Linda K. *The Politics of Tourism in Asia*. Honolulu: University of Hawai'i Press, 1989.

Rimmer, Peter J. and Howard Dick. *The City in Southeast Asia: Patterns, Processes and Policy.* Singapore: NUS Press, 2009.

Rizal, José. *El Filibusterismo: Subversion,* trans. Soledad Lacson-Locsin. Makati City: Bookmark, 1996.

Robb, Walter. "The Drab amid the Beautiful." *ACCJ* 10 (11), 1930: 8–9.

———. "The Growth of a City: Manila." *ACCJ* 10 (2), 1930: 9, 11.

———. "The Growth of Manila: Changing Ermita (Fourth Paper)." *ACCJ* 10 (5), 1930: 9, 11, 26–27.

———. "Santa Mesa Heights (Growth of Manila Series, 6th Paper)." ACCJ 10 (7), 1930: 5–7.

———. "Why Buy a Home? We May Not Be Here Long." *ACCJ* 7 (8), 1927: 12–13.

Robles, Raissa. *Marcos Martial Law: Never Again,* ed. Alan Robles. Quezon City: Filipinos for a Better Philippines, 2016.

Rodrigo, Raul. *Phoenix: The Saga of the Lopez Family,* vol. 1: *1800–1972.* Manila: Eugenio López Foundation, 2000.

Romani, John N. and M. Ladd Thomas. 1954. *A Survey of Local Government in the Philippines.* Manila: Institute of Public Administration, University of the Philippines, 1954.

Rondain, Celine Singson. *Vicente Singson Encarnacion: A Biography.* n.p.:n.p., n.d. Copy available at the Filipiniana Section, UP-Diliman Main Library.

Roosmalen, Pauline K. M. van. "Netherlands Indies Town Planning: An Agent of Modernization (1905–1957)." In *Cars, Conduits, and Kampongs: The Modernization of the Indonesian City, 1920–1960,* ed. Freek Colombijn and Joost Coté, 87–119. Leiden: Brill, 2015.

Rosenberg, Emily S. *Spreading the American Dream: American Economic and Cultural Expansion, 1890–1945.* New York: Hill and Wang, 1982.

Rotea, Hermie. *Behind the Barricades: I Saw Them Aim and Fire!* n.p.: Hermie Rotea, 1970.

———. *Marcos' Lovey Dovie.* Los Angeles: Liberty, 1983.

———. "Plan for a Greater Manila." *This Week* 16 (2), 8 Jan. 1961: 10–14.

Roth, Dennis Morrow. *The Friar Estates of the Philippines.* Albuquerque: University of New Mexico Press, 1977.

Roxas, Manuel. "Message on the State of the Nation to the Second Congress of the Philippines, June 3, 1946." In *Speeches, Addresses and Messages as President of the Philippines,* vol. 1: *Jan. 1946 – Feb. 1, 1947,* 71–101. Manila: Bureau of Printing, 1954.

Rüland, Jürgen. "The Dynamics of Metropolitan Management in Southeast Asia: An Introductory Note." In *The Dynamics of Metropolitan Management in Southeast Asia,* ed. Jürgen Rüland, 1–29. Singapore: Institute of Southeast Asian Studies, 1996.

———. "Metropolitan Government under Martial Law: The Metro Manila Commission Experiment." *Philippine Journal of Public Administration,* Jan. 1985: 27–41.

Salamanca, Bonifacio S. "Bocobo Fosters a Vibrant Nationalism (1934–1939): Reassertion of Filipino Values as an Underlying Concept of Academic Life." In *University of the Philippines: The first 75 years (1908–1983),* ed. Oscar M. Alfonso, 201–57. Quezon City: University of the Philippines Press, 1985.

Salazar, Z. A. *Agosto 29–30, 1896: Ang Pagsalakay ni Bonifacio sa Maynila,* trans. Monico M. Atienza. Quezon City: Miranda Bookstore, 1994.

Salonga, Isayas. *Rizal Province Directory, Vol. I: History, Government and General Information with the Full Text of the Philippine Independence Law.* Manila: General Printing Press, 1934.

———. *Rizal Province Today: A Souvenir of the Province of Rizal Depicting its History and Progress.* Manila: Salonga Publishing Company, 1940.

San Juan, E. Jr. "Encircle the Cities by the Countryside: The City in Philippine Writing." In *History and Form: Selected Essays,* 150–67. Quezon City: Ateneo de Manila University Press, 1996.

Santiago, Luciano P. R. "The Last Hacendera: Doña Teresa de la Paz, 1841–1890." *Philippine Studies* 46 (3), 1998: 340–60.

Santiago, Maria Lina A. *Araneta: A Love Affair with God and Country.* Quezon City: Sahara Heritage Foundation, 2007.

Santos, Angeles S. *Ang Malabon (Katipunan ng Mahahalagang Kasulatan tungkol sa Bayang Malabon, Lalawigan ng Rizal)* [Malabon (A Compilation of Important Writings about the Town of Malabon, Rizal Province)]. Malabon: Dalubhasaang Epifanio de los Santos Press, 1975.

Sarte, Alona H. and Veronica F. Agbayani. *Quezon City: The Promised City with a Glorious Past, a Tangible Present and a Bright Future.* Manila: Catholic Trade School, 1953.

Sastrón, Manuel. *La Insurrección en Filipinas* [The Insurrection in the Philippines], vol. I. Madrid: La Viuda de M. Minuesa de los Ríos, 1897.

Saulo, Alfredo B. *Communism in the Philippines: An Introduction*, rev. ed. Quezon City: Ateneo de Manila University Press, 1990.

———. *"Let George Do It": A Biography of Jorge B. Vargas.* Quezon City: University of the Philippines Press, 1990.

Sayre, Francis B. *Fourth Annual Report of the United States High Commissioner to the Philippine Islands to the President and Congress of the United States Covering the Fiscal Year July 1, 1939 to June 30, 1940.* Washington, DC: Government Printing Office, 1943.

Schoenstein, Erwin, OFM. "San Pedro Bautista in the Philippines." In *400 Years, 1578–1978: Franciscans in the Philippines*, ed. Jesús Galindo, 123–30. Manila: Franciscans in the Philippines, 1979.

Schumacher, John N. *The Propaganda Movement, 1880–1895: The Creation of a Filipino Consciousness, the Making of the Revolution.* Quezon City: Ateneo de Manila University Press, 1997.

Seagrave, Sterling. *The Marcos Dynasty.* New York: Harper & Row, 1988.

Seekins, Donald M. *State and Society in Modern Rangoon.* Abingdon: Routledge, 2011.

Sendut, Hamzah. "The Structure of Kuala Lumpur, Malaysia's Capital City." In *The City in Newly Developing Countries: Readings on Urbanism and Urbanization*, ed. Gerald Breese, 461–73. Englewood, NJ: Prentice-Hall, 1969.

Serrano, F. M. *Atoms-for-Peace in the Philippines: Official Report of the Philippine Delegation to the International Conference on the Peaceful Uses of Atomic Energy.* New York: Philippine Mission to the United Nations, [1955?].

Serrano, Leopoldo R. *A Brief History of Caloocan.* Manila: L. R. Serrano, 1960.

Shatkin, Gavin. "Colonial Capital, Modernist Capital, Global Capital: The Changing Political Symbolism of Urban Space in Metro Manila, the Philippines." *Pacific Affairs* 78 (4), 2005–2006: 577–600.

———. "Planning to Forget: Informal Settlements as 'Forgotten Places' in Globalising Metro Manila." *Urban Studies* 41 (12), 2004: 2469–84.

Shopping in Old Manila. Manila: n.p., [1934?].

Sicat, Gerardo P. *Cesar Virata: Life and Times through Four Decades of Philippine Economic History.* Quezon City: University of the Philippines Press, 2014.

Sidel, John. "Walking in the Shadow of the Big Man: Justiniano Montano and Failed Dynasty Building in Cavite, 1935–1972. In *An Anarchy of Families*, 109–61. Quezon City: Ateneo de Manila University Press, 1994.

Simbulan, Dante C. *The Modern Principalia: The Historical Evolution of the Philippine Ruling Oligarchy.* Quezon City: University of the Philippines Press, 2005.

Sioson-San Juan, Thelma. "Is 'Burgis' Power for Real?" *Sunday Times Magazine*, 9 Mar. 1986: 5–7.

Sirat, Morshidi. "Kuala Lumpur: Primacy, Urban System and Rationalizing Capital City Functions." In *Capital Cities in Asia-Pacific: Primacy and Diversity*, ed. K. C. Ho and Hsin-Huang Michael Hsiao, 71–88. Taipei: Center for Asia-Pacific Area Studies, Research Center for Humanities and Social Sciences, Academia Sinica, 2006.

Smith, David A. and Roger J. Nemeth. "Urban Development in Southeast Asia: An Historical Structural Analysis." In *Urbanisation in the Developing World*, ed. David Drakakis-Smith, 121–39. London: Croom Helm, 1986.

Social Welfare Administration. *Annual Report of the Social Welfare Administration for the Fiscal Year 1956–1957*. Manila: SWA, [1958?].

Soja, Edward W. *Postmodern Geographies: The Reassertion of Space in Critical Social Theory*. London: Verso, 1989.

Special Mission to the United States. *Report of the Special Mission to the United States, 1938– 1939*. Manila: Bureau of Printing, 1939.

Sta. Maria, Felice Prudente. "In the Steps of the Founder: A History of the City of Manuel Luis Quezon." In *Quezon City: The Rise of Asia's City of the Future*, ed. Regina A. Samson and Marily Y. Orosa, 46–85. Quezon City: Local Government of Quezon City, 2010.

Stevens, Joseph Earle. *The Philippines Circa 1900: Yesterdays in the Philippines*. Manila: Filipiniana Book Guild, 1968.

Storey, Donovan. "Housing the Urban Poor in Metro Manila." *Philippine Studies* 46 (3), 1998: 267–92.

———. "Whose Model City? Poverty, Prosperity and the Battle over 'Progress' in Quezon City." In *Asian Futures, Asian Traditions*, ed. Edwina Palmer, 176–95. Folkestone, Kent, UK: Global Oriental, 2005.

Sycip, Cynthia Y. *Memories of a Hero*. n.p.: n.p., 1984.

Tadiar, Neferti Xina M. *Fantasy-Production: Sexual Economies and Other Philippine Consequences for the New World Order*. Quezon City: Ateneo de Manila University Press, 2004.

———. *Things Fall Away: Philippine Historical Experience and the Makings of Globalization*. Quezon City: University of the Philippines Press, 2004.

Taguiwalo, Judy. "Babaeng 'Makibaka' sa Likod ng Rehas." [Makibaka Woman behind Bars] In *Tibak Rising: Activism in the Days of Martial Law*, ed. Ferdinand C. Llanes, 44–47. Mandaluyong City: Anvil, 2012.

———. "Pangkalahatang Welga sa UP, Pebrero 4, 1969: Militante at Matagumpay na Pagsulong sa Demokratisasyon ng Unibersidad" [General Strike in UP, February 4, 1969: The Militant and Successful Progress of Democratization in the University]. In *Serve the People: Ang Kasaysayan ng Radikal na Kilusan sa Unibersidad ng Pilipinas* [The History of the Radical Movement in the University of the Philippines], ed. Bienvenido Lumbera, Judy Taguiwalo, Roland Tolentino, Arnold Alamon, and Ramon Guillermo, 97–102. [Quezon City]: IBON; Congress of Teachers and Educators for Nationalism and Democracy; Alliance of Concerned Teachers, 2008.

Takagi, Yusuke. *Central Banking as State Building: Policymakers and their Nationalism in the Philippines, 1933–1964*. Quezon City: Ateneo de Manila University Press, 2016.

Taruc, Luis. *Born of the People*. New York: International Publishers, 1953.

Task Force on Human Settlements, Development Academy of the Philippines. *Technical Report: Housing Policy Guidelines for the MBMR*. Quezon City: Development Academy of the Philippines, 1975.

Taylor, George E. *The Philippines and the United States: Problems of Partnership*. New York: Frederick A. Praeger, 1964.

Taylor, John R. M. *The Philippine Insurrection against the United States: A Compilation of Documents*, vol. 1. Pasay City: Eugenio Lopez Foundation, 1971.

———. *The Philippine Insurrection against the United States: A Compilation of Documents with Notes and Introduction*, vol. 2: *May 19, 1898 to July 4, 1902*. Pasay City: Eugenio Lopez Foundation, 1971.

Teodoro, Luis V. "UP in the Sixties: Life in the 'Diliman Republic.'" In *The University Experience: Essays on the 82nd Anniversary of the University of the Philippines*, ed. Belinda A. Aquino, 57–63. Quezon City: University of the Philippines Press, 1991.

Terami-Wada, Motoe. *Sakdalistas' Struggle for Philippine Independence, 1930–1945*. Quezon City: Ateneo de Manila University Press, 2014.

REFERENCES 349

Thomas, David. "The Edge of the City." *Transactions of the Institute of British Geographers* 15 (2), 1990: 131–38.

Thompson, J. M. "Report of Col. J. M. Thompson." In *Annual Reports of the War Department for the Fiscal Year Ended June 30, 1901*, part 3. Washington, DC: Government Printing Office, 1901.

Thompson, Mark R. *The Anti-Marcos Struggle: Personalistic Rule and Democratic Transition in the Philippines*. Quezon City: New Day, 1996.

———. "The EDSAs: From Cross-class to Class-based." In *Remembering/Rethinking EDSA*, ed. JPaul S. Manzanilla and Caroline S. Hau, 310–24. Mandaluyong City: Anvil, 2016.

———. "Southeast Asia's Subversive Voters: A Philippine Perspective." *Philippine Studies: Historical and Ethnographic Viewpoints* 64 (2), 2016: 265–87.

Tiglao, Teodora V. *Health Practices in a Rural Community*. Quezon City: Community Development Research Council, University of the Philippines, 1964.

Timberman, David G. *A Changeless Land: Continuity and Change in Philippine Politics*. Makati: Bookmark, 1991.

Tirol, Lorna Kalaw. "Edgar Jopson: The 'Magis' Seeker." In *Six Young Filipino Martyrs*, ed. Asuncion David Maramba, 131–79. Pasig City: Anvil, 1997.

Tobias, Gaudencio V. *Priority Projects of the National Housing Authority*. Makati: Technology Resource Center, 1978.

Tolentino, Isagani V. "Sa Namarco Mayroon, Hulugan pa." *Filipinas: Magasing Tagapamansag ng Katarungang Panlipunan*, 16 Jan. 1958: 8–9.

Tolentino, Rolando B. *Almanak ng Isang Aktibista*. Quezon City: University of the Philippines Press, 2011.

———. *Contestable Nation-Space: Cinema, Cultural Politics, and Transnationalism in the Marcos–Brocka Philippines*. Quezon City: University of the Philippines Press, 2014.

———. *Sipat Kultura: Tungo sa Mapagpalayang Pagbabasa, Pag-aaral at Pagtuturo ng Panitikan* [A Look at Culture: Toward Liberating Ways of Reading, Studying, and Teaching Literature]. Quezon City: Ateneo de Manila University Press, 2007.

Torres, Cristina Evangelista. *The Americanization of Manila, 1898–1921*. Quezon City: University of the Philippines Press, 2010.

Torres, Jose Victor Z. *Ciudad Murada: A Walk through Historic Intramuros*. Manila: Intramuros Administration; Vibal, 2005.

Totanes, Stephen Henry S. "Student Activism in the Pre-Martial Law Era." In *Down from the Hill*, ed. Cristina Jayme Montiel and Susan Evangelista, 1–54. Quezon City: Ateneo de Manila University Press, 2005.

Toynbee, Arnold. *Cities on the Move*. London: Oxford University Press, 1970.

"Triumphant End for Lakbayan." *Malaya*, 8 Mar. 1984. In *Ninoy Aquino: The Man, the Legend*, ed. Asuncion David Maramba, 190–91. Mandaluyong: Cacho Hermanos, 1984.

Tupas, Rodolfo G. "The Exercise of Restraint." *Sunday Times Magazine*, 7 Mar. 1971: 10–11.

Tutay, Filemon V. "Charges and Counter-Charges." *PFP*, 13 Jan. 1971: 11, 30, 38.

———. "Gang Hideout Busted." *PFP*, 21 Aug. 1948: 6–7, 59.

———. "A Squatter for 70 Years." *PFP*, 24 May 1952: 6–7, 63.

———. "Squatter Trouble." *PFP*, 3 May 1952: 6–7, 27, 50.

———. "Worst Flood in Years." *PFP*, 4 June 1960: 6–7, 42–43, 79.

Ty, Leon. "Another Gardenia for Manila?" *PFP*, 31 Jan. 1948: 8, 41.

———. "Forced Migration." *PFP*, 20 Dec. 1941: 24–27.

———. "'Many of Our Countrymen are Homeless.'" *PFP*, 18 Sept. 1947: 4–5, 49.

———. "A Real Tenancy Problem." *PFP*, 29 July 1939: 20–23.

———. "'Royal Grant' to Royal Buses." *PFP*, 25 Feb. 1956: 10–11, 63.

———. "Scandalous and Shocking." *PFP*, 19 July 1958: 2–3, 32–33.

———. "Why Didn't I Also Die?" *PFP*, 4 June 1960: 4, 77.

University of the Philippines (UP). *Resurgence of the University.* Manila: University of the Philippines, 1948.

———. *University Perspectives: Reports of the President's Ad Hoc Committees.* Quezon City: University of the Philippines, 1962–63.

"Up from Ramshackles to Institute." *The Bulletin of the Quezon Institute* 1 (1), 1939: 93–103.

US Bureau of the Census. *Census of the Philippines, Taken under the Direction of the Philippine Commission in the Year 1903,* 4 vols. Washington: United States Bureau of the Census, 1905.

US Congress. *Mutual Security Act of 1958: Hearings before the Committee on Foreign Affairs, House of Representatives, Eighty-Fifth Congress, Second Session,* part 1. Washington, DC: Government Printing Office, 1958.

US Philippine Commission. *Report of the United States Philippine Commission to the Secretary of War for the Period from December 1, 1900, to October 15, 1901,* part 2. Washington, DC: Government Printing Office, 1901.

US Philippine War Damage Commission (PWDC). *Eighth Semiannual Report of the United States Philippine War Damage Commission, Manila, Philippines, for Period Ending June 30, 1950.* Washington, DC: Government Printing Office, 1950.

Varias, Antonio. "Real Estate." *ACCJ,* 31 (8), 1955: 349.

Veneracion, Jaime Balcos. *Kasaysayan ng Bulakan.* Cologne: Bahay-Saliksikan ng Kasaysayan, 1986.

———. *Sapang Palay: Hacienda, Urban Resettlement and Core of the City of San Jose del Monte, Bulacan.* Manila: National Commission for Culture and the Arts, 2011.

Versnel, Hans and Freek Colombijn. "Rückert and Hoesni Thamrin: Bureaucrat and Politician in Colonial Kampung Improvement." In *Cars, Conduits, and Kampongs: The Modernization of the Indonesian City, 1920–1960,* ed. Freek Colombijn and Joost Coté, 123–51. Leiden: Brill, 2015.

Villamor, Ignacio. *Criminality in the Philippine Islands, 1903–1908.* Manila: Bureau of Printing, 1909.

Villoria, Leandro A. "Manila." In *Rural–Urban Migrants and Metropolitan Development,* ed. Aprodicio A. Laquian, 135–50. Toronto: INTERMET, 1971.

Viloria, Julie G. and David Williams. "Evaluation of Community Upgrading Programs in Metro Manila." In *Shelter Upgrading for the Urban Poor: Evaluation of Third World Experiences,* ed. Reinhard J. Skinner, John L. Taylor, and Emiel A. Wegelin, 11–37. Manila: Island Publishing, 1987.

Wagner, Bernard. *Housing and Urban Development in the Philippines.* Manila: USAID, 1968.

Waller, Douglas. *Wild Bill Donovan: The Spymaster Who Created the OSS and Modern American Espionage.* New York: Free Press, 2011.

Watanabe, Akiko. "Representing Muslimness: Strategic Essentialism in a Land Dispute in Metro Manila." *Philippine Studies* 56 (3), 2008: 285–311.

Waterhouse, Alan. *Boundaries of the City: The Architecture of Western Urbanism.* Toronto: University of Toronto Press, 2015.

Weissblatt, Franz, ed. *Who's Who in the Philippines: A Biographical Dictionary of Notable Living Men of the Philippines,* vol. II, *1940–1941.* Manila: Franz Weissblatt, 1940.

Wheeler, Gerald E. The American Minority in the Philippines during the Prewar Commonwealth Period. *Asian Studies* 4 (2), 1966: 362–73.

Whitehand, J. W. R. "Fringe Belts: A Neglected Aspect of Urban Geography." *Transactions of the Institute of British Geographers* 41, 1967: 223–33.

Wickberg, Edgar. *The Chinese in Philippine Life, 1850–1898.* Quezon City: Ateneo de Manila University Press, 2000.

———. *The Chinese Mestizo in Philippine History.* Manila: Kaisa para sa Kaunlaran, 2001.

Wong Kwok-Chu. *The Chinese in the Philippine Economy, 1898–1941.* Quezon City: Ateneo de Manila University Press, 1999.

Wood, Leonard. *Message of Governor-General Leonard Wood to the Seventh Philippine Legislature, Delivered July 16, 1925 at the Opening of the First Session.* Manila: Bureau of Printing, 1925.

———. *Message of Governor-General Leonard Wood to the Seventh Philippine Legislature, Delivered July 16, 1926 at the Opening of the Second Session.* Manila: Bureau of Printing, 1926.

Yamaguchi, Kiyoko. "The New 'American' House in the Colonial Philippines and the Rise of the Urban Filipino Elite." *Philippine Studies* 54 (3), 2006: 412–51.

Yap Kioe Sheng. "Peri-Urban Transformations in Southeast Asia." In *Routledge Handbook of Urbanization in Southeast Asia*, ed. Rita Padawangi, 31–42. Abingdon and New York: Routledge, 2019.

Youngblood, Robert L. *Marcos against the Church: Economic Development and Political Repression in the Philippines.* Quezon City: New Day, 1993.

Yung Li Yuk-wai. *The Huaqiao Warriors: Chinese Resistance Movement in the Philippines, 1942–45.* Quezon City: Ateneo de Manila University Press, 1996.

Yuson, Alfred A. *Confessions of a Q.C. House-husband and Other Privacies.* Pasig: Anvil, 1991.

Zialcita, Fernando N. and Martin I. Tinio Jr. *Philippine Ancestral Houses (1810–1930).* Quezon City: GCF, 1980.

Periodicals and Other Serials

American Chamber of Commerce Journal 1921–1922, 1926–1927, 1930, 1937–1941, 1948, 1951, 1955
Bulletin Today 1976
Chronicle Magazine 1962
Congressional Record 1945–1948
The Diliman Star 1952
Examiner 1975
FOCUS Philippines 1976
Graphic 1971
The Guidon 1949, 1951–1952
Lipang Kalabaw 1949
Manila Daily Bulletin 1938–1941
Manila Times 1902–1905, 1920, 1926, 1929, 1945–1946, 1948, 1963
Manila Times Anniversary Issue 1910
Mr. & Ms. 1985
Philippine Graphic 1929, 1938
Philippine Magazine 1929, 1935, 1938, 1940
Philippine Panorama 1974–1976
Philippines 1940
Philippines Commonweal 1939–1940
Philippines Free Press 1932, 1939–1941, 1947–1948, 1952, 1956, 1958, 1960, 1963, 1966, 1971
Sunday Times Magazine 1952, 1956, 1963, 1971, 1986
This Week 1960–1961
The Weekly Nation 1965, 1970–1971
Tribune XIV Anniversary Issue 1939

Theses and Dissertations

Abalahin, Andrew Jimenez. "Prostitution Policy and the Project of Modernity: A Comparative Study of Colonial Indonesia and the Philippines, 1850–1940." PhD dissertation, Cornell University, 2003.

Ignacio, Louie Benedict R. "The Emergence of a Gated Community in the Philippines: The Case of Philam Homes Subdivision, Quezon City, Philippines." MA thesis, Ateneo de Manila University, 2010.

Rodriguez-Arcinas, Fe. "A Sociological Analysis of a Specialized Community—Diliman." MA thesis, University of the Philippines-Diliman, 1954.

Audiovisual Source
Diaz, Ramona S. *Imelda*. New York: CineDiaz, 2003.

Online Materials
Alcazaren, Paulo. "Requiem for a Master Architect." *Philippine Star*, 30 Aug. 2008. http://www.philstar.com/modern-living/82437/requiem-master-architect, accessed 3 Sept. 2016.

"Ang Depensa ng Diliman." *Bandilang Pula: Pahayagan ng Malayang Purok ng Diliman*, 12 Feb. 1971: 4–5, 8, *Arkibong Bayan, The Diliman Commune of 1971*, Part II. http://www.arkibongbayan.org/2010/2010-03March28-DilimanCommune2/bandilangpula/IMG_0219.jpg; http://www.arkibongbayan.org/2010/2010-03March28-DilimanCommune2/bandilangpula/IMG_0220.jpg; http://www.arkibongbayan.org/2010/2010-03March28-DilimanCommune2/bandilangpula/IMG_0223.jpg, accessed 16 Dec. 2015.

"Ang Leksiyon ng Pakikibaka." *Bandilang Pula: Pahayagan ng Malayang Purok ng Diliman*, 12 Feb. 1971: 1, 6, *Arkibong Bayan, The Diliman Commune of 1971*, Part II: "A Up Professor's View and Account of the Diliman Commune." http://www.arkibongbayan.org/2010/2010-03Marchs28-DilimanCommune2/bandilangpula/IMG_0216.jpg, accessed 16 Dec. 2015.

Baculinao, Ericson M. and June C. Pagaduan. "'Barricades are Fine': Resolution Endorsing the Barricades as a Form of Protest," 13 Feb. 1971. *Arkibong Bayan, The Diliman Commune of 1971*, Part II. http://www.arkibongbayan.org/2010/2010-03March28-DilimanCommune2/upsc/IMG_0201.jpg; http://www.arkibongbayan.org/2010/2010-03March28-DilimanCommune2/upsc/IMG_0202.jpg, accessed 16 Dec. 2015.

Chu, Richard T. and Teresita Ang See. "Toward a History of Chinese Burial Grounds in Manila during the Spanish Colonial Period." *Archipel: Études Interdisciplinaires sur le Monde Insulindien* 92 (2016): 63–90. http://archipel.revues.org/283, accessed 17 Oct. 2017.

De Joya, Preciosa. "Exorcising Communist Specters and Witch Philosophers: The Struggle for Academic Freedom of 1961." *Kritika Kultura* 26, 2016: 4–32. http://journals.ateneo.edu/ojs/kk/article/view/KK2016.02602/2220, accessed 13 Aug. 2016.

De las Alas, Antonio. Diary of Antonio de las Alas, 26 June 1945. *The Philippine Diary Project*. https://philippinediaryproject.wordpress.com/1945/06/27/june-26-1945-tuesday/, accessed 27 Aug. 2016.

———. Diary of Antonio de las Alas, 17 May 1945. *The Philippine Diary Project*. Online, https://philippinediaryproject.wordpress.com/1945/05/17/may-17-1945-thursday/, accessed 27 Aug. 2016.

Farrer, James. "Globalizing Asian Cuisines: From Eating for Strength to Culinary Cosmopolitanism—A Long History of Culinary Globalization." *Education about Asia* 16 (3), 2011: 33–37. http://s3.amazonaws.com/academia.edu.documents/6977629/Farrer_EAA-16-3.pdf?AWSAccessKeyId=AKIAJ56TQJRTWSMTNPEA&Expires=1478267784&Signature=B7yuAPAYbtZRBw7%2BZgLf%2FhdP%2FCs%3D&response-content-disposition=inline%3B%-20filename%3DGlobalizing_Asian_Cuisines_From_Eating_f.pdf, accessed 4 Nov. 2016.

Harrison, Francis Burton. Diary of Francis Burton Harrison, 24 Aug. 1942. *The Philippine Diary Project*. https://philippinediaryproject.wordpress.com/1942/08/24/august-24-1942/, accessed 27 Aug. 2016.

Issace, John Jebasingam. "Creating the Essence of Cities: The Planning & Development of Malaysia's New Federal Administrative Capital, Putrajaya." World Bank discussion paper, 2005. http://info.worldbank.org/etools/docs/library/235915/S5_p22paper.pdf, accessed 10 October 2013.

Magturo, Daphne J. "Quezon City Moves to Replace Manila as Country's Capital." *Philippine Daily Inquirer*, 24 May 2012. http://newsinfo.inquirer.net/199881/quezon-city-moves-to-replace-manila-as-country%E2%80%99s-capital accessed 2 Oct. 2013.

REFERENCES   353

Manto-Beltran, Lea. "Emil Jurado: A Man of Letters; A Father of Journalists." *The Manila Times*, 20 June 2015. http://www.manilatimes.net/a-man-of-letters-a-father-of-journalists/193533/, accessed 1 Dec. 2015;

Marcos, Ferdinand E. Diary of Ferdinand E. Marcos, 9 Feb. 1970. *The Philippine Diary Project*. https://philippinediaryproject.wordpress.com/1970/02/09/february-9-1970-monday/, accessed 27 Aug. 2016.

———. Presidential Decree No. 940, June 24, 1976, Establishing Manila as the Capital of the Philippines and as the Permanent Seat of the National Government. *The Lawphil Project*. http://www.lawphil.net/statutes/presdecs/pd1976/pd_940_1976.html, accessed 14 Jan. 2016.

———. Proclamation No. 1081, s. 1972: Proclaiming a State of Martial Law in the Philippines, *OG*. http://www.gov.ph/1972/09/21/proclamation-no-1081/, accessed 11 Sept. 2016.

Maung Aung Myoe. "The Road to Naypyitaw: Making Sense of the Myanmar Government's Decision to Move Its Capital." *Asia Research Institute Working Paper Series* no. 79, November 2006.

McGee, Terry. "The Spatiality of Urbanization: The Policy Challenges of Mega-Urban and Desakota Regions of Southeast Asia." UNU-IAS Working Papers No. 161, Apr. 2009. http://archive.ias.unu.edu/resource_centre/161%20Terry%20McGee.pdf, accessed 26 Oct. 2016.

Ocampo, Ambeth. "Bohol and the Blood Compact." *Philippine Daily Inquirer*, 18 Oct. 2013. http://opinion.inquirer.net/63541/bohol-and-the-blood-compact, accessed 14 Sept. 2016.

Office of the President. "Official Month in Review: March 1954." *OG* 50 (3), 1954: lxv–xcii. http://www.gov.ph/1954/03/01/official-month-in-review-march-1954/, accessed 24 Aug. 2016.

———. "Official Month in Review: February 1955." *OG* 51 (2), 1955: liii–xci. http://www.gov.ph/1955/02/01/official-month-in-review-february-1955/, accessed 24 Aug. 2016.

———. "Official Week in Review: June 16 – June 30, 1966." *OG* 62 (31), 1966: cclxi–cclxxvii. http://www.gov.ph/1966/08/01/official-week-in-review-june-16-june-30-1966/, accessed 5 Nov. 2016.

Philippine Commonwealth. Commonwealth Act No. 457 – An Act to Further Section One of Act Numbered Thirty-Five Hundred and Ninety-Seven, as Amended, 8 June 1939. *Chan Robles Virtual Law Library*. http://laws.chanrobles.com/commonwealthacts/2_commonwealthacts.php?id=83, accessed 7 Nov. 2016.

———. Commonwealth Act No. 502: An Act to Create Quezon City, 12 Oct. 1939. *Chan Robles Virtual Law Library*. http://www.chanrobles.com/commonwealthactno502.htm#.UIDpYmcv8sE, accessed 18 Oct 2012.

Philippine Congress. Republic Act 54: An Act to Repeal Executive Order Numbered Four Hundred Dated January Two Nineteen Hundred and Forty-Two and Executive Order Numbered Fifty-Eight Dated July Twenty-Six, Nineteen Hundred and Forty-Five, 10 Oct. 1946. *Chan Robles Virtual Law Library*. http://laws.chanrobles.com/republicacts/1_republicacts.php?id=54, accessed 3 Nov. 2016.

———. Republic Act 333 – An Act to Establish the Capital of the Philippines and the Permanent Seat of the National Government, 17 July 1948. *Official Gazette (OG)*. http://www.gov.ph/1948/07/17/republic-act-no-333/, accessed 27 Oct. 2015.

———. Republic Act 2140 – An Act Changing the Name of Highway 54 in the Province of Rizal to Epifanio de los Santos Avenue in Honor of Don Epifanio de los Santos, a Filipino Scholar, Jurist, and Historian, 7 Apr. 1959. *Chan Robles Virtual Law Library*. http://www.chanrobles.com/republicacts/republicactno2140.html#.WBQNVPp96Uk, accessed 29 Oct. 2016.

———. Republic Act 2259: An Act Making Elective the Offices of Mayor, Vice-Mayor and Councilors in Chartered Cities, Regulating the Election in Such Cities and Fixing the Salaries and Tenure of Such Offices, 19 June 1959. *The Lawphil Project*. http://www.lawphil.net/statutes/repacts/ra1959/ra_2259_1959.html, accessed 10 Sept. 2016.

"Philippines Population 2016." *World Population Review*. http:// worldpopulationreview.com/countries/philippines-population/, accessed 26 Oct. 2016.

Quezon, Manuel L. EO 400, s. 1942, Creating the City of Greater Manila, 1 Jan. 1942, Malacañang Records Office. http://www.gov.ph/1942/01/01/executive-order-no-400-s-1942/, accessed 8 Sept. 2016.

"Quezon City Rolls out Plans for 'Future Perfect' Diamond Jubilee Celebration." *Philippine Star,* 3 Apr. 2014. http://www.philstar.com/food-and-leisure/2014/04/03/1308011/quezon-city-rolls-out-plans-future-perfect-diamond-jubilee, accessed 15 Mar. 2016.

Roxas, Manuel A. "Third State of the Nation Address, January 26, 1948: The Nation on the Road to Prosperity." *Official Gazette (OG).* http://www.gov.ph/1948/01/26/manuel-roxas-the-nation-on-the-road-to-prosperity-third-state-of-the-nation-address-january-26-1948/, accessed 27 Oct. 2015.

Santos, Reynaldo, Jr. "1986 Comelec Walkout Not about Cory or Marcos." *Rappler,* 25 Feb. 2013. http://www.rappler.com/nation/politics/elections-2013/22582-1986-comelec-walkout-not-about-cory-or-marcos, accessed 4 Sept. 2016.

Schatz, Edward. "When Capital Cities Move: The Political Geography of Nation and State Building." The Helen Kellogg Institute for International Studies Working Paper #303, 2003. https://kellogg.nd.edu/publications/workingpapers/WPS/303.pdf, accessed 17 Aug. 2014.

Segundo, Fidel. Diary of Fidel Segundo, 3 Apr. 1940, *The Philippine Diary Project.* http://philippinediaryproject.com/1940/04/03/wednesday-april-3-1940/, accessed 27 Aug. 2016.

Supreme Court, en banc. "Sy Chiuco vs. Collector of Internal Revenue," G. R. no. L-13387, 28 Mar. 1960, *The Lawphil Project.* http://www.lawphil.net/judjuris/juri1960/mar1960/gr_l-13387_1960.html, accessed 18 May 2015.

——, en banc. "Pedro Casimiro vs. Leon Roque and Ernesto Gonzales," G. R. no. L-7643, 27 Apr. 1956, *The Lawphil Project.* http://www.lawphil.net/judjuris/juri1956/apr1956/gr_l-7643_1956.html, accessed 14 Sept. 2016.

——, en banc. "Vicente Fragante vs. PHHC," G. R. no. L-16020, 30 Jan. 1962, *Chan Robles Virtual Law Library.* http://www.chanrobles.com/scdecisions/jurisprudence1962/jan1962/gr_l-16020_1962.php, accessed 28 Aug. 2016.

——, en banc, "Constancio Joaquin vs. Godofredo B. Herrera, Lope K. Santos and the Provincial Board of Rizal, and Jose Javier," G.R. no. L-11217, 28 Feb. 1918. *The Lawphil Project.* http://www.lawphil.net/judjuris/juri1918/feb1918/gr_l-11217_1918.html, accessed 7 Nov. 2016.

——, first division. "La Vista Association, Inc. vs. Court of Appeals, et al," G. R. no. 95252, 5 Sept. 1997. http://sc.judiciary.gov.ph/jurisprudence/1997/sep1997/95252.htm, accessed 30 Nov. 2015.

University of the Philippines Board of Regents. *The University of the Philippines Gazette,* vol. 46, no. 5: *Decisions of the Board of Regents, 1318th Meeting, 27 May 2016.* Quezon City: Office of the Secretary, UP, 2016. http://osu.up.edu.ph/wp-content/uploads/2016/08/1318-GAZETTE.pdf, accessed 28 Aug. 2016.

Index

1901 charter of Manila (Act 183), 30, 248
1935 Constitution, 52, 91
1941 Philippine International Exposition, 82, 83
1942 Executive Order, 115
1949 Quezon City Master Plan, 17, 195, 250

A

Abrams, Charles, 11, 64, 157, 164
ABS-CBN, 176, 179
Acro Taxicab Co., 88
Act No. 1841 of 1908, 120
activism, 92, 210–12, 233, 252
Acuña, Sebastián Pérez de, 24
Addition Hills, 40, 46, 51, 53
agrarian unrest, 46, 54, 61, 112, 157, 249
Aguilar, Eusebio, 94
Aguinaldo, Emilio, 30, 46, 50, 70–72, 235, 270n102
Alabang, 75, 280n82
Algabre, Salud, 315
Ali Mall, 316
American Chamber of Commerce (ACC), 42–43
American colonial period, 3, 33–34, 65, 248, 263n18. *See also* American period
American period, 50, 56. *See also* American colonial period
Amilbangsa, S. Ombra, 157
Amoranto, Norberto, 201, 208, 213, 215
ancien régime, 9, 210
Angara, Edgardo, 233
Angat River Dam, 122
Anonas, 239
Antipolo, 22, 28, 119–20, 128, 207
Antonino, Magnolia, 172
Aquino, Alex, 211
Aquino, Corazon "Cory" Cojuangco, 170, 243, 252

Aquino Jr, Benigno "Ninoy", 147, 170, 242, 251
Aquino Sr, Benigno, 49, 143
Araneta Avenue, 129, 208
Araneta Center, 2, 147, 173–75, 316n152
Araneta Coliseum, 146–47, 173, 235, 297n195, 316n152
Araneta (family), 131, 173, 176, 179, 203, 235, 249, 252, 303n112, 315n135
Araneta, J. Amado "Amading", 146–47, 297n193, 318n176
Araneta, Salvador, 124, 224
Araneta subdivision, 155
Arceo, Liwayway, 237
architecture, 8, 10, 13, 26, 33, 85, 114, 127, 130, 147, 151, 182, 219–20, 253, 256
Arellano, Juan, 63, 80, 124, 130, 132, 151, 170
Arguelles, Carlos, 130, 182
Arias, Vicente, 72
Armed Forces of the Philippines (AFP), 2, 154
arrabal, 19, 21–22, 25–27, 29–30, 34, 55, 59, 148
Arranz, Melecio, 119, 143–44
Artiaga, Santiago, 43
artificiality, 7–8, 12, 148
Asistio, Macario B., 135, 137
Ateneo de Manila, 15, 130, 140–41, 172, 210–12, 236, 238, 243, 245, 250, 302n92
Augustinian (order), 21–22, 24–25, 46, 48–49, 263n17
Aurora (province), 64
Aurora Boulevard, 175–76, 214, 240, 242
authoritarianism, 7, 52, 62, 91, 231, 251, 253
Avelino, Jose, 143
Avenida de Rizal (Rizal Avenue), 35, 249
Ayala (family), 14
Ayala Technohub, 256
Azcarraga (Calle), 26

B

Baclaran, 54

Bacolod, 93
Baculinao, Ericson, 209–10
Baesa, 106, 135, 185
Bagbag, 135, 187
Bago Bantay, 28, 76, 160, 163, 185, 190–93, 195, 198
Bago Bantay Transmitter Area, 154
Bagong Barangay Housing Project, 159
Bagong Buhay Confederation, 165–66
Bagong Lipunan Sites and Services (BLISS), 217–18
Bagong Pag-asa, 160, 185, 192, 194–95
Baguio, 75, 81, 92, 96, 119–20, 128, 221, 284n146
Bagumbayan (Manila), 107, 109, 288n21
Bagumbayan (Quezon City), 122, 186, 231–32
Bagumbuhay, 107, 109, 288n21
Bagumpanahon, 107, 109, 288n21
Bagungdiwa, 107, 109, 288n21
bahay na bato, 26, 68
bailarina, 55–56
Balara, 29, 98, 122, 140–41, 155, 185, 211, 233, 265n36, 287n190
Balara Filters, 140
Balara Filters Park, 123
Baler, 63–64, 68–71, 155
Balete Drive, 103–4, 172, 318n174
Balintawak, 44–45, 72, 76, 97–98, 107, 109–10, 122, 173, 185, 236, 265n36, 287n190
Balintawak Cloverleaf (Balintawak Interchange), 2, 222
Balintawak Estate, 71–73
Balintawak Estate Corporation, 279n61
Balintawak Market, 222
Balut, 157
Balweg, Conrado, 241, 319n185
Bangkusay, 157
Banlat, 98, 135
Bantayog ng mga Bayani, 251
Baranca, 122. See also Barangka
barangay, 20, 107, 155
Barangka, 78. See also Baranca
Barilan, 122
Barrio Obrero (Kamuning), 90, 166, 283n139
barrio obrero (Tondo), 35
Barrio Vitas, 35
Basa, Jesus, 137
Bataan, 65, 118–19
Batasang Pambansa, 2, 217, 227, 231, 243, 316n137
Batasan Hills, 2, 251, 256
Battle for Manila, 128

Bautista, Herbert, 247
Belden, Henry, 172
Bell Mission, 163, 300n46
Bell Trade Act, 131
Beltran, Crispin, 232, 316n137
Benedicto, Roberto S., 91–92, 285n158
Benitez, Conrado, 94
Benton, Guy Potter, 75
Bernal, Ishmael, 237, 261n49
Bernardo, Gabriel, 153, 155
Binondo, 22, 26–28, 30, 34, 38, 50, 142, 172, 237
Biñan, 25
Blue Ridge, 183
Bocobo, Jorge, 92, 284n152
Bohol Avenue, 176, 303n103
Bonifacio, Andrés, 28, 45, 98, 107
Bonifacio Global City, 5, 255
Bonifacio Road, 135
border, 10–12, 17, 42, 44, 56, 80, 99, 133, 145, 148–149, 152, 220, 248, 250, 274n160
border area, 11, 99
border town, 55, 106
border zone, 1, 3, 10–13, 19, 57–61, 101–102, 105, 142–44, 146, 149, 248, 254
borderland, 11
Bosoboso, 28
boundary, 7, 10–11, 13, 18, 26, 30, 33, 42, 54, 56, 58, 61, 105, 110, 120, 124, 126, 133, 135, 142, 144–45, 148, 172, 237, 243, 248, 254
British occupation, 25, 50
Broadway Avenue, 49, 88, 110, 171
Brocka, Lino, 237, 249, 261n49
Buencamino, Victor, 69
buffer zone, 5, 10–11, 140, 152, 249
Bulacan, 2, 13, 25, 30, 39, 52, 120, 122, 138, 140, 142, 192, 225
Burnham, Daniel, 33, 84, 151
Burnham plan, 33, 37, 42, 62–63, 75, 120
Buscayno, Bernabe, 210

C

cabaret, 13, 19, 55–58, 68, 98–100, 102, 145–46, 149, 248, 274n158, 275n174
Cabarroguis, Leon C., 118, 284n146
Cabili, Tomas, 135
Cagayan, 221
Caloocan, 22, 25, 27–28, 37, 39–40, 42–44, 52, 57, 73, 77–78, 96, 99–100, 106–7, 109, 112, 129, 135, 137, 140, 142–144, 148–49, 157, 177–78, 192, 214, 216, 223, 228, 233, 248–49, 265n36, 269n92
Camp Aguinaldo, 2, 235–236, 243–244

Camp Crame, 2, 78, 81, 154, 184, 211, 236, 244
Camp Eldrige, 75
Camp Murphy, 80, 100, 114, 154, 184, 196, 235, 273n145
Campos, Inocente, 209
Canlubang, 119
capital city, 1, 3, 7–8, 13, 17–18, 33, 45, 62–63, 72, 84, 87, 101–2, 105–6, 114, 118, 120, 124, 127, 134–35, 138, 140, 145–46, 148, 152, 156, 190, 203, 206, 221, 223, 246–47, 249, 251–54, 260n41, 282n103, 296n182
Capital City Planning Commission, 124, 130, 170
Capitol Site Club, 128
Capitol Site Selection Committee, 119
Carmona, 198
Carmona, Vicente, 73
Carpenter Estate, 50
Carpenter, Frank, 50, 144, 271n119
Carroll, Earl, 180, 182–83, 190
carromata, 26, 58, 110
carruaje, 26
Casiana cronies, 94
Catholic Bishops Conference of the Philippines, 241
Cavite, 25, 46, 75, 93, 198, 230, 265n36, 272n137, 296n182
Cebu, 20, 93, 95, 174, 256, 279n63
Cenacle Retreat House, 243
Central, 185
central business district, 5, 26, 255
Central Intelligence Agency (CIA), 154, 180, 213
Chico River Dam, 241
Chinese Cemetery, 28, 57
Christ the King Seminary, 110, 239, 241–42
Circumferential Road, 91
Circumferential Road 3 (C3), 129
Circumferential Road 4 (C4), 107, 129
Circumferential Road 5 (C5), 129
Citizens League for Good Government, 250
city, 6, 14, 76, 147, 151, 179, 250, 256; chartered, 92–95, 200, 285n165; global, 247, 256; imagined, 76; industrial, 9; invented, 76; market port, 7; modern, 226; open, 106; planned, 8, 248; post-suburban, 10; primate, 14, 17, 21, 25, 114, 261; sacred inland, 7, 20; unplanned, 7, 8
City Beautiful, 33, 63, 84, 151
City of Greater Manila, 106, 115
City of Man, 220–21, 226
ciudad, 21

civitas, 76
cockfighting, 55, 58, 146–47, 297
cockpit, 13, 55–58, 98–99, 102, 145–46, 149, 248
Cold War, 7, 17–18, 151–53, 155, 157–58, 162, 182, 201, 213, 254, 299
colonialism, 8, 12, 17, 20–21, 30, 35, 45, 48, 52, 55, 65, 85, 109; Spanish, 12, 17, 20, 55; US, 30, 48, 55, 109
commercial hub, 13, 235
Commission on Elections (Comelec), 243
Committee on Anti-Filipino Activities, 153
Committee on Capital City Site, 16, 119, 121, 124, 127–28, 134–35, 143–44, 148
Commonwealth Act No. 502 (CA 502), 76
Commonwealth Act No. 659 (CA 659), 78
Commonwealth Avenue, 2, 125, 224, 232
Commonwealth government, 35, 54, 61–63, 73, 80–81, 90–91, 93, 113
Commonwealth period, 3, 17, 62, 94, 101–2, 201, 285
Communist Party of the Philippines (CPP), 205, 252
Compañía Agricola de Ultramar, 49
Constitution Hill, 2, 125–27, 198, 223–24, 227, 229, 231–33, 245–46, 251
Constitution Hills Committee, 232
consumerism, 19
consumption, 19, 36, 52, 61, 70, 73, 109, 128, 202–3, 248, 250, 254, 256
Cordner, G. F., 163–65
Corinthian Gardens, 183–84, 235, 248, 250
Corpuz, Jose, 157
Corregidor, 105, 118
corta fuego, 26, 34
Council of War, 105
criminality, 55, 214, 248, 273n144
Croft, Louis, 80, 128, 133, 163, 293n109
Cruz, Florencio, 106–7
Cruz, Jose, 211
Cruz na Ligas, 122. See also Krus na Ligas
Cry of Balintawak, 28, 98, 107
Cry of Pugad Lawin, 28
Cubao, 2, 77, 107, 111, 122, 136, 140, 173, 175–76, 185, 221–22, 232, 235–37, 244, 246, 306n166, 316n152
Cubao Heights, 40, 46
Culiat, 122, 142
Cultural Center of the Philippines (CCP), 220, 225
Cuneta, Pablo, 215

D

Damar Village, 172
Dancel, Arturo, 46, 49–50, 271n117
Dansalan, 93. *See* Marawi
Dario River, 198
Dasmariñas (Cavite), 230
Dasmariñas Village (Makati), 180, 304
Davao, 93, 95, 193
Davis, Dwight F., 42
de Guzman-Lingat, Rosario, 237–38, 249
de la Rama, Francisco C., 144
de Leon, Narcisa "Sisang", 49
decolonization, 7, 147–48, 151–52
del Pilar, Marcelo H., 8, 64
Delaney, John P., 153
Demerath, N. J., 163
democratization, 17, 33, 44–45, 52, 61, 75, 179, 202, 250
Department of Agriculture and Natural Resources (DANR), 223–24
desakota, 9, 259n24
Diaz, Ignacio Santos, 115, 155–56
Diaz, Manuel, 94–95
Diliman, 1–2, 18, 30, 44, 48–51, 55, 74, 76–77, 87–88, 90, 92, 94–95, 99, 102, 106–7, 109–10, 115–17, 130, 132–33, 136, 142–43, 149, 152, 155, 179, 185, 190, 205, 207–8, 212, 227, 239, 246, 250, 290n58
Diliman Commune, 209–13, 246, 309n14
Diliman quadrangle, 80, 82, 125, 159, 180, 191, 198–99, 222
Diokno, Jose, 172
Diokno, Ramon, 135
domestication, 17, 44–45, 61, 250
Dominican (order), 21–22, 24, 46, 173, 238, 244
Doña Imelda, 172
Doña Josefa, 172
Down from the Hill Manifesto, 211
Dulag, Macli-ing, 241
DZBB, 176

E

Eastwood City, 255–56
Echagüe, Rafaél, 27
Economic Cooperation Administration (ECA), 162
EDSA Shrine, 245, 251
Eisenhower, Dwight, 154, 286
elite, 8, 16–17, 19, 24, 34–35, 37, 40, 44–45, 48–49, 51–52, 59, 62, 64–65, 70, 88, 96, 101–2, 128, 131, 138, 147–49, 156, 171, 180,

183–84, 210, 235, 237, 249–50, 270n102, 277n14, 278n41, 304n116, 307n185
Elliot, Charles Edward, 75
Elliptical Road, 1, 2, 224
Elser, H. W., 46
Encarnacion, Vicente Singson, 72, 279n61, 283n132, 285n161
Engineering and Architectural Mission of the Philippines, 124–25, 130
Enrile, Juan Ponce, 184, 234, 243–44, 249, 251
Epifanio de los Santos Avenue (EDSA), 2, 129, 195, 207–8, 221–22, 240, 244–46
Episcopal Church, 241
Ermita, 8, 22, 28, 34–35, 37–38, 40, 63, 75, 80, 115, 260n40
E. Rodriguez Avenue, 110, 241–42
Escolta, 26, 249
Escopa, 186, 190, 196–97, 229
España Boulevard, 133
España Extension, 99, 110
estero, 21, 157, 197, 230, 238
Estrella, Conrado, 234
evangelization, 20, 22
Extramuros, 17, 21–22, 59, 248

F

Felipe, Gregorio, 106–7
Fernandez, Ramón, 42
Filinvest Corporate City, 255
Filipinization, 211
First Quarter Storm (FQS), 205, 208, 212, 214, 237, 242, 308n1
folklore, 103, 320n5
Forbes Park, 169, 180, 235, 304n117
Foreign Operations Administration (FOA), 162–63
Fort McKinley, 119
Fragante, Vicente, 74, 94, 165
Franciscan (order), 21–22, 24, 48, 263n18
friar estate, 3, 17, 20, 24, 45–46, 50, 52, 61, 263n17
Friar Lands Act, 46, 49–52, 271
Frieder, Alex, 111
fringe belt, 11
Frost, Harry T., 80–81, 90, 124, 128, 130
Frost plan, 80–81
Fugoso, 157

G

Gabriel Estate, 192, 195
Gagalañgin, 106
Galarraga, Pedro, 25

Galas, 99, 102, 107, 122, 185
galleon trade, 21–22, 26, 50
gambling, 11, 55–57, 98–99, 145, 297n193
Garcia, Carlos P., 169, 215
gated community, 18, 180–81, 201, 234
gender, 189–90, 236, 251
Gilmore Street, 172, 239
Gilmore, Eugene A., 42, 269n87
Gokhale, Vishnu, 153
Gonzalez, Bienvenido, 116, 170
Gonzalez, Florencio, 46
Gouger, Earl, 163
Government Service Insurance System (GSIS), 169, 179, 222
Grace Christian School, 172
Grace Park, 135, 142, 157
Grace Village, 172
Grayson, William, 44
greater Manila, 43, 59, 61, 107, 109–10, 145, 157, 176–77, 190, 193, 205–6, 210, 215–16, 269
greater Manila area (GMA), 152, 213, 216
Greenmeadows, 183
Gregorio Araneta, Inc., 40, 51, 88, 171, 179
guerrilla, 17, 44–45, 65, 110–13, 138, 145, 212, 232, 269n98
Guinto, Leon G., 106, 109

H

hacienda, 24, 28, 45–46, 48, 50–51, 59, 67, 71, 74, 96, 107, 143, 158, 225, 264n23, 270n162, 296n181
Hacienda de Diliman, 50–51, 73–74, 96, 122, 249
Hacienda de Magdalena, 49. *See also* Magdalena Estate
Hacienda de Payatas, 50, 271n118
Hacienda de Piedad, 25, 49, 271n118. *See also* Piedad
Hacienda de Tala, 24, 39, 50, 54, 144, 263. *See also* Tala
Halili Bus Company, 193
Halili Transit Company, 88
Hare–Hawes–Cutting Act (HHC), 279n65, 284n152
Harrison, Francis Burton, 42, 54, 58, 96
Harvey, David, 6, 255
health, 5, 15, 21, 33, 37, 40, 56, 79, 86, 94, 119, 122–23, 127–28, 131, 137, 222, 268n72
Hemady, K. H., 49
Hemady, Magdalena Ysmael, 49
Hemady Avenue, 172
Hernando, Eugenio, 74

Heroes' Hill, 154
Herrera, Arsenio Cruz, 30
Highway 54, 129, 207–8, 293n113
Hillcrest, 232
historical geography, 3, 5, 19, 149, 249, 251–52, 256
historiography, 7, 14–15
Home for Refugees, 111
Hoskins, C. M., 72
housing, 5, 18, 60, 63, 74–76, 85–86, 88, 90, 110, 114, 131, 151–52, 156–59, 162–65, 168, 170, 172–73, 179, 182, 184, 193, 195, 197, 201–2, 205, 218, 220, 229, 254
housing project, 2, 5, 13, 16, 18, 35, 75, 151, 154, 158–59, 162, 165, 168, 170, 172, 180–82, 184, 191, 201, 217–18, 249–50, 283n139
Hukbong Bayan Laban sa Hapon (HUKBALA-HAP), 112
Huk (under HUKBALAHAP), 138, 140, 142, 152, 156–57, 182, 195, 202, 207, 232, 249, 255
Human Settlements Development Corporation, 217

I

Ilocos, 221, 279n61
Iloilo, 93, 119
ilustrado, 8, 64, 201, 258n20
imagined community, 85
import-substitution industrialization (ISI), 156, 175–77, 298n21
inequality, 40, 52, 202, 226, 248, 254
informal settlement, 13, 35, 63, 90, 152, 157, 202, 206–8, 223, 225, 231, 251
informal settler, 35, 96, 149, 163, 191–92, 195, 198, 201–23, 227, 229, 251, 256
infrastructure, 11, 26, 76, 86, 97, 114, 156, 169, 193, 207, 253
Institute of National Language, 62
insurrecto, 65
Inter-Agency Committee on Metropolitan Manila (IACMM), 215–16
International Monetary Fund (IMF), 229
Intramuros, 8, 17, 19, 21–23, 25–27, 29–30, 33–35, 38, 59, 129, 133, 140, 173, 180, 191–92, 220
Ipo, 119–20, 127

J

J. M. Tuason and Co., Inc., 179
Jacinto, Nicanor, 128
Japanese occupation, 18, 103, 105–6, 109, 112–13, 145, 304n126

jeprox, 151, 203, 297
Jesuit, 21–22, 24–25, 110, 140–41, 153, 173, 210–11, 263n16, 310n23, 318n176
Jesus de la Peña, 77–78
Joaquin, Nick, 237, 249, 261n49
Joint US Military Advisory Group (JUSMAG), 114, 154
Jollibee, 175
Jones, H. M., 37
Jones Law, 66, 68, 72
Jopson, Edgar, 184, 235, 251
Jose Abad Santos Memorial School, 182
Jose, F. Sionil, 237, 249
Juan Ysmael Company, 87
Jurado, Emil, 184

K

Kabataang Makabayan (KM), 205, 211, 239
Kabuyao, 135
Kalayaan Avenue, 162
Kalipunang Makabayan ng mga Pilipino (Makapili), 110
Kamarin, 192–93
Kamias, 239
Kamuning, 88, 90, 110, 122, 159, 165–66, 186, 190, 200
Kamuning Road, 166
Kangkong, 97–98, 102
Kapisanan ng mga Brodkaster sa Pilipinas, 184
Karingal, Tomas, 210
Katipunan, 28, 107, 140, 236, 255
Katipunan Avenue, 129, 140, 211, 242
Kilusang Mayo Uno (May First Movement), 235
Koenigsberger, Otto, 164
Krus na Ligas, 55, 98, 140, 287n190, 290n61. *See also* Cruz na Ligas
Kuhlman, Richard N., 163

L

La Loma, 28, 44, 57, 76, 99, 102, 106–7, 122, 142, 146, 149, 179, 186, 248, 275n173, 275n174, 297n201
La Loma Cabaret, 145
La Loma Cemetery, 28, 110
La Loma Cockpit, 57
La Mesa, 138
La Mesa Dam, 122, 128
La Mesa Dam Park, 123
La Mesa watershed, 122

La Vanguardia, 72
La Vista, 173, 234
labor, 27, 35, 138, 184, 190, 195, 205, 231, 235–36, 239, 249, 254, 256, 259n24, 319n185, 320n5
Lacaba, Emmanuel, 211
Lacson, Arsenio, 169, 191, 215, 249
ladrones, 44, 54
Laguna, 22, 25, 52, 138, 198, 207
laissez-faire, 8
Lakbayan, 242
Lansdale, Edward, 154
Las Piñas, 27–28, 42, 110, 214, 216, 228, 230
Lava, Jesus, 153
Lava, Jose, 153
Lava, Vicente, 153
law enforcement, 98–99
layout, 7–8, 10, 21, 79, 84, 129, 148, 161
Le Corbusier, 151
Ledesma, Oscar, 172
Lefebvre, Henri, 6
Legazpi, Miguel López de, 20
Legazpi Village, 180
Lerma Cabaret, 57
Leyte, 184, 189, 305
Liberal Party (LP), 114, 134, 136–37, 143, 145
Liberty gang, 57
Libis, 244
Licaros, Gregorio, 234
Lichauco, Maur Aquino, 49
Light-a-Fire Movement (LAFM), 239
Local Autonomy Act of 1959 (RA 2264), 215
local government, 16, 56, 58, 98, 106, 131, 137, 214–15, 224, 229–31, 250
Lopez (family), 203, 249, 252
Lopez, Salvador, 210, 213, 224
Los Baños, 75, 119
low-cost housing (LCH), 13, 16–18, 75, 86, 151–52, 158–60, 162, 164–65, 168–69, 172, 182, 190, 197, 199, 202
Loyola Grand Villas, 173
Loyola Heights, 130, 141–42, 173, 185, 211, 233
Loyola House of Studies, 241, 243
Lung Center of the Philippines, 222
Luzon, 2, 9, 20, 28, 35, 112, 138, 142, 153, 155–56, 170, 184, 241–42, 249, 269n98, 282n108, 313n73

M

M. Morelos and Sons, Inc., 170
Macapagal, Diosdado, 169, 179, 200, 303n114
MacArthur, Douglas, 81, 95, 106, 286n173

Madrigal, Vicente, 48, 65, 270n108, 279n59, 279n81, 283n132
Magallanes Village, 180, 304n116
Magdalena Estate, 49, 72–74, 87–88, 96, 111, 270n112, 282n110. *See also* Hacienda de Magdalena
Magsaysay, Ambrosio, 74
Magsaysay, Ramon, 154, 170, 200, 215, 223–24
Maharlika, 172
Makati, 2, 5, 10, 13, 36, 39, 42–43, 54, 57, 68, 106–7, 109, 129, 169, 177, 180, 184, 201, 214, 216, 225, 228, 230, 235, 242, 249, 255–56. *See also* San Pedro Macati
Malabon, 37, 39–40, 43, 52, 54, 112, 173, 214, 228, 230. *See also* Tambobong
Malacañang, 27, 49, 63, 70, 73, 87, 134–35, 165, 169, 205, 212, 224–25, 238, 246, 255, 264n31, 310n27
Malamig, 122, 187
malaria, 114, 137–39
Malate, 8, 22, 28, 34, 37–38, 40, 191, 268n70, 288n21
Malaya Avenue, 161
Malaya Subdivision, 161
Malcolm, George, 58
Malibay, 27–28, 272n137
Malinta, 39, 46, 48
Malitlit, 122
Manalo, Felix, 49
Mandaloya Estate, 48, 72–74, 80, 96, 263, 279
Mandaluyong, 22, 36, 37, 39, 42–43, 52, 54, 59, 70, 72–73, 78, 80, 106–7, 109, 112, 129, 177, 214, 216, 228, 230, 255, 263n17, 275n173. *See also* San Felipe Neri
Manila, 1, 2, 5, 12, 17, 18, 20, 22, 23, 25, 28–31, 34–38, 43–45, 47, 52, 54, 56–57, 59–61, 64–65, 68, 73–76, 79–80, 84–85, 88, 92, 95–96, 99, 101–3, 105–7, 109–10, 113, 115, 117–18, 120, 129, 132–33, 135, 140, 142–43, 145, 148, 152, 156–59, 162–63, 172, 175–77, 184, 191, 194–95, 199, 205, 207, 211–16, 220, 223, 225, 227–30, 232, 238–39, 241, 245–46, 248, 250, 252, 256, 259n24, 260n40, 261n49, 263n17
Manila Bay, 21, 37, 118, 220
Manila Electric Railroad and Light Company (Meralco), 34, 201
Manila North Cemetery, 226
Manila Railroad Company, 74
Manila Times, 71–72
Manresa Site, 171
Marawi, 93

Marcos era, 3, 18, 184, 203, 205, 207, 212, 219, 220, 222, 227, 229, 243, 246–47, 251–52
Marcos (family), 18, 217–22, 226, 229, 235–36, 243, 313n73, 313n90, 319n189
Marcos, Ferdinand, 18, 205, 211, 213–18, 222–23, 226, 231, 235, 241, 246, 252
Marcos, Imelda, 216–18, 220–22, 225, 229, 243
marginalization, 57, 59, 138
Marikina, 17, 22, 27, 49, 50, 63, 69–70, 73, 75–78, 96, 105, 111, 137, 177, 214, 228, 230, 234, 263n16. *See also* Mariquina
Marikina River, 137–38, 140. *See also* Mariquina River
Marikina Valley, 22, 140, 225
Mariquina, 28, 48, 51, 76, 100, 263n16, 281n88. *See also* Marikina
Mariquina River, 70. *See also* Marikina River
Marsch Estate, 172
martial law, 151, 184, 214–17, 219, 221, 224–28, 232–37, 240, 242, 246, 249, 285n158, 309n8, 309n12, 311n43, 312n54, 316n145
Martínez, Miguel, 24
Maryknoll, 172–73, 211, 302
Masambong, 76, 112, 122
Massey, Doreen, 6
Masterson, SJ, William, 140
Matalahib, 122, 187
Mathay, Jr., Ismael, 216, 312
mayorazgo, 50
Maypajo Cabaret, 57
Maysilo Estate, 48, 74
Mendiola, 212, 225, 244–45, 310, 317
Metro Manila, 1–5, 8, 14–15, 18, 123, 216, 218, 221–22, 228–31, 233, 239, 241–43, 254–55, 261n50, 309n8, 321n10, 322n31
Metropolitan Command (Metrocom), 209–11, 213–14, 216, 230, 233
Metropolitan Manila Commission (MMC), 216, 218, 220, 229–30, 243
Metropolitan Manila Flood Control and Drainage Council (MMFCDC), 215–16
Metropolitan Police Force (Metropol), 214
Metropolitan Theater, 220
Metropolitan Transportation Service (METRAN), 193
Metropolitan Water District (MWD), 122–23, 138, 140
Middleton, George F., 164
migrant, 5, 9, 13, 26, 34, 143, 152, 156–57, 184, 188, 190, 202, 225, 305n143
migration, 9, 26, 110, 152, 156, 184, 305n143
Mijares, Primitivo, 234

Military Bases Agreement, 154
Ministry of Human Settlements (MHS), 216–18, 229, 233
Missionary Sisters of the Immaculate Heart of Mary, 173
Mitra, Ramon, 90
mobility, 21, 26–27, 58, 217, 277n14, 322n31
modernism, 130
modernity, 147, 176, 191, 195, 234, 294n148, 321n17
modernization, 13, 152, 156
monpai, 107
Montalban, 22, 27, 29, 45, 50, 52, 112, 119, 122, 137, 140, 149
Morató, Tomás, 68, 93–94, 107, 112
Morelos Housing Project, 170, 189
Moro National Liberation Front (MNLF), 205
Morong, 22, 25, 27, 29, 33
morphology, 3, 7–8, 21, 25–26, 85, 203, 252, 264n26
mujeres publicas, 55
Muntinlupa, 27–28, 228, 230, 255
Murphy, 122, 186
Murphy, Frank, 49
Mutual Security Agency (MSA), 162–63, 165
myth, 103, 219

N

Nacionalista Party (NP), 114, 135–36, 147, 290. *See also* Partido Nacionalista
Nagcarlan, 119
Nagtahan, 172, 191
Nakpil, Angel, 182
National Assembly, 65, 73, 76, 91, 93
National Development Company (NDC), 73
National Economic Council, 62
National Economic Protectionism Association, 62
National Government Center (NGC), 224–25, 232, 241, 256
National Housing Authority (NHA), 217, 229–30, 233
National Housing Commission (NHC), 158
National Kidney and Transplant Institute, 222
National Planning Commission (NPC), 215
National Urban Planning Commission, 128
nationalism, 8, 62, 110, 219–20, 253, 276n3, 321n17; official, 5, 8, 62, 85, 101, 248
nation-state, 3, 5, 7–8, 13, 21, 61, 82–83, 101, 125, 140, 152, 156, 245, 252
Navotas, 22, 27–28, 37, 39–40, 43, 52, 112, 214, 228, 230

Negros, 88
Nemenzo, Francisco, 140
New Manila, 40, 49, 87–88, 103, 110, 171, 176–77, 186, 189, 239, 243, 248, 269n87
New People's Army (NPA), 205, 210, 241
New Society, 215, 226
Ninoy Aquino International Airport, 2
North Avenue, 2, 208
North Cemetery, 275n173
North Luzon Expressway, 222
North Triangle, 195, 208, 256
Novaliches, 2–3, 22, 27, 29, 39, 45, 49–50, 54, 75, 106, 110, 112, 119–23, 127–28, 135–38, 140, 149, 155, 186, 190, 231, 249
Novaliches Poblacion, 135
Novaliches Subdivision, 192
Novaliches watershed, 122, 192
Nueno, Jose Topacio, 143–44

O

Oblation, 117
Olalia, Felixberto, 235
Old Balara, 233
Oppus, Tomas, 99
Orense, Eusebio, 46
Ortigas and Company, 48
Ortigas Center, 5, 255
Ortigas & Fisher, 48
Ortigas, Francisco, 48, 65, 72, 270n108
Ortigas, Julia Vargas, 270n108
Osmeña, Sergio, 8, 65–66, 80, 113, 128, 163
Our Lady of EDSA Shrine, 2–3, 252

P

Pacific War, 19, 34, 57. *See also* Second World War, World War II
Packer, Dean Paul C., 75
Paco, 22, 28, 37–38
Paco Park, 220
Padre Faura, 140
Paez, Jose, 74, 94, 119
Pag-asa, 218
Palacio, Perfecto R., 94
Palacio del Gobernador, 27
Palma, Cecilia Muñoz, 172
Palomar, 157
Pampanga, 71, 96, 156–57, 195
Panay, 20
Pandacan, 27–28, 38, 159
Pandacan Oil Depot, 208
Panel on Flood Control and Damage, 215

Pangkalahatang Sanggunian [General Council of] Manila and Suburbs Drivers Association, 208
Pansol, 122
Parañaque, 27–28, 42–43, 106–7, 109, 122, 214, 216, 228, 230, 303*n*106
Paredes, Quintin, 172
Parian, 22
Parsons, William, 62, 80, 84, 151
Partido Democrata, 43
Partido Demokratikong Sosyalista ng Pilipinas, 318*n*176
Partido Federal, 50, 65
Partido Komunista ng Pilipinas (Communist Party of the Philippines; PKP), 153–54, 308*n*2
Partido Nacionalista, 43, 65, 113, 290*n*45. *See also* Nacionalista Party
Pasay, 2, 17, 22, 28, 34, 36, 39–40, 42–43, 52, 54, 57, 59, 68, 70, 72, 106–7, 109, 129, 142, 201, 214–16, 220, 228, 230, 255, 272*n*137
Pasay Municipal Council, 43
Pasig, 5, 22, 27, 28, 36, 43, 52, 77–78, 177, 214, 228, 230, 232, 255
Pasig River, 21–22, 37
Pasong Putik, 135
Pasong Tamo, 29, 98, 135
Pateros, 3, 27–28, 43, 228
Payatas, 28, 48, 140, 231, 255–56
Payatas Estate Company, 50
peasant, 54
Pedrosa, Pio, 94
Pelaez, Emmanuel, 172
Pendatun, Salipada, 134
People Power, 2, 18, 244–46, 251–52, 255–56
People Power Monument, 251
People's Homesite and Housing Corporation (PHHC), 16, 154, 158–66, 168–70, 172, 179–80, 192–95, 197, 199, 202–3, 217, 224, 249, 301*n*67
People's Homesite Corporation (PHC), 74, 76, 86–88, 90, 95, 110, 112, 122, 158–59, 163, 165, 168, 280*n*70
People's March of March 1970, 208
Perez, Tony, 236, 249
periphery, 5, 10–11, 13, 15, 19, 25, 27, 34, 37, 61, 88, 99, 102, 105, 112, 142, 149, 203, 219, 248, 254
peri-urban, 6, 9–10, 13, 152, 202, 246, 251
Philamlife Homes, 18, 182–83, 189–91, 195, 234, 249, 251, 304*n*117
Philippine American Life Insurance Company (Philamlife), 180, 234

Philippine-American War, 12, 30, 65
Philippine Army, 80–81, 95, 154
Philippine Atomic Energy Commission, 153
Philippine Building Corporation, 173
Philippine Children's Hospital, 222
Philippine Commission Act No. 942, 43
Philippine Constabulary (PC), 81, 154–55, 211, 213–14
Philippine Council for United States Aid (PHILCUSA), 162–63, 165, 300*n*41
Philippine Heart Center, 222
Philippine Medical Center, 222
Philippine Military Academy (PMA), 81, 95
Philippine National Bank (PNB), 72–73, 97, 281*n*88, 283*n*132, 316*n*148
Philippine National Police, 2
Philippine Science High School (PSHS), 208
Philippines Free Press, 143
Philippine Women's University, 182
Piedad, 48, 74. *See also* Hacienda de Piedad
Piñahan Homeowners' Association, 200
Pineda, 27
Pink, Louis H., 163
planned capital, 7–9, 148, 253
Plaza Goiti, 34
Plaza Miranda, 208–9, 212, 225, 244–45, 249, 317*n*168
Plaza San Gabriel, 26
Plaza Santa Cruz, 110
political center, 3, 5, 7, 225, 252
political power, 90–91
population, 3, 5, 20, 26, 40, 42, 44, 49, 59, 77, 85, 90, 110, 117, 120, 122, 127, 135, 142, 155, 166, 172, 178, 184, 189, 191, 195, 212, 227–28, 238, 250, 253
Port Area, 191
Posadas Jr, Juan, 54, 92
Primcias, Cipriano, 172
principalía, 24, 46
private capital, 18, 170, 172, 178, 182, 226, 303*n*113
Project 1, 164, 193
Project 2, 164
Project 3, 163–65
Project 4, 159, 197
Project 4-A, 164
Project 4-B, 164
Project 5, 159
Project 6, 160, 164
Project 7, 160, 163
Project 8, 160, 164, 199
Project 9, 164

Project 11, 164
Project 12, 164
Project 13, 164
Project 14, 164
Project X-7, 164
Propaganda Movement, 8, 258n20
prostitution, 11, 55–58, 98–99, 145, 273n146, 274n149, 296n186
Provincia de Manila, 27–29, 33
Provincia de Tondo, 22, 24, 25, 27, 28
pueblo, 20, 22–23, 27–28, 39
Pugad Lawin, 98, 135, 265n36
Puyat, Gil, 88

Q

Quadrangle, 186
Quezon, Aurora, 68, 70, 96, 117, 155
Quezon, Manuel L., 1, 5, 8, 16, 17, 43–44, 48, 54, 58, 61–63, 65–66, 68–76, 82, 105, 118, 131, 148, 158, 207, 227, 262n61, 270n168, 284n152
Quezon Avenue, 1, 133, 155, 162, 170, 207–8, 239, 242, 244
Quezon City Central Business District, 256
Quezon City Citizens League, 200
Quezon Institute (QI), 88, 95, 110, 113
Quezon Memorial Circle (QMC), 1, 8, 198–99, 208, 224, 226
Quezon Memorial Shrine, 1, 8, 224, 226, 227
Quezon Province, 221. *See also* Tayabas
Quiapo, 22, 26–28, 207, 213
Quiapo Church, 208
Quiapo Mosque, 220
Quimpo, Jan, 208, 232
Quimpo, Susan, 238
Quirino, Elpidio, 124–25, 128, 131–32, 134–35, 137, 142, 144, 155, 162, 165–66, 170, 180, 215, 223–24
Quirino District, 159, 186
Quirino–Novaliches Highway, 135

R

radicalism, 158, 201, 205, 207, 210–11, 213, 233, 245, 252, 285n161
Rajah Sulayman, 20
Ramos, Emerito, 173, 179
Ramos, Fidel, 243
Ramos, Narciso, 90
real estate, 26, 34, 37, 40, 44, 54, 59, 61, 72–73, 77, 87–88, 96, 131, 135, 144–45, 156, 165, 169–70, 179, 248
real estate development, 12, 17, 40, 51, 61
Recollect (order), 21

Recto, Claro M., 88
reducción, 20, 22
remontados, 54
repression, 92, 209, 211–12, 232, 251
Republic Act 54 (RA 54), 115
Republic Act 333 (RA 333), 124, 135
Republic Act 537 (RA 537), 137
Republic Act 2259 (RA 2259), 200
Reyes, Edgardo, 261n49
Rivera, Fernando Primo de, 29–30
Rivera, Gines, 130
Rizal, José, 8, 33, 64, 107
Rizal monument, 63, 120
Rizal Park, 220, 242
Rizal (province), 2, 13, 32–33, 39, 42–44, 49–50, 55, 68, 75–78, 93–94, 96, 102, 120, 130, 138, 178
Roces, Alejandro, 73–74, 94
Roces, Ramon, 74, 95
Rodrigo, Soc, 172
Rodriguez, Jr, Eulogio, 43, 88
Rodriguez, Sr, Eulogio, 43, 88, 93, 172
Romulo, Carlos P., 280n65
Rosario Heights, 40, 43, 46
Rosenthal, Jacob, 94
Roxas, Baldomero, 72
Roxas, Gerardo "Gerry", 235
Roxas, Manuel, 73, 75, 79, 113–15, 118, 124, 138, 145
Roxas, Nicanor, 126, 155
Roxas Boulevard, 222
Roxas District, 159, 193, 198
Roy, Jose, 172
Royal Bus Company, 193
Rural Progress Administration (RPA), 133

S

Sacred Heart Novitiate, 110, 241
Saint Peter, 172
Sakay, Macario, 44
Sakdalista, 52, 54, 272n136, 315n135
Sakdal (peasant movement), 52, 54, 112, 249n136, 255n135
Salanga, Alfredo Navarro, 211
Salonga, Asiong, 249
Samahang Demokratiko ng Kabataan (SDK), 205, 211
Samahang Maralita para sa Makatao at Makatarungang Paninirahan (SAMA-SAMA), 232, 241
Samar, 184, 189
Sampagita Pictures, 176

Sampaloc, 22, 28–30, 37–38, 106, 238, 263
San Bartolome, 135, 187, 190
San Felipe Neri, 22, 27, 36, 70. *See also* Mandaluyong
San Francisco del Monte, 22, 24, 29–30, 40, 43–44, 48–49, 74, 77, 106–7, 112, 122, 136, 142, 154, 187, 263
San Francisco del Monte Subdivision, 40, 48
San Jose (Manila), 28
San Jose (Quezon City), 106, 122, 179, 187, 189
San Jose del Monte (Bulacan), 192
San Juan, 22, 27, 34, 36–37, 39, 42–44, 49, 52, 59, 70, 72–73, 75, 77–78, 99–100, 106–7, 109–10, 112, 129, 137, 140, 214, 216, 228, 230
San Juan Heights, 40, 46, 72
San Juan Heights Co., 88
San Mateo, 22, 25, 27–29, 44–45, 50, 112, 119, 137, 148–49, 265n36
San Miguel, 22, 26–28, 225
San Miguel Corporation, 172
San Nicolas, 22, 26, 38, 142
San Pablo, 93, 119
San Pedro Macati, 22, 27, 36. *See also* Makati
San Pedro Tunasan, 198
San Roque, 195
Santa Ana, 26–28, 37–38, 56, 220
Santa Ana Cabaret, 57, 68, 145
Santa Catalina Site, 171
Santa Clara Lumber Company, 95
Santa Cruz, 22, 26, 28, 34–35, 38, 110, 142
Santa Mesa, 37, 44, 48, 51, 68–69, 96, 110, 112, 171
Santa Mesa Estate, 74
Santa Mesa Heights, 40, 51, 88, 171, 187, 190, 238
Santa Mesa Subdivision, 133
Santo Domingo Church, 173, 238, 242–43
Santol, 76, 122, 187
Santol Tuberculosis Sanatorium, 88
Santolan, 99
Santos, Jose Abad, 73
Sapang Camias, 122
Sapang Palay, 192, 198
Sariaya, 72
Schwartzkopf, Sidney C., 49
Scott, William Henry, 241
Second People's March against Poverty, 212
Second World War, 7, 10, 17, 69, 103–4, 128, 133, 138, 156, 248, 289n35, 312n55. *See also* Pacific War, World War II
security, 80, 110, 114, 140, 142, 154–55, 157, 179, 181, 183, 201, 205, 209, 214–15, 237, 243, 253

Senate Committee on City Governments, 134
Sibul, 119
Sienna, 172
Simon Jr, Brigido "Jun", 247
Sin, Jaime Cardinal, 242
slum, 14, 34–35, 207, 218, 223, 227–29, 231–34, 248, 251, 256, 260n41, 266n54
Slum Clearance Committee, 163, 192
SM (Shoe Mart), 175
SM City North EDSA, 2
social justice, 46, 61–62, 85, 92, 101, 158, 203, 248, 255
Social Welfare Administration (SWA), 191, 195
Sociedad Agricola de Ultramar, 48
sociospatial, 3, 37, 58, 101–2, 180, 205, 208, 210–211, 220, 233, 238, 246, 251–52, 304n116
Soja, Edward, 6
South Bago Bantay Housing Project, 160
Southeast Asia, 7, 15, 20–21, 59, 147, 152, 252–54, 256, 257n12, 304n117, 322n26
space, 6, 8, 11, 148–49, 179, 212, 250, 252, 256
Spanish colonial period, 19, 37, 57, 180. *See also* colonialism
spatial turn, 6
St. Louis World's Fair, 282n108
St. Mary's College, 172
St. Theresa's College, 172, 239
state of the nation address (SONA), 82, 124, 222
Sto. Tomas, 119
subdivision, 17, 20, 37, 40, 49, 51, 59, 75, 86, 88, 101, 158, 172, 182–84, 193, 234
suburb, 10, 17, 25, 33, 35–37, 40, 43–44, 52, 54, 56–57, 59, 74, 99, 103, 106, 110, 138, 145–46, 148, 172, 184, 205, 225, 251
suburbanization, 14, 17, 19, 34, 37, 40, 42, 44–45, 59, 61, 183, 190, 202, 254
Sumulong, Juan, 43, 65, 94, 96, 137, 170
Sumulong, Lorenzo, 137
Supreme Court, 255
Sy, Henry, 175
Sycip, Alfonso, 144

T

Taft, William Howard, 45–46
Tagaytay, 75, 93, 119, 120, 128
Taguig, 2, 5, 27, 28, 43, 228, 255
Tala, 48. *See also* Hacienda de Tala
Tala Institute of Malariology, 122
Tala Leprosarium, 122
Talayan, 172
Talipapa, 135

Tambobong, 22, 25, 27–28, 37. *See also* Malabon
Tan Caktiong, Tony, 175
Tanauan, 119
Tanay, 22
Tandang Sora, 187, 200
Tañada, Lorenzo, 172
Tañong, 77
Tarlac, 156
Tatad, Francisco, 234
Tatalon, 30, 122, 190, 198, 208, 232, 241–45, 255–56, 305n143, 315n135
Tayabas, 65, 71, 93–94, 96. *See also* Quezon Province
Taytay, 22, 28
Teresa, 119
Teresa de la Paz Estate, 51
Times Street, 242
Timog Avenue, 2, 244
Tobias, Gaudencio, 230
Tondo, 20, 22, 25–28, 34–35, 38, 40, 149, 157, 232, 237–38, 283n139, 288n21
transportation, 34, 37, 40, 74, 88, 121, 155, 176, 193–94, 207, 221, 226
tranvia, 26, 34
trauma, 104, 128
Treaty of Paris, 30, 45
Trias, Mariano, 46
Trinoma, 2
Tuason (family), 173, 203, 252
Tuason, Antonio, 50
Tuason, Bobby, 73
Tuason, Teresa, 73
Ty (family), 255
Tydings–McDuffie Act, 62, 67, 91

U

Ugong, 44
Ugong Norte, 77, 122, 232
unemployment, 229
United Church of Christ in the Philippines (UCCP), 240
United States Agency for International Development (USAID), 164, 213
University of the Philippines (UP), 2, 5, 18, 37, 75, 77, 88, 91, 95, 99–100, 107, 111, 115–17, 124, 130, 132, 138, 140, 152, 154–55, 162, 198, 205, 207, 209–11, 217, 219, 222, 233, 236, 238–39, 242, 246, 250–51, 256, 284n152, 290n61
UP Teachers Village, 161

urban biography, 17, 63–64, 67, 93, 101
urban center, 22, 59, 93, 148, 218, 252, 254, 259n24
urban change, 7, 109
urban design, 33, 92, 114
urban development, 37, 54, 101, 114, 225
urban expansion, 14, 16, 101
urban form, 21
urban geography, 79, 255
urban history, 6, 14–15, 261n50
urban personality, 64
urban plan, 80, 84, 105, 114, 128, 202, 246
urban planning, 13, 17, 21, 33, 55, 79, 147, 191, 215, 255, 266n47
urban poor, 14, 35, 152, 157, 179, 190–91, 194–95, 197, 200–1, 203–5, 207–8, 218, 223, 229, 231–33, 244–45, 251, 255–56, 307n169
urban-rural, 5, 10, 13, 54, 103, 222, 254, 259n25
urban space, 34–35, 40, 84, 92, 218, 220, 226, 256
urban tradition, 17, 20
urbanism, 18–20, 25, 30, 33, 63–64, 114, 127, 151, 213, 219, 253, 255–56
urbanity, 64–65, 67, 109, 203
urbanization, 7, 9, 17, 19, 21, 25–27, 30, 55, 64, 246, 253
Urdaneta Village, 180
US Armed Forces Cemetery No. 2, 154
US Philippine War Damage Commission (PWDC), 114–15, 117, 132, 154, 159, 223, 302n92

V

Valenzuela, 228
Vargas, Jorge, 106
Varsity Hills, 173
Vera, Santiago de, 24
Vessels, 38
Villegas, Antonio, 208
Virata, Cesar, 184, 217, 234, 249
Visayas, 9, 20, 88, 203
Vitas Housing Project, 164

W

Wack Wack Golf and Country Club, 78, 275n173
Wagner, Bernard, 164
walis-walisan, 111
Waring, Frank A., 117

water, 21, 33, 35, 120–23, 135, 137, 140, 182, 191, 193, 214, 217, 222
Welcome Rotonda, 1–3, 133, 173, 208, 238, 243
West Avenue, 2
West Triangle, 170, 181, 189, 240, 242
White Lady, 103
White Plains, 183
Whoopee Cabaret, 57
Williams, Alpheus, 43, 80, 94
Winthrop-Stearns, 49
Wood, Leonard, 42
working class, 151
World Bank, 216, 218
World War II, 5, 154, 182, 231. See also Pacific War, Second World War

X

Xavierville Estate, 173
Xavierville Real Estate, Inc., 179
Xavierville Subdivision, 173, 180

Y

Young Christian Community, 233
Ysmael, Felipe, 49
Ysmael, Halim, 49

Z

Zamboanga, 93, 193
Zonal Improvement Program (ZIP), 229, 231